A GUIDE BOOK OF

# UNITED STATES COINS

## LARGE PRINT EDITION

R. S. YEOMAN

SENIOR EDITOR
JEFF GARRETT

RESEARCH EDITOR
Q. DAVID BOWERS

EDITOR EMERITUS
KENNETH BRESSETT

Fully Illustrated Catalog and
Retail Valuation List—1556 to Date

A Guide Book of United States Coins™ Large Print Edition
A Guide Book of United States Coins™
THE OFFICIAL RED BOOK OF UNITED STATES COINS™

THE OFFICIAL RED BOOK and THE OFFICIAL RED BOOK OF UNITED STATES COINS are trademarks of Whitman Publishing, LLC. Library of Congress Catalog Card No.: 47-22284

ISBN: 079484801X

Printed in the United States of America.


1974 Chandalar Drive • Suite D • Pelham, AL 35124

# CONTENTS

# CONTRIBUTORS TO THIS EDITION

*Senior Editor: Jeff Garrett. Research Editor: Q. David Bowers.*
*Editor Emeritus: Kenneth Bressett.*
*Special Consultants: Philip Bressett, Ben Garrett, Robert Rhue, Troy Thoreson, Ben Todd.*

Gary Adkins
John Albanese
Dominic Albert
Buddy Alleva
Richard M. August
Scott Barman
Mitchell Battino
Chris Berinato
Mark Borckardt
Larry Briggs
William Bugert
H. Robert Campbell
Elizabeth Coggan
Gary and Alan Cohen
Stephen M. Cohen
James H. Cohen
Steve Contursi
Adam Crum
Raymond Czahor
John Dannreuther
Sheridan Downey
Steven Ellsworth
Brant Fahnestock
Michael Fey
Gerry Fortin
Pierre Fricke
John Frost
Mike Fuljenz
Dennis M. Gillio
Ronald J. Gillio
Rusty Goe
Lawrence Goldberg
Ira Goldberg
Kenneth M. Goldman
Robert Green
Bob Grellman
Thomas Hallenbeck
James Halperin
Ash Harrison
Stephen Hayden
Brian Hendelson
John W. Highfill
Brian Hodge
Jack Howes
Steve Ivy
Amandeep Jassal
Joseph Jones
Mike Joyce
Donald H. Kagin
Bradley S. Karoleff
Jim Koenings
John Kraljevich
Richard A. Lecce
Julian M. Leidman
Denis W. Loring
Dwight N. Manley
Syd Martin
David McCarthy
Chris McCawley
Harry Miller
Lee S. Minshull
Scott P. Mitchell
Charles Morgan
Alex Nocerino
Paul Nugget
Mike Orlando
John M. Pack
Joseph Parrella
Robert M. Paul
Joel Rettew
Robert Rhue
Steve Roach
Greg Rohan
Maurice Rosen
Mark Salzberg
Gerald R. Scherer Jr.
Harry Schultz
Jeff Shevlin
Roger Siboni
James Simek
Scott Sparks
David M. Sundman
Anthony Terranova
Troy Thoreson
Frank Van Valen
Kevin Vinton
Fred Weinberg
Douglas Winter
Mark S. Yaffe

***Special credit is due to the following for service and data in this book:*** Charles Davis, David Fanning, Robert W. Julian, George F. Kolbe, Christopher McDowell, P. Scott Rubin, and William Spencer.

***Special credit is due to the following for service in past editions:*** Lee J. Bellisario, Stewart Blay, Roger W. Burdette, Frank J. Colletti, Tom DeLorey, Bill Fivaz, Chuck Furjanic, James C. Gray, Charles Hoskins, Richard Kelly, David W. Lange, G.J. Lawson, Andy Lustig, J.P. Martin, Eric P. Newman, Ken Potter, Paul Rynearson, Mary Sauvain, Richard J. Schwary, Robert W. Shippee, Craig Smith, Barry Sunshine, Jerry Treglia, Mark R. Vitunic, Holland Wallace, Weimar White, John Whitney, Raymond Williams, and John Wright.

***Special photo credits are due to the following:*** Al Adams, David Akers, James Bevill, Heritage Auctions (ha.com), Ira & Larry Goldberg Coins & Collectibles, Ron Karp, Massachusetts Historical Society, Christopher McDowell, Tom Mulvaney, Ken Potter, John Scanlon, Roger Siboni, the Smithsonian Institution, Stack's Bowers Galleries, Richard Stinchcomb, and the United States Mint.

Coin values shown in this book are retail prices figured from data from the listed contributors approximately two months prior to publication. The coin market is so active in some categories that values can easily change during that period. Values are shown as a guide and are not intended to serve as a price list for any dealer's stock. A dash appearing in a price column indicates that coins in that grade exist even though there are no current sales or auction records for them. The dash does not necessarily mean that such coins are exceedingly rare. Italicized prices indicate unsettled or speculative values. A number of listings of rare coins lack prices or dashes in certain grades, indicating that they are not available or not believed to exist in those grades.

Prices rise when (1) the economic trend is inflationary and speculators turn to tangible assets as a hedge, or when the number of collectors increases, while coin supplies remain stationary or decrease through attrition or melting; (2) dealers replace their stocks of coins only from collectors or other dealers, who expect a profit over what they originally paid; (3) speculators attempt to influence the market through selective buying; or (4) bullion (gold and silver) prices rise.

Prices decline when (1) changes in collecting habits or economic conditions alter demand for certain coins; (2) speculators sell in large quantities; (3) hoards or large holdings are suddenly released and cannot be quickly absorbed by the normal market; or (4) bullion (gold and silver) prices decline.

Those who edit, contribute to, and publish this book advocate the collecting of coins for pleasure and educational benefits. A secondary consideration is that of investment, the profits from which are usually realized over the long term based on careful purchases.

The *Handbook of United States Coins* (commonly called the Blue Book), by R.S. Yeoman, Whitman Publishing, contains average prices dealers will pay for these coins, and is obtainable through most coin dealers, hobby shops, bookstores, and the Internet.

**ABBREVIATIONS COMMONLY USED IN THIS BOOK**

| Abbreviation | Meaning | Abbreviation | Meaning | Abbreviation | Meaning |
|---|---|---|---|---|---|
| Arr | Arrows | HR | High Relief | Obv | Obverse |
| Cl | Close | Inv | Inverted | Pf | Proof |
| CN | Copper-Nickel | Knbd | Knobbed | Rev | Reverse |
| Dbl | Doubled | LE | Lettered Edge | SE | Small Eagle |
| Dbln | Doubloon | Lg | Large | Sm | Small |
| Drap | Drapery | Lib | Liberty | Sq | Square |
| Dt | Date | Ltrs | Letters | T | Type |
| FR | Flat Rim | Med | Medium | V, Var | Variety |
| HE | Heraldic Eagle | Mmk | Mintmark | WR | Wire Rim |
| Horiz | Horizontal | Nml | Normal | | |

A slash between words or letters represents an overdate or overmintmark: "3/2" is an abbreviation of "3 Over 2," "D/S" is "D Over S," etc.

### *Photographs in This Book*

Collectors should be aware that unofficial copies of certain American issues were made after 1850 to provide facsimiles of rarer issues that would otherwise have been unobtainable. Many crude imitations have also been made in recent years, as well as forgeries intended to deceive collectors. Photos herein, however, are of genuine specimens, except for certain modern issues, which may be U.S. Mint renderings.

## CONDITIONS OF COINS

*Essential Elements of the American Numismatic Association Grading Standards*

**Proof**—A specially made coin distinguished by sharpness of detail and usually with a brilliant, mirrorlike surface. *Proof* refers to the method of manufacture and is not a grade. The term implies superior condition unless otherwise noted. See page 363 for details.

**Gem Proof (PF-65)**—Surfaces are brilliant, with no noticeable blemishes or flaws. A few scattered, barely noticeable marks or hairlines.

**Choice Proof (PF-63)**—Surfaces are reflective, with only a few blemishes in secondary focal places. No major flaws.

**Proof (PF-60)**—Surfaces may have several contact marks, hairlines, or light rubs. Luster may be dull and eye appeal lacking.

**Mint State**—The terms *Mint State (MS)* and *Uncirculated (Unc.)* are interchangeable and refer to coins showing no trace of wear. Such coins may vary slightly due to minor surface imperfections, as described in the following subdivisions:

**Perfect Uncirculated (MS-70)**—Perfect new condition, showing no trace of wear. The finest quality possible, with no evidence of scratches, handling, or contact with other coins. Very few circulation-issue coins are ever found in this condition.

**Gem Uncirculated (MS-65)**—An above-average Uncirculated coin that may be brilliant or lightly toned and that has very few contact marks on the surface or rim.

**Choice Uncirculated (MS-63)**—A coin with some distracting contact marks or blemishes in prime focal areas. Luster may be impaired.

**Uncirculated (MS-60)**—A coin that has no trace of wear, but which may show a number of contact marks, and whose surface may be spotted or lack some luster.

**Choice About Uncirculated (AU-55)**—Evidence of friction on high points of design. Most of the mint luster remains.

**About Uncirculated (AU-50)**—Traces of light wear on many of the high points. At least half of the mint luster is still present.

**Choice Extremely Fine (EF-45)**—Light overall wear on the highest points. All design details are very sharp. Some of the mint luster is evident.

**Extremely Fine (EF-40)**—Light wear on the design throughout, but all features are sharp and well defined. Traces of luster may show.

**Choice Very Fine (VF-30)**—Light, even wear on the surface and highest parts of the design. All lettering and major features are sharp.

**Very Fine (VF-20)**—Moderate wear on design high points. All major details are clear.

**Fine (F-12)**—Moderate to considerable even wear. The entire design is bold with an overall pleasing appearance.

**Very Good (VG-8)**—Well worn with main features clear and bold, although rather flat.

**Good (G-4)**—Heavily worn, with the design visible but faint in areas. Many details are flat.

**About Good (AG-3)**—Very heavily worn with portions of the lettering, date, and legend worn smooth. The date may be barely readable.

A star (or similar notation) in the grade on a slab means "exceptional quality."

*Important:* Undamaged coins are worth more than bent, corroded, scratched, holed, nicked, stained, or mutilated ones. Flawless Uncirculated coins are generally worth more than values quoted in this book. Slightly worn coins ("sliders") that have been cleaned and conditioned ("buffed") to simulate Uncirculated luster are worth considerably less than perfect pieces.

Unlike damage inflicted after striking, manufacturing defects do not always lessen values. Examples include colonial coins with planchet flaws or weakly struck designs; early silver and gold coins with weight-adjustment "file marks" (parallel cuts made on the planchet prior to striking); and coins with "lint marks" (surface marks due to the presence of dust or other foreign matter during striking).

Brief guides to grading are placed before each major coin type. While grading *standards* strive to be precise, interpretations are subjective and often vary among collectors, dealers, and certification services.

## THIRD-PARTY GRADING AND AUTHENTICATION

In this guide book values from under $1 up to several hundred dollars are for "raw" coins—that is, coins that have *not* been graded and encapsulated by a professional third-party grading service. Coins valued near or above $500 are assumed to be third-party-graded. A high-value coin that has not been professionally certified as authentic, graded, and encapsulated by an independent firm is apt to be valued lower than the prices indicated.

What *is* third-party grading? This is a service providing, for a fee, an impartial, independent opinion of a coin's grade and its authenticity. The grader is neither buyer nor seller, and has no biased interest in the coin's market value. Third-party grading started in the late 1970s with ANACS (then a service of the American Numismatic Association; now privately owned and operated). ANACS graders would examine a coin and, after determining its authenticity, would assign separate grades to its obverse and reverse (such as MS-63/65) and return it to the sender, along with a certificate and photograph.

In 1986 a group of coin dealers launched the Professional Coin Grading Service (PCGS), which grades coins for a fee and hermetically seals them in plastic holders with interior labels. This "slabbing" helps guarantee that a coin and its grade certificate cannot be separated. In 1987 Numismatic Guaranty Corporation of America (NGC) was started, offering a similar encapsulation service. Both companies guarantee the authenticity and grades of the coins they certify. Coins are judged by consensus, with the graders having no knowledge of who submitted them.

From the 1970s to the present there have been more than 100 different commercial grading companies. Readers are cautioned to investigate the background of a TPG (third-party grader) before trusting in its services.

Today the hobby's leading third-party grading firms are NGC (Sarasota, Florida) and PCGS (Newport Beach, California).

Professional grading strives to be completely objective, but coins are graded by humans and not computers. This introduces a subjective element of *art* as opposed to *science.* A coin's grade, even if certified by a leading TPG, can be questioned by any collector or dealer—or even by the service that graded it, if resubmitted for a second look. Furthermore, within a given grade, a keen observer will find coins that are low-quality, average, and high-quality for that grade. Such factors as luster, color, strength of strike, and overall eye appeal can make, for example, one MS-65 1891 Morgan dollar more visually attractive than another with the same grade. This gives the smart collector the opportunity to "cherrypick," or examine multiple slabbed coins and select the highest-quality coin for the desired grade. This process builds a better collection than simply accepting a TPG's assigned grades, and is summed up in the guidance of "Buy the coin, not the slab." (Also note that a coin certified as, for example, MS-64 might have greater eye appeal—and therefore be more desirable to a greater number of collectors—than a less attractive coin graded MS-65.)

Over the years, collectors have observed a trend nicknamed "gradeflation": the reinterpretation, in practice, of the standards applied to a given grade over time. For example, a coin evaluated by a leading TPG in 1992 as MS-64 might be graded today as MS-65 or even MS-66.

The general effect of third-party grading and authentication has been to increase buyers' and sellers' comfort levels with the perceived quality of rare coins in the marketplace. And, as mentioned, there still exists the potential for keen-eyed collectors to cherrypick coins that are "exceptional for their grade."

## AN INTRODUCTION TO UNITED STATES COINS

### The Spanish Milled Dollar

The Spanish milled dollar, valued at 8 reales, and otherwise known as the *Pillar dollar* or *piece of eight,* has been given a place in romantic fiction unequaled by any other coin.

This time-honored piece and its fractional parts (one-half, one, two, and four reales) were the principal coins of the American colonists and were the forerunners of our own silver dollar and its fractional divisions. Thomas Jefferson even recommended to the Continental Congress on September 2, 1776, that the new country adopt the silver Spanish milled dollar as its monetary unit of value.

The coin shown above bears the M̊ mintmark for Mexico City. Similar pieces with other mintmarks were struck in Bolivia, Chile, Colombia, Guatemala, and Peru. Average value for an 8 reales Pillar dollar of common date and mint is about $200 in Fine condition. Dates range from 1732 to 1772. Bust-type 8 reales dollars, made from 1772 to 1825, also circulated widely. These are valued at $100 in Very Fine condition. *Note that many modern copies of the 8 reales exist. These are produced mostly as souvenirs and have little or no value.*

### Money of the Early Americans

The saga of American money covers a period of nearly four centuries, from 1620 to the present. It began when the early European settlers in New England started trading with Native Americans for furs and commodities that could be exported to Britain. The furs, tobacco, and lumber exports were used to purchase needed items that could not be produced locally. Trade was carried on with the Indians through the use of barter and strings of wampum, which were fashioned from clam shells in the form of beads. Beaver skins, wampum, and, in Virginia, tobacco, soon became the commonly accepted local media of exchange for all other available commodities that were not bartered. The immigrants, in fact, had little use for coined money at first; but when merchandise arrived from Europe, coins were usually demanded in payment for goods.

Nearly all foreign coins were accepted for purchases. The most popular were French louis, English guineas, German thalers, Dutch ducats, and various Spanish coins, including gold doubloons and, particularly, the Spanish milled dollar, or piece of eight. The piece of eight continued to be a standard money unit throughout the entire colonial period. Even after the Revolutionary War ended (in 1783) and the United States Mint was established (in 1792), the Spanish dollar and its fractional parts circulated in this country with official sanction until 1857. One real equaled 12-1/2 cents and was known as a *bit.* A quarter of the dollar thus became known as *two bits,* a term that is still understood to mean 25 cents.

Because of the shortage of small change, large coins were sometimes cut into smaller pieces for convenience. Spanish-American milled dollars were often chopped into halves, quarters, or eighths. Fraudulent cutting into five or six "quarters" caused many to distrust these cut pieces.

**Early Americans cut Spanish-American silver coins into pieces to make small change.**

England consistently ignored the plight of its American colonists and made no effort to provide gold or silver coins, or small change in any form, for their convenience. The English mercantile system relied on exports from the colonies, and sought to control trade by limiting the amount of "hard" money paid to them. Under these constraints, the colonists were able to trade for most necessities only with England, and were left with very little coinage for trade with other countries. The foreign coins that were sometimes available were a valuable commodity for purchases outside the normal English trade.

As a remedy for the dearth of circulating coinage, a wide assortment of foreign coins and tokens was pressed into use. Only a very few were made in America prior to 1783. Copper coins known as *Hogge Money* (from their design; see page 38) were privately made for the Sommer Islands, now known as Bermuda, about the year 1616. The first coins minted for the colonies in America were made by John Hull in Boston for the Massachusetts Bay Colony. The General Court of the colony granted him authority to begin coinage, despite the possibility of objection and recrimination by the king of England. Starting in 1652 the Massachusetts minter began producing the famous NE, Willow, Oak, and Pine Tree shillings, with their fractional parts, for the convenience of the colonists. This venture, which defied English law and lasted from 1652 to 1682, was in a sense the first declaration of independence for the colonies.

As time passed, coins and tokens of many types were introduced and employed by the colonists to supplement their use of barter. Lord Baltimore was responsible for a small issue of silver pieces struck in England in 1659 and sent to Maryland for use there. Mark Newby imported from Ireland coins known as *St. Patrick's halfpence,* for use in the province of New Jersey in 1682. Coins dated 1722 to 1724, known as *Rosa Americana* issues, were produced by William Wood in England and were widely circulated in America. In addition, many British and other European coppers circulated there.

Enterprising Americans were responsible for some of the other copper and brass pieces that circulated during the 18th century. The Gloucester token, about which little is known, was one of these. Samuel and John Higley of Granby, Connecticut, made an interesting series of threepence pieces during the period from 1737 to 1739. John Chalmers, a silversmith in Annapolis, Maryland, issued silver shillings, sixpence, and threepence pieces in 1783. In 1786 and 1787 Ephraim Brasher, a New York goldsmith, struck gold coins of the value of a doubloon (about $15 in New York currency). Standish Barry of Baltimore, Maryland, made a curious silver threepence token in 1790.

Still other tokens, struck in Britain, reached our shores in early times and were for the most part speculative ventures. These much-needed, small-denomination coppers were readily circulated because of the great scarcity of fractional coins. Included in this category were the Nova Constellatio coppers and various English merchants' tokens.

During the period of turmoil following America's War of Independence, from about 1781 to 1795, still more English- and American-made copper pieces were added to the great variety of coins and tokens employed in the new nation. It was a time when Americans were suffering from postwar economic depression, a shortage of currency, high taxes, and foreclosures from bankruptcies. In the 1780s the Nova Eborac pieces (known as *New York coppers*), the Georgivs Triumpho coppers, and the Auctori Plebis tokens found their way into circulation as small change, despite their unofficial nature.

Collectors of colonial coins also include other pieces that are interesting because of their close association with early America and its first president. These consist of the Kentucky, Myddelton, and Franklin Press tokens, and those pieces bearing the portrait of George Washington. Although most of these pieces are dated from 1783 to 1795, many of them were made in England around the turn of the 19th century. Few of them actually circulated in the United States.

## Coinage of the States

The Articles of Confederation, adopted March 1, 1781, provided that Congress should have the sole right to regulate the alloy and value of coin struck by its own authority or by that of the respective states. Each state, therefore, had the right to coin money, with Congress serving as a regulating authority. New Hampshire was the first state to consider coinage, but few if any of its copper coins were placed into circulation. The only specimens known bear the date 1776.

In the period from 1785 to 1788, Vermont, Connecticut, and New Jersey granted coining privileges to companies and individuals. Massachusetts erected its own mint in Boston, where copper coins were produced in 1787 and 1788. A number of interesting types and varieties of these state issues, most of which were struck in fairly large quantities, are still extant and form the basis for many present-day collections and museum exhibits of early American coins.

## The Beginnings of United States Coinage

Throughout the years from 1620 to 1776, colonists were forced to rely on numerous European coins and denominations that had to be converted to some common value to facilitate transactions. Further compounding this mathematical obstacle was the variation of values from one colony to another. Merchants became accustomed to using the Spanish dollar and its fractional parts, the real, the medio (half-real), and other, similar denominations. In time, those coins became more familiar to them than the old English coins, which were always scarce. It was only natural, therefore, that when a national coinage was under consideration a dollar-size coin was the first choice.

Contracts, currency statutes, and prices in the colonies were usually quoted in English pounds or Spanish dollars. In 1767 Maryland took the lead and produced paper money that was denominated in dollars. Connecticut, Massachusetts, and Virginia soon passed laws making Spanish coins legal tender. The first issue of Continental paper money, May 10, 1775, offers further evidence that the dollar was to be the basic American money unit, for it provided that the notes should be payable in "Spanish Milled Dollars or the value thereof in gold or silver."

The assistant financier of the Confederation, Gouverneur Morris, proposed a decimal coinage ratio designed to make conversion of various foreign currencies easier to compute in terms of a dollar-size unit. His plan was incorporated into a report presented by Robert Morris, superintendent of finance, to the Congress, January 15, 1782. Plans for a mint were advanced, and a uniform national currency to relieve the confused money conditions was outlined. Morris's unit, 1/1,440 of a dollar, was calculated to agree without a fraction with all the different valuations of the Spanish milled dollar in the various states. Although a government mint was approved on February 21, 1782, no immediate action was taken. During 1784, Thomas Jefferson, then a member of the House of Representatives, brought in a report concerning the plan and expressed disagreement with Morris's complicated money unit. He advocated the simple dollar unit because he believed the dollar was already as familiar and convenient a unit of value as the British pound. He favored the decimal system, and remarked, "The most easy ratio of multiplication and division is that of ten. George Washington referred to it as 'a measure, which in my opinion, has become indispensably necessary.'"

The Grand Committee in May 1785 recommended a gold five-dollar piece; a dollar of silver with fractional coins of the same metal (in denominations of half, quarter, 10th, and 20th parts of a dollar); and copper pieces valued at 1/100 and 1/200 of a dollar.

In 1783 Robert Morris submitted a series of pattern pieces in silver that were designed by Benjamin Dudley to carry out the decimal idea for United States money. These are known as the Nova Constellatio patterns and consist of the "mark," or 1,000 units; the "quint," or 500 units; the "bit," or 100 units; and a copper "five." The unit was to be a quarter grain of silver. This was not the first attempt at a dollar coin, for the Continental Currency piece of dollar size, dated 1776, had been struck in such metals as brass, pewter, and silver. The reason is unknown for making a very limited number of pieces in silver. The more-common pewter pieces were most likely intended as a substitute for the paper dollar, and saw considerable circulation.

Congress gave formal approval to the basic dollar unit and decimal coinage ratio in its resolution of July 1785 but other, more pressing matters delayed further action. Not until the Constitutional Convention of 1787 had placed the country on firm ground and the new nation had elected George Washington president did the Congress again turn attention to the subjects of currency, a mint, and a coinage system.

The Massachusetts cents and half cents struck in 1787 and 1788 were the first official coins in the United States to bear stated values in terms of decimal parts of the dollar unit. The cent represented a hundredth part of a Spanish dollar.

The first federally authorized coin for which we have extensive documentation was the Fugio copper (sometimes called the Franklin cent, as Benjamin Franklin is believed to have supplied the design and composed the legends). This piece, similar in design to the Continental Currency dollar of 1776, was privately struck in 1787 by contract with the government.

Ephraim Brasher was engaged to regulate foreign gold coins and certain silver issues. This was done by clipping or plugging coins in circulation to bring them up or down to the standards published in 1784 by the Bank of New York. Appropriate hallmarks were then added for verification. Various goldsmiths who participated in this function included Standish Barry, John Burger, Thomas Underhill, and others. Brasher used a counterstamp in the form of the letters EB in an oval. John Burger also used his initials in an oval. Most regulated coins are scarce or rare. See pages 67 and 76–77 for additional information.

Alexander Hamilton, then secretary of the Treasury, reported his views on monetary matters on January 21, 1791. He concurred in all essentials with the decimal subdivisions and multiples of the dollar contained in the earlier resolutions and urged the use of both gold and silver in U.S. standard money.

Congress passed a resolution on March 3, 1791, that a mint be established, and authorized President Washington to engage artists and procure machinery for the making of coins. No immediate steps were taken, but when Washington delivered his third annual address, he recommended immediate establishment of a mint.

On April 2, 1792, a bill was finally passed providing "that the money of account of the United States should be expressed in dollars or units, dismes or tenths, cents or hundredths, and milles or thousandths; a disme being the tenth part of a dollar, a cent the hundredth part of a dollar, a mille the thousandth part of a dollar. . . ."

Denominations specified in the act were as follows:

| | Value | Grains Pure | Grains Standard |
|---|---|---|---|
| Gold eagle | $10.00 | 247-4/8 | 270 |
| Gold half eagle | 5.00 | 123-6/8 | 135 |
| Gold quarter eagle | 2.50 | 61-7/8 | 67-4/8 |
| Silver dollar | 1.00 | 371-4/16 | 416 |
| Silver half dollar | .50 | 185-10/16 | 208 |
| Silver quarter dollar | .25 | 92-13/16 | 104 |
| Silver disme (dime) | .10 | 37-2/16 | 41-3/5 |
| Silver half disme | .05 | 18-9/16 | 20-4/5 |
| Copper cent | .01 | 264 | |
| Copper half cent | .005 | 132 | |

The word *pure* meant unalloyed metal; *standard* meant, in the case of gold, 11/12 fine, or 11 parts pure metal to one part alloy, which was mixed with the pure metal to improve the wearing qualities of the coins. The fineness for silver coins was 1,485/1,664, or approximately 892.43 thousandths, in contrast with the gold coins' fineness of 22 carats, or 916-2/3 thousandths.

The law also provided for free coinage of gold and silver coins at the fixed ratio of 15 to 1, and a token coinage of copper cents and half cents. Under the free-coinage provision no charge was to be made for converting gold or silver bullion into coins "weight for weight." At the depositor's option, however, he could demand an immediate exchange of coins for his bullion, for which privilege a deduction of one-half of 1% was to be imposed.

President Washington appointed David Rittenhouse, a well-known scientist, as the first director of the Mint. Construction began on a mint building nearly four months after the passage of the Act of April 2, 1792. The building was located on Seventh Street near Arch in Philadelphia.

The first coin struck by the government was the half disme. Fifteen hundred of these pieces were produced during the month of July 1792 before the mint was completed. Additional coins were probably made in early October. There is no historical evidence for the story that Washington donated his personal silverware for minting these coins. A few dismes were also struck at this time or a short while later. Silver and gold for coinage were to be supplied by the public, but copper for cents and half cents had to be provided by the government. This was accomplished by the Act of May 8, 1792, when the purchase of not more than 150 tons was authorized. On September 11, 1792, six pounds of old copper was purchased, and probably used for the striking of patterns. Thereafter, planchets with upset rims for cents and half cents were purchased from Boulton and Watt of Birmingham, England, from 1798 to 1838.

**David Rittenhouse—surveyor, astronomer, mathematician, and inventor—was named the first director of the U.S. Mint.**

Several pattern coins were prepared in 1792 before regular mint operations commenced. *Patterns* are test or trial pieces intended to show the size, form, and design of proposed coins. These included Henry Voigt's silver center cent, a piece smaller than that of regular issue. The small plug of silver, worth about three-quarters of a cent, was evidently intended to bring the intrinsic value of the coin up to the value of 1¢ and to permit production of a coin of more convenient size. Alexander Hamilton had mentioned a year before that the proposed "intrinsic value" cent would be too large, and suggested that the amount of copper could be reduced and a trace of silver added. The pattern cent with a silver center may have been designed to conform to this recommendation.

The cents by Robert Birch are equally interesting. These patterns are identified by their legends, which read LIBERTY PARENT OF SCIENCE AND INDUSTRY and TO BE ESTEEMED BE USEFUL. The quarter with an eagle on the reverse side (designer unknown) belongs among the 1792 patterns devised before regular issues were struck.

The Bank of Maryland deposited the first silver, sending $80,715.73-1/2 in French coins to the mint on July 18, 1794. Moses Brown, a Boston merchant, deposited the first gold in the form of ingots (February 12, 1795) amounting to $2,276.22, receiving silver coin in payment. The first coins transferred to the treasurer consisted of 11,178 cents on March 1, 1793. The first return of coined silver was made on October 15, 1794, and the first gold coins (744 half eagles) were delivered July 31, 1795. The early Mint was constantly vigilant to see that the weights of these coins were standard. Overweight blank planchets were filed and adjusted prior to striking, and many of the coins made prior to 1836 show file marks and blemishes from these adjustments.

## Regular Mint Issues

Cents and half cents, exclusively, were coined during the year 1793, and by 1799 approximately $50,000 in these coins had been placed into circulation. This amount proved insufficient for the requirements of commerce, and small-denomination coins of the states and of foreign countries continued in use well into the 19th century.

One of the most serious problems confronting commercial interests prior to 1857 was the failure of the government to provide a sufficient volume of circulating coins. The fault, contrary to popular opinion at the time, did not lie with any lack of effort on the part of the Mint. Other circumstances tended to interfere with the expected steady flow of new coinage into the channels of trade.

Free circulation of United States gold and silver coins was greatly hindered by speculators. For example, worn Spanish dollars of reduced weight and value were easily exchanged for U.S. silver dollars, which meant the export of most of the new dollars as fast as they were minted, and a complete loss to American trade channels.

Gold coins failed to circulate for similar reasons. The ratio of 15 to 1 between gold and silver was close to the world ratio when Alexander Hamilton recommended it in 1791, but by 1799 the ratio in European commercial centers had reached 15-3/4 to 1. At this rate, the undervalued gold coins tended to flow out of the country, or were melted for bullion. After 1800, therefore, United States gold coins were rarely seen in general circulation. As no remedy could be found, coinage of the gold eagle and the silver dollar was suspended by President Jefferson in 1804. It is generally held that the silver dollar was discontinued in 1804, although the last coins minted for the period were dated 1803.

With the lack of gold coins and silver dollars, the half dollar became America's desirable coin for large transactions and bank reserves. Until 1834, in fact, half dollars circulated very little as they were mainly transferred from bank to bank. This accounts for the relatively good supply of higher-condition half dollars of this period that is still available to collectors. A Senate committee of 1830 reported that United States silver coins were considered so much bullion and were accordingly "lost to the community as coins."

There was only a negligible coinage of quarters, dimes, and half dimes from 1794 to 1834. It has been estimated that there was less than one piece for each person in the country in the year 1830. This period has been described as one of chaotic currency made up of bank notes, underweight foreign gold coins, foreign silver coins of many varieties, and domestic fractional silver coins. Paper money of that time was equally bothersome. Privately issued bank notes sometimes had little or no backing and were apt to be worthless at the time of redemption. In this period, before national paper money commenced in 1861, notes of the state-chartered banks flooded the country and were much more common than silver coins.

On June 28, 1834, a law was passed reducing the weight and fineness of gold coins, which had the effect of placing American money on a new gold standard. Trade and finance greatly benefited from this act, which also proved a boon to the gold mines of Georgia and North Carolina. Branch mints in Dahlonega, Georgia; New Orleans; and Charlotte, North Carolina, began operations in 1838 to handle the newly mined gold near the source. The various issues of private gold coins were struck in these areas.

The law of January 18, 1837, completely revised and standardized the Mint and coinage laws. Legal standards, Mint charges, legal tender, Mint procedure, tolerance in coin weights, accounting methods, a bullion fund, standardization of gold and silver coins to 900 thousandths fineness, and other desirable regulations were covered by the new legislation. Results of importance to the collector were the changes in type for the various coin denominations and the resumption of coinage of the eagle in 1838 and larger quantities of silver dollars in 1840.

Prior to Andrew Jackson's election as president in 1828, the Second Bank of the United States had considerable control over the nation's currency. In 1832 Jackson vetoed a bill rechartering the bank and transferred government deposits to state banks. The action took away some stability from the economy and eventually led to a national financial collapse. By 1837 the country was so deprived of circulating coinage that merchants resorted to making their own "hard times tokens" to facilitate trade. The few available government coins were hoarded or traded at a premium for private paper money, which was often unreliable.

The California gold discovery in 1848 was responsible for an interesting series of private, state, and territorial gold issues in the western region, culminating in the establishment of a branch mint at San Francisco in 1854.

Two new regular gold issues were authorized in 1849. In that year the gold dollar joined the American family of coins, followed in 1850 by the double eagle. The California gold fields greatly influenced the world gold market, making the exportation of silver profitable. For example, the silver in two half dollars was worth $1.03-1/2 in gold. The newly introduced gold dollars soon took over the burden and hastened the disappearance of silver coins from trade channels. This was the situation when the new 3¢ postage rate brought about the bill authorized by Congress on March 3, 1851, calling for the coinage of a silver three-cent piece in 1851. This was the United States' first subsidiary coin in precious metals, for its silver value was intrinsically 86% of its face value, as an expedient designed to prevent its withdrawal from circulation.

The $3 gold piece was authorized by the Act of February 21, 1853. It was never a popular or necessary coin because of the existing $2.50 and $5 coins; it nevertheless was issued regularly from 1854 until 1889.

The California Gold Rush had a great influence on American coinage.

On February 21, 1853, fractional silver coins were made subsidiary by reduction of their weights. As the coins' face value now exceeded their bullion value, free coinage of silver was prohibited except for dollars, and the Mint was authorized to purchase its silver requirements on its own account using the bullion fund of the Mint, and, according to law, "the profit of said coinage shall be . . . transferred to the account of the treasury of the United States."

To identify the new lightweight pieces, arrows were placed at the date on all silver coins except three-cent pieces, for which arrows were added to the reverse. Dollars, which were not reduced in weight, were not marked in any way. On the quarters and half dollars of 1853, rays were added on the reverse to denote the change of weight. In 1854, the rays were removed, and in 1856, the arrows disappeared from all but the silver three-cent coins. Large-scale production of silver coins during this period greatly relieved the demands on gold dollars and three-cent pieces, and for the first time in U.S. history, enough fractional coins were in general circulation to facilitate commerce.

The Coinage Act of February 21, 1857, was designed primarily to reform the copper coinage. Although large cents and half cents are interesting and valuable in the eyes of the modern collector, they were unpopular with the American public in the 1850s because of their size. They also cost the Mint too much to produce.

The new law abolished the half cent, and reduced the size and changed the design of the cent. The new Flying Eagle cent contained 88% copper and 12% nickel. Nearly 1,000 pattern cents were stamped from dies bearing the date 1856, although no authority for the issue existed before 1857. Other important effects of the law were the retirement of Spanish silver coins from circulation, and dispersal of the new cents in such excessive quantities as to create a nuisance to business houses, particularly in the eastern cities. The Indian Head design replaced the Flying Eagle in 1859, and in 1864 the weight of the cent was further reduced and its composition changed to a proportion of 95% copper and 5% tin and zinc. (This bronze composition was the standard for the cent except for the years 1943 and 1944–1946. In 1962 the alloy was changed to 95% copper and 5% zinc. In 1982 the composition was changed to a core of 99.2% zinc and 0.8% copper, covered with an outer layer of pure copper.)

An abundance of coins turned to scarcity following the outbreak of the Civil War. Anticipation of a scarcity of hard money, and uncertainty as to the outcome of the war, induced hoarding. The large volume of greenbacks in circulation caused a premium for gold. Subsidiary silver coins, as a result of the sudden depreciation, quickly vanished from circulation. As an expediency, some people made use of postage stamps for small change. Merchants, banks, individuals, and even some towns and cities produced a wide array of small-denomination paper scrip and promissory notes to meet their needs. In 1862 the government released its first issue of "Postage Currency" and subsequent fractional notes. In 1863 many privately issued copper tokens appeared to help fill the void. They are of two general classes: tradesmen's tokens and imitations of official cents. Many of the latter were political or patriotic in character and carried slogans typical of the times. They not only served as a medium of exchange, but also often advertised merchants or products, and were usually produced at a profit.

The Civil War brought dramatic changes to our nation's coins.

The Coinage Act of April 22, 1864, which effected changes in the cent, provided also for the new bronze two-cent piece. The act, moreover, provided legal tender status for these two coins up to 10 times their face value. The two-cent piece was the first coin to bear the motto IN GOD WE TRUST. The new coin at first was readily accepted by the public, but it proved an unnecessary denomination because of the competing three-cent coins, and production was halted after only nine years. The secretary of the Treasury had issued a great many currency notes of the three-cent denomination early in 1865. American nickel interests seized upon this circumstance to fight for a new three-cent coin for redemption of the paper money. A law was quickly passed and signed by President Abraham Lincoln on March 3, 1865, providing for a three-cent coin of 75%-25% copper-nickel composition. The United States then possessed two types of three-cent pieces, although neither was seriously needed. The nickel three-cent piece was struck continuously until 1889, the silver three-cent piece until 1873.

The new copper-nickel alloy ratio was selected for the five-cent coin, adopted May 16, 1866, and thereafter known as a *nickel.* Again, the people had a coin denomination available to them in two forms. The silver half dime, like the three-cent piece, was retired from service in 1873 to curb the use of silver.

The great influx of silver from the Comstock Lode in Nevada, mainly in the 1860s and '70s, increased the nation's supply of silver for coins and taxed the Philadelphia Mint's capacity for production. Pressure from silver-mine interests in Nevada influenced the opening of a special mint in Carson City to assay and mint silver locally, rather than having it shipped to Philadelphia or San Francisco. Production was inefficient, costly, and slow. By 1893 the lode was virtually depleted, and minting activities at Carson City ceased.

The Law of March 3, 1871, was a redemption measure and was passed to provide the United States Treasury with means for the disposal of millions of minor coins, which had accumulated in the hands of postmasters, merchants, and others. Small-denomination coins, because of this new law, were placed on an equal footing with silver and could be redeemed when presented in lots of $20.

There was a general revision of the coinage laws in 1873. Several years of study and debate preceded the final enactment. The legislative history of the bill occupies hundreds of pages of the *Congressional Globe,* and the result was considered by many a clumsy attempt and a failure. The law has sometimes been referred to as the "Crime of '73." One consequence of the bill, which achieved final enactment on February 12, 1873, was the elimination of the silver dollar. In its stead, the trade dollar of greater weight was provided for use in commerce with the Orient in competition with the Mexican dollar. The legal tender provision, which gave the trade dollar currency within U.S. borders, was repealed in 1876 to avoid profiteers' buying them at a reduced rate. The trade dollar was thus the only United States coin ever demonetized. (Through an oversight, the legal tender status was reinstated under the Coinage Act of 1965.)

It may be a surprise to some collectors to learn that silver dollars did not circulate to any great extent after 1803 (except in the 1840s). The coin was turned out steadily since 1840, but for various reasons (such as exportation, melting, and holding in bank vaults), the dollar was virtually an unknown coin. The Act of February 21, 1853, in effect demonetized silver and committed the country to gold as a single standard. The silver-mining interests came to realize what had occurred in the 1870s, and the ensuing quarter century of political and monetary history was filled with their voluble protests. There was a constant bitter struggle for the return to bimetallism.

From an economic point of view, the abundant supply of gold was responsible for a steady decline in gold prices worldwide. This brought about a gradual business depression in the United States, particularly in the South and Midwest. Private silver interests influenced great sections of the West for bimetallism as a remedy for the failing price level. Worldwide adoption of bimetallism might have improved economic conditions; but, had the United States alone proceeded to place its money on a double standard at the old 16-to-1 ratio, the situation would only have worsened.

Of particular importance to collectors were those features of the Law of 1873 that affected the statuses and physical properties of the individual coins. The weights of the half dollar, quarter, and dime were slightly changed, and arrows were placed at the date for the ensuing two years to indicate the differences in weight. Silver three-cent pieces, half dimes, and two-cent pieces were abolished by the act, and the manufacture of minor coins was restricted to the Philadelphia Mint.

The short-lived twenty-cent piece was authorized March 3, 1875. It was created for the Western states, where the Spanish "bit" had become equivalent to a U.S. dime. The five-cent piece did not circulate there, so when a quarter was offered for a "bit" purchase, only a dime was returned in change. The so-called double dime was frequently confused with the quarter dollar and was issued for circulation only in 1875 and 1876.

On February 28, 1878, Congress passed the Bland-Allison Act, which restored coinage of silver dollars. It required the Treasury to purchase at market price two to four million dollars' worth of silver each month and to coin it into silver dollars at a ratio to gold of 16 to 1. Proponents of "free silver" contended that with more money in circulation, workers would receive higher wages. Business leaders argued for the gold standard and against free silver because they believed that inflation would cheapen the value of money. The act was called by some "a wretched compromise."

The North and East so avoided the silver dollars that the coins did not actively circulate there and eventually found their way back to the Treasury, mostly through tax payments. Treasury Secretary Daniel Manning transferred ownership to the people and the coins were specifically earmarked as backing for Silver Certificates.

The Bland-Allison Act was repealed in 1890 and the Sherman Silver Purchase Act took its place. Under this new law, 4,500,000 ounces of silver per month could be paid for with Treasury Notes that were to be legal tender, and redeemable in gold or silver dollars coined from the bullion purchased. Important in this case was the fact that the notes were constantly being redeemed for gold that mainly was exported. The measure was actually a government subsidy for a few influential silver miners, and as such it was marked for failure. It was hastily repealed. The Bland-Allison Act and the Sherman Act added a total of 570 million silver dollars to the nation's monetary stocks.

The Gold Standard Act of 1900 again gave the country a single standard, but reaffirmed the fiction that the silver dollar was a standard coin. It still enjoyed unlimited legal-tender status, but was as much a subsidiary coin, practically speaking, as the dime, for its value in terms of standard gold, even before the gold-surrender executive order several decades later, was far below its face value.

The lapse in silver dollar coinage after 1904 and until 1921 was due to lack of silver. Legislation authorizing further metal supplies for

**The silver dollar struck from 1878 to 1921 is named for its designer, U.S. Mint engraver George T. Morgan.**

silver dollars was not forthcoming until 1918, when the Pittman Act provided silver for more dollars.

Prior to March 1933, the metallic worth of U.S. gold coins was equal to their face value. In order to encourage a steady flow of gold to the mints, the government (with the exception of the period 1853–1873) had adopted a policy of gratuitous coinage. The cost of converting gold into coin had generally been considered an expense chargeable to the government.

In practice, the Mint made fine bars for commercial use, or mint bars for coinage, at its discretion. The bars in later years were stored in vaults and Gold or Silver Certificates issued in place of the coins.

On April 5, 1933, President Franklin Roosevelt issued an order prohibiting banks from paying out gold and Gold Certificates without permission, and gold coins were thus kept for reserve purposes. The law was intended to stabilize the value of gold. In effect, it removed all gold from circulation and prevented it from being hoarded. Gold imports and newly mined domestic gold could be sold only to the government. Today, gold bullion and coins may be collected and saved by anyone, as all restrictions were removed on December 31, 1974.

Under the Coinage Act of 1965, the compositions of dimes, quarters, and half dollars were changed to eliminate or reduce the silver content of these coins because the value of silver had risen above their face values. The replacement "clad" dimes and quarters were composed of an outer layer of copper-nickel (75%-25%) bonded to an inner core of pure copper. Beginning in 1971 the half dollar and dollar compositions were changed to that of the dime and quarter. All silver clad coins have an outer layer of 80% silver bonded to an inner core of 21% silver, for a total content of 40% silver.

By the Law of September 26, 1890, changes in designs of United States coins cannot be made more often than once every 25 years without congressional approval. Since that date, there have been design changes in all denominations, and there have been many gold and silver bullion and commemorative issues. In 1999, programs were started to honor each of the individual states and territories, and various national parks, by using special designs on the reverse of the quarter. The one-cent, five-cent, and dollar coins have also undergone several design changes. These factors, and a growing awareness of the value and historical importance of older coins, are largely responsible for the ever-increasing interest in coin collecting in the United States.

## MINTS AND MINTMARKS

Mintmarks are small letters designating where coins were made. Coins struck at Philadelphia before 1979 (except 1942–1945 five-cent pieces) do not have mintmarks. Starting in 1979, a letter P was used on the dollar, and thereafter on all other denominations except the cent. Mintmark position is on the reverse of nearly all coins prior to 1965 (the cent is an exception), and on the obverse after 1967.

C—Charlotte, North Carolina (gold coins only; 1838–1861)
CC—Carson City, Nevada (gold and silver coins only; 1870–1893)
D—Dahlonega, Georgia (gold coins only; 1838–1861)
D—Denver, Colorado (1906 to date)
O—New Orleans, Louisiana (gold and silver coins only; 1838–1861; 1879–1909)
P—Philadelphia, Pennsylvania (1793 to date; P not used in early years)
S—San Francisco, California (1854 to date)
W—West Point, New York (1984 to date)

Prior to 1996 all dies for United States coins were made at the Philadelphia Mint. Some dies are now made at the Denver Mint. Dies for use at other mints are made with the appropriate mintmarks before they are shipped to those mints. Because this was a hand operation prior to 1985, the exact positioning and size of the mintmarks may vary slightly, depending on where and how deeply the punches were impressed. This also accounts for double-punched and superimposed mintmarks such as the 1938 D Over D, and D Over S, Buffalo nickels. Polishing of dies may also alter the apparent size of fine details. Occasionally the mintmark is inadvertently left off a die sent to a branch mint, as was the case with some recent Proof cents, nickels, and dimes. Similarly, some 1982 dimes without mintmarks were made as circulation strikes. The mintmark M was used on coins made in Manila for the Philippines from 1925 through 1941.

Prior to 1900, punches for mintmarks varied greatly in size. This is particularly noticeable in the 1850 to 1880 period, in which the letters range from very small to very large. An attempt to standardize sizes started in 1892 with the Barber series, but exceptions are seen in the 1892-O half dollar and 1905-O dime, both of which have normal and "microscopic" mintmarks. A more or less standard-size, small mintmark was used on all minor coins starting in 1909, and on all dimes, quarters, and halves after the Barber series was replaced in 1916. Slight variations in mintmark size occur through 1945, with notable differences in 1928, when small and large S mintmarks were used.

In recent years a single D or S punch has been used to mark all branch-mint dies. The change to the larger D for Denver coins occurred in 1933. Nickels, dimes, quarter dollars, half dollars, and dollars of 1934 exist with either the old, smaller-size mintmark or the new, larger-size D. All other denominations of 1934 and after are standard. The San Francisco mintmark was changed to a larger size during 1941 and, with the exception of the half dollar, all 1941-S coins are known with either small or large mintmarks. Halves were not changed until 1942, and the 1942-S and 1943-S pieces exist both ways. The 1945-S dime with "microscopic" S is an unexplained use of a punch originally intended for Philippine coins of 1907 through 1920. In 1979, the punches were replaced. Varieties of some 1979 coins appear with either the old- or new-shaped S or D. The S punch was again replaced in 1981 with a punch that yielded a more distinct letter.

The mintmark application technique for Proof coins was changed in 1985, and for circulation-strike production in 1990 and 1991, when the letter was applied directly to the master die rather than being hand punched on each working die. At the same time, all the mintmark letters were made much larger and clearer than those of previous years.

## QUANTITIES OF COINS STRUCK, AND MINT DATA

Collectors are cautioned that Mint reports are not always reliable for estimating the rarities of coins. In the early years of the Mint, dies of previous years were often used until they became worn or broken. It should also be emphasized that certain quantities reported, particularly for gold and silver, cover the number of coins struck and have no reference to the quantity that actually reached circulation. Many issues were deposited in the Treasury as backing for paper currency and were later melted.

Gold coins struck before August 1, 1834, are rare today, because from 1821 onward (and at times before 1821), the gold in the coins was worth more than their face values, so they were struck as bullion and traded at a premium above face value.

The quantities reported by the Mint of three-dollar gold pieces from 1873 to 1877 and half cents from 1832 to 1835 are subject to doubt.

Coinage figures shown for 1964 through 1966 are for coins bearing those dates. Some of them were struck in more than one year and at various mints, both with and without mintmarks. In recent years, mintage figures reported by the Mint have been revised several times and remain uncertain as to precise amounts.

Mintage quantities are shown adjacent to each date throughout this book. Figures shown in italic are estimates based on the most accurate information available. Exact mintage figures for most pre-1878 Proof minor coins, and most pre-1860 silver and gold coins, are not known. Listed figures are occasionally revised when new information becomes available. Proof totals are shown in parentheses and are not included with coins made for circulation.

## TODAY'S RARE-COIN MARKET

Investing in rare coins can be a rewarding experience for anyone who approaches the calling armed with the right attitude and background knowledge about this exciting field. It can just as easily become a costly mistake for anyone who attempts to profit from coins without giving serious thought to the idiosyncrasies of this unique market.

For hundreds of years, rare coins and precious metals have proven themselves to be an excellent hedge against inflation and a source of ready money in times of crisis, provided that purchases are carefully made. There is little reason to think that this will change in the future. Gone are the days when coin collecting was only a passive hobby mainly for those who would study the history and artistry of these enjoyable objects. The activity has grown to the point that speculation on the future demand for rare coins has made them a part of many investment portfolios. Some people describe it as an "industry," no longer mainly a hobby. With this change in attitude about collecting has come a measure of concern for those who purchase coins without the background or experience necessary to avoid costly mistakes.

The best advice for investing in rare coins is to use common sense. No thinking person would expect to buy a genuine diamond ring from a street peddler, or an art masterpiece at a garage sale. It is just the same with rare coins, and the more careful you are in selecting a qualified dealer and making an educated evaluation of the coins you purchase, the greater will be your chance of making a profitable investment. If you have access to the Internet, visit the sites of the Professional Numismatists Guild (the leading nationwide association of rare coin dealers, at PNGdealers.com). Many of these dealers have web sites or issue catalogs. Reviewing them will give you much basic information that can be useful.

At any given time there are many advertisements, talks given by "experts," and the like on television, in magazines, and elsewhere stating that investment in gold, silver, rare coins, and related items is the best way to preserve and increase assets. Some of these promotions are by firms that are not part of established professional numismatics. Collectors and investors should investigate the background of a potential seller before making any significant purchases.

Take your time and go slowly. As is the case with art, securities, and other investments, coins can be bought instantly, but selling them at a profit may be another thing entirely. That said, for the careful buyer the opportunities for successful collecting and investing in quality numismatic items are as great today as at any time in the past. Inexperienced buyers can purchase coins that have been graded and authenticated by third-party services (see "Third-Party Grading and Authentication" on page 10), and services such as CAC (Certified Acceptance Corporation) offer additional professional opinions as to a coin's grade. There is also more written and digitized information available for beginners than ever before. And the pricing of rare coins is very competitive in today's widespread market.

The shift in emphasis from collecting to investing on the part of many buyers in recent decades has created a dynamic market and demand for coins, resulting in more stringent grading methods and in pricing geared to the perceived rarity of coins in various levels of Mint State or Proof perfection. Coins in high grades that have been certified (professionally graded and guaranteed authentic) and encapsulated ("slabbed") may be valued significantly higher than similar coins that have not been so treated. In this book, values above several hundred dollars are generally for coins certified by a reputable grading service. In today's marketplace, "raw" or non-certified coins, or coins certified by other services, are usually valued at less, except for modern U.S. Mint and bullion products. Some television promotions, investment pitches, and offers to sell coins to the general public are priced above what a knowledgeable collector would pay. Moreover, it is important to remember that popular coin magazines and newspapers give no guarantee that items advertised in certain grades will merit those grades if submitted to a reputable grading service. "Bargains" are often anything but. A bargain offering might actually be a loss leader designed to gather collector names for future offerings. On the Internet, auction sites do not examine coins offered for sale—and countless offerings range from overgraded to counterfeit.

Always buy from an established professional dealer or firm—as you would do if you were buying a valuable painting or antique.

The editors of the *Guide Book* reiterate and emphasize that buyers must beware of overpriced or overgraded coins that simply are not worth what is charged for them. This is especially true of coins that are offered for sale online or at electronic auctions, where it often is not possible to examine the items carefully enough to determine authenticity or grade. Extreme caution is advised for anyone considering an investment in expensive coins. Investigate the person or firm with whom you are dealing. Seek professional, unbiased help with grading determinations. Satisfy yourself that the coins you select are authentic and are not priced considerably higher than is being charged by other dealers. This takes time. Do not be in a hurry. Most coins that are available today will also be available next month. Take time to track the price history and trends of coins you are most interested in purchasing.

Protecting valuable coins from deterioration and theft is another important part of investing. The best protection for keeping coins pristine is to store them in inert, airtight plastic holders (the encapsulation slabs of third-party grading services are a good example), and away from paper products, cigarette smoke, wood, natural rubber, paint, and textiles such as wool and felt. Humidity greater than 75% can also be harmful and should be avoided. When you buy coins, take physical possession of them. They should be insured and kept in a secure place such as a bank safe deposit box. There have been many frauds in which sellers of gold, rare coins, and the like have offered to hold them for the buyer and later it was found that the coins did not exist or were other than described.

It is important to keep invoices and to maintain a listing of your purchases for identification and tax purposes. Digitally capturing the coins is easily enough done with an inexpensive camera or scanner and provides proof of identification should any become lost or stolen. Note that bank storage boxes are not automatically insured. Insurance costs very little and is highly recommended.

Beyond the financial aspect, collectors and investors alike can profit by investigating the background and history of the coins they buy. Coins are a mirror of history and art, telling the story of mankind over the past 2,600 years and reflecting the economic struggles, wars, prosperity, and creativity of every major nation on earth. Most traditional numismatists acquire coins for their historical, artistic, and similar appeals—as tangible links with early America, ancient Rome and Greece, the British Empire, and other connections. Today, the investigation of the motifs, issuance, and other aspects of a coin can be done easily on the Internet. The lives of presidents, monarchs, and other figures depicted on a coin are interesting to study. Often, a single coin can lead to a pleasant hour or two of research. Building a working library is also strongly recommended. Most popular series such as Morgan and Peace silver dollars, various denominations of gold coins, commemoratives, and the like can be studied and enjoyed by reading books, with the Whitman Publishing list of titles being a fine place to start.

Purchased with care and over a period of time, nearly all specialized collections have proved to be good financial investments as well—an instance of having your cake and eating it too. More than just a few enthusiasts have called it the world's greatest hobby.

We are but the custodians of these historical relics; we must appreciate and care for them while they are in our possession. Those who treat rare coins with the consideration and respect they deserve will profit in many ways, not the least of which can be in the form of a sound financial return on their investments of time and money.

Enjoy the experience!

## CHECKING YOUR COINS FOR AUTHENTICITY

Coin collectors occasionally encounter counterfeit coins, or coins that have been altered so that they appear to be something other than what they really are. Any coin that does not seem to fit the description of similar pieces listed in this guide book should be looked upon with suspicion. Experienced coin dealers can usually tell quickly whether a coin is genuine and would never knowingly sell spurious coins to a collector. Coins found in circulation or bought from a nonprofessional source should be examined carefully.

The risk of purchasing a spurious coin can be minimized through the use of common sense and an elementary knowledge of the techniques used by counterfeiters. It is well to keep in mind that the more popular a coin is among collectors and the public, the more likely it is that counterfeits and replicas will abound. Until recently, collector coins valued at under $100 were rarely replicated because of the high cost of making such items. The same was true of counterfeits made to deceive the public. Few counterfeit coins were made because it was more profitable for the fakers to print paper money. Today, however, counterfeiters in Asia and elsewhere create fakes of a surprising variety of coins, most notably silver dollar types, but also smaller denominations.

### Replicas

Reproductions of famous and historical coins have been distributed for decades by marketing firms and souvenir vendors. These pieces are often tucked away by the original recipients as curios, and later are found in old furniture by others who believe they have discovered objects of great value. Most replicas are poorly made by the casting method, and are virtually worthless. They can sometimes be identified by a seam that runs around the edge of the piece where the two halves of the casting mold were joined together. Genuine specimens of extremely rare or valuable coins are almost never found in unlikely places.

### Counterfeits

For many centuries, counterfeiters have produced base-metal forgeries of gold and silver coins to deceive the public in the normal course of trade. These pieces are usually crudely made and easily detected on close examination. Crudely cast counterfeit copies of older coins are the most prevalent. These can usually be detected by the casting bubbles or pimples that can be seen with low-power magnification. Pieces struck from handmade dies are more deceptive, but the engravings do not match those of genuine Mint products.

More recently, as coin collecting has gained popularity and rare coin prices have risen, "numismatic" counterfeits have become more common. The majority of these are die-struck gold coin counterfeits that have been mass produced overseas since 1950. Forgeries exist of most U.S. gold coins dated between 1870 and 1933, as well as all issues of the gold dollar and three-dollar gold piece. Most of these are very well made, as they were intended to pass the close scrutiny of collectors. Few gold coins of earlier dates have been counterfeited, but false 1799 ten-dollar gold pieces and 1811 five-dollar coins have been made. Gold coins in less than Extremely Fine condition are seldom counterfeited.

Silver dollars dated 1804, Lafayette dollars, several of the low-mintage commemorative half dollars, and the 1795 half dimes have been forged in quantity. Minor-coin forgeries made in recent years are the 1909-S V.D.B., 1914-D and 1955 doubled-die Lincoln cents, 1877 Indian Head cents, 1856 Flying Eagle cents, and, on a much smaller scale, a variety of dates of half cents and large cents. Nineteenth-century copies of colonial coins are also sometimes encountered.

## Alterations

Coins are occasionally altered by the addition, removal, or change of a design feature (such as a mintmark or date digit) or by the polishing, sandblasting, acid etching, toning, or plating of the surface of a genuine piece. Changes of this sort are usually done to deceive collectors. Among U.S. gold coins, only the 1927-D double eagle is commonly found with an added mintmark. On $2.50 and $5 gold coins, 1839 through 1856, New Orleans O mintmarks have been altered to C (for Charlotte, North Carolina) in a few instances.

Over a century ago, five-dollar gold pieces were imitated by gold plating 1883 Liberty Head five-cent coins without the word CENTS on the reverse. Other coins commonly created fraudulently through alteration include the 1799 large cent and the 1909-S; 1909-S V.D.B.; 1914-D; 1922, No D; and 1943, Copper, cents. The 1913 Liberty Head nickel has been extensively replicated by alteration of 1903 and 1912 nickels. Scarce, high-grade Denver and San Francisco Buffalo nickels of the 1920s; 1916-D and 1942, 42 Over 41, dimes; 1918-S, 8 Over 7, quarters; 1932-D and -S quarters; and 1804 silver dollars have all been made by the alteration of genuine coins of other dates or mints.

## Detection

The best way to detect counterfeit coins is to compare suspected pieces with others of the same issue. Carefully check size, color, luster, weight, edge devices, and design details. Replicas generally have less detail than their genuine counterparts when studied under magnification. Modern struck counterfeits made to deceive collectors are an exception to this rule. Any questionable gold coin should be referred to an expert for verification.

Cast forgeries are usually poorly made and of incorrect weight. Base metal is often used in place of gold or silver, and the coins are lightweight and often incorrect in color and luster. Deceptive cast pieces have been made using real metal content and modern dental techniques, but these too usually vary in quality and color.

Detection of alterations sometimes involves comparative examination of the suspected areas of a coin (usually mintmarks and date digits) at magnification ranging from 10x to 40x.

Coins of exceptional rarity or value should never be purchased without a written guarantee of authenticity. Professional authentication of rare coins for a fee is available with the services offered by commercial grading services, and by some coin dealers.

# COINS FROM TREASURES AND HOARDS: A KEY TO UNDERSTANDING RARITY AND VALUE

*by Q. David Bowers*

## Elements of Rarity

In many instances, the mintage of a coin can be a determinant of its present-day rarity and value. However, across American numismatics there are many important exceptions, some very dramatic. As an introduction and example, if you peruse this issue of the *Guide Book* you will find many listings of Morgan silver dollars of 1878 through 1921 for which the mintage figure does not seem to correlate with a coin's price. For example, among such coins the 1901, of which 6,962,000 were made for circulation, is valued at $350,000 in MS-65. In the same series the 1884-CC, of which only 1,136,000 were struck, is listed at $365, or only a tiny fraction of the value of a 1901.

Why the difference? The explanation is that nearly all of the 6,962,000 dollars of 1901 were either placed into circulation at the time, and became worn, or were melted generations ago. Very few were saved by collectors, and today MS-65 coins are extreme rarities. On the other hand, of the 1,136,000 1884-CC silver dollars minted, relatively few went into circulation. Vast quantities were sealed in 1,000-coin cloth bags and put into government storage. Generations later, as coin collecting became popular, thousands were paid out by the Treasury Department. Years after that, in the early 1960s, when silver metal rose in value, there was a "run" on long-stored silver dollars, and it was learned in March 1964 that 962,638 1884-CC dollars—84.7% of the original mintage—were still in the hands of the Treasury Department!

So, these price disparities make sense. Even though the 1901 had a high mintage, few were saved, and although worn coins are common, gem MS-65 coins are rarities. In contrast, nearly all of the low-mintage 1884-CC dollars were stored by the government, and today most of them still exist, including some in MS-65 grade.

There are many other situations in which mintages are not very relevant to the availability and prices of coins today. Often a special circumstance will lead to a coin being saved in especially large quantities, later dramatically affecting the availability and value of such pieces. The following are some of those circumstances.

## Excitement of a New Design

In the panorama of American coinage, some new designs have captured the fancy of the public, who saved them in large quantities when they were released. In many other instances new designs were ignored, and coins slipped into circulation unnoticed.

In 1909, much publicity was given to the new Lincoln portrait to be used on the one-cent piece, replacing the familiar Indian Head motif. On the reverse in tiny letters were the initials, V.D.B., of the coin's designer, Victor David Brenner. The occasion was the 100th anniversary of Lincoln's birth. Coinage commenced at the Philadelphia and San Francisco mints. In total, 27,995,000 1909 V.D.B. cents were struck and 484,000 of the 1909-S V.D.B.

On August 2, 1909, the new cents were released to the public. A mad scramble ensued, and banks had to ration the number paid out to any individual, particularly in the East. Interest in the West was less intense, and fewer coins were saved. A controversy arose as to the V.D.B. initials, and some newspaper notices complained that as Brenner had been paid for his work, there was no point in giving his initials a prominent place on the coins. Never mind that artists' initials had been used on other coins for a long time. As examples, the M initial of George T. Morgan appeared on both the obverse and reverse of silver dollars from 1878 onward; Chief Engraver Charles E. Barber was memorialized by a B on the neck of Miss Liberty on dimes, quarters, and half dollars from 1892 onward; and the recent (1907 onward) double eagles bore the monogram of Augustus Saint-Gaudens prominently on the obverse. In spite of these precedents, the offending V.D.B. initials were removed, and later 1909 and 1909-S cents were made without them.

Word spread that the cents with V.D.B. would be rare, and even more were saved. Today, the 1909 V.D.B. cents are readily available in Mint State. The 1909-S V.D.B., of lower mintage and of which far fewer were saved, lists for $1,350 in MS-63.

A few years later, at the Denver Mint, 1,193,000 1914-D cents were struck. Not much attention was paid to them, and today examples are rare, with an MS-63 listing for $3,000. Years later, only 866,000 1931-S cents were made. However, at this time there was a strong and growing interest in the numismatic hobby, and the low mintage figure was widely publicized; and although the mintage of the 1931-S is lower than for the 1914-D, an MS-63 1931-S is valued at just $195.

## Other Popular First-Year Coins

Among other United States coins struck since 1792, these first-year-of-issue varieties (a partial list) were saved in large numbers and are especially plentiful today:

- **1943 zinc-coated steel cent.** The novel appearance of this coin resulted in many being saved as curiosities.
- **1883 Liberty Head nickel without CENTS.** The Mint expressed the value of this new design simply as "V," without mention of cents—not particularly unusual, as three-cent pieces of the era were simply denominated as "III." Certain people gold-plated the new nickels and passed them off as five-dollar gold coins of similar diameter. Soon, the Mint added CENTS. News accounts were printed that the "mistake" coins without CENTS would be recalled and would become very rare. So many were saved that today this variety is the most plentiful in Mint State of any Liberty Head nickel in the entire series from 1883 to 1913.
- **1913 Buffalo nickel.** These were saved in large quantities. Today more Mint State coins of this year exist than for any other issue of the next 15 years.
- **1837 Liberty Seated, No Stars, half dime.** Several thousand or more were saved, a large number for a half dime of the era. Apparently, their cameo-like appearance made them attractive curiosities at the time, as was also true of dimes in 1837.
- **1837 Liberty Seated, No Stars, dime.** Somewhat over a thousand were saved, a large number for a dime of the era.
- **1916 "Mercury" dime.** Quantities were saved of the 1916 and 1916-S, the first year of issue. However, for some reason the low-mintage 1916-D was generally overlooked and today is very rare in Mint State.
- **1932 Washington quarter.** At the Philadelphia Mint, 5,504,000 were minted, and it is likely that several hundred thousand were saved, making them plentiful today. The 1932-D quarter was struck to the extent of 436,800, but for some reason was overlooked by the public, with the result that Mint State coins are rare today. On the other hand, of the 408,000 1932-S quarters struck, thousands were saved. Today, Mint State 1932-S quarters are at least 10 to 20 times more readily available than are equivalent examples of the higher-mintage 1932-D.
- **1999–2008 State quarters.** From 1999 to 2008, five different quarter dollar designs were produced each year, with motifs observing the states in the order that they joined the Union. These coins were highly publicized and collected.
- **1964 Kennedy half dollar.** The popularity of the assassinated president was such that although hundreds of millions were minted, it is likely that many were saved

as souvenirs both at home and abroad. This was also the last year of the 90% silver-content half dollar made for circulation, further increasing its popularity.

- **2000 Sacagawea "golden dollar."** These coins, intended to be a popular, wear-resistant substitute for paper dollars, were launched with much fanfare in 2000, and many were saved by the public. However, the coin did not catch on for general use in commerce. Later issues have been made for sale to collectors, not for circulation.
- **MCMVII (1907) High-Relief gold twenty-dollar coin.** Although only about 12,000 were minted, at least 6,000 survive today, mostly in Mint State. Released in December 1907, the coin, by famous sculptor Augustus Saint-Gaudens, created a sensation, and soon the coins were selling for $30 each. Today, Mint State coins are plentiful, but as the demand for them is extremely strong, choice specimens sell for strong prices. An MS-63 coin lists for $24,000.
- **1892 and 1893 World's Columbian Exposition commemorative half dollars.** These, the first U.S. commemorative half dollars, were widely publicized, and hundreds of thousands were saved. Today they are very common in used condition.

## Coins Few People Noticed

In contrast to the above, most coins of new designs attracted no particular notice, and examples were not saved in unusual quantities. In sharp contrast to the ultra-popular Kennedy half dollar of 1964, its predecessor design, the Franklin half dollar (launched in 1948), generated very little interest, and even numismatists generally ignored them—perhaps preferring the old Liberty Walking design that had been a favorite.

Here are some first-year-of-issue coins that were not noticed in their own time, for which specimens range from scarce to rare in Mint State today:

- **1793 cent and half cent.** Though popular today, there is no known instance in which a numismatist or museum in 1793 deliberately saved pieces as souvenirs.
- **1794–1795 half dime, half dollar, and silver dollar.** The Flowing Hair coins are highly desired today, but again there is no record of any having been deliberately saved.
- **1807 and related Capped Bust coinages.** The Capped Bust and related designs of John Reich, assistant engraver at the Mint, were first used in 1807 on the silver half dollar and gold five-dollar piece, and later on other denominations. Today these are extremely popular with collectors, but in their time few were saved in Mint State.
- **1840 Liberty Seated dollar.** Specimens are very scarce in Mint State today and are virtually unknown in gem preservation.
- **1892 Barber dime, quarter dollar, and half dollar.** In 1892 the new Liberty Head design by Charles E. Barber replaced the long-lived Liberty Seated motif. The new coins received bad press, and public interest was focused on commemorative half dollars for the World's Columbian Exposition. Few of the Barber coins were saved.
- **1938 Jefferson nickel.** The numismatic hobby was dynamic at the time, but the new design attracted little notice. The market was depressed by the burst bubble of the 1935 and 1936 commemorative craze, making coin investments less popular.

## The 1962–1964 Treasury Release

The Bland-Allison Act of February 28, 1878, a political boondoggle passed to accommodate silver-mining interests in the West, mandated that the Treasury Department buy millions of ounces of silver each year and convert it to silver dollars. At the time, the world price of silver bullion was dropping, and there were economic difficulties in the mining states. From 1878 to 1904 and again in 1921, silver dollars of the Morgan design were minted under this legislation and subsequent acts, to the extent of

656,989,387 pieces. From 1921 to 1928, and 1934–1935, silver dollars of the Peace design were produced in the amount of 190,577,279 pieces.

Although silver dollars were used in commerce in certain areas of the West, paper currency by and large served the needs of trade and exchange. As these hundreds of millions of newly minted dollars were not needed, most were put up in 1,000-coin canvas bags and stored in Treasury vaults. In 1918, under terms of the Pittman Act, 270,232,722 Morgan dollars were melted. At the time, the market for silver was temporarily strong, and there was a call for bullion to ship to India to shore up confidence in Britain's wartime government. No accounting was kept of the dates and mints involved in the destruction. Just the quantities were recorded (this procedure being typical when the Treasury melted old coins). However, hundreds of millions remained.

Now and again there was a call for silver dollars for circulation, especially in the West; and in the East and Midwest there was a modest demand for pieces for use as holiday and other gifts; in such instances many were paid out. The earlier example of the high-mintage 1901 dollar being rare in Mint State, as most were circulated, is reflective of this. Other coins were stored, such as the aforementioned low-mintage 1884-CC, of which 84.7% were still in the hands of the Treasury as late as 1964! At this time the Treasury decided to hold back bags that were marked as having Carson City dollars, although in records of storage no account was made of them earlier.

Beginning in a significant way in the 1950s, silver dollars became very popular with numismatists. The rarest of all Morgan silver dollars by 1962 was considered to be the 1903-O. In the *Guide Book,* an Uncirculated coin listed for $1,500, the highest price for any variety. Experts estimated that fewer than a dozen Mint State coins existed in all of numismatics. It was presumed that most had been melted in 1918 under the Pittman Act.

Then this—in November 1962, during the normal payout of silver dollars as gifts for the holiday season, some long-sealed bags of coins were taken from a Philadelphia Mint vault that had remained under seal since 1929. It was soon found that brilliant 1903-O dollars were among these! A treasure hunt ensued, and hundreds of thousands of these former rarities were found. The rush was on!

From then until March 1964, hundreds of millions of Morgan and Peace dollars were emptied from government and bank storage. At one time a long line of people, some with wheelbarrows, formed outside of the Treasury Building in Washington, D.C., to obtain bags of dollars. Finally, only about three million coins remained, mostly the aforementioned Carson City issues, which the Treasury decided to hold back. These were later sold at strong premiums in a series of auctions held by the General Services Administration.

In the meantime, Morgan and Peace dollars became very large and important sections of the coin hobby, as they remain today. However, as can be seen, the combined elements of some coins' having been melted in 1918, others having been placed into circulation generations ago, and still others existing in Mint State from long-stored hoards, results in silver dollar prices that often bear little relation to mintage figures.

## Other Famous Hoards

While the great Treasury release of 1962 through 1964 is the most famous of all hoards, quite a few others have attracted interest and attention over the years.

- **Castine Hoard of Early Silver Coins (discovered in the 1840s).** From November 1840 through April 1841, Captain Stephen Grindle and his son Samuel unearthed many silver coins on their farm on the Bagaduce River about six miles from the harbor of Castine, Maine. Between 500 and 2,000 pieces were buried in 1690 (the latest date observed) or soon afterward. Most pieces were foreign silver coins, but dozens of Massachusetts Pine Tree shillings and related silver coins were found. This hoard stands today as one of the most famous in American history.

- **Bank of New York Hoard (1856).** Circa 1856, a keg containing several thousand 1787 Fugio copper cents was found at the Bank of New York at 44 Wall Street. Each was in Mint State, most with brown toning. For many years these were given out as souvenirs and keepsakes to clients. By 1948, when numismatist Damon G. Douglas examined them, there were 1,641 remaining. Today, many remain at the bank and are appreciated for their history and value.
- **Nichols Find of Copper Cents (by 1859).** In the annals of American numismatics, one of the most famous hoards is the so-called Nichols Find, consisting of 1796 and 1797 copper cents, Mint State, perhaps about 1,000 in total. These were distributed in the late 1850s by David Nichols. All were gone as of 1863, by which time they were worth $3 to $4 each, or less than a thousandth of their present-day value.
- **Randall Hoard of Copper Cents (1860s).** Sometime soon after the Civil War, a wooden keg filled with as-new copper cents was located, said to have been beneath an old railroad platform in Georgia. Revealed were thousands of coins dated 1816 to 1820, with the 1818 and 1820 being the most numerous. Today, the Randall hoard accounts for most known Mint State examples of these particular dates.
- **Colonel Cohen Hoard of 1773 Virginia Halfpennies (by the 1870s).** Sometime in the 1870s or earlier, Colonel Mendes I. Cohen, a Baltimore numismatist, obtained a cache of at least 2,200 Uncirculated specimens of the 1773 Virginia halfpenny. These passed through several hands, and many pieces were dispersed along the way. As a result, today these are the only colonial (pre-1776) American coins that can be easily obtained in Mint State.
- **Exeter Hoard of Massachusetts Silver (1876).** During the excavation of a cellar near the railroad station in Exeter, New Hampshire, a group of 30 to 40 Massachusetts silver shillings was found in the sand, amid the remains of what seemed to be a wooden box. All bore the date 1652 and were of the Pine Tree and Oak Tree types, plus, possibly, a rare Willow Tree shilling.
- **Economite Treasure (1878).** In 1878 a remarkable hoard of silver coins was found in a subterranean storage area at Economy, Pennsylvania, in a building erected years earlier by the Harmony Society, a utopian work-share community. The March 1881 issue of the *Coin Collector's Journal* gave this inventory: Quarter dollars: 1818 through 1828, 400 pieces. Half dollars: 1794, 150; 1795, 650; 1796, 2; 1797, 1; 1801, 300; 1802, 200; 1803, 300; 1805 Over 04, 25; 1805, 600; 1806, 1,500; 1807, 2,000; 1815, 100. Common half dollars: 1808 through 1836, 111,356. Silver dollars: 1794, 1; 1795, 800; 1796, 125; 1797, 80; 1798 Small Eagle reverse, 30; 1798 Large Eagle reverse, 560; 1799 5 stars facing, 12; 1799, 1,250; 1800, 250; 1801, 1802, and 1803, 600. Foreign silver (French, Spanish, and Spanish-American), total face value: $12,600. Total face value of the hoard: $75,000.00. Other information indicates that most of the coins had been taken from circulation and showed different degrees of wear.
- **Hoard of Miser Aaron White (before 1888).** Aaron White, a Connecticut attorney, distrusted paper money, going so far as to issue a token inscribed NEVER KEEP A PAPER DOLLAR IN YOUR POCKET TILL TOMORROW. He had a passion for saving coins, accumulating more than 100,000 pieces. After his death the coins were moved to a warehouse, then placed in the hands of dealer Édouard Frossard, who sold most of them privately and others by auction on July 20, 1888, billing them as "18,000 American and foreign copper coins and tokens selected from the Aaron White hoard." An estimate of the White hoard before its dispersal, made by Benjamin P. Wright, included: "250 colonial and state copper coins, 60,000 copper

large cents (which were mainly 'rusted' and spotted; 5,000 of the nicest ones were picked out and sold for 2¢ each), 60,000 copper-nickel Flying Eagle and Indian cents (apparently most dated 1862 and 1863), 5,000 bronze two-cent pieces, 200 half dollars, 100 silver dollars, 350 gold dollars, and 20,000 to 30,000 foreign copper coins."

- **Collins Find of 1828 Half Cents (1894).** Benjamin H. Collins, a Washington, D.C., numismatist, acquired a bag of 1828, 13 Stars, half cents. Around 1,000 coins were involved, all bright Uncirculated. By the early 1950s all but a few hundred had been distributed in the marketplace, and by now it is likely that all have individual owners.
- **Chapman Hoard of 1806 Half Cents (1906).** About 1906, Philadelphia dealer Henry Chapman acquired a hoard of 1806 half cents. It is estimated that a couple hundred or so coins were involved. Most or all had much of their original mint red color, with toning to brown, and with light striking at the upper part of the wreath.
- **Baltimore Find (1934).** One of the most storied hoards in American numismatics is this cache of at least 3,558 gold coins, all dated before 1857. On August 31, 1934, two young boys playing in the cellar of a rented house at 132 South Eden Street, Baltimore, found these coins hidden in a wall. More were found later in the same location. On May 2, 1935, many of the coins were sold at auction, though others had been sold quietly, some unofficially. This hoard included many choice and gem coins of the 1850s.
- **New Orleans Bank Find (1982).** A few minutes past noon, on October 29, 1982, a bulldozer unearthed a cache of long-hidden silver coins, believed to have been stored in three wooden boxes in the early 1840s. Though mostly Spanish-American issues, hundreds of United States coins, including 1840-O and 1841-O Liberty Seated quarters, were also found. A scrabble in the dirt and mud ensued, as bank employees and bystanders scrambled to find treasure. The latest dated coin found was from 1842. This must have been a secret reserve of some long-forgotten merchant or bank.
- **Wells-Fargo Hoard of 1908 $20 (1990s).** In the 1990s, dealer Ron Gillio purchased a hoard of 19,900 1908 No Motto double eagles. These were stored in a Wells Fargo Bank branch, giving the cache its name. All were Mint State, and many were of choice and gem quality. They were dispersed in the market over a period of several years.
- **Gold coins from abroad (turn of the 21st century).** In the late 1900s and early 2000s, some exciting finds of Mint State double eagles were made in foreign banks: high-grade examples of some Carson City issues in the Liberty Head series and hundreds of scarce-mintmark varieties dated after 1923. As is often the case with hoards, pieces filtered into the market without any publicity or an accounting of varieties found.

## Sunken Treasure

Throughout American history, tens of thousands of ships have been lost at sea and on inland waters. Only a handful of these vessels were reported as having had significant quantities of coins aboard. In recent decades, numismatists have been front-row center as wrecks from several sidewheel steamers lost in the 1850s and 1860s have yielded rare coins.

The SS *New York* was launched in 1837, carrying passengers between New York City and Charleston, South Carolina. The steamer was carrying $30,000 or more in money when she encountered an unexpected hurricane in the Gulf of Mexico on September 5, 1846. Captain John D. Phillips ordered the anchor dropped, hoping to ride out the storm. The wind and waves increased, however, and for two days those aboard watched as the rigging and other parts of the ship were torn apart. On September 7 the storm prevailed and the *New York* was overwhelmed, sinking into water 60 feet deep. An estimated 17 people—about one third of the passengers and crew—lost their lives. Decades later, in 2006 and 2007, treasure seekers recovered more than 2,000 silver coins and several hundred gold coins from the shipwreck. Most of the silver was heavily etched from exposure to the salt water, but certain of the gold coins were in high grades, including some of the finest known examples of their date and mint.

Eight years after the loss of the *New York*, the SS *Yankee Blade* was off the coast of Santa Barbara, California, steaming at full speed in a heavy fog. Captain Henry T. Randall believed the ship was in deep water far out to sea, and he was trying to establish a speed record. In fact the steamer was amid the rockbound Channel Islands, and in the fog she smashed onto a rock and got hung up. The date was October 1, 1854. On board was some $152,000 in coins consigned by a banking house, plus other gold, and about 900 passengers and crew. Most of them escaped, but in the ensuing confusion before the *Yankee Blade* sank, between 17 and 50 lost their lives. Over the years most of the coins appear to have been recovered, under circumstances largely unknown. In 1948 the hull was found again and divers visited the wreck. Circa 1977 more recoveries were yielded, including 200 to 250 1854-S double eagles. All showed microscopic granularity, possibly from the action of sea-bottom sand, and all had die cracks on the reverse. Little in the way of facts has ever reached print.

The wreck and recovery of the SS *Central America* was much better documented. The steamer was lost on September 12, 1857, carrying about $2,600,000 in gold treasure, heading from Havana, Cuba, to New York City. A monster hurricane engulfed the ship on the 10th and 11th; Captain William Lewis Herndon enlisted the aid of male passengers to bail water, but their efforts proved futile. The ship was swamped, and the captain signaled distress. The nearby brig *Marine* approached and nearly all of the women and children were transferred over, along with some crew members, before the *Central America* went down, with Captain Herndon standing on the paddle box. The steamer ultimately settled 7,200 feet deep, and some 435 lives were lost. The wreck was found in 1987 and over time more than $150 million worth of treasure was brought to the surface. This included more than 6,500 mint-fresh 1857-S double eagles, hundreds of gold ingots (including one weighing 80 pounds), and other coins. Most of these were distributed beginning in 1999. The scientists and others who found the treasure have made many numismatic appearances.

In the 1990s another sidewheel steamer was found: the SS *Brother Jonathan*, lost with few survivors as she attempted to return to safe harbor in Crescent City, California, after hitting stormy weather on her way north to Oregon (January 30, 1865). More than 1,000 gold coins were recovered from the wreck, including many Mint State 1865-S double eagles. Detailed files and photographs recorded every step of the recovery.

In 2003 another 1865 shipwreck was located: that of the SS *Republic*, lost off the coast of Georgia while en route from New York City to New Orleans, October 25, just months after the Civil War ended. The steamer sank in a hurricane along with a reported $400,000 in silver and gold. Recovery efforts brought up 51,000 coins and 14,000 other artifacts (bottles, ceramics, personal items, etc.). The coins included 1,400 eagles dating from 1838 to 1865, and thousands of double eagles from the 1850s and 1860s; plus more than 180 different examples of Liberty Seated half dollars, including five 1861-O die combinations attributed to Confederate control of the New Orleans Mint. The most valuable single coin was a Mint State 1854-O $20 then valued at more than $500,000.

Shipwrecks continue to be found even today, and the hobby community eagerly awaits news of coins and treasure found amidst their watery resting places. More stories can be found in *Lost and Found Coin Hoards and Treasures* (Bowers).

## FOREIGN COINS IN THE COLONIES

Money had a rich history in America prior to the advent of the United States' national coinage in 1793. When coins tumbled off the presses from the first Philadelphia Mint the country was much more accustomed to coins from other lands. Prior to 1652 there was no local coinage and the only money in circulation was whatever came here from Europe through trade or travel. People were content to use currency, both old and new, whose value was based more on the metal content than on the issuer's reliability. Foreign money in America during the colonial period had become so embedded that it continued to be accepted as legal tender until discontinued by the Coinage Act of February 21, 1857. Coins of this era are so fundamental to American numismatics that every collection should include at least a sampling.

From the very beginning of commerce in America "hard money" was needed for trade with overseas nations. The largest quantity of coinage consisted of English crowns, shillings, and pence, and Spanish and Spanish-American silver pieces of eight, all of which circulated throughout colonial settlements until being sent back to England for critically needed supplies. Additional quantities of coins came from trading furs, lumber, and other exports that provided a limited but much needed supply of hard currency. Of equal importance to commerce were similar coins of other European countries. The large silver Dutch *leeuwendaalder* (Lyon or Lion dollar) and French *écu* saw extensive circulation, as did the Brazilian gold *peças*. Some New York bills of 1709 were even denominated in Lyon dollars. Distinguishing between the relative values of the multitude of different foreign currencies was not a simple task. To facilitate conversions, books and tables showed comparison prices for each currency.

The popular Spanish-American silver eight reales, Pillar dollar, or piece of eight, which was a radical departure from denominations in terms of English pounds, shillings, and pence, became a model for the American silver dollar, and its fractional parts morphed into the half-dollar and quarter-dollar coins that are now considered decimal fractions of the dollar. The American quarter dollar, which was similar in size and value to the Spanish two-real coin, took on the nickname "two bits"—a moniker that remains today. Similarly, the American one-cent coin has never totally lost its association with the English penny, and is still called that by anyone indifferent to numismatic accuracy.

Coins, tokens, paper money, and promissory notes were not the only media of exchange used during the early formation of the country. Many day-to-day transactions were carried on by barter and credit. Mixed into this financial morass were local trade items such as native wampum, hides, household goods, and tools. Records were kept in the traditional English pounds, shillings, and pence, but debts and taxes were paid in corn, beaver pelts, or money—money being whatever foreign coins were available. The terms "country pay" or "corn" referred to a number of different kinds of grain or even peas. Standard exchange rates were established and country pay was lawfully received at the colonial treasury for taxes.

Beyond these pre-federal considerations are the many kinds of private and state issues of coins and tokens that permeate the colonial period from 1616 to 1776. These are items that catch the attention and imagination of everyone interested in the history and development of early America. Yet, despite their enormous historical importance, forming a basic collection of such items is not nearly as daunting as one might expect.

The coins and tokens described in the next three sections of this book are fundamentally a major-type listing of the metallic money used throughout the pre-federal period. Many collectors use this as a guide to forming a basic set of these pieces. It is not encyclopedic in its scope. Beyond the basic types are numerous sub-varieties of some of the issues, and a wider range of European coins. Some collectors aim for the finest possible condition, while others find great enjoyment in pieces that saw actual circulation and use during the formative days of the country. There are no rules about how or what to collect other than to enjoy owning a genuine piece of early American history.

## Spanish-American Coinage of the New World

Values shown for these silver coins are for the most common dates and mintmarked pieces of each issue. Similar pieces were struck at Spanish-American mints in Bolivia, Chile, Colombia, Guatemala, Mexico, Panama, Peru, and Santo Domingo.

### *Cob Coinage – King Philip II (1556–1598) to King Charles III (1760–1772)*

**1 real cob of Mexico from the reign of Philip III**

**1668 2 reales cob struck in Potosi, from the reign of Charles II**

| | VG | F | VF | EF |
|---|---|---|---|---|
| Cob Type, 1/2 Real (1556–1773) | $40 | $90 | $150 | $400 |
| Cob Type, 1 Real (1556–1773) | 60 | 125 | 200 | 450 |
| Cob Type, 2 Reales (1556–1773) | 90 | 175 | 300 | 625 |
| Cob Type, 4 Reales (1556–1773) | 125 | 300 | 450 | 950 |
| Cob Type, 8 Reales (1556–1773) | 150 | 300 | 500 | 900 |

Values are for coins with partial or missing dates. Fully dated coins are valued much higher. Some cobs were also issued beyond these dates and until as late as 1773 in Bolivia.

### *Pillar Type – King Philip V (1732–1747), King Ferdinand VI (1747–1760), and King Charles III (1760–1772)*

**1739 4 reales, Pillar type, from the reign of Philip V**

**1761 2 reales "pistareen" from the reign of Charles III**

| | VG | F | VF | EF |
|---|---|---|---|---|
| Pillar Type, 1/2 Real (1732–1772) | $30 | $50 | $100 | $175 |
| Pillar Type, 1 Real (1732–1772) | 40 | 90 | 125 | 200 |
| Pillar Type, 2 Reales (1732–1772) | 50 | 100 | 150 | 300 |
| Pillar Type, 4 Reales (1732–1772) | 150 | 300 | 500 | 900 |
| Pillar Type, 8 Reales (1732–1772) | 120 | 225 | 450 | 700 |
| Spanish 2 Reales "pistareen" (1716–1771) | 30 | 50 | 125 | 200 |

### *Bust Type – King Charles III (1772–1789), King Charles IV (1789–1808), and King Ferdinand VII (1808–1825)*

**1807 8 reales Bust dollar from the reign of Charles IV**

| | VG | F | VF | EF |
|---|---|---|---|---|
| Bust Type, 1/2 Real (1772–1825) | $15 | $25 | $40 | $110 |
| Bust Type, 1 Real (1772–1825) | 20 | 35 | 60 | 125 |
| Bust Type, 2 Reales (1772–1825) | 35 | 60 | 100 | 200 |
| Bust Type, 4 Reales (1772–1825) | 100 | 250 | 475 | 800 |
| Bust Type, 8 Reales (1772–1825) | 50 | 75 | 100 | 220 |

The New World began its first coinage in 1536 in Mexico City. By 1732 the first round coins were made and the *columnario*, or Pillar coinage, became the coin of trade internationally. In 1772 the Bust dollars with the effigy of the king of Spain were placed in circulation. These coins and the Republican style of later Latin American countries circulated legally in the United States until 1857.

Parallel issues of Spanish-American gold coins were made during this period. They saw extensive use for international trade and somewhat lesser use in domestic transactions in America. The Spanish silver pistareen was also a popular and convenient coin in circulation.

## Typical World Coinage Used in Colonial America

### *Netherlands Silver Coinage, 1601–1693*

**1616 Leeuwendaalder**

| | VG | F | VF | EF |
|---|---|---|---|---|
| Netherlands, 1/2 Leeuwendaalder (1601–1653) | $100 | $250 | $500 | $1,000 |
| Netherlands, Leeuwendaalder "Lion Dollar" (1601–1693) | 70 | 150 | 275 | 600 |

## *French Silver Coinage of King Louis XV (1715–1774) and King Louis XVI (1774–1792)*

**1791 écu from the reign of Louis XVI**

| | VG | F | VF | EF |
|---|---|---|---|---|
| France, 1/2 Écu (1715–1792) . . . . . . . . . . . . . . . . . . . . . . . . . . . . . . . | $25 | $80 | $150 | $350 |
| France, Écu (1715–1792) . . . . . . . . . . . . . . . . . . . . . . . . . . . . . . . . . . | 50 | 100 | 225 | 400 |

See additional listings of silver, billon, and copper French coins authorized for use in North America on pages 53–55.

## *British Silver Coinage of King Charles I (1625–1649) to King George III (1760–1820)*

**1639 6 pence from the reign of Charles I**

**1787 Shilling from the reign of George III**

| | VG | F | VF | EF |
|---|---|---|---|---|
| England, Threepence (1625–1786) . . . . . . . . . . . . . . . . . . . . . . . . . . . | $15 | $25 | $60 | $100 |
| England, Sixpence (1625–1787) . . . . . . . . . . . . . . . . . . . . . . . . . . . . | 25 | 40 | 90 | 120 |
| England, Shilling (1625–1787). . . . . . . . . . . . . . . . . . . . . . . . . . . . . . | 35 | 60 | 125 | 225 |
| England, Half Crown (1625–1750). . . . . . . . . . . . . . . . . . . . . . . . . . . . | 90 | 160 | 350 | 625 |
| England, Crown (1625–1730) . . . . . . . . . . . . . . . . . . . . . . . . . . . . . . | 225 | 450 | 800 | 1,200 |

English copper coins and their imitations circulated extensively in early America and are described on pages 69–71.

Other items frequently used as money in early America included cut fractions of various silver coins. These were cut by private individuals. The quarter 8-reales coin was "two bits." Worn and cut portions of coins usually passed for change according to their weight.

# BRITISH NEW WORLD ISSUES

## Sommer Islands (Bermuda)

This coinage, the first struck for the English colonies in the New World, was issued circa 1616. The coins were known as *Hogge Money* or *Hoggies*.

The pieces were made of brass or copper, lightly silvered, in four denominations: shilling, sixpence, threepence, and twopence, each indicated by Roman numerals. The hog is the main device and appears on the obverse side of each. SOMMER ISLANDS is inscribed within beaded circles on the larger denominations. The reverse shows a full-rigged galleon with the flag of St. George on each of four masts. Many examples of these coins show signs of oxidation and pitting.

The islands were named for Sir George Sommers, who was shipwrecked there in 1609 while en route to the Virginia plantations. Shakespeare's *Tempest* was possibly based on this incident.

The Bermuda Islands, as they are known today, were named for Juan de Bermúdez, who is believed to have stopped there in 1515. A few hogs that he carried for delivery to the West Indies were left behind. When Sommers and his party arrived, the islands were overrun with the animals, which served as a welcome source of food.

Twopence — Threepence

Sixpence Obverse — Large Portholes Reverse — Small Portholes Reverse

Shilling Obverse — Small Sail Reverse — Large Sail Reverse

| | AG | G | VG | F | VF | EF |
|---|---|---|---|---|---|---|
| Twopence, Large Star Between Legs | $4,500 | $10,000 | $15,000 | $17,500 | $35,000 | $65,000 |
| Twopence, Small Star Between Legs | 4,500 | 10,000 | 15,000 | 20,000 | 40,000 | 65,000 |
| Threepence | — | — | 35,000 | 65,000 | 90,000 | — |
| Sixpence, Small Portholes | 3,500 | 7,500 | 10,000 | 20,000 | 30,000 | 50,000 |
| Sixpence, Large Portholes | 3,750 | 10,000 | 15,000 | 20,000 | 55,000 | 80,000 |
| Shilling, Small Sail | 4,750 | 6,500 | 10,000 | 30,000 | 55,000 | 75,000 |
| Shilling, Large Sail | 8,000 | 15,000 | 40,000 | 70,000 | 90,000 | — |

## Massachusetts

### *"New England" Coinage (1652)*

The earliest authorized medium of exchange in the New England settlements was wampum. The General Court of Massachusetts in 1637 ordered "that wampamege should passe at 6 a penny for any sume under 12 d." Wampum consisted of shells of various colors, ground to the size of kernels of corn. A hole was drilled through each piece so it could be strung on a leather thong for convenience and adornment.

Corn, pelts, and bullets were frequently used in lieu of coins, which were rarely available. Silver and gold coins brought over from England, Holland, and other countries tended to flow back across the Atlantic to purchase needed supplies. The colonists, thus left to their own resources, traded with the friendly Native Americans in kind. In 1661 the law making wampum legal tender was repealed.

Agitation for a standard coinage reached its height in 1651. England, recovering from a civil war between the Puritans and Royalists, ignored the colonists, who took matters into their own hands in 1652.

The Massachusetts General Court in 1652 ordered the first metallic currency—the New England silver threepence, sixpence, and shilling—to be struck in the English Americas (the Spaniards had established a mint in Mexico City in 1535). Silver bullion was procured principally from the West Indies. The mint was located in Boston, and John Hull was appointed mintmaster; his assistant was Robert Sanderson (or Saunderson). At first, Hull received as compensation one shilling threepence for every 20 shillings coined. This fee was adjusted several times during his term as mintmaster.

NE Threepence

NE Sixpence

NE Shilling

*Early American coins in conditions better than those listed are rare and are consequently valued much higher.*

| | G | VG | F | VF | EF | AU |
|---|---|---|---|---|---|---|
| NE Threepence *(unique)* | | | | — | | |
| NE Sixpence *(8 known)* | $55,000 | $90,000 | $135,000 | $250,000 | $350,000 | $650,000 |
| NE Shilling | 55,000 | 75,000 | 100,000 | 125,000 | 160,000 | 250,000 |
| *$152,750, EF-45, Stack's Bowers auction, March 2015* | | | | | | |

### *Willow Tree Coinage (1653–1660)*

The simplicity of the designs on the NE coins invited counterfeiting and clipping of the edges. Therefore, they were soon replaced by the Willow, Oak, and Pine Tree series. The Willow Tree coins were struck from 1653 to 1660, the Oak Trees from 1660 to 1667, and the Pine Trees from 1667 to 1682. All of them (with the exception of the Oak Tree twopence) bore the date 1652, which gives them the appearance of having been struck when Cromwell was in power, after the English civil war. The coinage was abandoned in 1682; a proposal to renew coinage in 1686 was rejected by the General Court.

These pieces, like all early American coins, were produced from handmade dies that are often individually distinctive. The great number of die varieties that can be found and identified are of interest to collectors who value each according to individual rarity. Values shown for type coins in this guide are for the most common die variety.

Threepence

Sixpence

Shilling

| | G | VG | F | VF | EF |
|---|---|---|---|---|---|
| 1652 Willow Tree Threepence *(3 known)*. . . . . . . . . . . . . . . | | — | — | — | |
| *$587,500, VF, Stack's Bowers auction, March 2015* | | | | | |
| 1652 Willow Tree Sixpence *(14 known)*. . . . . . . . . . . . . . . . | $17,500 | $30,000 | $60,000 | $100,000 | $200,000 |
| *$282,000, AU-58, Stack's Bowers auction, March 2015* | | | | | |
| 1652 Willow Tree Shilling . . . . . . . . . . . . . . . . . . . . . . . . . | 17,500 | 30,000 | 55,000 | 100,000 | 150,000 |
| *$164,500, MS-62, Stack's Bowers auction, March 2015* | | | | | |

## *Oak Tree Coinage (1660–1667)*

Twopence

Threepence

Sixpence

Shilling

| | G | VG | F | VF | EF | AU | Unc. |
|---|---|---|---|---|---|---|---|
| 1662 Oak Tree Twopence, Small 2 . . . . . . . . . . . . . | $600 | $850 | $1,200 | $2,700 | $4,500 | $6,500 | $10,000 |
| 1662 Oak Tree Twopence, Large 2 . . . . . . . . . . . . . | 600 | 850 | 1,200 | 2,700 | 4,500 | 6,500 | 10,000 |
| 1652 Oak Tree Threepence, No IN on Obverse . . . . | 700 | 1,100 | 2,500 | 5,000 | 10,000 | 17,500 | 30,000 |
| 1652 Oak Tree Threepence, IN on Obverse . . . . . . . | 650 | 1,100 | 2,800 | 6,500 | 12,000 | 18,000 | 45,000 |

| | G | VG | F | VF | EF | AU | Unc. |
|---|---|---|---|---|---|---|---|
| 1652 Oak Tree Sixpence, IN on Reverse | $800 | $1,300 | $2,500 | $6,000 | $10,000 | $15,000 | $35,000 |
| 1652 Oak Tree Sixpence, IN on Obverse | 800 | 1,300 | 3,000 | 6,000 | 10,000 | 14,000 | 32,000 |
| 1652 Oak Tree Shilling, IN at Left . . . . . | 700 | 1,200 | 2,200 | 6,000 | 9,000 | 12,500 | 25,000 |
| 1652 Oak Tree Shilling, IN at Bottom. . . | 750 | 1,250 | 2,500 | 6,000 | 9,000 | 13,500 | 27,500 |
| 1652 Oak Tree Shilling, ANDO. . . . . . . . | 750 | 1,500 | 3,000 | 6,500 | 10,000 | 15,000 | 30,000 |
| 1652 Oak Tree Shilling, Spiny Tree . . . . | 750 | 1,250 | 2,500 | 5,500 | 9,000 | 15,000 | 30,000 |

### *Pine Tree Coinage (1667–1682)*

The first Pine Tree coins were minted on the same size planchets as the Oak Tree pieces. Subsequent issues of the shilling were narrower and thicker to conform to the style of English coins. Large Planchet shillings ranged from 27 to 31 mm in diameter; Small Planchet shillings ranged from 22 to 26 mm in diameter.

Threepence Sixpence

Shilling, Large Planchet (1667–1674) Shilling, Small Planchet (1675–1682)

| | G | VG | F | VF | EF | AU | Unc. |
|---|---|---|---|---|---|---|---|
| 1652 Threepence, Pellets at Trunk . . . . . . | $600 | $950 | $1,600 | $2,500 | $4,500 | $7,500 | $17,000 |
| 1652 Threepence, Without Pellets . . . . . . . | 600 | 950 | 1,500 | 2,500 | 4,500 | 7,500 | 17,000 |
| 1652 Sixpence, Pellets at Trunk . . . . . . . . | 750 | 925 | 1,750 | 3,000 | 5,000 | 8,000 | 18,000 |
| 1652 Sixpence, Without Pellets . . . . . . . . . | 900 | 1,350 | 2,500 | 4,500 | 6,000 | 10,000 | 22,000 |
| 1652 Shilling, Large Planchet (27–31 mm) | | | | | | | |
| Pellets at Trunk. . . . . . . . . . . . . . . . . . . | 850 | 1,250 | 2,500 | 4,500 | 7,000 | 11,000 | 22,000 |
| Without Pellets at Trunk . . . . . . . . . . . . | 700 | 1,000 | 2,500 | 4,000 | 6,500 | 10,500 | 22,000 |
| No H in MASATUSETS . . . . . . . . . . . . . . | 800 | 1,400 | 2,700 | 6,000 | 10,000 | 15,000 | — |
| Ligatured NE in Legend. . . . . . . . . . . . . | 750 | 1,100 | 2,400 | 4,500 | 6,500 | 10,500 | 22,000 |
| 1652 Shilling, Small Planchet (22–26 mm) | 600 | 925 | 2,000 | 3,000 | 4,500 | 10,000 | 20,000 |

## Maryland

### *Lord Baltimore Coinage*

Cecil Calvert, the second Lord Baltimore, inherited from his father nearly absolute control over Maryland. Calvert believed he had the right to coin money for the colony, and in 1659 he ordered shillings, sixpences, and groats (four-penny pieces) from the Royal Mint in London and shipped samples to Maryland, to his brother Philip, who was then his secretary for the colony. Calvert's right to strike coins was upheld by Cromwell's government. The whole issue was small, and while his coins did circulate in Maryland at first, by 1700 they had largely disappeared from commerce.

Calvert's coins bear his portrait on the obverse, with a Latin legend calling him "Lord of Mary's Land." The reverses of the larger denominations bear his family coat of arms and the denomination in Roman numerals. There are several die varieties of each. Many of these coins are found holed and repaired. The copper penny, or denarium, is the rarest denomination, with only nine reported specimens.

**Penny (Denarium)** **Fourpence (Groat)**

**Sixpence** **Shilling**

| | G | VG | F | VF | EF | AU |
|---|---|---|---|---|---|---|
| Denarium copper *(extremely rare)* . . . . . . . . . . . | — | — | $75,000 | $125,000 | $150,000 | — |
| *$241,500, AU, Stack's Bowers auction, May 2004* | | | | | | |
| Fourpence . . . . . . . . . . . . . . . . . . . . . . . . . . . | $4,000 | $7,000 | 13,000 | 20,000 | 30,000 | $50,000 |
| Fourpence, Small Bust *(unique)* *$111,000, AU-53, Heritage auction, January 2015* | | | | | | — |
| Sixpence . . . . . . . . . . . . . . . . . . . . . . . . . . . . | 1,700 | 2,500 | 4,500 | 6,000 | 10,000 | 15,000 |
| Shilling . . . . . . . . . . . . . . . . . . . . . . . . . . . . | 2,500 | 4,500 | 6,500 | 12,000 | 17,000 | 30,000 |

## New Jersey

### *St. Patrick or Mark Newby Coinage*

Mark Newby, who came to America from Dublin, Ireland, in November 1681, brought copper pieces believed by numismatists to have been struck in Dublin circa 1663 to 1672. These are called *St. Patrick coppers.*

The coinage was made legal tender by the General Assembly of New Jersey in May 1682. The legislature did not specify which size piece could circulate, only that the coin was to be worth a halfpenny in trade. Some numismatists believe the larger-size coin was intended. However, as many more farthing-size pieces are known than halfpennies, most believe that the smaller-size piece was meant. Copper coins often circulated in the colonies at twice what they would have been worth in England.

The obverses show a crowned king kneeling and playing a harp. The legend FLOREAT REX ("May the King Prosper") is separated by a crown. The reverse side of the halfpence shows St. Patrick with a crozier in his left hand and a trefoil in his right, and surrounded by people. At his left side is a shield. The legend is ECCE GREX ("Behold the Flock"). The farthing reverse shows St. Patrick driving away serpents and a dragon as he holds a metropolitan cross in his left hand. The legend reads QUIESCAT PLEBS ("May the People Be at Ease").

The large-size piece, called by collectors a *halfpenny,* bears the arms of the City of Dublin on the shield on the reverse; the smaller-size piece, called a *farthing,* does not. Both denominations have a reeded edge.

The decorative brass insert found on the coinage, usually over the crown on the obverse, was put there to make counterfeiting more difficult. On some pieces this decoration has been removed or does not show. Numerous die variations exist.

St. Patrick "Farthing" St. Patrick "Halfpenny"

| | G | VG | F | VF | EF | AU |
|---|---|---|---|---|---|---|
| St. Patrick "Farthing" | $200 | $400 | $600 | $1,500 | $3,500 | $12,500 |
| Similar, Halo Around Saint's Head | 1,000 | 2,500 | 7,000 | 18,000 | 45,000 | — |
| Similar, No C in QUIESCAT | 1,000 | 5,000 | 10,000 | 20,000 | — | — |
| St. Patrick "Farthing," silver | 2,500 | 4,000 | 8,000 | 17,500 | 25,000 | 40,000 |
| St. Patrick "Farthing," gold *(unique)* *$184,000, AU, Stack's Bowers auction, January 2005* | | | | | | — |
| St. Patrick "Halfpenny" | 350 | 600 | 800 | 2,500 | 7,500 | 15,000 |

## COINAGE AUTHORIZED BY BRITISH ROYAL PATENT

### American Plantations Coins

These pieces, struck in nearly pure tin, were the first royally authorized coinage for the British colonies in America. They were made under a franchise granted in 1688 to Richard Holt. Most examples show black oxidation of the tin. Bright, unblemished specimens are more valuable. Restrikes were made about 1828 from original dies.

| | G | VG | F | VF | EF | AU | Unc. |
|---|---|---|---|---|---|---|---|
| (1688) James II Plantation 1/24 Real coinage | | | | | | | |
| 1/24 Part Real | $200 | $400 | $900 | $2,000 | $3,000 | $5,000 | $7,500 |
| 1/24 Part Real, ET. HB. REX. | 250 | 400 | 900 | 2,000 | 3,000 | 7,000 | 10,000 |
| 1/24 Part Real, Sidewise 4 in 24 | 500 | 1,000 | 2,000 | 4,000 | 5,500 | 7,500 | 20,000 |
| 1/24 Part Real, Arms Transposed | 500 | 1,500 | 2,750 | 7,000 | 10,000 | 15,000 | |
| 1/24 Part Real, Restrike | | | | | 500 | 1,000 | 2,000 |

### Coinage of William Wood

#### *Rosa Americana Coins*

William Wood, an Englishman, obtained a patent from King George I to make coins for Ireland and the American colonies.

The first pieces struck were undated; others bear the dates 1722, 1723, 1724, and 1733. The Rosa Americana pieces were issued in three denominations—half penny, penny, and twopence—and were intended for America. This type had a fully bloomed rose on the reverse with the words ROSA AMERICANA UTILE DULCI ("American Rose—Useful and Sweet").

The obverse, common to both Rosa Americana and Hibernia pieces, shows the head of George I and the legend GEORGIUS D:G MAG: BRI: FRA: ET. HIB: REX ("George, by the Grace of God, King of Great Britain, France, and Ireland") or abbreviations thereof. Rosa Americana coins, however, were rejected by the American colonists. The coins are made of a brass composition of copper and zinc (sometimes mistakenly referred to as *Bath metal*). Planchet quality is often rough and porous.

| | VG | F | VF | EF | AU | Unc. |
|---|---|---|---|---|---|---|
| (No date) Twopence, Motto in Ribbon *(illustrated)* . . . . . . | $200 | $400 | $700 | $1,000 | $2,500 | $5,000 |
| (No date) Twopence, Motto Without Ribbon *(3 known)*. . . | | — | — | — | | |

| | VG | F | VF | EF | AU | Unc. |
|---|---|---|---|---|---|---|
| 1722 Halfpenny, VTILE DVLCI . . . . . . . . . . . . . . . . . | $900 | $2,000 | $3,500 | $6,250 | $10,000 | |
| 1722 Halfpenny, D.G.REX ROSA AMERI. UTILE DULCI | 125 | 200 | 400 | 800 | 1,250 | $3,250 |
| 1722 Halfpenny, DEI GRATIA REX UTILE DULCI . . . . | 150 | 200 | 400 | 700 | 1,100 | 2,700 |

| | VG | F | VF | EF | AU | Unc. |
|---|---|---|---|---|---|---|
| 1722 Penny, GEORGIVS. . . . . . . . . . . . . . . . . . . | $2,500 | $5,000 | $12,000 | $17,500 | $20,000 | $30,000 |
| 1722 Penny, VTILE DVLCI . . . . . . . . . . . . . . . . | 170 | 300 | 500 | 850 | 2,250 | 5,000 |
| 1722 Penny, UTILE DULCI . . . . . . . . . . . . . . . . | 150 | 200 | 300 | 600 | 1,200 | 2,500 |

| | VG | F | VF | EF | AU | Unc. |
|---|---|---|---|---|---|---|
| 1722 Twopence, Period After REX. . . . . . . . . . . | $100 | $200 | $300 | $700 | $1,250 | $2,000 |
| 1722 Twopence, No Period After REX . . . . . . . . | 175 | 300 | 600 | 1,100 | 1,800 | 3,500 |

| | VG | F | VF | EF | AU | Unc. |
|---|---|---|---|---|---|---|
| 1723 Halfpenny, Uncrowned Rose. . . . . . . . . . . | $1,000 | $1,800 | $3,600 | $5,500 | $8,500 | $12,500 |
| 1723 Halfpenny, Crowned Rose. . . . . . . . . . . . . | 125 | 200 | 375 | 600 | 1,200 | 2,700 |

| | VG | F | VF | EF | AU | Unc. |
|---|---|---|---|---|---|---|
| 1723 Penny *(illustrated)*. . . . . . . . . . . . . . . . . . | $100 | $125 | $275 | $500 | $800 | $2,000 |
| 1723 Twopence. . . . . . . . . . . . . . . . . . . . . . . . | 85 | 150 | 250 | 350 | 700 | 1,250 |

| | EF | AU | Unc. |
|---|---|---|---|
| 1724, 4 Over 3 Penny (pattern), DEI GRATIA . . . . . . . . . . . . . . . . . . . . . . . . . . . . | | $20,000 | $27,500 |
| 1724, 4 Over 3 Penny (pattern), D GRATIA. . . . . . . . . . . . . . . . . . . . . . . . . . . . . . | $8,750 | 20,000 | 31,000 |
| (Undated) (1724) Penny, ROSA: SINE: SPINA. *(5 known)* . . . . . . . . . . . . . . . . . . . | 18,000 | 25,000 | 31,200 |

*$21,850, VF, Stack's Bowers auction, May 2005*

| | |
|---|---|
| 1724 Twopence (pattern) *$25,300, Choice AU, Stack's Bowers auction, May 2005* | . . . . . . . . . . . . . . . . |

The 1733 twopence is a pattern piece and bears the bust of George II facing to the left. It was issued by the successors to the coinage patent, as William Wood had died in 1730.

| | |
|---|---|
| 1733 Twopence (pattern), Proof *$63,250, Gem PF, Stack's Bowers auction, May 2005* | . . . . . . . . . . . . |

## *Wood's Hibernia Coinage*

The type intended for Ireland had a seated figure with a harp on the reverse side and the word HIBERNIA. Denominations struck were farthing and halfpenny, with dates 1722, 1723, and 1724. Hibernia coins were unpopular in Ireland, so some of them were sent to the American colonies. Numerous varieties exist.

First Type

Second Type

1723, 3 Over 2

| | VG | F | VF | EF | AU | Unc. |
|---|---|---|---|---|---|---|
| 1722 Farthing, D: G: REX. . . . . . . . . . . . . . . . . . . . . | $2,500 | $3,500 | $5,000 | $7,500 | $10,000 | $15,000 |
| 1722 Halfpenny, D: G: REX, Rocks at Right (pattern) | — | 5,000 | 8,000 | 12,000 | 20,000 | 40,000 |
| 1722 Halfpenny, First Type, Harp at Left . . . . . . . . . | 80 | 125 | 250 | 450 | 700 | 1,400 |
| 1722 Halfpenny, Second Type, Harp at Right. . . . . . | 70 | 100 | 200 | 400 | 700 | 1,200 |
| 1722 Halfpenny, Second Type, DEII (blunder) . . . . . | 150 | 375 | 800 | 1,400 | 1,800 | 3,000 |
| 1723 Farthing, D.G.REX. . . . . . . . . . . . . . . . . . . . . | 300 | 400 | 650 | 1,000 | 1,250 | 2,000 |
| 1723 Farthing, DEI. GRATIA. REX. . . . . . . . . . . . . . | 50 | 80 | 125 | 225 | 400 | 600 |
| 1723 Farthing (silver pattern) . . . . . . . . . . . . . . . . . | 600 | 1,200 | 2,500 | 4,000 | 5,000 | 7,500 |

1724, Hibernia Farthing

1724, Hibernia Halfpenny

| | G | VG | F | VF | EF | AU | Unc. |
|---|---|---|---|---|---|---|---|
| 1723 Halfpenny, 3 Over 2 (varieties exist) | $40 | $60 | $125 | $350 | $500 | $900 | $1,750 |
| 1723 Halfpenny | 25 | 45 | 75 | 125 | 250 | 375 | 700 |
| 1723 Halfpenny (silver pattern) | | | — | — | — | — | — |
| 1724 Farthing | 50 | 125 | 200 | 600 | 1,250 | 1,450 | 3,600 |
| 1724 Halfpenny | 45 | 100 | 150 | 350 | 600 | 900 | 2,000 |
| 1724 Halfpenny, DEI Above Head | | | | | — | — | |

## Virginia Halfpennies

In 1773, coinage of a copper halfpenny for Virginia was authorized by the Crown. The pattern, in Proof struck on a large planchet with a wide milled border, is often referred to as a penny. Most Mint State pieces are from the Colonel Cohen Hoard discussed on page 31.

The silver piece dated 1774 is referred to as a shilling, but may have been a pattern or trial for a halfpenny or a guinea.

*Red uncirculated pieces without spots are worth considerably more.*

| | G | VG | F | VF | EF | AU | Unc. |
|---|---|---|---|---|---|---|---|
| 1773 Halfpenny, Period After GEORGIVS | $25 | $50 | $100 | $150 | $350 | $500 | $1,100 |
| 1773 Halfpenny, No Period After GEORGIVS | 35 | 75 | 125 | 250 | 400 | 650 | 1,350 |

1773, "Penny" 1774, "Shilling"

| | PF |
|---|---|
| 1773 "Penny" | $27,000 |
| 1774 "Shilling" *(6 known)* | *110,000* |

# EARLY AMERICAN AND RELATED TOKENS

## Elephant Tokens

### *London Elephant Tokens*

The London Elephant tokens were struck circa 1672 to 1694. Although they were undated, two examples are known to have been struck over 1672 British halfpennies. Most were struck in copper, but one was made of brass. The legend on this piece, GOD PRESERVE LONDON, is probably just a general plea for divine aid and not a specific reference to the outbreak of plague in 1665 or the great fire of 1666.

These pieces were not struck for the colonies, and probably did not circulate widely in America, although a few may have been carried there by colonists. They are associated with the 1694 Carolina and New England Elephant tokens, through a shared obverse die.

| | VG | F | VF | EF | AU | Unc. |
|---|---|---|---|---|---|---|
| (1694) Halfpenny, GOD PRESERVE LONDON, Thick Planchet | $350 | $600 | $900 | $1,300 | $2,000 | $3,200 |
| (1694) Halfpenny, GOD PRESERVE LONDON, Thin Planchet . . | 750 | 1,250 | 2,500 | 5,000 | 8,500 | 25,000 |
| Similar, brass *(unique)*. . . . . . . . . . . . . . . . . . . . . . . . . . . . | | | | | — | |
| (1694) Halfpenny, GOD PRESERVE LONDON, Diagonals in Center of Shield . . . . . . . . . . . . . . . . . . . . | 700 | 1,800 | 4,000 | 7,500 | 11,000 | 25,000 |
| (1694) Halfpenny, Similar, Sword in Second Quarter of Shield | — | — | 20,000 | — | — | — |
| (1694) Halfpenny, LON DON . . . . . . . . . . . . . . . . . . . . . . . . . | 1,000 | 2,000 | 3,500 | 7,500 | 15,000 | 24,000 |

### *Carolina Elephant Tokens*

Although no law is known authorizing coinage for Carolina, two very interesting pieces known as Elephant tokens were made with the date 1694. These copper tokens were of halfpenny denomination. The reverse reads GOD PRESERVE CAROLINA AND THE LORDS PROPRIETERS 1694.

The second and more readily available variety has the last word spelled PROPRIETORS. The correction was made on the original die, for the E shows plainly beneath the O. The elephant's tusks nearly touch the milling on the second variety.

The Carolina pieces were probably struck in England and perhaps intended as advertising to heighten interest in the Carolina Plantation.

| | VG | F | VF | EF | AU | Unc. |
|---|---|---|---|---|---|---|
| 1694 PROPRIETERS | $10,000 | $30,000 | $50,000 | $60,000 | $80,000 | $125,000 |
| 1694 PROPRIETERS, O Over E | 6,500 | 11,000 | 20,000 | 40,000 | 65,000 | 100,000 |

### *New England Elephant Tokens*

Like the Carolina tokens, the New England Elephant tokens are believed to have been struck in England as promotional pieces to increase interest in the American colonies.

| | VG | F | VF | EF | AU |
|---|---|---|---|---|---|
| 1694 NEW ENGLAND | $140,000 | $160,000 | $180,000 | $220,000 | — |

## New Yorke in America Token

The New Yorke in America token is a farthing or halfpenny token intended for New York, issued by Francis Lovelace, who was governor from 1668 until 1673. The token uses the older spelling with a final "e" (YORKE), which predominated before 1710. The obverse shows Cupid pursuing the butterfly-winged Psyche—a rebus on the name Lovelace. The reverse shows a heraldic eagle, identical to the one displayed in fesse, raguly (i.e., on a crenellated bar) on the Lovelace coat of arms. In weight, fabric, and die axis the tokens are similar to the 1670 farthing tokens of Bristol, England, where they may have been struck. There is no evidence that any of these pieces ever circulated in America.

| | VG | F | VF | EF |
|---|---|---|---|---|
| (Undated) Brass or Copper | $10,000 | $20,000 | $30,000 | $60,000 |
| (Undated) Pewter | | 20,000 | 35,000 | 75,000 |

## Gloucester Tokens

S.S. Crosby, in his book *The Early Coins of America,* stated that this token appears to have been intended as a pattern for a shilling—a private coinage by Richard Dawson of Gloucester (county), Virginia. The only specimens known are struck in brass, although the denomination XII indicates that a silver coinage (one shilling) may have been planned. The building may represent some public building, possibly the courthouse.

Although neither of the two known examples shows the full legends, combining the pieces shows GLOVCESTER COVRTHOVSE VIRGINIA / RIGHAVLT DAWSON. ANNO.DOM. 1714. This recent discovery has provided a new interpretation of the legends, as a Righault family once owned land near the Gloucester courthouse. A similar, but somewhat smaller, piece possibly dated 1715 exists. The condition of this unique piece is too poor for positive attribution.

| | F |
|---|---|
| 1714 Shilling, brass *(2 known)* | $120,000 |

## Higley or Granby Coppers

Dr. Samuel Higley owned a private copper mine near Granby, Connecticut. He worked the mine as an individual, smelting his own ore and making his own dies for the coins that he issued. After his death in 1737 his brother John continued the coinage.

The Higley coppers were never officially authorized. All the pieces were made of pure copper. There were seven obverse and four reverse dies. The first issue, in 1737, bore the legend THE VALUE OF THREEPENCE. After a time, the quantity exceeded the local demand, and a protest arose against the stated value of the piece. Higley, a resourceful individual, promptly created a new design, still with the Roman III, but with the inscription VALUE ME AS YOU PLEASE. On the reverse appeared the words I AM GOOD COPPER. Electrotypes and cast copies exist.

| | AG | G | VG | F | VF |
|---|---|---|---|---|---|
| 1737 THE • VALVE • OF • THREE • PENCE, CONNECTICVT, 3 Hammers | $12,000 | $18,000 | $30,000 | $50,000 | $100,000 |
| 1737 THE • VALVE • OF • THREE • PENCE, I • AM • GOOD • COPPER, CONNECTICVT, 3 Hammers *(3 known)* | — | 35,000 | 50,000 | 80,000 | 175,000 |
| 1737 VALUE • ME • AS • YOU • PLEASE, I • AM • GOOD • COPPER, 3 Hammers | 12,000 | 18,000 | 30,000 | 50,000 | 100,000 |

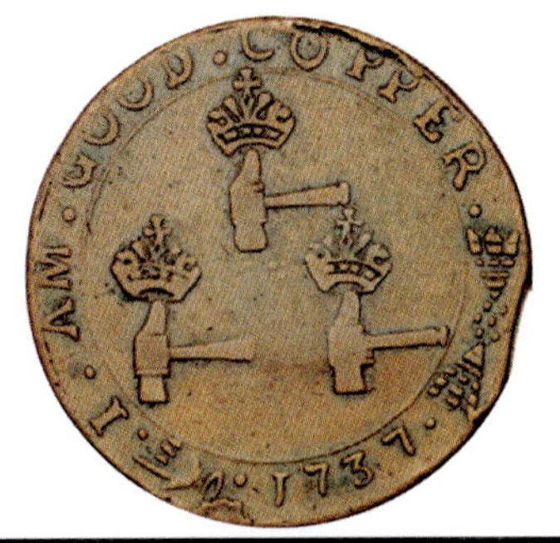

| | AG | G | VG | F | VF |
|---|---|---|---|---|---|
| 1737 VALVE • ME • AS • YOU • PLEASE, I • AM • GOOD • COPPER, 3 Hammers *(3 known)* | | | $75,000 | | |
| (1737) VALUE • ME • AS • YOU • PLEASE, J • CUT • MY • WAY • THROUGH, Broad Axe | $12,000 | $18,000 | 30,000 | $50,000 | $100,000 |
| (1737) THE • WHEELE • GOES • ROUND, Reverse as Above *(unique)* | | | | | 350,000 |
| 1739 VALUE • ME • AS • YOU • PLEASE, J • CUT • MY • WAY • THROUGH, Broad Axe | 15,000 | 20,000 | 37,500 | 60,000 | 125,000 |

## Hibernia–Voce Populi Coins

These coins, struck in the year 1760, were prepared by Roche, of King Street, Dublin, who was at that time engaged in the manufacture of buttons for the army. Like other Irish tokens, some could have found their way to colonial America and possibly circulated in the colonies with numerous other counterfeit halfpence and "bungtown tokens."

There are two distinct issues. Coins from the first, with a "short bust" on the obverse, range in weight from 87 to 120 grains. Those from the second, with a "long bust" on the obverse, range in weight from 129 to 154 grains. Most of the "long bust" varieties have the letter P on the obverse. None of the "short bust" varieties bear the letter P, and judging from their weight, may have been contemporary counterfeits.

**Large-Letter Variety Farthing**

**Halfpenny**

**Halfpenny, "P" Before Face**

**VOOE POPULI**

| | G | VG | F | VF | EF | AU | Unc. |
|---|---|---|---|---|---|---|---|
| 1760 Farthing, Large Letters | $200 | $300 | $500 | $1,250 | $2,000 | $3,000 | $5,500 |
| 1760 Farthing, Small Letters | | | 8,000 | 10,000 | 15,000 | 20,000 | 25,000 |
| 1760 Halfpenny | 80 | 110 | 180 | 300 | 500 | 700 | 1,250 |
| 1760 Halfpenny, VOOE POPULI | 90 | 150 | 200 | 400 | 550 | 1,000 | 3,000 |
| 1760 Halfpenny, P Below Bust | 110 | 200 | 300 | 600 | 900 | 1,600 | 4,500 |
| 1760 Halfpenny, P in Front of Face | 90 | 175 | 250 | 500 | 800 | 1,400 | 4,000 |

## Pitt Tokens

William Pitt, the British politician who endeared himself to America, is the subject of these pieces, probably intended as commemorative medalets. The so-called halfpenny served as currency during a shortage of regular coinage. The reverse legend (THANKS TO THE FRIENDS OF LIBERTY AND TRADE) refers to Pitt's efforts to have the Stamp Act repealed. The Pitt farthing-size tokens, struck in brass or copper, are rare.

Farthing Halfpenny

| | G | VG | F | VF | EF | AU | Unc. |
|---|---|---|---|---|---|---|---|
| 1766 Farthing | $2,500 | $5,000 | $10,000 | $22,000 | $30,000 | $50,000 | |
| 1766 Halfpenny | 300 | 450 | 650 | 1,100 | 1,700 | 2,700 | $8,000 |
| 1766 Halfpenny, silvered | | | | 1,600 | 3,500 | 5,000 | 12,000 |

## Rhode Island Ship Medals

The obverse shows the flagship of British admiral Lord Richard Howe at anchor, while the reverse depicts the retreat of American forces from Rhode Island in 1778. The inscriptions show that the coin was meant for a Dutch-speaking audience. It is believed the medal was struck in England circa 1779 for the Dutch market. Specimens are known in brass and pewter.

Rhode Island Ship Medal (1778–1779)

Wreath Below Ship

| | VF | EF | AU | Unc. |
|---|---|---|---|---|
| With "vlugtende" (fleeing) Below Ship, brass | | $90,000 | | |
| Wreath Below Ship, brass | $1,350 | 2,250 | $3,250 | $4,500 |
| Without Wreath Below Ship, brass | 900 | 1,700 | 2,700 | 5,000 |
| Similar, pewter | 3,000 | 4,500 | 6,500 | 10,000 |

## John Chalmers Issues

John Chalmers, a silversmith, struck a series of silver tokens at Annapolis in 1783. The shortage of change and the refusal of the people to use underweight cut Spanish coins, or "bits," prompted the issuance of these pieces.

On the Chalmers threepence and shilling obverses, two clasped hands are shown, symbolizing unity of the several states; the reverse of the threepence has a branch encircled by a wreath. A star within a wreath is on the obverse of the sixpence, with hands clasped upon a cross utilized as the reverse type. On this denomination, the designer's initials TS (for Thomas Sparrow, a fellow silversmith of Chalmers's) can be found in the crescents that terminate the horizontal arms of the cross. The reverse of the more common shilling varieties displays two doves competing for a worm underneath a hedge and a snake. There are only a few known examples of the shilling type with 13 interlinked rings, from which a liberty cap on a pole arises.

| | VG | F | VF | EF | AU |
|---|---|---|---|---|---|
| 1783 Threepence | $2,000 | $4,000 | $7,500 | $15,000 | $25,000 |
| 1783 Sixpence, Small Date | 2,600 | 7,500 | 15,000 | 20,000 | 27,500 |
| 1783 Sixpence, Large Date | 2,600 | 6,000 | 12,000 | 17,500 | 25,000 |

| | VG | F | VF | EF | AU |
|---|---|---|---|---|---|
| 1783 Shilling, Birds, Long Worm | $1,100 | $2,000 | $5,000 | $8,500 | $17,500 |
| 1783 Shilling, Birds, Short Worm *(illustrated)* | 1,100 | 2,000 | 5,000 | 8,500 | 17,500 |
| 1783 Shilling, Rings *(5 known)* | *50,000* | *100,000* | *200,000* | — | — |

## FRENCH NEW WORLD ISSUES

None of the coins of the French regime relate specifically to territories that later became part of the United States. They were all general issues for the French colonies of the New World. The coinage of 1670 was authorized by an edict of King Louis XIV for use in New France, Acadia, the French settlements in Newfoundland, and the French West Indies. The copper coinage of 1717 to 1722 was authorized by edicts of 1716 and 1721 for use in New France, Louisiana, and the French West Indies.

### Coinage of 1670

The coinage of 1670 consisted of silver 5 and 15 sols and copper 2 deniers (or "doubles"). A total of 200,000 of the 5 sols and 40,000 of the 15 sols was struck at Paris. Nantes was to have coined the copper, but did not; the reasons for this may never be known, since the archives of the Nantes Mint before 1700 were destroyed. The only known specimen is a pattern struck at Paris. The silver coins were raised in value by a third in 1672 to keep them circulating, but in vain. They rapidly disappeared, and by 1680 none were to be seen. Later they were restored to their original values. This rare issue should not be confused with the common 1670-A 1/12 écu with reverse legend SIT. NOMEN. DOMINI. BENEDICTUM.

The 1670-A double de l'Amerique Françoise was struck at the Paris Mint along with the 5- and 15-sols denominations of the same date. All three were intended to circulate in France's North American colonies, but very few doubles were ever struck.

Copper Double

Silver 5 Sols

| | VG | F | VF | EF | Unc. |
|---|---|---|---|---|---|
| 1670-A Copper Double *(unique)*. . . . . . . . . . . . . . . . . . . . . | | | $225,000 | | |
| 1670-A 5 Sols . . . . . . . . . . . . . . . . . . . . . . . . . . . . . . . . | $750 | $1,000 | 2,000 | $3,000 | $7,500 |
| 1670-A 15 Sols . . . . . . . . . . . . . . . . . . . . . . . . . . . . . . . | 13,000 | 35,000 | 75,000 | 125,000 | — |

## Coinage of 1717–1720

The copper 6 and 12 deniers of 1717 were authorized by an edict of King Louis XV dated December 1716, to be struck at Perpignan (mintmark Q). The order could not be carried out, for the supply of copper was too brassy. A 1720 attempt also failed. The issues of 1720, which were struck at multiple mints, are popularly collected for their association with the John Law "Mississippi Bubble" venture.

1720 6 Deniers

1720 20 Sols

| | F | VF | EF |
|---|---|---|---|
| 1717-Q 6 Deniers, No Crowned Arms on Reverse *(extremely rare)* . . . . . . . . . . . | | | — |
| 1717-Q 12 Deniers, No Crowned Arms on Reverse . . . . . . . . . . . . . . . . . . . . . . | | | — |
| 1720 Liard, Crowned Arms on Reverse, copper. . . . . . . . . . . . . . . . . . . . . . . . . | $350 | $500 | $900 |
| 1720 6 Deniers, Crowned Arms on Reverse, copper . . . . . . . . . . . . . . . . . . . . . | 550 | 900 | 1,750 |
| 1720 12 Deniers, Crowned Arms on Reverse, copper . . . . . . . . . . . . . . . . . . . . | 400 | 750 | 1,500 |
| 1720 20 Sols, silver. . . . . . . . . . . . . . . . . . . . . . . . . . . . . . . . . . . . . . . . . . . | 375 | 700 | 1,500 |

## Billon Coinage of 1709–1760

The piece of 30 deniers was called a *mousquetaire,* and was coined at Metz and Lyon. The 15 deniers was coined only at Metz. The sou marque and the half sou were coined at almost every French mint, those of Paris being most common. The half sou of 1740 is the only commonly available date. Specimens of the sou marque dated after 1760 were not used in North America. A unique specimen of the 1712-AA 30 deniers is known in the size and weight of the 15-denier coins.

30 Deniers "Mousquetaire"

Sou Marque (24 Deniers)

| | VG | F | VF | EF | AU | Unc. |
|---|---|---|---|---|---|---|
| 1711–1713-AA 15 Deniers | $150 | $300 | $500 | $1,000 | $1,750 | $4,000 |
| 1709–1713-AA 30 Deniers | 75 | 100 | 250 | 400 | 675 | 1,500 |
| 1709–1713-D 30 Deniers | 75 | 100 | 250 | 400 | 675 | 1,500 |
| 1738–1748 Half Sou Marque, various mints | 60 | 100 | 200 | 350 | 575 | 1,200 |
| 1738–1760 Sou Marque, various mints | 50 | 80 | 125 | 175 | 300 | 500 |

## Coinage of 1721–1722

The copper coinage of 1721 and 1722 was authorized by an edict of King Louis XV dated June 1721. The coins were struck on copper blanks imported from Sweden. Rouen and La Rochelle struck pieces of nine deniers in 1721 and 1722. New France received 534,000 pieces, mostly from the mint of La Rochelle, but only 8,180 were successfully put into circulation, as the colonists disliked copper. In 1726 the rest of the issue was sent back to France.

### *Copper Sou or Nine Deniers*

| | VG | F | VF | EF |
|---|---|---|---|---|
| 1721-B (Rouen) | $500 | $1,000 | $3,500 | $10,000 |
| 1721-H (La Rochelle) | 100 | 175 | 1,000 | 2,500 |
| 1722-H | 100 | 175 | 1,000 | 2,500 |
| 1722-H, 2 Over 1 | 175 | 275 | 1,200 | 4,000 |

## French Colonies in General

These were coined for use in the French colonies and only unofficially circulated in Louisiana along with other foreign coins and tokens. Most were counterstamped RF (République Française) for use in the West Indies. The mintmark A signifies the Paris Mint.

| | VG | VF | EF | AU |
|---|---|---|---|---|
| 1767 French Colonies, Sou | $120 | $250 | $600 | $1,400 |
| 1767 French Colonies, Sou, counterstamped RF | 100 | 200 | 250 | 600 |

# SPECULATIVE ISSUES, TOKENS, AND PATTERNS

## Nova Constellatio Coppers

The Nova Constellatio coppers, dated 1783 and 1785 and without denomination, were struck in fairly large quantities in Birmingham, England, and were shipped to New York where they entered circulation. Apparently they resulted from a private coinage venture undertaken by Constable, Rucker & Co., a trading business formed by William Constable, John Rucker, Robert Morris, and Gouverneur Morris as equal partners. The designs and legends were copied from the denominated patterns dated 1783 made in Philadelphia (see page 88). A few additional coppers dated 1786 were made by an inferior diesinker.

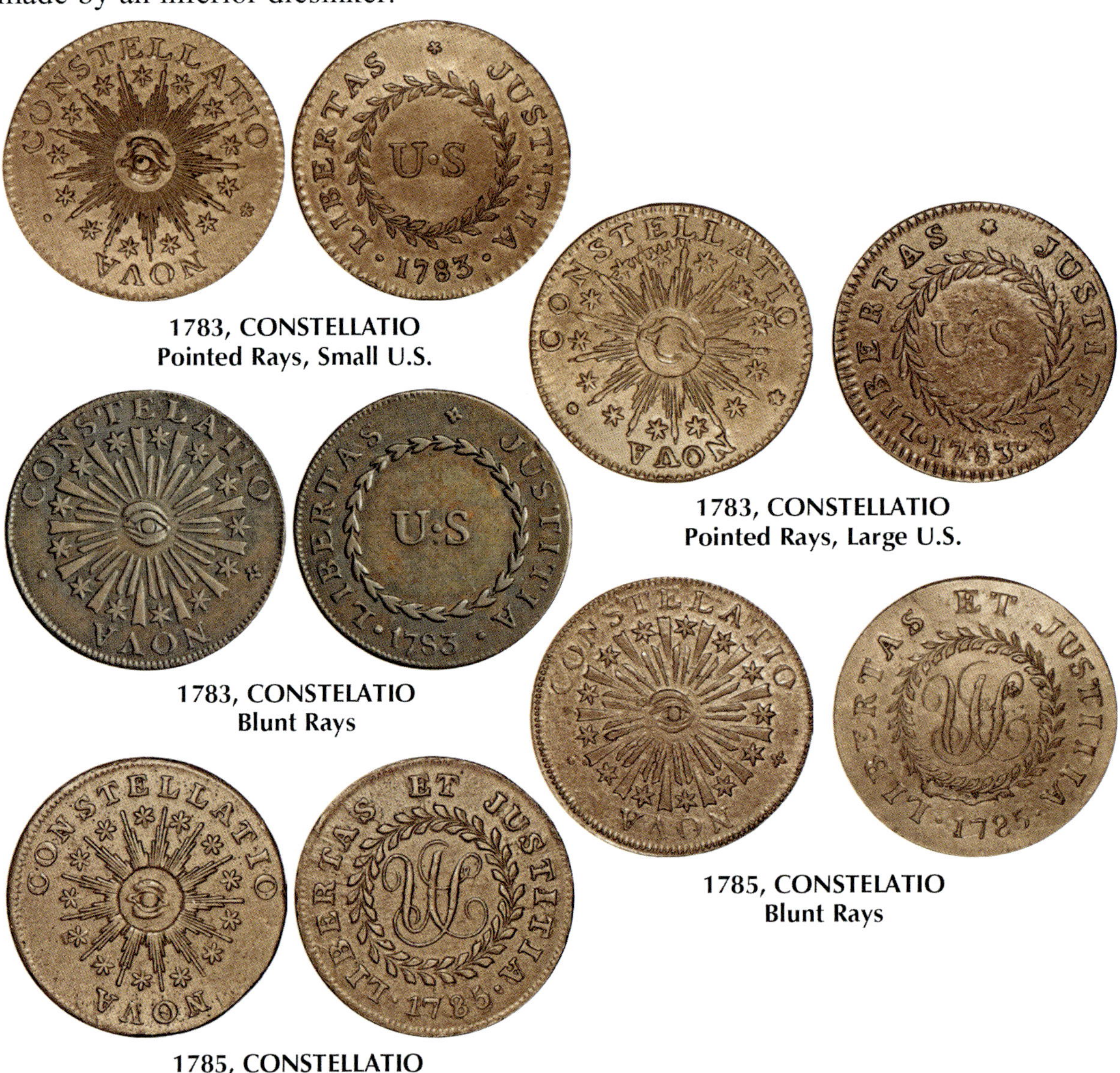

**1783, CONSTELLATIO**
**Pointed Rays, Small U.S.**

**1783, CONSTELLATIO**
**Pointed Rays, Large U.S.**

**1783, CONSTELATIO**
**Blunt Rays**

**1785, CONSTELATIO**
**Blunt Rays**

**1785, CONSTELLATIO**
**Pointed Rays**

| | VG | F | VF | EF | AU | Unc. |
|---|---|---|---|---|---|---|
| 1783, CONSTELLATIO, Pointed Rays, Small U.S. | $100 | $200 | $375 | $750 | $1,300 | $3,000 |
| 1783, CONSTELLATIO, Pointed Rays, Large U.S. | 100 | 500 | 750 | 2,000 | 4,500 | 10,000 |
| 1783, CONSTELATIO, Blunt Rays | 100 | 225 | 550 | 1,000 | 2,500 | 7,000 |
| 1785, CONSTELATIO, Blunt Rays | 100 | 225 | 550 | 1,000 | 2,500 | 6,000 |
| 1785, CONSTELLATIO, Pointed Rays | 100 | 200 | 375 | 750 | 1,300 | 3,000 |
| 1785, Similar, Small, Close Date | 300 | 500 | 1,800 | 3,500 | 5,500 | 15,000 |
| 1786, Similar, Small Date | 2,500 | 5,000 | 7,500 | 15,000 | | |

## Immune Columbia Pieces

These pieces are considered private or unofficial coins. No laws describing them are known. There are several types bearing the seated figure of Justice. The Immune Columbia device with liberty cap and scale replaced the LIBERTAS and JUSTITIA on the Nova Constellatio coppers.

1785, Silver, 13 Stars

1785, Pointed Rays, CONSTELLATIO

| | F | VF | EF |
|---|---|---|---|
| 1785, Copper, 13 Stars | $15,000 | $27,000 | $45,000 |
| 1785, Silver, 13 Stars | 25,000 | 50,000 | 75,000 |
| 1785, Pointed Rays, CONSTELLATIO, Extra Star in Reverse Legend, copper | 15,000 | 25,000 | 45,000 |
| 1785, Pointed Rays, CONSTELLATIO, gold *(unique)* | | | — |
| 1785, Blunt Rays, CONSTELATIO, copper *(2 known)* | | 50,000 | — |

*Note:* The gold specimen in the National Numismatic Collection (now in the Smithsonian) was acquired in 1843 from collector Matthew A. Stickney in exchange for an 1804 dollar.

1785, George III Obverse

| | G | VG | F | VF |
|---|---|---|---|---|
| 1785, George III Obverse | $5,500 | $8,500 | $12,500 | $25,000 |
| 1785, VERMON AUCTORI Obverse, IMMUNE COLUMBIA | 6,000 | 10,000 | 15,000 | 30,000 |

1787, IMMUNIS COLUMBIA, Eagle Reverse

| | VG | F | VF | EF | AU | Unc. |
|---|---|---|---|---|---|---|
| 1787, IMMUNIS COLUMBIA, Eagle Reverse | $600 | $1,000 | $3,000 | $4,500 | $9,000 | $25,000 |

*Note:* Believed to be a prototype for federal coinage; some were coined after 1787.

## Confederatio and Related Tokens

The Confederatio and associated coppers have patriotic motifs and were made in small quantities for circulation. The 1785, Inimica Tyrannis America, variety may owe its design to a sketch by Thomas Jefferson. In all, 12 dies were presumed struck in 13 combinations. No one knows for certain who made these pieces. The combination with a standard reverse die for a 1786 New Jersey copper is especially puzzling.

Inimica Tyrannis America

Inimica Tyrannis Americana

Gen. Washington

Immunis Columbia

Eagle

Libertas et Justitia

Large Circle

Small Circle

Pattern Shield

The 1786, Immunis Columbia, with scrawny-eagle reverse is a related piece probably made by a different engraver or mint.

| | VG | F | VF | EF | AU |
|---|---|---|---|---|---|
| 1785, Inimica Tyrannis America, Large Circle **(a)** | $40,000 | $70,000 | $100,000 | $150,000 | $225,000 |
| 1785, Inimica Tyrannis Americana, Small Circle **(b)** | 30,000 | 40,000 | 50,000 | 125,000 | 200,000 |
| 1785, Inimica Tyrannis Americana, Large Circle, Silver **(c)** | | 50,000 **(d)** | | | |
| 1785, Gen. Washington, Large Circle **(e)** | 50,000 | 75,000 | 125,000 | 250,000 | |
| 1786, Gen. Washington, Eagle **(f)** | | 40,000 | | | |
| (No Date) Gen. Washington, Pattern Shield **(g)** | | 75,000 | 100,000 | | 300,000 |
| 1786, Immunis, Pattern Shield **(h)** | | 25,000 | 50,000 | 75,000 | 95,000 |
| 1786, Immunis, 1785 Large Circle **(f)** | | | | | 100,000 |
| 1786, Eagle, Pattern Shield **(c)** | | | | | 200,000 |
| 1786, Eagle, 1785 Large Circle **(f)** | | 50,000 | 85,000 | | |
| 1785, Libertas et Justitia, 1785 Large Circle **(c)** | 25,000 | | | | |
| 1785, Small Circle, 1787 Excelsior Eagle **(f,i)** | | 35,000 | | | |
| 1786, Immunis Columbia, Scrawny Eagle **(g)** | | | 50,000 | 90,000 | |

**a.** 7 known. **b.** 9 known. **c.** 1 known. **d.** Damaged. **e.** 6 known. **f.** 2 known. **g.** 3 known. **h.** 17 known. **i.** Image of the 1787 Excelsior eagle (facing right) is on page 68.

## COINAGE OF THE STATES AND VERMONT

### Vermont

Reuben Harmon Jr., of Rupert, Vermont, was granted permission to coin copper pieces for a period of two years beginning July 1, 1785.(Vermont, then a republic, would not become a state until 1791.) The well-known Vermont "Landscape" coppers were first produced in that year. The franchise was extended for eight years in 1786.

Harmon's mint was located in the northeast corner of Rupert near a stream known as Millbrook. Colonel William Coley, a New York goldsmith, made the first dies. Some of the late issues were made near Newburgh, New York, by the Machin's Mills coiners.

Most Vermont coppers were struck on poor and defective planchets. Well-struck coins on smooth, full planchets command higher prices.

1785, IMMUNE COLUMBIA

1785, VERMONTS

1785, Reverse

1785, VERMONTIS

| | AG | G | VG | F | VF | EF | AU |
|---|---|---|---|---|---|---|---|
| 1785, IMMUNE COLUMBIA | $4,000 | $6,000 | $10,000 | $15,000 | $30,000 | $50,000 | $75,000 |
| 1785, VERMONTS | 150 | 275 | 450 | 750 | 2,500 | 6,000 | 15,000 |
| 1785, VERMONTIS | 175 | 325 | 600 | 1,300 | 3,500 | 12,000 | 20,000 |

1786, VERMONTENSIUM 1786, Baby Head

Bust Left

1786, Reverse

1787, Reverse

| | AG | G | VG | F | VF | EF | AU |
|---|---|---|---|---|---|---|---|
| 1786, VERMONTENSIUM . . . . . . . . . | $110 | $200 | $450 | $750 | $1,750 | $5,000 | $10,000 |
| 1786, Baby Head . . . . . . . . . . . . . . . | 150 | 275 | 400 | 800 | 3,000 | 7,500 | |
| 1786, Bust Left . . . . . . . . . . . . . . . . | | 300 | 500 | 750 | 1,250 | 2,000 | |
| 1787, Bust Left . . . . . . . . . . . . . . . . | | | 15,000 | 20,000 | 35,000 | — | |

1787, BRITANNIA

| | AG | G | VG | F | VF | EF | AU |
|---|---|---|---|---|---|---|---|
| 1787, BRITANNIA. . . . . . . . . . . . . . . . | $45 | $90 | $120 | $200 | $400 | $1,000 | $2,500 |

*Note:* The reverse of this coin is always weak.

1787, 1788, Bust Right (Several Varieties)

| | AG | G | VG | F | VF | EF | AU |
|---|---|---|---|---|---|---|---|
| 1787, Bust Right (several varieties) | $60 | $110 | $150 | $250 | $800 | $2,000 | $3,500 |
| 1788, Bust Right (several varieties) | 50 | 90 | 120 | 225 | 500 | 1,250 | 2,500 |
| 1788, Backward C in AUCTORI . . . . | | 5,000 | 10,000 | 25,000 | 40,000 | 55,000 | 85,000 |
| 1788, *ET LIB* *INDE. . . . . . . . . . . . | 175 | 300 | 550 | 1,250 | 4,000 | 10,000 | 15,000 |

**1788, GEORGIVS III REX / INDE+ ET•LIB+**

| | AG | G | VG | F | VF | EF | AU |
|---|---|---|---|---|---|---|---|
| 1788, GEORGIVS III REX. . . . . . . . . . | $300 | $500 | $900 | $2,000 | $4,000 | $10,000 | |

*Note:* This piece should not be confused with the common English halfpence with similar design and reverse legend BRITANNIA.

## New Hampshire

New Hampshire was the first of the states to consider the subject of coinage following the Declaration of Independence.

William Moulton was empowered to make a limited quantity of coins of pure copper authorized by the State House of Representatives in 1776. Although cast patterns were prepared, it is believed that they were not approved. Little of the proposed coinage was ever actually circulated.

Other purported patterns are of doubtful origin. These include a unique engraved piece and a rare struck piece with large initials WM on the reverse.

| | | G |
|---|---|---|
| 1776 New Hampshire Copper | *$172,500, VG-10, Stack's Bowers auction, March 2012* . . . . . . . . . . . . . | $100,000 |

## Massachusetts

### *Massachusetts Unofficial Coppers*

Nothing is known regarding the origin of the Pine Tree piece dated 1776. The obverse has a crude pine tree with "1d LM" at its base and the inscription MASSACHUSETTS STATE. The reverse has a figure probably intended to represent the Goddess of Liberty, seated on a globe and holding a liberty cap and staff. A dog sits at her feet. The legend LIBERTY AND VIRTUE surrounds the figure.

| | VF |
|---|---|
| 1776 Pine Tree Copper *(unique, in Massachusetts Historical Society collection)* . . . . . . . . . . . . . . . . . . . . | — |

A similar piece, probably from the same source, has a Native American with a bow on the obverse, and a seated figure on the reverse.

| | VG |
|---|---|
| 1776 Indian Copper *(unique)* . . . . . . . . . . . . . . . . . . . . . . . . . . . . . . . . . . . . . . . . . . . . . . . . . . . . . . . . . | — |

This piece is sometimes called the *Janus copper*. On the obverse are three heads, facing left, front, and right, with the inscription STATE OF MASSA. 1/2 D. The reverse shows the Goddess of Liberty facing right, resting against a globe. The legend is GODDESS LIBERTY 1776.

| | F |
|---|---|
| 1776 Halfpenny, 3 Heads on Obverse *(unique)* . . . . . . . . . . . . . . . . . . . . . . . . . . . . . . . . . . . . . . . . . . . . | — |

### *Massachusetts Authorized Issues*

An "Act for establishing a mint for the coinage of gold, silver and copper" was passed by the Massachusetts General Court on October 17, 1786. The next year, the council directed that the design should incorporate "the figure of an Indian with a bow & arrow & a star at one side, with the word 'Commonwealth,' the reverse a spread eagle with the words—'of Massachusetts A.D. 1787.' "

The coinage of Massachusetts copper cents and half cents in 1787 and 1788 was under the direction of Joshua Witherle. These were the first coins bearing the denomination *cent* as would later be established by Congress. Many varieties exist, the most valuable being that with arrows in the eagle's right talon.

Most of the dies for these coppers were made by Joseph Callender. Jacob Perkins of Newburyport also engraved some of the 1788 dies.

The mint was abandoned early in 1789, in compliance with the newly ratified Constitution, and because its production was unprofitable.

1787 Half Cent

1787 Cent, Obverse

Arrows in Right Talon

Arrows in Left Talon

| | G | VG | F | VF | EF | AU | Unc. |
|---|---|---|---|---|---|---|---|
| 1787 Half Cent | $100 | $125 | $225 | $450 | $650 | $1,250 | $2,500 |
| 1787 Cent, Arrows in Right Talon | 10,000 | 16,000 | 25,000 | 50,000 | 75,000 | 100,000 | 200,000 |
| 1787 Cent, Arrows in Left Talon | 250 | 100 | 150 | 200 | 650 | 1,100 | 2,250 |
| 1787 Cent, "Horned Eagle" (die break) | 110 | 135 | 235 | 650 | 1,100 | 2,250 | 6,000 |

1788 Half Cent

1788 Cent, Period After MASSACHUSETTS

| | G | VG | F | VF | EF | AU | Unc. |
|---|---|---|---|---|---|---|---|
| 1788 Half Cent | $100 | $125 | $225 | $500 | $700 | $1,400 | $4,500 |
| 1788 Cent, Period After MASSACHUSETTS | 100 | 110 | 200 | 600 | 1,250 | 2,500 | 6,000 |
| 1788 Cent, No Period After MASSACHUSETTS | 100 | 110 | 200 | 600 | 1,250 | 2,500 | 6,000 |

Early American coins were produced from handmade dies, which are often individually distinctive. The great number of die varieties that can be found and identified are of interest to collectors who value each according to individual rarity. Values shown for type coins in this book are for the most common die variety of each.

## Connecticut

Authority for establishing a mint near New Haven was granted by the state to Samuel Bishop, Joseph Hopkins, James Hillhouse, and John Goodrich in 1785.

Available records indicate that most of the Connecticut coppers were coined under a subcontract, by Samuel Broome and Jeremiah Platt, former New York merchants. Abel Buell was probably the principal diesinker.

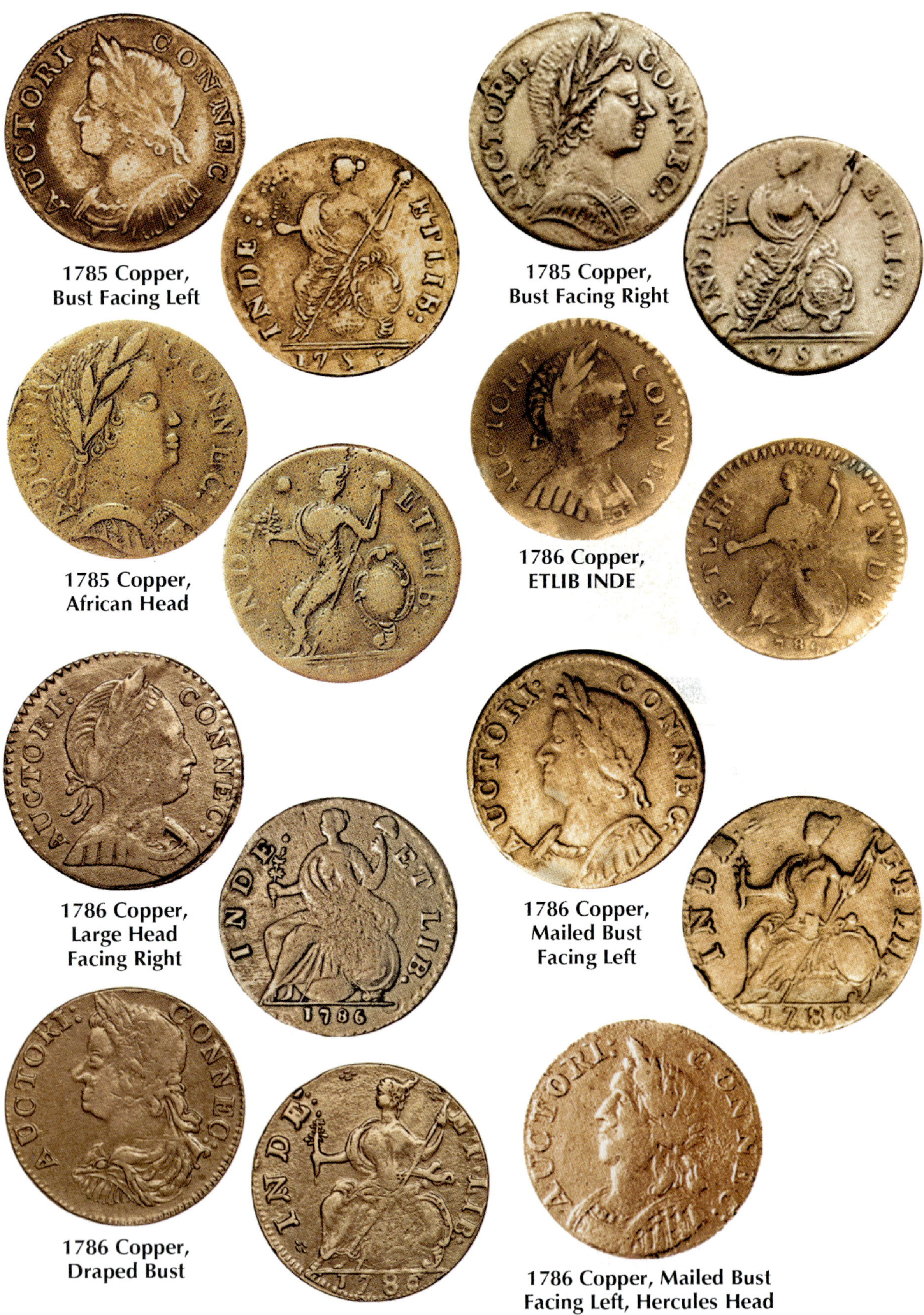

1785 Copper, Bust Facing Left

1785 Copper, Bust Facing Right

1785 Copper, African Head

1786 Copper, ETLIB INDE

1786 Copper, Large Head Facing Right

1786 Copper, Mailed Bust Facing Left

1786 Copper, Draped Bust

1786 Copper, Mailed Bust Facing Left, Hercules Head

| | G | VG | F | VF | EF | AU |
|---|---|---|---|---|---|---|
| 1785 Copper, Bust Facing Left . . . . . . . . . . . . . . . . . . | $200 | $325 | $650 | $1,750 | $3,750 | $8,000 |
| 1785 Copper, Bust Facing Right . . . . . . . . . . . . . . . . . | 50 | 90 | 150 | 500 | 1,250 | 3,500 |
| 1785 Copper, African Head . . . . . . . . . . . . . . . . . . . . . | 100 | 175 | 500 | 1,250 | 3,000 | 6,500 |
| 1786 Copper, ETLIB INDE . . . . . . . . . . . . . . . . . . . . . | 70 | 140 | 325 | 850 | 2,500 | 7,000 |
| 1786 Copper, Large Head Facing Right . . . . . . . . . . . . | 750 | 1,500 | 3,500 | 5,500 | 10,000 | 15,000 |
| 1786 Copper, Mailed Bust Facing Left. . . . . . . . . . . . . | 40 | 75 | 140 | 400 | 800 | 2,200 |
| 1786 Copper, Draped Bust . . . . . . . . . . . . . . . . . . . . | 125 | 200 | 500 | 1,200 | 3,000 | 5,000 |
| 1786 Copper, Mailed Bust Facing Left, Hercules Head | 110 | 200 | 450 | 1,350 | 3,250 | |

The Connecticut coppers were often crudely struck and on imperfect planchets.

1787 Copper, Small Head Facing Right, ETLIB INDE

1787 Copper, Muttonhead Variety

| | G | VG | F | VF | EF | AU |
|---|---|---|---|---|---|---|
| 1787 Copper, Small Head Facing Right, ETLIB INDE . . . . . . . | $110 | $200 | $400 | $1,300 | $2,500 | $5,000 |
| 1787 Copper, Liberty Seated Facing Right *(2 known)* . . . . . . | | — | | | | |
| 1787, Mailed Bust Facing Right, INDE ET LIB . . . . . . . . . . . . | 100 | 180 | 400 | 2,200 | 5,000 | |
| 1787 Copper, Muttonhead. . . . . . . . . . . . . . . . . . . . . . . . . . | 125 | 200 | 400 | 1,700 | 4,000 | 7,500 |

1787 Copper, Mailed Bust Facing Left

1787 Copper, Laughing Head

1787 Copper, Horned Bust

1787 Copper, Reverse

| | G | VG | F | VF | EF | AU |
|---|---|---|---|---|---|---|
| 1787 Copper, Mailed Bust Facing Left. . . . . . . . . . . . . . . . . . | $40 | $65 | $120 | $350 | $900 | $2,200 |
| 1787 Copper, Mailed Bust Facing Left, Laughing Head . . . . . | 65 | 125 | 250 | 550 | 1,000 | 2,250 |
| 1787 Copper, Mailed Bust Facing Left, Horned Bust . . . . . . . | 40 | 65 | 120 | 375 | 750 | 1,750 |
| 1787 Copper, Mailed Bust Facing Left, Hercules Head *(see 1786 for illustration)* . . . . . . . . . . . . . . . . . . . . . . . | 500 | 900 | 1,700 | 5,000 | 8,500 | — |
| 1787 Copper, Mailed Bust Facing Left, Dated 1787 Over 1877 . . . . . . . . . . . . . . . . . . . . . . . . | 80 | 180 | 600 | 1,400 | 4,200 | — |
| 1787 Copper, Mailed Bust Facing Left, 1787 Over 88 . . . . . . . . . . . . . . . . . . . . . . . . . . . . . . | 175 | 235 | 600 | 1,500 | 4,500 | — |
| 1787 Copper, Mailed Bust Facing Left, CONNECT, INDE . . . . | 50 | 100 | 175 | 475 | 1,200 | 2,500 |
| 1787 Copper, Mailed Bust Facing Left, CONNECT, INDL . . . . | 375 | 700 | 1,500 | 3,000 | 6,500 | |

1787 Copper, Draped Bust Facing Left

| | G | VG | F | VF | EF | AU |
|---|---|---|---|---|---|---|
| 1787 Copper, Draped Bust Facing Left | $30 | $50 | $90 | $250 | $650 | $1,200 |
| 1787 Copper, Draped Bust Facing Left, AUCIORI | 40 | 65 | 125 | 350 | 850 | 1,500 |
| 1787 Copper, Draped Bust Facing Left, AUCTOPI | 50 | 100 | 200 | 600 | 1,400 | 2,500 |
| 1787 Copper, Draped Bust Facing Left, AUCTOBI | 50 | 90 | 180 | 500 | 1,250 | 2,000 |
| 1787 Copper, Draped Bust Facing Left, CONNFC | 40 | 60 | 125 | 400 | 750 | 1,500 |
| 1787 Copper, Draped Bust Facing Left, CONNLC | 75 | 150 | 250 | 700 | 2,500 | — |
| 1787 Copper, Draped Bust Facing Left, FNDE | 40 | 65 | 150 | 400 | 1,300 | 2,400 |
| 1787 Copper, Draped Bust Facing Left, ETLIR | 40 | 60 | 125 | 300 | 800 | 1,400 |
| 1787 Copper, Draped Bust Facing Left, ETIIB | 40 | 60 | 125 | 300 | 800 | 1,400 |
| 1787 Copper, GEORGIVS III Obv, INDE•ET Reverse | 1,500 | 3,250 | 4,000 | — | — | — |

1788 Copper, Mailed Bust Facing Right

1788 Copper, Mailed Bust Facing Left

1788 Copper, Draped Bust Facing Left

| | G | VG | F | VF | EF | AU |
|---|---|---|---|---|---|---|
| 1788 Copper, Mailed Bust Facing Right | $75 | $125 | $250 | $650 | $1,500 | $3,000 |
| 1788 Copper, GEORGIVS III Obv (Reverse as Above) | 100 | 210 | 500 | 1,400 | 2,800 | — |
| 1788 Copper, Small Head *(see 1787 for illustration)* | 1,500 | 3,750 | 4,500 | 11,000 | 20,000 | — |
| 1788 Copper, Mailed Bust Facing Left | 45 | 70 | 175 | 350 | 1,000 | |
| 1788 Copper, Mailed Bust Facing Left, CONNLC | 55 | 130 | 200 | 500 | 1,500 | 2,800 |
| 1788 Copper, Draped Bust Facing Left | 55 | 85 | 200 | 450 | 1,350 | |
| 1788 Copper, Draped Bust Facing Left, CONNLC | 85 | 200 | 350 | 800 | 2,000 | 3,000 |
| 1788 Copper, Draped Bust Facing Left, INDL ET LIB | 80 | 140 | 250 | 700 | 1,800 | 3,400 |

## New York and Related Issues

### *Brasher Doubloons*

Among the most famous pieces coined before establishment of the U.S. Mint at Philadelphia were those produced by the well-known New York goldsmith and jeweler Ephraim Brasher, who was a neighbor and friend of George Washington.

The gold pieces Brasher made weighed about 408 grains and were valued at $15 in New York currency. They were approximately equal to the Spanish doubloon, which was equal to 16 Spanish dollars.

Pieces known as *Lima Style doubloons* were dated 1742, but it is almost certain that they were produced in 1786, and were the first efforts of Brasher to make a circulating coin for local use. Neither of the two known specimens shows the full legends; but weight, gold content, and punchmark are all identical to those for the other Brasher coins. An analogous cast imitation Lima style doubloon dated 1735 bears a hallmark attributed to Standish Barry of Baltimore, Maryland, circa 1787.

An original design was used on the 1787 Brasher doubloon with an eagle on one side and the arms of New York on the other. In addition to his impressed hallmark, Brasher's name appears in small letters on each of his coins. The unique 1787 gold half doubloon is struck from doubloon dies on an undersized planchet that weighs half as much as the larger coins.

It is uncertain why Brasher produced these pieces. He was later commissioned to test and verify other gold coins then in circulation. His hallmark EB was punched on each coin as evidence of his testing and its value. In some cases the foreign coins have been weight-adjusted by clipping.

| | |
|---|---|
| "1742" (1786) Lima Style gold doubloon *(2 known)* | $700,000 |
| *$690,000, EF-40, Heritage auction, January 2005* | |

| | | EF |
|---|---|---|
| 1787 New York gold doubloon, EB on Breast | *$2,990,000, EF-45, Heritage auction, January 2005* | *$5,000,000* |
| 1787 New York gold doubloon, EB on Wing | *$4,582,500, MS-63, Heritage auction, January 2014* | *4,000,000* |
| 1787 New York gold half doubloon *(unique, in Smithsonian Collection)* | | — |
| Various foreign gold coins with Brasher's EB hallmark | | *5,000–20,000* |

## *New York Copper Coinage*

Several individuals petitioned the New York legislature in early 1787 for the right to coin copper for the state, but a coinage was never authorized. Instead, a law was passed to regulate the copper coins already in use. Nevertheless, various unauthorized copper pieces were issued within the state, principally by two private mints.

One firm, known as Machin's Mills, was organized by Thomas Machin and situated near Newburgh. Shortly after this mint was formed, on April 18, 1787, it was merged with the Rupert, Vermont, mint operated by Reuben Harmon Jr. Harmon held a coinage grant from the Republic of Vermont. The combined partnership agreed to conduct their business in New York, Vermont, Connecticut, or elsewhere if they could benefit by it.

The operations at Machin's Mills were conducted in secret and were looked upon with suspicion by the local residents. They minted several varieties of imitation George III halfpence, as well as coppers of Connecticut, Vermont, and New Jersey.

The other mints, located in or near New York City, were operated by John Bailey and Ephraim Brasher. They had petitioned the legislature on February 12, 1787, for a franchise to coin copper. The extent of their partnership, if any, and details of their operation are unknown. Studies of the state coinage show that they produced primarily the EXCELSIOR and NOVA EBORAC pieces of New York, and possibly the "running fox" New Jersey coppers.

***Believed to be the bust of George Washington.***

| | G | VG | F | VF | EF | AU |
|---|---|---|---|---|---|---|
| 1786, NON VI VIRTUTE VICI | $3,500 | $7,500 | $12,500 | $25,000 | $50,000 | $85,000 |

**1787 EXCELSIOR Copper, Eagle on Globe Facing Left**

**1787 EXCELSIOR Copper, Large Eagle on Obverse**

| | G | VG | F | VF | EF |
|---|---|---|---|---|---|
| 1787 EXCELSIOR Copper, Eagle on Globe Facing Right | $2,750 | $4,000 | $8,500 | $25,000 | $60,000 |
| 1787 EXCELSIOR Copper, Eagle on Globe Facing Left | 2,750 | 3,500 | 8,000 | 18,000 | 40,000 |
| 1787 EXCELSIOR Copper, Large Eagle on Obverse, Arrows and Branch Transposed | 4,100 | 6,750 | 18,000 | 35,000 | 70,000 |

1787, George Clinton

1787, Indian and New York Arms

1787, Indian and Eagle on Globe

1787, Indian and George III Reverse

| | G | VG | F | VF | EF |
|---|---|---|---|---|---|
| 1787, George Clinton | $10,000 | $20,000 | $50,000 | $100,000 | $165,000 |
| 1787, Indian and New York Arms | 10,000 | 18,000 | 40,000 | 65,000 | 125,000 |
| 1787, Indian and Eagle on Globe | 10,000 | 20,000 | 40,000 | 70,000 | 135,000 |
| 1787, Indian and George III Reverse *(4 known)* | — | | | | |

## British Copper Coins and Their Imitations

### *(Including Machin's Mills, and Other Underweight Coinage of 1786–1789)*

The most common coin used for small transactions in early America was the British copper halfpenny. Wide acceptance and the non–legal tender status of these copper coins made them a prime choice for unauthorized reproduction by private individuals. Many such counterfeits were created in America by striking from locally made dies, or by casting or other crude methods. Some were made in England and imported into this country. Pieces dated 1781 and 1785 seem to have been made specifically for this purpose, while others were circulated in both countries.

Regal British halfpence and farthings dated 1749 are of special interest to collectors because they were specifically sent to the North American Colonies as reimbursement for participation in the expedition against Cape Breton, and circulated extensively throughout New England.

*Genuine British halfpenny coppers of both George II (1729–1754) and George III (1770–1775) show finely detailed features within a border of close dentils; the 1 in the date looks like a J. They are boldly struck on good-quality planchets. Their weight is approximately 9.5 grams; their diameter, 29 mm.*

*British-made lightweight imitation halfpence are generally smaller in diameter and thickness, and weigh less than genuine pieces. Details are crudely engraved or sometimes incomplete. Planchet quality may be poor.*

| | G | VG | F | VF | EF |
|---|---|---|---|---|---|
| 1749, George II British farthing | $20 | $40 | $75 | $175 | $250 |
| 1749, George II British halfpenny | 25 | 50 | 100 | 200 | 300 |
| 1770–1775, George III British halfpenny **(a)** | 15 | 20 | 50 | 100 | 250 |
| 1770–1775, British imitation halfpenny **(a)** | 15 | 20 | 25 | 100 | 250 |

**a.** Values shown are for the most common variety. Rare pieces are sometimes worth significantly more.

During the era of American state coinage, James F. Atlee and/or other coiners minted unauthorized, lightweight, imitation British halfpence. These American-made false coins have the same devices, legends, and, in some cases, dates as genuine regal halfpence, but contain less copper. Overall quality of these pieces is similar to that of the British-made imitations, but details are more often poorly rendered or missing. Identification of American-made imitations has been confirmed by identifying punch marks and matching them to those of known engravers.

There are four distinct groups of these halfpence, all linked to the regular state coinage. The first group was probably struck in New York City prior to 1786. The second group was minted in New York City in association with John Bailey and Ephraim Brasher during the first half of 1787. The third group was struck at Machin's Mills during the second half of 1787 and into 1788 or later. A fourth group, made by the Machin's coiners, consists of pieces made from dies that were muled with those of the state coinages of Connecticut, Vermont, and New York. Pieces with very crude designs and other dates are believed to have been struck elsewhere in New England.

## Georgivs/Britannia

### *"Machin's Mills" Copper Halfpennies Made in America*

Dates used on these pieces were often evasive, and are as follows: 1771, 1772, and 1774 through 1776 for the first group; 1747 and 1787 for the second group; and 1776, 1778, 1787, and 1788 for the third group. Pieces generally attributed to Atlee can be identified by a single outline in the crosses (British Union) of Britannia's shield and large triangular dentils along the coin circumference. The more-valuable American-made pieces are not to be confused with the similar English-made George III counterfeits (some of which have identical dates), or with genuine British halfpence dated 1770 to 1775.

*Group I coins dated 1771, 1772, and 1774 through 1776 have distinctive bold designs but lack the fine details of the original coins. Planchets are generally of high quality.*

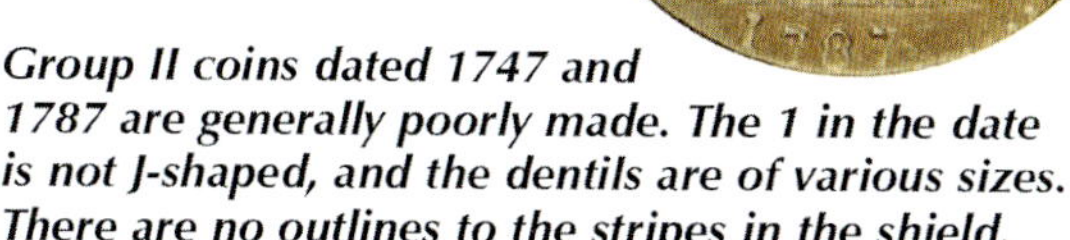

*Group II coins dated 1747 and 1787 are generally poorly made. The 1 in the date is not J-shaped, and the dentils are of various sizes. There are no outlines to the stripes in the shield.*

*Group III coins dated 1776, 1778, 1787, and 1788, struck at Machin's Mills in Newburgh, New York, are similar to coins of Group II, with their triangular-shaped dentils. Most have large dates and berries in obverse wreath.*

| | AG | G | VG | F | VF | EF | AU |
|---|---|---|---|---|---|---|---|
| 1747, GEORGIVS II. Group II. . . . . . . | $150 | $350 | $600 | $1,500 | $3,500 | $8,500 | |
| 1771, GEORGIVS III. Group I. . . . . . . | 150 | 350 | 600 | 1,500 | 3,500 | 8,500 | |
| 1772, GEORGIVS III. Group I. . . . . . . | 150 | 350 | 1,000 | 1,500 | 3,500 | 6,000 | |
| 1772, GEORGIUS III. Group I. . . . . . . | 85 | 200 | 300 | 750 | 2,300 | 4,500 | — |
| 1774, GEORGIVS III. Group I. . . . . . . | 50 | 100 | 250 | 750 | 1,500 | 3,500 | |
| 1774, GEORGIUS III. Group I. . . . . . . | 100 | 250 | 800 | 2,000 | 4,000 | 6,500 | |
| 1775, GEORGIVS III. Group I. . . . . . . | 50 | 100 | 200 | 750 | 1,500 | 3,500 | |
| 1776, GEORGIVS III. Group III. . . . . . | 100 | 200 | 500 | 1,000 | 3,000 | 7,000 | |
| 1776, GEORCIVS III, Small Date . . . . | 1,000 | 2,000 | 4,500 | 9,000 | 18,000 | 25,000 | $35,000 |
| 1778, GEORGIVS III. Group III. . . . . . | 40 | 70 | 125 | 275 | 700 | 2,000 | 3,200 |
| 1784, GEORGIVS III . . . . . . . . . . . . . | 150 | 400 | 1,000 | 2,500 | 4,500 | 6,500 | |
| 1787, GEORGIVS III. Group II . . . . . . | 30 | 75 | 100 | 200 | 600 | 1,200 | 2,500 |
| 1787, GEORGIVS III. Group III. . . . . . | 30 | 75 | 100 | 200 | 600 | 1,200 | 2,500 |
| 1788, GEORGIVS III. Group III. . . . . . | 50 | 100 | 200 | 650 | 1,200 | 2,750 | |

*Note:* Values shown are for the most common varieties in each category. Rare pieces can be worth significantly more. Also see related George III combinations under Connecticut, Vermont, and New York.

The muled coins of Group IV are listed separately with the Immune Columbia pieces and with the coins of Connecticut, Vermont, and New York. Other imitation coppers made by unidentified American makers are generally very crude and excessively rare. Cast copies of British coins probably circulated along with the imitations without being questioned. Counterfeit copies of silver Spanish-American coins and Massachusetts tree coins may have also been coined by American minters.

### *Nova Eborac Coinage for New York*

1787, NOVA EBORAC, Reverse: Seated Figure Facing Right

1787, NOVA EBORAC, Reverse: Seated Figure Facing Left

1787, NOVA EBORAC, Small Head

1787, NOVA EBORAC, Large Head

| | AG | G | F | VF | EF | AU |
|---|---|---|---|---|---|---|
| 1787, NOVA EBORAC, Seated Figure Facing Right. . . . | $50 | $110 | $300 | $700 | $1,200 | $2,000 |
| 1787, NOVA EBORAC, Seated Figure Facing Left. . . . . | 50 | 125 | 300 | 600 | 1,000 | 1,500 |
| 1787, NOVA EBORAC, Small Head . . . . . . . . . . . . . . . . | 3,000 | 6,500 | 25,000 | 45,000 | | |
| 1787, NOVA EBORAC, Large Head . . . . . . . . . . . . . . . . | 500 | 900 | 2,000 | 4,250 | 8,000 | |

## New Jersey

On June 1, 1786, the New Jersey General Assembly granted to Thomas Goadsby, Albion Cox, and Walter Mould authority to coin three million coppers weighing six pennyweight and six grains (150 grains total, or 9.72 grams) apiece, to be completed by June 1788, on condition that they deliver to the state treasurer "one Tenth Part of the full Sum they shall strike." These coppers were to pass current at 15 to the shilling. Matthias Ogden also played a significant financial and political role in the operation.

In an undertaking of this kind, the contractors purchased the metal and assumed all expenses of coining. The difference between these expenses and the total face value of the coins issued represented the profit.

Later, Goadsby and Cox asked authority to coin two-thirds of the total independently of Mould. Their petition was granted November 22, 1786. Mould was known to have produced his coins at Morristown, while Cox and Goadsby operated in Rahway. Coins with a diameter of 30 mm or more are generally considered Morristown products. Coins were also minted in Elizabethtown by Ogden and by others in New York.

The obverse shows design elements of the state seal, a horse's head with plow, and the legend NOVA CÆSAREA (New Jersey). The reverse has a United States shield and, for the first time on a coin, the legend E PLURIBUS UNUM (One Composed of Many).

More than 140 varieties exist. The majority have the horse's head facing to the right; however, three show the head facing left. Other variations have a sprig beneath the head, branches below the shield, stars, cinquefoils, and other ornaments.

**1786, Date Under Plow Beam**

**1786 and 1787, Pattern Shield**

**1786, Date Under Plow, No Coulter**

| | AG | G | F | VF | EF |
|---|---|---|---|---|---|
| 1786, Date Under Plow Beam | | | $85,000 | $125,000 | $200,000 |
| 1786, Date Under Plow, No Coulter | | $600 | 1,100 | 2,000 | 5,500 |
| 1787, Pattern Shield **(a)** | | 200 | 400 | 900 | 2,000 |

a. The so-called Pattern Shield reverse was also used on several speculative patterns. See pages 58 and 59.

**1786, Straight Plow Beam, Protruding Tongue**

**1786, Wide Shield**

**1786, Curved Plow Beam, Bridle Variety**

| | AG | G | F | VF | EF | AU |
|---|---|---|---|---|---|---|
| 1786, Straight Plow Beam (common varieties) | | $60 | $200 | $500 | $850 | $1,250 |
| 1786, Curved Plow Beam (common varieties) | | 60 | 220 | 650 | 1,000 | 1,750 |
| 1786, Protruding Tongue | $50 | 90 | 275 | 600 | 1,750 | 6,000 |
| 1786, Wide Shield | | 70 | 240 | 675 | 2,000 | 4,000 |
| 1786, Bridle variety | | 100 | 300 | 700 | 1,500 | 5,000 |

**1787, U Over S in PLURIBUS**

**1787, PLURIBS Error**

**1787, PLURIRUS Error**

| | AG | G | F | VF | EF | AU |
|---|---|---|---|---|---|---|
| 1786, PLUKIBUS error | | $120 | $500 | $750 | $2,000 | $5,500 |
| 1787, PLURIBS error | $150 | 300 | 2,000 | 3,500 | 9,000 | 12,500 |
| 1787, Second U Over S in PLURIBUS | 40 | 160 | 470 | 1,000 | 2,700 | 5,000 |
| 1787, PLURIRUS error | 100 | 250 | 900 | 1,800 | 3,500 | 7,000 |

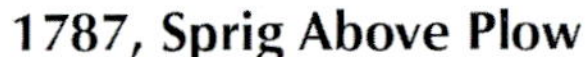
1787, Sprig Above Plow

1787, WM Above Plow

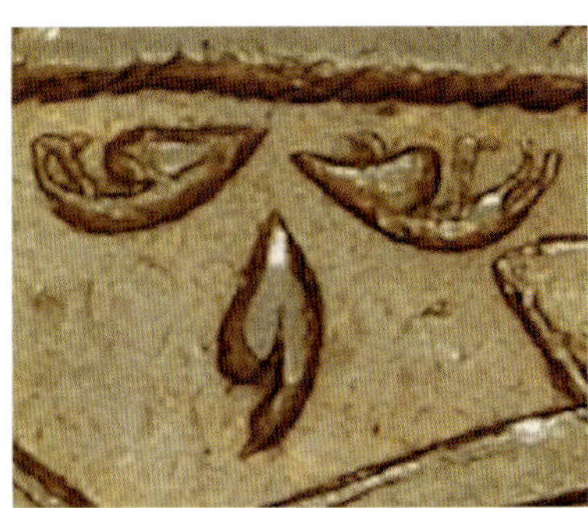
1787, Hidden WM

| | AG | G | F | VF | EF | AU |
|---|---|---|---|---|---|---|
| 1787, Sprig Above Plow (common varieties) . . . | | $80 | $275 | $600 | $1,200 | $2,500 |
| 1787, No Sprig Above Plow (common varieties) | | 65 | 200 | 550 | 800 | 1,250 |
| 1787, WM Above Plow *(unique)*. . . . . . . . . . . . . | | | | — | | |
| 1787, Hidden WM in Sprig. . . . . . . . . . . . . . . . . | | 90 | 350 | 850 | 2,200 | 4,500 |

1787 Over 1887

1787, Camel Head

1787, Serpent Head

| | AG | G | F | VF | EF | AU |
|---|---|---|---|---|---|---|
| 1787, Date Over 1887. . . . . . . . . . . . . . . . . . . . | | $800 | $4,000 | $9,000 | $20,000 | — |
| 1787, Camel Head (snout in high relief) . . . . . . | $40 | 85 | 250 | 600 | 1,000 | $2,250 |
| 1787, Serpent Head. . . . . . . . . . . . . . . . . . . . . . | 50 | 120 | 400 | 1,200 | 2,500 | 6,000 |
| 1787, Goiter Variety. . . . . . . . . . . . . . . . . . . . . | | 120 | 500 | 1,500 | 3,500 | 7,500 |

1788, Fox Before Legend

1788, Indistinct Coulter

1788, Fox After Legend

1788, Braided Mane

1788, Head Facing Left

| | AG | G | F | VF | EF | AU |
|---|---|---|---|---|---|---|
| 1788, Horse's Head Facing Right, several varieties | | $60 | $200 | $500 | $1,100 | $2,400 |
| 1788, Horse's Head Facing Right, Running Fox Before Legend | $75 | 150 | 500 | 1,400 | 3,500 | 8,000 |
| 1788, Similar, Indistinct Coulter | 150 | 650 | 2,500 | 6,500 | 15,000 | — |
| 1788, Horse's Head Facing Right, Running Fox After Legend | | | | 50,000 | 75,000 | |
| 1788, Braided Mane | 250 | 600 | 3,000 | 5,500 | 10,000 | 15,000 |
| 1788, Horse's Head Facing Left | | 250 | 1,200 | 3,500 | 12,000 | 22,000 |

# PRIVATE TOKENS AFTER CONFEDERATION

## North American Tokens

This piece was struck in Dublin, Ireland. The obverse shows the seated figure of Hibernia facing left. The date of issue is believed to have been much later than that shown on the token. Like many Irish tokens, this issue found its way to America in limited quantities and was accepted near the Canadian border.

| | VG | F | VF | EF | AU |
|---|---|---|---|---|---|
| 1781, copper or brass | $60 | $100 | $200 | $600 | $1,500 |

## Bar Coppers

The Bar copper is undated and of uncertain origin. It has 13 parallel and unconnected bars on one side. On the other side is the large roman-letter USA monogram. The design is virtually identical to that used on a Continental Army uniform button.

The significance of the design is clearly defined by its extreme simplicity. The separate 13 states (bars) unite into a single entity as symbolized by the interlocking letters (USA).

This piece is believed to have first circulated in New York during November 1785, and may have been made in England.

John Adams Bolen (1826–1907), a numismatist and a master diesinker in Springfield, Massachusetts, struck copies of the Bar copper around 1862. On these copies, the letter A passes under, instead of over, the S. Bolen's intent was not to deceive, and he advertised his copies plainly as reproductions. But his skills were such that W. Elliot Woodward, a leading auctioneer of tokens and medals in the 1860s, vacillated between selling Bolen's copies and describing them as "dangerous counterfeits." Bolen copies of the Bar copper are highly collectible in their own right, but they are less valuable than the originals.

| | G | VG | F | VF | EF | AU | Unc. |
|---|---|---|---|---|---|---|---|
| (Undated) (Circa 1785) Bar Copper . . | $1,000 | $1,800 | $3,000 | $6,000 | $8,000 | $12,000 | $25,000 |

## Auctori Plebis Tokens

This token is sometimes included with the coins of Connecticut, as it greatly resembles issues of that state. It was struck in England by an unknown maker, possibly for use in America.

| | G | VG | F | VF | EF | AU | Unc. |
|---|---|---|---|---|---|---|---|
| 1787, AUCTORI PLEBIS . . . . . . . . . . | $75 | $100 | $175 | $350 | $550 | $1,000 | $5,500 |

## Mott Store Cards

This 19th century store card has long been considered an early token because of its date (1789). Most scholars believe it was produced no earlier than 1807 (possibly in the Hard Times era of the late 1830s) as a commemorative of the founding of the Mott Company, and served as a business card. The firm, operated by Jordan Mott, was located at 240 Water Street, a fashionable section of New York at that time.

| | VG | F | VF | EF | AU | Unc. |
|---|---|---|---|---|---|---|
| "1789," Mott Token, Thick Planchet . . . . . . . . . | $80 | $175 | $300 | $400 | $500 | $1,000 |
| "1789," Mott Token, Thin Planchet . . . . . . . . . . | 80 | 200 | 350 | 600 | 1,200 | 2,200 |
| "1789," Mott Token, Entire Edge Engrailed . . . . | 80 | 300 | 450 | 900 | 1,400 | 3,000 |

## Standish Barry Threepence

Standish Barry, of Baltimore, circulated a silver threepence in 1790. He was a watch- and clockmaker, an engraver, and, later, a silversmith. The tokens are believed to have been an advertising venture at a time when small change was scarce. The precise date on this piece may indicate that Barry intended to commemorate Independence Day, but there are no records to prove this. The head on the obverse is probably that of James Calhoun, who was active in Baltimore politics in the 1790s. The legend BALTIMORE TOWN JULY 4, 90, appears in the border. An enigmatic gold doubloon is also attributed to Barry (see page 67).

| | VG | F | VF | EF | AU |
|---|---|---|---|---|---|
| 1790 Threepence | $10,000 | $20,000 | $40,000 | $65,000 | $80,000 |

## Albany Church Pennies

The First Presbyterian Church of Albany, New York, authorized an issue of 1,000 copper uniface tokens in 1790. These passed at 12 to a shilling and were used to stop contributions of worn and counterfeit coppers. Two varieties were made, one with the addition of a large D (the British abbreviation for penny) above the word CHURCH.

| | VG | F | VF | EF |
|---|---|---|---|---|
| (Undated) (1790) Without D | $10,000 | $12,500 | $25,000 | $40,000 |
| (Undated) (1790) With D Added | 10,000 | 15,000 | 30,000 | 50,000 |

## Kentucky Tokens

These tokens were struck in England circa 1792 to 1794. Each star in the triangle represents a state, identified by its initial letter. These pieces are usually called *Kentucky cents* because the letter K (for Kentucky) happens to be at the top. Some of the edges are plain; others are milled with a diagonal reeding; and some have edge lettering that reads PAYABLE IN LANCASTER LONDON OR BRISTOL, PAYABLE AT BEDWORTH NUNEATON OR HINKLEY, or PAYABLE AT I. FIELDING, etc.

| | VF | EF | AU | Unc. |
|---|---|---|---|---|
| (1792–1794) Copper, Plain Edge | $175 | $275 | $450 | $850 |
| (1792–1794) Copper, Engrailed Edge | 500 | 800 | 1,200 | 2,000 |
| (1792–1794) Copper, Lettered Edge, PAYABLE AT BEDWORTH, etc. | — | — | — | — |
| (1792–1794) Copper, Lettered Edge, PAYABLE IN LANCASTER, etc. | 225 | 300 | 500 | 700 |
| (1792–1794) Copper, Lettered Edge, PAYABLE AT I. FIELDING, etc. | — | — | — | — |

## Franklin Press Tokens

This piece is an English tradesman's token, but, being associated with the Franklin name, has accordingly been included in American collections.

| | VF | EF | AU | Unc. | MS-63 |
|---|---|---|---|---|---|
| 1794 Franklin Press Token | $250 | $350 | $550 | $750 | $1,000 |
| Similar, Edge Reads AN ASYLUM FOR THE OPPRESS'D OF ALL NATIONS *(unique)* | | | | | |
| Similar, Edge Diagonally Reeded *(unique)* | | | | | |

## Talbot, Allum & Lee Cents

Talbot, Allum & Lee, engaged in the India trade and located at 241 Pearl Street, New York, placed a large quantity of English-made coppers in circulation during 1794 and 1795. ONE CENT appears on the 1794 issue, and the legend PAYABLE AT THE STORE OF on the edge. The denomination is not found on the 1795 reverse but the edge legend was changed to read WE PROMISE TO PAY THE BEARER ONE CENT. Rare plain-edged specimens of both dates exist. Exceptional pieces have edges ornamented or with lettering CAMBRIDGE BEDFORD AND HUNTINGDON.X.X. Many of these tokens were later cut down and used by the U.S. Mint as planchets for coining 1795 and 1797 half cents.

1794 Cent, With NEW YORK

1795 Cent

| | VG | F | VF | EF | AU | Unc. |
|---|---|---|---|---|---|---|
| 1794 Cent, With NEW YORK | $65 | $80 | $225 | $350 | $500 | $1,000 |
| 1794 Cent, Without NEW YORK | 500 | 850 | 1,500 | 2,500 | 4,500 | 6,500 |
| 1795 Cent | 50 | 75 | 150 | 250 | 350 | 550 |

## Myddelton Tokens

These tokens were struck at the Soho Mint of Boulton and Watt near Birmingham, England, but they were never actually issued for circulation in Kentucky. Many believe they are unsurpassed in beauty and design by any piece of this period.

| | PF |
|---|---|
| 1796, Copper | $20,000 |

| | PF |
|---|---|
| 1796, Silver | $25,000 |

## Copper Company of Upper Canada Tokens

The obverse of this piece is the same as that of the Myddelton token. The new reverse refers to a Canadian firm and may have been made for numismatic purposes, or as part of the coiner's samples.

| | PF |
|---|---|
| 1796, Copper | $15,000 |

## Castorland Medals

These medals, or "jetons," are dated 1796 and allude to a proposed French settlement known as Castorland in Carthage, New York, at the time of the French Revolution. They were given to directors of the colonizing company for their attendance at board meetings.

Copy dies are still available and have been used at the Paris Mint for restriking throughout the years. Restrikes have a more modern look; their metallic content (in French) is impressed on the edge: ARGENT (silver), CUIVRE (copper), or OR (gold).

| | EF | AU | Unc. |
|---|---|---|---|
| 1796, Original, silver (reeded edge, unbroken dies) | $3,000 | $4,500 | $7,500 |
| 1796, Original, silver (reverse rusted and broken) | 300 | 600 | 1,500 |
| 1796, Original, bronze (reverse rusted and broken) | 200 | 300 | 700 |
| (1796) Undated, Restrike, silver (Paris Mint edge marks) | | 30 | 70 |
| (1796) Undated, Restrike, bronze (Paris Mint edge marks) | | 20 | 40 |

## Theatre at New York Tokens

These token pennies were issued by Skidmore of London and illustrate The Theatre, New York, circa 1797.

| | EF | PF |
|---|---|---|
| Penny, THE THEATRE AT NEW YORK AMERICA | $10,000 | $22,500 |

## New Spain (Texas) Jola Tokens

In 1817 the Spanish governor of Texas, Manuel Pardo, authorized Manuel Barrera to coin 8,000 copper coins known as jolas. These crudely made pieces show the denomination ½ (real), the maker's initials and the date on the obverse, and a five-pointed star on the reverse.

The 1817 coins were withdrawn from circulation the following year and replaced by a similar issue of 8,000 pieces bearing the date 1818 and the initials JAG of the maker, José Antonio de la Garza. Several varieties of each issue are known. All are rare.

| | F | VF | EF |
|---|---|---|---|
| 1817 1/2 Real | $6,000 | $12,500 | $25,000 |
| 1818 1/2 Real, Large or Small Size | 10,000 | 15,000 | 25,000 |

## North West Company Tokens

These tokens were probably valued at one beaver skin and struck in Birmingham in 1820 by John Walker & Co. All but two known specimens are holed, and most have been found in the region of the Columbia and Umpqua river valleys.

| | AG | G | VG | F | VF |
|---|---|---|---|---|---|
| 1820, Copper or Brass (with hole) | $375 | $800 | $2,000 | $3,500 | $7,500 |

## WASHINGTON PIECES

Medals, tokens, and coinage proposals in this interesting series dated from 1783 to 1795 bear the portrait of George Washington. The likenesses in most instances were faithfully reproduced and were designed to honor the first president. Many of these pieces were of English origin and were made later than their dates indicate.

The legends generally signify a strong unity among the states and the marked display of patriotism that pervaded the new nation during that period. We find among these tokens an employment of what were soon to become the nation's official coin devices, namely, the American eagle, the United States shield, and stars. The denomination ONE CENT is used in several instances, while on some of the English pieces HALFPENNY will be found. Several of these pieces were private patterns for proposed coinage contracts.

### Georgivs Triumpho Tokens

Although the head shown on this token bears a strong resemblance to that on some coins of George III, many collectors consider the Georgivs Triumpho ("Triumphant George") a token intended to commemorate America's victory in the Revolutionary War.

The reverse side shows the Goddess of Liberty behind a framework of 13 bars and fleurs-de-lis. Holding an olive branch in her right hand and staff of liberty in her left, she is partially encircled by the words VOCE POPOLI ("By the Voice of the People") 1783. An example is known used as an undertype for a 1787 New Jersey copper (Maris 73-aa).

| | VG | F | VF | EF | AU |
|---|---|---|---|---|---|
| 1783, GEORGIVS TRIUMPHO . . . . . . . . . . . . . . . . . . . . . . . . | $110 | $225 | $500 | $700 | $1,000 |

### Washington Portrait Pieces

Large Military Bust, Point of Bust Close to W

Small Military Bust

| | F | VF | EF | AU | Unc. |
|---|---|---|---|---|---|
| 1783, Large Military Bust . . . . . . . . . . . . . . . . . . . . . . . . . . | | | $250 | $500 | $1,500 |
| 1783, Small Military Bust, Plain Edge . . . . . . . . . . . . . . . . . | $80 | $175 | 450 | 650 | 1,800 |
| 1783, Small Military Bust, Engrailed Edge . . . . . . . . . . . . . . | 100 | 200 | 550 | 1,000 | 2,750 |

No Button

With Button

| | F | VF | EF | AU | Unc. | PF |
|---|---|---|---|---|---|---|
| 1783, Draped Bust, No Button *(illustrated)* | $80 | $160 | $300 | $500 | $1,500 | |
| 1783, Draped Bust, With Button (on Drapery at Neck) | 125 | 225 | 350 | 700 | 3,200 | |
| 1783, Draped Bust, Copper Restrike, Plain Edge | 125 | 225 | 350 | 550 | 650 | $850 |
| 1783, Draped Bust, Copper Restrike, Engrailed Edge | | | | | | 750 |
| 1783, Draped Bust, Silver Restrike, Engrailed Edge | | | | | | 3,500 |

| | VG | F | VF | EF | AU | Unc. |
|---|---|---|---|---|---|---|
| 1783, UNITY STATES | $100 | $150 | $200 | $250 | $450 | $1,250 |

| | F | VF | EF | AU | Unc. |
|---|---|---|---|---|---|
| (Undated) Double-Head Cent | $100 | $250 | $425 | $500 | $2,000 |

Satirical Medal Presumably of American Origin

| | |
|---|---|
| 1784, Ugly Head, Copper *$20,000, Crude Good, Stack's Bowers auction, December 1983* | — |
| 1784, Ugly Head, Pewter *(unique)* | |

1791 Cent, Edge Lettered UNITED STATES OF AMERICA

| | F | VF | EF | AU | Unc. |
|---|---|---|---|---|---|
| 1791 Cent, Small Eagle (Date on Reverse). . . . . . . . . . . . . . | $475 | $650 | $800 | $1,200 | $2,500 |

1791 Cent, Large Eagle Reverse

Obverse (Cent and Halfpenny)

1791 Halfpenny, Reverse

| | VG | F | VF | EF | AU | Unc. |
|---|---|---|---|---|---|---|
| 1791 Cent, Large Eagle (Date on Obverse) . . . . | $150 | $350 | $550 | $750 | $1,100 | $2,250 |
| 1791 Liverpool Halfpenny, Lettered Edge. . . . . . | 700 | 900 | 1,250 | 1,500 | 2,500 | — |

1792, Eagle With 13 Stars Reverse

| | VG | F | VF | EF |
|---|---|---|---|---|
| 1792, WASHINGTON PRESIDENT, Eagle With 13 Stars Reverse | | | | |
| PRESIDENT at Side of Bust, copper . . . . . . . . . . . . . . . . . . . . . . . . | | | | — |
| PRESIDENT, silver . . . . . . . . . . . . . . . . . . . . . . . . . . . . . . . . . . . . . . . | | | $125,000 | — |
| PRESIDENT, gold *(unique)* . . . . . . . . . . . . . . . . . . . . . . . . . . . . . . . | | | — | |
| *$1,740,000, EF-45★, Heritage auction, August 2018* | | | | |
| PRESIDENT Extends Below Bust, copper *(unique)* . . . . . . . . . . . . . . | | | | $125,000 |

1792,
WASHINGTON PRESIDENT

Legend Reverse

(1792) Undated,
WASHINGTON BORN VIRGINIA

| | VG | F | VF | EF |
|---|---|---|---|---|
| 1792, WASHINGTON PRESIDENT, Legend on Reverse | | | | |
| Plain Edge, copper | $2,750 | $7,500 | $18,000 | $50,000 |
| Lettered Edge, copper | — | — | — | — |
| (1792) Undated, WASHINGTON BORN VIRGINIA, Eagle With 13 Stars Reverse *(reverse illustrated on previous page)*, copper *(3 known)* | | — | | |
| (1792) Undated, WASHINGTON BORN VIRGINIA, Legend on Reverse | | | | |
| Copper | 1,000 | 1,500 | 3,000 | 5,000 |
| Copper, edge lettered UNITED STATES OF AMERICA *(1 known)* | | | | |
| Silver | — | — | — | — |

*Note:* Uniface restrike of undated obverse exists, made from transfer dies by Albert Collis, 1959.

### *Getz Patterns*

Dies engraved by Peter Getz of Lancaster, Pennsylvania, are believed to have been made to produce a half dollar and cent as a proposal to Congress for a private contract coinage before the Philadelphia Mint became a reality.

| | VG | F | VF | EF | AU | Unc. |
|---|---|---|---|---|---|---|
| 1792, Small Eagle, silver<br>*$241,500, AU, Stack's Bowers auction, May 2004* | — | — | — | $125,000 | | |
| 1792, Small Eagle, copper<br>*$165,000, MS-64BN, Heritage auction, November 2014* | $6,000 | $12,000 | $30,000 | 50,000 | $75,000 | $100,000 |
| 1792, Small Eagle, Ornamented Edge (Circles and Squares), copper<br>*$207,000, AU, Stack's Bowers auction, November 2006* | — | — | — | 150,000 | | |
| 1792, Small Eagle, Ornamented Edge, silver *(4 known)*<br>*$391,000, Gem BU PL, Stack's Bowers auction, May 2004* | — | — | 100,000 | 175,000 | | |
| 1792, Large Eagle, silver<br>*$34,500, EF, Stack's Bowers auction, May 2004* | | | — | — | | |

**1792 Cent, Roman Head, Lettered Edge: UNITED STATES OF AMERICA**

| | PF |
|---|---|
| 1792 Cent, Roman Head, Lettered Edge UNITED STATES OF AMERICA, Proof | $75,000 |

**1793 Ship Halfpenny**

| | VG | F | VF | EF | AU | Unc. |
|---|---|---|---|---|---|---|
| 1793 Ship Halfpenny, Lettered Edge | $100 | $200 | $400 | $600 | $850 | $3,250 |
| 1793 Ship Halfpenny, Plain Edge *(rare)* | | | — | — | | |

**1795 Halfpenny, Grate Token**
***Large Coat Buttons variety shown.***

| | F | VF | EF | AU | Unc. |
|---|---|---|---|---|---|
| 1795, Large Buttons, Lettered Edge | $180 | $300 | $650 | $1,000 | $1,500 |
| 1795, Large Buttons, Reeded Edge | 80 | 175 | 300 | 400 | 700 |
| 1795, Small Buttons, Reeded Edge | 80 | 200 | 400 | 550 | 1,250 |

## *Liberty and Security Tokens*

*See next page for chart.*

| | F | VF | EF | AU | Unc. |
|---|---|---|---|---|---|
| 1795 Halfpenny, Plain Edge | $110 | $200 | $500 | $850 | $2,500 |
| 1795 Halfpenny, LONDON Edge | 100 | 210 | 500 | 700 | 2,500 |
| 1795 Halfpenny, BIRMINGHAM Edge | 125 | 250 | 500 | 900 | 2,500 |
| 1795 Halfpenny, ASYLUM Edge | 200 | 400 | 1,000 | 1,500 | 3,000 |
| 1795 Penny, ASYLUM Edge | | | 10,000 | 15,000 | 25,000 |

**(1795) Undated, Liberty and Security Penny, ASYLUM Edge**

| | F | VF | EF | AU | Unc. |
|---|---|---|---|---|---|
| (1795) Undated, Liberty and Security Penny | $275 | $450 | $600 | $1,000 | $1,700 |
| Same, Corded Outer Rims | 600 | 1,000 | 2,500 | 5,000 | 7,500 |

## *North Wales Halfpennies*

| | G | F | VF | EF | AU |
|---|---|---|---|---|---|
| (1795) Undated, NORTH WALES Halfpenny | $90 | $200 | $500 | $750 | $1,000 |
| (1795) Undated, Lettered Edge | 450 | 1,200 | 4,000 | 6,000 | 7,500 |
| (1795) Undated, Two Stars at Each Side of Harp | 2,000 | 5,000 | 7,500 | 25,000 | |

## *Success Medals*

| | VF | EF | AU | Unc. | MS-63 |
|---|---|---|---|---|---|
| (Undated) SUCCESS Medal, Large, Plain or Reeded Edge | $250 | $450 | $750 | $1,400 | $2,750 |
| (Undated) SUCCESS Medal, Small, Plain or Reeded Edge | 300 | 500 | 800 | 1,250 | 3,000 |

*Note:* These pieces are struck in copper or brass and are believed to have been made in the late 18th century. Specimens with original silvering are rare and are valued 20% to 50% higher. Varieties exist.

## CONTINENTAL CURRENCY

The Continental Currency pieces were made to serve in lieu of a paper dollar, but the exact nature of their monetary role is still unclear. They were the first silver dollar–sized coins ever proposed for the United States and may have been intended as a substitute for the paper dollar. One obverse die was engraved by someone whose initials were E.G. (undoubtedly Elisha Gallaudet) and is marked EG FECIT ("EG Made It"). Studies of the coinage show that there may have been two separate emissions made at different mints. The link design on the reverse was suggested by Benjamin Franklin.

Varieties result from differences in the spelling of the word CURRENCY and the addition of EG FECIT on the obverse. These coins were struck in pewter, brass, and silver. Pewter pieces served as a dollar, substituting for paper currency of this design that was never issued. Brass and silver pieces may have been experimental or patterns. Pewter pieces in original bright Uncirculated condition are worth an additional premium.

Numerous copies and replicas of these coins have been made over the years. Authentication is recommended for all pieces.

CURRENCY CURENCY

| | G | F | VF | EF | AU | Unc. |
|---|---|---|---|---|---|---|
| 1776 CURENCY, Pewter *(2 varieties)* . . . . . . . . . . . . | $7,750 | $12,000 | $25,000 | $35,000 | $50,000 | $70,000 |
| 1776 CURENCY, Brass *(2 varieties)* . . . . . . . . . . . . . | | 35,000 | 65,000 | 115,000 | | |
| *$299,000, MS-63, Heritage auction, July 2009* | | | | | | |
| 1776 CURENCY, Silver *(2 known)*. . . . . . . . . . . . . . . | | | | *1,527,000* | | |
| *$1,527,500, EF-40, Heritage auction, January 2015* | | | | | | |
| 1776 CURRENCY, Pewter. . . . . . . . . . . . . . . . . . . . . | 8,000 | 13,000 | 25,000 | 35,000 | 50,000 | 75,000 |
| 1776 CURRENCY, EG FECIT, Pewter. . . . . . . . . . . . . | 8,500 | 15,000 | 27,500 | 40,000 | 55,000 | 80,000 |
| *$546,250, MS-67, Heritage auction, January 2012* | | | | | | |
| 1776 CURRENCY, EG FECIT, Silver *(2 known)* . . . . . | | — | — | — | — | 1,500,000 |
| *$1,410,000, MS-63, Heritage auction, May 2014* | | | | | | |
| 1776 CURRENCEY, Pewter. . . . . . . . . . . . . . . . . . . | — | — | 65,000 | | 175,000 | — |
| 1776 CURRENCY, Pewter, Ornamented Date *(3 known)* | | | | 276,000 | 329,000 | |
| *$276,000, EF-45, Heritage auction, July 2009* | | | | | | |

## NOVA CONSTELLATIO PATTERNS

These Nova Constellatio pieces undoubtedly represent the first patterns for a coinage of the United States. They were designed by Benjamin Dudley for Gouverneur Morris to carry out his ideas for a decimal coinage system. The 1,000-unit designation he called a mark, the 500 a quint. These denominations, together with the small 100-unit piece, were designed to standardize the many different coin values among the several states. These pattern pieces represent the first attempt at a decimal ratio, and were the forerunners of our present system of money values. Neither the proposed denominations nor the coins advanced beyond the pattern stage. These unique pieces are all dated 1783. There are two types of the quint. The copper "five" was first brought to the attention of collectors in 1980. Electrotype copies exist.

5 Units

Bit (100 Units)

Quint (Plain Obverse)

Quint Reverse

Quint (Legend on Obverse)

Mark

| | |
|---|---|
| 1783 (Five) "5," Copper | (unique) |
| 1783 (Bit) "100," Silver, Decorated Edge *$97,500, Unc., B&R auction, November 1979* | (2 known) |
| 1783 (Bit) "100," Silver, Plain Edge *$705,000, AU-55, Heritage auction, May 2014* | (unique) |
| 1783 (Quint) "500," Silver, Plain Obverse *$1,175,000, AU-53, Heritage auction, April 2013* | (unique) |
| 1783 (Quint) "500," Silver, Legend on Obverse *$165,000, Unc., B&R auction, November 1979* | (unique) |
| 1783 (Mark) "1000," Silver *$190,000, Unc., B&R auction, November 1979* | (unique) |

## FUGIO COPPERS

The first coins issued under U.S. authority for which contract information is known today were the Fugio pieces, which were valued at one cent each. They were made under contract with James Jarvis, owner of a a controlling interest in the Connecticut mint, which was then striking Connecticut coppers in New Haven. Jarvis obtained the federal contract with a $10,000 bribe to Col. William Duer, then head of the Board of Treasury. The contract called for Jarvis to deliver 345 tons of copper coins to the federal government. Congress, which was ignorant of the bribe, directed on July 7, 1787, "that the Board of Treasury direct the contractor for the copper coinage to stamp on one side of each piece the following device, viz: thirteen circles linked together, a small circle in the middle, with the words 'United States,' around it; and in the centre, the words 'We are one'; on the other side of the same piece the following device, viz: a dial with the hours expressed on the face of it; a meridian sun above on one side of which is the word 'Fugio,' ["time flies"] and on the other the year in figures '1787,' below the dial, the words 'Mind Your Business.'"

Jarvis was only able to mint 11,910 pounds of Fugios (equal to around 554,741 coins). Not all of these were shipped to the government, which cancelled the contract for failure to meet the delivery schedule.

All Fugios were minted in 1788 and back-dated 1787. The dies were engraved by Abel Buell.

## 1787 With Pointed Rays

American Congress Pattern — Cross After Date — Label With Raised Rims

| | G | VG | F | VF | EF | AU | Unc. |
|---|---|---|---|---|---|---|---|
| Obverse Cross After Date, No Cinquefoils | | | | | | | |
| Reverse Rays and AMERICAN CONGRESS . . . . . . | | | | $200,000 | $300,000 | $500,000 | |
| Reverse Label with Raised Rims *(extremely rare)* | | | $10,000 | 15,000 | 35,000 | | |
| Reverse STATES UNITED . . . . . . . . . . . . . . . . . . | $325 | $500 | 1,000 | 2,500 | 6,000 | 12,000 | — |
| Reverse UNITED STATES . . . . . . . . . . . . . . . . . . . | 300 | 450 | 800 | 1,500 | 4,000 | 9,000 | — |

Cinquefoil After Date

***These types, with pointed rays, have regular obverses punctuated with four cinquefoils (five-leafed ornaments).***

| | G | VG | F | VF | EF | AU | Unc. |
|---|---|---|---|---|---|---|---|
| STATES UNITED at Sides of Circle, Cinquefoils on Label . . . . . . . . | $225 | $375 | $600 | $1,100 | $1,600 | | |
| STATES UNITED, 1 Over Horizontal 1 | 300 | 500 | 1,000 | 3,000 | 8,000 | $22,500 | |
| UNITED STATES, 1 Over Horizontal 1 | 225 | 375 | 600 | 1,000 | 1,500 | 1,800 | $2,300 |
| UNITED STATES at Sides of Circle . . | 225 | 375 | 600 | 1,000 | 1,500 | 1,800 | |

*Chart continued on next page.*

| | G | VG | F | VF | EF | AU | Unc. |
|---|---|---|---|---|---|---|---|
| STATES UNITED, Label With Raised Rims, Large Letters in WE ARE ONE .... | $250 | $400 | $700 | $1,700 | $3,500 | $6,000 | $12,000 |
| STATES UNITED, 8-Pointed Star on Label | 225 | 375 | 600 | 1,100 | 1,800 | 3,200 | 7,500 |
| UNITED Above, STATES Below........ | 850 | 1,750 | 3,750 | 8,000 | 11,500 | 15,000 | 18,000 |

## 1787 With Club Rays

Rounded Ends

Concave Ends

| | G | VG | F | VF | EF | AU |
|---|---|---|---|---|---|---|
| Club Rays, Rounded Ends ...................... | $275 | $400 | $800 | $1,500 | $2,500 | $4,500 |
| Club Rays, Concave Ends to Rays, FUCIO (C instead of G) *(extremely rare)* .............. | 1,500 | 3,000 | 6,000 | 20,000 | 30,000 | |
| Club Rays, Concave Ends, FUGIO, UNITED STATES .... | 2,200 | 5,000 | 10,000 | 30,000 | 40,000 | 90,000 |
| Club Rays, Similar, STATES UNITED Reverse......... | | — | — | | — | — |

The so-called New Haven "restrikes" were made for Horatio N. Rust from dies recreated in 1859, partially through use of hubs or other devices supposedly obtained (though the story is discredited by modern scholars) by 14-year-old C. Wyllis Betts in 1858 on the site of the Broome & Platt store in New Haven, where the original coins had been made.

**New Haven Restrike.** *Note narrow rings.*

| | EF | AU | Unc. |
|---|---|---|---|
| Gold *(2 known)* ............................................. | | — | — |
| Silver......................................................... | $3,200 | $4,750 | $7,500 |
| Copper or Brass............................................. | 500 | 600 | 900 |

## 1792 PROPOSED COINAGE

Many members of the House favored a representation of the president's head on the obverse of each coin; others considered the idea a monarchical practice. Washington is believed to have expressed disapproval of the use of his portrait on American coins.

The majority considered a figure emblematic of Liberty more appropriate, and the Senate finally concurred in this opinion. Robert Birch was an engraver employed to design proposed devices for American coins. He, perhaps together with others, engraved the dies for the disme and half disme. He also cut the dies for the large copper patterns known today as *Birch cents.* Many 1792 half dismes circulated.

## 1792 Silver Center Cent

| | F | VF | EF | AU |
|---|---|---|---|---|
| Cent, Silver Center *(14 known, including one unique specimen without plug) $1,997,500, MS-64BN, Heritage auction, August 2014* | $200,000 | $275,000 | $350,000 | $600,000 |
| Cent, Without Silver Center *(9 known)* | 250,000 | 375,000 | 475,000 | 650,000 |

## 1792 Birch Cent

G★W.Pt.

| | F | VF | EF |
|---|---|---|---|
| Copper, Lettered Edge, TO BE ESTEEMED * BE USEFUL* *(6–7 known)* *$2,585,000, MS-65★RB, Heritage auction, January 2015* | $225,000 | $550,000 | $675,000 |
| Copper, Plain Edge *(2 known)* | | 700,000 | |
| Copper, Lettered Edge, TO BE ESTEEMED BE USEFUL * *(2 known)* | | — | |
| White Metal, G*W.Pt. (George Washington President) Below Wreath *(unique)* | | | — |

## 1792 Half Disme

| | Mintage | AG | G | VG | F | VF | EF | AU | Unc. |
|---|---|---|---|---|---|---|---|---|---|
| Silver *$1,410,000, SP-67, Heritage auction, January 2013* | 1,500 | $9,500 | $22,000 | $27,500 | $40,000 | $80,000 | $110,000 | $175,000 | $300,000 |

## 1792 Disme

| | F | EF | AU | Unc. |
|---|---|---|---|---|
| Silver *(3 known)* | $300,000 | $450,000 | $850,000 | |
| Copper *(about 15 known; illustrated)* *$1,057,500, MS-64RB, Heritage auction, January 2015* | 135,000 | 225,000 | 450,000 | $950,000 |

## 1792 Quarter Dollar

Little is known of this pattern coin's origins, except that it was added to the Mint Cabinet by Chief Coiner Adam Eckfeldt. In the 19th century it was often called a "cent," but the eagle design is more appropriate for a silver or gold issue than a copper. It is commonly called a "quarter" today. Unique uniface trials of the obverse and reverse also exist.

| | EF |
|---|---|
| 1792, Copper *(illustrated) (2 known)* | $750,000 |
| *$2,232,500, MS-63, Heritage auction, January 2015* | |
| 1792, White Metal *(4 known)* | 325,000 |

## THE LIBERTAS AMERICANA MEDAL

The Liberty Cap coinage of the fledgling United States was inspired by the famous Libertas Americana medal, whose dies were engraved by Augustin Dupré in Paris in 1782 from a concept and mottoes proposed by Benjamin Franklin. To Franklin (then U.S. minister to France), the infant Hercules symbolized America, strangling two serpents representing the British armies at Saratoga and Yorktown. Minerva, with shield and spear, symbolized France as America's ally, keeping the British Lion at bay. Franklin presented examples of the medal to the French king and queen (in gold) and to their ministers (in silver), "as a monumental acknowledgment, which may go down to future ages, of the obligations we are under to this nation."

Between 100 and 125 original copper medals exist, and two dozen or more silver; the location of the two gold medals is unknown. Over the years the Paris Mint has issued additional medals that have a more modest value as mementos.

| | PF-50 | PF-60 | PF-63 | PF-65 |
|---|---|---|---|---|
| Libertas Americana medal, copper *(100–125 known)* | $10,000 | $15,000 | $27,500 | $50,000 |
| Libertas Americana medal, silver *(24+ known)* | 60,000 | 100,000 | 175,000 | 300,000 |

The half cent is the lowest face value coin struck by the United States. All half cents are scarce.

This denomination was authorized on April 2, 1792. Originally the weight was to have been 132 grains, but this was changed to 104 grains by the Act of January 14, 1793, before coinage commenced. The weight was again changed, to 84 grains, on January 26, 1796, by presidential proclamation in conformity with the Act of March 3, 1795. Coinage was discontinued by the Act of February 21, 1857. All were coined at the Philadelphia Mint.

There were various intermissions in coinage. During the period from 1836 through 1848, coinage consisted entirely of Proofs and in very small quantities, causing a very noticeable lapse in the series for most collectors. While 1796 is the most valuable date, the original and restrike Proofs of 1831, 1836, 1840 through 1848, and 1852, along with other rare varieties, are all difficult to obtain.

## LIBERTY CAP, HEAD FACING LEFT (1793)

*Designer unknown; engraver Henry Voigt; weight 6.74 grams; composition, copper; approx. diameter 22 mm; edge: TWO HUNDRED FOR A DOLLAR.*

**AG-3 About Good**—Clear enough to identify.
**G-4 Good**—Outline of bust of Liberty clear, no details. Date readable. Reverse lettering incomplete.
**VG-8 Very Good**—Some hair details. Reverse lettering complete.
**F-12 Fine**—Most of hair detail visible. Leaves worn, but all visible.
**VF-20 Very Fine**—Hair near ear and forehead worn, other areas distinct. Some details in leaves visible.
**EF-40 Extremely Fine**—Light wear on highest parts of head and wreath.
**AU-50 About Uncirculated**—Only a trace of wear on Liberty's face.

*Values shown are for coins with attractive surfaces and color consistent with the amount of normal wear. Minor imperfections are permissible for grades below Fine. Coins that are porous, corroded, or similarly defective are worth significantly lower prices.*

| | Mintage | AG-3 | G-4 | VG-8 | F-12 | VF-20 | EF-40 | AU-50 |
|---|---|---|---|---|---|---|---|---|
| 1793 | 35,334 | $2,500 | $3,500 | $5,250 | $8,750 | $11,000 | $16,500 | $25,000 |
| *$920,000, MS-66BN, Goldberg auction, January 2014* | | | | | | | | |

## LIBERTY CAP, HEAD FACING RIGHT (1794–1797)

*1794—Designer and engraver Robert Scot; weight 6.74 grams; composition, copper; approx. diameter 23.5 mm; edge: TWO HUNDRED FOR A DOLLAR. 1795—Designer John Smith Gardner; weight 6.74 grams; composition, copper; approx. diameter 23.5 mm; edge: TWO HUNDRED FOR A DOLLAR. 1795–1797 (thin planchet)—Weight 5.44 grams; composition, copper; approx. diameter 23.5 mm; edge: plain (some 1797 are either lettered or gripped).*

**AG-3 About Good**—Clear enough to identify.
**G-4 Good**—Outline of bust of Liberty clear, no details. Date readable. Reverse lettering incomplete.
**VG-8 Very Good**—Some hair details. Reverse lettering complete.
**F-12 Fine**—Most of hair detail visible. Leaves worn, but all visible.
**VF-20 Very Fine**—Hair near ear and forehead worn, other areas distinct. Some details in leaves visible.
**EF-40 Extremely Fine**—Light wear on highest parts of head and wreath.
**AU-50 About Uncirculated**—Only a trace of wear on Liberty's face.

Normal Head

High-Relief Head

| | Mintage | AG-3 | G-4 | VG-8 | F-12 | VF-20 | EF-40 | AU-50 |
|---|---|---|---|---|---|---|---|---|
| 1794, All kinds | 81,600 | | | | | | | |
| 1794, Normal Head | | $425 | $575 | $950 | $1,800 | $2,250 | $5,000 | $11,000 |
| 1794, High-Relief Head | | 475 | 600 | 975 | 1,850 | 3,200 | 6,200 | 14,500 |
| *$1,150,000, MS-67RB, Goldberg auction, January 2014* | | | | | | | | |

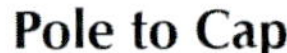

Pole to Cap

Punctuated Date

No Pole to Cap

| | Mintage | AG-3 | G-4 | VG-8 | F-12 | VF-20 | EF-40 | AU-50 |
|---|---|---|---|---|---|---|---|---|
| 1795, All kinds | 139,690 | | | | | | | |
| 1795, Lettered Edge, With Pole | | $325 | $600 | $825 | $1,300 | $2,250 | $4,500 | $8,000 |
| 1795, Lettered Edge, Punctuated Date | | 350 | 675 | 875 | 1,750 | 2,850 | 7,000 | 11,000 |
| 1795, Plain Edge, Punctuated Date | | 275 | 550 | 725 | 1,250 | 2,350 | 5,500 | 9,500 |
| 1795, Plain Edge, No Pole **(a)** | | 220 | 500 | 675 | 1,250 | 2,000 | 4,000 | 7,500 |
| 1796, With Pole **(b)** | 1,390 | 10,500 | 20,000 | 27,500 | 37,500 | 55,000 | 75,000 | 95,000 |
| *$630,000, MS-66+, Heritage auction, August 2018* | | | | | | | | |
| 1796, No Pole | * | 20,000 | 35,000 | 45,000 | 105,000 | 150,000 | 210,000 | 300,000 |
| *$891,250, MS-65BN, Goldberg auction, January 2014* | | | | | | | | |

* Included in number above. **a.** Many are struck on cut-down cents, or are on planchets cut from Talbot, Allum & Lee cents (see page 78). **b.** The deceptive "Dr. Edwards" struck copy of this coin has a different head and larger letters.

1797, 1 Above 1

1797, Low Head

| | Mintage | AG-3 | G-4 | VG-8 | F-12 | VF-20 | EF-40 | AU-50 |
|---|---|---|---|---|---|---|---|---|
| 1797, All kinds **(a)** | 127,840 | | | | | | | |
| 1797, 1 Above 1, Plain Edge | | $250 | $500 | $650 | $1,100 | $1,800 | $4,000 | $6,500 |
| 1797, Plain Edge, Low Head | | 350 | 575 | 975 | 2,000 | 4,000 | 14,000 | — |
| 1797, Plain Edge | | 275 | 500 | 750 | 1,250 | 3,500 | 6,000 | 8,500 |
| 1797, Lettered Edge | | 700 | 1,400 | 2,500 | 6,000 | 15,000 | 50,000 | |
| 1797, Gripped Edge | | 22,500 | 50,000 | 75,000 | 145,000 | — | — | — |

**a.** Many are struck on cut-down cents, or are on planchets cut from Talbot, Allum & Lee cents (see page 78).

## DRAPED BUST (1800–1808)

*Designer probably Gilbert Stuart; engraver Robert Scot; weight 5.44 grams; composition, copper; diameter 23.5 mm; plain edge.*

**AG-3 About Good**—Clear enough to identify.
**G-4 Good**—Outline of bust of Liberty clear, few details, date readable. Reverse lettering worn and incomplete.
**VG-8 Very Good**—Some drapery visible. Date and legends complete.
**F-12 Fine**—Shoulder drapery and hair over brow worn smooth.
**VF-20 Very Fine**—Only slight wear in previously mentioned areas. Slight wear on reverse.
**EF-40 Extremely Fine**—Light wear on highest parts of head and wreath.
**AU-50 About Uncirculated**—Wear slight on hair above forehead.

1st Reverse (Style of 1800)

2nd Reverse (Style of 1803)

| | Mintage | AG-3 | G-4 | VG-8 | F-12 | VF-20 | EF-40 | AU-50 |
|---|---|---|---|---|---|---|---|---|
| 1800 | 202,908 | $55 | $110 | $150 | $175 | $300 | $675 | $850 |
| 1802, 2 Over 0, Reverse of 1800 | * | 10,000 | 22,000 | 32,500 | 55,000 | 75,000 | 115,000 | — |
| 1802, 2 Over 0, Second Reverse | 20,266 | 475 | 950 | 2,250 | 4,750 | 11,000 | 20,000 | — |
| 1803 | * | 45 | 95 | 120 | 175 | 325 | 950 | 1,500 |
| 1803, Widely Spaced 3 | 92,000 | 50 | 100 | 135 | 185 | 325 | 950 | 1,500 |

* Included in number below.

Plain 4

Crosslet 4

"Spiked Chin"

Stems to Wreath

Stemless Wreath

| | Mintage | AG-3 | G-4 | VG-8 | F-12 | VF-20 | EF-40 | AU-50 |
|---|---|---|---|---|---|---|---|---|
| 1804, All kinds | 1,055,312 | | | | | | | |
| 1804, Plain 4, Stems to Wreath | | $55 | $100 | $125 | $200 | $475 | $1,300 | $2,200 |
| 1804, Plain 4, Stemless Wreath | | 40 | 85 | 125 | 145 | 225 | 385 | 675 |
| 1804, Crosslet 4, Stemless | | 40 | 85 | 125 | 145 | 225 | 385 | 675 |
| 1804, Crosslet 4, Stems | | 40 | 85 | 125 | 145 | 225 | 400 | 675 |
| 1804, "Spiked Chin" | | 40 | 95 | 125 | 225 | 350 | 600 | 950 |

Medium 5

Small 5

Large 5

| | Mintage | AG-3 | G-4 | VG-8 | F-12 | VF-20 | EF-40 | AU-50 |
|---|---|---|---|---|---|---|---|---|
| 1805, All kinds | 814,464 | | | | | | | |
| 1805, Medium 5, Stemless | | $40 | $85 | $125 | $145 | $225 | $400 | $750 |
| 1805, Small 5, Stems | | 500 | 1,000 | 1,600 | 4,000 | 8,000 | 17,000 | 50,000 |
| 1805, Large 5, Stems | | 40 | 85 | 125 | 145 | 225 | 425 | 850 |

Small 6

Large 6

1808, 8 Over 7

Normal Date

| | Mintage | AG-3 | G-4 | VG-8 | F-12 | VF-20 | EF-40 | AU-50 |
|---|---|---|---|---|---|---|---|---|
| 1806, All kinds | 356,000 | | | | | | | |
| 1806, Small 6, Stems | | $100 | $235 | $425 | $750 | $1,650 | $3,500 | $6,500 |
| 1806, Small 6, Stemless | | 40 | 85 | 125 | 145 | 175 | 325 | 675 |
| 1806, Large 6, Stems | | 40 | 85 | 125 | 145 | 175 | 325 | 675 |
| 1807 | 476,000 | 40 | 85 | 125 | 145 | 200 | 500 | 1,000 |
| 1808, All kinds | 400,000 | | | | | | | |
| 1808, Normal Date | | 40 | 85 | 125 | 145 | 220 | 525 | 1,200 |
| 1808, 8 Over 7 | | 80 | 150 | 350 | 750 | 2,000 | 4,000 | 10,000 |
| *$483,000, MS-65BN+, Goldberg auction, January 2014* | | | | | | | | |

## CLASSIC HEAD (1809–1836)

*Designer John Reich. Standards same as for previous issue.*

**G-4 Good**—LIBERTY only partly visible on hair band. Lettering, date, and stars worn but visible.
**VG-8 Very Good**—LIBERTY entirely visible on hair band. Lower curls worn.
**F-12 Fine**—Only partial wear on LIBERTY, and hair at top worn in spots.
**VF-20 Very Fine**—Lettering clear-cut. Hair only slightly worn.
**EF-40 Extremely Fine**—Light wear on highest points of hair and leaves.
**AU-50 About Uncirculated**—Sharp hair detail with only a trace of wear on higher points.
**MS-60 Uncirculated**—Typical brown to red surface. No trace of wear.
**MS-63 Choice Uncirculated**—Well-defined color, brown to red. No traces of wear.

1809, Small o Inside 0

1811, Wide Date

1809, 9 Over Inverted 9

1809, Normal Date

1811, Close Date

| | Mintage | G-4 | VG-8 | F-12 | VF-20 | EF-40 | AU-50 | MS-60 | MS-63BN |
|---|---|---|---|---|---|---|---|---|---|
| 1809, All kinds | 1,154,572 | | | | | | | | |
| 1809, Normal Date | | $55 | $95 | $115 | $125 | $150 | $275 | $750 | $1,350 |
| 1809, Small o Inside 0 | | 65 | 85 | 135 | 325 | 450 | 900 | 3,250 | |
| 1809, 9 Over Inverted 9 | | 65 | 85 | 125 | 150 | 375 | 750 | 1,300 | 2,200 |
| 1810 | 215,000 | 70 | 100 | 150 | 270 | 575 | 1,000 | 2,000 | 3,200 |
| 1811, All kinds | 63,140 | | | | | | | | |
| 1811, Wide Date | | 450 | 850 | 1,900 | 2,750 | 6,500 | 10,000 | 32,500 | 75,000 |
| *$1,121,250, MS-66RB, Goldberg auction, January 2014* | | | | | | | | | |
| 1811, Close Date | | 400 | 725 | 1,750 | 2,500 | 6,500 | 10,000 | 32,500 | 75,000 |
| 1811, Reverse of 1802, Unofficial Restrike *(extremely rare)* | | | | | | — | — | 16,000 | 20,000 |
| 1825 | 63,000 | 55 | 90 | 100 | 115 | 200 | 325 | 900 | 1,800 |
| 1826 | 234,000 | 55 | 90 | 100 | 115 | 150 | 300 | 600 | 1,000 |

13 Stars

12 Stars

| | Mintage | G-4 | VG-8 | F-12 | VF-20 | EF-40 | AU-50 | MS-60 | MS-63BN |
|---|---|---|---|---|---|---|---|---|---|
| 1828, All kinds | 606,000 | | | | | | | | |
| 1828, 13 Stars | | $50 | $90 | $100 | $115 | $120 | $200 | $325 | $600 |
| 1828, 12 Stars | | 50 | 90 | 115 | 120 | 250 | 425 | 1,150 | 1,850 |
| 1829 | 487,000 | 50 | 90 | 100 | 115 | 140 | 220 | 400 | 700 |

Beginning in 1831, new coinage equipment and modified dies produced a raised rim on each side of these coins. Proofs and restrikes were made at the Mint for sale to collectors. Restrikes are believed to have been struck circa 1858 through 1861.

Reverse (1831–1836)

Reverse (1840–1857)

| | Mintage | PF-40 | PF-60BN | PF-63BN |
|---|---|---|---|---|
| 1831, Original *(beware of altered date)* | 2,200 | $50,000 | $85,000 | $125,000 |
| 1831, Restrike, Large Berries (Reverse of 1836) | | 5,000 | 10,000 | 15,000 |
| 1831, Restrike, Small Berries (Reverse of 1840–1857) | | 7,000 | 14,000 | 21,500 |

| | Mintage | VG-8 | F-12 | VF-20 | EF-40 | AU-50 | MS-60 | PF-63BN |
|---|---|---|---|---|---|---|---|---|
| 1832 **(a)** | 51,000 | $65 | $90 | $110 | $125 | $200 | $325 | $12,500 |
| 1833 **(a)** | 103,000 | 65 | 90 | 110 | 125 | 200 | 325 | 6,000 |
| 1834 **(a)** | 141,000 | 65 | 90 | 110 | 125 | 200 | 300 | 6,000 |
| 1835 **(a)** | 398,000 | 65 | 85 | 110 | 125 | 200 | 325 | 6,000 |
| 1836, Original | | | | | | | | 8,000 |
| 1836, Restrike (Reverse of 1840–1857) | | | | | | | | 17,000 |

**a.** The figures given here are thought to be correct, although official Mint records report these quantities for 1833 through 1836 rather than 1832 through 1835.

No half cents were struck in 1837. Because of the great need for small change, however, a large number of tokens similar in size to current large cents were issued privately by businessmen who needed them in commerce. Additionally, thousands of half cent tokens were issued of the variety listed and illustrated below.

| | G-4 | VG-8 | F-12 | VF-20 | EF-40 | AU-50 | MS-60 |
|---|---|---|---|---|---|---|---|
| 1837 Token *(not a coin)* | $45 | $65 | $75 | $110 | $200 | $375 | $700 |

## BRAIDED HAIR (1840–1857)

Both originals and restrikes use the reverse of 1840 to 1857. Most originals have large berries and most restrikes have small berries in the wreath.

*Designer Christian Gobrecht; weight 5.44 grams; composition, copper; diameter 23 mm; plain edge.*

**VG-8 Very Good**—Beads in hair uniformly distinct. Hair lines visible in spots.
**F-12 Fine**—Hair lines above ear worn. Beads sharp.
**VF-20 Very Fine**—Lowest curl worn; hair otherwise distinct.
**EF-40 Extremely Fine**—Light wear on highest points of hair and on leaves.
**AU-50 About Uncirculated**—Very slight trace of wear on hair above Liberty's ear.
**MS-60 Uncirculated**—No trace of wear. Clear luster.
**MS-63 Choice Uncirculated**—No trace of wear.
**PF-63 Choice Proof**—Nearly perfect; only light blemishes.

Large Berries

Small Berries

*Brilliant red Proof half cents are worth more than the prices shown.*

| | PF-63BN | PF-65BN |
|---|---|---|
| 1840, Original | $6,500 | $10,000 |
| 1840, Restrike | 6,500 | 9,250 |
| 1841, Original | 5,500 | 10,000 |
| 1841, Restrike | 5,500 | 8,750 |
| 1842, Original | 7,000 | 10,000 |
| 1842, Restrike | 5,500 | 8,750 |
| 1843, Original | 5,500 | 10,000 |
| 1843, Restrike | 5,700 | 8,750 |
| 1844, Original | 6,000 | 12,500 |
| 1844, Restrike | 5,750 | 8,750 |
| 1845, Original | $6,000 | $15,000 |
| 1845, Restrike | 5,400 | 9,000 |
| 1846, Original | 6,000 | 12,500 |
| 1846, Restrike | 5,750 | 8,750 |
| 1847, Original | 6,000 | 12,500 |
| 1847, Restrike | 5,500 | 8,500 |
| 1848, Original | 6,250 | 15,000 |
| 1848, Restrike | 5,600 | 8,500 |
| 1849, Original, Small Date | 5,500 | 10,000 |
| 1849, Restrike, Small Date | 5,750 | 9,750 |

1849, Small Date

1849, Large Date

*Brilliant red Uncirculated half cents are worth more than the prices shown.*

| | Mintage | VG-8 | F-12 | VF-20 | EF-40 | AU-50 | MS-60 | MS-63BN | PF-63BN |
|---|---|---|---|---|---|---|---|---|---|
| 1849, Large Date | 39,864 | $60 | $75 | $90 | $150 | $240 | $500 | $700 | — |
| 1850 | 39,812 | 60 | 75 | 125 | 175 | 275 | 600 | 800 | $7,000 |
| 1851 | 147,672 | 60 | 75 | 90 | 115 | 175 | 275 | 500 | 10,000 |
| 1852, Original<br>*$603,750, PF-65RD, Goldberg auction, January 2014* | | | | | | | | | — |
| 1852, Restrike | | | | | | | | | 6,000 |
| 1853 | 129,694 | 60 | 75 | 90 | 115 | 175 | 275 | 500 | |
| 1854 | 55,358 | 60 | 75 | 90 | 115 | 165 | 275 | 500 | 4,500 |
| 1855 | 56,500 | 60 | 75 | 90 | 100 | 165 | 275 | 500 | 4,500 |
| 1856 | 40,430 | 60 | 75 | 90 | 125 | 185 | 275 | 575 | 4,500 |
| 1857 | 35,180 | 95 | 115 | 130 | 185 | 260 | 400 | 650 | 4,500 |

Cents and half cents were the first coins struck for circulation by the United States Mint. Coinage began in 1793 with laws specifying that the cent should weigh exactly twice as much as the half cent. Large cents are dated every year from 1793 to 1857 with the exception of 1815, when a lack of copper prevented production. All were coined at the Philadelphia Mint. Mintage records in some cases may be inaccurate, as many of the early pieces were struck later than the dates shown on the coins. Varieties listed are those most significant to collectors. Numerous other die varieties may be found because each of the early dies was individually made. Values of varieties not listed in this guide depend on collector interest, rarity, and demand. Proof large cents were first made in 1817; all Proofs are rare, as they were not made available to the general public before the mid-1850s.

## FLOWING HAIR

**AG-3 About Good**—Date and devices clear enough to identify.
**G-4 Good**—Lettering worn but readable. No detail on bust.
**VG-8 Very Good**—Date and lettering distinct, some details of head visible.
**F-12 Fine**—About half of hair and other details visible.
**VF-20 Very Fine**—Ear visible, most details visible.
**EF-40 Extremely Fine**—Wear evident on highest points of hair and back of temple.

### Chain Reverse (1793)

*Designer unknown; engraver Henry Voigt; weight 13.48 grams; composition, copper; approx. diameter 26–27 mm; edge: bars and slender vine with leaves.*

AMERI. Reverse

Obverse

AMERICA Reverse

*Values shown for Fine and better copper coins are for those with attractive surfaces and color consistent with the amount of normal wear. Coins that are porous, corroded, or similarly defective are worth significantly lower prices.*

| | Mintage | AG-3 | G-4 | VG-8 | F-12 | VF-20 | EF-40 | AU-50 |
|---|---|---|---|---|---|---|---|---|
| 1793, Chain, All kinds | 36,103 | | | | | | | |
| 1793, AMERI. in Legend | | $5,500 | $9,000 | $17,500 | $26,500 | $45,000 | $85,000 | $175,000 |
| *$1,500,000, MS-64BN+, Heritage auction, January 2019* | | | | | | | | |
| 1793, AMERICA, With Periods | | 4,750 | 7,750 | 15,000 | 21,000 | 35,000 | 65,000 | 120,000 |
| *$2,350,000, MS-66BN, $990,000, MS-65BN, Heritage auction, June 2018* | | | | | | | | |
| 1793, AMERICA, Without Periods | | 4,750 | 7,500 | 14,000 | 19,500 | 32,000 | 60,000 | 100,000 |
| *$998,750, MS-65RB, Sotheby's / Stack's Bowers auction, February 2016* | | | | | | | | |

### Wreath Reverse (1793)

The reverse of this type bears a single-bow wreath, as distinguished from the wreath tied with a double bow on the following type. A three-leaf sprig appears above the date on the obverse, and both sides have borders of small beads.

Introduction of this reverse answered criticism of the chain design, which critics saw as symbolic of slavery rather than strength in unity, but the stronger modeling of the face and hair still failed to gain acceptance as representative of Liberty. After three months' production the design was abandoned in favor of the Liberty Cap type.

Instead of the normal sprig above the date, the rare strawberry-leaf variety has a spray of trefoil leaves and a small blossom. The trefoils match those found on the normal wreath reverse. It is not clear why this variety was created. All four known specimens are well worn.

*Designer unknown; engraver Henry Voigt; weight 13.48 grams; composition, copper; approx. diameter 26–28 mm; edge: vine and bars, or lettered ONE HUNDRED FOR A DOLLAR followed by either a single or a double leaf.*

Wreath Type

Strawberry Leaf Variety

| | Mintage | AG-3 | G-4 | VG-8 | F-12 | VF-20 | EF-40 | AU-50 |
|---|---|---|---|---|---|---|---|---|
| 1793, Wreath, All kinds | 63,353 | | | | | | | |
| 1793, Vine/Bars Edge<br>*$528,750, MS-66BN, Heritage, August 2014* | | $1,600 | $3,250 | $4,700 | $7,500 | $12,000 | $21,000 | $30,000 |
| 1793, Lettered Edge<br>*$270,250, MS-64BN, Stack's Bowers auction, August 2014* | | 1,800 | 3,500 | 5,000 | 8,500 | 15,000 | 25,000 | 36,000 |
| 1793, Strawberry Leaf *(4 known)*<br>*$862,500, F-12, Stack's Bowers auction, January 2009* | | 350,000 | 500,000 | 650,000 | 1,000,000 | | | |

## LIBERTY CAP (1793–1796)

Another major change was made in 1793 to satisfy continuing objections to the obverse portrait. This version appears to have been more popular, as it was continued into 1796. The 1793 pieces had beaded borders, but a border of denticles (or "teeth") was adopted in 1794. A famous 1794 variety is the probably whimsical "starred" reverse, with a border of 94 tiny, five-pointed stars among the denticles.

Portrait variations listed for 1794 are the result of several changes of die engravers. The so-called Jefferson Head of 1795 is now thought to be a sample for a proposed coinage contract by a private manufacturer, John Harper.

Planchets became too thin for edge lettering after the weight reduction ordered in late 1795. The variety with reeded edge was probably an experimental substitute, rejected in favor of a plain edge.

*1793–1795 (thick planchet)—Designer probably Henry Voigt; weight 13.48 grams; composition, copper; approx. diameter 29 mm; edge: ONE HUNDRED FOR A DOLLAR followed by a single leaf. 1795–1796 (thin planchet)—Designer John Smith Gardner; weight 10.89 grams; composition, copper; approx. diameter 29 mm; plain edge.*

**1793, Vine and Bars Edge**
*Chain and Wreath types only.*

**Lettered Edge (1793–1795)**
**ONE HUNDRED FOR A DOLLAR**

Beaded Border (1793)

"Jefferson" Head

**Head of 1793 (1793–1794)**
*Head in high, rounded relief.*

**Head of 1794 (1794)**
*Well-defined hair; hook on lowest curl. (a)*

**Head of 1795 (1794–1796)**
*Head in low relief; no hook on lowest curl. (a)*

**1794, Starred Reverse**

**Reeded Edge**

| | Mintage | AG-3 | G-4 | VG-8 | F-12 | VF-20 | EF-40 |
|---|---|---|---|---|---|---|---|
| 1793, Liberty Cap | 11,056 | $7,000 | $12,000 | $16,500 | $24,000 | $40,000 | $115,000 |
| *$940,000, AU-58, Sotheby's/ Stack's Bowers auction, March 2017* | | | | | | | |
| 1794, All kinds | 918,521 | | | | | | |
| 1794, Head of 1793 | | 800 | 1,800 | 3,600 | 5,000 | 12,000 | 25,000 |
| *$881,250, MS-64BN, Stack's Bowers auction, January 2013* | | | | | | | |
| 1794, Head of 1794 | | 275 | 425 | 700 | 1,250 | 2,300 | 4,500 |
| 1794, Head in Low Relief **(a)** | | 250 | 400 | 650 | 1,200 | 2,100 | 4,250 |
| 1794, Exact Head of 1795 **(a)** | | 300 | 475 | 750 | 1,350 | 2,750 | 5,250 |
| *$499,375, MS-67RB, Stack's Bowers auction, January 2013* | | | | | | | |
| 1794, Starred Reverse | | 13,500 | 18,500 | 25,000 | 50,000 | 90,000 | 300,000 |
| *$632,500, AU-50, Heritage auction, February 2008* | | | | | | | |
| 1794, No Fraction Bar | | 300 | 500 | 900 | 1,500 | 3,000 | 6,500 |
| 1795, Lettered Edge | 37,000 | 275 | 500 | 900 | 1,250 | 2,750 | 5,500 |
| 1795, Plain Edge | 501,500 | 200 | 375 | 600 | 1,000 | 1,800 | 3,300 |
| 1795, Reeded Edge *(9 known)* | | 110,000 | 225,000 | 450,000 | 750,000 | | |
| *$1,265,000, VG-10, Goldberg auction, September 2009* | | | | | | | |
| 1795, Jefferson Head *(not a regular Mint issue)*, Plain Edge | | 11,000 | 25,000 | 37,500 | 55,000 | 110,000 | 225,000 |
| 1795, Jefferson Head, Lettered Edge *(3 known)* | | | — | 100,000 | 150,000 | 300,000 | |
| 1796, Liberty Cap | 109,825 | 300 | 475 | 850 | 1,750 | 3,500 | 7,000 |
| *$705,000, MS-66+RB, Sotheby's/ Stack's Bowers auction, March 2017* | | | | | | | |

**a.** The 1794 coin with Head of 1795 has a hooked curl but is in low relief.

## DRAPED BUST (1796–1807)

*Designer Robert Scot; weight 10.89 grams; composition, copper; approx. diameter 29 mm; plain edge.*

**AG-3 About Good**—Clear enough to identify.
**G-4 Good**—Lettering worn, but clear; date clear. Bust lacking in detail.
**VG-8 Very Good**—Drapery on Liberty partly visible. Less wear in date and lettering.
**F-12 Fine**—Hair over brow smooth; some detail showing in other parts of hair.
**VF-20 Very Fine**—Hair lines slightly worn. Hair over brow better defined.
**EF-40 Extremely Fine**—Hair above forehead and left of eye outlined and detailed. Only slight wear on olive leaves.

**1796–1807**
***This head was modified slightly in 1798.*** ***See page 103 for details.***

**LIHERTY Error**

**Reverse of 1794 (1794–1796)**
***Note double leaf at top right; 14–16 leaves on left, 16–18 leaves on right.***

**Reverse of 1795 (1795–1798)**
***Note single leaf at top right; 17–21 leaves on left, 16–20 leaves on right.***

**Reverse of 1797 (1796–1807)**
***Note double leaf at top right; 16 leaves on left, 19 leaves on right.***

| | Mintage | AG-3 | G-4 | VG-8 | F-12 | VF-20 | EF-40 |
|---|---|---|---|---|---|---|---|
| 1796, Draped Bust, All kinds | 363,375 | | | | | | |
| 1796, Reverse of 1794 | | $275 | $425 | $700 | $1,500 | $2,750 | $6,250 |
| 1796, Reverse of 1795 | | 225 | 375 | 600 | 1,150 | 3,000 | 6,500 |
| 1796, Reverse of 1797 | | 200 | 350 | 500 | 1,000 | 2,250 | 4,500 |
| 1796, LIHERTY Error | | 450 | 850 | 1,600 | 3,500 | 6,000 | 13,500 |
| 1796, Stemless Reverse *(3 known)* | | | 25,000 | | | | |

**With Stems**

**Gripped Edge**

**Stemless**

| | Mintage | AG-3 | G-4 | VG-8 | F-12 | VF-20 | EF-40 |
|---|---|---|---|---|---|---|---|
| 1797, All kinds | 897,510 | | | | | | |
| 1797, Gripped Edge, 1795-Style Reverse | | $130 | $225 | $400 | $750 | $1,500 | $3,700 |
| 1797, Plain Edge, 1795-Style Reverse | | 150 | 275 | 500 | 1,200 | 2,500 | 4,500 |
| 1797, 1797 Reverse, With Stems | | 125 | 200 | 300 | 650 | 1,400 | 2,400 |
| 1797, 1797 Reverse, Stemless | | 150 | 275 | 650 | 1,400 | 3,000 | 7,000 |

**Style 1 Hair**
*All 1796–1797, many 1798 varieties, and on 1800 Over 1798.*

**Style 2 Hair**
*1798–1807 (extra curl near shoulder).*

**1798, 8 Over 7**

| | Mintage | AG-3 | G-4 | VG-8 | F-12 | VF-20 | EF-40 |
|---|---|---|---|---|---|---|---|
| 1798, All kinds | 1,841,745 | | | | | | |
| 1798, 8 Over 7 | | $200 | $375 | $650 | $1,500 | $3,500 | $8,000 |
| 1798, Reverse of 1796 | | 250 | 500 | 1,250 | 3,000 | 5,500 | 12,000 |
| 1798, Style 1 Hair | | 95 | 150 | 275 | 600 | 1,100 | 2,200 |
| 1798, Style 2 Hair | | 70 | 120 | 200 | 475 | 750 | 1,650 |

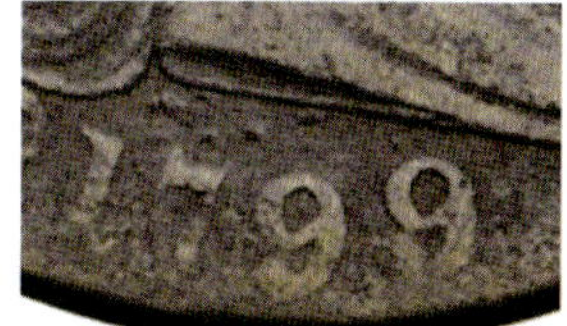
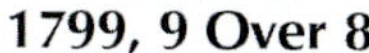

**1799, 9 Over 8**

**1800, 1800 Over 1798**

**1800, 80 Over 79**

| | Mintage | AG-3 | G-4 | VG-8 | F-12 | VF-20 | EF-40 |
|---|---|---|---|---|---|---|---|
| 1799, 9 Over 8 | **(a)** | $3,750 | $6,500 | $11,500 | $25,000 | $40,000 | $135,000 |
| *$368,000, EF-45, Goldberg auction, September 2009* | | | | | | | |
| 1799, Normal Date | **(a)** | 3,000 | 5,000 | 9,000 | 15,000 | 30,000 | 95,000 |
| *$977,500, MS-62BN, Goldberg auction, September 2009* | | | | | | | |
| 1800, All kinds | 2,822,175 | | | | | | |
| 1800, 1800 Over 1798, Style 1 Hair | | 65 | 130 | 250 | 550 | 1,400 | 3,850 |
| 1800, 80 Over 79, Style 2 Hair | | 65 | 125 | 200 | 400 | 1,000 | 2,500 |
| 1800, Normal Date | | 65 | 100 | 160 | 325 | 800 | 2,000 |

**a.** Included in "1798, All kinds" mintage.

**Fraction 1/000**

**Corrected Fraction**

**1801 Reverse, 3 Errors**

*Error-fraction dies appear on 1801–1803 cents; all these dies originated in 1801, possibly from same engraver.*

| | Mintage | AG-3 | G-4 | VG-8 | F-12 | VF-20 | EF-40 |
|---|---|---|---|---|---|---|---|
| 1801, All kinds | 1,362,837 | | | | | | |
| 1801, Normal Reverse | | $55 | $85 | $140 | $275 | $600 | $1,500 |
| 1801, 3 Errors: 1/000, One Stem, and IINITED | | 125 | 225 | 550 | 1,400 | 3,000 | 7,500 |
| 1801, Fraction 1/000 | | 95 | 150 | 325 | 575 | 1,300 | 4,250 |
| 1801, 1/100 Over 1/000 | | 105 | 180 | 375 | 675 | 1,600 | 5,500 |
| 1802, All kinds | 3,435,100 | | | | | | |
| 1802, Normal Reverse | | 55 | 100 | 125 | 250 | 500 | 1,200 |
| 1802, Fraction 1/000 | | 75 | 125 | 200 | 375 | 650 | 1,750 |
| 1802, Stemless Wreath | | 60 | 100 | 135 | 250 | 550 | 1,300 |

1803, Small Date, Blunt 1 — 1803, Large Date, Pointed 1 — Small Fraction — Large Fraction

*All Small Date varieties have blunt 1 in date.*
*Large Dates have pointed 1 and noticeably larger 3.*

*Values shown for Fine and better copper coins are for those with attractive surfaces and color consistent with the amount of normal wear. Coins that are porous, corroded, or similarly defective are worth significantly lower prices.*

| | Mintage | AG-3 | G-4 | VG-8 | F-12 | VF-20 | EF-40 |
|---|---|---|---|---|---|---|---|
| 1803, All kinds | 3,131,691 | | | | | | |
| 1803, Small Date, Small Fraction | | $55 | $85 | $125 | $250 | $500 | $1,200 |
| 1803, Small Date, Large Fraction | | 55 | 85 | 130 | 250 | 500 | 1,100 |
| 1803, Large Date, Small Fraction | | 5,000 | 8,500 | 12,000 | 25,000 | 40,000 | 115,000 |
| 1803, Large Date, Large Fraction | | 160 | 265 | 500 | 900 | 2,200 | 3,700 |
| 1803, 1/100 Over 1/000 | | 75 | 150 | 250 | 475 | 950 | 2,250 |
| 1803, Stemless Wreath | | 65 | 125 | 150 | 325 | 800 | 1,800 |

**Broken Dies**

*All genuine 1804 cents have crosslet 4 in date and a large fraction. The 0 in date is in line with O in OF on reverse.*

| | Mintage | AG-3 | G-4 | VG-8 | F-12 | VF-20 | EF-40 |
|---|---|---|---|---|---|---|---|
| 1804 **(a)** | *96,500* | $1,200 | $2,500 | $4,000 | $5,500 | $9,500 | $17,000 |
| *$661,250, MS-63BN, Goldberg auction, September 2009* | | | | | | | |

**a.** Values shown are for coins with normal or broken dies.

A "restrike" 1804 was manufactured from discarded Mint dies. An altered 1803 die was used for the obverse and a die of the 1820 cent used for the reverse. They were struck circa 1860 to satisfy the demand for this rare date. Known as the "restrike," the product actually is a combination of two unrelated dies and cannot be confused with the genuine.

**Unofficial 1804 "Restrike"**

| | Mintage | AG-3 | G-4 | VG-8 | F-12 | VF-20 | EF-40 |
|---|---|---|---|---|---|---|---|
| 1804, Unofficial Restrike of 1860 *(Uncirculated)* | | | | | | | $1,000 |
| 1805 | 941,116 | $55 | $85 | $115 | $225 | $500 | 1,200 |
| 1806 | 348,000 | 75 | 125 | 180 | 400 | 700 | 2,000 |

Small 1807, 7 Over 6
(Blunt 1)

Large 1807, 7 Over 6
(Pointed 1)

"Comet" Variety
*Note die break behind head.*

| | Mintage | AG-3 | G-4 | VG-8 | F-12 | VF-20 | EF-40 |
|---|---|---|---|---|---|---|---|
| 1807, All kinds | 829,221 | | | | | | |
| 1807, Small 1807, 7 Over 6, Blunt 1 | | $1,500 | $3,250 | $5,000 | $9,500 | $22,500 | $65,000 |
| 1807, Large 1807, 7 Over 6, Pointed 1 | | 65 | 100 | 200 | 400 | 700 | 1,500 |
| 1807, Small Fraction | | 65 | 110 | 225 | 450 | 600 | 2,500 |
| 1807, Large Fraction | | 55 | 100 | 200 | 350 | 550 | 1,250 |
| 1807, "Comet" Variety | | 100 | 175 | 300 | 550 | 1,200 | 2,850 |

## CLASSIC HEAD (1808–1814)

This group (1808–1814) does not compare in sharpness and quality to those struck previously (1793–1807) nor to those struck later (from 1816 on). The copper used was softer, having more metallic impurity. This impaired the wearing quality of the series. For this reason, collectors find greater difficulty in obtaining these dates in choice condition.

*Designer John Reich; weight 10.89 grams; composition, copper; approx. diameter 29 mm; plain edge.*

**AG-3 About Good**—Details clear enough to identify.
**G-4 Good**—Legends, stars, and date worn, but plain.
**VG-8 Very Good**—LIBERTY all readable. Liberty's ear visible. Details worn but plain.
**F-12 Fine**—Hair on forehead and before ear nearly smooth. Ear and hair under ear sharp.
**VF-20 Very Fine**—Some detail in all hair lines. Slight wear on leaves on reverse.
**EF-40 Extremely Fine**—All hair lines sharp. Very slight wear on high points.

| | Mintage | AG-3 | G-4 | VG-8 | F-12 | VF-20 | EF-40 |
|---|---|---|---|---|---|---|---|
| 1808 | 1,007,000 | $75 | $125 | $235 | $550 | $1,100 | $2,200 |
| 1809 | 222,867 | 200 | 275 | 600 | 950 | 1,700 | 3,750 |

1810, 10 Over 09

1810, Normal Date

1811, Last 1 Over 0

1811, Normal Date

| | Mintage | AG-3 | G-4 | VG-8 | F-12 | VF-20 | EF-40 |
|---|---|---|---|---|---|---|---|
| 1810, All kinds | 1,458,500 | | | | | | |
| 1810, 10 Over 09 | | $65 | $110 | $225 | $550 | $1,000 | $2,000 |
| 1810, Normal Date | | 60 | 100 | 200 | 450 | 900 | 1,900 |
| 1811, All kinds | 218,025 | | | | | | |
| 1811, Last 1 Over 0 | | 140 | 225 | 500 | 800 | 2,000 | 6,000 |
| 1811, Normal Date | | 110 | 200 | 350 | 700 | 1,400 | 2,800 |

1812, Small Date

1812, Large Date

1814, Plain 4

1814, Crosslet 4

| | Mintage | AG-3 | G-4 | VG-8 | F-12 | VF-20 | EF-40 |
|---|---|---|---|---|---|---|---|
| 1812, All kinds | 1,075,500 | | | | | | |
| 1812, Small Date | | $60 | $100 | $200 | $450 | $900 | $1,900 |
| 1812, Large Date | | 60 | 100 | 200 | 450 | 900 | 1,900 |
| 1813 | 418,000 | 80 | 140 | 275 | 500 | 900 | 2,300 |
| 1814, All kinds | 357,830 | | | | | | |
| 1814, Plain 4 | | 60 | 100 | 200 | 400 | 700 | 1,700 |
| 1814, Crosslet 4 | | 60 | 100 | 200 | 400 | 700 | 1,700 |

## LIBERTY HEAD (1816–1857)

**G-4 Good**—Details on Liberty's head partly visible. Even wear in date and legends.
**VG-8 Very Good**—LIBERTY, date, stars, and legends clear. Part of hair cord visible.
**F-12 Fine**—All hair lines visible. Hair cords uniformly visible.
**VF-20 Very Fine**—Hair cords only slightly worn. Hair lines only partly worn, all well defined.
**EF-40 Extremely Fine**—Both hair cords stand out sharply. All hair lines sharp.
**AU-50 About Uncirculated**—Only traces of wear on hair and highest points on leaves and bow.
**MS-60 Uncirculated**—Typical brown surface. No trace of wear.
**MS-63 Choice Uncirculated**—Some distracting contact marks or blemishes in prime focal areas. Impaired luster possible.

## Matron Head (1816–1835)

*Designer Robert Scot or John Reich; weight 10.89 grams; composition, copper; approx. diameter 28–29 mm; plain edge.*

**Standard Design**

**15 Stars**

*The values shown for all MS-60 and MS-63 Matron Head large cents are for average condition; red to bright red Uncirculated pieces with attractive surfaces (not cleaned) command higher prices. Beware of slightly worn copper coins that have been cleaned and recolored to simulate Uncirculated luster. Cents in VF or better condition with attractive surfaces and toning may also command higher prices than those listed here.*

| | Mintage | G-4 | VG-8 | F-12 | VF-20 | EF-40 | AU-50 | MS-60 | MS-63BN |
|---|---|---|---|---|---|---|---|---|---|
| 1816 | 2,820,982 | $30 | $40 | $60 | $120 | $300 | $475 | $675 | $1,000 |
| 1817, All kinds | 3,948,400 | | | | | | | | |
| 1817, 13 Stars | | 30 | 40 | 60 | 110 | 225 | 375 | 625 | 1,000 |
| 1817, 15 Stars | | 50 | 75 | 150 | 225 | 700 | 1,200 | 3,000 | 5,500 |
| 1818 | 3,167,000 | 30 | 40 | 45 | 85 | 175 | 300 | 450 | 600 |

**1819, 9 Over 8**

**1819, Large Date**

**1819, Small Date**

| | Mintage | G-4 | VG-8 | F-12 | VF-20 | EF-40 | AU-50 | MS-60 | MS-63BN |
|---|---|---|---|---|---|---|---|---|---|
| 1819, All kinds | 2,671,000 | | | | | | | | |
| 1819, 9 Over 8 | | $30 | $40 | $55 | $100 | $325 | $375 | $850 | $1,300 |
| 1819, Large Date | | 30 | 40 | 45 | 85 | 175 | 300 | 550 | 950 |
| 1819, Small Date | | 30 | 40 | 45 | 85 | 200 | 350 | 550 | 1,000 |

**1820, 20 Over 19**
*Note 1 under 2.*

**1820, Large Date**
*Note plain-topped 2.*

**1820, Small Date**
*Note curl-topped 2.*

| | Mintage | G-4 | VG-8 | F-12 | VF-20 | EF-40 | AU-50 | MS-60 | MS-63BN |
|---|---|---|---|---|---|---|---|---|---|
| 1820, All kinds | 4,407,550 | | | | | | | | |
| 1820, 20 Over 19 | | $30 | $50 | $55 | $110 | $400 | $550 | $1,350 | $1,600 |
| 1820, Large Date | | 30 | 40 | 45 | 85 | 175 | 300 | 400 | 650 |
| 1820, Small Date | | 30 | 40 | 120 | 180 | 450 | 850 | 1,500 | 2,250 |
| 1821 **(a)** | 389,000 | 60 | 100 | 210 | 450 | 1,500 | 2,600 | 9,000 | 20,000 |
| 1822 | 2,072,339 | 30 | 45 | 55 | 150 | 425 | 700 | 1,200 | 2,300 |

**a.** Wide and closely spaced AMER varieties are valued the same.

1823, 3 Over 2

Unofficial 1823 "Restrike"

| | Mintage | G-4 | VG-8 | F-12 | VF-20 | EF-40 | AU-50 | MS-60 | MS-63BN |
|---|---|---|---|---|---|---|---|---|---|
| 1823, 3 Over 2 . . . . . . . . . . . . .(a) | | $135 | $250 | $600 | $1,200 | $3,000 | $6,500 | $20,000 | — |
| 1823, Normal Date . . . . . . . . .(a) | | 135 | 285 | 700 | 1,650 | 4,000 | 8,500 | 23,000 | $30,000 |
| 1823, Unofficial Restrike, from broken obverse die . . . . . . . | | | | | 450 | 550 | 925 | 1,250 | 1,500 |

**a.** Included in "1824, All kinds" mintage.

The 1823 unofficial "restrike" was made at the same time and by the same people as the 1804 "restrike" (see page 104), using a discarded 1823 obverse and an 1813 reverse die. The dies are heavily rusted (producing lumps on the coins) and most examples have both dies cracked across.

1824, 4 Over 2

1826, 6 Over 5

| | Mintage | G-4 | VG-8 | F-12 | VF-20 | EF-40 | AU-50 | MS-60 | MS-63BN |
|---|---|---|---|---|---|---|---|---|---|
| 1824, All kinds . . . . . . | 1,262,000 | | | | | | | | |
| 1824, 4 Over 2 . . . . . . . . . . . . | | $50 | $80 | $115 | $350 | $1,200 | $2,500 | $6,000 | $25,000 |
| 1824, Normal Date . . . . . . . . . | | 35 | 60 | 75 | 200 | 550 | 850 | 3,000 | 4,600 |
| 1825 . . . . . . . . . . . . . . | 1,461,100 | 30 | 50 | 60 | 150 | 450 | 750 | 1,750 | 2,750 |
| 1826, All kinds . . . . . . | 1,517,425 | | | | | | | | |
| 1826, 6 Over 5 . . . . . . . . . . . . | | 30 | 70 | 100 | 275 | 975 | 1,500 | 2,800 | 5,500 |
| 1826, Normal Date . . . . . . . . . | | 30 | 40 | 50 | 100 | 250 | 450 | 900 | 1,500 |
| 1827 . . . . . . . . . . . . . . | 2,357,732 | 30 | 40 | 60 | 100 | 225 | 425 | 775 | 1,400 |

Date Size, Through 1828

Date Size, 1828 and Later

| | Mintage | G-4 | VG-8 | F-12 | VF-20 | EF-40 | AU-50 | MS-60 | MS-63BN |
|---|---|---|---|---|---|---|---|---|---|
| 1828, All kinds . . . . . . . . . . . | 2,260,624 | | | | | | | | |
| 1828, Large Narrow Date . . . . . . . . . | | $30 | $40 | $50 | $90 | $210 | $400 | $1,250 | $1,750 |
| 1828, Small Wide Date . . . . . . . . . . . | | 30 | 40 | 50 | 190 | 275 | 650 | 1,950 | 3,500 |

**Large Letters (1808–1834)**
*Note individual letter size and proximity.*

**Medium Letters (1829–1837)**
*Note isolation of letters, especially* STATES.

| | Mintage | G-4 | VG-8 | F-12 | VF-20 | EF-40 | AU-50 | MS-60 | MS-63BN |
|---|---|---|---|---|---|---|---|---|---|
| 1829, All kinds | 1,414,500 | | | | | | | | |
| 1829, Large Letters | | $30 | $40 | $50 | $110 | $200 | $385 | $650 | $1,500 |
| 1829, Medium Letters | | 30 | 40 | 110 | 325 | 800 | 2,250 | 6,500 | 10,500 |
| 1830, All kinds | 1,711,500 | | | | | | | | |
| 1830, Large Letters | | 30 | 40 | 50 | 70 | 190 | 300 | 550 | 1,000 |
| 1830, Medium Letters | | 30 | 40 | 160 | 500 | 2,000 | 5,000 | 15,000 | 25,000 |
| 1831, All kinds | 3,359,260 | | | | | | | | |
| 1831, Large Letters | | 30 | 40 | 50 | 70 | 150 | 250 | 400 | 700 |
| 1831, Medium Letters | | 30 | 40 | 50 | 70 | 200 | 350 | 750 | 1,600 |
| 1832, All kinds | 2,362,000 | | | | | | | | |
| 1832, Large Letters | | 30 | 40 | 50 | 70 | 150 | 250 | 375 | 650 |
| 1832, Medium Letters | | 30 | 40 | 50 | 85 | 200 | 550 | 900 | 1,200 |
| 1833 | 2,739,000 | 30 | 40 | 50 | 70 | 150 | 250 | 375 | 750 |

**Large 8 and Stars**

**Large 8, Small Stars**

**Small 8, Large Stars**

| | Mintage | G-4 | VG-8 | F-12 | VF-20 | EF-40 | AU-50 | MS-60 | MS-63BN |
|---|---|---|---|---|---|---|---|---|---|
| 1834, All kinds | 1,855,100 | | | | | | | | |
| 1834, Large 8, Stars, and Reverse Letters | | $30 | $40 | $75 | $200 | $550 | $1,200 | $2,250 | $4,000 |
| 1834, Large 8 and Stars, Medium Letters | | 200 | 375 | 500 | 1,000 | 3,500 | 6,500 | 9,000 | 12,000 |
| 1834, Large 8, Small Stars, Medium Letters | | 30 | 40 | 55 | 65 | 140 | 240 | 500 | 800 |
| 1834, Small 8, Large Stars, Medium Letters | | 30 | 40 | 55 | 65 | 140 | 240 | 350 | 625 |

Small 8 and Stars, Matron Head

Large 8 and Stars, Matron Head

1835, Head of 1836

| | Mintage | G-4 | VG-8 | F-12 | VF-20 | EF-40 | AU-50 | MS-60 | MS-63BN |
|---|---|---|---|---|---|---|---|---|---|
| 1835, All kinds | 3,878,400 | | | | | | | | |
| 1835, Large 8 and Stars | | $30 | $40 | $55 | $75 | $225 | $400 | $750 | $1,400 |
| 1835, Small 8 and Stars | | 30 | 40 | 55 | 65 | 175 | 375 | 475 | 675 |

## Matron Head Modified (1835–1839): The "Young Head"

*Designer Christian Gobrecht; weight 10.89 grams; composition, copper; diameter 27.5 mm; plain edge.*

**G-4 Good**—Considerably worn. LIBERTY readable.
**VG-8 Very Good**—Hairlines smooth but visible; outline of ear clearly defined.
**F-12 Fine**—Hairlines at top of head and behind ear worn but visible. Braid over brow plain; ear clear.
**VF-20 Very Fine**—All details sharper than for F-12. Only slight wear on hair over brow.
**EF-40 Extremely Fine**—Hair above ear detailed, but slightly worn.
**AU-50 About Uncirculated**—Trace of wear on high points of hair above ear and eye and on highest points on leaves and bow.
**MS-60 Uncirculated**—Typical brown surface. No trace of wear.
**MS-63 Choice Uncirculated**—Some distracting contact marks or blemishes in prime focal areas. Impaired luster possible.

**1829–1837**
*Medium letters; note letter spacing.*

**Head of 1838**
*Note slim bust with beaded cords.*

**1837–1839**
*Small letters; note letter spacing.*

*The values shown for all MS-60 and MS-63 Young Head large cents are for average condition; red to bright red Uncirculated large cents with attractive surfaces (not cleaned) command higher prices. Beware of slightly worn copper coins that have been cleaned and recolored to simulate Uncirculated luster. Cents in VF or better condition with attractive surfaces and toning may also command higher prices than those listed here.*

| | Mintage | G-4 | VG-8 | F-12 | VF-20 | EF-40 | AU-50 | MS-60 | MS-63BN |
|---|---|---|---|---|---|---|---|---|---|
| 1835, Head of 1836 | (a) | $30 | $40 | $50 | $65 | $125 | $250 | $350 | $550 |
| 1836 | 2,111,000 | 30 | 40 | 50 | 65 | 125 | 250 | 350 | 550 |
| 1837, All kinds | 5,558,300 | | | | | | | | |
| 1837, Plain Cord, Medium Letters | | 27 | 35 | 50 | 65 | 125 | 250 | 350 | 550 |
| 1837, Plain Cord, Small Letters | | 27 | 35 | 50 | 65 | 125 | 250 | 375 | 600 |
| 1837, Head of 1838 | | 27 | 35 | 50 | 65 | 110 | 200 | 325 | 500 |
| 1838 | 6,370,200 | 27 | 35 | 50 | 65 | 120 | 225 | 335 | 575 |

**a.** Included in "1835, All kinds" mintage.

| Silly Head | 1839 Over 1836 | Booby Head |
|---|---|---|
| *Note lock at forehead.* | *Note closed 9, plain cords.* | *Note shoulder tip.* |

| | Mintage | G-4 | VG-8 | F-12 | VF-20 | EF-40 | AU-50 | MS-60 | MS-63BN |
|---|---|---|---|---|---|---|---|---|---|
| 1839, All kinds | 3,128,661 | | | | | | | | |
| 1839, 1839 Over 1836, Plain Cords | | $500 | $800 | $1,400 | $3,250 | $7,000 | $22,500 | $60,000 | $100,000 |
| 1839, Head of 1838, Beaded Cords | | 40 | 50 | 75 | 100 | 150 | 250 | 350 | 550 |
| 1839, Silly Head | | 40 | 50 | 75 | 125 | 250 | 550 | 800 | 1,500 |
| 1839, Booby Head **(a)** | | 30 | 50 | 60 | 90 | 225 | 500 | 950 | 1,600 |

**a.** The 1839 Booby Head variety has a modified reverse that omits the line under CENT (see 1837–1839 Small Letters photo on page 110).

## Braided Hair (1839–1857)

**1840, Large Date**

**1840, Small Date**

**1840, Small Date Over Large 18**

| | Mintage | G-4 | VG-8 | F-12 | VF-20 | EF-40 | AU-50 | MS-60 | MS-63BN |
|---|---|---|---|---|---|---|---|---|---|
| 1839 | **(a)** | $35 | $50 | $80 | $110 | $225 | $440 | $800 | $1,600 |
| 1840, All kinds | 2,462,700 | | | | | | | | |
| 1840, Large Date | | 25 | 35 | 40 | 55 | 110 | 250 | 600 | 1,150 |
| 1840, Small Date | | 25 | 35 | 40 | 55 | 110 | 250 | 600 | 1,150 |
| 1840, Small Date Over Large 18 | | 25 | 35 | 40 | 75 | 200 | 400 | 900 | 1,600 |
| 1841 | 1,597,367 | 30 | 50 | 80 | 125 | 175 | 300 | 800 | 1,500 |

**a.** Included in "1839, All kinds" mintage.

1842, Small Date

1842, Large Date

Small Letters
(1839–1843)

| | Mintage | G-4 | VG-8 | F-12 | VF-20 | EF-40 | AU-50 | MS-60 | MS-63BN |
|---|---|---|---|---|---|---|---|---|---|
| 1842, All kinds | 2,383,390 | | | | | | | | |
| 1842, Small Date | | $25 | $30 | $35 | $50 | $100 | $220 | $625 | $1,200 |
| 1842, Large Date | | 25 | 30 | 35 | 50 | 100 | 200 | 550 | 1,100 |

Head of 1840
*Petite head (1839–1843)*

Head of 1844
*Mature head (1843–1857)*

Large Letters
(1843–1857)

| | Mintage | G-4 | VG-8 | F-12 | VF-20 | EF-40 | AU-50 | MS-60 | MS-63BN |
|---|---|---|---|---|---|---|---|---|---|
| 1843, All kinds | 2,425,342 | | | | | | | | |
| 1843, Petite, Small Letters | | $25 | $30 | $35 | $50 | $100 | $200 | $500 | $950 |
| 1843, Petite, Large Letters | | 25 | 35 | 45 | 100 | 250 | 320 | 825 | 1,500 |
| 1843, Mature, Large Letters | | 25 | 30 | 35 | 50 | 150 | 275 | 550 | 1,100 |
| 1844, Normal Date | 2,398,752 | 25 | 30 | 35 | 40 | 100 | 200 | 550 | 1,000 |
| 1844, 44 Over 81 **(b)** | * | 75 | 125 | 165 | 235 | 400 | 750 | 1,500 | 3,500 |

* Included in number above. **b.** See discussion of date-punch blunders, with images, on the following page.

1846, Small Date
*Note squat date, closed 6.*

1846, Medium Date
*Note medium height, ball-top 6.*

1846, Tall Date
*Note vertically stretched date, open-mouthed 6.*

| | Mintage | G-4 | VG-8 | F-12 | VF-20 | EF-40 | AU-50 | MS-60 | MS-63BN |
|---|---|---|---|---|---|---|---|---|---|
| 1845 | 3,894,804 | $25 | $30 | $35 | $40 | $75 | $135 | $225 | $375 |
| 1846, All kinds | 4,120,800 | | | | | | | | |
| 1846, Small Date | | 25 | 30 | 35 | 40 | 75 | 135 | 225 | 350 |
| 1846, Medium Date | | 25 | 30 | 35 | 40 | 85 | 150 | 250 | 400 |
| 1846, Tall Date | | 25 | 35 | 40 | 50 | 150 | 250 | 650 | 1,000 |
| 1847 | 6,183,669 | 20 | 25 | 35 | 40 | 75 | 135 | 225 | 350 |
| 1847, 7 Over "Small 7" **(b)** | * | 50 | 75 | 125 | 175 | 350 | 420 | 1,350 | 2,000 |

* Included in number above. **b.** See discussion of date-punch blunders, with images, below.

| | Mintage | G-4 | VG-8 | F-12 | VF-20 | EF-40 | AU-50 | MS-60 | MS-63BN |
|---|---|---|---|---|---|---|---|---|---|
| 1848 **(c)** | 6,415,799 | $20 | $25 | $35 | $40 | $75 | $130 | $225 | $350 |
| 1849 | 4,178,500 | 20 | 25 | 35 | 40 | 85 | 150 | 250 | 450 |
| 1850 | 4,426,844 | 20 | 25 | 35 | 40 | 65 | 125 | 180 | 230 |

**c.** The 1848 Small Date cent is a rare contemporary counterfeit.

The following are not true overdates, but are some of the more spectacular of several date-punch blunders of the 1844 through 1854 period. The so-called overdates of 1844 and 1851 each have the date punched upside down, then corrected normally.

**1844, 44 Over 81**

**1847, 7 Over "Small" 7**

**1851, 51 Over 81**

| | Mintage | G-4 | VG-8 | F-12 | VF-20 | EF-40 | AU-50 | MS-60 | MS-63BN |
|---|---|---|---|---|---|---|---|---|---|
| 1851, Normal Date | 9,889,707 | $20 | $25 | $35 | $40 | $65 | $125 | $180 | $230 |
| 1851, 51 Over 81 | * | 40 | 60 | 100 | 150 | 250 | 375 | 575 | 1,000 |
| 1852 | 5,063,094 | 20 | 25 | 35 | 40 | 65 | 125 | 180 | 230 |
| 1853 | 6,641,131 | 20 | 25 | 35 | 40 | 65 | 125 | 180 | 230 |
| 1854 | 4,236,156 | 20 | 25 | 35 | 40 | 65 | 125 | 180 | 230 |

* Included in number above.

Original sketches of engraver James B. Longacre's work reveal that the slanting 5's in the following pieces were a peculiarity of his. The figure punch for an upright 5 was probably the work of an apprentice.

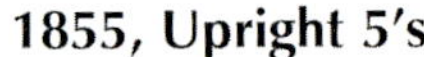

1855, Upright 5's

1855, Slanting 5's

Knob on Ear

| Mintage | G-4 | VG-8 | F-12 | VF-20 | EF-40 | AU-50 | MS-60 | MS-63BN |
|---|---|---|---|---|---|---|---|---|
| 1855, All kinds . . . . . . . . . . . 1,574,829 | | | | | | | | |
| 1855, Upright 5's . . . . . . . . . . . . . . . | $20 | $25 | $35 | $40 | $65 | $125 | $180 | $230 |
| 1855, Slanting 5's. . . . . . . . . . . . . . . | 20 | 25 | 35 | 45 | 65 | 130 | 200 | 275 |
| 1855, Slanting 5's, Knob on Ear . . . . | 30 | 40 | 50 | 75 | 140 | 250 | 400 | 550 |
| 1856, All kinds . . . . . . . . . . . 2,690,463 | | | | | | | | |
| 1856, Upright 5. . . . . . . . . . . . . . . . . | 20 | 25 | 35 | 40 | 65 | 130 | 200 | 270 |
| 1856, Slanting 5 . . . . . . . . . . . . . . . . | 20 | 25 | 35 | 40 | 65 | 130 | 200 | 270 |

1857, Large Date

1857, Small Date

| Mintage | G-4 | VG-8 | F-12 | VF-20 | EF-40 | AU-50 | MS-60 | MS-63BN |
|---|---|---|---|---|---|---|---|---|
| 1857, All kinds . . . . . . . . . . 333,546 | | | | | | | | |
| 1857, Large Date . . . . . . . . . . . . . | $100 | $150 | $225 | $325 | $400 | $550 | $800 | $1,000 |
| 1857, Small Date . . . . . . . . . . . . . | 75 | 150 | 225 | 325 | 400 | 600 | 750 | 900 |

## PASSING OF THE LARGE CENT AND HALF CENT

By 1857, the cost of making and distributing copper coins had risen. Mint Director James Ross Snowden reported that they "barely paid expenses." Both cents and half cents had become unpopular; in fact, they hardly circulated outside the larger cities. The practice of issuing subsidiary silver coins, which began in 1853, brought about a reform of the copper coinage. The half cent was abandoned and a smaller cent was introduced in 1857.

The law of 1857 brought important benefits to the citizens. By its terms, Spanish coins were redeemed and melted at the mint in exchange for new, small cents. The decimal system became popular and official thereafter, and the old method of reckoning in reales, medios, shillings, and so on was gradually given up (although the terms *two bits* and *penny* were still commonly used). The new, convenient small cent won popular favor and soon became a useful instrument of retail trade and a boon to commerce.

The Act of February 21, 1857, provided for the coinage of the new copper-nickel small cent. It also called for Spanish and Mexican coins and old copper cents and half cents in circulation to be brought in and exchanged for U.S. silver coins and the new cents. The cent weighed 72 grains, with a metallic composition of 88% copper and 12% nickel.

The 1856 Flying Eagle cent, a pattern, was made to show Congress how the new cent would look. Additional Proof pieces were struck for sale to collectors. It is believed that between 2,000 and 3,000 pieces were struck in all. These have always been collected along with regular issues because of their early widespread popularity.

Some 1858-dated cents have been deceptively altered to read 1856. They are easy to spot because the shape of the 5 is different on the 1858 than it is on the 1856.

Many varieties are known for 1857 and 1858. In particular, 1858 is found with two major variations. In the Large Letters design, the A and M in AMERICA are joined, while in the Small Letters design they are separated; minor variations of the reverse designs of corn, wheat, cotton, and tobacco also appear. The 1858, 8 Over 7, variety can be identified by a small dot in the field above the first 8—during production, the die was ground down until the 7 was invisible. Coins with the 7 showing are more desirable.

## FLYING EAGLE (1856–1858)

*Designer James B. Longacre; weight 4.67 grams; composition .880 copper, .120 nickel; diameter 19 mm; plain edge. All coined at Philadelphia Mint.*

**G-4 Good**—All details worn, but readable.
**VG-8 Very Good**—Details in eagle's feathers and eye evident, but worn.
**F-12 Fine**—Eagle-head details and feather tips sharp.
**VF-20 Very Fine**—Considerable detail visible in feathers in right wing and tail.
**EF-40 Extremely Fine**—Slight wear, all details sharp.
**AU-50 About Uncirculated**—Slight wear on eagle's left wing and breast.
**MS-60 Uncirculated**—No trace of wear. Light blemishes.
**MS-63 Choice Uncirculated**—Some distracting contact marks or blemishes in prime focal areas. Some impairment of luster possible.
**PF-63 Choice Proof**—Nearly perfect.

*Circulation strike.* *Proof strike.*

1858, 8 Over 7 — Large Letters — Small Letters

| | Mintage | G-4 | VG-8 | F-12 | VF-20 | EF-40 | AU-50 | MS-60 | MS-63 | PF-63 |
|---|---|---|---|---|---|---|---|---|---|---|
| 1856 . . . . . . . . *(1,500)*. . . . . | *2,000* | $7,000 | $7,750 | $9,500 | $11,000 | $13,000 | $13,500 | $15,000 | $20,000 | $16,000 |
| 1857 . . . . . . . . . . *(100)* | 17,450,000 | 25 | 40 | 50 | 60 | 140 | 215 | 450 | 1,000 | 8,000 |
| 1858, All kinds . . . . . . . | 24,600,000 | | | | | | | | | |
| 1858, Lg Ltrs. . *(100)*. . . . . . . . . | | 25 | 40 | 50 | 60 | 140 | 215 | 450 | 1,000 | 8,000 |
| 1858, 8/7 . . . . . . . . . . . . . . . . . | | 75 | 100 | 200 | 400 | 850 | 1,500 | 3,650 | 11,000 | |
| 1858, Sm Ltrs *(200)*. . . . . . . . . | | 25 | 40 | 50 | 60 | 150 | 250 | 500 | 1,150 | 8,000 |

# INDIAN HEAD (1859–1909)

The "Indian Head" design first issued in 1859 is actually a representation of Liberty wearing an Indian headdress, not an actual Native American. The first year featured a laurel wreath on the reverse. This was changed after one year to the oak wreath with a small shield. Coins of 1859 and early 1860 show a pointed bust. Those made from late 1860 until 1864 have a more rounded bust. Prior to the issuance of nickel five-cent pieces in 1866, these coins were popularly referred to as *nickels* or *nicks*. Later, they were called *white cents*.

**G-4 Good**—No LIBERTY visible.
**VG-8 Very Good**—At least some letters of LIBERTY readable on headband.
**F-12 Fine**—LIBERTY mostly visible.
**VF-20 Very Fine**—Slight but even wear on LIBERTY.
**EF-40 Extremely Fine**—LIBERTY sharp. All other details sharp. Only slight wear on ribbon end.
**AU-50 About Uncirculated**—Very slight trace of wear above the ear and the lowest curl of hair.
**MS-60 Uncirculated**—No trace of wear. Light blemishes. Values shown are for brown-color coins.
**MS-63 Choice Uncirculated**—Some distracting contact marks or blemishes in prime focal areas. Impaired luster possible. Values shown are for brown-color coins. Red-brown to red coins are valued higher.

## Variety 1 – Copper-Nickel, Laurel Wreath Reverse (1859)

*Designer James B. Longacre; weight 4.67 grams; composition .880 copper, .120 nickel; diameter 19 mm; plain edge. All coined at Philadelphia Mint.*

**Laurel Wreath Reverse, Without Shield (1859 Only)**

***Proof strike.***

*Spotted, cleaned, or discolored pieces are worth less than the values shown.*

| | Mintage | G-4 | VG-8 | F-12 | VF-20 | EF-40 | AU-50 | MS-60 | MS-63 | PF-63 |
|---|---|---|---|---|---|---|---|---|---|---|
| 1859 . . . . . . . *(800)* . . | 36,400,000 | $15 | $20 | $25 | $55 | $110 | $200 | $285 | $700 | $1,600 |
| 1859, Oak Wreath Rev, With Shield **(a)** . . . . . . . . . . | | | | | | | | | 1,100 | |

**a.** 1,000 pieces made but never released for circulation.

## Variety 2 – Copper-Nickel, Oak Wreath With Shield (1860–1864)

*Standards same as for Variety 1.*

**Oak Wreath Reverse, With Shield (1860–1909)**
***Circulation strike.***

***Proof strike.***

| | Mintage | G-4 | VG-8 | F-12 | VF-20 | EF-40 | AU-50 | MS-60 | MS-63 | PF-63 |
|---|---|---|---|---|---|---|---|---|---|---|
| 1860 . . . . . . *(1,000)* . | 20,566,000 | $10 | $15 | $20 | $35 | $70 | $110 | $185 | $250 | $900 |
| 1860, Pointed Bust . . . . . . . . . . | * | 20 | 25 | 30 | 50 | 100 | 165 | 300 | 575 | |
| 1861 . . . . . . *(1,000)* . . | 10,100,000 | 25 | 35 | 45 | 60 | 110 | 175 | 225 | 400 | 1,200 |
| 1862 *(1,500–2,000)* . . | 28,075,000 | 10 | 15 | 20 | 30 | 50 | 75 | 110 | 200 | 850 |
| 1863 . . *(800–1,000)* . . | 49,840,000 | 10 | 15 | 20 | 30 | 50 | 75 | 110 | 200 | 850 |
| 1864 . . *(800–1,000)* . . | 13,740,000 | 20 | 30 | 40 | 55 | 100 | 150 | 200 | 325 | 850 |

* Included in number above.

## Variety 3 – Bronze (1864–1909)

*Designer James B. Longacre; weight 3.11 grams; composition .950 copper, .050 tin and zinc; diameter 19 mm; plain edge; mints: Philadelphia, San Francisco.*

During the Civil War, nearly all gold and silver, and eventually the copper-nickel cent, disappeared from circulation in the Midwest and East. In larger cities, thin, copper, cent-sized tokens began to be issued by merchants to fill the void left by the missing cents. The government stepped in and with the Act of April 22, 1864, issued its own thin, bronze coin and made the issuance of the merchants' tokens illegal.

The obverse was redesigned near the end of 1864. A slightly sharper portrait included the designer's initial L (for Longacre) on the lower ribbon behind the neck. If the coin is turned slightly (so Indian faces observer) the highlighted details of the L will appear to better advantage. The tip of the bust is pointed on the variety with L, and rounded on the variety without L. This design continued until 1909, when the design was replaced with the Lincoln cent.

**1864, With L on Ribbon**

**1873, Close 3**

**1873, Open 3**

| | Mintage | G-4 | VG-8 | F-12 | VF-20 | EF-40 | AU-50 | MS-60 | MS-63 | PF-63 |
|---|---|---|---|---|---|---|---|---|---|---|
| 1864, All kinds | 39,233,714 | | | | | | | | | |
| 1864, No L . . *(150+)* | | $15 | $20 | $25 | $45 | $70 | $90 | $115 | $150 | $500 |
| 1864, With L . . *(20+)* | | 55 | 80 | 150 | 200 | 275 | 375 | 425 | 575 | 20,000 |
| *$161,000, PF-65 RB, Heritage auction, September 2012* | | | | | | | | | | |
| 1865 **(a)** . . *(750–1,000)* | 35,429,286 | 15 | 20 | 25 | 30 | 45 | 65 | 90 | 150 | 375 |
| 1866 . . . . *(725–1,000)* | 9,826,500 | 50 | 65 | 80 | 100 | 190 | 250 | 275 | 380 | 400 |
| 1867 . . . . *(850–1,100)* | 9,821,000 | 50 | 70 | 90 | 135 | 230 | 275 | 300 | 400 | 400 |
| 1868 . . . . *(750–1,000)* | 10,266,500 | 40 | 50 | 70 | 125 | 170 | 220 | 250 | 360 | 375 |
| 1869 **(a)** . . *(850–1,100)* | 6,420,000 | 85 | 120 | 235 | 335 | 445 | 550 | 600 | 700 | 380 |
| 1869, 9 Over 9 | * | 125 | 225 | 450 | 575 | 725 | 825 | 975 | 1,200 | |
| 1870, Shallow N **(b)** . . . . . . . *(1,000+)* | 5,275,000 | 80 | 100 | 220 | 320 | 400 | 500 | 550 | 900 | 425 |
| 1870, Bold N **(b)** | * | 55 | 75 | 200 | 280 | 375 | 450 | 500 | 850 | 325 |
| 1871, Shallow N **(b)** . . . . . . . . . *(960+)* | 3,929,500 | 130 | 180 | 325 | 450 | 575 | 650 | 775 | 1,000 | 500 |
| 1871, Bold N **(b)** | * | 70 | 85 | 250 | 350 | 475 | 525 | 550 | 800 | 325 |
| 1872, Shallow N **(b)** | 4,042,000 | 100 | 170 | 370 | 425 | 575 | 700 | 950 | 1,250 | |
| 1872, Bold N **(b)** . . . . . . *(850–1,100)* | * | 90 | 140 | 300 | 375 | 500 | 650 | 785 | 1,150 | 400 |
| 1873, All kinds | 11,676,500 | | | | | | | | | |
| 1873, Cl 3 *(1,500–2,000)* | | 25 | 35 | 65 | 125 | 185 | 235 | 410 | 550 | 265 |
| 1873, Doubled LIBERTY | | 200 | 350 | 825 | 1,750 | 2,500 | 5,250 | 7,500 | 13,500 | |
| 1873, Open 3 | | 20 | 30 | 50 | 85 | 160 | 190 | 250 | 325 | |

* Included in number above. **a.** One variety of 1865 appears to show traces of a 4 under the 5 in the date. On other varieties, the tip of the 5 is either plain or curved. The 9 is doubled on some varieties of the 1869; on others it appears to be over an 8, although it is actually a doubled 9. None of these varieties is a true overdate. **b.** Cents dated 1869 and earlier have a shallow N in ONE. Those dated 1870, 1871, or 1872 have either shallow N or bold N. Those dated 1873 to 1876 all have the bold N. Circulation strikes of 1877 have the shallow N, while Proofs have the bold N.

On coins minted from 1859 through mid-1886, the last feather of the headdress points between I and C (Variety 1); on those minted from mid-1886 through 1909, it points between C and A (Variety 2; both varieties illustrated on the next page).

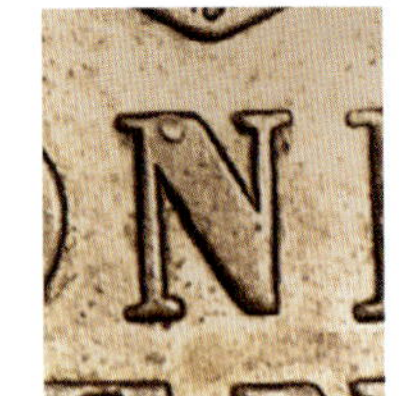

1875, Dot Reverse

1886, Variety 1

1886, Variety 2

| Mintage | G-4 | VG-8 | F-12 | VF-20 | EF-40 | AU-50 | MS-60 | MS-63 | PF-63 |
|---|---|---|---|---|---|---|---|---|---|
| 1874 . . . *(1,000–1,200)*. . 14,187,500 | $20 | $25 | $45 | $65 | $100 | $150 | $225 | $250 | $250 |
| 1875 . . . *(1,000–1,250)*. . 13,528,000 | 20 | 35 | 60 | 75 | 120 | 160 | 235 | 260 | 250 |
| 1875, Dot Reverse **(a)** . . . . . . . . . . . . . . . . | | | | | | | | — | |
| 1876 . . . *(1,500–2,000)*. . . 7,944,000 | 35 | 40 | 70 | 135 | 225 | 240 | 300 | 390 | 250 |
| 1877 . . . *(1,250–1,500)*. . . . .852,500 | 900 | 1,100 | 1,550 | 2,000 | 2,500 | 3,000 | 3,800 | 4,500 | 3,000 |
| 1878 . . . . . . . . (2,350). . . 5,797,500 | 35 | 45 | 60 | 110 | 200 | 275 | 325 | 380 | 235 |
| 1879 . . . . . . . . (3,200). . 16,228,000 | 8 | 12 | 20 | 40 | 70 | 80 | 90 | 140 | 150 |
| 1880 . . . . . . . . (3,955). . 38,961,000 | 5 | 7 | 9 | 12 | 30 | 60 | 80 | 130 | 150 |
| 1881 . . . . . . . . (3,575). . 39,208,000 | 5 | 6 | 8 | 10 | 25 | 35 | 60 | 90 | 150 |
| 1882 . . . . . . . . (3,100). . 38,578,000 | 5 | 6 | 8 | 10 | 25 | 35 | 60 | 90 | 150 |
| 1883 . . . . . . . . (6,609). . 45,591,500 | 5 | 6 | 8 | 10 | 25 | 35 | 60 | 90 | 150 |
| 1884 . . . . . . . . (3,942). . 23,257,800 | 5 | 7 | 10 | 14 | 27 | 40 | 75 | 120 | 150 |
| 1885 . . . . . . . . (3,790). . 11,761,594 | 8 | 9 | 15 | 30 | 65 | 80 | 110 | 200 | 150 |
| 1886, All kinds (4,290). . 17,650,000 | | | | | | | | | |
| 1886, Var 1 . . . . . . . . . . . . . . . . . . | 6 | 8 | 20 | 50 | 140 | 175 | 200 | 250 | 150 |
| 1886, Var 2 . . . . . . . . . . . . . . . . . . | 7 | 12 | 25 | 75 | 175 | 220 | 325 | 500 | 350 |

**a.** This variety has a small, raised dot near the left top of N in ONE. It is believed by some to be a secret mark added to the die in a successful plan to apprehend a Mint employee suspected of stealing coins.

**1888, Last 8 Over 7.**
*The tail of the 7 is slightly visible; the cud to the left of UNITED is diagnostic. A less prominent similar variety exists but is valued lower than the clear overdate.*

**1894, Doubled Die Obverse**

| Mintage | G-4 | VG-8 | F-12 | VF-20 | EF-40 | AU-50 | MS-60 | MS-63 | PF-63 |
|---|---|---|---|---|---|---|---|---|---|
| 1887 . . . . . (2,960) . . 45,223,523 | $3 | $4 | $5 | $8 | $18 | $28 | $55 | $80 | $150 |
| 1888 . . . . . (4,582) . . 37,489,832 | 3 | 4 | 5 | 8 | 22 | 27 | 65 | 130 | 150 |
| 1888, Last 8/7 . . . . . . . . . . . . . . * | 1,250 | 1,500 | 2,000 | 3,500 | 7,500 | 17,500 | 30,000 | 50,000 | |
| 1889 . . . . . (3,336) . . 48,866,025 | 3 | 4 | 5 | 7 | 18 | 27 | 60 | 80 | 150 |
| 1890 . . . . . (2,740) . . 57,180,114 | 3 | 4 | 5 | 7 | 16 | 27 | 60 | 80 | 150 |
| 1891 . . . . . (2,350) . . 47,070,000 | 3 | 4 | 5 | 7 | 15 | 27 | 60 | 80 | 150 |
| 1892 . . . . . (2,745) . . 37,647,087 | 3 | 4 | 5 | 8 | 20 | 27 | 60 | 80 | 150 |
| 1893 . . . . . (2,195) . . 46,640,000 | 3 | 4 | 5 | 8 | 20 | 27 | 60 | 80 | 150 |
| 1894 . . . . . (2,632) . . 16,749,500 | 5 | 6 | 15 | 20 | 50 | 70 | 85 | 115 | 150 |
| 1894, Dbl Date . . . . . . . . . . . . . * | 30 | 40 | 65 | 130 | 225 | 385 | 675 | 1,200 | |
| 1895 . . . . . (2,062) . . 38,341,574 | 3 | 4 | 5 | 8 | 15 | 25 | 45 | 65 | 160 |
| 1896 . . . . . (1,862) . . 39,055,431 | 3 | 4 | 5 | 8 | 15 | 25 | 45 | 65 | 150 |
| 1897 . . . . . (1,938) . . 50,464,392 | 3 | 4 | 5 | 8 | 15 | 25 | 45 | 65 | 150 |

* Included in number above.

Location of Mintmark S on Reverse of Indian Head Cent (1908 and 1909 Only)

| | Mintage | G-4 | VG-8 | F-12 | VF-20 | EF-40 | AU-50 | MS-60 | MS-63 | PF-63 |
|---|---|---|---|---|---|---|---|---|---|---|
| 1898 | (1,795). . .49,821,284 | $3 | $4 | $5 | $8 | $15 | $25 | $45 | $65 | $150 |
| 1899 | (2,031). . .53,598,000 | 3 | 4 | 5 | 8 | 15 | 25 | 45 | 65 | 150 |
| 1900 | (2,262). . .66,831,502 | 2 | 3 | 5 | 6 | 10 | 20 | 40 | 60 | 150 |
| 1901 | (1,985). . .79,609,158 | 2 | 3 | 5 | 6 | 10 | 20 | 40 | 60 | 150 |
| 1902 | (2,018). . .87,374,704 | 2 | 3 | 5 | 6 | 10 | 20 | 40 | 60 | 150 |
| 1903 | (1,790). . .85,092,703 | 2 | 3 | 5 | 6 | 10 | 20 | 40 | 60 | 150 |
| 1904 | (1,817). . .61,326,198 | 2 | 3 | 5 | 6 | 10 | 20 | 40 | 60 | 150 |
| 1905 | (2,152). . .80,717,011 | 2 | 3 | 5 | 6 | 10 | 20 | 40 | 60 | 150 |
| 1906 | (1,725). . .96,020,530 | 2 | 3 | 5 | 6 | 10 | 20 | 40 | 60 | 150 |
| 1907 | (1,475). .108,137,143 | 2 | 3 | 5 | 6 | 10 | 20 | 40 | 60 | 150 |
| 1908 | (1,620). . .32,326,367 | 2 | 3 | 5 | 6 | 10 | 20 | 40 | 60 | 150 |
| 1908S | 1,115,000 | 90 | 100 | 125 | 145 | 175 | 250 | 290 | 400 | |
| 1909 | (2,175). . .14,368,470 | 12 | 15 | 17 | 20 | 25 | 30 | 45 | 65 | 150 |
| 1909S | 309,000 | 300 | 325 | 400 | 475 | 600 | 700 | 1,000 | 1,200 | |

## LINCOLN, WHEAT EARS REVERSE (1909–1958)

Victor D. Brenner designed this cent, which was issued to commemorate the 100th anniversary of Abraham Lincoln's birth. The designer's initials (V.D.B.) appear on the reverse of a limited quantity of cents of 1909. The initials were restored, in 1918, to the obverse side on Lincoln's shoulder, as illustrated on page 120. The Lincoln type was the first cent to have the motto IN GOD WE TRUST.

Matte Proof coins were made for collectors from 1909 through 1916, and an exceptional specimen dated 1917 is also reported to exist.

**G-4 Good**—Date worn but apparent. Lines in wheat heads missing. Full rims.
**VG-8 Very Good**—Half of lines visible in upper wheat heads.
**F-12 Fine**—Wheat lines worn but visible.
**VF-20 Very Fine**—Lincoln's cheekbone and jawbone worn but separated. No worn spots on wheat heads.
**EF-40 Extremely Fine**—Slight wear. All details sharp.
**AU-50 About Uncirculated**—Slight wear on cheek and jaw and on wheat stalks.
**MS-60 Uncirculated**—No trace of wear. Light blemishes. Brown or red-brown color.
**MS-63 Uncirculated**—No trace of wear. Slight blemishes. Red-brown color.
**MS-65 Uncirculated**—No trace of wear. Barely noticeable blemishes. Red-brown color.

*Circulation strike.*

*Matte Proof.*

*Mirror Proof.*

Designer's Initials V.D.B. (1909 Reverse Only)

No V.D.B. on Reverse (1909–1958)

Mintmark Location

## Variety 1 – Bronze (1909–1942)

*Designer Victor D. Brenner; weight 3.11 grams; composition .950 copper, .050 tin and zinc; diameter 19 mm; plain edge; mints: Philadelphia, Denver, San Francisco.*

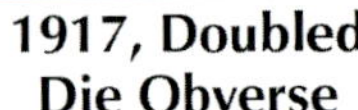

**1917, Doubled Die Obverse**

***Designer's initials placed on Lincoln's shoulder next to rim, starting 1918.***

*Brilliant red Uncirculated cents command higher prices. Discolored or weakly struck pieces are valued lower.*

| | Mintage | G-4 | VG-8 | F-12 | VF-20 | EF-40 | AU-50 | MS-60 | MS-63 |
|---|---|---|---|---|---|---|---|---|---|
| 1909, V.D.B. | 27,995,000 | $10.00 | $12.00 | $15.00 | $17.00 | $19 | $20 | $25 | $30 |
| 1909, V.D.B., Pf **(a)**(1,194) **(b)** | | | | | | | | | 8,500 |
| 1909S, V.D.B. | 484,000 | 625.00 | 700.00 | 725.00 | 750.00 | 850 | 1,050 | 1,200 | 1,350 |
| 1909 | 72,702,618 | 4.00 | 5.00 | 6.00 | 7.00 | 8 | 12 | 17 | 20 |
| 1909, Proof **(a)** (2,618) | | | | | | | | | 550 |
| 1909S | 1,825,000 | 80.00 | 90.00 | 100.00 | 130.00 | 150 | 225 | 300 | 350 |
| 1909S, S Over Horiz S | * | 95.00 | 100.00 | 120.00 | 150.00 | 200 | 275 | 325 | 370 |
| 1910 | 146,801,218 | 0.40 | 0.55 | 1.00 | 1.50 | 4 | 10 | 18 | 25 |
| 1910, Proof **(a)** (4,083) | | | | | | | | | 500 |
| 1910S | 6,045,000 | 17.00 | 20.00 | 22.00 | 25.00 | 45 | 80 | 100 | 120 |
| 1911 | 101,177,787 | 0.50 | 0.70 | 1.50 | 2.50 | 6 | 11 | 21 | 50 |
| 1911, Proof **(a)** (1,725) | | | | | | | | | 500 |
| 1911D | 12,672,000 | 6.00 | 7.00 | 10.00 | 20.00 | 50 | 75 | 95 | 125 |
| 1911S | 4,026,000 | 35.00 | 45.00 | 55.00 | 60.00 | 75 | 110 | 185 | 235 |
| 1912 | 68,153,060 | 1.25 | 1.65 | 2.25 | 5.50 | 13 | 25 | 35 | 50 |
| 1912, Proof **(a)** (2,172) | | | | | | | | | 500 |
| 1912D | 10,411,000 | 7.00 | 9.00 | 11.00 | 25.00 | 65 | 100 | 170 | 250 |
| 1912S | 4,431,000 | 20.00 | 25.00 | 30.00 | 40.00 | 75 | 110 | 180 | 255 |
| 1913 | 76,532,352 | 0.85 | 1.00 | 2.00 | 4.00 | 18 | 27 | 35 | 55 |
| 1913, Proof **(a)** (2,983) | | | | | | | | | 500 |
| 1913D | 15,804,000 | 3.00 | 3.50 | 4.50 | 10.00 | 50 | 70 | 110 | 175 |
| 1913S | 6,101,000 | 10.00 | 15.00 | 20.00 | 30.00 | 60 | 100 | 175 | 225 |
| 1914 | 75,238,432 | 0.75 | 1.00 | 2.00 | 6.00 | 20 | 40 | 55 | 70 |
| 1914, Proof **(a)** (1,365) | | | | | | | | | 500 |
| 1914D **(c)** | 1,193,000 | 150.00 | 175.00 | 225.00 | 250.00 | 700 | 1,450 | 2,000 | 3,000 |
| 1914S | 4,137,000 | 20.00 | 25.00 | 30.00 | 40.00 | 85 | 175 | 325 | 460 |
| 1915 | 29,092,120 | 1.75 | 2.75 | 5.00 | 18.00 | 60 | 70 | 90 | 105 |
| 1915, Proof **(a)** (1,150) | | | | | | | | | 500 |
| 1915D | 22,050,000 | 2.00 | 3.00 | 4.00 | 7.00 | 22 | 45 | 85 | 120 |
| 1915S | 4,833,000 | 20.00 | 25.00 | 30.00 | 35.00 | 70 | 135 | 200 | 235 |
| 1916 | 131,833,677 | 0.50 | 0.55 | 0.75 | 2.00 | 8 | 13 | 18 | 35 |
| 1916, Proof **(a)** (1,050) | | | | | | | | | 1,100 |
| 1916D | 35,956,000 | 1.00 | 1.75 | 3.00 | 6.00 | 15 | 35 | 75 | 150 |
| 1916S | 22,510,000 | 1.75 | 2.25 | 3.50 | 8.00 | 25 | 50 | 105 | 175 |
| 1917 | 196,429,785 | 0.30 | 0.40 | 0.50 | 2.00 | 4 | 10 | 16 | 32 |
| 1917, Doubled Die Obverse | * | 100.00 | 150.00 | 225.00 | 450.00 | 1,000 | 1,600 | 2,750 | 5,750 |
| 1917D | 55,120,000 | 0.90 | 1.10 | 2.50 | 4.50 | 35 | 50 | 80 | 125 |
| 1917S | 32,620,000 | 0.50 | 0.70 | 1.20 | 2.50 | 10 | 25 | 75 | 160 |
| 1918 | 288,104,634 | 0.20 | 0.30 | 0.50 | 1.50 | 3 | 8 | 16 | 27 |
| 1918D | 47,830,000 | 0.75 | 1.25 | 2.50 | 4.00 | 12 | 35 | 80 | 140 |
| 1918S | 34,680,000 | 0.50 | 1.00 | 2.00 | 3.00 | 11 | 32 | 80 | 185 |

* Included in number above. **a.** Matte Proof; valuations are for PF-63 coins. **b.** Reported struck; 400–600 estimated issued. **c.** Beware of altered date or mintmark. No V.D.B. on shoulder of genuine 1914-D cent.

1922-D, Normal D

1922-D, No D

1922-D, Weak D

| | Mintage | G-4 | VG-8 | F-12 | VF-20 | EF-40 | AU-50 | MS-60 | MS-63 | PF-63 |
|---|---|---|---|---|---|---|---|---|---|---|
| 1919 | 392,021,000 | $0.20 | $0.30 | $0.40 | $1.00 | $3.25 | $5.00 | $14 | $28 | |
| 1919D | 57,154,000 | 0.50 | 0.75 | 1.00 | 4.00 | 10.00 | 32.00 | 65 | 110 | |
| 1919S | 139,760,000 | 0.20 | 0.40 | 1.00 | 2.50 | 6.00 | 18.00 | 50 | 115 | |
| 1920 | 310,165,000 | 0.20 | 0.30 | 0.45 | 0.75 | 2.50 | 6.00 | 15 | 28 | |
| 1920D | 49,280,000 | 1.00 | 2.00 | 3.00 | 6.50 | 19.00 | 40.00 | 80 | 110 | |
| 1920S | 46,220,000 | 0.50 | 0.65 | 1.50 | 2.25 | 10.00 | 35.00 | 110 | 185 | |
| 1921 | 39,157,000 | 0.50 | 0.60 | 1.30 | 2.10 | 9.00 | 22.00 | 50 | 80 | |
| 1921S | 15,274,000 | 1.50 | 2.25 | 3.50 | 7.00 | 35.00 | 75.00 | 135 | 190 | |
| 1922D | 7,160,000 | 20.00 | 21.00 | 25.00 | 27.00 | 40.00 | 75.00 | 110 | 165 | |
| 1922, No D **(d)** | * | 450.00 | 550.00 | 650.00 | 750.00 | 1,500.00 | 3,500.00 | 8,500 | 18,500 | |
| 1922, Weak D | * | 25.00 | 35.00 | 50.00 | 70.00 | 160.00 | 200.00 | 350 | 1,000 | |
| 1923 | 74,723,000 | 0.35 | 0.45 | 0.65 | 1.00 | 5.00 | 9.50 | 15 | 30 | |
| 1923S | 8,700,000 | 5.00 | 7.00 | 8.00 | 12.00 | 40.00 | 90.00 | 220 | 390 | |
| 1924 | 75,178,000 | 0.20 | 0.30 | 0.40 | 0.85 | 5.00 | 10.00 | 24 | 50 | |
| 1924D | 2,520,000 | 35.00 | 45.00 | 50.00 | 60.00 | 125.00 | 175.00 | 300 | 350 | |
| 1924S | 11,696,000 | 2.00 | 2.50 | 3.50 | 5.50 | 20.00 | 75.00 | 125 | 225 | |
| 1925 | 139,949,000 | 0.20 | 0.25 | 0.35 | 0.60 | 3.00 | 6.50 | 10 | 20 | |
| 1925D | 22,580,000 | 1.00 | 1.30 | 2.50 | 5.00 | 13.00 | 30.00 | 75 | 90 | |
| 1925S | 26,380,000 | 1.00 | 1.50 | 2.00 | 4.00 | 12.00 | 30.00 | 90 | 200 | |
| 1926 | 157,088,000 | 0.20 | 0.25 | 0.30 | 0.50 | 2.00 | 4.00 | 8 | 18 | |
| 1926D | 28,020,000 | 1.35 | 1.75 | 3.50 | 5.25 | 14.00 | 32.00 | 85 | 125 | |
| 1926S | 4,550,000 | 9.00 | 11.00 | 13.00 | 17.00 | 35.00 | 75.00 | 155 | 325 | |
| 1927 | 144,440,000 | 0.20 | 0.25 | 0.30 | 0.60 | 2.00 | 3.50 | 10 | 20 | |
| 1927D | 27,170,000 | 1.25 | 1.75 | 2.75 | 3.75 | 7.50 | 25.00 | 62 | 85 | |
| 1927S | 14,276,000 | 1.50 | 2.00 | 3.00 | 5.00 | 15.00 | 40.00 | 85 | 140 | |
| 1928 | 134,116,000 | 0.20 | 0.25 | 0.30 | 0.60 | 2.00 | 3.00 | 9 | 13 | |
| 1928D | 31,170,000 | 0.75 | 1.00 | 1.75 | 3.00 | 5.50 | 17.00 | 37 | 80 | |
| 1928S **(e)** | 17,266,000 | 1.00 | 1.60 | 2.75 | 3.75 | 9.50 | 30.00 | 75 | 100 | |
| 1929 | 185,262,000 | 0.20 | 0.25 | 0.30 | 0.75 | 2.00 | 4.00 | 8 | 14 | |
| 1929D | 41,730,000 | 0.40 | 0.85 | 1.25 | 2.25 | 5.50 | 13.00 | 25 | 37 | |
| 1929S | 50,148,000 | 0.50 | 0.90 | 1.70 | 2.35 | 5.80 | 14.00 | 21 | 29 | |
| 1930 | 157,415,000 | 0.15 | 0.20 | 0.25 | 0.50 | 1.25 | 2.00 | 6 | 10 | |
| 1930D | 40,100,000 | 0.20 | 0.25 | 0.30 | 0.55 | 2.50 | 4.00 | 12 | 28 | |
| 1930S | 24,286,000 | 0.20 | 0.25 | 0.30 | 0.60 | 1.75 | 6.00 | 10 | 12 | |
| 1931 | 19,396,000 | 0.50 | 0.75 | 1.00 | 1.50 | 4.00 | 9.00 | 20 | 35 | |
| 1931D | 4,480,000 | 5.00 | 6.00 | 7.00 | 8.50 | 13.50 | 37.00 | 60 | 70 | |
| 1931S | 866,000 | 60.00 | 75.00 | 85.00 | 100.00 | 125.00 | 150.00 | 175 | 195 | |
| 1932 | 9,062,000 | 1.50 | 1.80 | 2.00 | 2.50 | 4.50 | 12.00 | 20 | 28 | |
| 1932D | 10,500,000 | 1.50 | 1.75 | 2.50 | 2.75 | 4.50 | 11.00 | 19 | 28 | |
| 1933 | 14,360,000 | 1.50 | 1.75 | 2.50 | 3.00 | 6.25 | 13.00 | 20 | 30 | |
| 1933D | 6,200,000 | 3.50 | 3.75 | 5.50 | 7.25 | 12.00 | 19.00 | 23 | 25 | |
| 1934 | 219,080,000 | 0.15 | 0.18 | 0.20 | 0.30 | 1.00 | 4.00 | 7 | 8 | |

* Included in number above. **d.** 1922 cents with a weak or missing mintmark were made from extremely worn dies that originally struck normal 1922-D cents. Three different die pairs were involved; two of them produced "Weak D" coins. One die pair (no. 2, identified by a "strong reverse") is acknowledged as striking "No D" coins. Weak D cents are worth considerably less. Beware of removed mintmark. **e.** Large and small mintmark varieties; see page 22.

1936, Doubled Die Obverse

| | Mintage | G-4 | VG-8 | F-12 | VF-20 | EF-40 | AU-50 | MS-60 | MS-63 | PF-63 |
|---|---|---|---|---|---|---|---|---|---|---|
| 1934D | 28,446,000 | $0.20 | $0.25 | $0.50 | $0.75 | $2.25 | $7.50 | $20 | $22 | |
| 1935 | 245,388,000 | 0.15 | 0.18 | 0.20 | 0.25 | 0.50 | 1.00 | 3 | 5 | |
| 1935D | 47,000,000 | 0.15 | 0.18 | 0.20 | 0.25 | 0.50 | 2.00 | 5 | 6 | |
| 1935S | 38,702,000 | 0.15 | 0.18 | 0.25 | 0.50 | 2.00 | 5.00 | 12 | 17 | |
| 1936 | (5,569) 309,632,000 | 0.15 | 0.18 | 0.25 | 0.50 | 1.50 | 2.60 | 3 | 4 | $125 **(f)** |
| 1936, DblDie Obv **(g)** | * | | | 75.00 | 125.00 | 200.00 | 350.00 | 500 | 1,500 | |
| 1936D | 40,620,000 | 0.15 | 0.20 | 0.30 | 0.50 | 1.00 | 2.00 | 3 | 4 | |
| 1936S | 29,130,000 | 0.15 | 0.25 | 0.40 | 0.55 | 1.00 | 3.00 | 5 | 6 | |
| 1937 | (9,320) 309,170,000 | 0.15 | 0.20 | 0.30 | 0.50 | 1.00 | 2.00 | 3 | 4 | 55 |
| 1937D | 50,430,000 | 0.15 | 0.20 | 0.25 | 0.40 | 1.00 | 3.00 | 5 | 6 | |
| 1937S | 34,500,000 | 0.15 | 0.20 | 0.30 | 0.40 | 1.00 | 3.00 | 5 | 8 | |
| 1938 | (14,734) 156,682,000 | 0.15 | 0.20 | 0.30 | 0.40 | 1.00 | 2.00 | 4 | 7 | 50 |
| 1938D | 20,010,000 | 0.20 | 0.30 | 0.50 | 0.80 | 1.25 | 3.00 | 4 | 7 | |
| 1938S | 15,180,000 | 0.40 | 0.50 | 0.60 | 0.75 | 1.10 | 3.00 | 4 | 6 | |
| 1939 | (13,520) 316,466,000 | 0.15 | 0.18 | 0.20 | 0.25 | 0.50 | 1.00 | 2 | 3 | 45 |
| 1939D | 15,160,000 | 0.50 | 0.60 | 0.65 | 0.85 | 1.25 | 3.00 | 4 | 5 | |
| 1939S | 52,070,000 | 0.15 | 0.20 | 0.30 | 0.75 | 1.00 | 2.50 | 3 | 4 | |
| 1940 | (15,872) 586,810,000 | 0.15 | 0.18 | 0.20 | 0.40 | 0.60 | 1.00 | 2 | 3 | 40 |
| 1940D | 81,390,000 | 0.15 | 0.18 | 0.25 | 0.60 | 0.75 | 2.00 | 3 | 4 | |
| 1940S | 112,940,000 | 0.15 | 0.18 | 0.20 | 0.50 | 1.00 | 1.75 | 3 | 4 | |
| 1941 | (21,100) 887,018,000 | 0.15 | 0.18 | 0.20 | 0.30 | 0.60 | 1.50 | 2 | 3 | 35 |
| 1941D | 128,700,000 | 0.15 | 0.18 | 0.20 | 0.50 | 1.00 | 3.00 | 4 | 5 | |
| 1941S **(e)** | 92,360,000 | 0.15 | 0.18 | 0.30 | 0.50 | 1.00 | 3.00 | 4 | 5 | |
| 1942 | (32,600) 657,796,000 | 0.15 | 0.18 | 0.20 | 0.25 | 0.50 | 0.75 | 1 | 2 | 35 |
| 1942D | 206,698,000 | 0.15 | 0.18 | 0.20 | 0.25 | 0.50 | 0.85 | 1 | 2 | |
| 1942S | 85,590,000 | 0.20 | 0.25 | 0.30 | 0.85 | 1.25 | 5.50 | 7 | 8 | |

* Included in number above. **e.** Large and small mintmark varieties; see page 22. **f.** Value is for Brilliant Proof; Satin Proof value in PF-63 is $100. **g.** Values are for pieces with strong doubling, as illustrated above.

## Variety 2 – Zinc-Coated Steel (1943)

Due to a copper shortage during the critical war year 1943, the Treasury used zinc-coated steel to make cents. Although no bronze cents were officially issued that year, a few specimens struck in error on bronze or silver planchets are known to exist; bronze examples have sold for over $200,000 in recent years. Through a similar error, a few 1944 cents were struck on steel planchets. Beware the many regular steel cents of 1943 that were later plated with copper, either as novelties or to deceive; a magnet will reveal their true nature. For more on the 1943 bronze cent, see appendix A.

*1943—Weight 2.70 grams; composition, steel coated with zinc; diameter 19 mm; plain edge.*

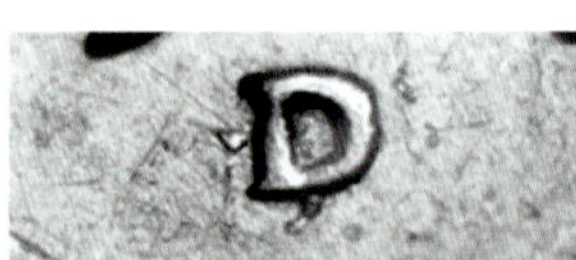

1943-D, Boldly Doubled Mintmark

| | Mintage | F-12 | VF-20 | EF-40 | AU-50 | MS-63 | MS-65 |
|---|---|---|---|---|---|---|---|
| 1943 | 684,628,670 | $0.30 | $0.35 | $0.40 | $0.50 | $2.50 | $8 |
| 1943D | 217,660,000 | 0.35 | 0.40 | 0.50 | 0.75 | 3.00 | 10 |
| 1943D, Boldly Doubled Mintmark | * | 40.00 | 50.00 | 60.00 | 70.00 | 100.00 | 1,000 |
| 1943S | 191,550,000 | 0.40 | 0.65 | 0.75 | 1.00 | 6.00 | 20 |

* Included in number above.

## Variety 1 (Bronze) Resumed (1944–1958)

Cartridge cases were salvaged for coinage of 1944 through 1946. Although the color was slightly different for Uncirculated specimens, the coins were satisfactory overall.

*1944–1946—Weight, 3.11 grams; composition .950 copper, .050 zinc; diameter 19 mm; plain edge.*
*1947–1958—Weight 3.11 grams; composition .950 copper, .050 tin and zinc; diameter 19 mm; plain edge.*

1944-D, D Over S

1946-S, S Over D

| | Mintage | VF-20 | EF-40 | AU-50 | MS-63RB | MS-65RB | PF-65 |
|---|---|---|---|---|---|---|---|
| 1944 | 1,435,400,000 | $0.10 | $0.20 | $0.35 | $1.00 | $5 | |
| 1944D | 430,578,000 | 0.10 | 0.20 | 0.35 | 0.85 | 4 | |
| 1944D, D Over S **(a)** | * | 100.00 | 175.00 | 235.00 | 450.00 | 700 | |
| 1944S | 282,760,000 | 0.15 | 0.20 | 0.35 | 0.85 | 4 | |
| 1945 | 1,040,515,000 | 0.10 | 0.20 | 0.35 | 0.85 | 2 | |
| 1945D | 266,268,000 | 0.10 | 0.20 | 0.35 | 0.85 | 2 | |
| 1945S | 181,770,000 | 0.15 | 0.20 | 0.35 | 0.85 | 2 | |
| 1946 | 991,655,000 | 0.10 | 0.20 | 0.35 | 0.60 | 2 | |
| 1946D | 315,690,000 | 0.10 | 0.20 | 0.35 | 0.60 | 2 | |
| 1946S | 198,100,000 | 0.15 | 0.20 | 0.35 | 0.60 | 2 | |
| 1946S, S Over D | * | 35.00 | 75.00 | 125.00 | 225.00 | 400 | |
| 1947 | 190,555,000 | 0.10 | 0.20 | 0.40 | 1.00 | 3 | |
| 1947D | 194,750,000 | 0.10 | 0.20 | 0.40 | 0.60 | 2 | |
| 1947S | 99,000,000 | 0.20 | 0.25 | 0.50 | 0.85 | 2 | |
| 1948 | 317,570,000 | 0.10 | 0.20 | 0.35 | 0.85 | 2 | |
| 1948D | 172,637,500 | 0.10 | 0.20 | 0.35 | 0.60 | 2 | |
| 1948S | 81,735,000 | 0.20 | 0.30 | 0.35 | 1.00 | 3 | |
| 1949 | 217,775,000 | 0.10 | 0.20 | 0.35 | 1.00 | 3 | |
| 1949D | 153,132,500 | 0.10 | 0.20 | 0.35 | 1.00 | 3 | |
| 1949S | 64,290,000 | 0.25 | 0.30 | 0.35 | 2.00 | 4 | |
| 1950 (51,386) | 272,635,000 | 0.10 | 0.20 | 0.35 | 0.85 | 2 | $70 |
| 1950D | 334,950,000 | 0.10 | 0.20 | 0.35 | 0.60 | 2 | |
| 1950S | 118,505,000 | 0.15 | 0.25 | 0.35 | 0.85 | 2 | |
| 1951 (57,500) | 284,576,000 | 0.10 | 0.25 | 0.35 | 0.70 | 2 | 65 |
| 1951D | 625,355,000 | 0.10 | 0.12 | 0.35 | 0.60 | 2 | |
| 1951S | 136,010,000 | 0.25 | 0.30 | 0.50 | 1.00 | 3 | |
| 1952 (81,980) | 186,775,000 | 0.10 | 0.15 | 0.35 | 1.00 | 3 | 50 |
| 1952D | 746,130,000 | 0.10 | 0.15 | 0.25 | 0.75 | 2 | |
| 1952S | 137,800,004 | 0.15 | 0.20 | 0.35 | 2.00 | 4 | |
| 1953 (128,800) | 256,755,000 | 0.10 | 0.15 | 0.20 | 0.50 | 1 | 30 |
| 1953D | 700,515,000 | 0.10 | 0.15 | 0.20 | 0.50 | 1 | |
| 1953S | 181,835,000 | 0.10 | 0.15 | 0.20 | 0.60 | 2 | |
| 1954 (233,300) | 71,640,050 | 0.25 | 0.35 | 0.45 | 0.60 | 2 | 20 |
| 1954D | 251,552,500 | 0.10 | 0.12 | 0.20 | 0.50 | 1 | |
| 1954S | 96,190,000 | 0.10 | 0.12 | 0.20 | 0.50 | 1 | |

* Included in number above. **a.** Varieties exist.

The popular 1955 doubled-die error coins (illustrated on the following page) were made from improperly prepared dies that show a fully doubled outline of the date and legend. Do not confuse these with less-valuable pieces showing only minor traces of doubling. Counterfeits exist.

1955, Doubled Die Obverse

| | Mintage | VF-20 | EF-40 | AU-50 | MS-63RB | MS-65RB | PF-65 |
|---|---|---|---|---|---|---|---|
| 1955 . . . . . . . . . . . . . (378,200) . . . | 330,958,200 | $0.10 | $0.12 | $0.15 | $0.35 | $1 | $18 |
| 1955, Doubled Die Obverse . . . . . . . . . . . . . . . . | * | 1,400.00 | 1,600.00 | 1,750.00 | 4,000 **(a)** | 10,000 | |
| 1955D . . . . . . . . . . . . . . . . . . . . . . | 563,257,500 | 0.10 | 0.12 | 0.15 | 0.35 | 1 | |
| 1955S . . . . . . . . . . . . . . . . . . . . . . . | 44,610,000 | 0.20 | 0.30 | 0.40 | 0.85 | 3 | |
| 1956 . . . . . . . . . . . . . (669,384) . . . | 420,745,000 | 0.10 | 0.12 | 0.15 | 0.35 | 1 | 10 |
| 1956D . . . . . . . . . . . . . . . . . . . . | 1,098,201,100 | 0.10 | 0.12 | 0.15 | 0.30 | 1 | |
| 1956D, D Above Shadow D . . . . . . . . . . . . . . . . | * | 10.00 | 25.00 | 30.00 | 35.00 | | |
| 1957 . . . . . . . . . . . (1,247,952) . . . | 282,540,000 | 0.10 | 0.12 | 0.15 | 0.30 | 1 | 10 |
| 1957D . . . . . . . . . . . . . . . . . . . . | 1,051,342,000 | 0.10 | 0.12 | 0.15 | 0.30 | 1 | |
| 1958 . . . . . . . . . . . . . (875,652) . . . | 252,525,000 | 0.10 | 0.12 | 0.15 | 0.30 | 1 | 8 |
| 1958, DblDie Obv *(3 known)* . . . . . . . . . . . . . . . | * | | | | | | |
| 1958D . . . . . . . . . . . . . . . . . . . . . . | 800,953,300 | 0.10 | 0.12 | 0.15 | 0.30 | 1 | |

* Included in number above. **a.** Value for MS-60 is $2,700.

## LINCOLN, MEMORIAL REVERSE (1959–2008)

Frank Gasparro designed the Lincoln Memorial reverse, which was introduced in 1959 on the 150th anniversary of Abraham Lincoln's birth.

### Copper Alloy (1959–1982)

*Designer Victor D. Brenner (obv), Frank Gasparro (rev); 1959–1962—Weight 3.11 grams; composition .950 copper, .050 tin and zinc; diameter 19 mm; plain edge. 1962–1982—Weight 3.11 grams; composition .950 copper, .050 zinc. 1982 to date—Weight 2.5 grams; composition copper-plated zinc (core: .992 zinc, .008 copper, with a plating of pure copper; total content .975 zinc, .025 copper). Mints: Philadelphia, Denver, San Francisco.*

*Circulation strike.*

*Proof strike.*

1960, Small Date

1960, Large Date

1960-D, D Over D, Small Date Over Large Date

| | Mintage | MS-63RB | MS-65RD | PF-65 |
|---|---|---|---|---|
| 1959 . . . . . . . . . . . . . . . . . . . . . . . . . . . . . . . . (1,149,291) . . . . | 609,715,000 | $0.20 | $0.30 | $3 |
| 1959D . . . . . . . . . . . . . . . . . . . . . . . . . . . . . . . . . . . . . . . . . . | 1,279,760,000 | 0.50 | 0.55 | |
| 1960, Large Date . . . . . . . . . . . . . . . . . . . . . . . . (1,691,602) . . . . | 586,405,000 | 0.20 | 0.30 | 2 |
| 1960, Small Date . . . . . . . . . . . . . . . . . . . . . . . . . . . . . . . . . . . . | * | 3.00 | 7.00 | 22 |
| 1960, Large Date Over Small Date . . . . . . . . . . . . . . . . . . . . . . . . . . . . . | * | | | — |
| 1960, Small Date Over Large Date . . . . . . . . . . . . . . . . . . . . . . . . . . . . . | * | | | — |
| 1960D, Large Date . . . . . . . . . . . . . . . . . . . . . . . . . . . . . . . . . | 1,580,884,000 | 0.20 | 0.30 | |
| 1960D, Small Date . . . . . . . . . . . . . . . . . . . . . . . . . . . . . . . . . . . . . . . | * | 0.20 | 0.30 | |
| 1960D, D Over D, Small Date Over Large Date . . . . . . . . . . . . . . . . . . . . . . . . | * | 150.00 | 300.00 | |

* Included in number above.

| | Mintage | MS-63RB | MS-65RD | PF-65 |
|---|---|---|---|---|
| 1961 | (3,028,244) . . . 753,345,000 | $0.15 | $0.30 | $2 |
| 1961D | 1,753,266,700 | 0.15 | 0.30 | |
| 1962 | (3,218,019) . . . 606,045,000 | 0.15 | 0.30 | 2 |
| 1962D | 1,793,148,140 | 0.15 | 0.30 | |
| 1963 | (3,075,645) . . . 754,110,000 | 0.15 | 0.30 | 2 |
| 1963D | 1,774,020,400 | 0.15 | 0.30 | |
| 1964 | (3,950,762) . . 2,648,575,000 | 0.15 | 0.30 | 2 |
| 1964D | 3,799,071,500 | 0.15 | 0.30 | |
| 1965 | 1,497,224,900 | 0.20 | 0.50 | |
| 1966 | 2,188,147,783 | 0.20 | 0.50 | |
| 1967 | 3,048,667,100 | 0.20 | 0.50 | |
| 1968 | 1,707,880,970 | 0.25 | 0.60 | |
| 1968D | 2,886,269,600 | 0.15 | 0.40 | |
| 1968S | (3,041,506) . . . 258,270,001 | 0.15 | 0.40 | 1 |

In 1969, the dies were modified to strengthen the design, and Lincoln's head was made slightly smaller. In 1973, dies were further modified and the engraver's initials FG made larger. The initials were reduced slightly in 1974. During 1982 the dies were again modified and the bust, lettering, and date made slightly smaller. One variety of the 1984 cent shows Lincoln's ear doubled. Some 1,579,324 cents dated 1974 were struck in aluminum as experimental pieces. None were placed in circulation, and most were later destroyed. One was preserved for the National Numismatic Collection in the Smithsonian Institution. Other 1974 experimental cents were struck in bronze-clad steel.

**1969-S, Doubled Die Obverse**

**1970-S, Small Date (High 7)**

**1970-S, Large Date (Low 7)**

**1971-S, Proof Doubled Die Obverse**

**1972, Doubled Die Obverse**

**1982, Large Date**

**1982, Small Date**

| | Mintage | MS-65 | PF-65 |
|---|---|---|---|
| 1969 | 1,136,910,000 | $0.70 | |
| 1969D | 4,002,832,200 | 0.30 | |
| 1969S | (2,934,631) | | $1 |
| | 544,375,000 | 0.50 | |
| 1969S, DblDie Obv | * | **(a)** | |
| 1970 | 1,898,315,000 | 0.65 | |
| 1970D | 2,891,438,900 | 0.30 | |
| 1970S, All kinds | (2,632,810) | | |
| | 690,560,004 | | |
| 1970S, Sm Dt (High 7) | | 55.00 | 40 |
| 1970S, Lg Dt (Low 7) | | 0.50 | 1 |
| 1970S, DblDie Obv | | — | |
| 1971 | 1,919,490,000 | 0.60 | |
| 1971, DblDie Obv | * | 50.00 | |

| | Mintage | MS-65 | PF-65 |
|---|---|---|---|
| 1971D | 2,911,045,600 | $0.50 | |
| 1971S | (3,220,733) | | $1 |
| | 525,133,459 | 0.50 | |
| 1971S, DblDie Obv | * | | 500 |
| 1972 | 2,933,255,000 | 0.30 | |
| 1972, DblDie Obv **(b)** | * | 600.00 | |
| 1972D | 2,665,071,400 | 0.30 | |
| 1972S | (3,260,996) | | 1 |
| | 376,939,108 | 0.75 | |
| 1973 | 3,728,245,000 | 0.30 | |
| 1973D | 3,549,576,588 | 0.30 | |
| 1973S | (2,760,339) | | 1 |
| | 317,177,295 | 0.85 | |
| 1974 | 4,232,140,523 | 0.30 | |

* Included in number above. **a.** Value for an MS-63RB coin is $75,000. **b.** Other slightly doubled varieties (worth far less) exist.

*Chart continued on next page.*

| | Mintage | MS-65 | PF-65 |
|---|---|---|---|
| 1974D | 4,235,098,000 | $0.30 | |
| 1974S | (2,612,568) | | $1.00 |
| | 409,426,660 | 0.75 | |
| 1975 | 5,451,476,142 | 0.30 | |
| 1975D | 4,505,275,300 | 0.30 | |
| 1975S | (2,845,450) | | 3.50 |
| 1976 | 4,674,292,426 | 0.30 | |
| 1976D | 4,221,592,455 | 0.30 | |
| 1976S | (4,149,730) | | 3.20 |
| 1977 | 4,469,930,000 | 0.30 | |
| 1977D | 4,194,062,300 | 0.30 | |
| 1977S | (3,251,152) | | 2.50 |
| 1978 | 5,558,605,000 | 0.30 | |
| 1978D | 4,280,233,400 | 0.30 | |
| 1978S | (3,127,781) | | 2.50 |
| 1979 | 6,018,515,000 | $0.30 | |
| 1979D | 4,139,357,254 | 0.30 | |
| 1979S, Type 1 **(c)** | (3,677,175) | | $5.00 |
| 1979S, Type 2 **(c)** | * | | 6.00 |
| 1980 | 7,414,705,000 | 0.30 | |
| 1980D | 5,140,098,660 | 0.30 | |
| 1980S | (3,554,806) | | 2.50 |
| 1981 | 7,491,750,000 | 0.30 | |
| 1981D | 5,373,235,677 | 0.30 | |
| 1981S, Type 1 **(c)** | (4,063,083) | | 3.00 |
| 1981S, Type 2 **(c)** | * | | 15.00 |
| 1982, Large Date | 10,712,525,000 | 0.35 | |
| 1982, Small Date | * | 0.50 | |
| 1982D, Large Date | 6,012,979,368 | 0.30 | |
| 1982S, Small Date | (3,857,479) | | 2.50 |

**c.** See page 246 for illustrations of Type 1 and Type 2 varieties.

## Copper-Plated Zinc (1982–2008)

*The composition for this period changed to copper-plated zinc. The core is 99.2% zinc, 0.8% copper, with a plating of pure copper; the weight is 2.5 grams (approximately 20% lighter than the copper alloy cents).*

**1983, Doubled Die Reverse**

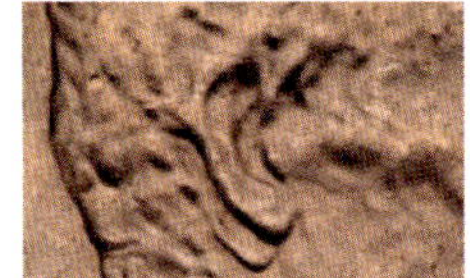

**1984, Doubled Ear Variety**

**1990, Proof, No S**

**1995, Doubled Die Obverse**

| | Mintage | MS-65 | PF-65 |
|---|---|---|---|
| 1982, Large Date | **(a)** | $0.50 | |
| 1982, Small Date | **(a)** | 0.85 | |
| 1982D, Large Date | **(a)** | 0.40 | |
| 1982D, Small Date | **(a)** | 0.30 | |
| 1983 | 7,752,355,000 | 0.30 | |
| 1983, DblDie Rev. | * | 375.00 | |
| 1983D | 6,467,199,428 | 0.30 | |
| 1983S | (3,279,126) | | $3 |
| 1984 | 8,151,079,000 | 0.30 | |
| 1984, Doubled Ear | * | 225.00 | |
| 1984D | 5,569,238,906 | 0.30 | |
| 1984S | (3,065,110) | | 4 |
| 1985 | 5,648,489,887 | 0.30 | |
| 1985D | 5,287,339,926 | 0.30 | |
| 1985S | (3,362,821) | | 5 |
| 1986 | 4,491,395,493 | 0.30 | |
| 1986D | 4,442,866,698 | 0.30 | |
| 1986S | (3,010,497) | | 7 |
| 1987 | 4,682,466,931 | 0.30 | |
| 1987D | 4,879,389,514 | $0.30 | |
| 1987S | (4,227,728) | | $5 |
| 1988 | 6,092,810,000 | 0.30 | |
| 1988D | 5,253,740,443 | 0.30 | |
| 1988S | (3,262,948) | | 9 |
| 1989 | 7,261,535,000 | 0.30 | |
| 1989D | 5,345,467,111 | 0.30 | |
| 1989S | (3,220,194) | | 9 |
| 1990 | 6,851,765,000 | 0.30 | |
| 1990D | 4,922,894,533 | 0.30 | |
| 1990S | (3,299,559) | | 5 |
| 1990, Proof, No S | * | | 2,250 |
| 1991 | 5,165,940,000 | 0.30 | |
| 1991D | 4,158,446,076 | 0.30 | |
| 1991S | (2,867,787) | | 12 |
| 1992 | 4,648,905,000 | 0.30 | |
| 1992, Close AM **(b)** | * | — | |
| 1992D | 4,448,673,300 | 0.30 | |
| 1992D, Close AM **(b)** | * | — | |

* Included in number above. **a.** Included in previous chart. **b.** Varieties were made using Proof dies that have a wide space between A and M in AMERICA. The letters nearly touch on other circulation-strike cents after 1993.

| | Mintage | MS-65 | PF-65 |
|---|---|---|---|
| 1992S | (4,176,560) | | $5.00 |
| 1993 | 5,684,705,000 | $0.30 | |
| 1993D | 6,426,650,571 | 0.30 | |
| 1993S | (3,394,792) | | 9.00 |
| 1994 | 6,500,850,000 | 0.30 | |
| 1994D | 7,131,765,000 | 0.30 | |
| 1994S | (3,269,923) | | 9.00 |
| 1995 | 6,411,440,000 | 0.30 | |
| 1995, DblDie Obv | * | 50.00 | |
| 1995D | 7,128,560,000 | 0.30 | |
| 1995S | (2,797,481) | | 9.00 |
| 1996 | 6,612,465,000 | 0.30 | |
| 1996D | 6,510,795,000 | 0.30 | |
| 1996S | (2,525,265) | | 4.50 |
| 1997 | 4,622,800,000 | 0.30 | |
| 1997D | 4,576,555,000 | 0.30 | |
| 1997S | (2,796,678) | | 10.00 |
| 1998 | 5,032,155,000 | 0.30 | |
| 1998, Wide AM **(b)** | * | 25.00 | |
| 1998D | 5,225,353,500 | 0.30 | |
| 1998S | (2,086,507) | | 9.00 |
| 1998S, Close AM **(c)** | * | | 150.00 |
| 1999 | 5,237,600,000 | 0.30 | |
| 1999, Wide AM **(b)** | * | 500.00 | |
| 1999D | 6,360,065,000 | 0.30 | |
| 1999S | (3,347,966) | | 6.00 |
| 1999S, Close AM **(c)** | * | | 80.00 |
| 2000 | 5,503,200,000 | 0.30 | |
| 2000, Wide AM **(b)** | * | $20.00 | |
| 2000D | 8,774,220,000 | 0.30 | |
| 2000S | (4,047,993) | | $4 |
| 2001 | 4,959,600,000 | 0.30 | |
| 2001D | 5,374,990,000 | 0.30 | |
| 2001S | (3,184,606) | | 4 |
| 2002 | 3,260,800,000 | 0.30 | |
| 2002D | 4,028,055,000 | 0.30 | |
| 2002S | (3,211,995) | | 4 |
| 2003 | 3,300,000,000 | 0.30 | |
| 2003D | 3,548,000,000 | 0.30 | |
| 2003S | (3,298,439) | | 4 |
| 2004 | 3,379,600,000 | 0.30 | |
| 2004D | 3,456,400,000 | 0.30 | |
| 2004S | (2,965,422) | | 4 |
| 2005 | 3,953,600,000 | 0.30 | |
| 2005D | 3,764,450,500 | 0.30 | |
| 2005S | (3,344,679) | | 4 |
| 2006 | 4,290,000,000 | 0.30 | |
| 2006D | 3,944,000,000 | 0.30 | |
| 2006S | (3,054,436) | | 4 |
| 2007 | 3,762,400,000 | 0.30 | |
| 2007D | 3,638,800,000 | 0.30 | |
| 2007S | (2,577,166) | | 4 |
| 2008 | 2,558,800,000 | 0.30 | |
| 2008D | 2,849,600,000 | 0.30 | |
| 2008S | (2,169,561) | | 4 |

*Note:* Uncirculated Mint Sets for 2005–2010 were made with Satin Finish coins not included in the listings here. See page 369 for their mintages. * Included in number above. **b.** Varieties were made using Proof dies that have a wide space between A and M in AMERICA. The letters nearly touch on other circulation-strike cents after 1993. **c.** The reverse design for circulation strikes of 1993 was inadvertently used on some circulation-strike coins of 1992. This same design was accidentally used on some Proof coins from 1998 and 1999.

Some of the cents minted since 1994 show the faint trace of a mintmark, believed to be the result of the letter's having been removed from the master hub during production of working dies for coinage. So-called phantom mintmark pieces were produced in Philadelphia but show traces of either a D or an S. Values for such pieces vary according to date and condition but are not significantly higher than for normal pieces.

## LINCOLN, BICENTENNIAL (2009)

One-cent coins issued during 2009 are a unique tribute to President Abraham Lincoln, recognizing the bicentennial of his birth and the 100th anniversary of the first issuance of the Lincoln cent. These coins use four different design themes on the reverse to represent the four major aspects of President Lincoln's life. The obverse of each of these coins carries the traditional portrait of Lincoln that has been in use since 1909.

The special reverse designs, released as quarterly issues throughout 2009, are as follows. The first, Birth and Early Childhood in Kentucky (designer, Richard Masters; sculptor, Jim Licaretz), depicts a small log cabin like the one in which Lincoln was born. The second, Formative Years in Indiana (designer and sculptor, Charles Vickers), shows a youthful Abe Lincoln taking a break from rail-splitting to read a book. On the third coin, Professional Life in Illinois (designer, Joel Iskowitz; sculptor, Don Everhart),

Lincoln stands in front of the state capitol of Illinois. The design commemorates his pre-presidential career in law and politics. Finally, Presidency in Washington (designer, Susan Gamble; sculptor, Joseph Menna), depicts the partially completed U.S. Capitol dome as it appeared when Lincoln held office. The state of the Capitol represents "the unfinished business of a nation torn apart by slavery and the Civil War." Lincoln Bicentennial cents issued for commercial circulation are made of the exact same copper-plated composition used since 1982. Special versions included in satin-finish collector sets are made of the same metallic composition as was used for the original 1909 cents (95% copper, 5% tin and zinc).

The Mint-packaged Abraham Lincoln Coin and Chronicles set of four 2009-S Proof cents and the Lincoln commemorative silver dollar is listed on page 361.

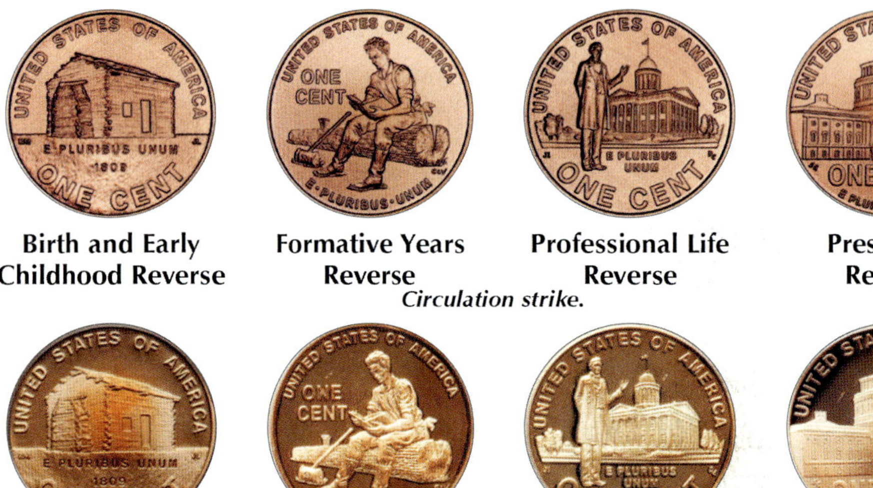


**Birth and Early Childhood Reverse** | **Formative Years Reverse** | **Professional Life Reverse** | **Presidency Reverse**

*Circulation strike.*

**Birth and Early Childhood Reverse** | **Formative Years Reverse** | **Professional Life Reverse** | **Presidency Reverse**

*Proof strike.*

| | Mintage | MS-65 | PF-65 |
|---|---|---|---|
| 2009, Birth and Early Childhood | 284,400,000 | $0.30 | |
| 2009, Birth and Early Childhood, copper, Satin Finish | 784,614 | 10.00 | |
| 2009D, Birth and Early Childhood | 350,400,000 | 0.30 | |
| 2009D, Birth and Early Childhood, copper, Satin Finish | 784,614 | 10.00 | |
| 2009S, Birth and Early Childhood, copper | (2,995,615) | | $4 |
| 2009, Formative Years | 376,000,000 | 0.30 | |
| 2009, Formative Years, copper, Satin Finish | 784,614 | 10.00 | |
| 2009D, Formative Years | 363,600,000 | 0.30 | |
| 2009D, Formative Years, copper, Satin Finish | 784,614 | 10.00 | |
| 2009S, Formative Years, copper | (2,995,615) | | 4 |
| 2009, Professional Life | 316,000,000 | 0.30 | |
| 2009, Professional Life, copper, Satin Finish | 784,614 | 10.00 | |
| 2009D, Professional Life | 336,000,000 | 0.30 | |
| 2009D, Professional Life, copper, Satin Finish | 784,614 | 10.00 | |
| 2009S, Professional Life, copper | (2,995,615) | | 4 |
| 2009, Presidency | 129,600,000 | 0.30 | |
| 2009, Presidency, copper, Satin Finish | 784,614 | 10.00 | |
| 2009D, Presidency | 198,000,000 | 0.30 | |
| 2009D, Presidency, copper, Satin Finish | 784,614 | 10.00 | |
| 2009S, Presidency, copper | (2,995,615) | | 4 |

*Note:* Several varieties with minor die doubling exist. Values vary according to the severity of the doubling.

## LINCOLN, SHIELD REVERSE (2010 TO DATE)

Since the conclusion of the 2009 Bicentennial One-Cent Program, one-cent coins feature a reverse that has "an image emblematic of President Lincoln's preservation of the United States of America as a single and united country."

Circulation strike.

Proof strike.

*Designer Victor D. Brenner (obv.), Lyndall Bass (rev.); weight 2.5 grams; composition copper-plated zinc (core: .992 zinc, .008 copper, with a plating of pure copper; total content .975 zinc, .025 copper); diameter 19 mm; plain edge; mints: Philadelphia, Denver, San Francisco, West Point.*

| | Mintage | MS-65 | PF-65 |
|---|---|---|---|
| 2010 | 1,963,630,000 | $0.30 | |
| 2010D | 2,047,200,000 | 0.30 | |
| 2010S | *(1,689,216)* | | $4 |
| 2011 | 2,402,400,000 | 0.30 | |
| 2011D | 2,536,140,000 | 0.30 | |
| 2011S | *(1,673,010)* | | 5 |
| 2012 | 3,132,000,000 | 0.30 | |
| 2012D | 2,883,200,000 | 0.30 | |
| 2012S | (1,239,148) | | 5 |
| 2013 | 3,750,400,000 | 0.30 | |
| 2013D | 3,319,600,000 | 0.30 | |
| 2013S | *(1,274,505)* | | 5 |
| 2014 | 3,990,800,000 | 0.30 | |
| 2014D | 4,155,600,000 | 0.30 | |
| 2014S | *(1,190,369)* | | 5 |
| 2015 | 4,691,300,000 | 0.30 | |
| 2015D | 4,674,000,000 | 0.30 | |
| 2015S | *(1,050,164)* | | 5 |
| 2016 | 4,698,000,000 | $0.30 | |
| 2016D | 4,420,400,000 | 0.30 | |
| 2016S | *(1,011,624)* | | $5 |
| 2017P **(a)** | 4,361,220,000 | 0.30 | |
| 2017D | 4,272,800,000 | 0.30 | |
| 2017S **(b)** | *(979,477)* | | 5 |
| 2018 | *4,066,800,000* | 0.30 | |
| 2018D | *3,736,400,000* | 0.30 | |
| 2018S | *(844,220)* | | 5 |
| 2019 | *3,542,800,000* | 0.30 | |
| 2019D | *3,497,600,000* | 0.30 | |
| 2019S | | | 5 |
| 2019W **(c)** | | 10.00 | |
| 2019W, Proof **(d)** | | | 10 |
| 2019W, Reverse Proof **(e)** | | | 10 |
| 2020 | | 0.30 | |
| 2020D | | 0.30 | |
| 2020S | | | 5 |

*Note:* Uncirculated Mint Sets for 2005–2010 were made with Satin Finish coins not included in the listings here. See page 369 for their mintages. **a.** All 2017-dated cents struck at the Philadelphia Mint bear a P mintmark in honor of the 225th anniversary of U.S. coinage. **b.** For its 225th anniversary, the Mint issued a special set of Enhanced Uncirculated coins from the San Francisco Mint; they are not included in the listings here. **c.** Included as a premium in the U.S. Mint 2019 Uncirculated Coin Set. **d.** Included as a premium in the U.S. Mint 2019 Proof Set. **e.** Included as a premium in the 2019 U.S. Mint Silver Proof Set.

The Act of April 22, 1864, which changed the weight and composition of the cent, included a provision for a bronze two-cent piece. The weight was specified as 96 grains, the alloy being the same as for the cent. The two-cent piece is one of the shortest-lived issues of United States coinage. The motto IN GOD WE TRUST appeared for the first time on the new coin, with the personal support of Treasury Secretary Salmon P. Chase. There are two varieties for the first year of issue, 1864: the Small Motto, which is scarce, and the Large Motto. See illustrations below. On the obverse, the D in GOD is narrow on the Large Motto. The stem to the leaf shows plainly on the Small Motto variety. There is no stem on the Large Motto. The first T in TRUST is very close to the ribbon crease at left on the Small Motto variety; there is a 1 mm gap on the Large Motto variety.

The shield device is very similar to that on the nickel five-cent piece introduced in 1866. Listed Proof mintages are estimates.

*Designer James B. Longacre; weight 6.22 grams; composition .950 copper, .050 tin and zinc; diameter 23 mm; plain edge. All coined at Philadelphia Mint.*

**G-4 Good**—At least part of IN GOD visible.
**F-12 Fine**—Complete motto visible. The word WE weak.
**VF-20 Very Fine**—WE is clear, but not strong.
**EF-40 Extremely Fine**—The word WE bold.
**AU-50 About Uncirculated**—Traces of wear visible on leaf tips, arrow points, and the word WE.
**MS-60 Uncirculated**—No trace of wear. Light blemishes.
**MS-63 Choice Uncirculated**—Some distracting contact marks or blemishes in prime focal areas. Some impairment of luster possible.
**PF-63 Choice Proof**—Attractive, mirrorlike fields. Minimal hairlines. Only a few blemishes in secondary focal areas.

*Circulation strike.*

*Proof strike.*

**1864, Small Motto**

**1864, Large Motto**

*Brilliant red choice Uncirculated and Proof coins command higher prices. Spotted, cleaned, or discolored pieces are valued lower.*

| | Mintage | G-4 | F-12 | VF-20 | EF-40 | AU-50 | MS-60 | MS-63BN | PF-63BN |
|---|---|---|---|---|---|---|---|---|---|
| 1864, Small Motto | * | $225 | $350 | $500 | $600 | $1,000 | $1,200 | $1,500 | $25,000 |
| 1864, Large Motto . . *(100+)* | 19,822,500 | 13 | 20 | 30 | 50 | 80 | 110 | 175 | 750 |
| 1865 **(a)** . . *(500+)* | 13,640,000 | 13 | 20 | 30 | 50 | 80 | 110 | 175 | 450 |
| 1866 . . *(725+)* | 3,177,000 | | | | | | 120 | 175 | 450 |
| 1867 . . *(625+)* | 2,938,750 | 15 | 25 | 35 | 50 | 80 | 130 | 190 | 450 |
| 1867, DblDie Obv | ** | 125 | 185 | 350 | 700 | 1,150 | 2,000 | 3,200 | |
| 1868 . . *(600+)* | 2,803,750 | 15 | 35 | 50 | 75 | 110 | 150 | 250 | 450 |
| 1869 . . *(600+)* | 1,546,500 | 20 | 40 | 55 | 80 | 125 | 160 | 250 | 450 |
| 1870 . . *(1,000+)* | 861,250 | 35 | 55 | 85 | 150 | 200 | 275 | 300 | 450 |
| 1871 . . *(960+)* | 721,250 | 40 | 75 | 100 | 155 | 200 | 275 | 325 | 450 |
| 1872 . . *(950+)* | 65,000 | 300 | 450 | 700 | 1,000 | 1,650 | 2,800 | 3,750 | 900 |
| 1873, Close 3, Proof only . . . . *(600)* | | | 1,400 | 1,500 | 1,650 | | | | 2,500 |
| 1873, Open 3, Alleged Restrike . . . . ** | | | 1,250 | 1,500 | 1,750 | | | | 2,750 |

* Included in number below. ** Included in number above. **a.** Varieties show the tip of the 5 either plain or curved.

# SILVER THREE-CENT PIECES (TRIMES) (1851–1873)

This smallest of United States silver coins, called the *trime* by the Treasury Department, was authorized by Congress March 3, 1851. The first three-cent silver pieces had no lines bordering the six-pointed star. From 1854 through 1858 there were two lines, while issues of the final 15 years show only one line. Issues from 1854 through 1873 have an olive sprig over the III and a bundle of three arrows beneath. Nearly the entire production of non-Proof coins from 1863 to 1872 was melted in 1873.

*Designer James B. Longacre. 1851–1853—Weight .80 gram; composition .750 silver, .250 copper; diameter 14 mm; plain edge; 1854–1873—Weight .75 gram; composition .900 silver, .100 copper; diameter 14 mm; plain edge. Mints: Philadelphia, New Orleans.*

**G-4 Good**—Star worn smooth. Legend and date readable.
**VG-8 Very Good**—Outline of shield defined. Legend and date clear.
**F-12 Fine**—Only star points worn smooth.
**VF-20 Very Fine**—Only partial wear on star ridges.
**EF-40 Extremely Fine**—Ridges on star points (coins of 1854 onward) visible.
**AU-50 About Uncirculated**—Trace of wear visible at each star point. Center of shield possibly weak.
**MS-60 Uncirculated**—No trace of wear. Light blemishes.
**MS-63 Choice Uncirculated**—Some distracting contact marks or blemishes in prime focal areas. Some impairment of luster possible.

*Proof strike.*

*Mintmark location.*

Variety 1 (1851–1853)

Variety 2 (1854–1858)

Variety 3 (1859–1873)

*Circulation strikes.*

1862, 2 Over 1

*Well-struck specimens of Variety 2 command higher prices.*

| | Mintage | G-4 | VG-8 | F-12 | VF-20 | EF-40 | AU-50 | MS-60 | MS-63 | PF-63 |
|---|---|---|---|---|---|---|---|---|---|---|
| 1851 | 5,447,400 | $25 | $35 | $50 | $65 | $80 | $165 | $200 | $275 | — |
| 1851O | 720,000 | 45 | 65 | 75 | 120 | 200 | 275 | 550 | 1,000 | |
| 1852, 1 Over Inverted 2 | * | | | | — | 775 | 950 | 1,150 | 1,425 | |
| 1852 | 18,663,500 | 25 | 35 | 50 | 65 | 80 | 165 | 200 | 275 | — |
| 1853 | 11,400,000 | 25 | 35 | 50 | 65 | 80 | 165 | 200 | 275 | |
| 1854 | 671,000 | 40 | 55 | 60 | 75 | 120 | 225 | 350 | 700 | $10,000 |
| 1855 | 139,000 | 40 | 65 | 75 | 125 | 200 | 350 | 600 | 1,450 | 5,000 |
| 1856 | 1,458,000 | 40 | 45 | 50 | 70 | 120 | 235 | 360 | 700 | 5,000 |
| 1857 | 1,042,000 | 40 | 45 | 50 | 70 | 120 | 235 | 360 | 800 | 3,500 |
| 1858 *(210)* | 1,603,700 | 40 | 45 | 50 | 70 | 120 | 235 | 360 | 700 | 2,500 |
| 1859 (800) | 364,200 | 35 | 40 | 50 | 60 | 90 | 175 | 215 | 300 | 800 |
| 1860 (1,000) | 286,000 | 35 | 40 | 50 | 60 | 90 | 175 | 215 | 300 | 900 |
| 1861 (1,000) | 497,000 | 35 | 40 | 50 | 60 | 90 | 175 | 215 | 300 | 750 |
| 1862, 2 Over 1 | * | 40 | 45 | 50 | 60 | 95 | 190 | 240 | 350 | |
| 1862 (550) | 343,000 | 35 | 40 | 50 | 60 | 90 | 175 | 215 | 285 | 750 |
| 1863, So-called 3 Over 2 | * | | | | | | | | | 2,850 |
| 1863 (460) | 21,000 | 475 | 550 | 600 | 650 | 750 | 1,000 | 1,400 | 1,800 | 750 |
| 1864 (470) | 12,000 | 475 | 525 | 625 | 650 | 750 | 900 | 1,200 | 1,400 | 750 |
| 1865 (500) | 8,000 | 475 | 525 | 575 | 650 | 800 | 1,100 | 1,700 | 2,350 | 750 |
| 1866 (725) | 22,000 | 450 | 525 | 575 | 625 | 800 | 1,100 | 1,600 | 2,000 | 750 |
| 1867 (625) | 4,000 | 450 | 525 | 575 | 650 | 850 | 1,200 | 1,700 | 3,000 | 750 |

* Included in number below.

*Chart continued on next page.*

| | Mintage | F-12 | VF-20 | EF-40 | AU-50 | MS-60 | MS-63 | PF-63 |
|---|---|---|---|---|---|---|---|---|
| 1868 . . . . . . . . . . . . . . . . . . . . . . . .(600) | 3,500 | $850 | $1,150 | $1,750 | $2,500 | $4,000 | $5,500 | $750 |
| 1869 . . . . . . . . . . . . . . . . . . . . . . . .(600) | 4,500 | 600 | 850 | 1,200 | 1,400 | 1,750 | 2,200 | 750 |
| 1870 . . . . . . . . . . . . . . . . . . . . . . (1,000) | 3,000 | 550 | 650 | 750 | 950 | 1,200 | 1,800 | 750 |
| 1871 . . . . . . . . . . . . . . . . . . . . . . . .(960) | 3,400 | 550 | 650 | 950 | 1,050 | 1,100 | 1,200 | 750 |
| 1872 . . . . . . . . . . . . . . . . . . . . . . . .(950) | 1,000 | 1,000 | 1,250 | 1,800 | 2,500 | 2,750 | 4,000 | 750 |
| 1873 (Close 3, Proof only) . . . . . . . .(600) | | | | | | | | 2,000 |

## NICKEL THREE-CENT PIECES (1865–1889)

Nickel three-cent pieces were issued because their silver counterpart was hoarded by the public.

Circulation strike.

Proof strike.

*Designer James B. Longacre; weight 1.94 grams; composition .750 copper, .250 nickel; diameter 17.9 mm; plain edge. All coined at Philadelphia Mint.*

**G-4 Good**—Date and legends complete though worn. III smooth.
**VG-8 Very Good**—III half worn. Rims complete.
**VF-20 Very Fine**—Three-quarters of hair details visible.
**EF-40 Extremely Fine**—Slight, even wear.
**AU-50 About Uncirculated**—Slight wear on hair curls, above forehead, and on wreath and numeral III.
**MS-60 Uncirculated**—No trace of wear. Light blemishes.
**MS-63 Choice Uncirculated**—Some distracting contact marks or blemishes in prime focal areas. Some impairment of luster possible.

| | Mintage | G-4 | VG-8 | VF-20 | EF-40 | AU-50 | MS-60 | MS-63 | PF-63 |
|---|---|---|---|---|---|---|---|---|---|
| 1865 . . . . . . . . . . . . . *(500+)* | 11,382,000 | $18 | $20 | $30 | $40 | $65 | $100 | $160 | $1,500 |
| 1866 . . . . . . . . . . . . . *(725+)* | 4,801,000 | 18 | 20 | 28 | 40 | 65 | 100 | 160 | 325 |
| 1867 . . . . . . . . . . . . . *(625+)* | 3,915,000 | 15 | 20 | 30 | 40 | 65 | 100 | 160 | 325 |
| 1868 . . . . . . . . . . . . . *(600+)* | 3,252,000 | 15 | 20 | 30 | 40 | 65 | 100 | 160 | 325 |
| 1869 . . . . . . . . . . . . . *(600+)* | 1,604,000 | 15 | 20 | 30 | 40 | 65 | 125 | 185 | 325 |
| 1870 . . . . . . . . . . . . *(1,000+)* | 1,335,000 | 20 | 25 | 30 | 40 | 65 | 140 | 195 | 325 |
| 1871 . . . . . . . . . . . . . *(960+)* | 604,000 | 20 | 25 | 30 | 40 | 65 | 140 | 195 | 325 |
| 1872 . . . . . . . . . . . . . *(950+)* | 862,000 | 20 | 25 | 30 | 40 | 65 | 150 | 210 | 325 |
| 1873, Close 3 . . . . . *(1,100+)* | 390,000 | 20 | 25 | 30 | 40 | 65 | 150 | 210 | 325 |
| 1873, Open 3 . . . . . . . . . . . . . . . . | 783,000 | 20 | 25 | 30 | 40 | 70 | 160 | 350 | |
| 1874 . . . . . . . . . . . . . *(700+)* | 790,000 | 20 | 25 | 30 | 40 | 65 | 150 | 210 | 325 |
| 1875 . . . . . . . . . . . . . *(700+)* | 228,000 | 20 | 25 | 35 | 45 | 80 | 175 | 225 | 325 |
| 1876 . . . . . . . . . . . . *(1,150+)* | 162,000 | 20 | 25 | 35 | 65 | 110 | 200 | 260 | 325 |
| 1877, Proof only . . . . .(900) . . . . . . . . . . . | | | | 1,400 | 1,500 | | | | 2,000 |
| 1878, Proof only . . . (2,350) . . . . . . . . . . . | | | | 725 | 750 | | | | 775 |
| 1879 . . . . . . . . . . . . (3,200) | 38,000 | 60 | 70 | 100 | 125 | 175 | 300 | 400 | 325 |
| 1880 . . . . . . . . . . . . (3,955) | 21,000 | 100 | 120 | 150 | 200 | 220 | 350 | 450 | 325 |
| 1881 . . . . . . . . . . . . (3,575) | 1,077,000 | 20 | 25 | 30 | 40 | 65 | 125 | 185 | 325 |
| 1882 . . . . . . . . . . . . (3,100) | 22,200 | 125 | 135 | 200 | 225 | 275 | 450 | 600 | 325 |
| 1883 . . . . . . . . . . . . (6,609) | 4,000 | 275 | 350 | 500 | 600 | 850 | 1,500 | 2,750 | 325 |
| 1884 . . . . . . . . . . . . (3,942) | 1,700 | 550 | 875 | 1,450 | 2,000 | 3,750 | 4,750 | 6,500 | 325 |
| 1885 . . . . . . . . . . . . (3,790) | 1,000 | 875 | 1,100 | 1,750 | 2,500 | 3,000 | 4,500 | 6,500 | 325 |
| 1886, Proof only . . . (4,290) . . . . . . . . . . . | | | | 350 | 375 | | | | 400 |
| 1887 . . . . . . . . . . . . (2,960) | 5,001 | 275 | 325 | 450 | 525 | 625 | 700 | 850 | 325 |
| 1887, 7 Over 6, Proof . . . . . . . . . . . . . . . | * | | | 400 | 425 | | | | 450 |
| 1888 . . . . . . . . . . . . (4,582) | 36,501 | 50 | 65 | 75 | 90 | 150 | 300 | 400 | 325 |
| 1889 . . . . . . . . . . . . (3,436) | 18,125 | 80 | 120 | 165 | 235 | 265 | 350 | 450 | 325 |

* Included in number above.

## SHIELD (1866–1883)

The Shield type nickel was made possible by the Act of May 16, 1866. Its weight was set at 77-16/100 grains (5 grams), with the same composition as the nickel three-cent piece that was authorized in 1865, and an obverse design similar to that of the two-cent coin. In 1866 the coin was designed with rays between the stars on the reverse. Some of the pieces minted in 1867 have the same details, but later the rays were eliminated, creating two varieties for that year. There was no further change in the type until it was replaced by the Liberty Head design in 1883. Only Proof pieces were struck in 1877 and 1878.

*Designer James B. Longacre; weight 5 grams; composition .750 copper, .250 nickel; diameter 20.5 mm; plain edge. All coined at Philadelphia Mint.*

**G-4 Good**—All letters in motto readable.
**VG-8 Very Good**—Motto clear and stands out. Rims slightly worn but even. Part of shield lines visible.
**F-12 Fine**—Half of each olive leaf worn smooth.
**EF-40 Extremely Fine**—Slight wear to leaf tips and cross over shield.
**AU-50 About Uncirculated**—Traces of light wear on only the high points of the design. Half of mint luster present.
**MS-60 Uncirculated**—No trace of wear. Light blemishes.
**MS-63 Choice Uncirculated**—Some distracting contact marks or blemishes in prime focal areas. Impaired luster possible.

Variety 1, Rays Between Stars (1866–1867)

1866, Repunched Date

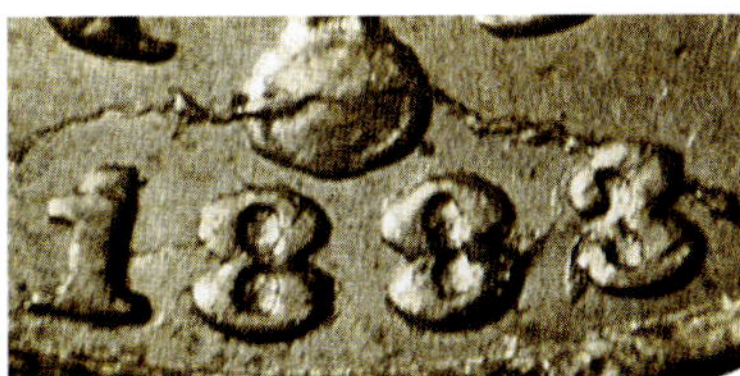


Example of 1883, 3 Over 2
*Other varieties exist, as well as pieces with recut 3.*

Variety 2, Without Rays (1867–1883)

*Sharply struck Uncirculated coins are valued higher than the prices shown here.*

| | Mintage | G-4 | VG-8 | F-12 | VF-20 | EF-40 | AU-50 | MS-60 | MS-63 | PF-63 |
|---|---|---|---|---|---|---|---|---|---|---|
| 1866, Rays . . . . . . . . *(600+)* | 14,742,500 | $30 | $45 | $60 | $90 | $165 | $240 | $300 | $500 | $1,750 |
| 1866, Repunched Date . . . . . . . . . . . . . . | * | 60 | 100 | 175 | 250 | 450 | 1,000 | 1,500 | 3,250 | |
| 1867, Rays . . . . . . . . . *(25+)* | 2,019,000 | 35 | 50 | 75 | 120 | 190 | 285 | 400 | 500 | 30,000 |
| 1867, Without Rays . . *(600+)* | 28,890,500 | 25 | 30 | 35 | 40 | 70 | 110 | 140 | 225 | 475 |
| 1867, Without Rays, Pattern Reverse. . . . . . . . . . . . . . . . . | | | | | | | | | | 6,500 |
| 1868 . . . . . . . . . . . . . *(600+)* | 28,817,000 | 25 | 30 | 35 | 40 | 70 | 110 | 140 | 225 | 350 |
| 1869 . . . . . . . . . . . . . *(600+)* | 16,395,000 | 25 | 30 | 35 | 40 | 70 | 110 | 140 | 225 | 350 |
| 1870 . . . . . . . . . . . *(1,000+)* | 4,806,000 | 30 | 35 | 60 | 80 | 95 | 140 | 225 | 300 | 350 |
| 1871 . . . . . . . . . . . . . *(960+)* | 561,000 | 80 | 100 | 150 | 210 | 285 | 375 | 525 | 675 | 350 |
| 1872 . . . . . . . . . . . . . *(950+)* | 6,036,000 | 40 | 50 | 85 | 105 | 130 | 175 | 235 | 300 | 350 |
| 1873, Close 3 . . . . *(1,100+)* | 436,050 | 30 | 40 | 80 | 100 | 150 | 200 | 350 | 750 | 350 |
| 1873, Open 3 . . . . . . . . . . . . . . | 4,113,950 | 30 | 40 | 60 | 80 | 100 | 145 | 210 | 300 | |
| 1873, Lg Over Sm 3 . . . . . . . . . . . . . . . . | * | | | | | | | | — | |
| 1874 . . . . . . . . . . . . . *(700+)* | 3,538,000 | 30 | 40 | 75 | 95 | 120 | 170 | 250 | 325 | 350 |
| 1875 . . . . . . . . . . . . . *(700+)* | 2,097,000 | 45 | 65 | 100 | 130 | 160 | 220 | 275 | 360 | 350 |
| 1876 . . . . . . . . . . . *(1,150+)* | 2,530,000 | 40 | 55 | 85 | 130 | 145 | 200 | 260 | 325 | 350 |
| 1877, Proof only . . . . (900) . . . . . . . . . . . . | | | | | | 2,200 | | | | 3,250 |
| 1878, Proof only . . (2,350) . . . . . . . . . . . . | | | | | | 1,000 | | | | 1,200 |

* Included in number above.

*Chart continued on next page.*

| | Mintage | G-4 | VG-8 | F-12 | VF-20 | EF-40 | AU-50 | MS-60 | MS-63 | PF-63 |
|---|---|---|---|---|---|---|---|---|---|---|
| 1879 . . . . . . . . . . . . (3,200) | 25,900 | $400 | $500 | $600 | $660 | $850 | $1,075 | $1,850 | $2,200 | $350 |
| 1879, 9 Over 8 **(a)** | * | | | | | | | | | 500 |
| 1880 . . . . . . . . . . . . (3,955) | 16,000 | 1,700 | 2,200 | 2,600 | 3,000 | 6,000 | 7,700 | 13,000 | 20,000 | 350 |
| 1881 . . . . . . . . . . . . (3,575) | 68,800 | 250 | 350 | 425 | 510 | 600 | 775 | 1,150 | 1,350 | 350 |
| 1882 . . . . . . . . . . . . (3,100) | 11,472,900 | 25 | 30 | 35 | 45 | 65 | 110 | 150 | 225 | 350 |
| 1883 . . . . . . . . . . . . (5,419) | 1,451,500 | 25 | 30 | 35 | 45 | 65 | 110 | 150 | 225 | 350 |
| 1883, 3 Over 2 | * | 250 | 325 | 650 | 950 | 1,250 | 1,500 | 2,100 | 2,500 | |

* Included in number above. **a.** Some consider this variety to be 1879, 9 Over 9.

## LIBERTY HEAD (1883–1913)

In early 1883, the nickel design was changed to the Liberty Head. This type first appeared without the word CENTS on the coin, merely a large letter V. Some of these "CENTS-less" coins were gold plated and passed for $5. Later in that year the word CENTS was added to discourage the fraudulent practice.

Liberty Head nickels dated 1913 were first revealed when a former Mint worker showed an example at the 1920 American Numismatic Association convention. Soon after that, five specimens are known to have been in the hands of a Philadelphia coin dealer. The coins were sold in 1924 to another dealer, and thence to Col. E.H.R. Green (son of the famous Wall Street investor Hetty Green). These have since been dispersed and are now held in various public and private collections. As they were not a regular issue, they were never placed in circulation.

*Designer Charles E. Barber; weight 5 grams; composition .750 copper, .250 nickel; diameter 21.2 mm; plain edge; mints: Philadelphia, Denver, San Francisco.*

**G-4 Good**—No details in head. LIBERTY obliterated.
**VG-8 Very Good**—Some letters in LIBERTY legible.
**F-12 Fine**—All letters in LIBERTY legible.
**VF-20 Very Fine**—LIBERTY bold, including letter L.
**EF-40 Extremely Fine**—LIBERTY sharp. Corn grains at bottom of wreath visible on reverse.
**AU-50 About Uncirculated**—Traces of light wear on only high points of design. Half of mint luster present.
**MS-60 Uncirculated**—No trace of wear, but many contact marks possible. Surface may be spotted, or luster faded.
**MS-63 Choice Uncirculated**—No trace of wear. Light blemishes.

Variety 1, Without CENTS (1883)

Mintmark Location

Variety 2, With CENTS (1883–1913)

*Sharply struck Uncirculated coins are valued higher than the prices shown; dull or weakly struck pieces are worth less.*

| | Mintage | G-4 | VG-8 | F-12 | VF-20 | EF-40 | AU-50 | MS-60 | MS-63 | PF-63 |
|---|---|---|---|---|---|---|---|---|---|---|
| 1883, Without CENTS. . (5,219) | 5,474,300 | $7 | $8 | $9 | $11 | $15 | $20 | $35 | $50 | $300 |
| 1883, With CENTS. . (6,783) | 16,026,200 | 20 | 30 | 35 | 55 | 85 | 120 | 150 | 200 | 275 |
| 1884 . . . . . . . (3,942) | 11,270,000 | 20 | 30 | 35 | 55 | 85 | 130 | 190 | 300 | 250 |
| 1885 . . . . . . . (3,790) | 1,472,700 | 375 | 550 | 750 | 1,000 | 1,200 | 1,600 | 2,000 | 3,250 | 1,150 |
| 1886 . . . . . . . (4,290) | 3,326,000 | 225 | 265 | 425 | 500 | 700 | 825 | 1,250 | 2,100 | 650 |
| 1887 . . . . . . . (2,960) | 15,260,692 | 15 | 20 | 35 | 50 | 75 | 110 | 140 | 195 | 250 |
| 1888 . . . . . . . (4,582) | 10,167,901 | 30 | 40 | 65 | 120 | 175 | 220 | 275 | 350 | 250 |
| 1889 . . . . . . . (3,336) | 15,878,025 | 15 | 20 | 30 | 55 | 80 | 120 | 140 | 175 | 250 |
| 1890 . . . . . . . (2,740) | 16,256,532 | 10 | 20 | 25 | 40 | 70 | 110 | 160 | 220 | 250 |

| | Mintage | G-4 | VG-8 | F-12 | VF-20 | EF-40 | AU-50 | MS-60 | MS-63 | PF-63 |
|---|---|---|---|---|---|---|---|---|---|---|
| 1891 | (2,350). . 16,832,000 | $7 | $12 | $25 | $45 | $70 | $125 | $160 | $220 | $250 |
| 1892 | (2,745). . 11,696,897 | 6 | 10 | 20 | 40 | 65 | 110 | 145 | 180 | 250 |
| 1893 | (2,195). . 13,368,000 | 6 | 10 | 20 | 40 | 65 | 110 | 140 | 160 | 250 |
| 1894 | (2,632). . . 5,410,500 | 20 | 35 | 100 | 165 | 230 | 300 | 350 | 425 | 250 |
| 1895 | (2,062). . . 9,977,822 | 6 | 8 | 22 | 45 | 75 | 115 | 140 | 230 | 250 |
| 1896 | (1,862). . . 8,841,058 | 9 | 20 | 35 | 65 | 100 | 150 | 190 | 265 | 250 |
| 1897 | (1,938). . 20,426,797 | 4 | 5 | 12 | 27 | 50 | 75 | 100 | 160 | 250 |
| 1898 | (1,795). . 12,530,292 | 4 | 5 | 12 | 27 | 50 | 75 | 150 | 190 | 250 |
| 1899 | (2,031). . 26,027,000 | 2 | 3 | 8 | 20 | 30 | 60 | 90 | 140 | 250 |
| 1900 | (2,262). . 27,253,733 | 2 | 3 | 8 | 15 | 30 | 65 | 90 | 140 | 250 |
| 1901 | (1,985). . 26,478,228 | 2 | 3 | 5 | 15 | 30 | 60 | 85 | 125 | 250 |
| 1902 | (2,018). . 31,487,561 | 2 | 3 | 4 | 15 | 30 | 60 | 85 | 125 | 250 |
| 1903 | (1,790). . 28,004,935 | 2 | 3 | 4 | 15 | 30 | 60 | 85 | 125 | 250 |
| 1904 | (1,817). . 21,403,167 | 2 | 3 | 4 | 15 | 30 | 60 | 85 | 125 | 250 |
| 1905 | (2,152). . 29,825,124 | 2 | 3 | 4 | 15 | 30 | 60 | 85 | 125 | 250 |
| 1906 | (1,725). . 38,612,000 | 2 | 3 | 4 | 15 | 30 | 60 | 85 | 125 | 250 |
| 1907 | (1,475). . 39,213,325 | 2 | 3 | 4 | 15 | 30 | 60 | 85 | 125 | 250 |
| 1908 | (1,620). . 22,684,557 | 2 | 3 | 4 | 15 | 30 | 60 | 85 | 125 | 250 |
| 1909 | (4,763). . 11,585,763 | 3 | 4 | 5 | 18 | 35 | 75 | 100 | 140 | 250 |
| 1910 | (2,405). . 30,166,948 | 2 | 3 | 4 | 15 | 30 | 60 | 85 | 125 | 250 |
| 1911 | (1,733). . 39,557,639 | 2 | 3 | 4 | 15 | 30 | 60 | 85 | 125 | 250 |
| 1912 | (2,145). . 26,234,569 | 2 | 3 | 4 | 15 | 30 | 60 | 85 | 125 | 250 |
| 1912D | 8,474,000 | 3 | 4 | 10 | 40 | 95 | 180 | 300 | 400 | |
| 1912S | 238,000 | 145 | 155 | 175 | 450 | 850 | 1,250 | 1,500 | 1,850 | |
| 1913 Liberty Head *(5 known)* | *$4,560,000, PF-66, Stack's Bowers auction, August 2018* | | | | | | | | | 3,000,000 |

## INDIAN HEAD OR BUFFALO (1913–1938)

These pieces are known as Buffalo (usually) or Indian Head nickels. In the first year of issue, 1913, there were two distinct varieties, the first showing the bison on a mound, and the second with the base redesigned to a thinner, straight line.

James Earle Fraser designed this nickel, employing three different Native Americans as models. His initial F is beneath the date. The bison was supposedly modeled after "Black Diamond" in the New York Central Park Zoo.

Matte Proof coins were made for collectors from 1913 to 1916.

*Designer James Earle Fraser; weight 5 grams; composition .750 copper, .250 nickel; diameter 21.2 mm; plain edge; mints: Philadelphia, Denver, San Francisco.*

**G-4 Good**—Legends and date readable. Buffalo's horn does not show.
**VG-8 Very Good**—Horn worn nearly flat.
**F-12 Fine**—Horn and tail smooth but partially visible. Obverse rim intact.
**VF-20 Very Fine**—Much of horn visible. Indian's cheekbone worn.
**EF-40 Extremely Fine**—Horn lightly worn. Slight wear on Indian's hair ribbon.
**AU-50 About Uncirculated**—Traces of light wear on only the high points of the design. Half of mint luster present.
**MS-60 Uncirculated**—No trace of wear. May have several blemishes.
**MS-63 Choice Uncirculated**—No trace of wear. Light blemishes.

*Circulation strike.*

*Matte Proof.*

*Mirror Proof.*

## Variety 1 – FIVE CENTS on Raised Ground (1913)

| | Mintage | G-4 | VG-8 | F-12 | VF-20 | EF-40 | AU-50 | MS-60 | MS-63 | MATTE PF-63 |
|---|---|---|---|---|---|---|---|---|---|---|
| 1913, Variety 1 . . (1,520) | 30,992,000 | $12 | $15 | $17 | $20 | $25 | $35 | $45 | $60 | $1,350 |
| 1913D, Variety 1 | 5,337,000 | 15 | 20 | 25 | 35 | 40 | 60 | 75 | 80 | |
| 1913S, Variety 1 | 2,105,000 | 45 | 50 | 60 | 70 | 85 | 110 | 130 | 150 | |

## Variety 2 – FIVE CENTS in Recess (1913–1938)

Mintmark Below FIVE CENTS

1914, 4 Over 3

1916, Doubled Die Obverse

1918-D, 8 Over 7

| | Mintage | G-4 | VG-8 | F-12 | VF-20 | EF-40 | AU-50 | MS-60 | MS-63 | PF-63 |
|---|---|---|---|---|---|---|---|---|---|---|
| 1913, Var 2 (1,514) | 29,857,186 | $10.00 | $12.00 | $16.00 | $20 | $25 | $30 | $40 | $65 | $1,000 |
| 1913D, Var 2 | 4,156,000 | 120.00 | 150.00 | 175.00 | 200 | 235 | 250 | 300 | 400 | |
| 1913S, Var 2 | 1,209,000 | 250.00 | 325.00 | 375.00 | 475 | 550 | 750 | 800 | 975 | |
| 1914 . . . . . . (1,275) | 20,664,463 | 20.00 | 22.00 | 25.00 | 30 | 35 | 45 | 60 | 85 | 900 |
| 1914, 4 Over 3 | * | 200.00 | 250.00 | 325.00 | 525 | 700 | 1,000 | 2,250 | 5,000 | |
| 1914D | 3,912,000 | 90.00 | 125.00 | 160.00 | 220 | 325 | 350 | 450 | 550 | |
| 1914S | 3,470,000 | 26.00 | 38.00 | 45.00 | 65 | 90 | 160 | 200 | 425 | |
| 1915 . . . . . . (1,050) | 20,986,220 | 6.00 | 8.00 | 9.00 | 15 | 25 | 45 | 60 | 100 | 1,000 |
| 1915D | 7,569,000 | 20.00 | 35.00 | 40.00 | 70 | 130 | 160 | 270 | 350 | |
| 1915S | 1,505,000 | 45.00 | 75.00 | 100.00 | 200 | 400 | 500 | 650 | 1,100 | |
| 1916 . . . . . . . .(600) | 63,497,466 | 6.00 | 7.00 | 8.00 | 10 | 15 | 25 | 50 | 85 | 1,500 |
| 1916, DblDie Obv | * | 4,500.00 | 6,000.00 | 8,500.00 | 12,000 | 18,000 | 30,000 | 60,000 | 150,000 | |
| *$316,250, MS-64, Stack's Bowers auction, November 2007* | | | | | | | | | | |
| 1916D | 13,333,000 | 16.00 | 28.00 | 30.00 | 45 | 90 | 120 | 175 | 260 | |
| 1916S | 11,860,000 | 10.00 | 15.00 | 20.00 | 40 | 90 | 125 | 200 | 275 | |
| 1917 | 51,424,019 | 8.00 | 9.00 | 10.00 | 12 | 15 | 35 | 60 | 150 | |
| 1917D | 9,910,000 | 18.00 | 30.00 | 50.00 | 85 | 150 | 275 | 375 | 750 | |
| 1917S | 4,193,000 | 22.00 | 45.00 | 80.00 | 120 | 200 | 325 | 650 | 1,550 | |
| 1918 | 32,086,314 | 6.00 | 7.00 | 8.00 | 15 | 35 | 50 | 125 | 325 | |
| 1918D, 8 Over 7 | ** | 800.00 | 1,250.00 | 2,500.00 | 4,500 | 8,500 | 11,000 | 35,000 | 57,500 | |
| *$350,750, MS-65, Stack's Bowers auction, August 2006* | | | | | | | | | | |
| 1918D | 8,362,000 | 22.00 | 40.00 | 70.00 | 135 | 225 | 350 | 550 | 1,050 | |
| 1918S | 4,882,000 | 15.00 | 30.00 | 60.00 | 110 | 200 | 325 | 585 | 2,500 | |
| 1919 | 60,868,000 | 2.25 | 3.00 | 3.50 | 8 | 15 | 35 | 55 | 125 | |
| 1919D **(a)** | 8,006,000 | 15.00 | 30.00 | 75.00 | 135 | 250 | 450 | 700 | 1,500 | |
| 1919S **(a)** | 7,521,000 | 9.00 | 20.00 | 50.00 | 125 | 250 | 375 | 675 | 1,800 | |
| 1920 | 63,093,000 | 1.50 | 2.50 | 3.00 | 7 | 15 | 30 | 65 | 145 | |
| 1920D **(a)** | 9,418,000 | 9.00 | 18.00 | 40.00 | 120 | 275 | 350 | 600 | 1,400 | |
| 1920S | 9,689,000 | 5.00 | 14.00 | 30.00 | 100 | 200 | 300 | 650 | 1,750 | |
| 1921 | 10,663,000 | 4.00 | 6.00 | 8.00 | 24 | 50 | 75 | 150 | 320 | |
| 1921S | 1,557,000 | 65.00 | 115.00 | 155.00 | 375 | 950 | 1,100 | 1,750 | 2,500 | |

*Note:* Matte Proof through 1916; mirror Proof thereafter. * Included in number above. ** Included in number below.
**a.** Uncirculated pieces with full, sharp details are worth considerably more.

1935, Doubled Die Reverse

1936-D, "3-1/2 Legged" Variety

| | Mintage | G-4 | VG-8 | F-12 | VF-20 | EF-40 | AU-50 | MS-60 | MS-63 | PF-63 |
|---|---|---|---|---|---|---|---|---|---|---|
| 1923 | 35,715,000 | $2.00 | $3.00 | $4.00 | $6.00 | $15 | $35 | $65 | $160 | |
| 1923S **(a)** | 6,142,000 | 8.00 | 10.00 | 30.00 | 135.00 | 250 | 400 | 600 | 900 | |
| 1924 | 21,620,000 | 1.50 | 2.00 | 5.00 | 10.00 | 25 | 45 | 75 | 175 | |
| 1924D | 5,258,000 | 8.50 | 12.00 | 30.00 | 85.00 | 235 | 325 | 450 | 800 | |
| 1924S | 1,437,000 | 17.00 | 40.00 | 110.00 | 475.00 | 1,000 | 1,700 | 2,500 | 4,500 | |
| 1925 | 35,565,100 | 3.00 | 3.50 | 4.00 | 8.00 | 15 | 35 | 45 | 100 | |
| 1925D **(a)** | 4,450,000 | 10.00 | 20.00 | 40.00 | 95.00 | 165 | 300 | 450 | 800 | |
| 1925S | 6,256,000 | 5.00 | 10.00 | 20.00 | 90.00 | 180 | 275 | 600 | 1,850 | |
| 1926 | 44,693,000 | 1.25 | 1.75 | 2.50 | 5.00 | 10 | 20 | 35 | 75 | |
| 1926D **(a)** | 5,638,000 | 10.00 | 18.00 | 28.00 | 110.00 | 185 | 300 | 350 | 600 | |
| 1926S | 970,000 | 25.00 | 45.00 | 100.00 | 275.00 | 900 | 2,500 | 4,500 | 8,500 | |
| 1927 | 37,981,000 | 1.25 | 1.75 | 2.50 | 5.00 | 15 | 20 | 35 | 80 | |
| 1927D | 5,730,000 | 2.50 | 6.00 | 10.00 | 35.00 | 80 | 135 | 165 | 375 | |
| 1927S | 3,430,000 | 1.50 | 3.00 | 5.00 | 35.00 | 95 | 185 | 850 | 2,250 | |
| 1928 | 23,411,000 | 1.25 | 1.75 | 2.50 | 5.00 | 15 | 25 | 35 | 90 | |
| 1928D | 6,436,000 | 1.50 | 2.50 | 5.00 | 15.00 | 45 | 50 | 60 | 110 | |
| 1928S | 6,936,000 | 1.75 | 2.00 | 2.50 | 11.00 | 26 | 110 | 260 | 550 | |
| 1929 | 36,446,000 | 1.25 | 1.50 | 2.50 | 5.00 | 15 | 20 | 40 | 75 | |
| 1929D | 8,370,000 | 1.25 | 2.00 | 2.50 | 7.00 | 32 | 45 | 60 | 130 | |
| 1929S | 7,754,000 | 1.25 | 1.50 | 2.00 | 4.00 | 12 | 25 | 55 | 90 | |
| 1930 | 22,849,000 | 1.25 | 1.50 | 2.50 | 4.00 | 11 | 20 | 35 | 75 | |
| 1930S | 5,435,000 | 1.25 | 1.50 | 2.50 | 4.00 | 15 | 35 | 65 | 120 | |
| 1931S | 1,200,000 | 15.00 | 16.00 | 20.00 | 25.00 | 35 | 55 | 65 | 100 | |
| 1934 | 20,213,003 | 1.25 | 1.50 | 2.50 | 4.00 | 10 | 18 | 50 | 65 | |
| 1934D **(b)** | 7,480,000 | 1.50 | 2.50 | 4.00 | 9.00 | 20 | 45 | 80 | 125 | |
| 1935 | 58,264,000 | 1.00 | 1.50 | 1.75 | 2.00 | 5 | 10 | 22 | 45 | |
| 1935, DblDie Rev. | * | 45.00 | 65.00 | 100.00 | 160.00 | 500 | 1,300 | 4,000 | 6,000 | |
| 1935D | 12,092,000 | 1.00 | 1.50 | 2.50 | 6.00 | 18 | 42 | 75 | 90 | |
| 1935S | 10,300,000 | 1.00 | 1.50 | 2.00 | 2.50 | 4 | 18 | 55 | 70 | |
| 1936 (4,420) | 118,997,000 | 1.00 | 1.50 | 1.75 | 2.00 | 3 | 9 | 25 | 40 | 1,150 |
| 1936D | 24,814,000 | 1.00 | 1.50 | 1.75 | 2.00 | 4 | 12.00 | 40.00 | 45 | |
| 1936D, 3-1/2 Legs | * | 400.00 | 600.00 | 1,000.00 | 1,500.00 | 3,000 | 4,250 | 12,500 | | |
| 1936S | 14,930,000 | 1.00 | 1.50 | 1.75 | 2.00 | 4 | 12 | 38 | 45 | |
| 1937 (5,769) | 79,480,000 | 1.00 | 1.50 | 1.75 | 2.00 | 3 | 9 | 25 | 40 | 1,000 |

*Note:* Matte Proof through 1916; regular Proof thereafter. * Included in number above. **a.** Uncirculated pieces with full, sharp details are worth considerably more. **b.** Large and small mintmark varieties exist; see page 22.

1937-D, "3-Legged" Variety

1938-D, D Over S

| | Mintage | G-4 | VG-8 | F-12 | VF-20 | EF-40 | AU-50 | MS-60 | MS-63 |
|---|---|---|---|---|---|---|---|---|---|
| 1937D | 17,826,000 | $1 | $1.50 | $1.75 | $3 | $4 | $10 | $35 | $45 |
| 1937D, 3-Legged | * | 450 | 475.00 | 550.00 | 600 | 675 | 850 | 1,850 | 4,250 |

* Included in number above.

*Chart continued on next page.*

| | Mintage | G-4 | VG-8 | F-12 | VF-20 | EF-40 | AU-50 | MS-60 | MS-63 |
|---|---|---|---|---|---|---|---|---|---|
| 1937S | 5,635,000 | $1.00 | $1.50 | $1.75 | $3.00 | $6 | $9 | $32 | $42 |
| 1938D | 7,020,000 | 3.50 | 4.00 | 4.50 | 4.75 | 5 | 8 | 22 | 35 |
| 1938D, D Over S | * | 5.50 | 8.00 | 10.00 | 14.00 | 20 | 32 | 55 | 80 |

* Included in number above.

## JEFFERSON (1938–2003)

This nickel was originally designed by Felix Schlag, who won an award of $1,000 in a competition with some 390 artists. His design confirmed the definite public approval of portrait and pictorial themes rather than symbolic devices on our coinage.

*Designer Felix Schlag; weight 5 grams; composition (1938–1942, 1946 to date), .750 copper, .250 nickel, (1942–1945), .560 copper, .350 silver, .090 manganese, with net weight .05626 oz. pure silver; diameter 21.2 mm; plain edge; mints: Philadelphia, Denver, San Francisco.*

**VG-8 Very Good**—Second porch pillar from right nearly gone, other three still visible but weak.
**F-12 Fine**—Jefferson's cheekbone worn flat. Hair lines and eyebrow faint. Second pillar weak, especially at bottom.
**VF-20 Very Fine**—Second pillar plain and complete on both sides.
**EF-40 Extremely Fine**—Cheekbone, hair lines, eyebrow slightly worn but well defined. Base of triangle above pillars visible but weak.
**AU-50 About Uncirculated**—Traces of light wear on only high points of design. Half of mint luster present.
**MS-60 Uncirculated**—No trace of wear. Light blemishes.
**MS-65 Gem Uncirculated**—No trace of wear. Barely noticeable blemishes.

*Circulation strike.*

**1939, Doubled MONTICELLO and FIVE CENTS**

**1942-D, D Over Horizontal D**

*Proof strike.*

*Uncirculated pieces with fully struck steps on Monticello have higher values.*

| | Mintage | VF-20 | EF-40 | AU-50 | MS-60 | MS-63 | MS-65 | PF-65 |
|---|---|---|---|---|---|---|---|---|
| 1938 | (19,365). . .19,496,000 | $0.50 | $1.00 | $1.50 | $3.00 | $5.00 | $16 | $100 |
| 1938D | 5,376,000 | 1.50 | 2.00 | 3.00 | 7.00 | 10.00 | 15 | |
| 1938S | 4,105,000 | 2.50 | 3.00 | 3.50 | 4.50 | 8.00 | 16 | |
| 1939 | (12,535). .120,615,000 | 0.25 | 0.50 | 1.00 | 2.00 | 2.50 | 12 | 120 |
| 1939, Doubled MONTICELLO, FIVE CENTS | * | 100.00 | 135.00 | 165.00 | 200.00 | 375.00 | 900 | |
| 1939D | 3,514,000 | 10.00 | 13.00 | 30.00 | 60.00 | 70.00 | 80 | |
| 1939S | 6,630,000 | 2.00 | 5.00 | 10.00 | 18.00 | 35.00 | 70 | |
| 1940 | (14,158). .176,485,000 | 0.25 | 0.40 | 0.75 | 1.00 | 1.50 | 15 | 100 |
| 1940D | 43,540,000 | 0.35 | 0.50 | 1.00 | 2.00 | 2.50 | 15 | |
| 1940S | 39,690,000 | 0.35 | 0.50 | 1.00 | 2.25 | 3.00 | 12 | |
| 1941 | (18,720). .203,265,000 | 0.20 | 0.30 | 0.50 | 0.75 | 1.50 | 12 | 75 |
| 1941D | 53,432,000 | 0.25 | 0.40 | 1.50 | 2.50 | 3.50 | 12 | |
| 1941S **(a)** | 43,445,000 | 0.30 | 0.50 | 1.50 | 3.00 | 4.00 | 12 | |
| 1942 | (29,600). . .49,789,000 | 0.30 | 0.45 | 1.25 | 4.00 | 6.00 | 15 | 90 |
| 1942D | 13,938,000 | 1.00 | 2.00 | 5.00 | 28.00 | 38.00 | 60 | |
| 1942D, D Over Horizontal D | * | 75.00 | 200.00 | 500.00 | 1,500.00 | 3,000.00 | 8,000 | |

* Included in number above. **a.** Large and small mintmark varieties; see page 22.

## Wartime Silver Alloy (1942–1945)

On October 8, 1942, the wartime five-cent piece composed of copper (56%), silver (35%), and manganese (9%) was introduced to eliminate nickel, a critical war material. A larger mintmark was placed above the dome of Monticello, indicating the change of alloy. The letter P (Philadelphia) was used for the first time.

Mintmark Location

1943-P, 3 Over 2

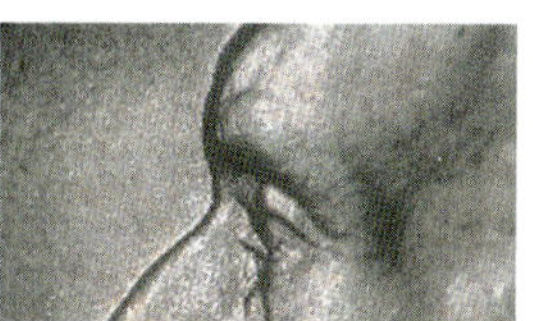
1943-P, Doubled Eye

1945-P, Doubled Die Reverse

| | Mintage | VF-20 | EF-40 | AU-50 | MS-60 | MS-63 | MS-65 | PF-65 |
|---|---|---|---|---|---|---|---|---|
| 1942P . . . . (27,600) . . . | 57,873,000 | $2 | $2.50 | $3.25 | $7 | $12 | $20 | $110 |
| 1942S . . . . . . . . . . . . . . | 32,900,000 | 2 | 2.50 | 3.25 | 7 | 12 | 25 | |
| 1943P, 3 Over 2 . . . . . . . . . . . . . . | * | 50 | 100.00 | 165.00 | 225 | 260 | 700 | |
| 1943P . . . . . . . . . . . . | 271,165,000 | 2 | 2.50 | 3.00 | 5 | 8 | 20 | |
| 1943P, Doubled Eye . . . . . . . . . . | ** | 25 | 40.00 | 60.00 | 90 | 160 | 650 | |
| 1943D . . . . . . . . . . . . . . | 15,294,000 | 2 | 3.50 | 4.00 | 6 | 12 | 20 | |
| 1943S . . . . . . . . . . . . | 104,060,000 | 2 | 2.50 | 3.00 | 5 | 8 | 20 | |
| 1944P . . . . . . . . . . . . | 119,150,000 | 2 | 2.50 | 3.25 | 7 | 12 | 30 | |
| 1944D . . . . . . . . . . . . . . | 32,309,000 | 2 | 2.50 | 3.00 | 6 | 12 | 25 | |
| 1944S . . . . . . . . . . . . . . | 21,640,000 | 2 | 2.50 | 3.00 | 5 | 10 | 22 | |
| 1945P . . . . . . . . . . . . | 119,408,100 | 2 | 2.50 | 3.00 | 5 | 8 | 20 | |
| 1945P, DblDie Reverse . . . . . . . . | ** | 20 | 30.00 | 50.00 | 75 | 130 | 800 | |
| 1945D . . . . . . . . . . . . . . | 37,158,000 | 2 | 2.50 | 3.00 | 5 | 8 | 20 | |
| 1945S . . . . . . . . . . . . . . | 58,939,000 | 2 | 2.50 | 3.00 | 5 | 8 | 20 | |

*Note:* 1944 nickels without mintmarks are counterfeits. Genuine pieces of other wartime dates struck in nickel by error are known to exist. * Included in number below. ** Included in number above.

## Prewar Composition, Mintmark Style Resumed (1946–1965)

| | Mintage | VF-20 | EF-40 | AU-50 | MS-60 | MS-63 | MS-65 |
|---|---|---|---|---|---|---|---|
| 1946 . . . . . . . . . . . . . . . . . . . . . | 161,116,000 | $0.25 | $0.30 | $0.35 | $0.75 | $2.50 | $15 |
| 1946D . . . . . . . . . . . . . . . . . . . . . | 45,292,200 | 0.35 | 0.40 | 0.45 | 1.00 | 2.50 | 12 |
| 1946S . . . . . . . . . . . . . . . . . . . . . | 13,560,000 | 0.40 | 0.45 | 0.50 | 1.00 | 2.00 | 11 |
| 1947 . . . . . . . . . . . . . . . . . . . . . . | 95,000,000 | 0.25 | 0.30 | 0.35 | 0.75 | 1.75 | 12 |
| 1947D . . . . . . . . . . . . . . . . . . . . . | 37,822,000 | 0.30 | 0.35 | 0.40 | 0.90 | 1.75 | 11 |
| 1947S . . . . . . . . . . . . . . . . . . . . . | 24,720,000 | 0.40 | 0.45 | 0.50 | 1.00 | 1.75 | 12 |

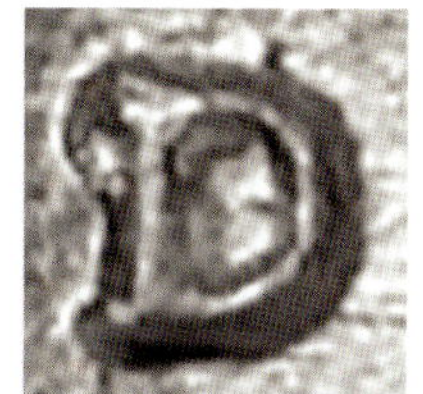
1949-D, D Over S

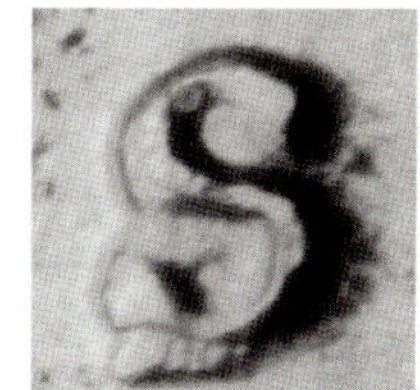
1954-S, S Over D

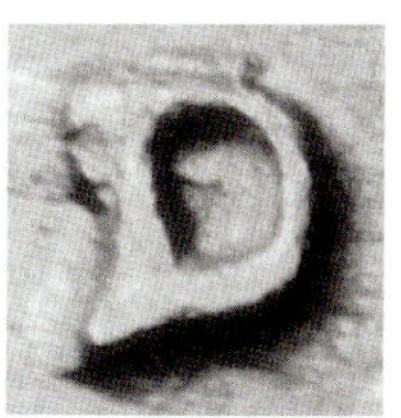
1955-D, D Over S

| | Mintage | MS-60 | MS-63 | MS-65 | PF-65 |
|---|---|---|---|---|---|
| 1948 . . . . . . . . . . . . . . . . . . . . . . . . . . . . . . . . . . . . . . | 89,348,000 | $1.00 | $1.50 | $10 | |
| 1948D . . . . . . . . . . . . . . . . . . . . . . . . . . . . . . . . . . . . . | 44,734,000 | 1.60 | 4.00 | 10 | |
| 1948S . . . . . . . . . . . . . . . . . . . . . . . . . . . . . . . . . . . . . | 11,300,000 | 1.50 | 2.50 | 9 | |
| 1949 . . . . . . . . . . . . . . . . . . . . . . . . . . . . . . . . . . . . . . | 60,652,000 | 2.50 | 9.00 | 12 | |
| 1949D . . . . . . . . . . . . . . . . . . . . . . . . . . . . . . . . . . . . . | 36,498,000 | 1.50 | 6.00 | 10 | |
| 1949D, D Over S . . . . . . . . . . . . . . . . . . . . . . . . . . . . . . . . . . | * | 150.00 | 200.00 | 500 | |

* Included in number above.

*Chart continued on next page.*

| | Mintage | MS-60 | MS-63 | MS-65 | PF-65 |
|---|---|---|---|---|---|
| 1949S | 9,716,000 | $1.75 | $5.00 | $10 | |
| 1950 (51,386) | 9,796,000 | 2.00 | 3.25 | 8 | $75 |
| 1950D | 2,630,030 | 14.00 | 16.00 | 25 | |
| 1951 (57,500) | 28,552,000 | 3.00 | 6.50 | 15 | 65 |
| 1951D | 20,460,000 | 4.00 | 7.00 | 11 | |
| 1951S | 7,776,000 | 1.50 | 2.00 | 12 | |
| 1952 (81,980) | 63,988,000 | 1.00 | 4.00 | 9 | 45 |
| 1952D | 30,638,000 | 3.50 | 6.25 | 15 | |
| 1952S | 20,572,000 | 1.00 | 1.50 | 12 | |
| 1953 (128,800) | 46,644,000 | 0.25 | 0.75 | 8 | 45 |
| 1953D | 59,878,600 | 0.25 | 0.75 | 9 | |
| 1953S | 19,210,900 | 0.75 | 1.00 | 10 | |
| 1954 (233,300) | 47,684,050 | 1.00 | 1.50 | 15 | 22 |
| 1954D | 117,183,060 | 0.60 | 1.00 | 30 | |
| 1954S | 29,384,000 | 1.75 | 2.00 | 15 | |
| 1954S, S Over D | * | 26.00 | 40.00 | 145 | |
| 1955 (378,200) | 7,888,000 | 0.75 | 1.00 | 15 | 18 |
| 1955D | 74,464,100 | 0.50 | 0.75 | 20 | |
| 1955D, D Over S **(a)** | * | 36.00 | 57.50 | 175 | |
| 1956 (669,384) | 35,216,000 | 0.50 | 0.75 | 20 | 5 |
| 1956D | 67,222,940 | 0.50 | 0.75 | 20 | |
| 1957 (1,247,952) | 38,408,000 | 0.50 | 0.75 | 15 | 4 |
| 1957D | 136,828,900 | 0.50 | 0.70 | 15 | |
| 1958 (875,652) | 17,088,000 | 0.60 | 0.80 | 12 | 8 |
| 1958D | 168,249,120 | 0.40 | 0.50 | 12 | |
| 1959 (1,149,291) | 27,248,000 | 0.25 | 0.50 | 10 | 3 |
| 1959D | 160,738,240 | 0.25 | 0.50 | 8 | |
| 1960 (1,691,602) | 55,416,000 | 0.25 | 0.50 | 8 | 3 |
| 1960D | 192,582,180 | 0.25 | 0.50 | 10 | |
| 1961 (3,028,144) | 73,640,100 | 0.25 | 0.50 | 20 | 3 |
| 1961D | 229,342,760 | 0.25 | 0.50 | 20 | |
| 1962 (3,218,019) | 97,384,000 | 0.25 | 0.50 | 10 | 3 |
| 1962D | 280,195,720 | 0.25 | 0.50 | 30 | |
| 1963 (3,075,645) | 175,776,000 | 0.25 | 0.50 | 10 | 3 |
| 1963D | 276,829,460 | 0.25 | 0.50 | 25 | |
| 1964 (3,950,762) | 1,024,672,000 | 0.25 | 0.50 | 8 | 3 |
| 1964D | 1,787,297,160 | 0.25 | 0.50 | 5 | |
| 1965 | 136,131,380 | 0.25 | 0.50 | 5 | |

* Included in number above. **a.** Varieties exist; value is for the variety illustrated.

## 1966–2003

*The designer's initials, FS, were added below the bust starting in 1966, and dies were further remodeled to strengthen the design in 1971, 1972, 1977, and 1982. The mintmark position was moved to the obverse starting in 1968. At this time appropriate mintmarks were hand-punched into the dies at the Philadelphia Mint. During this operation the exact position of the mintmark occasionally varied to some degree. One extreme exception is on some coins of 1975-D, where the D is located near the date. This variation has a premium value.*

| | Mintage | MS-63 | MS-65 | PF-65 |
|---|---|---|---|---|
| 1966 | 156,208,283 | $0.25 | $5 | **(a)** |
| 1967 | 107,325,800 | 0.25 | 5 | |
| 1968D | 91,227,880 | 0.25 | 4 | |
| 1968S | (3,041,506) | | | $3.00 |
| | 100,396,004 | 0.25 | 5 | |
| 1969D | 202,807,500 | 0.25 | 4 | |
| 1969S | (2,934,631) | | | 3.00 |
| | 120,165,000 | 0.25 | 2 | |
| 1970D | 515,485,380 | 0.25 | 10 | |
| 1970S | (2,632,810) | | | 2.00 |
| | 238,832,004 | 0.25 | 8 | |
| 1971 | 106,884,000 | 0.75 | 3 | |
| 1971D | 316,144,800 | 0.30 | 3 | |
| 1971, No S **(b)** | | | | 1,000.00 |
| 1971S | (3,220,733) | | | 2.50 |
| 1972 | 202,036,000 | 0.25 | 3 | |
| 1972D | 351,694,600 | 0.25 | 3 | |
| 1972S | (3,260,996) | | | 2.50 |
| 1973 | 384,396,000 | 0.25 | 3 | |
| 1973D | 261,405,000 | 0.25 | 3 | |
| 1973S | (2,760,339) | | | 2.00 |
| 1974 | 601,752,000 | 0.25 | 3 | |
| 1974D | 277,373,000 | 0.25 | 3 | |
| 1974S | (2,612,568) | | | 2.50 |
| 1975 | 181,772,000 | 0.50 | 3 | |
| 1975D | 401,875,300 | 0.25 | 3 | |
| 1975S | (2,845,450) | | | 2.50 |
| 1976 | 367,124,000 | 0.45 | 3 | |
| 1976D | 563,964,147 | 0.45 | 3 | |
| 1976S | (4,149,730) | | | 2.50 |
| 1977 | 585,376,000 | 0.25 | 3 | |
| 1977D | 297,313,422 | 0.50 | 3 | |
| 1977S | (3,251,152) | | | 2.00 |
| 1978 | 391,308,000 | 0.25 | 3 | |
| 1978D | 313,092,780 | 0.25 | 3 | |
| 1978S | (3,127,781) | | | 2.00 |
| 1979 | 463,188,000 | 0.25 | 3 | |
| 1979D | 325,867,672 | 0.25 | 4 | |
| 1979S, All kinds | (3,677,175) | | | |
| 1979S, Type 1 **(c)** | | | | 4.00 |
| 1979S, Type 2 **(c)** | | | | 5.00 |
| 1980P | 593,004,000 | 0.25 | 4 | |
| 1980D | 502,323,448 | 0.25 | 3 | |
| 1980S | (3,554,806) | | | 2.00 |
| 1981P | 657,504,000 | 0.25 | 3 | |
| 1981D | 364,801,843 | 0.25 | 3 | |
| 1981S, All kinds | (4,063,083) | | | |
| 1981S, Type 1 **(c)** | | | | 3.00 |
| 1981S, Type 2 **(c)** | | | | 5.00 |

| | Mintage | MS-63 | MS-65 | PF-65 |
|---|---|---|---|---|
| 1982P | 292,355,000 | $5.00 | $10.00 | |
| 1982D | 373,726,544 | 2.00 | 6.00 | |
| 1982S | (3,857,479) | | | $2.50 |
| 1983P | 561,615,000 | 2.00 | 9.00 | |
| 1983D | 536,726,276 | 1.50 | 4.00 | |
| 1983S | (3,279,126) | | | 2.50 |
| 1984P | 746,769,000 | 1.00 | 3.00 | |
| 1984D | 517,675,146 | 0.25 | 3.00 | |
| 1984S | (3,065,110) | | | 5.00 |
| 1985P | 647,114,962 | 0.50 | 3.00 | |
| 1985D | 459,747,446 | 0.50 | 3.00 | |
| 1985S | (3,362,821) | | | 3.00 |
| 1986P | 536,883,483 | 0.50 | 3.00 | |
| 1986D | 361,819,140 | 1.00 | 3.00 | |
| 1986S | (3,010,497) | | | 7.00 |
| 1987P | 371,499,481 | 0.25 | 2.75 | |
| 1987D | 410,590,604 | 0.25 | 3.50 | |
| 1987S | (4,227,728) | | | 3.00 |
| 1988P | 771,360,000 | 0.25 | 3.00 | |
| 1988D | 663,771,652 | 0.25 | 3.00 | |
| 1988S | (3,262,948) | | | 5.00 |
| 1989P | 898,812,000 | 0.25 | 2.75 | |
| 1989D | 570,842,474 | 0.25 | 2.75 | |
| 1989S | (3,220,194) | | | 4.00 |
| 1990P | 661,636,000 | 0.25 | 2.75 | |
| 1990D | 663,938,503 | 0.25 | 2.75 | |
| 1990S | (3,299,559) | | | 4.00 |
| 1991P | 614,104,000 | 0.30 | 2.75 | |
| 1991D | 436,496,678 | 0.30 | 2.75 | |
| 1991S | (2,867,787) | | | 4.50 |
| 1992P | 399,552,000 | 1.50 | 3.00 | |
| 1992D | 450,565,113 | 0.25 | 2.75 | |
| 1992S | (4,176,560) | | | 3.50 |
| 1993P | 412,076,000 | 0.25 | 1.00 | |
| 1993D | 406,084,135 | 0.25 | 1.00 | |
| 1993S | (3,394,792) | | | 4.00 |
| 1994P | 722,160,000 | 0.25 | 2.50 | |
| 1994P, Special Unc. **(d)** | 167,703 | 50.00 | 100.00 | |
| 1994D | 715,762,110 | 0.25 | 1.00 | |
| 1994S | (3,269,923) | | | 3.50 |
| 1995P | 774,156,000 | 0.25 | 1.00 | |
| 1995D | 888,112,000 | 0.50 | 1.00 | |
| 1995S | (2,797,481) | | | 5.00 |
| 1996P | 829,332,000 | 0.25 | 1.00 | |
| 1996D | 817,736,000 | 0.25 | 1.00 | |
| 1996S | (2,525,265) | | | 3.00 |
| 1997P | 470,972,000 | 0.50 | 2.00 | |
| 1997P, Special Unc. **(d)** | 25,000 | 55.00 | 75.00 | |

**a.** Two presentation pieces were given to the designer. **b.** 1971 Proof nickels without mintmark were made in error. See discussion on page 22. **c.** See page 246 for illustrations of Type 1 and Type 2 varieties. **d.** Special "frosted" Uncirculated pieces were included in the 1993 Thomas Jefferson commemorative dollar packaging (sold in 1994) and the 1997 Botanic Garden sets. They resemble Matte Proof coins.

*Chart continued on next page.*

| | Mintage | MS-63 | MS-65 | PF-65 |
|---|---|---|---|---|
| 1997D | 466,640,000 | $1.00 | $2 | |
| 1997S | (2,796,678) | | | $3.00 |
| 1998P | 688,272,000 | 0.35 | 1 | |
| 1998D | 635,360,000 | 0.35 | 1 | |
| 1998S | (2,086,507) | | | 3.00 |
| 1999P | 1,212,000,000 | 0.25 | 1 | |
| 1999D | 1,066,720,000 | 0.25 | 1 | |
| 1999S | (3,347,966) | | | 3.50 |
| 2000P | 846,240,000 | 0.25 | 1 | |
| 2000D | 1,509,520,000 | 0.25 | 1 | |
| 2000S | (4,047,993) | | | 2.50 |
| 2001P | 675,704,000 | 0.25 | 1 | |
| 2001D | 627,680,000 | 0.25 | 1 | |
| 2001S | (3,184,606) | | | 2.50 |
| 2002P | 539,280,000 | 0.25 | 1 | |
| 2002D | 691,200,000 | 0.25 | 1 | |
| 2002S | (3,211,995) | | | 2.50 |
| 2003P | 441,840,000 | 0.25 | 1 | |
| 2003D | 383,040,000 | 0.25 | 1 | |
| 2003S | (3,298,439) | | | 3.00 |

## WESTWARD JOURNEY (2004–2005)

The Westward Journey Nickel Series™ (2004–2005) commemorated the bicentennial of the Louisiana Purchase and the journey of Meriwether Lewis and William Clark to explore that vast territory.

*2004:* The Louisiana Purchase / Peace Medal reverse, by Mint sculptor Norman E. Nemeth, was adapted from the reverse of certain of the original Indian Peace medals commissioned for the expedition. These medals bore a portrait of President Thomas Jefferson on one side, and symbols of peace and friendship on the other. They were presented to Native American chiefs and other important leaders as tokens of the goodwill of the United States. The Keelboat reverse, by Mint sculptor Al Maletsky, depicts the boat that transported the Lewis and Clark expedition and their supplies through the rivers of the Louisiana Territory. Built to Captain Lewis's specifications, this 55-foot craft could be sailed, rowed, poled like a raft, or towed from the riverbank.

*2005:* The new obverse portrait of President Jefferson was inspired by a 1789 marble bust by Jean-Antoine Houdon; the inscription "Liberty" was based on Jefferson's handwriting. Joe Fitzgerald designed the new obverse, which was rendered by Mint sculptor Don Everhart. The American Bison reverse, designed by Jamie Franki and produced by Norman E. Nemeth, features a bison in profile. Described in journals from the expedition, bison held great significance for many American Indian cultures. (The design also recalls the popular Indian Head / Buffalo nickel design of 1913–1938.) The "Ocean in View" reverse, designed by Joe Fitzgerald and produced by Mint sculptor Donna Weaver, depicts cliffs over the Pacific Ocean and an inscription inspired by a November 7, 1805, entry in Clark's journal: "Ocean in view! O! The joy!"

The Mint also produced Westward Journey Nickel Series™ Coin Sets for 2004 and 2005 (see page 360).

*Weight 5 grams; composition, .750 copper, .250 nickel; diameter 21.2 mm; plain edge; mints: Philadelphia, Denver, San Francisco.*

2004 Obverse

2005 Obverse

*Circulation strike.*

Peace Medal Keelboat American Bison Ocean in View

2004 Obverse

2005 Obverse

*Proof strike.*

Peace Medal Keelboat American Bison Ocean in View

| | Mintage | MS-63 | MS-65 | PF-65 |
|---|---|---|---|---|
| 2004P, Peace Medal | 361,440,000 | $0.25 | $0.75 | |
| 2004D, Peace Medal | 372,000,000 | 0.25 | 0.75 | |
| 2004S, Peace Medal | (2,992,069) | | | $8 |
| 2004P, Keelboat | 366,720,000 | 0.25 | 0.75 | |
| 2004D, Keelboat | 344,880,000 | 0.25 | 0.75 | |
| 2004S, Keelboat | (2,965,422) | | | 8 |
| 2005P, American Bison | 448,320,000 | 0.35 | 1.25 | |
| 2005D, American Bison | 487,680,000 | 0.35 | 1.25 | |
| 2005S, American Bison | (3,344,679) | | | 10 |
| 2005P, Ocean in View | 394,080,000 | 0.25 | 0.75 | |
| 2005D, Ocean in View | 411,120,000 | 0.25 | 0.75 | |
| 2005S, Ocean in View | (3,344,679) | | | 8 |

*Note:* Uncirculated Mint Sets for 2005–2010 were made with Satin Finish coins not included in the listings here. See page 369 for their mintages.

## MODIFIED (2006 TO DATE)

Following the Westward Journey series, the Mint returned to the Monticello reverse, but revised the Jefferson portrait yet again. This modified design shows a facing portrait of Jefferson, designed by Jamie Franki and sculpted by Donna Weaver.

*Weight 5 grams; composition, .750 copper, .250 nickel; diameter 21.2 mm; plain edge; mints: Philadelphia, Denver, San Francisco.*

*Circulation strike.*

*Proof strike.*

*Felix Schlag's initials moved to reverse.*

| | Mintage | MS-63 | MS-65 | PF-65 |
|---|---|---|---|---|
| 2006P | 693,120,000 | $0.25 | $0.75 | |
| 2006D | 809,280,000 | 0.25 | 0.75 | |
| 2006S | (3,054,436) | | | $5 |
| 2007P | 571,680,000 | 0.25 | 0.50 | |
| 2007D | 626,160,000 | 0.25 | 0.50 | |
| 2007S | (2,577,166) | | | 4 |
| 2008P | 279,840,000 | 0.25 | 0.50 | |
| 2008D | 345,600,000 | 0.25 | 0.50 | |
| 2008S | (2,169,561) | | | 4 |
| 2009P | 39,840,000 | 0.30 | 0.70 | |
| 2009D | 46,800,000 | 0.30 | 0.70 | |
| 2009S | (2,179,867) | | | 4 |
| 2010P | 260,640,000 | 0.25 | 0.50 | |
| 2010D | 229,920,000 | 0.25 | 0.50 | |
| 2010S | *(1,689,216)* | | | 4 |
| 2011P | 450,000,000 | 0.25 | 0.50 | |
| 2011D | 540,240,000 | 0.25 | 0.50 | |
| 2011S | *(1,673,010)* | | | 4 |
| 2012P | 464,640,000 | 0.25 | 0.50 | |
| 2012D | 558,960,000 | 0.25 | 0.50 | |
| 2012S | (1,239,148) | | | 4 |
| 2013P | 607,440,000 | 0.25 | 0.50 | |
| 2013D | 615,600,000 | 0.25 | 0.50 | |
| 2013S | *(1,274,505)* | | | $4 |
| 2014P | 635,520,000 | $0.25 | $0.50 | |
| 2014D | 570,720,000 | 0.25 | 0.50 | |
| 2014S | *(1,190,369)* | | | 4 |
| 2015P | 752,880,000 | 0.25 | 0.50 | |
| 2015D | 846,720,000 | 0.25 | 0.50 | |
| 2015S | *(1,050,164)* | | | 4 |
| 2016P | 786,960,000 | 0.25 | 0.50 | |
| 2016D | 759,600,000 | 0.25 | 0.50 | |
| 2016S | *(1,011,624)* | | | 4 |
| 2017P | 710,160,000 | 0.25 | 0.50 | |
| 2017D | 663,120,000 | 0.25 | 0.50 | |
| 2017S **(a)** | *(979,477)* | | | 4 |
| 2018P | *629,520,000* | 0.25 | 0.50 | |
| 2018D | *626,880,000* | 0.25 | 0.50 | |
| 2018S | *(844,220)* | | | 4 |
| 2019P | *567,854,400* | 0.25 | 0.50 | |
| 2019D | *527,040,000* | 0.25 | 0.50 | |
| 2019S | | | | 4 |
| 2020P | | 0.25 | 0.50 | |
| 2020D | | 0.25 | 0.50 | |
| 2020S | | | | 4 |

*Note:* Uncirculated Mint Sets for 2005–2010 were made with Satin Finish coins not included in the listings here. See page 369 for their mintages. **a.** For its 225th anniversary, the Mint issued a special set of Enhanced Uncirculated coins from the San Francisco Mint; they are not included in the listings here.

Half dimes have the same general designs as larger United States silver coins. Authorized by the Act of April 2, 1792, they were not struck until February 1795, although some were dated 1794. At first the weight was 20.8 grains, and fineness .8924. By the Act of January 18, 1837, the weight was reduced to 20-5/8 grains and the fineness changed to .900. The weight was later reduced to 19.2 grains by the Act of February 21, 1853. Half dimes offer many varieties in the early dates.

## FLOWING HAIR (1794–1795)

*Designer unknown; engraver Robert Scot; weight 1.35 grams; composition .8924 silver, .1076 copper; approx. diameter 16.5 mm; reeded edge. All coined at Philadelphia Mint.*

**AG-3 About Good**—Details clear enough to identify.
**G-4 Good**—Eagle, wreath, bust outlined but lack details.
**VG-8 Very Good**—Some details on face. All lettering legible.
**F-12 Fine**—Hair ends visible. Hair at top smooth.
**VF-20 Very Fine**—Hair lines at top visible. Hair about ear defined.
**EF-40 Extremely Fine**—Hair above forehead and at neck well defined but shows some wear.
**AU-50 About Uncirculated**—Slight wear on high waves of hair, near ear and face, and on head and tips of eagle's wings.
**MS-60 Uncirculated**—No trace of wear. Light blemishes.
**MS-63 Choice Uncirculated**—Some distracting marks or blemishes in prime focal areas. Some impairment of luster possible.

| | Mintage | AG-3 | G-4 | VG-8 | F-12 | VF-20 | EF-40 | AU-50 | MS-60 | MS-63 |
|---|---|---|---|---|---|---|---|---|---|---|
| 1792 | * | $15,000 | $30,000 | $45,000 | $52,500 | $80,000 | $115,000 | $135,000 | $155,000 | $275,000 |
| 1794 | * | 1,000 | 1,750 | 2,200 | 3,000 | 4,000 | 7,500 | 11,000 | 17,500 | 32,500 |
| *$367,775, SP-67, Heritage auction, October 2012* | | | | | | | | | | |
| 1795 | 86,416 | 650 | 1,350 | 1,600 | 2,000 | 3,250 | 6,000 | 8,000 | 11,500 | 18,000 |

* Included in number below.

## DRAPED BUST (1796–1805)

*Designer probably Gilbert Stuart; engraver Robert Scot; weight 1.35 grams; composition .8924 silver, .1076 copper; approx. diameter 16.5 mm; reeded edge. All coined at Philadelphia Mint.*

**AG-3 About Good**—Details clear enough to identify.
**G-4 Good**—Date, stars, LIBERTY readable. Bust of Liberty outlined, but no details.
**VG-8 Very Good**—Some details visible.
**F-12 Fine**—Hair and drapery lines worn, but visible.
**VF-20 Very Fine**—Only left side of drapery indistinct.
**EF-40 Extremely Fine**—Details visible in all hair lines.
**AU-50 About Uncirculated**—Slight wear on bust, shoulder, and hair; wear on eagle's head and top of wings.
**MS-60 Uncirculated**—No trace of wear. Light blemishes.
**MS-63 Choice Uncirculated**—Some distracting marks or blemishes in prime focal areas. Impaired luster possible.

### Small Eagle Reverse (1796–1797)

*See next page for chart.*

| | Mintage | AG-3 | G-4 | VG-8 | F-12 | VF-20 | EF-40 | AU-50 | MS-60 | MS-63 |
|---|---|---|---|---|---|---|---|---|---|---|
| 1796, 6 Over 5 | 10,230 | $1,000 | $2,500 | $3,250 | $4,000 | $5,250 | $9,500 | $15,000 | $25,000 | $40,000 |
| *$345,000, MS-66, Heritage auction, January 2008* | | | | | | | | | | |
| 1796 | | 850 | 1,800 | 2,000 | 3,500 | 5,000 | 8,750 | 13,500 | 18,500 | 35,000 |
| 1796, LIKERTY | * | 850 | 1,500 | 2,000 | 3,450 | 4,750 | 8,750 | 11,500 | 16,000 | 35,000 |
| 1797, 15 Stars | 44,527 | 850 | 1,500 | 1,800 | 3,450 | 4,750 | 8,750 | 10,500 | 15,000 | 25,000 |
| 1797, 16 Stars | * | 1,000 | 1,750 | 2,400 | 3,600 | 4,750 | 8,750 | 12,500 | 16,000 | 25,000 |
| 1797, 13 Stars | * | 1,250 | 2,250 | 3,500 | 5,000 | 6,500 | 13,500 | 25,000 | 42,500 | 65,000 |

* Included in number above.

## Heraldic Eagle Reverse (1800–1805)

1800, LIBEKTY
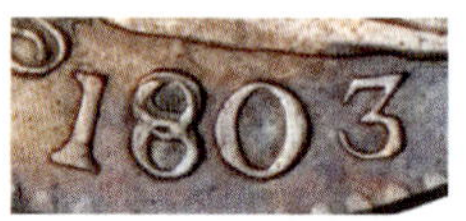
1803, Large 8

1803, Small 8

| | Mintage | AG-3 | G-4 | VG-8 | F-12 | VF-20 | EF-40 | AU-50 | MS-60 | MS-63 |
|---|---|---|---|---|---|---|---|---|---|---|
| 1800 | 24,000 | $600 | $1,100 | $1,500 | $2,000 | $3,000 | $6,000 | $8,000 | $12,500 | $20,000 |
| 1800, LIBEKTY | 16,000 | 600 | 1,200 | 1,750 | 2,500 | 3,250 | 6,200 | 8,500 | 13,000 | 22,000 |
| 1801 | 27,760 | 600 | 1,450 | 1,750 | 2,500 | 4,000 | 6,500 | 10,000 | 17,500 | 27,500 |
| 1802 | 3,060 | 35,000 | 70,000 | 115,000 | 130,000 | 150,000 | 225,000 | 350,000 | | |
| 1803, Large 8 | 37,850 | 750 | 1,250 | 1,500 | 2,000 | 3,000 | 6,500 | 9,000 | 14,000 | 25,000 |
| 1803, Small 8 | * | 1,000 | 1,750 | 2,500 | 3,500 | 5,000 | 9,000 | 17,500 | 55,000 | 90,000 |
| 1805 | 15,600 | 800 | 1,450 | 1,500 | 2,750 | 3,750 | 10,000 | 25,000 | | |

* Included in number above.

## CAPPED BUST (1829–1837)

*Engraver William Kneass, after a design by John Reich; weight 1.35 grams; composition .8924 silver, .1076 copper; approx. diameter 15.5 mm; reeded edge. Changed to 1.34 grams, .900 fine in 1837. All coined at Philadelphia Mint.*

**G-4 Good**—Bust of Liberty outlined, no detail. Date and legend legible.
**VG-8 Very Good**—Complete legend and date plain. At least three letters of LIBERTY on edge of cap show clearly.
**F-12 Fine**—All letters in LIBERTY visible.
**VF-20 Very Fine**—Full rims. Ear and shoulder clasp show plainly.
**EF-40 Extremely Fine**—Ear very distinct; eyebrow and hair well defined.
**AU-50 About Uncirculated**—Traces of light wear on many of the high points. At least half of mint luster still present.
**MS-60 Uncirculated**—No trace of wear. Light blemishes.
**MS-63 Choice Uncirculated**—No trace of wear. Light blemishes. Attractive mint luster.

| | Mintage | G-4 | VG-8 | F-12 | VF-20 | EF-40 | AU-50 | MS-60 | MS-63 |
|---|---|---|---|---|---|---|---|---|---|
| 1829 | 1,230,000 | $60 | $75 | $100 | $125 | $200 | $300 | $425 | $925 |
| 1830 | 1,240,000 | 50 | 65 | 80 | 115 | 175 | 275 | 400 | 875 |
| 1831 | 1,242,700 | 50 | 65 | 80 | 115 | 175 | 250 | 400 | 875 |
| 1832 | 965,000 | 50 | 65 | 80 | 115 | 175 | 250 | 400 | 875 |

1835, Large Date

1835, Small Date

| | Mintage | G-4 | VG-8 | F-12 | VF-20 | EF-40 | AU-50 | MS-60 | MS-63 |
|---|---|---|---|---|---|---|---|---|---|
| 1833 | 1,370,000 | $50 | $65 | $80 | $115 | $175 | $250 | $400 | $875 |
| 1834 | 1,480,000 | 50 | 65 | 80 | 115 | 175 | 250 | 400 | 875 |
| 1834, 3 Over Inverted 3 | * | 50 | 65 | 80 | 135 | 200 | 350 | 550 | 1,200 |
| 1835, All kinds | 2,760,000 | | | | | | | | |
| 1835, Large Date and 5 C. | | 50 | 65 | 80 | 115 | 175 | 250 | 400 | 850 |
| 1835, Large Date, Small 5 C. | | 50 | 65 | 80 | 115 | 175 | 250 | 400 | 850 |
| 1835, Small Date, Large 5 C. | | 50 | 65 | 80 | 115 | 175 | 250 | 400 | 850 |
| 1835, Small Date and 5 C. | | 50 | 65 | 80 | 115 | 175 | 250 | 400 | 850 |
| 1836, Small 5 C. | 1,900,000 | 50 | 65 | 80 | 115 | 175 | 250 | 400 | 850 |
| 1836, Large 5 C. | * | 50 | 65 | 80 | 115 | 175 | 250 | 400 | 850 |
| 1836, 3 Over Inverted 3 | * | 55 | 75 | 100 | 135 | 200 | 350 | 675 | 1,200 |
| 1837, Small 5 C. | 871,000 | 85 | 100 | 150 | 185 | 300 | 500 | 1,000 | 2,500 |
| 1837, Large 5 C. | * | 55 | 75 | 80 | 125 | 185 | 250 | 450 | 850 |

* Included in number above.

## LIBERTY SEATED (1837–1873)

The Liberty Seated design without stars on the obverse was used on the half dime and dime only at the Philadelphia Mint in 1837 and the New Orleans Mint in 1838. On those coins, Liberty has no drapery fold at her elbow. Starting in 1838 on the Philadelphia coinage, stars were added around the obverse border. During 1840 and thereafter, an additional fold of drapery was added at the elbow of Liberty.

**G-4 Good**—LIBERTY on shield smooth. Date and letters legible.
**VG-8 Very Good**—At least three letters in LIBERTY visible.
**F-12 Fine**—Entire LIBERTY visible, weak spots.
**VF-20 Very Fine**—Entire LIBERTY strong and even.
**EF-40 Extremely Fine**—LIBERTY and scroll edges distinct.
**AU-50 About Uncirculated**—Traces of light wear on many of the high points. At least half of mint luster still present.
**MS-60 Uncirculated**—No trace of wear. Light blemishes.
**MS-63 Choice Uncirculated**—No trace of wear. Light blemishes. Attractive mint luster.

### Variety 1 – No Stars on Obverse (1837–1838)

*Designer Christian Gobrecht; weight 1.34 grams; composition .900 silver, .100 copper; diameter 15.5 mm; reeded edge; mints: Philadelphia, New Orleans.*

| | Mintage | G-4 | VG-8 | F-12 | VF-20 | EF-40 | AU-50 | MS-60 | MS-63 |
|---|---|---|---|---|---|---|---|---|---|
| 1837, Small Date | 1,405,000 | $40 | $55 | $90 | $145 | $250 | $450 | $600 | $950 |
| 1837, Large Date | * | 40 | 55 | 80 | 145 | 250 | 450 | 600 | 950 |
| 1838O, No Stars | 70,000 | 150 | 215 | 400 | 750 | 2,000 | 3,000 | 5,250 | 10,750 |

* Included in number above.

## Variety 2 – Stars on Obverse (1838–1853)

From 1838 through 1859, the mintmark was located above the bow on the reverse. Large, medium, or small mintmark varieties occur for several dates.

*Designer Christian Gobrecht; weight 1.34 grams; composition .900 silver, .100 copper; diameter 15.5 mm; reeded edge; mints: Philadelphia, New Orleans.*

No Drapery From Elbow (1837–1840)

Drapery From Elbow (Starting 1840)

| | Mintage | G-4 | VG-8 | F-12 | VF-20 | EF-40 | AU-50 | MS-60 | MS-63 |
|---|---|---|---|---|---|---|---|---|---|
| 1838, No Drapery, Large Stars | 2,225,000 | $18 | $21 | $28 | $45 | $125 | $200 | $280 | $475 |
| 1838, No Drapery, Small Stars | * | 22 | 40 | 70 | 175 | 250 | 375 | 625 | 1,000 |
| 1839, No Drapery | 1,069,150 | 20 | 25 | 35 | 50 | 100 | 185 | 275 | 450 |
| 1839O, No Drapery | 1,291,600 | 20 | 25 | 40 | 85 | 200 | 325 | 850 | 2,100 |
| 1840, No Drapery | 1,034,000 | 20 | 25 | 30 | 45 | 100 | 185 | 275 | 450 |
| 1840O, No Drapery | 695,000 | 40 | 55 | 85 | 125 | 220 | 475 | 1,200 | 3,750 |
| 1840, Drapery | 310,085 | 35 | 50 | 70 | 140 | 210 | 360 | 500 | 900 |
| 1840O, Drapery | 240,000 | 45 | 75 | 150 | 300 | 750 | 1,550 | 10,000 | 22,000 |
| 1841 | 1,150,000 | 16 | 20 | 30 | 35 | 70 | 150 | 190 | 325 |
| 1841O | 815,000 | 60 | 90 | 140 | 200 | 325 | 500 | 1,000 | 3,250 |
| 1842 | 815,000 | 16 | 20 | 27 | 35 | 75 | 150 | 225 | 400 |
| 1842O | 350,000 | 55 | 75 | 125 | 215 | 550 | 900 | 1,275 | 2,250 |
| 1843 | 815,000 | 25 | 35 | 40 | 60 | 90 | 160 | 225 | 400 |
| 1844 | 430,000 | 20 | 25 | 35 | 55 | 115 | 200 | 275 | 500 |
| 1844O | 220,000 | 80 | 160 | 300 | 750 | 1,250 | 2,750 | 5,000 | 10,000 |
| 1845 | 1,564,000 | 16 | 20 | 27 | 35 | 60 | 145 | 225 | 365 |
| 1846 | 27,000 | 850 | 1,275 | 1,650 | 2,350 | 4,250 | 7,500 | 12,500 | 30,000 |
| 1847 | 1,274,000 | 20 | 25 | 35 | 70 | 95 | 150 | 225 | 400 |
| 1848, Medium Date | 668,000 | 16 | 25 | 40 | 60 | 95 | 180 | 285 | 600 |
| 1848, Large Date | * | 35 | 50 | 80 | 150 | 190 | 350 | 750 | 2,500 |
| 1848O | 600,000 | 22 | 25 | 45 | 85 | 210 | 325 | 650 | 1,400 |
| 1849, All kinds | 1,309,000 | | | | | | | | |
| 1849, 9 Over 6 **(a)** | | 35 | 50 | 75 | 120 | 200 | 350 | 700 | 1,200 |
| 1849, 9 Over Widely Placed 6 | | 50 | 70 | 100 | 150 | 275 | 380 | 620 | 1,400 |
| 1849, Normal Date | | 25 | 30 | 40 | 58 | 100 | 175 | 265 | 750 |
| 1849O | 140,000 | 45 | 75 | 145 | 285 | 625 | 1,200 | 2,175 | 4,000 |
| 1850 | 955,000 | 22 | 30 | 40 | 60 | 90 | 180 | 220 | 375 |
| 1850O | 690,000 | 30 | 40 | 60 | 100 | 200 | 275 | 675 | 1,400 |
| 1851 | 781,000 | 18 | 22 | 28 | 40 | 75 | 140 | 190 | 325 |
| 1851O | 860,000 | 25 | 30 | 35 | 50 | 110 | 235 | 450 | 925 |
| 1852 | 1,000,500 | 18 | 22 | 28 | 40 | 75 | 140 | 190 | 325 |
| 1852O | 260,000 | 30 | 40 | 75 | 150 | 275 | 500 | 950 | 2,250 |
| 1853, No Arrows | 135,000 | 60 | 85 | 140 | 225 | 325 | 500 | 750 | 1,200 |
| 1853O, No Arrows | 160,000 | 350 | 600 | 775 | 1,200 | 2,400 | 3,850 | 6,200 | 12,500 |

* Included in number above. **a.** Some 1849 half dime overdates have been called "9 Over 8" rather than "9 Over 6," but no indisputable image of an 8 underdate has come to light.

## Variety 3 – Arrows at Date (1853–1855)

As on the dimes, quarters, and halves, arrows were placed at the sides of the date for a short period starting in 1853. They were placed there to denote the reduction of weight under the terms of the Act of February 21, 1853.

*Weight 1.24 grams; composition .900 silver, .100 copper; diameter 15.5 mm; reeded edge; mints: Philadelphia, New Orleans.*

*Circulation strike.* *Proof strike.*

| | Mintage | G-4 | VG-8 | F-12 | VF-20 | EF-40 | AU-50 | MS-60 | MS-63 | PF-63 |
|---|---|---|---|---|---|---|---|---|---|---|
| 1853 | 13,210,020 | $20 | $25 | $30 | $35 | $70 | $150 | $200 | $325 | $60,000 |
| 1853O | 2,200,000 | 25 | 30 | 40 | 65 | 100 | 240 | 350 | 1,250 | |
| 1854 | 5,740,000 | 20 | 25 | 30 | 35 | 65 | 150 | 200 | 300 | 7,500 |
| 1854O | 1,560,000 | 20 | 24 | 35 | 45 | 90 | 200 | 300 | 900 | |
| 1855 | 1,750,000 | 20 | 25 | 30 | 35 | 75 | 150 | 210 | 375 | 7,500 |
| 1855O | 600,000 | 30 | 40 | 55 | 85 | 200 | 380 | 850 | 1,500 | |

## Variety 2 Resumed, With Weight Standard of Variety 3 (1856–1859)

*Circulation strike.* *Proof strike.* **1858 Over Inverted Date**

| | Mintage | G-4 | VG-8 | F-12 | VF-20 | EF-40 | AU-50 | MS-60 | MS-63 | PF-63 |
|---|---|---|---|---|---|---|---|---|---|---|
| 1856 | 4,880,000 | $18 | $22 | $25 | $35 | $60 | $115 | $175 | $285 | $4,000 |
| 1856O | 1,100,000 | 18 | 22 | 25 | 55 | 135 | 285 | 550 | 1,000 | |
| 1857 | 7,280,000 | 18 | 22 | 25 | 35 | 60 | 115 | 175 | 285 | 3,000 |
| 1857O | 1,380,000 | 18 | 22 | 25 | 45 | 80 | 175 | 300 | 500 | |
| 1858 . . . . . . . . . . . *(300)* | 3,500,000 | 18 | 22 | 25 | 35 | 60 | 125 | 170 | 320 | 1,200 |
| 1858, Repunched High Dt | * | 35 | 50 | 80 | 125 | 200 | 325 | 650 | 1,300 | |
| 1858, Over Inverted Dt. | * | 40 | 60 | 100 | 150 | 250 | 350 | 800 | 1,600 | |
| 1858O | 1,660,000 | 18 | 22 | 30 | 50 | 80 | 155 | 240 | 480 | |
| 1859 . . . . . . . . . . . *(800)* | 340,000 | 18 | 22 | 30 | 45 | 80 | 135 | 200 | 425 | 1,100 |
| 1859O | 560,000 | 25 | 35 | 65 | 90 | 165 | 225 | 285 | 500 | |

* Included in number above.

### *Transitional Patterns*

A new die was utilized in 1859 at the Philadelphia Mint, in which the stars are hollow in the center and the arms of Liberty are slimmer. During the years 1859 and 1860 interesting half dime patterns were made which do not bear our nation's identity. These are transitional pieces, not made for circulation, but struck at the time the inscription UNITED STATES OF AMERICA was being transferred from the reverse to the obverse.

| | Mintage | MS-60 | MS-63 | PF-63 |
|---|---|---|---|---|
| 1859, Obverse of 1859, Reverse of 1860<br>*$66,700, PF-65, Stack's Bowers auction, May 2005* | *20* | | | $35,000 |
| 1860, Obverse of 1859 (With Stars), Reverse of 1860<br>*$9,200, MS-67, Stack's Bowers auction, August 2009* | *100* | $3,500 | $5,500 | |

## Variety 4 – Legend on Obverse (1860–1873)

*Weight 1.24 grams; composition .900 silver, .100 copper; diameter 15.5 mm; reeded edge; mints: Philadelphia, New Orleans, San Francisco.*

*Circulation strike.*

*Proof strike.*

1861, So-Called 1 Over 0

Mintmark Below Bow (1860–1869, 1872–1873)

Mintmark Above Bow (1870–1872)

| | Mintage | G-4 | VG-8 | F-12 | VF-20 | EF-40 | AU-50 | MS-60 | MS-63 | PF-63 |
|---|---|---|---|---|---|---|---|---|---|---|
| 1860, Legend . . (1,000) | 798,000 | $16 | $20 | $25 | $30 | $50 | $85 | $175 | $300 | $550 |
| 1860O | 1,060,000 | 20 | 25 | 30 | 45 | 80 | 120 | 170 | 320 | |
| 1861 . . . . . . . . . (1,000) | 3,360,000 | 20 | 25 | 30 | 40 | 70 | 120 | 160 | 275 | 550 |
| 1861, "1 Over 0" **(a)** | * | 35 | 45 | 50 | 90 | 200 | 325 | 525 | 800 | |
| 1862 . . . . . . . . . . . (550) | 1,492,000 | 25 | 30 | 45 | 55 | 70 | 100 | 160 | 300 | 550 |
| 1863 . . . . . . . . . . . (460) | 18,000 | 200 | 280 | 330 | 425 | 600 | 750 | 825 | 975 | 550 |
| 1863S | 100,000 | 45 | 60 | 100 | 200 | 300 | 400 | 750 | 1,175 | |
| 1864 . . . . . . . . . . . (470) | 48,000 | 325 | 440 | 675 | 850 | 1,100 | 1,200 | 1,300 | 1,475 | 550 |
| 1864S | 90,000 | 65 | 100 | 175 | 250 | 400 | 750 | 1,100 | 1,850 | |
| 1865 . . . . . . . . . . . (500) | 13,000 | 400 | 475 | 550 | 750 | 900 | 1,200 | 1,300 | 1,650 | 550 |
| 1865S | 120,000 | 50 | 80 | 125 | 200 | 350 | 550 | 1,100 | 2,450 | |
| 1866 . . . . . . . . . . . (725) | 10,000 | 325 | 400 | 500 | 650 | 850 | 1,000 | 1,100 | 1,225 | 550 |
| 1866S | 120,000 | 45 | 60 | 90 | 150 | 225 | 325 | 500 | 900 | |
| 1867 . . . . . . . . . . . (625) | 8,000 | 450 | 525 | 625 | 750 | 850 | 1,000 | 1,200 | 1,500 | 550 |
| 1867S | 120,000 | 30 | 40 | 60 | 90 | 250 | 345 | 575 | 1,150 | |
| 1868 . . . . . . . . . . . (600) | 88,600 | 55 | 65 | 120 | 185 | 325 | 475 | 675 | 800 | 550 |
| 1868S | 280,000 | 16 | 25 | 40 | 50 | 85 | 145 | 320 | 700 | |
| 1869 . . . . . . . . . . . (600) | 208,000 | 30 | 40 | 50 | 70 | 110 | 175 | 275 | 450 | 550 |
| 1869S | 230,000 | 30 | 40 | 50 | 90 | 150 | 250 | 335 | 500 | |
| 1870 . . . . . . . . . (1,000) | 535,000 | 16 | 20 | 25 | 30 | 45 | 80 | 175 | 400 | 550 |
| 1870S *(unique)* . . . . . . . . . . . . . . . . *$661,250, MS-63, Stack's Bowers auction, July 2004* | | | | | | | | | *2,000,000* | |
| 1871 . . . . . . . . . . . (960) | 1,873,000 | 16 | 20 | 25 | 30 | 60 | 80 | 150 | 250 | 550 |
| 1871S | 161,000 | 18 | 22 | 32 | 65 | 80 | 180 | 250 | 450 | |
| 1872 . . . . . . . . . . . (950) | 2,947,000 | 16 | 20 | 25 | 30 | 45 | 80 | 150 | 300 | 550 |
| 1872S, All kinds | 837,000 | | | | | | | | | |
| 1872S, Mmk above bow | | 20 | 25 | 30 | 45 | 55 | 100 | 180 | 300 | |
| 1872S, Mmk below bow | | 20 | 25 | 30 | 45 | 55 | 120 | 160 | 285 | |
| 1873 (Close 3 only) . . . . . . . (600) | 712,000 | 16 | 20 | 25 | 30 | 45 | 80 | 150 | 350 | 550 |
| 1873S (Close 3 only) | 324,000 | 16 | 20 | 25 | 30 | 65 | 125 | 150 | 300 | |

* Included in number above. **a.** Not an actual overdate.

The designs of the dimes, first coined in 1796, follow closely those of the half dimes up through the Liberty Seated type. The dimes in each instance weigh twice as much as the half dimes.

*Note: Values of common-date silver coins have been based on a silver bullion price of $18 per ounce, and may vary with the prevailing spot price. To determine the intrinsic value of common silver coins, see page 445.*

# DRAPED BUST (1796–1807)

## Small Eagle Reverse (1796–1797)

*Designer probably Gilbert Stuart; engraver Robert Scot; weight 2.70 grams; composition .8924 silver, .1076 copper; approx. diameter 19 mm; reeded edge. All coined at Philadelphia Mint.*

**AG-3 About Good**—Details clear enough to identify.
**G-4 Good**—Date legible. Bust outlined, but no detail.
**VG-8 Very Good**—All but deepest drapery folds worn smooth. Hair lines nearly gone and curls lacking in detail.
**F-12 Fine**—All drapery lines visible. Hair partly worn.
**VF-20 Very Fine**—Only left side of drapery indistinct.
**EF-40 Extremely Fine**—Hair well outlined with details visible.
**AU-50 About Uncirculated**—Traces of light wear on many of the high points. At least half of mint luster still present.
**MS-60 Uncirculated**—No trace of wear. Light blemishes.
**MS-63 Choice Uncirculated**—Some distracting marks or blemishes in prime focal areas. Impaired luster possible.

1796

1797, 16 Stars

1797, 13 Stars

| | Mintage | AG-3 | G-4 | VG-8 | F-12 | VF-20 | EF-40 | AU-50 | MS-60 | MS-63 |
|---|---|---|---|---|---|---|---|---|---|---|
| 1796 | 22,135 | $1,100 | $2,750 | $3,500 | $5,000 | $6,500 | $9,500 | $15,000 | $23,000 | $35,000 |
| *$881,250, MS-67, Heritage auction, June 2014* | | | | | | | | | | |
| 1797, All kinds | 25,261 | | | | | | | | | |
| 1797, 16 Stars | | 1,100 | 2,750 | 4,000 | 5,000 | 7,000 | 10,000 | 16,500 | 32,500 | 50,000 |
| 1797, 13 Stars | | 1,200 | 2,850 | 4,000 | 6,500 | 8,250 | 16,500 | 21,000 | 52,500 | 85,000 |

## Heraldic Eagle Reverse (1798–1807)

1805, 4 Berries

1805, 5 Berries

| | Mintage | AG-3 | G-4 | VG-8 | F-12 | VF-20 | EF-40 | AU-50 | MS-60 | MS-63 |
|---|---|---|---|---|---|---|---|---|---|---|
| 1798, All kinds | 27,550 | | | | | | | | | |
| 1798, 8 Over 7, 16 Stars on Reverse | | $350 | $850 | $1,200 | $1,750 | $2,500 | $3,500 | $5,000 | $8,500 | $18,000 |
| 1798, 8 Over 7, 13 Stars on Reverse | | 750 | 2,000 | 4,500 | 6,000 | 7,000 | 12,500 | 27,500 | 50,000 | |
| 1798, Large 8 | | 325 | 850 | 1,200 | 1,650 | 2,500 | 3,750 | 4,750 | 9,500 | 32,500 |
| 1798, Small 8 | | 350 | 1,250 | 2,250 | 3,000 | 5,500 | 9,500 | 15,000 | 35,000 | 65,000 |
| 1800 | 21,760 | 325 | 1,000 | 1,050 | 1,650 | 2,750 | 4,000 | 9,000 | 22,500 | 45,000 |

*Chart continued on next page.*

| | Mintage | AG-3 | G-4 | VG-8 | F-12 | VF-20 | EF-40 | AU-50 | MS-60 | MS-63 |
|---|---|---|---|---|---|---|---|---|---|---|
| 1801 | 34,640 | $325 | $1,150 | $1,250 | $2,000 | $3,750 | $6,000 | $11,000 | $40,000 | $55,000 |
| 1802 | 10,975 | 650 | 1,500 | 2,250 | 3,000 | 4,500 | 8,750 | 16,500 | 35,000 | |
| 1803 | 33,040 | 350 | 1,100 | 1,500 | 1,800 | 3,000 | 6,000 | 11,500 | 55,000 | |
| 1804, All kinds | 8,265 | | | | | | | | | |
| 1804, 13 Stars on Rev. | | 1,250 | 3,250 | 5,500 | 9,500 | 15,000 | 35,000 | 70,000 | — | |
| 1804, 14 Stars on Rev. *$632,500, AU-58, Heritage auction, July 2008* | | 2,000 | 6,500 | 13,500 | 22,500 | 27,500 | 55,000 | 85,000 | — | |
| 1805, All kinds | 120,780 | | | | | | | | | |
| 1805, 4 Berries | | 250 | 600 | 1,000 | 1,400 | 1,850 | 3,000 | 3,500 | 7,500 | 9,000 |
| 1805, 5 Berries | | 250 | 600 | 1,000 | 1,400 | 1,900 | 3,000 | 3,750 | 8,000 | 17,500 |
| 1807 | 165,000 | 250 | 550 | 850 | 1,300 | 1,750 | 2,750 | 3,250 | 5,500 | 9,500 |

## CAPPED BUST (1809–1837)

*Designer John Reich; weight 2.70 grams; composition .8924 silver, .1076 copper; approx. diameter (1809–1827) 18.8 mm, (1828–1837) 18.5 mm; reeded edge. All coined at Philadelphia Mint. Changed to 2.67 grams, .900 fine in 1837.*

**AG-3 About Good**—Details clear enough to identify.
**G-4 Good**—Date, letters, and stars discernible. Bust outlined, no details.
**VG-8 Very Good**—Legends and date plain. Some letters in LIBERTY visible.
**F-12 Fine**—Clear LIBERTY. Ear and shoulder clasp visible. Part of rim visible on both sides.
**VF-20 Very Fine**—LIBERTY distinct. Full rim. Ear and clasp plain and distinct.
**EF-40 Extremely Fine**—LIBERTY sharp. Ear distinct. Hair above eye well defined.
**AU-50 About Uncirculated**—Traces of light wear on only the high points of the design. Half of mint luster present.
**MS-60 Uncirculated**—No trace of wear. Light blemishes.
**MS-63 Choice Uncirculated**—Some distracting marks or blemishes in prime focal areas. Impaired luster possible.

### Variety 1 – Wide Border (1809–1828)

1811, 11 Over 09

| | Mintage | G-4 | VG-8 | F-12 | VF-20 | EF-40 | AU-50 | MS-60 | MS-63 |
|---|---|---|---|---|---|---|---|---|---|
| 1809 | 51,065 | $750 | $950 | $1,400 | $2,250 | $3,500 | $4,500 | $5,500 | $8,000 |
| 1811, 11 Over 09 | 65,180 | 200 | 350 | 1,000 | 1,150 | 1,700 | 2,350 | 4,000 | 7,000 |

1814, Small Date

1814, Large Date

| | Mintage | G-4 | VG-8 | F-12 | VF-20 | EF-40 | AU-50 | MS-60 | MS-63 |
|---|---|---|---|---|---|---|---|---|---|
| 1814, All kinds | 421,500 | | | | | | | | |
| 1814, Small Date | | $70 | $115 | $145 | $275 | $725 | $1,200 | $2,200 | $5,000 |
| 1814, Large Date | | 65 | 125 | 135 | 250 | 650 | 1,000 | 2,000 | 4,000 |
| 1814, STATESOFAMERICA | | 225 | 500 | 750 | 1,000 | 1,650 | 2,250 | 3,000 | 7,000 |

1820, Large 0

1820, Small 0

| | Mintage | G-4 | VG-8 | F-12 | VF-20 | EF-40 | AU-50 | MS-60 | MS-63 |
|---|---|---|---|---|---|---|---|---|---|
| 1820, All kinds. . . . . . . . | 942,587 | | | | | | | | |
| 1820, Large 0 . . . . . . . . . . . . . | | $65 | $115 | $150 | $225 | $550 | $675 | $1,400 | $2,750 |
| 1820, Small 0 . . . . . . . . . . . . . | | 65 | 115 | 150 | 225 | 650 | 1,200 | 1,500 | 3,500 |
| 1820, STATESOFAMERICA **(a)**. . | | 150 | 300 | 450 | 700 | 1,200 | 1,750 | 3,000 | 5,250 |

**a.** This is identical to the die used in 1814.

1821, Small Date

1821, Large Date

| | Mintage | G-4 | VG-8 | F-12 | VF-20 | EF-40 | AU-50 | MS-60 | MS-63 |
|---|---|---|---|---|---|---|---|---|---|
| 1821, All kinds. . . . . . . | 1,186,512 | | | | | | | | |
| 1821, Small Date. . . . . . . . . . . | | $75 | $115 | $150 | $225 | $525 | $1,000 | $1,750 | $4,000 |
| 1821, Large Date . . . . . . . . . . | | 75 | 115 | 150 | 225 | 525 | 800 | 1,700 | 3,250 |
| 1822 . . . . . . . . . . . . . . . | 100,000 | 2,500 | 3,000 | 4,250 | 7,500 | 9,500 | 12,500 | 20,000 | 28,500 |

1823, 3 Over 2

Small E's

Large E's

| | Mintage | G-4 | VG-8 | F-12 | VF-20 | EF-40 | AU-50 | MS-60 | MS-63 |
|---|---|---|---|---|---|---|---|---|---|
| 1823, 3 Over 2, All kinds . . . . . . . | 440,000 | | | | | | | | |
| 1823, 3 Over 2, Small E's . . . . . . . . . . . | | $100 | $150 | $225 | $400 | $700 | $1,100 | $1,650 | $3,250 |
| 1823, 3 Over 2, Large E's . . . . . . . . . . . | | 100 | 150 | 225 | 400 | 700 | 1,100 | 1,650 | 3,250 |

1824, 4 Over 2

1824 and 1827, Flat Top 1

1824 and 1827, Pointed Top 1

1828, Large Date

1828, Small Date

| | Mintage | G-4 | VG-8 | F-12 | VF-20 | EF-40 | AU-50 | MS-60 | MS-63 |
|---|---|---|---|---|---|---|---|---|---|
| 1824, 4 Over 2, Flat Top 1 . . . . . . | 510,000 | $100 | $150 | $225 | $400 | $1,000 | $1,500 | $2,250 | $4,000 |
| 1824, 4 Over 2, Pointed Top 1 . . . . . . . . . | * | 325 | 750 | 1,500 | 5,500 | 7,500 | | | |
| 1825 . . . . . . . . . . . . . . . . . . . . . . . . . . . | * | 65 | 115 | 150 | 225 | 525 | 950 | 1,800 | 3,250 |
| 1827, Flat Top 1 in 10 C. . . . . . | 1,215,000 | 225 | 375 | 1,000 | 1,800 | 3,000 | 4,500 | | |
| 1827, Pointed Top 1 in 10 C. . . . . . . . . . | * | 65 | 115 | 165 | 250 | 525 | 700 | 1,400 | 3,000 |
| 1828, Both varieties. . . . . . . . . . . | 125,000 | | | | | | | | |
| 1828, Large Date, Curl Base 2. . . . . . . . | | 115 | 175 | 275 | 650 | 1,000 | 1,200 | 3,750 | 6,000 |

* Included in number above.

## Variety 2 – Modified Design (1828–1837)

New Mint equipment was used to make the Small Date 1828 dimes and subsequent issues. Unlike earlier coinage, these have beaded borders and a uniform diameter. Large Date has curl base knob 2; Small Date has square base knob 2.

1829, Curl Base 2

1829, Small 10 C.

1829, Large 10 C.

1830, 30 Over 29

| | Mintage | G-4 | VG-8 | F-12 | VF-20 | EF-40 | AU-50 | MS-60 | MS-63 |
|---|---|---|---|---|---|---|---|---|---|
| 1828, Sm Date, Square Base 2 | * | $65 | $100 | $175 | $250 | $475 | $750 | $1,300 | $2,500 |
| 1829, All kinds | 770,000 | | | | | | | | |
| 1829, Curl Base 2 | | 5,000 | 7,500 | 16,500 | 22,500 | | | | |
| 1829, Square Base 2 | | | | | | | | | |
| 1829, Small 10 C. | | 45 | 50 | 55 | 120 | 375 | 475 | 1,200 | 2,000 |
| 1829, Medium 10 C. | | 45 | 50 | 55 | 120 | 350 | 450 | 1,000 | 2,000 |
| 1829, Large 10 C. | | 45 | 50 | 55 | 125 | 400 | 750 | 2,000 | 4,000 |
| 1830, All kinds | 510,000 | | | | | | | | |
| 1830, 30 Over 29 | | 55 | 65 | 100 | 140 | 400 | 650 | 1,300 | 4,000 |
| 1830, Large 10 C. | | 45 | 55 | 65 | 100 | 275 | 500 | 1,200 | 2,500 |
| 1830, Small 10 C. | | 45 | 55 | 85 | 125 | 375 | 650 | 1,200 | 2,500 |
| 1831 | 771,350 | 35 | 45 | 50 | 100 | 275 | 450 | 1,000 | 2,000 |
| 1832 | 522,500 | 35 | 45 | 50 | 100 | 275 | 450 | 1,000 | 2,000 |
| 1833, All kinds | 485,000 | | | | | | | | |
| 1833 | | 35 | 45 | 50 | 100 | 275 | 450 | 1,000 | 2,000 |
| 1833, Last 3 High | | 35 | 45 | 50 | 100 | 275 | 450 | 1,000 | 2,000 |
| 1834, All kinds | 635,000 | | | | | | | | |
| 1834, Small 4 | | 30 | 45 | 50 | 100 | 275 | 450 | 1,500 | 2,250 |
| 1834, Large 4 | | 30 | 45 | 50 | 100 | 275 | 450 | 1,000 | 2,000 |
| 1835 | 1,410,000 | 30 | 45 | 50 | 100 | 275 | 450 | 1,000 | 2,000 |
| 1836 | 1,190,000 | 30 | 45 | 50 | 100 | 275 | 450 | 1,000 | 2,000 |
| 1837 | 359,500 | 30 | 45 | 50 | 100 | 275 | 450 | 1,000 | 2,000 |

* Included in "1828, Both varieties" mintage.

## LIBERTY SEATED (1837–1891)

**G-4 Good**—LIBERTY on shield not readable. Date and letters legible.
**F-12 Fine**—LIBERTY visible, weak spots.
**VF-20 Very Fine**—LIBERTY strong and even.
**EF-40 Extremely Fine**—LIBERTY and scroll edges distinct.
**AU-50 About Uncirculated**—Wear on Liberty's shoulder and hair high points.
**MS-60 Uncirculated**—No trace of wear. Light blemishes.
**MS-63 Choice Uncirculated**—Some distracting contact marks or blemishes in prime focal areas. Impaired luster possible.

### Variety 1 – No Stars on Obverse (1837–1838)

*Designer Christian Gobrecht; weight 2.67 grams; composition .900 silver, .100 copper; diameter 17.9 mm; reeded edge; mints: Philadelphia, New Orleans.*

No Drapery From Elbow, No Stars on Obverse

*Mintmarks on Liberty Seated dimes on reverse, within or below the wreath. Size of mintmark varies on many dates.*

| | Mintage | G-4 | F-12 | VF-20 | EF-40 | AU-50 | MS-60 | MS-63 |
|---|---|---|---|---|---|---|---|---|
| 1837, All kinds. . . . . . . . . . | 682,500 | | | | | | | |
| 1837, Large Date . . . . . . . . . . . . | | $45 | $100 | $275 | $500 | $750 | $1,100 | $1,800 |
| 1837, Small Date. . . . . . . . . . . . . | | 50 | 120 | 325 | 500 | 750 | 1,200 | 2,000 |
| 1838O . . . . . . . . . . . . . . . . | 489,034 | 100 | 180 | 400 | 800 | 1,200 | 3,600 | 5,500 |

## Variety 2 – Stars on Obverse (1838–1853)

No Drapery From Elbow, Tilted Shield (1838–1840)

Drapery From Elbow, Upright Shield (1840–1891)

1838, Small Stars

1838, Large Stars

| | Mintage | G-4 | F-12 | VF-20 | EF-40 | AU-50 | MS-60 | MS-63 |
|---|---|---|---|---|---|---|---|---|
| 1838, All kinds. . . . . . . . . . . | 1,992,500 | | | | | | | |
| 1838, Small Stars . . . . . . . . . . . . . . | | $25 | $55 | $85 | $175 | $400 | $700 | $1,350 |
| 1838, Large Stars . . . . . . . . . . . . . . | | 30 | 40 | 48 | 150 | 300 | 500 | 850 |
| 1838, Partial Drapery . . . . . . . . . . . | | 30 | 60 | 100 | 200 | 500 | 850 | 1,500 |
| 1839, No Drapery . . . . . . . . | 1,053,115 | 20 | 30 | 48 | 145 | 300 | 475 | 850 |
| 1839O, No Drapery . . . . . . . | 1,291,600 | 25 | 75 | 145 | 240 | 425 | 800 | |
| 1840, No Drapery . . . . . . . . . . | 981,500 | 20 | 30 | 48 | 150 | 300 | 425 | 850 |
| 1840O, No Drapery . . . . . . . | 1,175,000 | 60 | 120 | 180 | 480 | 1,025 | 7,000 | 14,500 |
| 1840, Drapery . . . . . . . . . . . . . | 377,500 | 90 | 180 | 300 | 800 | 1,300 | 3,000 | 12,000 |
| 1841, Drapery . . . . . . . . . . . | 1,622,500 | 20 | 30 | 35 | 60 | 140 | 425 | 775 |
| 1841, No Drapery, Small Stars . . . . . . | | | | | | | | |
| 1841O . . . . . . . . . . . . . . . . . | 2,007,500 | 25 | 45 | 100 | 150 | 325 | 850 | 1,400 |
| 1842 . . . . . . . . . . . . . . . . . . | 1,887,500 | 20 | 30 | 35 | 50 | 125 | 400 | 650 |
| 1842O . . . . . . . . . . . . . . . . . | 2,020,000 | 35 | 90 | 175 | 475 | 1,500 | 2,750 | 5,000 |
| 1843 . . . . . . . . . . . . . . . . . . | 1,370,000 | 20 | 30 | 35 | 50 | 125 | 475 | 800 |
| 1843O . . . . . . . . . . . . . . . . . . | 150,000 | 175 | 600 | 1,350 | 3,500 | 11,000 | 70,000 | |
| 1844 . . . . . . . . . . . . . . . . . . . . | 72,500 | 150 | 375 | 600 | 1,000 | 1,750 | 4,000 | 11,500 |
| 1845 . . . . . . . . . . . . . . . . . . | 1,755,000 | 20 | 30 | 35 | 50 | 150 | 400 | 800 |
| 1845O . . . . . . . . . . . . . . . . . . | 230,000 | 90 | 240 | 550 | 1,000 | 3,000 | 12,000 | 24,000 |
| 1846 . . . . . . . . . . . . . . . . . . . . | 31,300 | 200 | 600 | 1,150 | 2,500 | 7,000 | 22,500 | 45,000 |
| 1847 . . . . . . . . . . . . . . . . . . . | 245,000 | 20 | 40 | 70 | 180 | 425 | 1,550 | 4,000 |
| 1848 . . . . . . . . . . . . . . . . . . . | 451,500 | 20 | 32 | 50 | 85 | 180 | 725 | 975 |
| 1849 . . . . . . . . . . . . . . . . . . . | 839,000 | 20 | 30 | 40 | 75 | 180 | 375 | 900 |
| 1849O . . . . . . . . . . . . . . . . . . | 300,000 | 25 | 75 | 150 | 375 | 950 | 2,500 | 5,500 |
| 1850 . . . . . . . . . . . . . . . . . . | 1,931,500 | 20 | 30 | 40 | 60 | 150 | 300 | 700 |
| 1850O . . . . . . . . . . . . . . . . . . | 510,000 | 25 | 100 | 120 | 300 | 900 | 2,000 | 3,600 |
| 1851 . . . . . . . . . . . . . . . . . . | 1,026,500 | 20 | 30 | 40 | 70 | 200 | 425 | 850 |
| 1851O . . . . . . . . . . . . . . . . . . | 400,000 | 25 | 40 | 120 | 300 | 1,000 | 2,500 | 3,750 |
| 1852 . . . . . . . . . . . . . . . . . . | 1,535,500 | 20 | 30 | 40 | 60 | 125 | 300 | 650 |
| 1852O . . . . . . . . . . . . . . . . . . | 430,000 | 30 | 90 | 180 | 325 | 550 | 1,800 | 3,600 |
| 1853, No Arrows . . . . . . . . . . . | 95,000 | 110 | 300 | 500 | 650 | 800 | 950 | 1,500 |

## Variety 3 – Arrows at Date (1853–1855)

*Weight 2.49 grams; composition .900 silver, .100 copper; diameter 17.9 mm; reeded edge; mints: Philadelphia, New Orleans.*

Arrows at Date (1853–1855) *Circulation strikes.* Small Date, Arrows Removed (1856–1860) *Proof strike.*

| | Mintage | G-4 | F-12 | VF-20 | EF-40 | AU-50 | MS-60 | MS-63 | PF-63 |
|---|---|---|---|---|---|---|---|---|---|
| 1853, With Arrows | 12,173,000 | $20 | $25 | $30 | $50 | $150 | $325 | $650 | $20,000 |
| 1853O | 1,100,000 | 25 | 85 | 125 | 300 | 650 | 2,000 | 4,500 | |
| 1854 | 4,470,000 | 20 | 25 | 30 | 50 | 175 | 325 | 675 | 8,500 |
| 1854O | 1,770,000 | 20 | 25 | 45 | 85 | 225 | 425 | 1,000 | |
| 1855 | 2,075,000 | 20 | 25 | 30 | 60 | 185 | 325 | 850 | 8,500 |

## Variety 2 Resumed, With Weight Standard of Variety 3 (1856–1860)

*Weight 2.49 grams; composition .900 silver, .100 copper; diameter 17.9 mm; reeded edge; mints: Philadelphia, New Orleans, San Francisco.*

| | Mintage | G-4 | F-12 | VF-20 | EF-40 | AU-50 | MS-60 | MS-63 | PF-63 |
|---|---|---|---|---|---|---|---|---|---|
| 1856, All kinds | 5,780,000 | | | | | | | | |
| 1856, Large Date | | $40 | $90 | $120 | $180 | $300 | $600 | $2,100 | |
| 1856, Small Date | | 16 | 20 | 30 | 60 | 145 | 300 | 550 | $3,500 |
| 1856O | 1,180,000 | 20 | 60 | 90 | 150 | 360 | 800 | 1,350 | |
| 1856S | 70,000 | 250 | 650 | 1,200 | 1,700 | 2,500 | 7,250 | 15,000 | |
| 1857 | 5,580,000 | 16 | 20 | 30 | 50 | 130 | 300 | 550 | 3,000 |
| 1857O | 1,540,000 | 18 | 25 | 35 | 70 | 200 | 425 | 750 | |
| 1858 *(300+)* | 1,540,000 | 16 | 20 | 30 | 50 | 130 | 300 | 550 | 1,750 |
| 1858O | 200,000 | 25 | 40 | 85 | 150 | 360 | 900 | 2,000 | |
| 1858S | 60,000 | 150 | 325 | 825 | 1,250 | 2,000 | 7,000 | 17,000 | |
| 1859 (800) | 429,200 | 20 | 22 | 32 | 60 | 140 | 300 | 650 | 1,250 |
| 1859O | 480,000 | 20 | 25 | 60 | 95 | 275 | 400 | 850 | |
| 1859S | 60,000 | 250 | 475 | 1,050 | 2,750 | 5,500 | 18,000 | 30,000 | |
| 1860S | 140,000 | 60 | 150 | 300 | 480 | 950 | 2,500 | 8,100 | |

In 1859 (see the first row of the chart below), an interesting dime pattern was made that does not bear the nation's identity. It is a "transitional" piece, not made for circulation, but struck at the time the inscription UNITED STATES OF AMERICA was being transferred from the reverse to the obverse.

## Variety 4 – Legend on Obverse (1860–1873)

*Weight 2.49 grams; composition .900 silver, .100 copper; diameter 17.9 mm; reeded edge; mints: Philadelphia, New Orleans, San Francisco, Carson City.*

1873, Close 3

1873, Open 3

| | Mintage | G-4 | F-12 | VF-20 | EF-40 | AU-50 | MS-60 | MS-63 | PF-63 |
|---|---|---|---|---|---|---|---|---|---|
| 1859, Obv of 1859 (With Stars), Rev of 1860 | *20+* | | | | | | $10,000 | | $15,000 |

| | Mintage | G-4 | F-12 | VF-20 | EF-40 | AU-50 | MS-60 | MS-63 | PF-63 |
|---|---|---|---|---|---|---|---|---|---|
| 1860 | (1,000) . . . 606,000 | $16 | $20 | $32 | $40 | $100 | $200 | $325 | $600 |
| 1860O | 40,000 | 650 | 1,500 | 2,500 | 5,000 | 8,500 | 18,000 | 35,000 | |
| 1861 **(a)** | (1,000) . . 1,883,000 | 16 | 22 | 30 | 40 | 100 | 200 | 325 | 650 |
| 1861S | 172,500 | 165 | 425 | 650 | 900 | 1,200 | 5,500 | 18,000 | |
| 1862 | (550) . . . 847,000 | 16 | 25 | 30 | 40 | 100 | 185 | 350 | 650 |
| 1862S | 180,750 | 150 | 300 | 550 | 1,000 | 2,400 | 4,250 | 9,000 | |
| 1863 | (460) . . . . 14,000 | 750 | 1,050 | 1,150 | 1,200 | 1,300 | 1,500 | 2,400 | 600 |
| 1863S | 157,500 | 120 | 300 | 480 | 900 | 1,200 | 3,600 | 9,500 | |
| 1864 | (470) . . . . 11,000 | 300 | 650 | 925 | 1,000 | 1,150 | 1,200 | 2,150 | 600 |
| 1864S | 230,000 | 120 | 240 | 360 | 800 | 1,000 | 1,300 | 2,000 | |
| 1865 | (500) . . . . 10,000 | 425 | 750 | 900 | 1,000 | 1,150 | 1,300 | 2,100 | 650 |
| 1865S | 175,000 | 120 | 360 | 725 | 1,200 | 3,000 | 7,000 | 16,500 | |
| 1866 | (725) . . . . . 8,000 | 750 | 1,100 | 1,250 | 1,400 | 1,750 | 1,850 | 2,500 | 600 |
| 1866S | 135,000 | 120 | 240 | 425 | 625 | 1,500 | 3,500 | 6,500 | |
| 1867 | (625) . . . . . 6,000 | 600 | 925 | 1,200 | 1,300 | 1,400 | 1,500 | 2,000 | 600 |
| 1867S | 140,000 | 120 | 240 | 400 | 725 | 1,550 | 2,000 | 5,000 | |
| 1868 | (600) . . . 464,000 | 18 | 30 | 40 | 65 | 150 | 300 | 850 | 600 |
| 1868S | 260,000 | 60 | 150 | 250 | 550 | 650 | 1,000 | 1,500 | |
| 1869 | (600) . . . 256,000 | 22 | 40 | 85 | 150 | 200 | 400 | 900 | 600 |
| 1869S | 450,000 | 18 | 25 | 50 | 225 | 250 | 450 | 800 | |
| 1870 | (1,000) . . . 470,500 | 16 | 25 | 30 | 50 | 100 | 225 | 450 | 600 |
| 1870S | 50,000 | 250 | 575 | 725 | 900 | 1,200 | 1,800 | 2,750 | |
| 1871 | (960) . . . 906,750 | 16 | 25 | 30 | 50 | 150 | 250 | 425 | 600 |
| 1871CC | 20,100 | 2,500 | 5,000 | 7,000 | 14,500 | 22,500 | 45,000 | 125,000 | |
| 1871S | 320,000 | 25 | 120 | 180 | 325 | 750 | 1,600 | 3,600 | |
| 1872 | (950) . . 2,395,500 | 18 | 25 | 30 | 40 | 90 | 175 | 300 | 600 |
| 1872, DblDie Rev *(rare)* | * | 100 | 350 | 550 | 850 | 1,500 | 1,750 | | |
| 1872CC | 35,480 | 1,450 | 3,000 | 4,500 | 11,500 | 16,000 | 65,000 | 200,000 | |
| 1872S | 190,000 | 25 | 120 | 180 | 325 | 500 | 1,800 | 3,500 | |
| 1873, Close 3 | (600) . . *1,507,400* | 16 | 30 | 48 | 70 | 120 | 240 | 480 | 600 |
| 1873, Open 3 | *60,000* | 20 | 50 | 75 | 130 | 200 | 600 | 1,500 | |
| 1873CC *(unique)* **(b)** | 12,400 | | | | | | | *3,000,000* **(c)** | |
| *$1,840,000, MS-65, Stack's Bowers auction, August 2012* | | | | | | | | | |

* Included in number above. **a.** Dies modified slightly during 1861. First variety with only five vertical lines in top of shield is scarcer than the later variety. **b.** Most of the mintage was melted after the law of 1873 was passed. **c.** Value is for MS-65.

## Variety 5 – Arrows at Date (1873–1874)

In 1873 the dime was increased in weight to 2.50 grams. Arrows at the date in 1873 and 1874 indicate this change.

*Weight 2.50 grams; composition .900 silver, .100 copper; diameter 17.9 mm; reeded edge; mints: Philadelphia, San Francisco, Carson City.*

*Circulation strike.*

*Proof strike.*

| | Mintage | G-4 | F-12 | VF-20 | EF-40 | AU-50 | MS-60 | MS-63 | PF-63 |
|---|---|---|---|---|---|---|---|---|---|
| 1873 | (500) . . 2,337,700 | $18 | $25 | $55 | $150 | $300 | $550 | $900 | $850 |
| 1873, Doubled Die Obverse | * | 500 | 1,200 | 1,700 | 3,300 | 7,500 | 20,000 | | |

* Included in number above.

*Chart continued on next page.*

| | Mintage | G-4 | F-12 | VF-20 | EF-40 | AU-50 | MS-60 | MS-63 | PF-63 |
|---|---|---|---|---|---|---|---|---|---|
| 1873CC | *18,791* | $2,850 | $5,000 | $7,250 | $14,000 | $42,500 | $57,500 | $150,000 | |
| 1873S | 455,000 | 22 | 35 | 60 | 175 | 450 | 1,000 | 2,000 | |
| 1874 | (700) . . 2,940,000 | 18 | 25 | 55 | 150 | 310 | 600 | 1,000 | $850 |
| 1874CC | 10,817 | 8,000 | 15,000 | 20,000 | 32,500 | 45,000 | 100,000 | 150,000 | |
| 1874S | 240,000 | 25 | 65 | 110 | 225 | 500 | 900 | 2,000 | |

## Variety 4 Resumed, With Weight Standard of Variety 5 (1875–1891)

*Weight 2.50 grams; composition .900 silver, .100 copper; diameter 17.9 mm; reeded edge; mints: Philadelphia, New Orleans, San Francisco, Carson City.*

| | Mintage | G-4 | F-12 | VF-20 | EF-40 | AU-50 | MS-60 | MS-63 | PF-63 |
|---|---|---|---|---|---|---|---|---|---|
| 1875 | (700) . . 10,350,000 | $15 | $20 | $25 | $35 | $80 | $150 | $250 | $600 |
| 1875CC, All kinds | 4,645,000 | | | | | | | | |
| 1875CC, Above Bow | | 45 | 75 | 95 | 145 | 220 | 400 | 950 | |
| 1875CC, Below Bow | | 60 | 95 | 165 | 250 | 315 | 550 | 1,550 | |
| 1875S, All kinds | 9,070,000 | | | | | | | | |
| 1875S, Below Bow | | 15 | 20 | 25 | 40 | 95 | 175 | 285 | |
| 1875S, Above Bow | | 15 | 20 | 25 | 35 | 85 | 160 | 275 | |
| 1876 | (1,250) . . 11,460,000 | 15 | 20 | 25 | 35 | 80 | 150 | 250 | 600 |
| 1876CC | 8,270,000 | 30 | 50 | 70 | 100 | 150 | 350 | 700 | |
| 1876S | 10,420,000 | 15 | 20 | 25 | 35 | 80 | 150 | 250 | |
| 1877 | (510) . . . 7,310,000 | 15 | 20 | 25 | 35 | 80 | 150 | 250 | 600 |
| 1877CC | 7,700,000 | 30 | 45 | 60 | 90 | 130 | 280 | 650 | |
| 1877S | 2,340,000 | 15 | 20 | 25 | 35 | 80 | 150 | 300 | |
| 1878 | (800) . . . 1,677,200 | 15 | 20 | 25 | 35 | 80 | 150 | 250 | 600 |
| 1878CC | 200,000 | 160 | 300 | 330 | 475 | 900 | 1,350 | 2,500 | |
| 1879 | (1,100) . . . . . 14,000 | 200 | 325 | 400 | 500 | 550 | 575 | 650 | 600 |
| 1880 | (1,355) . . . . . 36,000 | 150 | 250 | 350 | 400 | 500 | 650 | 700 | 600 |
| 1881 | (975) . . . . . 24,000 | 160 | 260 | 375 | 425 | 525 | 675 | 775 | 600 |
| 1882 | (1,100) . . . 3,910,000 | 15 | 20 | 25 | 35 | 80 | 150 | 250 | 600 |
| 1883 | (1,039) . . . 7,674,673 | 15 | 20 | 25 | 35 | 80 | 150 | 250 | 600 |
| 1884 | (875) . . . 3,365,505 | 15 | 20 | 25 | 35 | 80 | 150 | 250 | 600 |
| 1884S | 564,969 | 20 | 32 | 60 | 100 | 300 | 750 | 1,100 | |
| 1885 | (930) . . . 2,532,497 | 15 | 20 | 25 | 35 | 80 | 150 | 250 | 600 |
| 1885S | 43,690 | 550 | 1,000 | 1,400 | 2,250 | 4,000 | 5,500 | 8,500 | |
| 1886 | (886) . . . 6,376,684 | 15 | 20 | 25 | 35 | 80 | 150 | 250 | 600 |
| 1886S | 206,524 | 30 | 50 | 75 | 135 | 200 | 550 | 1,000 | |
| 1887 | (710) . . 11,283,229 | 15 | 20 | 25 | 35 | 80 | 150 | 250 | 600 |
| 1887S | 4,454,450 | 15 | 20 | 25 | 35 | 80 | 150 | 300 | |
| 1888 | (832) . . . 5,495,655 | 15 | 20 | 25 | 35 | 80 | 150 | 250 | 600 |
| 1888S | 1,720,000 | 15 | 20 | 25 | 35 | 100 | 250 | 850 | |
| 1889 | (711) . . . 7,380,000 | 15 | 20 | 25 | 35 | 80 | 150 | 250 | 600 |
| 1889S | 972,678 | 20 | 30 | 50 | 80 | 150 | 450 | 1,000 | |
| 1890 | (590) . . . 9,910,951 | 15 | 20 | 25 | 35 | 80 | 150 | 250 | 600 |
| 1890S, Large S | 1,423,076 | 18 | 25 | 55 | 85 | 150 | 350 | 700 | |
| 1890S, Small S *(rare)* | * | | | | — | — | — | | |
| 1891 | (600) . . 15,310,000 | 15 | 20 | 25 | 35 | 80 | 150 | 250 | 600 |
| 1891O | 4,540,000 | 15 | 20 | 30 | 50 | 100 | 175 | 350 | |
| 1891O, O Over Horizontal O | * | 60 | 120 | 150 | 225 | 1,000 | 3,000 | | |
| 1891S | 3,196,116 | 15 | 20 | 25 | 35 | 80 | 175 | 300 | |

* Included in number above.

## BARBER OR LIBERTY HEAD (1892–1916)

Designed by Charles E. Barber, chief engraver of the Mint, who also designed the twenty-five- and fifty-cent pieces. His initial B is at the truncation of the neck.

*Designer Charles E. Barber; weight 2.50 grams; composition .900 silver, .100 copper (net weight: .07234 oz. pure silver); diameter 17.9 mm; reeded edge; mints: Philadelphia, Denver, New Orleans, San Francisco.*

**G-4 Good**—Date and letters plain. LIBERTY obliterated.
**VG-8 Very Good**—Some letters visible in LIBERTY.
**F-12 Fine**—Letters in LIBERTY visible, though some weak.
**VF-20 Very Fine**—Letters of LIBERTY evenly plain.
**EF-40 Extremely Fine**—All letters in LIBERTY sharp, distinct. Headband edges distinct.
**AU-50 About Uncirculated**—Slight traces of wear on hair and cheekbone, and on leaf tips in wreath.
**MS-60 Uncirculated**—No trace of wear. Light blemishes.
**MS-63 Choice Uncirculated**—Some distracting marks or blemishes in prime focal areas. Impaired luster possible.

*Circulation strike.*

*Proof strike.*

***Mintmark location is on reverse, below wreath.***

| | Mintage | G-4 | VG-8 | F-12 | VF-20 | EF-40 | AU-50 | MS-60 | MS-63 | PF-63 |
|---|---|---|---|---|---|---|---|---|---|---|
| 1892 (1,245) | 12,120,000 | $7.00 | $7.50 | $18 | $25 | $30 | $75 | $125 | $185 | $500 |
| 1892O | 3,841,700 | 12.00 | 15.00 | 35 | 55 | 75 | 95 | 175 | 350 | |
| 1892S | 990,710 | 65.00 | 115.00 | 200 | 240 | 280 | 330 | 425 | 775 | |
| 1893, "3 Over 2" **(a)** | * | 140.00 | 155.00 | 200 | 250 | 350 | 650 | 1,350 | 1,800 | — |
| 1893 (792) | 3,339,940 | 8.00 | 12.00 | 20 | 30 | 45 | 80 | 150 | 250 | 500 |
| 1893O | 1,760,000 | 30.00 | 45.00 | 120 | 150 | 190 | 230 | 325 | 500 | |
| 1893S **(b)** | 2,491,401 | 15.00 | 25.00 | 40 | 60 | 90 | 150 | 325 | 750 | |
| 1894 (972) | 1,330,000 | 30.00 | 45.00 | 120 | 160 | 180 | 220 | 300 | 400 | 500 |
| 1894O | 720,000 | 70.00 | 95.00 | 220 | 300 | 425 | 750 | 1,950 | 3,000 | |
| 1894S | 24 **(c)** | | | | | | | | | *1,500,000* |
| *$1,997,500, PF-66, Heritage auction, January 2016* | | | | | | | | | | |
| 1895 (880) | 690,000 | 80.00 | 160.00 | 350 | 500 | 550 | 650 | 725 | 900 | 500 |
| 1895O | 440,000 | 475.00 | 600.00 | 900 | 1,350 | 2,500 | 3,500 | 6,000 | 11,000 | |
| 1895S | 1,120,000 | 42.00 | 60.00 | 135 | 190 | 240 | 325 | 500 | 1,050 | |
| 1896 (762) | 2,000,000 | 10.00 | 22.00 | 50 | 75 | 100 | 125 | 175 | 375 | 500 |
| 1896O | 610,000 | 80.00 | 160.00 | 290 | 375 | 475 | 800 | 1,200 | 2,400 | |
| 1896S | 575,056 | 80.00 | 175.00 | 280 | 350 | 400 | 550 | 750 | 1,350 | |
| 1897 (731) | 10,868,533 | 4.00 | 5.00 | 8 | 15 | 32 | 75 | 135 | 200 | 500 |
| 1897O | 666,000 | 65.00 | 115.00 | 300 | 375 | 475 | 600 | 1,100 | 1,500 | |
| 1897S | 1,342,844 | 18.00 | 40.00 | 100 | 120 | 175 | 300 | 500 | 800 | |
| 1898 (735) | 16,320,000 | 4.00 | 5.00 | 8 | 12 | 26 | 75 | 130 | 200 | 500 |
| 1898O | 2,130,000 | 12.00 | 30.00 | 90 | 150 | 200 | 300 | 475 | 1,050 | |
| 1898S | 1,702,507 | 8.00 | 15.00 | 32 | 45 | 80 | 150 | 500 | 1,200 | |
| 1899 (846) | 19,580,000 | 4.00 | 5.00 | 8 | 12 | 25 | 75 | 130 | 200 | 500 |
| 1899O | 2,650,000 | 10.00 | 20.00 | 75 | 100 | 150 | 225 | 400 | 900 | |
| 1899S | 1,867,493 | 8.50 | 16.00 | 32 | 35 | 45 | 110 | 300 | 650 | |
| 1900 (912) | 17,600,000 | 4.00 | 5.00 | 8 | 12 | 25 | 75 | 125 | 225 | 500 |
| 1900O | 2,010,000 | 18.00 | 38.00 | 115 | 160 | 220 | 350 | 650 | 1,000 | |
| 1900S | 5,168,270 | 5.00 | 6.00 | 12 | 20 | 30 | 75 | 175 | 375 | |
| 1901 (813) | 18,859,665 | 4.00 | 5.00 | 7 | 10 | 26 | 75 | 125 | 225 | 500 |

* Included in number below. **a.** Overlaid photographs indicate this is not a true overdate. **b.** Boldly doubled mintmark variety is valued slightly higher. **c.** Five of these were reserved for assay.

*Chart continued on next page.*

1905-O, Normal O

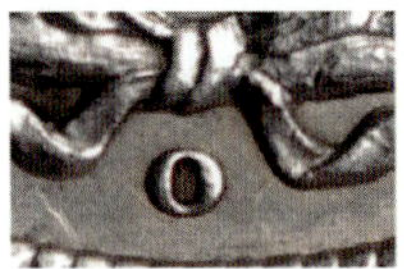
1905-O, Micro O

| | Mintage | G-4 | VG-8 | F-12 | VF-20 | EF-40 | AU-50 | MS-60 | MS-63 | PF-63 |
|---|---|---|---|---|---|---|---|---|---|---|
| 1901O | 5,620,000 | $4 | $5.50 | $16 | $28 | $75 | $180 | $600 | $1,100 | |
| 1901S | 593,022 | 80 | 135.00 | 375 | 500 | 550 | 750 | 1,300 | 2,100 | |
| 1902 | (777). .21,380,000 | 4 | 5.00 | 6 | 8 | 25 | 75 | 125 | 225 | $500 |
| 1902O | 4,500,000 | 4 | 6.00 | 15 | 32 | 65 | 175 | 425 | 750 | |
| 1902S | 2,070,000 | 9 | 20.00 | 55 | 80 | 140 | 200 | 400 | 750 | |
| 1903 | (755). .19,500,000 | 4 | 5.00 | 6 | 8 | 25 | 75 | 125 | 225 | 500 |
| 1903O | 8,180,000 | 5 | 6.00 | 14 | 25 | 55 | 110 | 275 | 550 | |
| 1903S | 613,300 | 85 | 130.00 | 375 | 500 | 675 | 825 | 1,100 | 1,350 | |
| 1904 | (670). .14,600,357 | 4 | 5.00 | 6 | 9 | 25 | 75 | 125 | 240 | 500 |
| 1904S | 800,000 | 45 | 75.00 | 160 | 250 | 325 | 500 | 850 | 1,800 | |
| 1905 | (727). .14,551,623 | 4 | 5.00 | 6 | 10 | 25 | 75 | 125 | 240 | 500 |
| 1905O | 3,400,000 | 5 | 10.00 | 35 | 60 | 100 | 150 | 300 | 425 | |
| 1905O, Micro O **(a)** | * | 60 | 90.00 | 150 | 300 | 725 | 1,150 | 2,700 | 5,500 | |
| 1905S | 6,855,199 | 4 | 6.00 | 9 | 20 | 40 | 95 | 250 | 325 | |
| 1906 | (675). .19,957,731 | 4 | 5.00 | 6 | 10 | 25 | 75 | 125 | 200 | 500 |
| 1906D | 4,060,000 | 4 | 5.00 | 8 | 15 | 35 | 80 | 175 | 350 | |
| 1906O | 2,610,000 | 6 | 14.00 | 45 | 75 | 110 | 130 | 200 | 380 | |
| 1906S | 3,136,640 | 4 | 6.00 | 13 | 25 | 45 | 130 | 275 | 450 | |
| 1907 | (575). .22,220,000 | 4 | 5.00 | 6 | 10 | 25 | 55 | 125 | 190 | 500 |
| 1907D | 4,080,000 | 4 | 5.00 | 10 | 20 | 45 | 110 | 250 | 700 | |
| 1907O | 5,058,000 | 4 | 7.00 | 30 | 45 | 70 | 110 | 200 | 325 | |
| 1907S | 3,178,470 | 4 | 6.00 | 15 | 27 | 75 | 150 | 400 | 700 | |
| 1908 | (545). .10,600,000 | 4 | 5.00 | 6 | 10 | 25 | 75 | 125 | 225 | 500 |
| 1908D | 7,490,000 | 4 | 5.00 | 6 | 10 | 30 | 75 | 130 | 300 | |
| 1908O | 1,789,000 | 6 | 12.00 | 45 | 65 | 95 | 150 | 300 | 650 | |
| 1908S | 3,220,000 | 4 | 6.00 | 15 | 25 | 45 | 170 | 350 | 650 | |
| 1909 | (650). .10,240,000 | 4 | 5.00 | 6 | 10 | 25 | 75 | 125 | 225 | 500 |
| 1909D | 954,000 | 8 | 20.00 | 60 | 90 | 140 | 225 | 500 | 800 | |
| 1909O | 2,287,000 | 5 | 8.00 | 13 | 25 | 70 | 160 | 275 | 600 | |
| 1909S | 1,000,000 | 9 | 20.00 | 80 | 130 | 180 | 310 | 450 | 975 | |
| 1910 | (551). .11,520,000 | 4 | 5.00 | 6 | 10 | 24 | 75 | 125 | 225 | 500 |
| 1910D | 3,490,000 | 4 | 5.00 | 10 | 20 | 48 | 95 | 220 | 375 | |
| 1910S | 1,240,000 | 6 | 9.00 | 50 | 70 | 110 | 180 | 425 | 600 | |
| 1911 | (543). .18,870,000 | 4 | 5.00 | 6 | 10 | 24 | 75 | 125 | 225 | 500 |
| 1911D | 11,209,000 | 4 | 5.00 | 6 | 10 | 24 | 75 | 125 | 225 | |
| 1911S | 3,520,000 | 4 | 5.00 | 10 | 20 | 40 | 100 | 200 | 375 | |
| 1912 | (700). .19,349,300 | 4 | 5.00 | 6 | 10 | 24 | 75 | 125 | 225 | 500 |
| 1912D | 11,760,000 | 4 | 5.00 | 6 | 10 | 24 | 75 | 125 | 225 | |
| 1912S | 3,420,000 | 4 | 5.00 | 6 | 12 | 32 | 90 | 170 | 300 | |
| 1913 | (622). .19,760,000 | 4 | 5.00 | 6 | 10 | 24 | 75 | 125 | 225 | 500 |
| 1913S | 510,000 | 35 | 55.00 | 125 | 190 | 250 | 325 | 725 | 1,200 | |
| 1914 | (425). .17,360,230 | 4 | 5.00 | 6 | 10 | 24 | 75 | 125 | 200 | 500 |
| 1914D | 11,908,000 | 4 | 5.00 | 6 | 10 | 24 | 75 | 125 | 200 | |
| 1914S | 2,100,000 | 4 | 5.00 | 10 | 18 | 40 | 80 | 125 | 250 | |
| 1915 | (450). . .5,620,000 | 4 | 5.00 | 6 | 10 | 24 | 75 | 125 | 225 | 500 |
| 1915S | 960,000 | 7 | 12.00 | 35 | 50 | 70 | 140 | 275 | 400 | |
| 1916 | 18,490,000 | 4 | 5.00 | 6 | 10 | 24 | 75 | 125 | 225 | |
| 1916S | 5,820,000 | 4 | 5.00 | 6 | 10 | 24 | 75 | 125 | 240 | |

* Included in number above. **a.** Normal and "microscopic" mintmark varieties; see page 22.

## WINGED LIBERTY HEAD OR "MERCURY" (1916–1945)

Although this coin is commonly called the *Mercury dime,* the main device is in fact a representation of Liberty. The wings crowning her cap are intended to symbolize liberty of thought. The designer's monogram AW is to the right of the neck. The Mint also created a 2016 gold Mercury dime at a smaller dimension. See page 167.

*Designer Adolph A. Weinman; weight 2.50 grams; composition .900 silver, .100 copper (net weight: .07234 oz. pure silver); diameter 17.9 mm; reeded edge; mints: Philadelphia, Denver, San Francisco.*

**G-4 Good**—Letters and date clear. Lines and bands in fasces obliterated.
**VG-8 Very Good**—Half of sticks discernible in fasces.
**F-12 Fine**—All sticks in fasces defined. Diagonal bands worn nearly flat.
**VF-20 Very Fine**—Diagonal bands definitely visible.
**EF-40 Extremely Fine**—Only slight wear on diagonal bands. Braids and hair before ear clearly visible.
**AU-50 About Uncirculated**—Slight trace of wear. Most mint luster present.
**MS-63 Choice Uncirculated**—No trace of wear. Light blemishes. Attractive mint luster.
**MS-65 Gem Uncirculated**—Only light, scattered marks that are not distracting. Strong luster, good eye appeal.

*Circulation strike.*

*Proof strike.*

***Mintmark location is on reverse, left of fasces.***

*Uncirculated values shown are for average pieces with minimum blemishes; those with sharp strikes and split horizontal bands on reverse are worth much more.*

| | Mintage | G-4 | VG-8 | F-12 | VF-20 | EF-40 | AU-50 | MS-60 | MS-63 | MS-65 |
|---|---|---|---|---|---|---|---|---|---|---|
| 1916 | 22,180,080 | $4.00 | $5.00 | $7.00 | $8 | $15 | $25 | $35 | $48 | $150 |
| 1916D | 264,000 | 800.00 | 1,500.00 | 2,500.00 | 4,000 | 6,000 | 8,250 | 12,500 | 16,000 | 25,000 |
| 1916S | 10,450,000 | 4.00 | 6.00 | 9.00 | 12 | 20 | 25 | 42 | 65 | 215 |
| 1917 | 55,230,000 | 3.00 | 3.25 | 3.50 | 6 | 8 | 12 | 30 | 60 | 170 |
| 1917D | 9,402,000 | 4.50 | 6.00 | 11.00 | 22 | 45 | 95 | 145 | 350 | 900 |
| 1917S | 27,330,000 | 3.00 | 3.25 | 4.00 | 7 | 12 | 30 | 60 | 180 | 425 |
| 1918 | 26,680,000 | 3.00 | 4.00 | 6.00 | 12 | 25 | 40 | 70 | 125 | 350 |
| 1918D | 22,674,800 | 3.00 | 4.00 | 6.00 | 12 | 24 | 50 | 125 | 250 | 800 |
| 1918S | 19,300,000 | 3.00 | 3.25 | 5.00 | 10 | 18 | 40 | 120 | 275 | 725 |
| 1919 | 35,740,000 | 3.00 | 3.25 | 4.00 | 6 | 10 | 30 | 45 | 150 | 350 |
| 1919D | 9,939,000 | 4.00 | 7.00 | 12.00 | 24 | 35 | 75 | 200 | 450 | 1,350 |
| 1919S | 8,850,000 | 3.50 | 4.00 | 8.00 | 16 | 35 | 75 | 200 | 450 | 1,500 |
| 1920 | 59,030,000 | 3.00 | 3.25 | 3.50 | 5 | 8 | 15 | 35 | 75 | 250 |
| 1920D | 19,171,000 | 3.00 | 3.50 | 4.50 | 8 | 20 | 45 | 145 | 350 | 625 |
| 1920S | 13,820,000 | 3.25 | 4.00 | 5.00 | 8 | 18 | 45 | 145 | 325 | 1,300 |
| 1921 | 1,230,000 | 45.00 | 75.00 | 125.00 | 250 | 550 | 850 | 1,250 | 2,250 | 3,250 |
| 1921D | 1,080,000 | 60.00 | 130.00 | 200.00 | 350 | 675 | 1,200 | 1,450 | 2,500 | 3,500 |
| 1923 **(a)** | 50,130,000 | 3.00 | 3.25 | 3.50 | 5 | 7 | 16 | 30 | 45 | 130 |
| 1923S | 6,440,000 | 3.00 | 4.00 | 8.00 | 18 | 65 | 105 | 160 | 400 | 1,250 |
| 1924 | 24,010,000 | 3.00 | 3.25 | 4.00 | 6 | 15 | 30 | 45 | 100 | 175 |
| 1924D | 6,810,000 | 3.50 | 4.50 | 8.00 | 24 | 70 | 110 | 175 | 500 | 950 |
| 1924S | 7,120,000 | 3.50 | 4.00 | 6.00 | 10 | 60 | 110 | 200 | 525 | 1,250 |
| 1925 | 25,610,000 | 3.00 | 3.25 | 4.00 | 5 | 10 | 20 | 30 | 85 | 250 |
| 1925D | 5,117,000 | 4.00 | 5.00 | 12.00 | 45 | 120 | 200 | 375 | 750 | 1,700 |
| 1925S | 5,850,000 | 3.25 | 4.00 | 8.00 | 18 | 70 | 110 | 180 | 500 | 1,250 |
| 1926 | 32,160,000 | 3.00 | 3.25 | 3.50 | 5 | 7 | 16 | 25 | 65 | 250 |
| 1926D | 6,828,000 | 3.25 | 4.50 | 6.00 | 10 | 28 | 50 | 125 | 275 | 500 |
| 1926S | 1,520,000 | 13.00 | 15.00 | 26.00 | 60 | 250 | 450 | 1,100 | 1,750 | 3,500 |

**a.** Dimes dated 1923-D or 1930-D are counterfeit.

*Chart continued on next page.*

| | Mintage | G-4 | VG-8 | F-12 | VF-20 | EF-40 | AU-50 | MS-60 | MS-63 | MS-65 |
|---|---|---|---|---|---|---|---|---|---|---|
| 1927 | 28,080,000 | $3.00 | $3.25 | $3.50 | $5 | $7 | $15 | $30 | $60 | $150 |
| 1927D | 4,812,000 | 3.50 | 5.50 | 8.00 | 25 | 80 | 100 | 200 | 400 | 1,200 |
| 1927S | 4,770,000 | 3.25 | 4.00 | 6.00 | 12 | 28 | 50 | 275 | 550 | 1,400 |
| 1928 | 19,480,000 | 3.00 | 3.25 | 3.50 | 5 | 7 | 18 | 30 | 55 | 130 |
| 1928D | 4,161,000 | 4.00 | 5.00 | 8.00 | 20 | 50 | 95 | 175 | 360 | 850 |
| 1928S **(b)** | 7,400,000 | 3.00 | 3.25 | 4.00 | 6 | 16 | 45 | 150 | 320 | 425 |
| 1929 | 25,970,000 | 3.00 | 3.25 | 3.50 | 5 | 6 | 12 | 22 | 35 | 75 |
| 1929D | 5,034,000 | 3.00 | 3.50 | 5.00 | 8 | 15 | 24 | 30 | 36 | 75 |
| 1929S | 4,730,000 | 3.00 | 3.25 | 3.75 | 5 | 10 | 20 | 35 | 45 | 125 |
| 1930 **(a)** | 6,770,000 | 3.00 | 3.25 | 3.50 | 5 | 8 | 16 | 30 | 50 | 125 |
| 1930S | 1,843,000 | 3.00 | 4.00 | 5.00 | 7 | 15 | 45 | 80 | 150 | 210 |
| 1931 | 3,150,000 | 3.00 | 3.10 | 4.00 | 6 | 10 | 22 | 35 | 70 | 150 |
| 1931D | 1,260,000 | 8.00 | 9.00 | 12.00 | 20 | 35 | 60 | 90 | 140 | 300 |
| 1931S | 1,800,000 | 4.00 | 5.00 | 6.00 | 10 | 16 | 45 | 90 | 150 | 275 |

**a.** Dimes dated 1923-D or 1930-D are counterfeit. **b.** Large and small mintmarks; see page 22.

**1942, 42 Over 41**

**1942-D, 42 Over 41**

| | Mintage | F-12 | VF-20 | EF-40 | MS-60 | MS-63 | MS-65 | PF-65 |
|---|---|---|---|---|---|---|---|---|
| 1934 | 24,080,000 | $2.75 | $3 | $3.25 | $25 | $35 | $50 | |
| 1934D **(b)** | 6,772,000 | 2.75 | 3 | 8.00 | 50 | 60 | 85 | |
| 1935 | 58,830,000 | 2.75 | 3 | 3.25 | 10 | 15 | 35 | |
| 1935D | 10,477,000 | 2.75 | 3 | 8.00 | 35 | 50 | 90 | |
| 1935S | 15,840,000 | 2.75 | 3 | 5.00 | 22 | 30 | 40 | |
| 1936 (4,130) | 87,500,000 | 2.75 | 3 | 3.25 | 10 | 18 | 30 | $1,050 |
| 1936D | 16,132,000 | 2.75 | 3 | 6.00 | 25 | 40 | 55 | |
| 1936S | 9,210,000 | 2.75 | 3 | 3.25 | 23 | 30 | 38 | |
| 1937 (5,756) | 56,860,000 | 2.75 | 3 | 3.25 | 10 | 15 | 30 | 525 |
| 1937D | 14,146,000 | 2.75 | 3 | 4.00 | 21 | 30 | 45 | |
| 1937S | 9,740,000 | 2.75 | 3 | 3.25 | 20 | 30 | 40 | |
| 1938 (8,728) | 22,190,000 | 2.75 | 3 | 3.25 | 10 | 15 | 30 | 300 |
| 1938D | 5,537,000 | 2.75 | 3 | 4.00 | 18 | 25 | 35 | |
| 1938S | 8,090,000 | 2.75 | 3 | 3.50 | 20 | 28 | 42 | |
| 1939 (9,321) | 67,740,000 | 2.75 | 3 | 3.25 | 8 | 12 | 26 | 225 |
| 1939D | 24,394,000 | 2.75 | 3 | 3.25 | 8 | 12 | 32 | |
| 1939S | 10,540,000 | 2.75 | 3 | 4.00 | 23 | 30 | 42 | |
| 1940 (11,827) | 65,350,000 | 2.75 | 3 | 3.25 | 7 | 12 | 30 | 180 |
| 1940D | 21,198,000 | 2.75 | 3 | 3.25 | 7 | 14 | 35 | |
| 1940S | 21,560,000 | 2.75 | 3 | 3.25 | 8 | 15 | 35 | |
| 1941 (16,557) | 175,090,000 | 2.75 | 3 | 3.25 | 7 | 12 | 30 | 175 |
| 1941D | 45,634,000 | 2.75 | 3 | 3.25 | 8 | 14 | 25 | |
| 1941S **(b)** | 43,090,000 | 2.75 | 3 | 3.25 | 7 | 12 | 30 | |
| 1942, 42 Over 41 | * | 450 | 550 | 650.00 | 2,500 | 4,750 | 15,000 | |
| 1942 (22,329) | 205,410,000 | 2.75 | 3 | 3.25 | 6 | 12 | 30 | 175 |
| 1942D, 42 Over 41 | * | 425 | 525 | 600.00 | 2,500 | 4,750 | 10,000 | |
| 1942D | 60,740,000 | 2.75 | 3 | 3.25 | 6 | 12 | 28 | |

* Included in number below. **b.** Large and small mintmarks; see page 22.

1945-S, Normal S

1945-S, Micro S

| | Mintage | F-12 | VF-20 | EF-40 | MS-60 | MS-63 | MS-65 | PF-65 |
|---|---|---|---|---|---|---|---|---|
| 1942S | 49,300,000 | $2.75 | $3.00 | $3.25 | $8 | $20 | $30 | |
| 1943 | 191,710,000 | 2.75 | 3.00 | 3.25 | 6 | 12 | 27 | |
| 1943D | 71,949,000 | 2.75 | 3.00 | 3.25 | 6 | 15 | 30 | |
| 1943S | 60,400,000 | 2.75 | 3.00 | 3.25 | 7 | 16 | 30 | |
| 1944 | 231,410,000 | 2.75 | 3.00 | 3.25 | 6 | 12 | 25 | |
| 1944D | 62,224,000 | 2.75 | 3.00 | 3.25 | 7 | 15 | 30 | |
| 1944S | 49,490,000 | 2.75 | 3.00 | 3.25 | 7 | 15 | 30 | |
| 1945 | 159,130,000 | 2.75 | 3.00 | 3.25 | 6 | 12 | 30 | |
| 1945D | 40,245,000 | 2.75 | 3.00 | 3.25 | 6 | 12 | 26 | |
| 1945S | 41,920,000 | 2.75 | 3.00 | 3.25 | 6 | 12 | 30 | |
| 1945S, Micro S | * | 3.25 | 3.50 | 6.00 | 30 | 40 | 100 | |

* Included in number above.

## ROOSEVELT (1946 TO DATE)

John R. Sinnock (whose initials, JS, are at the truncation of the neck) designed this dime showing a portrait of Franklin D. Roosevelt. The design has heavier lettering and a more modernistic character than preceding types.

Circulation strike.

Proof strike.

Mintmark on reverse, 1946–1964.

Mintmark on obverse, starting 1968.

### Silver Coinage (1946–1964)

*Designer John R. Sinnock; weight 2.50 grams; composition .900 silver, .100 copper (net weight .07234 oz. pure silver); diameter 17.9 mm; reeded edge; mints: Philadelphia, Denver, San Francisco.*

**EF-40 Extremely Fine**—All lines of torch, flame, and hair very plain.
**MS-63 Choice Uncirculated**—Some distracting contact marks or blemishes in prime focal areas. Impaired luster possible.
**MS-65 Gem Uncirculated**—Only light scattered marks that are not distracting. Strong luster, good eye appeal.
**PF-65 Gem Proof**—Nearly perfect.

| | Mintage | EF-40 | MS-63 | MS-65 | PF-65 |
|---|---|---|---|---|---|
| 1946 | 255,250,000 | $2 | $4.25 | $12 | |
| 1946D | 61,043,500 | 2 | 4.25 | 14 | |
| 1946S | 27,900,000 | 2 | 4.50 | 20 | |
| 1947 | 121,520,000 | 2 | 6.00 | 12 | |
| 1947D | 46,835,000 | 2 | 6.50 | 12 | |
| 1947S | 34,840,000 | 2 | 6.00 | 12 | |
| 1948 | 74,950,000 | 2 | 4.25 | 12 | |
| 1948D | 52,841,000 | 2 | 6.00 | 12 | |
| 1948S | 35,520,000 | 2 | 5.50 | 12 | |
| 1949 | 30,940,000 | 3 | 27.00 | 38 | |
| 1949D | 26,034,000 | 3 | 12.00 | 20 | |
| 1949S | 13,510,000 | 5 | 45.00 | 55 | |

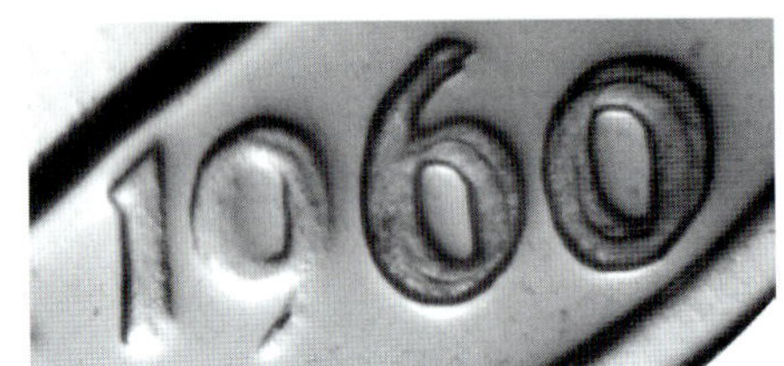
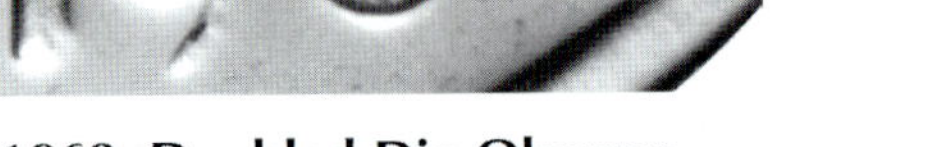

1960, Doubled Die Obverse

1964-D, Doubled Die Reverse

| | Mintage | EF-40 | MS-63 | MS-65 | PF-65 |
|---|---|---|---|---|---|
| 1950 | (51,386) . . . 50,130,114 | $3 | $13.00 | $16 | $50 |
| 1950D | 46,803,000 | 2 | 6.00 | 12 | |
| 1950S | 20,440,000 | 5 | 38.00 | 55 | |
| 1951 | (57,500) . . 103,880,102 | 2 | 4.25 | 10 | 50 |
| 1951D | 56,529,000 | 2 | 4.00 | 10 | |
| 1951S | 31,630,000 | 3 | 14.00 | 25 | |
| 1952 | (81,980) . . . 99,040,093 | 2 | 4.25 | 10 | 35 |
| 1952D | 122,100,000 | 2 | 4.25 | 9 | |
| 1952S | 44,419,500 | 3 | 8.00 | 12 | |
| 1953 | (128,800) . . . 53,490,120 | 2 | 4.00 | 8 | 38 |
| 1953D | 136,433,000 | 2 | 4.00 | 9 | |
| 1953S | 39,180,000 | 3 | 4.00 | 9 | |
| 1954 | (233,300) . . 114,010,203 | 2 | 4.00 | 8 | 18 |
| 1954D | 106,397,000 | 2 | 4.00 | 9 | |
| 1954S | 22,860,000 | 2 | 4.00 | 9 | |
| 1955 | (378,200) . . . 12,450,181 | 2 | 4.00 | 8 | 15 |
| 1955D | 13,959,000 | 2 | 4.00 | 8 | |
| 1955S | 18,510,000 | 2 | 4.00 | 8 | |
| 1956 | (669,384) . . 108,640,000 | 2 | 3.00 | 6 | 8 |
| 1956D | 108,015,100 | 2 | 3.00 | 6 | |
| 1957 | (1,247,952) . . 160,160,000 | 2 | 3.00 | 6 | 5 |
| 1957D | 113,354,330 | 2 | 3.00 | 6 | |
| 1958 | (875,652) . . . 31,910,000 | 2 | 3.00 | 7 | 5 |
| 1958D | 136,564,600 | 2 | 3.00 | 7 | |
| 1959 | (1,149,291) . . . 85,780,000 | 2 | 3.00 | 6 | 5 |
| 1959D | 164,919,790 | 2 | 3.00 | 6 | |
| 1960 | (1,691,602) . . . 70,390,000 | 2 | 3.00 | 6 | 5 |
| 1960, Doubled Die Obverse | * | | | | 150 |
| 1960D | 200,160,400 | 2 | 3.00 | 5 | |
| 1961 | (3,028,244) . . . 93,730,000 | 2 | 3.00 | 5 | 5 |
| 1961D | 209,146,550 | 2 | 3.00 | 5 | |
| 1962 | (3,218,019) . . . 72,450,000 | 2 | 3.00 | 5 | 5 |
| 1962D | 334,948,380 | 2 | 3.00 | 5 | |
| 1963 | (3,075,645) . . 123,650,000 | 2 | 3.00 | 5 | 5 |
| 1963, Doubled Die Reverse | * | | 25.00 | 38 | 150 |
| 1963D | 421,476,530 | 2 | 3.00 | 5 | |
| 1964 **(a)** | (3,950,762) . . 929,360,000 | 2 | 3.00 | 5 | 5 |
| 1964D **(a)** | 1,357,517,180 | 2 | 3.00 | 5 | |
| 1964D, Doubled Die Reverse | * | 35 | 100.00 | 160 | |

* Included in number above. **a.** Variations of 9 in date have pointed or straight tail.

## Clad Coinage and Silver Proofs (1965 to Date)

*Designer: John R. Sinnock; weight 2.27 grams; composition, outer layers of copper-nickel (.750 copper, .250 nickel) bonded to inner core of pure copper; diameter 17.9 mm; reeded edge; mints: Philadelphia, Denver, San Francisco, West Point. Silver Proofs: 1965–2018—weight 2.50 grams; composition .900 silver, .100 copper (net weight .07234 oz. pure silver); 2019 to date—weight 2.537 grams; composition .999 silver, .001 copper (net weight .0728 oz. pure silver); mints: Philadelphia, San Francisco, West Point.*

| | Mintage | MS-65 | PF-65 |
|---|---|---|---|
| 1965 | 1,652,140,570 | $2.00 | |
| 1966 | 1,382,734,540 | 2.25 | |
| 1967 | 2,244,007,320 | 2.00 | |
| 1968 | 424,470,400 | 2.00 | |
| 1968D | 480,748,280 | 2.00 | |
| 1968S **(a)** | (3,041,506) | | $2.00 |
| 1969 | 145,790,000 | 3.00 | |
| 1969D | 563,323,870 | 2.00 | |
| 1969S | (2,394,631) | | 2.00 |
| 1970 | 345,570,000 | 2.00 | |
| 1970D | 754,942,100 | 2.00 | |
| 1970S **(a)** | (2,632,810) | | 2.00 |
| 1971 | 162,690,000 | 2.50 | |
| 1971D | 377,914,240 | 2.25 | |
| 1971S | (3,220,733) | | 2.00 |
| 1972 | 431,540,000 | 2.00 | |
| 1972D | 330,290,000 | 2.00 | |
| 1972S | (3,260,996) | | 2.00 |
| 1973 | 315,670,000 | 2.00 | |
| 1973D | 455,032,426 | 2.00 | |
| 1973S | (2,760,339) | | 2.00 |
| 1974 | 470,248,000 | 2.00 | |
| 1974D | 571,083,000 | 2.00 | |
| 1974S | (2,612,568) | | 2.00 |
| 1975 | 585,673,900 | 2.00 | |
| 1975D | 313,705,300 | 2.00 | |
| 1975S **(a)** | (2,845,450) | | 2.50 |
| 1976 | 568,760,000 | 2.00 | |
| 1976D | 695,222,774 | 2.00 | |
| 1976S | (4,149,730) | | 2.75 |
| 1977 | 796,930,000 | 2.00 | |
| 1977D | 376,607,228 | 2.00 | |
| 1977S | (3,251,152) | | 2.50 |
| 1978 | 663,980,000 | 2.00 | |
| 1978D | 282,847,540 | 2.00 | |
| 1978S | (3,127,781) | | 2.50 |
| 1979 | 315,440,000 | 2.00 | |
| 1979D | 390,921,184 | 2.00 | |
| 1979S, Type 1 **(b)** | (3,677,175) | | 2.50 |
| 1979S, Type 2 **(b)** | * | | 5.00 |
| 1980P | 735,170,000 | 2.00 | |
| 1980D | 719,354,321 | 2.00 | |
| 1980S | (3,554,806) | | 2.50 |
| 1981P | 676,650,000 | $2.00 | |
| 1981D | 712,284,143 | 2.00 | |
| 1981S, Type 1 **(b)** | (4,063,083) | | $2.50 |
| 1981S, Type 2 **(b)** | * | | 5.50 |
| 1982, No Mintmark, Strong Strike **(a)** | | 200.00 | |
| 1982, No Mintmark, Weak Strike **(a)** | | 65.00 | |
| 1982P | 519,475,000 | 7.50 | |
| 1982D | 542,713,584 | 2.50 | |
| 1982S | (3,857,479) | | 2.50 |
| 1983P | 647,025,000 | 6.50 | |
| 1983D | 730,129,224 | 3.25 | |
| 1983S **(a)** | (3,279,126) | | 3.00 |
| 1984P | 856,669,000 | 2.00 | |
| 1984D | 704,803,976 | 2.25 | |
| 1984S | (3,065,110) | | 2.50 |
| 1985P | 705,200,962 | 2.25 | |
| 1985D | 587,979,970 | 2.25 | |
| 1985S | (3,362,821) | | 3.00 |
| 1986P | 682,649,693 | 2.50 | |
| 1986D | 473,326,970 | 2.50 | |
| 1986S | (3,010,497) | | 4.00 |
| 1987P | 762,709,481 | 2.00 | |
| 1987D | 653,203,402 | 2.00 | |
| 1987S | (4,227,728) | | 3.00 |
| 1988P | 1,030,550,000 | 2.00 | |
| 1988D | 962,385,489 | 2.00 | |
| 1988S | (3,262,948) | | 4.00 |
| 1989P | 1,298,400,000 | 2.00 | |
| 1989D | 896,535,597 | 2.00 | |
| 1989S | (3,220,194) | | 3.00 |
| 1990P | 1,034,340,000 | 2.00 | |
| 1990D | 839,995,824 | 2.00 | |
| 1990S | (3,299,559) | | 2.50 |
| 1991P | 927,220,000 | 2.00 | |
| 1991D | 601,241,114 | 2.00 | |
| 1991S | (2,867,787) | | 4.00 |
| 1992P | 593,500,000 | 2.00 | |
| 1992D | 616,273,932 | 2.00 | |
| 1992S | (2,858,981) | | 3.00 |
| 1992S, Silver | (1,317,579) | | 6.00 |
| 1993P | 766,180,000 | 2.00 | |

* Included in number above. **a.** Some 1968, 1970, 1975, and 1983 Proof dimes without S mintmark were made in error, as were some circulation-strike 1982 dimes. See page 22 for discussion. **b.** See page 246 for illustrations of Type 1 and Type 2 varieties.

*Chart continued on next page.*

| | Mintage | MS-65 | PF-65 |
|---|---|---|---|
| 1993D | 750,110,166 | $2 | |
| 1993S | (2,633,439) | | $5.00 |
| 1993S, Silver | (761,353) | | 7.00 |
| 1994P | 1,189,000,000 | 2 | |
| 1994D | 1,303,268,110 | 2 | |
| 1994S | (2,484,594) | | 5.00 |
| 1994S, Silver | (785,329) | | 8.00 |
| 1995P | 1,125,500,000 | 2 | |
| 1995D | 1,274,890,000 | 2 | |
| 1995S | (2,117,496) | | 10.00 |
| 1995S, Silver | (679,985) | | 14.00 |
| 1996P | 1,421,163,000 | 2 | |
| 1996D | 1,400,300,000 | 2 | |
| 1996W **(c)** | 1,457,000 | 20 | |
| 1996S | (1,750,244) | | 3.00 |
| 1996S, Silver | (775,021) | | 8.00 |
| 1997P | 991,640,000 | 2 | |
| 1997D | 979,810,000 | 2 | |
| 1997S | (2,055,000) | | 8.00 |
| 1997S, Silver | (741,678) | | 12.00 |
| 1998P | 1,163,000,000 | 2 | |
| 1998D | 1,172,250,000 | 2 | |
| 1998S | (2,086,507) | | 4.00 |
| 1998S, Silver | (878,792) | | 6.00 |
| 1999P | 2,164,000,000 | 2 | |
| 1999D | 1,397,750,000 | 2 | |
| 1999S | (2,543,401) | | 4.00 |
| 1999S, Silver | (804,565) | | 7.00 |
| 2000P | 1,842,500,000 | 2 | |
| 2000D | 1,818,700,000 | 2 | |
| 2000S | (3,082,572) | | 2.50 |
| 2000S, Silver | (965,421) | | 5.00 |
| 2001P | 1,369,590,000 | 2 | |
| 2001D | 1,412,800,000 | 2 | |
| 2001S | (2,294,909) | | 2.50 |
| 2001S, Silver | (889,697) | | 5.00 |
| 2002P | 1,187,500,000 | 2 | |
| 2002D | 1,379,500,000 | 2 | |
| 2002S | (2,319,766) | | 2.50 |
| 2002S, Silver | (892,229) | | 5.00 |
| 2003P | 1,085,500,000 | 2 | |
| 2003D | 986,500,000 | 2 | |
| 2003S | (2,172,684) | | 2.50 |
| 2003S, Silver | (1,125,755) | | 4.50 |
| 2004P | 1,328,000,000 | 2 | |
| 2004D | 1,159,500,000 | 2 | |
| 2004S | (1,789,488) | | 3.00 |
| 2004S, Silver | (1,175,934) | | $5.00 |
| 2005P | 1,412,000,000 | $2 | |
| 2005D | 1,423,500,000 | 2 | |
| 2005S | (2,275,000) | | 2.50 |
| 2005S, Silver | (1,069,679) | | 5.00 |
| 2006P | 1,381,000,000 | 2 | |
| 2006D | 1,447,000,000 | 2 | |
| 2006S | (2,000,428) | | 2.50 |
| 2006S, Silver | (1,054,008) | | 5.00 |
| 2007P | 1,047,500,000 | 2 | |
| 2007D | 1,042,000,000 | 2 | |
| 2007S | (1,702,116) | | 2.50 |
| 2007S, Silver | (875,050) | | 5.00 |
| 2008P | 391,000,000 | 2 | |
| 2008D | 624,500,000 | 2 | |
| 2008S | (1,405,674) | | 2.50 |
| 2008S, Silver | (763,887) | | 5.00 |
| 2009P | 96,500,000 | 2 | |
| 2009D | 49,500,000 | 2 | |
| 2009S | (1,482,502) | | 2.50 |
| 2009S, Silver | (697,365) | | 5.00 |
| 2010P | 557,000,000 | 2 | |
| 2010D | 562,000,000 | 2 | |
| 2010S | (1,103,815) | | 2.50 |
| 2010S, Silver | (585,401) | | 5.00 |
| 2011P | 748,000,000 | 2 | |
| 2011D | 754,000,000 | 2 | |
| 2011S | *(1,098,835)* | | 2.50 |
| 2011S, Silver | *(574,175)* | | 5.00 |
| 2012P | 808,000,000 | 2 | |
| 2012D | 868,000,000 | 2 | |
| 2012S | (794,002) | | 2.50 |
| 2012S, Silver | (495,315) | | 5.00 |
| 2013P | 1,086,500,000 | 2 | |
| 2013D | 1,025,500,000 | 2 | |
| 2013S | *(854,785)* | | 2.50 |
| 2013S, Silver | (467,691) | | 5.00 |
| 2014P | 1,125,500,000 | 2 | |
| 2014D | 1,177,000,000 | 2 | |
| 2014S | *(760,876)* | | 2.50 |
| 2014S, Silver | (491,157) | | 5.00 |
| 2015P | 1,497,510,000 | 2 | |
| 2015P, RevPf, Silv **(d)** | (74,430) | | 20.00 |
| 2015D | 1,543,500,000 | 2 | |
| 2015S | *(662,854)* | | 2.50 |
| 2015S, Silver | *(387,310)* | | 5.00 |
| 2015W, Silver **(d)** | (74,430) | | 15.00 |

*Note:* Uncirculated Mint Sets for 2005–2010 were made with Satin Finish coins not included in the listings here. See page 369 for their mintages. **c.** Issued in Mint sets only, to mark the 50th anniversary of the design. **d.** Included in March of Dimes commemorative Proof set.

Along with the regular Roosevelt dime of the year, in 2016 a special gold striking of the Mercury dime was created to celebrate the 100th anniversary of its introduction. Similar strikings were made for the 1916 quarter and half dollar designs.

*Designer Adolph A. Weinman; weight 3.11 grams; composition .9999 gold; diameter 16.5 mm; reeded edge; mint: West Point.*

| | Mintage | SP-67 | SP-70 |
|---|---|---|---|
| 2016W, Mercury Dime Centennial Gold Coin | 124,885 | $250 | $300 |

Normally scheduled production of clad and silver Roosevelt dimes continued in 2016 and beyond, and was not disrupted by the gold Mercury dime.

| | Mintage | MS-65 | PF-65 |
|---|---|---|---|
| 2016P | 1,517,000,000 | $2 | |
| 2016D | 1,437,000,000 | 2 | |
| 2016S | *(641,775)* | | $2.50 |
| 2016S, Silver | *(419,496)* | | 5.00 |
| 2017P | 1,437,500,000 | 2 | |
| 2017D | 1,290,500,000 | 2 | |
| 2017S **(a)** | *(621,384)* | | 2.50 |
| 2017S, Silver | *(406,994)* | | 5.00 |
| 2018P | *1,193,000,000* | 2 | |
| 2018D | *1,006,000,000* | 2 | |

| | Mintage | MS-65 | PF-65 |
|---|---|---|---|
| 2018S | *(535,221)* | | $2.50 |
| 2018S, Silver | *(350,820)* | | 5.00 |
| 2019P | *1,147,500,000* | $2 | |
| 2019D | *1,001,500,000* | 2 | |
| 2019S | | | 2.50 |
| 2019S, Silver | | | 5.00 |
| 2020P | | 2 | |
| 2020D | | 2 | |
| 2020S | | | 2.50 |
| 2020S, Silver | | | 5.00 |

**a.** For its 225th anniversary, the Mint issued a special set of Enhanced Uncirculated coins from the San Francisco Mint; they are not included in the listings here.

## LIBERTY SEATED (1875–1878)

This short-lived coin was authorized by the Act of March 3, 1875. Soon after the appearance of the first twenty-cent pieces, people complained about the similarity in design and size to the quarter dollar. The eagle is very similar to that used on the trade dollar, but the edge of this coin is plain. The mintmark is on the reverse below the eagle.

In the denomination's first year, more than one million pieces were struck at the San Francisco Mint; about 133,000 at the Carson City Mint; and roughly 37,000 at Philadelphia (not including about 1,200 Proofs struck there as well). These numbers dropped sharply in 1876. (Most of the Carson City coins of that year were melted at the mint and never released, a fate likely met by most of the Philadelphia twenty-cent pieces of 1876 as well.) In 1877 and 1878, only Proof examples were minted. None were struck for circulation.

Various factors caused the demise of the twenty-cent piece: the public was confused over the coin's similarity to the quarter dollar, which was better established as a foundation of American commerce; in the eastern United States, small-change transactions were largely satisfied by Fractional Currency notes; and the twenty-cent coin was essentially just a substitute for two dimes.

*Designer William Barber; weight 5 grams; composition .900 silver, .100 copper; diameter 22 mm; plain edge; mints: Philadelphia, Carson City, San Francisco.*

**G-4 Good**—LIBERTY on shield obliterated. Letters and date legible.
**VG-8 Very Good**—One or two letters in LIBERTY barely visible. Other details bold.
**F-12 Fine**—Some letters of LIBERTY possibly visible.
**VF-20 Very Fine**—LIBERTY readable, but partly weak.
**EF-40 Extremely Fine**—LIBERTY mostly sharp. Only slight wear on high points of coin.
**AU-50 About Uncirculated**—Slight trace of wear on breast, head, and knees.
**MS-60 Uncirculated**—No trace of wear. Light blemishes.
**MS-63 Choice Uncirculated**—Some distracting blemishes in prime focal areas. Some impairment of luster possible.

*Circulation strike.*

*Proof strike.*

*Mintmark location is below eagle.*

| | Mintage | G-4 | VG-8 | F-12 | VF-20 | EF-40 | AU-50 | MS-60 | MS-63 | PF-63 |
|---|---|---|---|---|---|---|---|---|---|---|
| 1875 . . . . . . (1,200) . . . . | 38,500 | $220 | $250 | $300 | $360 | $400 | $525 | $775 | $1,350 | $2,750 |
| 1875CC . . . . . . . . . . . . . | 133,290 | 200 | 240 | 325 | 475 | 650 | 950 | 1,600 | 2,750 | |
| 1875S . . . . . . . . . . . . | 1,155,000 | 85 | 100 | 130 | 150 | 250 | 360 | 575 | 1,050 | 55,000 |
| 1876 . . . . . . (1,150) . . . . | 14,750 | 235 | 275 | 350 | 400 | 475 | 600 | 850 | 1,600 | 2,800 |
| 1876CC . . . . . . . . . . . . . . | 10,000 | | | | | | 175,000 | 250,000 | 350,000 | |
| *$564,000, MS-65, Stack's Bowers auction, January 2013* | | | | | | | | | | |
| 1877 . . . . . . . . (510) . . . . . . . . . | | | | | 3,500 | 4,500 | | | | 8,500 |
| 1878 . . . . . . . . (600) . . . . . . . . . | | | | | 2,500 | 2,800 | | | | 4,250 |

Authorized in 1792, this denomination was not issued until 1796. The first coinage follows the design of the early half dimes and dimes by the absence of a mark of value. In 1804 the value "25 C." was added to the reverse. Figures were used until 1838, when the term QUAR. DOL. appeared. In 1892 the value was spelled out entirely.

The first type weighed 104 grains, which remained standard until modified to 103-1/8 grains by the Act of January 18, 1837. As with the dime and half dime, the weight was reduced and arrows placed at the date in 1853. Rays were placed in the field of the reverse during that year only. The law of 1873 slightly increased the weight, and arrows were again placed at the date.

Proofs of some dates prior to 1856 are known to exist, and all are rare.

*Note: Values of common-date silver coins have been based on a silver bullion price of $18 per ounce, and may vary with the prevailing spot price. To determine the intrinsic value of common silver coins, see page 445.*

## DRAPED BUST (1796–1807)

*Designer probably Gilbert Stuart; engraver Robert Scot; weight 6.74 grams; composition .8924 silver, .1076 copper; approx. diameter 27.5 mm; reeded edge. All coined at Philadelphia.*

**AG-3 About Good**—Details clear enough to identify.
**G-4 Good**—Date readable. Bust outlined, but no detail.
**VG-8 Very Good**—All but deepest drapery folds worn smooth. Hairlines nearly gone and curls lacking in detail.
**F-12 Fine**—All drapery lines visible. Hair partly worn.
**VF-20 Very Fine**—Only left side of drapery indistinct.
**EF-40 Extremely Fine**—Hair well outlined and detailed.
**AU-50 About Uncirculated**—Slight trace of wear on shoulder and highest waves of hair.
**MS-60 Uncirculated**—No trace of wear. Light blemishes.
**MS-63 Choice Uncirculated**—Some distracting marks or blemishes in focal areas. Impaired luster possible.

### Small Eagle Reverse (1796)

| | Mintage | AG-3 | G-4 | VG-8 | F-12 | VF-20 | EF-40 | AU-50 | MS-60 | MS-63 |
|---|---|---|---|---|---|---|---|---|---|---|
| 1796 | 6,146 | $7,500 | $11,000 | $17,000 | $25,000 | $32,500 | $48,500 | $60,000 | $80,000 | $125,000 |
| *$1,527,500, MS-66, Sotheby's / Stack's Bowers auction, May 2015* | | | | | | | | | | |

### Heraldic Eagle Reverse (1804–1807)

**1806, 6 Over 5**

| | Mintage | AG-3 | G-4 | VG-8 | F-12 | VF-20 | EF-40 | AU-50 | MS-60 | MS-63 |
|---|---|---|---|---|---|---|---|---|---|---|
| 1804 | 6,738 | $2,500 | $4,250 | $6,500 | $9,500 | $13,000 | $30,000 | $47,000 | $95,000 | $175,000 |
| 1805 | 121,394 | 250 | 500 | 650 | 950 | 1,800 | 3,750 | 5,500 | 11,000 | 20,000 |

*Chart continued on next page.*

| | Mintage | AG-3 | G-4 | VG-8 | F-12 | VF-20 | EF-40 | AU-50 | MS-60 | MS-63 |
|---|---|---|---|---|---|---|---|---|---|---|
| 1806, All kinds | 206,124 | | | | | | | | | |
| 1806, 6 Over 5 | | $300 | $550 | $700 | $1,100 | $2,000 | $4,250 | $6,000 | $13,500 | $25,000 |
| 1806 | | 225 | 500 | 650 | 950 | 1,800 | 3,750 | 5,500 | 11,000 | 20,000 |
| 1807 | 220,643 | 225 | 500 | 700 | 1,000 | 1,750 | 3,850 | 5,500 | 11,000 | 20,000 |

## CAPPED BUST (1815–1838)

### Variety 1 – Large Diameter (1815–1828)

*Designer John Reich; weight 6.74 grams; composition .8924 silver, .1076 copper; approx. diameter 27 mm; reeded edge. All coined at Philadelphia.*

**AG-3 About Good**—Details clear enough to identify.
**G-4 Good**—Date, letters, stars legible. Hair under Liberty's headband smooth. Cap lines worn smooth.
**VG-8 Very Good**—Rim well defined. Main details visible. Full LIBERTY on cap. Hair above eye nearly smooth.
**F-12 Fine**—All hair lines visible, but only partial detail visible in drapery. Shoulder clasp distinct.
**VF-20 Very Fine**—All details visible, but some wear evident. Clasp and ear sharp.
**EF-40 Extremely Fine**—All details distinct. Hair well outlined.
**AU-50 About Uncirculated**—Slight trace of wear on tips of curls and above the eye, and on the wing and claw tips.
**MS-60 Uncirculated**—No trace of wear. Light blemishes.
**MS-63 Choice Uncirculated**—Some distracting contact marks or blemishes in prime focal areas. Impaired luster possible.

1818, 8 Over 5 — 1819, Small 9 — 1819, Large 9

1820, Small 0 — 1820, Large 0 — 1822, 25 Over 50c

1823, 3 Over 2

1824, 4 Over 2

1825, 5 Over 2 (Wide Date)

1825, 5 Over 4 (Close Date)

| | Mintage | AG-3 | G-4 | VG-8 | F-12 | VF-20 | EF-40 | AU-50 | MS-60 | MS-63 |
|---|---|---|---|---|---|---|---|---|---|---|
| 1815 | 89,235 | $150 | $250 | $400 | $600 | $850 | $2,200 | $3,000 | $5,000 | $8,000 |
| 1818, 8 Over 5 | 361,174 | 100 | 125 | 200 | 350 | 650 | 1,700 | 2,350 | 4,000 | 7,250 |
| 1818, Normal Date | * | 70 | 125 | 200 | 300 | 600 | 1,600 | 2,250 | 4,000 | 7,250 |
| 1819, Small 9 | 144,000 | 70 | 125 | 200 | 300 | 600 | 1,600 | 2,250 | 4,250 | 8,500 |
| 1819, Large 9 | * | 70 | 125 | 200 | 300 | 600 | 1,600 | 2,450 | 5,000 | 10,000 |

* Included in number above.

| | Mintage | AG-3 | G-4 | VG-8 | F-12 | VF-20 | EF-40 | AU-50 | MS-60 | MS-63 |
|---|---|---|---|---|---|---|---|---|---|---|
| 1820, Small 0 | 127,444 | $70 | $125 | $200 | $300 | $600 | $1,750 | $2,450 | $4,000 | $6,000 |
| 1820, Large 0 | * | 70 | 125 | 200 | 300 | 600 | 1,600 | 3,250 | 6,500 | 10,000 |
| 1821 | 216,851 | 70 | 125 | 200 | 300 | 600 | 1,600 | 2,250 | 3,500 | 7,000 |
| 1822 | 64,080 | 200 | 300 | 375 | 750 | 1,100 | 1,800 | 3,000 | 7,250 | 11,500 |
| 1822, 25 Over 50 C. | * | 4,250 | 6,000 | 10,000 | 16,500 | 25,000 | 33,000 | 40,000 | 55,000 | 75,000 |
| 1823, 3 Over 2 | 17,800 | 25,000 | 42,500 | 55,000 | 75,000 | 95,000 | 135,000 | 165,000 | 300,000 | |
| 1824, 4 Over 2 | 168,000 | 500 | 800 | 1,100 | 2,000 | 2,750 | 5,250 | 7,500 | 25,000 | 55,000 |
| 1825, 5 Over 2 **(a)** | * | 75 | 125 | 200 | 325 | 600 | 1,700 | 2,200 | 3,500 | 6,000 |
| 1825, 5 Over 4 **(a)** | * | 350 | 500 | 750 | 1,000 | 1,350 | 2,500 | 5,000 | 10,000 | 27,000 |
| 1827, Original (Curl Base 2 in 25 C.) **(b)** | 4,000 | | | | | | 75,000 | 85,000 | 125,000 | 225,000 |
| *$705,000, PF-66+Cam, Sotheby's / Stack's Bowers auction, May 2015* | | | | | | | | | | |
| 1827, Restrike (Square Base 2 in 25 C.) **(b)** | | | | | | | | | | 65,000 |
| 1828 | 102,000 | 75 | 115 | 180 | 300 | 550 | 1,500 | 2,500 | 3,500 | 7,500 |
| 1828, 25 Over 50 C. | * | 750 | 1,250 | 1,750 | 2,250 | 3,500 | 7,000 | 10,000 | 17,500 | 90,000 |

* Included in number above. **a.** The date appears to be 5 over 4 over 2. The wide-date variety is the scarcer of the two. **b.** The 7 is punched over a 3, which is punched over an earlier 2.

## Variety 2 – Reduced Diameter (1831–1838), Motto Removed

*Designer William Kneass; weight 6.74 grams; composition .8924 silver, .1076 copper; diameter 24.3 mm; reeded edge. All coined at Philadelphia. Changed to 6.68 grams, .900 fine in 1837.*

**G-4 Good**—Bust of Liberty well defined. Hair under headband smooth. Date, letters, stars legible. Scant rims.
**VG-8 Very Good**—Details apparent but worn on high spots. Rims strong. Full LIBERTY.
**F-12 Fine**—All hair lines visible. Drapery partly worn. Shoulder clasp distinct.
**VF-20 Very Fine**—Only top spots worn. Clasp sharp. Ear distinct.
**EF-40 Extremely Fine**—Hair details and clasp bold and clear.
**AU-50 About Uncirculated**—Slight trace of wear on hair around forehead, on cheek, and at top and bottom tips of eagle's wings and left claw.
**MS-60 Uncirculated**—No trace of wear. Light blemishes.
**MS-63 Choice Uncirculated**—Some distracting contact marks or blemishes in prime focal areas. Impaired luster possible.

Small Letters (1831)

Large Letters

O Over F in OF

| | Mintage | G-4 | VG-8 | F-12 | VF-20 | EF-40 | AU-50 | MS-60 | MS-63 |
|---|---|---|---|---|---|---|---|---|---|
| 1831, Small Letters | 398,000 | $70 | $100 | $125 | $150 | $375 | $750 | $2,000 | $3,750 |
| 1831, Large Letters | * | 70 | 100 | 125 | 150 | 400 | 750 | 2,400 | 4,250 |
| 1832 | 320,000 | 70 | 100 | 125 | 150 | 375 | 750 | 2,000 | 3,750 |
| 1833 | 156,000 | 80 | 110 | 135 | 200 | 400 | 850 | 2,150 | 4,000 |
| 1833, O Over F in OF | * | 85 | 120 | 165 | 235 | 500 | 900 | 2,000 | 5,000 |
| 1834 | 286,000 | 70 | 100 | 125 | 150 | 375 | 750 | 2,000 | 4,000 |
| 1834, O Over F in OF | * | 80 | 110 | 150 | 200 | 450 | 850 | 2,000 | 5,000 |
| 1835 | 1,952,000 | 70 | 100 | 125 | 150 | 375 | 750 | 2,000 | 3,750 |
| 1836 | 472,000 | 70 | 100 | 125 | 150 | 375 | 750 | 2,000 | 3,750 |
| 1837 | 252,400 | 70 | 100 | 125 | 150 | 375 | 750 | 2,000 | 3,750 |
| 1838 | 366,000 | 70 | 100 | 125 | 150 | 375 | 750 | 2,000 | 3,750 |

* Included in number above.

## LIBERTY SEATED (1838–1891)

*Designer Christian Gobrecht.*

**G-4 Good**—Scant rim. LIBERTY on shield worn off. Date and letters legible.
**VG-8 Very Good**—Rim fairly defined, at least three letters in LIBERTY evident.
**F-12 Fine**—LIBERTY complete, but partly weak.
**VF-20 Very Fine**—LIBERTY strong.
**EF-40 Extremely Fine**—Complete LIBERTY and edges of scroll. Shoulder clasp on Liberty's gown clear.
**AU-50 About Uncirculated**—Slight wear on Liberty's knees and breast and on eagle's neck, wing tips, and claws.
**MS-60 Uncirculated**—No trace of wear. Light blemishes.
**MS-63 Choice Uncirculated**—Some distracting contact marks or blemishes in prime focal areas. Impaired luster possible.

### Variety 1 – No Motto Above Eagle (1838–1853)

*Weight 6.68 grams; composition .900 silver, .100 copper; diameter 24.3 mm; reeded edge; mints: Philadelphia, New Orleans.*

No Drapery From Elbow
*Mintmark location is on reverse, below eagle.*

Drapery From Elbow

Small Date

Large Date

| | Mintage | G-4 | VG-8 | F-12 | VF-20 | EF-40 | AU-50 | MS-60 | MS-63 |
|---|---|---|---|---|---|---|---|---|---|
| 1838, No Drapery | 466,000 | $35 | $50 | $75 | $175 | $450 | $950 | $1,700 | $4,000 |
| 1839, No Drapery | 491,146 | 35 | 50 | 75 | 175 | 450 | 1,050 | 1,750 | 4,250 |
| *$517,500, PF-65, Heritage auction, April 2008* | | | | | | | | | |
| 1840O, No Drapery | 382,200 | 40 | 60 | 85 | 195 | 450 | 950 | 2,200 | 5,500 |
| 1840, Drapery | 188,127 | 35 | 45 | 70 | 175 | 425 | 750 | 1,650 | 4,800 |
| 1840O, Drapery | 43,000 | 40 | 60 | 115 | 215 | 450 | 800 | 1,400 | 3,800 |
| 1841 | 120,000 | 65 | 100 | 125 | 225 | 400 | 750 | 1,200 | 2,250 |
| 1841O | 452,000 | 35 | 50 | 75 | 165 | 315 | 425 | 850 | 1,900 |
| 1842, Sm Date (Pf only) | | | | | | | | | |
| 1842, Large Date | 88,000 | 75 | 100 | 150 | 250 | 450 | 850 | 1,600 | 4,500 |
| 1842O, All kinds | 769,000 | | | | | | | | |
| 1842O, Small Date | | 600 | 1,150 | 1,600 | 3,000 | 7,500 | 11,000 | 32,500 | 70,000 |
| 1842O, Large Date | | 35 | 45 | 55 | 125 | 275 | 600 | 1,750 | 4,500 |
| 1843 | 645,600 | 30 | 35 | 45 | 75 | 200 | 350 | 675 | 1,300 |
| 1843O | 968,000 | 35 | 75 | 150 | 450 | 1,000 | 1,350 | 3,500 | 6,500 |
| 1844 | 421,200 | 30 | 40 | 50 | 80 | 165 | 325 | 650 | 1,650 |
| 1844O | 740,000 | 35 | 45 | 65 | 115 | 250 | 475 | 1,250 | 2,500 |
| 1845 | 922,000 | 30 | 35 | 45 | 80 | 165 | 235 | 500 | 1,250 |
| 1846 | 510,000 | 45 | 75 | 100 | 125 | 225 | 425 | 800 | 1,850 |
| 1847 | 734,000 | 35 | 50 | 70 | 95 | 160 | 275 | 600 | 1,650 |
| 1847O | 368,000 | 100 | 175 | 300 | 600 | 1,000 | 2,000 | 6,500 | 12,500 |
| 1848 | 146,000 | 45 | 95 | 150 | 275 | 450 | 650 | 1,250 | 4,750 |
| 1849 | 340,000 | 35 | 75 | 95 | 115 | 250 | 400 | 1,000 | 1,850 |
| 1849O | * | 1,250 | 1,750 | 2,250 | 3,000 | 7,000 | 8,500 | 17,500 | 20,000 |
| 1850 | 190,800 | 50 | 95 | 185 | 275 | 400 | 650 | 1,350 | 2,500 |
| *$460,000, PF-68, Heritage auction, January 2008* | | | | | | | | | |
| 1850O | 412,000 | 75 | 115 | 150 | 225 | 500 | 750 | 1,600 | 4,000 |

* Included in 1850-O mintage.

| | Mintage | G-4 | VG-8 | F-12 | VF-20 | EF-40 | AU-50 | MS-60 | MS-63 |
|---|---|---|---|---|---|---|---|---|---|
| 1851 | 160,000 | $100 | $175 | $275 | $400 | $700 | $1,000 | $1,450 | $2,350 |
| 1851O | 88,000 | 375 | 600 | 900 | 1,100 | 2,500 | 3,350 | 6,700 | 32,500 |
| 1852 | 177,060 | 125 | 225 | 325 | 450 | 600 | 750 | 1,100 | 2,100 |
| 1852O | 96,000 | 350 | 500 | 850 | 1,500 | 2,250 | 5,500 | 9,500 | 40,000 |
| 1853, Recut Dt, No Arrows or Rays **(a)** | 44,200 | 1,250 | 2,000 | 2,500 | 3,250 | 4,000 | 4,500 | 6,250 | 7,500 |

**a.** Beware of altered 1858, or removed arrows and rays.

## Variety 2 – Arrows at Date, Rays Around Eagle (1853)

The reduction in weight is indicated by the arrows at the date. Rays were added on the reverse side in the field around the eagle. The arrows were retained through 1855, but the rays were omitted after 1853.

*Weight 6.22 grams; composition .900 silver, .100 copper; diameter 24.3 mm; reeded edge; mints: Philadelphia, New Orleans.*

**1853, 3 Over 4**

| | Mintage | G-4 | VG-8 | F-12 | VF-20 | EF-40 | AU-50 | MS-60 | MS-63 |
|---|---|---|---|---|---|---|---|---|---|
| 1853 | 15,210,020 | $25 | $30 | $35 | $50 | $175 | $350 | $1,000 | $2,000 |
| 1853, 3 Over 4 | * | 55 | 100 | 175 | 250 | 350 | 675 | 1,850 | 4,000 |
| 1853O | 1,332,000 | 35 | 70 | 100 | 150 | 400 | 1,100 | 4,250 | 10,000 |

* Included in number above.

## Variety 3 – Arrows at Date, No Rays (1854–1855)

*Weight 6.22 grams; composition .900 silver, .100 copper; diameter 24.3 mm; reeded edge; mints: Philadelphia, New Orleans, San Francisco.*

**1854-O, Normal O**

**1854-O, Huge O**

| | Mintage | G-4 | VG-8 | F-12 | VF-20 | EF-40 | AU-50 | MS-60 | MS-63 |
|---|---|---|---|---|---|---|---|---|---|
| 1854 | 12,380,000 | $25 | $30 | $35 | $45 | $85 | $250 | $625 | $1,200 |
| 1854O | 1,484,000 | 35 | 40 | 50 | 55 | 125 | 300 | 1,100 | 1,750 |
| 1854O, Huge O | * | 600 | 1,150 | 1,450 | 1,850 | 3,850 | 6,500 | — | — |
| 1855 | 2,857,000 | 25 | 30 | 40 | 50 | 125 | 250 | 625 | 1,300 |
| 1855O | 176,000 | 125 | 185 | 300 | 550 | 850 | 2,000 | 3,000 | 12,500 |
| 1855S | 396,400 | 100 | 225 | 350 | 600 | 1,000 | 1,450 | 2,850 | 7,500 |

* Included in number above.

## Variety 1 Resumed, With Weight Standard of Variety 2 (1856–1865)

| | Mintage | G-4 | VG-8 | F-12 | VF-20 | EF-40 | AU-50 | MS-60 | MS-63 | PF-63 |
|---|---|---|---|---|---|---|---|---|---|---|
| 1856 | 7,264,000 | $25 | $30 | $35 | $45 | $75 | $185 | $350 | $650 | $4,500 |
| 1856O | 968,000 | 30 | 40 | 75 | 125 | 250 | 475 | 1,000 | 2,500 | |
| 1856S, All kinds | 286,000 | | | | | | | | | |
| 1856S | | 250 | 325 | 500 | 800 | 2,250 | 3,500 | 7,500 | 13,500 | |
| 1856S, S Over Sm S | | 500 | 850 | 1,500 | 3,000 | 6,500 | | — | | |
| 1857 | 9,644,000 | 25 | 30 | 35 | 45 | 75 | 185 | 350 | 600 | 4,000 |
| 1857O | 1,180,000 | 35 | 50 | 90 | 150 | 300 | 500 | 1,200 | 3,000 | |
| 1857S | 82,000 | 175 | 300 | 425 | 800 | 1,150 | 1,850 | 3,500 | 6,000 | |
| 1858 *(300)* | 7,368,000 | 25 | 30 | 35 | 45 | 75 | 185 | 350 | 600 | 2,000 |

*Chart continued on next page.*

| | Mintage | G-4 | VG-8 | F-12 | VF-20 | EF-40 | AU-50 | MS-60 | MS-63 | PF-63 |
|---|---|---|---|---|---|---|---|---|---|---|
| 1858O | 520,000 | $30 | $40 | $75 | $125 | $350 | $650 | $3,250 | $10,000 | |
| 1858S | 121,000 | 250 | 400 | 600 | 1,000 | 3,500 | 5,000 | 20,000 | — | |
| 1859 (800) | 1,343,200 | 25 | 30 | 45 | 65 | 90 | 200 | 425 | 900 | $1,500 |
| 1859O | 260,000 | 50 | 75 | 100 | 150 | 300 | 550 | 2,500 | 6,500 | |
| 1859S | 80,000 | 375 | 625 | 950 | 1,450 | 4,500 | 12,000 | | — | |
| 1860 (1,000) | 804,400 | 25 | 30 | 35 | 65 | 100 | 195 | 500 | 850 | 1,200 |
| 1860O | 388,000 | 30 | 45 | 55 | 85 | 250 | 475 | 1,000 | 1,750 | |
| 1860S | 56,000 | 1,000 | 1,500 | 3,000 | 5,000 | 9,000 | 18,500 | | — | |
| 1861 (1,000) | 4,853,600 | 25 | 30 | 35 | 65 | 100 | 200 | 350 | 725 | 1,200 |
| 1861S | 96,000 | 600 | 900 | 1,250 | 2,000 | 4,500 | 8,500 | | — | |
| 1862 (550) | 932,000 | 25 | 35 | 50 | 75 | 115 | 210 | 400 | 750 | 1,200 |
| 1862S | 67,000 | 175 | 300 | 450 | 600 | 1,250 | 2,500 | 4,250 | 7,500 | |
| 1863 (460) | 191,600 | 75 | 110 | 175 | 275 | 450 | 550 | 800 | 1,350 | 1,200 |
| 1864 (470) | 93,600 | 125 | 215 | 300 | 425 | 575 | 700 | 1,250 | 2,500 | 1,200 |
| 1864S | 20,000 | 875 | 1,000 | 1,500 | 2,000 | 4,000 | 5,500 | 12,000 | 20,000 | |
| 1865 (500) | 58,800 | 100 | 165 | 250 | 350 | 450 | 750 | 1,250 | 1,850 | 1,200 |
| 1865S | 41,000 | 225 | 350 | 475 | 650 | 1,100 | 1,600 | 3,500 | 5,500 | |
| 1866 *(unique, not a regular issue)* | | | | | | | | | | — |

*Note:* The 1866 Proof quarter, half, and dollar without motto are not mentioned in the Mint director's report and were not issued for circulation.

## Variety 4 – Motto Above Eagle (1866–1873)

The motto IN GOD WE TRUST was added to the reverse side in 1866. As with the half dollar and silver dollar, the motto has been retained since that time.

*Circulation strike.*

*Proof strike.*

| | Mintage | G-4 | VG-8 | F-12 | VF-20 | EF-40 | AU-50 | MS-60 | MS-63 | PF-63 |
|---|---|---|---|---|---|---|---|---|---|---|
| 1866 (725) | 16,800 | $750 | $1,000 | $1,250 | $1,500 | $2,000 | $2,450 | $2,800 | $3,150 | $850 |
| 1866S | 28,000 | 450 | 750 | 1,200 | 1,650 | 2,300 | 3,500 | 5,000 | 10,000 | |
| 1867 (625) | 20,000 | 350 | 550 | 700 | 1,000 | 1,500 | 1,850 | 2,250 | 4,500 | 850 |
| 1867S | 48,000 | 600 | 750 | 1,150 | 1,750 | 3,500 | 7,000 | 10,500 | 15,000 | |
| 1868 (600) | 29,400 | 185 | 275 | 400 | 500 | 700 | 850 | 1,750 | 3,500 | 850 |
| 1868S | 96,000 | 125 | 175 | 350 | 750 | 1,000 | 1,750 | 5,500 | 9,500 | |
| 1869 (600) | 16,000 | 500 | 650 | 850 | 1,000 | 1,250 | 1,500 | 2,250 | 4,500 | 850 |
| 1869S | 76,000 | 175 | 250 | 425 | 650 | 1,250 | 1,650 | 4,500 | 7,000 | |
| 1870 (1,000) | 86,400 | 65 | 100 | 150 | 250 | 450 | 600 | 1,000 | 1,750 | 850 |
| 1870CC | 8,340 | 10,500 | 13,500 | 18,500 | 25,000 | 45,000 | 85,000 | | — | |
| 1871 (960) | 118,200 | 50 | 75 | 125 | 175 | 325 | 450 | 750 | 1,500 | 850 |
| 1871CC | 10,890 | 8,000 | 12,500 | 17,500 | 25,000 | 37,500 | 55,000 | | | |
| 1871S | 30,900 | 900 | 1,400 | 2,350 | 3,200 | 4,000 | 5,500 | 7,250 | 10,000 | |
| 1872 (950) | 182,000 | 50 | 85 | 115 | 185 | 300 | 500 | 900 | 2,250 | 850 |
| 1872CC | 22,850 | 2,250 | 2,800 | 4,500 | 8,500 | 13,500 | 20,000 | 55,000 | | |
| 1872S | 83,000 | 2,000 | 2,600 | 3,200 | 4,750 | 6,000 | 7,000 | 10,000 | 13,000 | |
| 1873, Close 3 (600) | 40,000 | 450 | 700 | 900 | 1,300 | 3,500 | 4,500 | 18,000 | 35,000 | 850 |
| 1873, Open 3 | 172,000 | 30 | 45 | 85 | 150 | 300 | 425 | 675 | 1,850 | |
| 1873CC *(6 known)* | 4,000 | | | 150,000 | 175,000 | 200,000 | | 300,000 | 400,000 | |
| *$460,000, MS-64, Stack's Bowers auction, August 2012* | | | | | | | | | | |

## Variety 5 – Arrows at Date (1873–1874)

Arrows were placed at the date in the years 1873 and 1874 to denote the change of weight from 6.22 to 6.25 grams.

*Weight 6.25 grams; composition .900 silver, .100 copper; diameter 24.3 mm; reeded edge; mints: Philadelphia, San Francisco, Carson City.*

Circulation strike.

Proof strike.

| | Mintage | G-4 | VG-8 | F-12 | VF-20 | EF-40 | AU-50 | MS-60 | MS-63 | PF-63 |
|---|---|---|---|---|---|---|---|---|---|---|
| 1873 | (500)..1,271,200 | $25 | $30 | $45 | $60 | $225 | $425 | $850 | $1,650 | $1,350 |
| 1873CC | 12,462 | 5,000 | 9,500 | 13,000 | 19,000 | 27,500 | 45,000 | 85,000 | 125,000 | |
| 1873S | 156,000 | 100 | 125 | 175 | 250 | 450 | 650 | 1,750 | 4,500 | |
| 1874 | (700)... 471,200 | 25 | 30 | 40 | 65 | 200 | 450 | 850 | 1,100 | 1,350 |
| 1874S | 392,000 | 25 | 35 | 65 | 100 | 265 | 485 | 850 | 1,100 | |

## Variety 4 Resumed, With Weight Standard of Variety 5 (1875–1891)

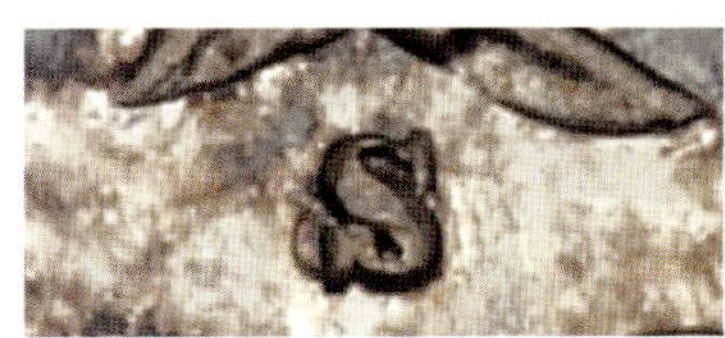

1877-S, S Over Horizontal S

| | Mintage | G-4 | VG-8 | F-12 | VF-20 | EF-40 | AU-50 | MS-60 | MS-63 | PF-63 |
|---|---|---|---|---|---|---|---|---|---|---|
| 1875 | (700)...4,292,800 | $25 | $30 | $35 | $45 | $65 | $160 | $275 | $550 | $750 |
| 1875CC | 140,000 | 200 | 275 | 550 | 800 | 1,350 | 2,500 | 4,500 | 7,500 | |
| 1875S | 680,000 | 45 | 60 | 95 | 130 | 250 | 325 | 600 | 1,000 | |
| 1876 | (1,150)..17,816,000 | 25 | 30 | 35 | 45 | 65 | 160 | 275 | 550 | 750 |
| 1876CC | 4,944,000 | 45 | 85 | 115 | 135 | 175 | 325 | 500 | 1,250 | |
| 1876S | 8,596,000 | 25 | 30 | 35 | 45 | 65 | 160 | 275 | 550 | |
| 1877 | (510)..10,911,200 | 25 | 30 | 35 | 45 | 65 | 160 | 275 | 550 | 750 |
| 1877CC **(a)** | 4,192,000 | 50 | 90 | 110 | 125 | 175 | 275 | 475 | 1,150 | |
| 1877S | 8,996,000 | 25 | 30 | 35 | 45 | 65 | 160 | 275 | 550 | |
| 1877S, S/Horiz S | * | 30 | 45 | 85 | 150 | 285 | 500 | 850 | 2,000 | |
| 1878 | (800)...2,260,000 | 25 | 30 | 35 | 45 | 65 | 160 | 275 | 550 | 750 |
| 1878CC | 996,000 | 75 | 95 | 120 | 150 | 275 | 425 | 750 | 1,650 | |
| 1878S | 140,000 | 250 | 400 | 600 | 900 | 1,250 | 1,700 | 3,500 | 6,000 | |
| 1879 | (1,100)..... 13,600 | 200 | 275 | 350 | 425 | 475 | 550 | 675 | 850 | 750 |
| 1880 | (1,355)..... 13,600 | 200 | 275 | 350 | 425 | 475 | 550 | 675 | 850 | 750 |
| 1881 | (975)..... 12,000 | 200 | 275 | 350 | 425 | 475 | 550 | 675 | 850 | 750 |
| 1882 | (1,100)..... 15,200 | 200 | 275 | 350 | 425 | 475 | 550 | 675 | 850 | 750 |
| 1883 | (1,039)..... 14,400 | 200 | 275 | 350 | 425 | 475 | 550 | 675 | 850 | 750 |
| 1884 | (875)...... 8,000 | 300 | 400 | 500 | 625 | 725 | 800 | 900 | 1,150 | 750 |
| 1885 | (930)..... 13,600 | 200 | 250 | 350 | 500 | 575 | 700 | 850 | 1,100 | 750 |
| 1886 | (886)...... 5,000 | 400 | 550 | 750 | 950 | 1,100 | 1,250 | 1,500 | 1,900 | 750 |

* Included in number above. **a.** Variety with fine edge-reeding is scarcer than that with normally spaced reeding.

*Chart continued on next page.*

| | Mintage | G-4 | VG-8 | F-12 | VF-20 | EF-40 | AU-50 | MS-60 | MS-63 | PF-63 |
|---|---|---|---|---|---|---|---|---|---|---|
| 1887 . . . . . . . . (710) | . . . . 10,000 | $250 | $350 | $425 | $500 | $575 | $625 | $850 | $1,150 | $750 |
| 1888 . . . . . . . . (832) | . . . . 10,001 | 250 | 350 | 425 | 500 | 550 | 600 | 700 | 900 | 750 |
| 1888S | . . . . . . . . . . . . . 1,216,000 | 25 | 30 | 35 | 45 | 70 | 200 | 360 | 750 | |
| 1889 . . . . . . . . (711) | . . . . 12,000 | 200 | 275 | 425 | 500 | 550 | 600 | 700 | 900 | 750 |
| 1890 . . . . . . . . (590) | . . . . 80,000 | 95 | 135 | 180 | 275 | 325 | 375 | 485 | 900 | 750 |
| 1891 . . . . . . . . (600) | . . 3,920,000 | 25 | 30 | 35 | 45 | 65 | 160 | 260 | 550 | 750 |
| 1891O | . . . . . . . . . . . . . . . 68,000 | 350 | 550 | 1,000 | 1,650 | 2,500 | 3,350 | 5,000 | 12,500 | |
| 1891S | . . . . . . . . . . . . . 2,216,000 | 25 | 30 | 35 | 45 | 70 | 160 | 260 | 550 | |

## BARBER OR LIBERTY HEAD (1892–1916)

Like other silver coins of this type, the quarter dollars minted from 1892 to 1916 were designed by Charles E. Barber. His initial B is found at the truncation of the neck of Liberty. There are two varieties of the 1892 reverse: (1) the eagle's wing covers only half of the E in UNITED; (2) the eagle's wing covers most of the E. Coins of the first variety reverse are somewhat scarcer than those of the second variety.

*Designer Charles E. Barber; weight 6.25 grams; composition .900 silver, .100 copper (net weight: .18084 oz. pure silver); diameter 24.3 mm; reeded edge; mints: Philadelphia, Denver, New Orleans, San Francisco.*

**G-4 Good**—Date and legends legible. LIBERTY worn off headband.
**VG-8 Very Good**—Some letters in LIBERTY legible.
**F-12 Fine**—LIBERTY completely legible but not sharp.
**VF-20 Very Fine**—All letters in LIBERTY evenly plain.
**EF-40 Extremely Fine**—LIBERTY bold, and its ribbon distinct.
**AU-50 About Uncirculated**—Slight trace of wear above forehead, on cheek, and on eagle's head, wings, and tail.
**MS-60 Uncirculated**—No trace of wear. Light blemishes.
**MS-63 Choice Uncirculated**—Some distracting contact marks or blemishes in prime focal areas. Impaired luster possible.
**PF-63 Choice Proof**—Reflective surfaces with only a few blemishes in secondary focal places. No major flaws.

*Mintmark location is on reverse, below eagle.*

| | Mintage | G-4 | VG-8 | F-12 | VF-20 | EF-40 | AU-50 | MS-60 | MS-63 | PF-63 |
|---|---|---|---|---|---|---|---|---|---|---|
| 1892 . . . . . . (1,245) | . . . 8,236,000 | $10 | $12 | $26 | $45 | $75 | $130 | $250 | $375 | $650 |
| 1892O | . . . . . . . . . . . . . 2,460,000 | 15 | 20 | 45 | 60 | 95 | 180 | 320 | 425 | |
| 1892S | . . . . . . . . . . . . . . 964,079 | 30 | 65 | 95 | 135 | 215 | 325 | 600 | 1,150 | |
| 1893 . . . . . . . (792) | . . . 5,444,023 | 10 | 12 | 20 | 30 | 55 | 130 | 240 | 400 | 650 |
| 1893O | . . . . . . . . . . . . . 3,396,000 | 10 | 14 | 35 | 60 | 110 | 180 | 300 | 450 | |
| 1893S | . . . . . . . . . . . . . 1,454,535 | 20 | 35 | 70 | 120 | 180 | 325 | 425 | 1,000 | |
| 1894 . . . . . . . (972) | . . . 3,432,000 | 10 | 12 | 35 | 50 | 95 | 150 | 240 | 425 | 650 |
| 1894O | . . . . . . . . . . . . . 2,852,000 | 10 | 20 | 45 | 80 | 130 | 230 | 325 | 550 | |
| 1894S | . . . . . . . . . . . . . 2,648,821 | 10 | 15 | 40 | 65 | 135 | 210 | 325 | 525 | |
| 1895 . . . . . . . (880) | . . . 4,440,000 | 10 | 14 | 30 | 45 | 80 | 140 | 275 | 450 | 650 |
| 1895O | . . . . . . . . . . . . . 2,816,000 | 12 | 20 | 50 | 70 | 140 | 230 | 400 | 900 | |
| 1895S | . . . . . . . . . . . . . 1,764,681 | 20 | 35 | 80 | 120 | 170 | 275 | 420 | 950 | |
| 1896 . . . . . . . (762) | . . . 3,874,000 | 10 | 14 | 30 | 45 | 80 | 135 | 250 | 325 | 650 |
| 1896O | . . . . . . . . . . . . . 1,484,000 | 60 | 85 | 200 | 320 | 600 | 900 | 1,100 | 1,600 | |
| 1896S | . . . . . . . . . . . . . . 188,039 | 650 | 1,200 | 2,100 | 3,500 | 5,000 | 6,500 | 12,500 | 15,000 | |
| 1897 . . . . . . . (731) | . . . 8,140,000 | 9 | 14 | 26 | 40 | 70 | 120 | 240 | 350 | 650 |
| 1897O | . . . . . . . . . . . . . 1,414,800 | 45 | 85 | 200 | 350 | 400 | 650 | 850 | 1,750 | |
| 1897S | . . . . . . . . . . . . . . 542,229 | 110 | 160 | 300 | 600 | 900 | 1,250 | 1,600 | 2,200 | |
| 1898 . . . . . . . (735) | . . 11,100,000 | 9 | 10 | 26 | 45 | 70 | 125 | 225 | 350 | 650 |
| 1898O | . . . . . . . . . . . . . 1,868,000 | 15 | 30 | 80 | 140 | 300 | 425 | 750 | 1,600 | |
| 1898S | . . . . . . . . . . . . . 1,020,592 | 11 | 25 | 45 | 75 | 125 | 350 | 900 | 2,250 | |

| | Mintage | G-4 | VG-8 | F-12 | VF-20 | EF-40 | AU-50 | MS-60 | MS-63 | PF-63 |
|---|---|---|---|---|---|---|---|---|---|---|
| 1899 | (846). . 12,624,000 | $9 | $10 | $26 | $45 | $75 | $125 | $240 | $375 | $650 |
| 1899O | 2,644,000 | 12 | 20 | 35 | 70 | 130 | 260 | 500 | 1,000 | |
| 1899S | 708,000 | 27 | 40 | 95 | 125 | 180 | 400 | 1,200 | 1,750 | |
| 1900 | (912). . 10,016,000 | 9 | 10 | 26 | 45 | 75 | 125 | 240 | 375 | 650 |
| 1900O | 3,416,000 | 15 | 28 | 75 | 120 | 160 | 350 | 650 | 1,000 | |
| 1900S | 1,858,585 | 10 | 15 | 35 | 55 | 80 | 200 | 550 | 1,100 | |
| 1901 | (813). . . 8,892,000 | 9 | 10 | 26 | 45 | 80 | 135 | 250 | 425 | 650 |
| 1901O | 1,612,000 | 55 | 85 | 165 | 350 | 750 | 1,000 | 1,650 | 2,500 | |
| 1901S | 72,664 | 3,750 | 8,000 | 13,500 | 20,000 | 27,500 | 32,500 | 40,000 | 50,000 | |
| *$550,000, MS-68, Superior auction, May 1990* | | | | | | | | | | |
| 1902 | (777). . 12,196,967 | 9 | 10 | 26 | 45 | 65 | 120 | 240 | 375 | 650 |
| 1902O | 4,748,000 | 10 | 16 | 50 | 85 | 140 | 240 | 500 | 1,100 | |
| 1902S | 1,524,612 | 14 | 22 | 55 | 90 | 160 | 240 | 500 | 850 | |
| 1903 | (755). . . 9,759,309 | 9 | 10 | 26 | 45 | 65 | 120 | 240 | 450 | 650 |
| 1903O | 3,500,000 | 10 | 12 | 40 | 60 | 120 | 250 | 475 | 900 | |
| 1903S | 1,036,000 | 15 | 25 | 45 | 85 | 150 | 275 | 425 | 725 | |
| 1904 | (670). . . 9,588,143 | 9 | 10 | 26 | 45 | 70 | 120 | 240 | 375 | 650 |
| 1904O | 2,456,000 | 30 | 40 | 90 | 160 | 240 | 400 | 850 | 1,350 | |
| 1905 | (727). . . 4,967,523 | 30 | 35 | 50 | 65 | 70 | 120 | 240 | 425 | 650 |
| 1905O | 1,230,000 | 35 | 60 | 130 | 220 | 260 | 350 | 550 | 1,300 | |
| 1905S | 1,884,000 | 30 | 40 | 75 | 100 | 105 | 225 | 350 | 1,000 | |
| 1906 | (675). . . 3,655,760 | 9 | 10 | 26 | 45 | 70 | 120 | 240 | 375 | 650 |
| 1906D | 3,280,000 | 9 | 10 | 30 | 50 | 70 | 145 | 250 | 425 | |
| 1906O | 2,056,000 | 9 | 10 | 40 | 60 | 100 | 200 | 300 | 500 | |
| 1907 | (575). . . 7,132,000 | 9 | 10 | 26 | 40 | 65 | 120 | 240 | 375 | 650 |
| 1907D | 2,484,000 | 9 | 10 | 26 | 48 | 70 | 200 | 300 | 600 | |
| 1907O | 4,560,000 | 9 | 10 | 26 | 45 | 70 | 135 | 250 | 450 | |
| 1907S | 1,360,000 | 10 | 20 | 45 | 75 | 140 | 280 | 475 | 900 | |
| 1908 | (545). . . 4,232,000 | 9 | 10 | 26 | 45 | 70 | 120 | 240 | 375 | 650 |
| 1908D | 5,788,000 | 9 | 10 | 26 | 45 | 70 | 120 | 240 | 375 | |
| 1908O | 6,244,000 | 9 | 10 | 26 | 45 | 65 | 120 | 240 | 375 | |
| 1908S | 784,000 | 25 | 50 | 115 | 165 | 325 | 500 | 800 | 1,200 | |
| 1909 | (650). . . 9,268,000 | 9 | 10 | 26 | 45 | 65 | 120 | 240 | 375 | 650 |
| 1909D | 5,114,000 | 9 | 10 | 26 | 45 | 85 | 150 | 240 | 375 | |
| 1909O | 712,000 | 55 | 140 | 425 | 900 | 1,500 | 3,100 | 3,600 | 4,300 | |
| 1909S | 1,348,000 | 9 | 10 | 35 | 55 | 90 | 225 | 350 | 750 | |
| 1910 | (551). . . 2,244,000 | 9 | 10 | 26 | 45 | 80 | 140 | 240 | 375 | 650 |
| 1910D | 1,500,000 | 10 | 11 | 45 | 70 | 125 | 240 | 375 | 800 | |
| 1911 | (543). . . 3,720,000 | 9 | 10 | 26 | 45 | 70 | 125 | 240 | 375 | 650 |
| 1911D | 933,600 | 30 | 45 | 150 | 300 | 425 | 625 | 850 | 1,200 | |
| 1911S | 988,000 | 9 | 10 | 55 | 85 | 180 | 280 | 475 | 775 | |
| 1912 | (700). . . 4,400,000 | 9 | 10 | 26 | 45 | 70 | 120 | 240 | 375 | 650 |
| 1912S | 708,000 | 20 | 30 | 65 | 90 | 125 | 225 | 400 | 900 | |
| 1913 | (613). . . . 484,000 | 30 | 45 | 100 | 180 | 400 | 525 | 700 | 850 | 650 |
| 1913D | 1,450,800 | 12 | 15 | 35 | 60 | 85 | 175 | 275 | 400 | |
| 1913S | 40,000 | 1,200 | 2,000 | 4,750 | 7,000 | 10,000 | 12,500 | 15,000 | 18,500 | |
| 1914 | (380). . . 6,244,230 | 9 | 10 | 22 | 40 | 65 | 120 | 240 | 375 | 650 |
| 1914D | 3,046,000 | 9 | 10 | 22 | 40 | 65 | 120 | 240 | 375 | |
| 1914S | 264,000 | 85 | 130 | 425 | 525 | 900 | 1,100 | 1,500 | 2,500 | |
| 1915 | (450). . . 3,480,000 | 9 | 10 | 22 | 40 | 65 | 120 | 240 | 375 | 750 |
| 1915D | 3,694,000 | 9 | 10 | 22 | 40 | 70 | 120 | 240 | 375 | |
| 1915S | 704,000 | 25 | 40 | 60 | 85 | 115 | 200 | 285 | 425 | |
| 1916 | 1,788,000 | 9 | 10 | 22 | 40 | 70 | 120 | 240 | 375 | |
| 1916D | 6,540,800 | 9 | 10 | 22 | 40 | 70 | 120 | 240 | 375 | |

## STANDING LIBERTY (1916–1930)

This type quarter was designed by Hermon A. MacNeil. The left arm of Liberty is upraised, uncovering a shield in the attitude of protection. Her right hand bears the olive branch of peace. MacNeil's initial M is located above and to the right of the date.

There was a modification in 1917 to cover Liberty's exposed breast. The reverse has a new arrangement of the stars, and the eagle is higher. In 1925 a depression was made in the pedestal on which Liberty stands and that bears the date. On the earlier issues the dates wore off easily because they were too high and were not protected by other features of the coin. The new "recessed" dates proved more durable as a result of this change.

No Proof coins of this type were officially issued, but specimen strikings of the first variety, dated 1917, are known to exist.

The Mint also created a 2016 gold Standing Liberty quarter at a smaller dimension. See page 197.

*Designer Hermon A. MacNeil; standards same as for previous issue; mints: Philadelphia, Denver, San Francisco.*

**G-4 Good**—Date and lettering legible. Top of date worn. Liberty's right leg and toes worn off. Much wear evident on left leg and drapery lines.
**VG-8 Very Good**—Distinct date. Toes faintly visible. Drapery lines visible above Liberty's left leg.
**F-12 Fine**—High curve of right leg flat from thigh to ankle. Only slight wear evident on left leg. Drapery lines over right thigh seen only at sides of leg.
**VF-20 Very Fine**—Garment line across right leg worn, but visible at sides.
**EF-40 Extremely Fine**—Flattened only at high spots. Liberty's toes are sharp. Drapery lines across right leg evident.
**AU-50 About Uncirculated**—Slight trace of wear on head, kneecap, shield's center, and highest point on eagle's body.
**MS-60 Uncirculated**—No trace of wear, but contact marks, surface spots, or faded luster possible.
**MS-63 Choice Uncirculated**—No trace of wear. Light blemishes. Attractive mint luster.

*Some modifications must be made for grading Variety 2.*

### Variety 1 – No Stars Below Eagle (1916–1917)

*Mintmark location is on obverse, to left of date.*

*Uncirculated pieces with fully struck head of Liberty are worth more than double the values listed below.*

| | Mintage | G-4 | VG-8 | F-12 | VF-20 | EF-40 | AU-50 | MS-60 | MS-63 |
|---|---|---|---|---|---|---|---|---|---|
| 1916 | 52,000 | $3,000 | $4,750 | $6,000 | $7,000 | $9,000 | $11,000 | $12,500 | $15,000 |
| 1917, Variety 1 | 8,740,000 | 20 | 40 | 50 | 80 | 110 | 150 | 225 | 325 |
| 1917D, Variety 1 | 1,509,200 | 25 | 65 | 95 | 125 | 175 | 225 | 300 | 375 |
| 1917S, Variety 1 | 1,952,000 | 30 | 75 | 115 | 150 | 200 | 275 | 350 | 425 |

### Variety 2 – Stars Below Eagle (1917–1930)

#### *Pedestal Date (1917–1924)*

1918-S, 8 Over 7

| | Mintage | G-4 | VG-8 | F-12 | VF-20 | EF-40 | AU-50 | MS-60 | MS-63 |
|---|---|---|---|---|---|---|---|---|---|
| 1917, Variety 2 | 13,880,000 | $20 | $32 | $45 | $55 | $75 | $110 | $150 | $275 |
| 1917D, Variety 2 | 6,224,400 | 30 | 45 | 65 | 90 | 110 | 150 | 225 | 300 |
| 1917S, Variety 2 | 5,552,000 | 35 | 50 | 75 | 105 | 125 | 165 | 235 | 325 |
| 1918 | 14,240,000 | 20 | 25 | 30 | 35 | 55 | 95 | 150 | 250 |
| 1918D | 7,380,000 | 22 | 30 | 60 | 75 | 120 | 150 | 200 | 360 |
| 1918S, Normal Date | 11,072,000 | 20 | 25 | 35 | 45 | 60 | 120 | 180 | 300 |
| 1918S, 8 Over 7 | * | 1,600 | 2,200 | 3,500 | 4,500 | 7,500 | 10,000 | 17,500 | 27,500 |
| 1919 | 11,324,000 | 25 | 40 | 55 | 65 | 80 | 105 | 150 | 210 |
| 1919D | 1,944,000 | 65 | 110 | 200 | 350 | 550 | 700 | 1,200 | 1,800 |
| 1919S | 1,836,000 | 65 | 90 | 160 | 300 | 500 | 600 | 1,000 | 2,000 |
| 1920 | 27,860,000 | 12 | 16 | 25 | 30 | 45 | 75 | 125 | 210 |
| 1920D | 3,586,400 | 50 | 60 | 80 | 120 | 165 | 235 | 400 | 1,000 |
| 1920S | 6,380,000 | 20 | 25 | 35 | 50 | 70 | 150 | 275 | 700 |
| 1921 | 1,916,000 | 150 | 250 | 385 | 550 | 700 | 900 | 1,200 | 1,900 |
| 1923 | 9,716,000 | 12 | 18 | 25 | 35 | 45 | 80 | 150 | 200 |
| 1923S | 1,360,000 | 250 | 350 | 625 | 875 | 1,200 | 1,700 | 2,100 | 3,000 |
| 1924 | 10,920,000 | 12 | 16 | 22 | 35 | 45 | 80 | 150 | 225 |
| 1924D | 3,112,000 | 40 | 45 | 70 | 110 | 160 | 195 | 240 | 350 |
| 1924S | 2,860,000 | 18 | 28 | 35 | 55 | 110 | 225 | 300 | 800 |

* Included in number above.

*Recessed Date (1925–1930)*

| | Mintage | G-4 | VG-8 | F-12 | VF-20 | EF-40 | AU-50 | MS-60 | MS-63 |
|---|---|---|---|---|---|---|---|---|---|
| 1925 | 12,280,000 | $6 | $8 | $10 | $20 | $40 | $70 | $130 | $200 |
| 1926 | 11,316,000 | 6 | 8 | 9 | 20 | 40 | 70 | 130 | 150 |
| 1926D | 1,716,000 | 8 | 11 | 24 | 38 | 70 | 110 | 150 | 225 |
| 1926S | 2,700,000 | 6 | 9 | 15 | 28 | 90 | 150 | 375 | 800 |
| 1927 | 11,912,000 | 6 | 8 | 9 | 17 | 35 | 70 | 130 | 200 |
| 1927D | 976,000 | 15 | 20 | 30 | 75 | 140 | 190 | 225 | 330 |
| 1927S | 396,000 | 35 | 45 | 110 | 325 | 1,000 | 2,250 | 4,750 | 7,000 |
| 1928 | 6,336,000 | 6 | 8 | 9 | 17 | 35 | 65 | 120 | 175 |
| 1928D | 1,627,600 | 6 | 8 | 9 | 17 | 35 | 65 | 120 | 175 |
| 1928S **(a)** | 2,644,000 | 6 | 8 | 9 | 22 | 40 | 70 | 120 | 190 |
| 1929 | 11,140,000 | 6 | 8 | 9 | 17 | 35 | 65 | 120 | 175 |
| 1929D | 1,358,000 | 6 | 8 | 10 | 17 | 35 | 65 | 120 | 175 |
| 1929S | 1,764,000 | 6 | 8 | 9 | 17 | 35 | 65 | 120 | 175 |
| 1930 | 5,632,000 | 6 | 8 | 9 | 17 | 35 | 65 | 120 | 175 |
| 1930S | 1,556,000 | 6 | 8 | 10 | 17 | 35 | 65 | 120 | 175 |

**a.** Large and small mintmark varieties; see page 22.

## WASHINGTON (1932 TO DATE)

This type was intended to be a commemorative issue marking the 200th anniversary of George Washington's birth. John Flanagan, a New York sculptor, was the designer; his initials, JF, can be found at the base of Washington's neck. The mintmark is on the reverse below the wreath (1932–1964).

**F-12 Fine**—Hair lines about Washington's ear visible. Tiny feathers on eagle's breast faintly visible.
**VF-20 Very Fine**—Most hair details visible. Wing feathers clear.
**EF-40 Extremely Fine**—Hair lines sharp. Wear spots confined to top of eagle's legs and center of breast.
**MS-60 Uncirculated**—No trace of wear, but many contact marks, surface spotting, or faded luster possible.
**MS-63 Choice Uncirculated**—No trace of wear. Light blemishes. Attractive mint luster.
**MS-65 Gem Uncirculated**—Only light, scattered contact marks that are not distracting. Strong luster, good eye appeal.
**PF-65 Gem Proof**—Hardly any blemishes, and no flaws.

*Circulation strike.* *Proof strike.*

1934, Doubled Die 1934, Light Motto 1934, Heavy Motto

## Silver Coinage (1932–1964)

*Designer John Flanagan; weight 6.25 grams; composition .900 silver, .100 copper (net weight .18084 oz. pure silver); diameter 24.3 mm; reeded edge; mints: Philadelphia, Denver, San Francisco.*

| | Mintage | VG-8 | F-12 | VF-20 | EF-40 | AU-50 | MS-60 | MS-63 | MS-65 |
|---|---|---|---|---|---|---|---|---|---|
| 1932 | 5,404,000 | $6 | $9 | $10 | $11 | $15 | $25 | $60 | $275 |
| 1932D | 436,800 | 90 | 100 | 135 | 175 | 300 | 1,000 | 1,500 | 7,500 |
| 1932S | 408,000 | 85 | 95 | 115 | 135 | 200 | 400 | 600 | 2,500 |
| 1934, All kinds | 31,912,052 | | | | | | | | |
| 1934, DblDie | | 55 | 85 | 150 | 225 | 600 | 1,000 | 1,700 | 3,250 |
| 1934, Light Motto | | 6 | 7 | 8 | 10 | 24 | 60 | 135 | 200 |
| 1934, Heavy Motto | | 6 | 7 | 8 | 10 | 15 | 30 | 50 | 165 |
| 1934D **(a)** | 3,527,200 | 6 | 7 | 12 | 25 | 85 | 250 | 340 | 475 |
| 1935 | 32,484,000 | 6 | 7 | 8 | 9 | 10 | 22 | 35 | 70 |
| 1935D | 5,780,000 | 6 | 7 | 10 | 20 | 125 | 240 | 275 | 425 |
| 1935S | 5,660,000 | 6 | 7 | 9 | 15 | 38 | 100 | 135 | 215 |

**a.** Large and small mintmark varieties; see page 22.

1937, Doubled Die Obverse

1942-D, Doubled Die Obverse

1943, Doubled Die Obverse

| | | Mintage | EF-40 | AU-50 | MS-60 | MS-63 | MS-65 | PF-65 |
|---|---|---|---|---|---|---|---|---|
| 1936 | (3,837) | 41,300,000 | $6 | $10 | $25 | $35 | $90 | $1,000 |
| 1936D | | 5,374,000 | 55 | 250 | 525 | 850 | 1,000 | |
| 1936S | | 3,828,000 | 15 | 50 | 120 | 140 | 235 | |
| 1937 | (5,542) | 19,696,000 | 6 | 12 | 25 | 35 | 95 | 425 |
| 1937, Doubled Die Obverse | | * | 700 | 1,500 | 2,450 | 3,200 | 9,000 | |
| 1937D | | 7,189,600 | 15 | 30 | 70 | 90 | 135 | |
| 1937S | | 1,652,000 | 35 | 95 | 150 | 250 | 335 | |

* Included in number above.

| | Mintage | EF-40 | AU-50 | MS-60 | MS-63 | MS-65 | PF-65 |
|---|---|---|---|---|---|---|---|
| 1938 | (8,045)....9,472,000 | $15 | $45 | $95 | $110 | $190 | $200 |
| 1938S | 2,832,000 | 20 | 55 | 105 | 140 | 155 | |
| 1939 | (8,795)...33,540,000 | 6 | 10 | 15 | 25 | 60 | 200 |
| 1939D | 7,092,000 | 11 | 20 | 40 | 50 | 85 | |
| 1939S | 2,628,000 | 20 | 60 | 95 | 135 | 250 | |
| 1940 | (11,246)...35,704,000 | 5 | 9 | 17 | 35 | 50 | 120 |
| 1940D | 2,797,600 | 24 | 65 | 120 | 165 | 250 | |
| 1940S | 8,244,000 | 9 | 16 | 21 | 32 | 45 | |
| 1941 | (15,287)...79,032,000 | 5 | 6 | 10 | 14 | 33 | 115 |
| 1941D | 16,714,800 | 5 | 13 | 32 | 55 | 65 | |
| 1941S **(a)** | 16,080,000 | 5 | 11 | 28 | 50 | 65 | |
| 1942 | (21,123)..102,096,000 | 5 | 6 | 9 | 10 | 27 | 100 |
| 1942D | 17,487,200 | 5 | 8 | 17 | 20 | 27 | |
| 1942D, Doubled Die Obverse | * | 350 | 750 | 1,800 | 3,500 | 7,000 | |
| 1942S | 19,384,000 | 10 | 20 | 70 | 115 | 150 | |
| 1943 | 99,700,000 | 5 | 6 | 9 | 10 | 37 | |
| 1943, Doubled Die Obverse | * | 2,500 | 3,500 | 5,000 | 7,500 | 12,000 | |
| 1943D | 16,095,600 | 8 | 10 | 28 | 39 | 55 | |
| 1943S | 21,700,000 | 9 | 13 | 26 | 42 | 55 | |
| 1943S, Doubled Die Obverse | * | 200 | 350 | 500 | 1,000 | 1,650 | |
| 1944 | 104,956,000 | 5 | 6 | 8 | 9 | 26 | |
| 1944D | 14,600,800 | 5 | 10 | 17 | 20 | 37 | |
| 1944S | 12,560,000 | 5 | 10 | 14 | 20 | 30 | |
| 1945 | 74,372,000 | 5 | 6 | 8 | 9 | 33 | |
| 1945D | 12,341,600 | 5 | 10 | 18 | 25 | 40 | |
| 1945S | 17,004,001 | 5 | 6 | 8 | 13 | 33 | |
| 1946 | 53,436,000 | 5 | 6 | 8 | 9 | 35 | |
| 1946D | 9,072,800 | 5 | 6 | 8 | 9 | 33 | |
| 1946S | 4,204,000 | 5 | 6 | 8 | 9 | 30 | |
| 1947 | 22,556,000 | 5 | 6 | 11 | 19 | 32 | |
| 1947D | 15,338,400 | 5 | 6 | 11 | 17 | 32 | |
| 1947S | 5,532,000 | 5 | 6 | 8 | 15 | 25 | |
| 1948 | 35,196,000 | 5 | 6 | 8 | 9 | 24 | |
| 1948D | 16,766,800 | 5 | 6 | 13 | 18 | 45 | |
| 1948S | 15,960,000 | 5 | 6 | 8 | 10 | 37 | |
| 1949 | 9,312,000 | 10 | 14 | 35 | 47 | 65 | |
| 1949D | 10,068,400 | 5 | 10 | 16 | 38 | 55 | |
| 1950 | (51,386)...24,920,126 | 5 | 6 | 8 | 9 | 32 | 65 |
| 1950D | 21,075,600 | 5 | 6 | 8 | 9 | 34 | |
| 1950D, D Over S | * | 150 | 225 | 325 | 550 | 2,900 | |
| 1950S | 10,284,004 | 5 | 6 | 12 | 16 | 35 | |
| 1950S, S Over D | * | 150 | 250 | 350 | 500 | 1,150 | |
| 1951 | (57,500)...43,448,102 | 5 | 6 | 8 | 9 | 26 | 65 |
| 1951D | 35,354,800 | 5 | 6 | 8 | 9 | 32 | |
| 1951S | 9,048,000 | 5 | 6 | 10 | 15 | 35 | |
| 1952 | (81,980)...38,780,093 | 5 | 6 | 8 | 9 | 24 | 45 |
| 1952D | 49,795,200 | 5 | 6 | 8 | 9 | 28 | |
| 1952S | 13,707,800 | 5 | 6 | 12 | 20 | 36 | |
| 1953 | (128,800)...18,536,120 | 5 | 6 | 8 | 9 | 25 | 45 |
| 1953D | 56,112,400 | 5 | 6 | 8 | 9 | 32 | |

* Included in number above. **a.** Large and small mintmark varieties; see page 22.

*Chart continued on next page.*

| | Mintage | EF-40 | AU-50 | MS-60 | MS-63 | MS-65 | PF-65 |
|---|---|---|---|---|---|---|---|
| 1953S | 14,016,000 | $5 | $6 | $8 | $9 | $25 | |
| 1954 | (233,300) . . . 54,412,203 | 5 | 6 | 8 | 9 | 24 | $25 |
| 1954D | 42,305,500 | 5 | 6 | 8 | 9 | 25 | |
| 1954S | 11,834,722 | 5 | 6 | 8 | 9 | 23 | |
| 1955 | (378,200) . . . 18,180,181 | 5 | 6 | 8 | 9 | 25 | 25 |
| 1955D | 3,182,400 | 5 | 6 | 8 | 9 | 40 | |
| 1956 | (669,384) . . . 44,144,000 | 5 | 6 | 8 | 9 | 18 | 20 |
| 1956D | 32,334,500 | 5 | 6 | 8 | 9 | 25 | |
| 1957 | (1,247,952) . . . 46,532,000 | 5 | 6 | 8 | 9 | 20 | 15 |
| 1957D | 77,924,160 | 5 | 6 | 8 | 9 | 23 | |
| 1958 | (875,652) . . . 6,360,000 | 5 | 6 | 8 | 9 | 18 | 15 |
| 1958D | 78,124,900 | 5 | 6 | 8 | 9 | 23 | |
| 1959 | (1,149,291) . . . 24,384,000 | 5 | 6 | 8 | 9 | 20 | 12 |
| 1959D | 62,054,232 | 5 | 6 | 8 | 9 | 20 | |
| 1960 | (1,691,602) . . . 29,164,000 | 5 | 6 | 8 | 9 | 16 | 11 |
| 1960D | 63,000,324 | 5 | 6 | 8 | 9 | 18 | |
| 1961 | (3,028,244) . . . 37,036,000 | 5 | 6 | 8 | 9 | 15 | 11 |
| 1961D | 83,656,928 | 5 | 6 | 8 | 9 | 17 | |
| 1962 | (3,218,019) . . . 36,156,000 | 5 | 6 | 8 | 9 | 15 | 11 |
| 1962D | 127,554,756 | 5 | 6 | 8 | 9 | 17 | |
| 1963 | (3,075,645) . . . 74,316,000 | 5 | 6 | 8 | 9 | 15 | 11 |
| 1963D | 135,288,184 | 5 | 6 | 8 | 9 | 17 | |
| 1964 | (3,950,762) . . 560,390,585 | 5 | 6 | 8 | 9 | 15 | 11 |
| 1964D | 704,135,528 | 5 | 6 | 8 | 9 | 15 | |

## Clad Coinage and Silver Proofs (1965–1998)

Proof coins from 1937 through 1972 were made from special dies with high relief and minor detail differences. Some of the circulation coins of 1956 through 1964 and 1969-D through 1972-D were also made from reverse dies with these same features. A variety of the 1964-D quarter occurs with the modified reverse normally found only on the clad coins.

*Weight 5.67 grams; composition, outer layers of copper-nickel (.750 copper, .250 nickel) bonded to inner core of pure copper; diameter 24.3 mm; reeded edge. Silver Proofs: weight 6.25 grams; composition .900 silver, .100 copper (net weight .18084 oz. pure silver); diameter 24.3 mm; reeded edge; mints: Philadelphia, Denver, San Francisco.*

**Starting in 1968 mintmark is on obverse, to right of ribbon.**

| | Mintage | MS-63 | MS-65 | PF-65 |
|---|---|---|---|---|
| 1965 | 1,819,717,540 | $1.00 | $9 | |
| 1966 | 821,101,500 | 1.00 | 7 | |
| 1967 | 1,524,031,848 | 1.00 | 6 | |
| 1968 | 220,731,500 | 1.25 | 8 | |
| 1968D | 101,534,000 | 1.10 | 6 | |
| 1968S | (3,041,506) | | | $5 |
| 1969 | 176,212,000 | 3.00 | 10 | |
| 1969D | 114,372,000 | 2.50 | 10 | |
| 1969S | (2,934,631) | | | 5 |
| 1970 | 136,420,000 | 1.00 | 10 | |
| 1970D **(a)** | 417,341,364 | 1.00 | 6 | |
| 1970S | (2,632,810) | | | 5 |

| | Mintage | MS-63 | MS-65 | PF-65 |
|---|---|---|---|---|
| 1971 | 109,284,000 | $1 | $6 | |
| 1971D | 258,634,428 | 1 | 6 | |
| 1971S | (3,220,733) | | | $5 |
| 1972 | 215,048,000 | 1 | 6 | |
| 1972D | 311,067,732 | 1 | 6 | |
| 1972S | (3,260,996) | | | 5 |
| 1973 | 346,924,000 | 1 | 6 | |
| 1973D | 232,977,400 | 1 | 6 | |
| 1973S | (2,760,339) | | | 5 |
| 1974 | 801,456,000 | 1 | 6 | |
| 1974D | 353,160,300 | 1 | 7 | |
| 1974S | (2,612,568) | | | 5 |

**a.** Lightweight, thin quarters of 1970-D are errors struck on metal intended for dimes.

### *Bicentennial (1776–1976)*

In October of 1973, the Treasury announced an open contest for the selection of suitable designs for the Bicentennial reverses of the quarter, half dollar, and dollar, with $5,000 to be awarded to each winner. Twelve semifinalists were chosen, and from these the symbolic entry of Jack L. Ahr was selected for the quarter reverse. It features a military drummer facing left, with a victory torch encircled by 13 stars at the upper left. Except for the dual dating, "1776–1976," the obverse remained unchanged. Pieces with this dual dating were coined during 1975 and 1976. They were struck for general circulation and included in all the Mint's offerings of Proof and Uncirculated sets.

*Designers John Flanagan and Jack L. Ahr; diameter 24.3 mm; reeded edge. Silver issue—Weight 5.75 grams; composition, outer layers of .800 silver, .200 copper bonded to inner core of .209 silver, .791 copper (net weight .0739 oz. pure silver). Copper-nickel issue—Weight 5.67 grams; composition, outer layers of .750 copper, .250 nickel bonded to inner core of pure copper.*

| | Mintage | MS-63 | MS-65 | PF-65 |
|---|---|---|---|---|
| 1776–1976, Copper-Nickel Clad | 809,784,016 | $1.25 | $6 | |
| 1776–1976D, Copper-Nickel Clad | 860,118,839 | 1.25 | 6 | |
| 1776–1976S, Copper-Nickel Clad | (7,059,099) | | | $5 |
| 1776–1976S, Silver Clad **(a)** | *11,000,000* | 4.00 | 7 | |
| 1776–1976S, Silver Clad **(a)** | *(4,000,000)* | | | 8 |

**a.** Mintages are approximate. Several million were melted in 1982.

### *Eagle Reverse Resumed (1977–1998) (Dies Slightly Modified to Lower Relief)*

| | Mintage | MS-63 | MS-65 | PF-65 |
|---|---|---|---|---|
| 1977 | 468,556,000 | $1 | $6 | |
| 1977D | 256,524,978 | 1 | 6 | |
| 1977S | (3,251,152) | | | $5 |
| 1978 | 521,452,000 | 1 | 6 | |
| 1978D | 287,373,152 | 1 | 6 | |
| 1978S | (3,127,781) | | | 5 |
| 1979 | 515,708,000 | 1 | 6 | |
| 1979D | 489,789,780 | 1 | 6 | |
| 1979S, T1 **(a)** | (3,677,175) | | | 5 |
| 1979S, T2 **(a)** | * | | | 6 |
| 1980P | 635,832,000 | 1 | 6 | |
| 1980D | 518,327,487 | 1 | 6 | |
| 1980S | (3,554,806) | | | 5 |
| 1981P | 601,716,000 | 1 | 6 | |
| 1981D | 575,722,833 | 1 | 6 | |
| 1981S, T1 **(a)** | (4,063,083) | | | 4 |
| 1981S, T2 **(a)** | * | | | 6 |
| 1982P | 500,931,000 | 7 | 30 | |
| 1982D | 480,042,788 | 5 | 18 | |
| 1982S | (3,857,479) | | | 4 |
| 1983P | 673,535,000 | 30 | 65 | |
| 1983D | 617,806,446 | 10 | 45 | |
| 1983S | (3,279,126) | | | 4 |
| 1984P | 676,545,000 | 2 | 10 | |
| 1984D | 546,483,064 | 2 | 12 | |
| 1984S | (3,065,110) | | | $4 |
| 1985P | 775,818,962 | $2.00 | $15 | |
| 1985D | 519,962,888 | 1.00 | 9 | |
| 1985S | (3,362,821) | | | 4 |
| 1986P | 551,199,333 | 2.50 | 12 | |
| 1986D | 504,298,660 | 6.00 | 18 | |
| 1986S | (3,010,497) | | | 4 |
| 1987P | 582,499,481 | 1.00 | 9 | |
| 1987D | 655,594,696 | 1.00 | 6 | |
| 1987S | (4,227,728) | | | 4 |
| 1988P | 562,052,000 | 1.25 | 15 | |
| 1988D | 596,810,688 | 1.00 | 10 | |
| 1988S | (3,262,948) | | | 4 |
| 1989P | 512,868,000 | 1.00 | 12 | |
| 1989D | 896,535,597 | 1.00 | 7 | |
| 1989S | (3,220,194) | | | 4 |
| 1990P | 613,792,000 | 1.00 | 10 | |
| 1990D | 927,638,181 | 1.00 | 10 | |
| 1990S | (3,299,559) | | | 4 |
| 1991P | 570,968,000 | 1.00 | 12 | |
| 1991D | 630,966,693 | 1.00 | 12 | |
| 1991S | (2,867,787) | | | 4 |
| 1992P | 384,764,000 | 1.50 | 16 | |
| 1992D | 389,777,107 | 1.00 | 16 | |
| 1992S | (2,858,981) | | | 4 |

* Included in number above. **a.** See page 246 for illustrations of Type 1 and Type 2 varieties.

*Chart continued on next page.*

| | Mintage | MS-63 | MS-65 | PF-65 |
|---|---|---|---|---|
| 1992S, Silver | (1,317,579) | | | $9 |
| 1993P | 639,276,000 | $1.00 | $7 | |
| 1993D | 645,476,128 | 1.00 | 7 | |
| 1993S | (2,633,439) | | | 4 |
| 1993S, Silver | (761,353) | | | 9 |
| 1994P | 825,600,000 | 1.00 | 10 | |
| 1994D | 880,034,110 | 1.00 | 10 | |
| 1994S | (2,484,594) | | | 4 |
| 1994S, Silver | (785,329) | | | 9 |
| 1995P | 1,004,336,000 | 1.25 | 14 | |
| 1995D | 1,103,216,000 | 1.00 | 13 | |
| 1995S | (2,117,496) | | | 8 |
| 1995S, Silver | (679,985) | | | 9 |
| 1996P | 925,040,000 | $1 | $10 | |
| 1996D | 906,868,000 | 1 | 10 | |
| 1996S | (1,750,244) | | | $5 |
| 1996S, Silver | (775,021) | | | 9 |
| 1997P | 595,740,000 | 1 | 11 | |
| 1997D | 599,680,000 | 1 | 12 | |
| 1997S | (2,055,000) | | | 5 |
| 1997S, Silver | (741,678) | | | 9 |
| 1998P | 896,268,000 | 1 | 7 | |
| 1998D | 821,000,000 | 1 | 7 | |
| 1998S | (2,086,507) | | | 6 |
| 1998S, Silver | (878,792) | | | 9 |

## *State Quarters (1999–2008)*

The United States Mint 50 State Quarters® Program begun in 1999 produced a series of 50 quarter dollar coins with special designs honoring each state. Five different designs were issued each year from 1999 through 2008. States were commemorated in the order of their entrance into statehood.

These are all legal tender coins of standard weight and composition. The obverse side depicting President George Washington was modified to include some of the wording previously used on the reverse. The modification was authorized by special legislation, and carried out by Mint sculptor-engraver William Cousins, whose initials were added to the truncation of Washington's neck adjacent to those of the original designer, John Flanagan.

Each state theme was proposed, and approved, by the governor of that state. Final designs were created by Mint personnel.

Circulation coins were made at the Philadelphia and Denver mints. Proof coins were made in San Francisco.

**Circulation strike.** **Proof strike.**

*Weight 5.67 grams; composition, outer layers of copper-nickel (.750 copper, .250 nickel) bonded to inner core of pure copper. Silver Proofs: weight 6.25 grams; composition .900 silver, .100 copper (net weight .18084 oz. pure silver); diameter 24.3 mm; reeded edge; mints: Philadelphia, Denver, San Francisco.*

| | Mintage | AU-50 | MS-63 | MS-65 | PF-65 |
|---|---|---|---|---|---|
| 1999P, Delaware | 373,400,000 | $0.50 | $2.00 | $5 | |
| 1999D, Delaware | 401,424,000 | 0.50 | 2.00 | 5 | |
| 1999S, Delaware | (3,713,359) | | | | $7 |
| 1999S, Delaware, Silver | (804,565) | | | | 25 |
| 1999P, Pennsylvania | 349,000,000 | 0.50 | 2.00 | 5 | |
| 1999D, Pennsylvania | 358,332,000 | 0.50 | 2.00 | 5 | |
| 1999S, Pennsylvania | (3,713,359) | | | | 7 |
| 1999S, Pennsylvania, Silver | (804,565) | | | | 25 |
| 1999P, New Jersey | 363,200,000 | 0.50 | 2.00 | 5 | |
| 1999D, New Jersey | 299,028,000 | 0.50 | 2.00 | 5 | |
| 1999S, New Jersey | (3,713,359) | | | | 7 |
| 1999S, New Jersey, Silver | (804,565) | | | | 25 |
| 1999P, Georgia | 451,188,000 | 0.50 | 2.00 | 5 | |
| 1999D, Georgia | 488,744,000 | 0.50 | 2.00 | 5 | |
| 1999S, Georgia | (3,713,359) | | | | 7 |
| 1999S, Georgia, Silver | (804,565) | | | | 25 |
| 1999P, Connecticut | 688,744,000 | 0.50 | 1.50 | 5 | |
| 1999D, Connecticut | 657,880,000 | 0.50 | 1.50 | 5 | |
| 1999S, Connecticut | (3,713,359) | | | | 7 |
| 1999S, Connecticut, Silver | (804,565) | | | | 25 |

| | Mintage | AU-50 | MS-63 | MS-65 | PF-65 |
|---|---|---|---|---|---|
| 2000P, Massachusetts | 628,600,000 | $0.35 | $1 | $4 | |
| 2000D, Massachusetts | 535,184,000 | 0.35 | 1 | 4 | |
| 2000S, Massachusetts | (4,020,172) | | | | $3 |
| 2000S, Massachusetts, Silver | (965,421) | | | | 8 |
| 2000P, Maryland | 678,200,000 | 0.35 | 1 | 4 | |
| 2000D, Maryland | 556,532,000 | 0.35 | 1 | 4 | |
| 2000S, Maryland | (4,020,172) | | | | 3 |
| 2000S, Maryland, Silver | (965,421) | | | | 8 |
| 2000P, South Carolina | 742,576,000 | 0.35 | 1 | 4 | |
| 2000D, South Carolina | 566,208,000 | 0.35 | 1 | 4 | |
| 2000S, South Carolina | (4,020,172) | | | | 3 |
| 2000S, South Carolina, Silver | (965,421) | | | | 8 |
| 2000P, New Hampshire | 673,040,000 | 0.35 | 1 | 4 | |
| 2000D, New Hampshire | 495,976,000 | 0.35 | 1 | 4 | |
| 2000S, New Hampshire | (4,020,172) | | | | 3 |
| 2000S, New Hampshire, Silver | (965,421) | | | | 8 |
| 2000P, Virginia | 943,000,000 | 0.35 | 1 | 4 | |
| 2000D, Virginia | 651,616,000 | 0.35 | 1 | 4 | |

*Chart continued on next page.*

| | Mintage | AU-50 | MS-63 | MS-65 | PF-65 |
|---|---|---|---|---|---|
| 2000S, Virginia | (4,020,172) | | | | $3 |
| 2000S, Virginia, Silver | (965,421) | | | | 8 |

| | Mintage | AU-50 | MS-63 | MS-65 | PF-65 |
|---|---|---|---|---|---|
| 2001P, New York | 655,400,000 | $0.35 | $1.00 | $4 | |
| 2001D, New York | 619,640,000 | 0.35 | 1.00 | 4 | |
| 2001S, New York | (3,094,140) | | | | $3 |
| 2001S, New York, Silver | (889,697) | | | | 10 |
| 2001P, North Carolina | 627,600,000 | 0.35 | 1.00 | 4 | |
| 2001D, North Carolina | 427,876,000 | 0.35 | 1.00 | 4 | |
| 2001S, North Carolina | (3,094,140) | | | | 3 |
| 2001S, North Carolina, Silver | (889,697) | | | | 10 |
| 2001P, Rhode Island | 423,000,000 | 0.35 | 1.00 | 4 | |
| 2001D, Rhode Island | 447,100,000 | 0.35 | 1.00 | 4 | |
| 2001S, Rhode Island | (3,094,140) | | | | 3 |
| 2001S, Rhode Island, Silver | (889,697) | | | | 10 |
| 2001P, Vermont | 423,400,000 | 0.35 | 1.00 | 4 | |
| 2001D, Vermont | 459,404,000 | 0.35 | 1.00 | 4 | |
| 2001S, Vermont | (3,094,140) | | | | 3 |
| 2001S, Vermont, Silver | (889,697) | | | | 10 |
| 2001P, Kentucky | 353,000,000 | 0.35 | 1.25 | 5 | |
| 2001D, Kentucky | 370,564,000 | 0.35 | 1.25 | 5 | |
| 2001S, Kentucky | (3,094,140) | | | | 3 |
| 2001S, Kentucky, Silver | (889,697) | | | | 10 |

| | Mintage | AU-50 | MS-63 | MS-65 | PF-65 |
|---|---|---|---|---|---|
| 2002P, Tennessee | 361,600,000 | $0.75 | $1.75 | $3 | |
| 2002D, Tennessee | 286,468,000 | 0.75 | 1.75 | 3 | |

| | Mintage | AU-50 | MS-63 | MS-65 | PF-65 |
|---|---|---|---|---|---|
| 2002S, Tennessee | (3,084,245) | | | | $3 |
| 2002S, Tennessee, Silver | (892,229) | | | | 8 |
| 2002P, Ohio | 217,200,000 | $0.35 | $1 | $1.50 | |
| 2002D, Ohio | 414,832,000 | 0.35 | 1 | 1.50 | |
| 2002S, Ohio | (3,084,245) | | | | 3 |
| 2002S, Ohio, Silver | (892,229) | | | | 8 |
| 2002P, Louisiana | 362,000,000 | 0.35 | 1 | 1.50 | |
| 2002D, Louisiana | 402,204,000 | 0.35 | 1 | 1.50 | |
| 2002S, Louisiana | (3,084,245) | | | | 3 |
| 2002S, Louisiana, Silver | (892,229) | | | | 8 |
| 2002P, Indiana | 362,600,000 | 0.35 | 1 | 1.50 | |
| 2002D, Indiana | 327,200,000 | 0.35 | 1 | 1.50 | |
| 2002S, Indiana | (3,084,245) | | | | 3 |
| 2002S, Indiana, Silver | (892,229) | | | | 8 |
| 2002P, Mississippi | 290,000,000 | 0.35 | 1 | 1.50 | |
| 2002D, Mississippi | 289,600,000 | 0.35 | 1 | 1.50 | |
| 2002S, Mississippi | (3,084,245) | | | | 3 |
| 2002S, Mississippi, Silver | (892,229) | | | | 8 |

| | Mintage | AU-50 | MS-63 | MS-65 | PF-65 |
|---|---|---|---|---|---|
| 2003P, Illinois | 225,800,000 | $0.50 | $1.50 | $2.00 | |
| 2003D, Illinois | 237,400,000 | 0.50 | 1.50 | 2.00 | |
| 2003S, Illinois | (3,408,516) | | | | $3 |
| 2003S, Illinois, Silver | (1,125,755) | | | | 8 |
| 2003P, Alabama | 225,000,000 | 0.35 | 1.00 | 1.50 | |
| 2003D, Alabama | 232,400,000 | 0.35 | 1.00 | 1.50 | |
| 2003S, Alabama | (3,408,516) | | | | 3 |
| 2003S, Alabama, Silver | (1,125,755) | | | | 8 |
| 2003P, Maine | 217,400,000 | 0.35 | 1.00 | 1.50 | |
| 2003D, Maine | 231,400,000 | 0.35 | 1.00 | 1.50 | |
| 2003S, Maine | (3,408,516) | | | | 3 |
| 2003S, Maine, Silver | (1,125,755) | | | | 8 |
| 2003P, Missouri | 225,000,000 | 0.35 | 1.00 | 1.50 | |
| 2003D, Missouri | 228,200,000 | 0.35 | 1.00 | 1.50 | |
| 2003S, Missouri | (3,408,516) | | | | 3 |
| 2003S, Missouri, Silver | (1,125,755) | | | | 8 |
| 2003P, Arkansas | 228,000,000 | 0.35 | 1.00 | 1.50 | |
| 2003D, Arkansas | 229,800,000 | 0.40 | 1.00 | 1.50 | |
| 2003S, Arkansas | (3,408,516) | | | | 3 |
| 2003S, Arkansas, Silver | (1,125,755) | | | | 8 |

*Some 2004-D Wisconsin quarters show one of two different die flaws on the reverse, in the shape of an extra leaf on the corn. On one (middle), the extra leaf extends upward; on the other (right), it bends low. The normal die is shown at left.*

| | Mintage | AU-50 | MS-63 | MS-65 | PF-65 |
|---|---|---|---|---|---|
| 2004P, Michigan | 233,800,000 | $0.35 | $0.75 | $3 | |
| 2004D, Michigan | 225,800,000 | 0.35 | 0.75 | 3 | |
| 2004S, Michigan | (2,740,684) | | | | $3 |
| 2004S, Michigan, Silver | (1,769,786) | | | | 8 |
| 2004P, Florida | 240,200,000 | 0.35 | 0.75 | 3 | |
| 2004D, Florida | 241,600,000 | 0.35 | 0.75 | 3 | |
| 2004S, Florida | (2,740,684) | | | | 3 |
| 2004S, Florida, Silver | (1,769,786) | | | | 8 |
| 2004P, Texas | 278,800,000 | 0.35 | 0.75 | 3 | |
| 2004D, Texas | 263,000,000 | 0.35 | 0.75 | 3 | |
| 2004S, Texas | (2,740,684) | | | | 3 |
| 2004S, Texas, Silver | (1,769,786) | | | | 8 |
| 2004P, Iowa | 213,800,000 | 0.35 | 0.75 | 3 | |
| 2004D, Iowa | 251,400,000 | 0.35 | 0.75 | 3 | |
| 2004S, Iowa | (2,740,684) | | | | 3 |
| 2004S, Iowa, Silver | (1,769,786) | | | | 8 |
| 2004P, Wisconsin | 226,400,000 | 0.35 | 0.75 | 3 | |
| 2004D, Wisconsin | 226,800,000 | 0.35 | 0.75 | 10 | |
| 2004D, Wisconsin, Extra Leaf High | * | 75.00 | 150.00 | 200 | |
| 2004D, Wisconsin, Extra Leaf Low | * | 50.00 | 130.00 | 165 | |
| 2004S, Wisconsin | (2,740,684) | | | | 3 |
| 2004S, Wisconsin, Silver | (1,769,786) | | | | 8 |

* Included in number above.

**Note: Uncirculated Mint Sets for 2005–2010 were made with Satin Finish coins not included in the listings here. See page 369 for their mintages.**

| | Mintage | AU-50 | MS-63 | MS-65 | PF-65 |
|---|---|---|---|---|---|
| 2005P, California | 257,200,000 | $0.30 | $0.75 | $5 | |
| 2005D, California | 263,200,000 | 0.30 | 0.75 | 5 | |
| 2005S, California | (3,262,960) | | | | $3 |
| 2005S, California, Silver | (1,678,649) | | | | 8 |
| 2005P, Minnesota | 239,600,000 | 0.30 | 0.75 | 5 | |
| 2005D, Minnesota | 248,400,000 | 0.30 | 0.75 | 5 | |
| 2005S, Minnesota | (3,262,960) | | | | 3 |
| 2005S, Minnesota, Silver | (1,678,649) | | | | 8 |
| 2005P, Oregon | 316,200,000 | 0.30 | 0.75 | 5 | |
| 2005D, Oregon | 404,000,000 | 0.30 | 0.75 | 5 | |
| 2005S, Oregon | (3,262,960) | | | | 3 |
| 2005S, Oregon, Silver | (1,678,649) | | | | 8 |
| 2005P, Kansas | 263,400,000 | 0.30 | 0.75 | 5 | |
| 2005D, Kansas | 300,000,000 | 0.30 | 0.75 | 5 | |
| 2005S, Kansas | (3,262,960) | | | | 3 |
| 2005S, Kansas, Silver | (1,678,649) | | | | 8 |
| 2005P, West Virginia | 365,400,000 | 0.30 | 0.75 | 5 | |
| 2005D, West Virginia | 356,200,000 | 0.30 | 0.75 | 5 | |
| 2005S, West Virginia | (3,262,960) | | | | 3 |
| 2005S, West Virginia, Silver | (1,678,649) | | | | 8 |

| | Mintage | AU-50 | MS-63 | MS-65 | PF-65 |
|---|---|---|---|---|---|
| 2006P, Nevada | 277,000,000 | $0.30 | $0.75 | $1 | |
| 2006D, Nevada | 312,800,000 | 0.30 | 0.75 | 1 | |
| 2006S, Nevada | (2,882,428) | | | | $3 |
| 2006S, Nevada, Silver | (1,585,008) | | | | 8 |
| 2006P, Nebraska | 318,000,000 | 0.30 | 0.75 | 2 | |
| 2006D, Nebraska | 273,000,000 | 0.30 | 0.75 | 2 | |
| 2006S, Nebraska | (2,882,428) | | | | 3 |
| 2006S, Nebraska, Silver | (1,585,008) | | | | 8 |
| 2006P, Colorado | 274,800,000 | 0.30 | 0.75 | 2 | |
| 2006D, Colorado | 294,200,000 | 0.30 | 0.75 | 2 | |
| 2006S, Colorado | (2,882,428) | | | | 3 |
| 2006S, Colorado, Silver | (1,585,008) | | | | 8 |
| 2006P, North Dakota | 305,800,000 | 0.30 | 0.75 | 2 | |
| 2006D, North Dakota | 359,000,000 | 0.30 | 0.75 | 2 | |
| 2006S, North Dakota | (2,882,428) | | | | 3 |
| 2006S, North Dakota, Silver | (1,585,008) | | | | 8 |

*Chart continued on next page.*

**Note: Uncirculated Mint Sets for 2005–2010 were made with Satin Finish coins not included in the listings here. See page 369 for their mintages.**

| | Mintage | AU-50 | MS-63 | MS-65 | PF-65 |
|---|---|---|---|---|---|
| 2006P, South Dakota | 245,000,000 | $0.30 | $0.75 | $2 | |
| 2006D, South Dakota | 265,800,000 | 0.30 | 0.75 | 2 | |
| 2006S, South Dakota | (2,882,428) | | | | $3 |
| 2006S, South Dakota, Silver | (1,585,008) | | | | 8 |

| | Mintage | AU-50 | MS-63 | MS-65 | PF-65 |
|---|---|---|---|---|---|
| 2007P, Montana | 257,000,000 | $0.30 | $0.75 | $4 | |
| 2007D, Montana | 256,240,000 | 0.30 | 0.75 | 4 | |
| 2007S, Montana | (2,374,778) | | | | $3 |
| 2007S, Montana, Silver | (1,313,481) | | | | 8 |
| 2007P, Washington | 265,200,000 | 0.30 | 0.75 | 4 | |
| 2007D, Washington | 280,000,000 | 0.30 | 0.75 | 4 | |
| 2007S, Washington | (2,374,778) | | | | 3 |
| 2007S, Washington, Silver | (1,313,481) | | | | 8 |
| 2007P, Idaho | 294,600,000 | 0.30 | 0.75 | 4 | |
| 2007D, Idaho | 286,800,000 | 0.30 | 0.75 | 4 | |
| 2007S, Idaho | (2,374,778) | | | | 3 |
| 2007S, Idaho, Silver | (1,313,481) | | | | 8 |
| 2007P, Wyoming | 243,600,000 | 0.30 | 0.75 | 4 | |
| 2007D, Wyoming | 320,800,000 | 0.30 | 0.75 | 4 | |
| 2007S, Wyoming | (2,374,778) | | | | 3 |
| 2007S, Wyoming, Silver | (1,313,481) | | | | 8 |
| 2007P, Utah | 255,000,000 | 0.30 | 0.75 | 4 | |
| 2007D, Utah | 253,200,000 | 0.30 | 0.75 | 4 | |
| 2007S, Utah | (2,374,778) | | | | 3 |
| 2007S, Utah, Silver | (1,313,481) | | | | 8 |

**Note: Uncirculated Mint Sets for 2005–2010 were made with Satin Finish coins not included in the listings here. See page 369 for their mintages.**

| | Mintage | AU-50 | MS-63 | MS-65 | PF-65 |
|---|---|---|---|---|---|
| 2008P, Oklahoma | 222,000,000 | $0.30 | $0.75 | $2 | |
| 2008D, Oklahoma | 194,600,000 | 0.30 | 0.75 | 2 | |
| 2008S, Oklahoma (2,078,112) | | | | | $3 |
| 2008S, Oklahoma, Silver (1,192,908) | | | | | 8 |
| 2008P, New Mexico | 244,200,000 | 0.30 | 0.75 | 2 | |
| 2008D, New Mexico | 244,400,000 | 0.30 | 0.75 | 2 | |
| 2008S, New Mexico (2,078,112) | | | | | 3 |
| 2008S, New Mexico, Silver (1,192,908) | | | | | 8 |
| 2008P, Arizona | 244,600,000 | 0.30 | 0.75 | 2 | |
| 2008D, Arizona | 265,000,000 | 0.30 | 0.75 | 2 | |
| 2008S, Arizona (2,078,112) | | | | | 3 |
| 2008S, Arizona, Silver (1,192,908) | | | | | 8 |
| 2008P, Alaska | 251,800,000 | 0.30 | 0.75 | 2 | |
| 2008D, Alaska | 254,000,000 | 0.30 | 0.75 | 2 | |
| 2008S, Alaska (2,078,112) | | | | | 3 |
| 2008S, Alaska, Silver (1,192,908) | | | | | 8 |
| 2008P, Hawaii | 254,000,000 | 0.30 | 0.75 | 2 | |
| 2008D, Hawaii | 263,600,000 | 0.30 | 0.75 | 2 | |
| 2008S, Hawaii (2,078,112) | | | | | 3 |
| 2008S, Hawaii, Silver *(1,192,908)* | | | | | 8 |

Some State quarters were accidentally made with "dis-oriented" dies and are valued higher than ordinary pieces. Normal United States coins have dies oriented in "coin alignment," such that the reverse appears upside down when the coin is rotated from right to left. Values for the rotated-die quarters vary according to the amount of shifting. The most valuable are those that are shifted 180 degrees, so that both sides appear upright when the coin is turned over (called *medal alignment*).

**Manufacturing varieties showing die doubling or other minor, unintentional characteristics are of interest to collectors and are often worth premium prices.**

### *District of Columbia and U.S. Territories Quarters (2009)*

At the ending of the U.S. Mint 50 State Quarters® Program a new series of quarter-dollar reverse designs was authorized to recognize the District of Columbia and the five U.S. territories: the Commonwealth of Puerto Rico, Guam, American Samoa, the U.S. Virgin Islands, and the Commonwealth of the Northern Mariana Islands. Each of these coins, issued sequentially during 2009, has the portrait of George Washington, as in the past, and is made of the same weight and composition. Each coin commemorates the history, geography, or traditions of the place it represents.

*See next page for chart.*

**Note: Uncirculated Mint Sets for 2005–2010 were made with Satin Finish coins not included in the listings here. See page 369 for their mintages.**

| | Mintage | AU-50 | MS-63 | MS-65 | PF-65 |
|---|---|---|---|---|---|
| 2009P, District of Columbia | 83,600,000 | $0.50 | $1 | $2 | |
| 2009D, District of Columbia | 88,800,000 | 0.50 | 1 | 2 | |
| 2009S, District of Columbia | (2,113,478) | | | | $3 |
| 2009S, District of Columbia, Silver | (996,548) | | | | 8 |
| 2009P, Puerto Rico | 53,200,000 | 0.50 | 1 | 2 | |
| 2009D, Puerto Rico | 86,000,000 | 0.50 | 1 | 2 | |
| 2009S, Puerto Rico | (2,113,478) | | | | 3 |
| 2009S, Puerto Rico, Silver | (996,548) | | | | 8 |
| 2009P, Guam | 45,000,000 | 0.50 | 1 | 2 | |
| 2009D, Guam | 42,600,000 | 0.50 | 1 | 2 | |
| 2009S, Guam | (2,113,478) | | | | 3 |
| 2009S, Guam, Silver | (996,548) | | | | 8 |
| 2009P, American Samoa | 42,600,000 | 0.50 | 1 | 2 | |
| 2009D, American Samoa | 39,600,000 | 0.50 | 1 | 2 | |
| 2009S, American Samoa | (2,113,478) | | | | 3 |
| 2009S, American Samoa, Silver | (996,548) | | | | 8 |
| 2009P, U.S. Virgin Islands | 41,000,000 | 0.75 | 1 | 2 | |
| 2009D, U.S. Virgin Islands | 41,000,000 | 0.75 | 1 | 2 | |
| 2009S, U.S. Virgin Islands | (2,113,478) | | | | 3 |
| 2009S, U.S. Virgin Islands, Silver | (996,548) | | | | 8 |
| 2009P, Northern Mariana Islands | 35,200,000 | 0.50 | 1 | 2 | |
| 2009D, Northern Mariana Islands | 37,600,000 | 0.50 | 1 | 2 | |
| 2009S, Northern Mariana Islands | (2,113,478) | | | | 3 |
| 2009S, Northern Mariana Islands, Silver | (996,548) | | | | 8 |

### *America the Beautiful™ Quarters Program (2010–2021)*

Following up on the popularity of the 50 State Quarters® Program, Congress authorized the production of new circulating commemorative quarters from 2010 to 2021. The coins honor a site of "natural or historic significance" from each of the 50 states, five U.S. territories, and the District of Columbia. They continue to bear George Washington's portrait on the obverse. In 2019, the silver Proof composition was changed to .999 silver, .001 copper (weight 6.343 grams; net weight .182 oz. pure silver).

Five designs are released each year, in the order the coins' featured locations were designated national parks or national sites. At the discretion of the secretary of the Treasury, after 2021 this series could be extended an additional 11 years by featuring a second national park or site from each state, district, and territory.

In addition to the circulating quarters, a series of five-ounce silver bullion pieces are being coined each year with designs nearly identical to those of the America the Beautiful™ quarters; see pages 371–373 for more information.

**Note: Uncirculated Mint Sets for 2005–2010 were made with Satin Finish coins not included in the listings here. See page 369 for their mintages.**

| | Mintage | AU-50 | MS-63 | MS-65 | PF-65 |
|---|---|---|---|---|---|
| 2010P, Hot Springs National Park (Arkansas) | 35,600,000 | $0.45 | $0.50 | $1 | |
| 2010D, Hot Springs National Park (Arkansas) | 34,000,000 | 0.45 | 0.50 | 1 | |
| 2010S, Hot Springs National Park (Arkansas) | *(1,402,889)* | | | | $3 |
| 2010S, Hot Springs National Park (Arkansas), Silver | (859,417) | | | | 8 |
| 2010P, Yellowstone National Park (Wyoming) | 33,600,000 | 0.45 | 0.50 | 2 | |
| 2010D, Yellowstone National Park (Wyoming) | 34,800,000 | 0.45 | 0.50 | 2 | |
| 2010S, Yellowstone National Park (Wyoming) | *(1,404,259)* | | | | 3 |
| 2010S, Yellowstone National Park (Wyoming), Silver | (859,417) | | | | 8 |
| 2010P, Yosemite National Park (California) | 35,200,000 | 0.50 | 0.75 | 2 | |
| 2010D, Yosemite National Park (California) | 34,800,000 | 0.50 | 0.75 | 2 | |
| 2010S, Yosemite National Park (California) | *(1,401,522)* | | | | 3 |
| 2010S, Yosemite National Park (California), Silver | (859,417) | | | | 8 |
| 2010P, Grand Canyon National Park (Arizona) | 34,800,000 | 0.45 | 0.50 | 1 | |
| 2010D, Grand Canyon National Park (Arizona) | 35,400,000 | 0.45 | 0.50 | 1 | |
| 2010S, Grand Canyon National Park (Arizona) | *(1,401,462)* | | | | 3 |
| 2010S, Grand Canyon National Park (Arizona), Silver | (859,417) | | | | 8 |
| 2010P, Mount Hood National Forest (Oregon) | 34,400,000 | 0.45 | 0.50 | 2 | |
| 2010D, Mount Hood National Forest (Oregon) | 34,400,000 | 0.45 | 0.50 | 2 | |
| 2010S, Mount Hood National Forest (Oregon) | *(1,398,106)* | | | | 3 |
| 2010S, Mount Hood National Forest (Oregon), Silver | (859,417) | | | | 8 |

| | Mintage | AU-50 | MS-63 | MS-65 | PF-65 |
|---|---|---|---|---|---|
| 2011P, Gettysburg National Military Park (Pennsylvania) | 30,800,000 | $0.50 | $0.75 | $1.25 | |
| 2011D, Gettysburg National Military Park (Pennsylvania) | 30,400,000 | 0.50 | 0.75 | 1.25 | |
| 2011S, Gettysburg National Military Park (Pennsylvania) | *(1,273,068)* | | | | $3 |
| 2011S, Gettysburg National Military Park (Pennsylvania), Silver | (722,076) | | | | 8 |
| 2011P, Glacier National Park (Montana) | 30,400,000 | 0.45 | 0.50 | 1.00 | |
| 2011D, Glacier National Park (Montana) | 31,200,000 | 0.45 | 0.50 | 1.00 | |
| 2011S, Glacier National Park (Montana) | *(1,269,422)* | | | | 3 |
| 2011S, Glacier National Park (Montana), Silver | (722,076) | | | | 8 |
| 2011P, Olympic National Park (Washington) | 30,400,000 | 0.45 | 0.50 | 2.00 | |
| 2011D, Olympic National Park (Washington) | 30,600,000 | 0.45 | 0.50 | 2.00 | |
| 2011S, Olympic National Park (Washington) | *(1,268,231)* | | | | 3 |
| 2011S, Olympic National Park (Washington), Silver | (722,076) | | | | 8 |
| 2011P, Vicksburg National Military Park (Mississippi) | 30,800,000 | 0.45 | 0.50 | 1.00 | |
| 2011D, Vicksburg National Military Park (Mississippi) | 33,400,000 | 0.45 | 0.50 | 1.00 | |
| 2011S, Vicksburg National Military Park (Mississippi) | *(1,268,623)* | | | | 3 |
| 2011S, Vicksburg National Military Park (Mississippi), Silver | (722,076) | | | | 8 |

*Chart continued on next page.*

| | Mintage | AU-50 | MS-63 | MS-65 | PF-65 |
|---|---|---|---|---|---|
| 2011P, Chickasaw National Recreation Area (Oklahoma) | 73,800,000 | $0.45 | $0.50 | $1 | |
| 2011D, Chickasaw National Recreation Area (Oklahoma) | 69,400,000 | 0.45 | 0.50 | 1 | |
| 2011S, Chickasaw National Recreation Area (Oklahoma) | *(1,266,825)* | | | | $3 |
| 2011S, Chickasaw National Recreation Area (Oklahoma), Silver | (722,076) | | | | 8 |

| | Mintage | AU-50 | MS-63 | MS-65 | PF-65 |
|---|---|---|---|---|---|
| 2012P, El Yunque National Forest (Puerto Rico) | 25,800,000 | $0.45 | $0.50 | $2 | |
| 2012D, El Yunque National Forest (Puerto Rico) | 25,000,000 | 0.45 | 0.50 | 2 | |
| 2012S, El Yunque National Forest (Puerto Rico) **(a)** | 1,680,140 | | 1.00 | 8 | |
| 2012S, El Yunque National Forest (Puerto Rico) | (1,012,094) | | | | $3 |
| 2012S, El Yunque National Forest (Puerto Rico), Silver | (608,060) | | | | 8 |
| 2012P, Chaco Culture National Historical Park (New Mexico) | 22,000,000 | 0.45 | 0.50 | 2 | |
| 2012D, Chaco Culture National Historical Park (New Mexico) | 22,000,000 | 0.45 | 0.50 | 2 | |
| 2012S, Chaco Culture National Historical Park (New Mexico) **(a)** | 1,389,020 | | 2.00 | 8 | |
| 2012S, Chaco Culture National Historical Park (New Mexico) | *(961,464)* | | | | 3 |
| 2012S, Chaco Culture National Historical Park (New Mexico), Silver | (608,060) | | | | 8 |
| 2012P, Acadia National Park (Maine) | 24,800,000 | 0.45 | 0.50 | 1 | |
| 2012D, Acadia National Park (Maine) | 21,606,000 | 0.45 | 0.50 | 1 | |
| 2012S, Acadia National Park (Maine) **(a)** | 1,409,120 | | 2.00 | 8 | |
| 2012S, Acadia National Park (Maine) | *(962,038)* | | | | 3 |
| 2012S, Acadia National Park (Maine), Silver | (608,060) | | | | 8 |
| 2012P, Hawai'i Volcanoes National Park (Hawaii) | 46,200,000 | 0.45 | 0.50 | 1 | |
| 2012D, Hawai'i Volcanoes National Park (Hawaii) | 78,600,000 | 0.45 | 0.50 | 1 | |
| 2012S, Hawai'i Volcanoes National Park (Hawaii) **(a)** | 1,409,120 | | 2.00 | 8 | |
| 2012S, Hawai'i Volcanoes National Park (Hawaii) | *(962,447)* | | | | 3 |
| 2012S, Hawai'i Volcanoes National Park (Hawaii), Silver | (608,060) | | | | 8 |
| 2012P, Denali National Park and Preserve (Alaska) | 135,400,000 | 0.40 | 0.50 | 1 | |
| 2012D, Denali National Park and Preserve (Alaska) | 166,600,000 | 0.40 | 0.50 | 1 | |
| 2012S, Denali National Park and Preserve (Alaska) **(a)** | 1,409,220 | | 1.00 | 8 | |
| 2012S, Denali National Park and Preserve (Alaska) | *(959,602)* | | | | 3 |
| 2012S, Denali National Park and Preserve (Alaska), Silver | (608,060) | | | | 8 |

**a.** The San Francisco Mint made Uncirculated S-mintmark quarters in relatively small quantities for collectors, who must purchase them directly from the Mint for a premium above face value. Unlike the Uncirculated S-mintmark Bicentennial quarters, which were silver clad and sold only in sets, S-Mint America the Beautiful™ quarters are of normal composition and are sold in bags and rolls. Thus, the 2012-S coins are considered the first circulation-strike quarters made at San Francisco since 1954.

| | Mintage | AU-50 | MS-63 | MS-65 | PF-65 |
|---|---|---|---|---|---|
| 2013P, White Mountain National Forest (New Hampshire) | 68,800,000 | $0.45 | $0.50 | $1 | |
| 2013D, White Mountain National Forest (New Hampshire) | 107,600,000 | 0.45 | 0.50 | 1 | |
| 2013S, White Mountain National Forest (New Hampshire) **(a)** | 1,606,900 | | 1.50 | 8 | |
| 2013S, White Mountain National Forest (New Hampshire) | *(989,803)* | | | | $3 |
| 2013S, White Mountain National Forest (New Hampshire), Silver | (467,691) | | | | 8 |
| 2013P, Perry's Victory and Int'l Peace Memorial (Ohio) | 107,800,000 | 0.45 | 0.50 | 2 | |
| 2013D, Perry's Victory and Int'l Peace Memorial (Ohio) | 131,600,000 | 0.45 | 0.50 | 2 | |
| 2013S, Perry's Victory and Int'l Peace Memorial (Ohio) **(a)** | 1,425,860 | | 1.50 | 8 | |
| 2013S, Perry's Victory and Int'l Peace Memorial (Ohio) | *(947,815)* | | | | 3 |
| 2013S, Perry's Victory and Int'l Peace Memorial (Ohio), Silver | (467,691) | | | | 8 |
| 2013P, Great Basin National Park (Nevada) | 122,400,000 | 0.45 | 0.50 | 1 | |
| 2013D, Great Basin National Park (Nevada) | 141,400,000 | 0.45 | 0.50 | 1 | |
| 2013S, Great Basin National Park (Nevada) **(a)** | 1,316,500 | | 1.50 | 8 | |
| 2013S, Great Basin National Park (Nevada) | *(945,777)* | | | | 3 |
| 2013S, Great Basin National Park (Nevada), Silver | (467,691) | | | | 8 |
| 2013P, Ft McHenry Nat'l Mon't / Historic Shrine (Maryland) | 120,000,000 | 0.45 | 0.50 | 1 | |
| 2013D, Ft McHenry Nat'l Mon't / Historic Shrine (Maryland) | 151,400,000 | 0.45 | 0.50 | 1 | |
| 2013S, Ft McHenry Nat'l Mon't / Historic Shrine (Maryland) **(a)** | 1,313,680 | | 1.50 | 8 | |
| 2013S, Ft McHenry Nat'l Mon't / Historic Shrine (Maryland) | *(946,380)* | | | | 3 |
| 2013S, Ft McHenry Nat'l Mon't / Historic Shrine (Maryland), Silver | (467,691) | | | | 8 |
| 2013P, Mount Rushmore Nat'l Memorial (South Dakota) | 231,800,000 | 0.45 | 0.50 | 1 | |
| 2013D, Mount Rushmore Nat'l Memorial (South Dakota) | 272,400,000 | 0.45 | 0.50 | 1 | |
| 2013S, Mount Rushmore Nat'l Memorial (South Dakota) **(a)** | 1,373,260 | | 1.50 | 8 | |
| 2013S, Mount Rushmore Nat'l Memorial (South Dakota) | *(958,853)* | | | | 3 |
| 2013S, Mount Rushmore Nat'l Memorial (South Dakota), Silver | (467,691) | | | | 8 |

**a.** Not issued for circulation; see chart note on page 194.

*See next page for chart.*

| | Mintage | AU-50 | MS-63 | MS-65 | PF-65 |
|---|---|---|---|---|---|
| 2014P, Great Smoky Mountains National Park (Tennessee) | 73,200,000 | $0.45 | $0.50 | $1 | |
| 2014D, Great Smoky Mountains National Park (Tennessee) | 99,400,000 | 0.45 | 0.50 | 1 | |
| 2014S, Great Smoky Mountains National Park (Tennessee) **(a)** | 1,360,780 | | 2.00 | 8 | |
| 2014S, Great Smoky Mountains National Park (Tennessee) | *(881,896)* | | | | $3 |
| 2014S, Great Smoky Mountains National Park (Tennessee), Silver | (472,107) | | | | 8 |
| 2014P, Shenandoah National Park (Virginia) | 112,800,000 | 0.45 | 0.50 | 1 | |
| 2014D, Shenandoah National Park (Virginia) | 197,800,000 | 0.45 | 0.50 | 1 | |
| 2014S, Shenandoah National Park (Virginia) **(a)** | 1,266,720 | | 1.50 | 8 | |
| 2014S, Shenandoah National Park (Virginia) | *(846,441)* | | | | 3 |
| 2014S, Shenandoah National Park (Virginia), Silver | (472,107) | | | | 8 |
| 2014P, Arches National Park (Utah) | 214,200,000 | 0.45 | 0.50 | 1 | |
| 2014D, Arches National Park (Utah) | 251,400,000 | 0.45 | 0.50 | 1 | |
| 2014S, Arches National Park (Utah) **(a)** | 1,235,940 | | 1.50 | 8 | |
| 2014S, Arches National Park (Utah) | *(844,775)* | | | | 3 |
| 2014S, Arches National Park (Utah), Silver | (472,107) | | | | 8 |
| 2014P, Great Sand Dunes National Park (Colorado) | 159,600,000 | 0.45 | 0.50 | 2 | |
| 2014D, Great Sand Dunes National Park (Colorado) | 171,800,000 | 0.45 | 0.50 | 2 | |
| 2014S, Great Sand Dunes National Park (Colorado) **(a)** | 1,176,760 | | 1.50 | 8 | |
| 2014S, Great Sand Dunes National Park (Colorado) | *(843,238)* | | | | 3 |
| 2014S, Great Sand Dunes National Park (Colorado), Silver | (472,107) | | | | 8 |
| 2014P, Everglades National Park (Florida) | 157,601,200 | 0.45 | 0.50 | 1 | |
| 2014D, Everglades National Park (Florida) | 142,400,000 | 0.45 | 0.50 | 1 | |
| 2014S, Everglades National Park (Florida) **(a)** | 1,180,900 | | 1.50 | 8 | |
| 2014S, Everglades National Park (Florida) | *(856,139)* | | | | 3 |
| 2014S, Everglades National Park (Florida), Silver | (472,107) | | | | 8 |

**a.** Not issued for circulation; see chart note on page 194.

| | Mintage | AU-50 | MS-63 | MS-65 | PF-65 |
|---|---|---|---|---|---|
| 2015P, Homestead National Monument of America (Nebraska) | 214,400,000 | $0.50 | $0.75 | $1 | |
| 2015D, Homestead National Monument of America (Nebraska) | 248,600,000 | 0.50 | 0.75 | 1 | |
| 2015S, Homestead National Monument of America (Nebraska) **(a)** | 1,153,840 | | 2.00 | 8 | |
| 2015S, Homestead National Monument of America (Nebraska) | *(831,503)* | | | | $3 |
| 2015S, Homestead National Monument of America (Nebraska), Silver | *(490,829)* | | | | 8 |
| 2015P, Kisatchie National Forest (Louisiana) | 397,200,000 | 0.50 | 0.75 | 1 | |
| 2015D, Kisatchie National Forest (Louisiana) | 379,600,000 | 0.50 | 0.75 | 1 | |
| 2015S, Kisatchie National Forest (Louisiana) **(a)** | 1,099,380 | | 2.00 | 8 | |
| 2015S, Kisatchie National Forest (Louisiana) | *(762,407)* | | | | 3 |
| 2015S, Kisatchie National Forest (Louisiana), Silver | *(490,829)* | | | | 8 |
| 2015P, Blue Ridge Parkway (North Carolina) | 325,616,000 | 0.50 | 0.75 | 1 | |
| 2015D, Blue Ridge Parkway (North Carolina) | 505,200,000 | 0.50 | 0.75 | 1 | |
| 2015S, Blue Ridge Parkway (North Carolina) **(a)** | 1,096,620 | | 2.00 | 8 | |

**a.** Not issued for circulation; see chart note on page 194.

| | Mintage | AU-50 | MS-63 | MS-65 | PF-65 |
|---|---|---|---|---|---|
| 2015S, Blue Ridge Parkway (North Carolina) | *(762,407)* | | | | $3 |
| 2015S, Blue Ridge Parkway (North Carolina), Silver | *(490,829)* | | | | 8 |
| 2015P, Bombay Hook National Wildlife Refuge (Delaware) | 275,000,000 | $0.50 | $0.75 | $1 | |
| 2015D, Bombay Hook National Wildlife Refuge (Delaware) | 206,400,000 | 0.50 | 0.75 | 1 | |
| 2015S, Bombay Hook National Wildlife Refuge (Delaware) **(a)** | 1,013,920 | | 2.00 | 8 | |
| 2015S, Bombay Hook National Wildlife Refuge (Delaware) | *(762,407)* | | | | 3 |
| 2015S, Bombay Hook National Wildlife Refuge (Delaware), Silver | *(490,829)* | | | | 8 |
| 2015P, Saratoga National Historical Park (New York) | 223,000,000 | 0.50 | 0.75 | 1 | |
| 2015D, Saratoga National Historical Park (New York) | 215,800,000 | 0.50 | 0.75 | 1 | |
| 2015S, Saratoga National Historical Park (New York) **(a)** | 1,045,500 | | 2.00 | 8 | |
| 2015S, Saratoga National Historical Park (New York) | *(791,347)* | | | | 3 |
| 2015S, Saratoga National Historical Park (New York), Silver | *(490,829)* | | | | 8 |

**a.** Not issued for circulation; see chart note on page 194.

Along with the regular America the Beautiful quarters of the year, in 2016 a special gold striking of the Standing Liberty quarter was created to celebrate the 100th anniversary of its introduction. Similar strikings were made for the 1916 dime and half dollar designs.

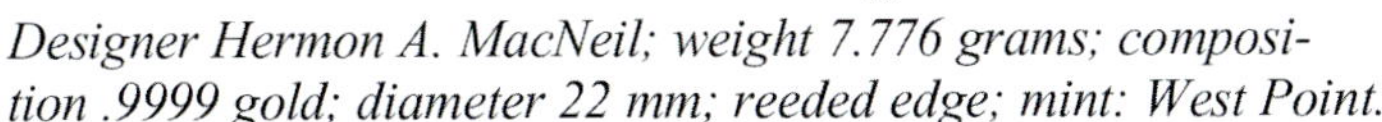

*Designer Hermon A. MacNeil; weight 7.776 grams; composition .9999 gold; diameter 22 mm; reeded edge; mint: West Point.*

| | Mintage | SP-67 | SP-70 |
|---|---|---|---|
| 2016W, Standing Liberty Centennial Gold Coin | *91,752* | $450 | $550 |

Normally scheduled production of clad and silver America the Beautiful quarters continued in 2016 and beyond, and was not disrupted by the gold Standing Liberty quarter.

| | Mintage | AU-50 | MS-63 | MS-65 | PF-65 |
|---|---|---|---|---|---|
| 2016P, Shawnee National Forest (Illinois) | 155,600,000 | $0.50 | $0.75 | $1 | |
| 2016D, Shawnee National Forest (Illinois) | 151,800,000 | 0.50 | 0.75 | 1 | |
| 2016S, Shawnee National Forest (Illinois) **(a)** | *1,066,440* | | 2.00 | 3 | |
| 2016S, Shawnee National Forest (Illinois) | *(732,039)* | | | | $3 |
| 2016S, Shawnee National Forest (Illinois), Silver | *(515,205)* | | | | 8 |
| 2016P, Cumberland Gap National Historical Park (Kentucky) | 215,400,000 | 0.50 | 0.75 | 1 | |
| 2016D, Cumberland Gap National Historical Park (Kentucky) | 223,200,000 | 0.50 | 0.75 | 1 | |
| 2016S, Cumberland Gap National Historical Park (Kentucky) **(a)** | *1,021,120* | | 2.00 | 3 | |
| 2016S, Cumberland Gap National Historical Park (Kentucky) | *(701,831)* | | | | 3 |
| 2016S, Cumberland Gap National Historical Park (Kentucky), Silver | *(515,205)* | | | | 8 |

**a.** Not issued for circulation; see chart note on page 194.

*Chart continued on next page.*

| | Mintage | AU-50 | MS-63 | MS-65 | PF-65 |
|---|---|---|---|---|---|
| 2016P, Harpers Ferry National Historical Park (West Virginia) | 434,630,000 | $0.50 | $0.75 | $1 | |
| 2016D, Harpers Ferry National Historical Park (West Virginia) | 424,000,000 | 0.50 | 0.75 | 1 | |
| 2016S, Harpers Ferry National Historical Park (West Virginia) **(a)** | *1,035,840* | | 2.00 | 3 | |
| 2016S, Harpers Ferry National Historical Park (West Virginia) | *(701,203)* | | | | $3 |
| 2016S, Harpers Ferry National Historical Park (West Virginia), Silver | *(515,205)* | | | | 8 |
| 2016P, Theodore Roosevelt National Park (North Dakota) | 231,600,000 | 0.50 | 0.75 | 1 | |
| 2016D, Theodore Roosevelt National Park (North Dakota) | 223,200,000 | 0.50 | 0.75 | 1 | |
| 2016S, Theodore Roosevelt National Park (North Dakota) **(a)** | *1,057,020* | | 2.00 | 3 | |
| 2016S, Theodore Roosevelt National Park (North Dakota) | *(702,930)* | | | | 3 |
| 2016S, Theodore Roosevelt National Park (North Dakota), Silver | *(515,205)* | | | | 8 |
| 2016P, Fort Moultrie at Fort Sumter Nat'l Mon't (SC) | 154,400,000 | 0.50 | 0.75 | 1 | |
| 2016D, Fort Moultrie at Fort Sumter Nat'l Mon't (SC) | 142,200,000 | 0.50 | 0.75 | 1 | |
| 2016S, Fort Moultrie at Fort Sumter Nat'l Mon't (SC) **(a)** | *966,260* | | 2.00 | 3 | |
| 2016S, Fort Moultrie at Fort Sumter Nat'l Mon't (SC) | *(717,049)* | | | | 3 |
| 2016S, Fort Moultrie at Fort Sumter Nat'l Mon't (SC), Silver | *(515,205)* | | | | 8 |

**a.** Not issued for circulation; see chart note on page 194.

| | Mintage | AU-50 | MS-63 | MS-65 | PF-65 |
|---|---|---|---|---|---|
| 2017P, Effigy Mounds National Monument (Iowa) | 271,200,000 | $0.50 | $0.75 | $1 | |
| 2017D, Effigy Mounds National Monument (Iowa) | 210,800,000 | 0.50 | 0.75 | 1 | |
| 2017S, Effigy Mounds National Monument (Iowa) **(a)** | 931,340 | | 2.00 | 3 | |
| 2017S, Effigy Mounds National Monument (Iowa) **(b)** | (706,042) | | | | $3 |
| 2017S, Effigy Mounds National Monument (Iowa), Silver | (496,626) | | | | 8 |
| 2017P, Frederick Douglass National Historic Site (DC) | 184,800,000 | 0.50 | 0.75 | 1 | |
| 2017D, Frederick Douglass National Historic Site (DC) | 185,800,000 | | | | |
| 2017S, Frederick Douglass National Historic Site (DC) **(a)** | 934,940 | | 2.00 | 3 | |
| 2017S, Frederick Douglass National Historic Site (DC) **(b)** | (672,188) | | | | 3 |
| 2017S, Frederick Douglass National Historic Site (DC), Silver | (496,626) | | | | 8 |
| 2017P, Ozark National Scenic Riverways (Missouri) | 203,000,000 | 0.50 | 0.75 | 1 | |
| 2017D, Ozark National Scenic Riverways (Missouri) | 200,000,000 | 0.50 | 0.75 | 1 | |
| 2017S, Ozark National Scenic Riverways (Missouri) **(a)** | 906,840 | | 2.00 | 3 | |
| 2017S, Ozark National Scenic Riverways (Missouri) **(b)** | (671,902) | | | | 3 |
| 2017S, Ozark National Scenic Riverways (Missouri), Silver | (496,626) | | | | 8 |
| 2017P, Ellis Island (Statue of Liberty Nat'l Monument) (NJ) | 234,000,000 | 0.50 | 0.75 | 1 | |
| 2017D, Ellis Island (Statue of Liberty Nat'l Monument) (NJ) | 254,000,000 | | | | |
| 2017S, Ellis Island (Statue of Liberty Nat'l Monument) (NJ) **(a)** | 956,200 | | 2.00 | 3 | |
| 2017S, Ellis Island (Statue of Liberty Nat'l Monument) (NJ) **(b)** | (674,537) | | | | 3 |
| 2017S, Ellis Island (Statue of Liberty Nat'l Monument) (NJ), Silver | (496,626) | | | | 8 |

**a.** Not issued for circulation; see chart note on page 194. **b.** For its 225th anniversary, the Mint issued a special set of Enhanced Uncirculated coins from the San Francisco Mint; these are not included in the listings here.

| | Mintage | AU-50 | MS-63 | MS-65 | PF-65 |
|---|---|---|---|---|---|
| 2017P, George Rogers Clark National Historical Park (IN) | 191,600,000 | $0.50 | $0.75 | $1 | |
| 2017D, George Rogers Clark National Historical Park (IN) | 180,800,000 | 0.50 | 0.75 | 1 | |
| 2017S, George Rogers Clark National Historical Park (IN) **(a)** | 919,060 | | 2.00 | 3 | |
| 2017S, George Rogers Clark National Historical Park (IN) **(b)** | (689,235) | | | | $3 |
| 2017S, George Rogers Clark National Historical Park (IN), Silver | (496,626) | | | | 8 |

**a.** Not issued for circulation; see chart note on page 194. **b.** For its 225th anniversary, the Mint issued a special set of Enhanced Uncirculated coins from the San Francisco Mint; these are not included in the listings here.

| | Mintage | AU-50 | MS-63 | MS-65 | PF-65 |
|---|---|---|---|---|---|
| 2018P, Pictured Rocks National Lakeshore (Michigan) | *186,714,000* | $0.50 | $0.75 | $1 | |
| 2018D, Pictured Rocks National Lakeshore (Michigan) | *182,600,000* | 0.50 | 0.75 | 1 | |
| 2018S, Pictured Rocks National Lakeshore (Michigan) **(a)** | *917,580* | | 2.00 | 3 | |
| 2018S, Pictured Rocks National Lakeshore (Michigan) | *(688,538)* | | | | $3 |
| 2018S, Pictured Rocks National Lakeshore (Michigan), Silver | *(350,820)* | | | | 10 |
| 2018P, Apostle Islands National Lakeshore (Wisconsin) | *223,200,000* | 0.50 | 0.75 | 1 | |
| 2018D, Apostle Islands National Lakeshore (Wisconsin) | *216,600,000* | 0.50 | 0.75 | 1 | |
| 2018S, Apostle Islands National Lakeshore (Wisconsin) **(a)** | *871,820* | | 2.00 | 3 | |
| 2018S, Apostle Islands National Lakeshore (Wisconsin) | *(659,633)* | | | | 3 |
| 2018S, Apostle Islands National Lakeshore (Wisconsin), Silver | *(350,820)* | | | | 10 |
| 2018P, Voyageurs National Park (Minnesota) | *237,400,000* | 0.50 | 0.75 | 1 | |
| 2018D, Voyageurs National Park (Minnesota) | *197,800,000* | 0.50 | 0.75 | 1 | |
| 2018S, Voyageurs National Park (Minnesota) **(a)** | *831,560* | | 2.00 | 3 | |
| 2018S, Voyageurs National Park (Minnesota) | *(659,448)* | | | | 3 |
| 2018S, Voyageurs National Park (Minnesota), Silver | *(350,820)* | | | | 10 |
| 2018P, Cumberland Island National Seashore (Georgia) | *138,000,000* | 0.50 | 0.75 | 1 | |
| 2018D, Cumberland Island National Seashore (Georgia) | *151,600,000* | 0.50 | 0.75 | 1 | |
| 2018S, Cumberland Island National Seashore (Georgia) **(a)** | *816,660* | | 2.00 | 3 | |
| 2018S, Cumberland Island National Seashore (Georgia) | *(658,438)* | | | | 3 |
| 2018S, Cumberland Island National Seashore (Georgia), Silver | *(350,820)* | | | | 10 |
| 2018P, Block Island National Wildlife Refuge (Rhode Island) | *159,600,000* | 0.50 | 0.75 | 1 | |
| 2018D, Block Island National Wildlife Refuge (Rhode Island) | *159,600,000* | 0.50 | 0.75 | 1 | |
| 2018S, Block Island National Wildlife Refuge (Rhode Island) **(a)** | *764,660* | | 2.00 | 3 | |
| 2018S, Block Island National Wildlife Refuge (Rhode Island) | *(675,567)* | | | | 3 |
| 2018S, Block Island National Wildlife Refuge (Rhode Island), Silver | *(350,820)* | | | | 10 |

**a.** Not issued for circulation; see chart note on page 194.

| | Mintage | AU-50 | MS-63 | MS-65 | PF-65 |
|---|---|---|---|---|---|
| 2019P, Lowell National Historical Park (Massachusetts) | *165,800,000* | $0.50 | $0.75 | $1 | |
| 2019D, Lowell National Historical Park (Massachusetts) | *182,200,000* | 0.50 | 0.75 | 1 | |
| 2019S, Lowell National Historical Park (Massachusetts) **(a)** | | | 2.00 | 3 | |
| 2019S, Lowell National Historical Park (Massachusetts) | | | | | $3 |
| 2019S, Lowell National Historical Park (Massachusetts), Silver **(c)** | | | | | 8 |
| 2019W, Lowell National Historical Park (Massachusetts) **(d)** | | | 10.00 | 25 | |
| 2019P, American Memorial Park (Northern Mariana Islands) | *142,800,000* | 0.50 | 0.75 | 1 | |
| 2019D, American Memorial Park (Northern Mariana Islands) | *182,600,000* | 0.50 | 0.75 | 1 | |
| 2019S, American Memorial Park (Northern Mariana Islands) **(a)** | | | 2.00 | 3 | |
| 2019S, American Memorial Park (Northern Mariana Islands) | | | 10.00 | 25 | 3 |
| 2019S, American Memorial Park (Northern Mariana Islands), Silver **(c)** | | | | | 8 |
| 2019W, American Memorial Park (Northern Mariana Islands) **(d)** | | | 10.00 | 25 | |
| 2019P, War in the Pacific National Historical Park (Guam) | *116,600,000* | 0.50 | 0.75 | 1 | |
| 2019D, War in the Pacific National Historical Park (Guam) | *114,400,000* | 0.50 | 0.75 | 1 | |
| 2019S, War in the Pacific National Historical Park (Guam) **(a)** | | | 2.00 | 3 | |
| 2019S, War in the Pacific National Historical Park (Guam) | | | | | 3 |
| 2019S, War in the Pacific National Historical Park (Guam), Silver **(c)** | | | | | 8 |
| 2019W, War in the Pacific National Historical Park (Guam) **(d)** | | | 10.00 | 25 | |
| 2019P, San Antonio Missions National Historical Park (Texas) | *142,800,000* | 0.50 | 0.75 | 1 | |
| 2019D, San Antonio Missions National Historical Park (Texas) | *129,400,000* | 0.50 | 0.75 | 1 | |
| 2019S, San Antonio Missions National Historical Park (Texas) **(a)** | | | 2.00 | 3 | |
| 2019S, San Antonio Missions National Historical Park (Texas) | | | | | 3 |
| 2019S, San Antonio Missions National Historical Park (Texas), Silver **(c)** | | | | | 8 |
| 2019W, San Antonio Missions National Historical Park (Texas) **(d)** | | | 10.00 | 25 | |
| 2019P, Frank Church River of No Return Wilderness (Idaho) | *223,400,000* | 0.50 | 0.75 | 1 | |
| 2019D, Frank Church River of No Return Wilderness (Idaho) | *251,600,000* | 0.50 | 0.75 | 1 | |
| 2019S, Frank Church River of No Return Wilderness (Idaho) **(a)** | | | 2.00 | 3 | |
| 2019S, Frank Church River of No Return Wilderness (Idaho) | | | | | 3 |
| 2019S, Frank Church River of No Return Wilderness (Idaho), Silver **(c)** | | | | | 8 |
| 2019W, Frank Church River of No Return Wilderness (Idaho) **(d)** | | | 10.00 | 25 | |

**a.** Not issued for circulation; see chart note on page 194. **c.** In 2019, fineness of silver Proofs was changed from .900 to .999. **d.** In 2019, 10 million quarters (2 million of each of the five America the Beautiful Designs) were struck at the West Point Mint and released into circulation, as part of an effort to stimulate public interest in coin collecting.

| | Mintage | AU-50 | MS-63 | MS-65 | PF-65 |
|---|---|---|---|---|---|
| 2020P, National Park of American Samoa (American Samoa) | | $0.50 | $0.75 | $1 | |
| 2020D, National Park of American Samoa (American Samoa) | | 0.50 | 0.75 | 1 | |
| 2020S, National Park of American Samoa (American Samoa) **(a)** | | | 2.00 | 3 | |
| 2020S, National Park of American Samoa (American Samoa) | | | | | $3 |
| 2020S, National Park of American Samoa (American Samoa), Silver **(c)** | | | | | 8 |
| 2020W, National Park of American Samoa (American Samoa) **(e)** | | | 10.00 | 25 | |
| 2020P, Weir Farm National Historic Site (Connecticut) | | 0.50 | 0.75 | 1 | |
| 2020D, Weir Farm National Historic Site (Connecticut) | | 0.50 | 0.75 | 1 | |
| 2020S, Weir Farm National Historic Site (Connecticut) **(a)** | | | 2.00 | 3 | |
| 2020S, Weir Farm National Historic Site (Connecticut) | | | | | 3 |
| 2020S, Weir Farm National Historic Site (Connecticut), Silver **(c)** | | | | | 8 |
| 2020W, Weir Farm National Historic Site (Connecticut) **(e)** | | | 10.00 | 25 | |
| 2020P, Salt River Bay Nat'l Hist'l Park/Ecological Preserve (USVI) | | 0.50 | 0.75 | 1 | |
| 2020D, Salt River Bay Nat'l Hist'l Park/Ecological Preserve (USVI) | | 0.50 | 0.75 | 1 | |
| 2020S, Salt River Bay Nat'l Hist'l Park/Ecological Preserve (USVI) **(a)** | | | 2.00 | 3 | |
| 2020S, Salt River Bay Nat'l Hist'l Park/Ecological Preserve (USVI) | | | | | 3 |
| 2020S, Salt River Bay Nat'l Hist'l Park/Ecological Preserve (USVI), Silver **(c)** | | | | | 8 |
| 2020W, Salt River Bay Nat'l Hist'l Park/Ecological Preserve (USVI) **(e)** | | | 10.00 | 25 | |
| 2020P, Marsh-Billings-Rockefeller Nat'l Hist'l Park (Vermont) | | 0.50 | 0.75 | 1 | |
| 2020D, Marsh-Billings-Rockefeller Nat'l Hist'l Park (Vermont) | | 0.50 | 0.75 | 1 | |
| 2020S, Marsh-Billings-Rockefeller Nat'l Hist'l Park (Vermont) **(a)** | | | 2.00 | 3 | |
| 2020S, Marsh-Billings-Rockefeller Nat'l Hist'l Park (Vermont) | | | | | 3 |
| 2020S, Marsh-Billings-Rockefeller Nat'l Hist'l Park (Vermont), Silver **(c)** | | | | | 8 |
| 2020W, Marsh-Billings-Rockefeller Nat'l Hist'l Park (Vermont) **(e)** | | | 10.00 | 25 | |
| 2020P, Tallgrass Prairie National Preserve (Kansas) | | 0.50 | 0.75 | 1 | |
| 2020D, Tallgrass Prairie National Preserve (Kansas) | | 0.50 | 0.75 | 1 | |
| 2020S, Tallgrass Prairie National Preserve (Kansas) **(a)** | | | 2.00 | 3 | |
| 2020S, Tallgrass Prairie National Preserve (Kansas) | | | | | 3 |
| 2020S, Tallgrass Prairie National Preserve (Kansas), Silver **(c)** | | | | | 8 |
| 2020W, Tallgrass Prairie National Preserve (Kansas) **(e)** | | | 10.00 | 25 | |

**a.** Not issued for circulation; see chart note on page 194. **c.** In 2019, fineness of silver Proofs was changed from .900 to .999. **e.** In 2020, the Mint produced 2 million of each of that year's America the Beautiful quarter designs at West Point with a "V75" privy mark on the obverse commemorating the 75th anniversary of the end of World War II.

The half dollar, authorized by the Act of April 2, 1792, was not minted until December 1794. The early types of this series have been extensively collected by die varieties, of which many exist for most dates. Valuations given below are in each case for the most common variety; scarcer ones as listed by Overton (see the bibliography at the end of the book) generally command higher prices.

When the half dollar was first issued, its weight was 208 grains and its fineness .8924. This standard was not changed until 1837, when the law of January 18, 1837, specified 206-1/4 grains, .900 fine. This fineness continued in use until 1965.

Arrows at the date in 1853 indicate the reduction of weight to 192 grains, in conformity with the Act of February 21, 1853. During that year only, rays were added to the field on the reverse side to identify the lighter coins. Arrows remained in 1854 and 1855.

The 1866 Proof quarter, half, and dollar without motto are not mentioned in the Mint director's report and were not issued for circulation. In 1873 the weight was raised by law to 192.9 grains and arrows were again placed at the date, to be removed in 1875.

*Note: Values of common-date silver coins have been based on a silver bullion price of $18 per ounce, and may vary with the prevailing spot price. To determine the intrinsic value of common silver coins, see page 445.*

## FLOWING HAIR (1794–1795)

*Engraver Robert Scot; weight 13.48 grams; composition .8924 silver, .1076 copper; approx. diameter 32.5 mm; edge: FIFTY CENTS OR HALF A DOLLAR with decorations between words.*

**AG-3 About Good**—Clear enough to identify.
**G-4 Good**—Date and letters sufficient to be legible. Main devices outlined, but lacking in detail.
**VG-8 Very Good**—Major details discernible. Letters well formed but worn.
**F-12 Fine**—Hair ends distinguishable. Top hair lines visible, but otherwise worn smooth.
**VF-20 Very Fine**—Some detail visible in hair in center; other details more bold.
**EF-40 Extremely Fine**—Hair above head and down neck detailed, with slight wear.
**AU-50 About Uncirculated**—All hair visible; slight wear on bust of Liberty and on top edges of eagle's wings, head, and breast.

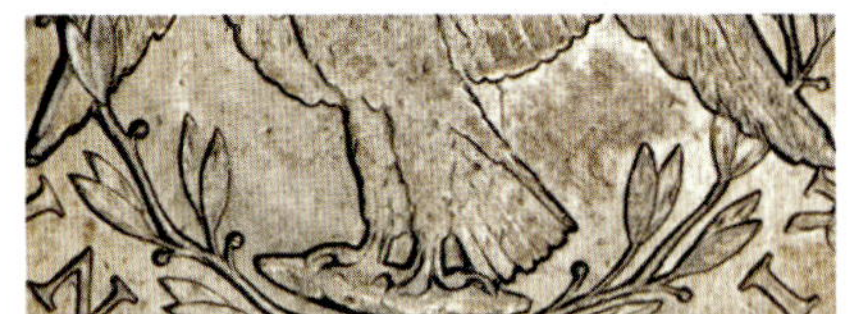

1795, 2 Leaves Under Each Wing

1795, 3 Leaves Under Each Wing

| | Mintage | AG-3 | G-4 | VG-8 | F-12 | VF-20 | EF-40 | AU-50 |
|---|---|---|---|---|---|---|---|---|
| 1794 | 23,464 | $2,500 | $4,500 | $7,000 | $12,000 | $23,000 | $40,000 | $65,000 |
| 1795, All kinds | 299,680 | | | | | | | |
| 1795, Normal Date | | 650 | 1,100 | 1,500 | 2,750 | 3,900 | 11,000 | 17,500 |
| 1795, Recut Date | | 650 | 1,150 | 1,550 | 2,750 | 4,250 | 11,000 | 20,500 |
| 1795, 3 Leaves Under Each Wing | | 1,100 | 2,350 | 3,250 | 4,600 | 8,500 | 20,000 | 40,000 |

*Note:* Varieties of 1795 are known with small, or narrow, head, with the final S in STATES over a D, with the A in STATES over an E, and with the Y in LIBERTY over a star. All are scarce. Some half dollars of 1794 and 1795 were weight-adjusted by insertion of a silver plug in the center of the blank planchet before the coin was struck.

## DRAPED BUST (1796–1807)

*Designer probably Gilbert Stuart; engraver Robert Scot; weight 13.48 grams; composition .8924 silver, .1076 copper; approx. diameter 32.5 mm; edge: FIFTY CENTS OR HALF A DOLLAR with decorations between words.*

**AG-3 About Good**—Clear enough to identify.
**G-4 Good**—Date and letters sufficiently clear to be legible. Main devices outlined, but lacking in detail.
**VG-8 Very Good**—Major details discernible. Letters well formed but worn.
**F-12 Fine**—Hair ends distinguishable. Top hair lines visible, but otherwise worn smooth.
**VF-20 Very Fine**—Right side of drapery slightly worn. Left side to curls smooth.
**EF-40 Extremely Fine**—All lines in drapery on bust distinctly visible around to hair curls.
**AU-50 About Uncirculated**—Slight trace of wear on cheek, hair, and shoulder.

### Small Eagle Reverse (1796–1797)

1796, 15 Stars

1796, 16 Stars

| | Mintage | AG-3 | G-4 | VG-8 | F-12 | VF-20 | EF-40 | AU-50 |
|---|---|---|---|---|---|---|---|---|
| 1796, 15 Stars | * | $23,000 | $35,000 | $43,500 | $52,000 | $75,000 | $125,000 | $165,000 |
| *$587,500, SP-63, Sotheby's/ Stack's Bowers auction, May 2015* | | | | | | | | |
| 1796, 16 Stars | * | 23,000 | 36,500 | 45,000 | 56,000 | 71,000 | 125,000 | 170,000 |
| *$822,500, MS-66, Sotheby's/ Stack's Bowers auction, May 2015* | | | | | | | | |
| 1797, 15 Stars | 3,918 | 23,000 | 37,500 | 47,500 | 57,500 | 75,000 | 125,000 | 165,000 |
| *$1,527,500, MS-66, Sotheby's/ Stack's Bowers auction, May 2015* | | | | | | | | |

* Included in number below.

### Heraldic Eagle Reverse (1801–1807)

| | Mintage | G-4 | VG-8 | F-12 | VF-20 | EF-40 | AU-50 | MS-60 |
|---|---|---|---|---|---|---|---|---|
| 1801 | 30,289 | $875 | $1,350 | $2,200 | $3,100 | $5,250 | $15,000 | $75,000 |
| 1802 | 29,890 | 900 | 1,400 | 2,300 | 3,200 | 5,750 | 17,000 | 60,000 |
| 1803, All kinds | 188,234 | | | | | | | |
| 1803, Small 3 | | 350 | 475 | 650 | 1,000 | 2,200 | 5,500 | 25,000 |
| 1803, Large 3 | | 275 | 425 | 500 | 900 | 1,850 | 5,000 | 22,500 |

1805, 5 Over 4

1806, 6 Over 5

Branch Stem Not Through Claw

Knobbed-Top 6, Small Stars

Pointed-Top 6

Branch Stem Through Claw

| | Mintage | G-4 | VG-8 | F-12 | VF-20 | EF-40 | AU-50 | MS-60 |
|---|---|---|---|---|---|---|---|---|
| 1805, All kinds | 211,722 | | | | | | | |
| 1805, 5 Over 4 | | $400 | $800 | $1,000 | $1,650 | $3,500 | $7,500 | $35,000 |
| 1805, Normal Date | | 260 | 350 | 475 | 850 | 2,100 | 5,000 | 22,500 |
| 1806, All kinds | 839,576 | | | | | | | |
| 1806, 6 Over 5 | | 300 | 400 | 600 | 900 | 2,100 | 5,000 | 13,500 |
| 1806, 6 Over Inverted 6 | | 350 | 500 | 925 | 1,500 | 3,500 | 8,500 | 27,500 |
| 1806, Knbd 6, Lg Stars (Traces of Overdate) | | 225 | 275 | 400 | 700 | 2,000 | 5,000 | |
| 1806, Knbd 6, Sm Stars | | 250 | 325 | 500 | 700 | 2,000 | 5,000 | 12,000 |
| 1806, Knbd 6, Stem Not Through Claw | | 65,000 | 80,000 | 85,000 | 95,000 | 125,000 | | |
| 1806, Pointed 6, Stem Through Claw | | 225 | 275 | 400 | 700 | 1,700 | 3,500 | 8,000 |
| 1806, E Over A in STATES | | 400 | 900 | 1,600 | 3,200 | 7,500 | 20,000 | |
| 1806, Pointed 6, Stem Not Through Claw | | 225 | 275 | 400 | 700 | 1,600 | 3,500 | 8,000 |
| 1807 | 301,076 | 225 | 275 | 400 | 700 | 1,700 | 3,500 | 8,000 |

## CAPPED BUST, LETTERED EDGE (1807–1836)

John Reich designed this capped-head concept of Liberty. The Capped Bust style was used on most other silver coin denominations for the next 30 years. A German immigrant, Reich became an engraver for the Mint, and served from 1807 to 1817, after having been freed from a bond of servitude by a Mint official. He was the first artist to consistently include the denomination on U.S. gold and silver coins.

*Designer John Reich; weight 13.48 grams; composition .8924 silver, .1076 copper; approx. diameter 32.5 mm. 1807–1814—Edge: FIFTY CENTS OR HALF A DOLLAR. 1814–1831—Edge: Star added between DOLLAR and FIFTY. 1832–1836—Edge: Vertical lines added between words.*

**G-4 Good**—Date and letters legible. Bust worn smooth with outline distinct.
**VG-8 Very Good**—LIBERTY faint. Legends distinguishable. Clasp at shoulder visible; curl above it nearly smooth.
**F-12 Fine**—Clasp and adjacent curl clearly outlined with slight details.
**VF-20 Very Fine**—Clasp at shoulder clear. Wear visible on highest point of curl. Hair over brow distinguishable.
**EF-40 Extremely Fine**—Clasp and adjacent curl fairly sharp. Brow and hair above distinct. Curls well defined.
**AU-50 About Uncirculated**—Trace of wear on hair over eye and over ear.
**MS-60 Uncirculated**—No trace of wear. Light blemishes. Possible slide marks from storage handling.
**MS-63 Choice Uncirculated**—Some distracting contact marks or blemishes in prime focal areas. Impaired luster possible.

## First Style (1807–1808)

1807, Small Stars

1807, Large Stars

1807, 50 Over 20

| | Mintage | G-4 | F-12 | VF-20 | EF-40 | AU-50 | MS-60 | MS-63 |
|---|---|---|---|---|---|---|---|---|
| 1807, All kinds | 750,500 | | | | | | | |
| 1807, Small Stars | | $225 | $650 | $1,000 | $2,200 | $4,500 | $20,000 | $35,000 |
| 1807, Large Stars | | 175 | 500 | 750 | 2,000 | 3,500 | 15,000 | 35,000 |
| 1807, Large Stars, 50 Over 20 | | 185 | 450 | 700 | 1,400 | 2,700 | 5,750 | 11,000 |
| 1807, "Bearded" Liberty | | 700 | 2,000 | 3,500 | 6,500 | 12,500 | | |
| 1808, All kinds | 1,368,600 | | | | | | | |
| 1808, 8 Over 7 | | 100 | 185 | 350 | 650 | 1,500 | 4,500 | 10,000 |
| 1808 | | 75 | 150 | 250 | 450 | 1,150 | 3,250 | 6,000 |

## Remodeled Portrait and Eagle (1809–1836)

1809, Experimental Edge, xxxx Between Words

1809, Experimental Edge, IIIII Between Words

| | Mintage | G-4 | F-12 | VF-20 | EF-40 | AU-50 | MS-60 | MS-63 |
|---|---|---|---|---|---|---|---|---|
| 1809, All kinds | 1,405,810 | | | | | | | |
| 1809, Normal Edge | | $100 | $175 | $250 | $500 | $900 | $3,000 | $8,500 |
| 1809, xxxx Edge | | 150 | 250 | 425 | 1,100 | 2,000 | 8,500 | 20,000 |
| 1809, IIIII Edge | | 100 | 150 | 250 | 650 | 1,200 | 4,750 | 12,500 |
| 1810 | 1,276,276 | 75 | 135 | 200 | 400 | 800 | 2,750 | 7,000 |

"Punctuated" Date 18.11

1811, Small 8

1811, Large 8

1812, 2 Over 1, Small 8

1812, 2 Over 1, Large 8

Single Leaf Below Wing

| | Mintage | G-4 | F-12 | VF-20 | EF-40 | AU-50 | MS-60 | MS-63 |
|---|---|---|---|---|---|---|---|---|
| 1811, All kinds | 1,203,644 | | | | | | | |
| 1811, (18.11), 11 Over 10 | | $100 | $250 | $400 | $650 | $1,400 | $5,500 | $14,000 |
| 1811, Small 8 | | 75 | 135 | 200 | 385 | 950 | 3,000 | 5,500 |
| 1811, Large 8 | | 75 | 125 | 170 | 325 | 800 | 2,750 | 5,000 |
| 1812, All kinds | 1,628,059 | | | | | | | |
| 1812, 2 Over 1, Small 8 | | 115 | 200 | 300 | 650 | 1,200 | 3,500 | 8,500 |
| 1812, 2 Over 1, Large 8 | | 2,000 | 5,500 | 10,000 | 13,000 | 24,000 | | |
| 1812 | | 75 | 135 | 175 | 450 | 750 | 2,200 | 4,000 |
| 1812, Single Leaf Below Wing | | 750 | 1,300 | 2,400 | 3,750 | 7,000 | 17,000 | 30,000 |

1813, 50 C. Over UNI

1814, 4 Over 3

1814, E Over A in STATES

| | Mintage | G-4 | F-12 | VF-20 | EF-40 | AU-50 | MS-60 | MS-63 |
|---|---|---|---|---|---|---|---|---|
| 1813, All kinds | 1,241,903 | | | | | | | |
| 1813 | | $75 | $115 | $160 | $400 | $750 | $2,500 | $4,500 |
| 1813, 50 C. Over UNI | | 115 | 250 | 400 | 800 | 1,400 | 4,000 | 7,500 |
| 1814, All kinds | 1,039,075 | | | | | | | |
| 1814, 4 Over 3 | | 135 | 250 | 400 | 800 | 2,000 | 4,500 | 8,500 |
| 1814, E Over A in STATES | | 115 | 200 | 450 | 1,500 | 2,750 | 8,500 | 15,000 |
| 1814 | | 85 | 150 | 225 | 600 | 800 | 2,750 | 5,250 |
| 1814, Single Leaf Below Wing | | 85 | 150 | 500 | 1,250 | 2,500 | 4,500 | 8,000 |

1817, 7 Over 3

1817, 7 Over 4

1817, "Punctuated Date"

| | Mintage | G-4 | F-12 | VF-20 | EF-40 | AU-50 | MS-60 | MS-63 |
|---|---|---|---|---|---|---|---|---|
| 1815, 5 Over 2 | 47,150 | $1,450 | $3,250 | $4,500 | $5,500 | $10,000 | $22,500 | $50,000 |
| 1817, All kinds | 1,215,567 | | | | | | | |
| 1817, 7 Over 3 | | 165 | 450 | 650 | 1,250 | 3,000 | 8,500 | 17,500 |
| 1817, 7 Over 4 *(8 known)* | | 67,500 | 150,000 | 200,000 | 275,000 | 375,000 | | |
| *$356,500, AU-50, Stack's Bowers auction, July 2009* | | | | | | | | |
| 1817, Dated 181.7 | | 100 | 200 | 300 | 650 | 1,750 | 4,000 | 8,000 |
| 1817 | | 100 | 145 | 200 | 400 | 750 | 2,500 | 4,750 |
| 1817, Single Leaf Below Wing | | 100 | 150 | 200 | 475 | 1,000 | 2,750 | 4,500 |

1818, First 8 Small, Second 8 Over 7

1818, First 8 Large, Second 8 Over 7

1819, Small 9 Over 8

1819, Large 9 Over 8

| Mintage | G-4 | F-12 | VF-20 | EF-40 | AU-50 | MS-60 | MS-63 |
|---|---|---|---|---|---|---|---|
| 1818, All kinds. . . . . . . . . . . 1,960,322 | | | | | | | |
| 1818, 8 Over 7, Small 8 . . . . . . . . . | $90 | $145 | $250 | $500 | $1,350 | $3,250 | $8,500 |
| 1818, 8 Over 7, Large 8 . . . . . . . . . | 90 | 145 | 225 | 475 | 1,250 | 3,250 | 7,500 |
| 1818 . . . . . . . . . . . . . . . . . . . . . . . | 70 | 100 | 155 | 300 | 650 | 2,750 | 4,500 |
| 1819, All kinds. . . . . . . . . . . 2,208,000 | | | | | | | |
| 1819, Small 9 Over 8 . . . . . . . . . . . | 75 | 120 | 200 | 375 | 825 | 3,000 | 5,750 |
| 1819, Large 9 Over 8 . . . . . . . . . . . | 75 | 120 | 175 | 350 | 750 | 3,000 | 5,750 |
| 1819 . . . . . . . . . . . . . . . . . . . . . . . | 75 | 100 | 150 | 325 | 650 | 2,500 | 5,000 |

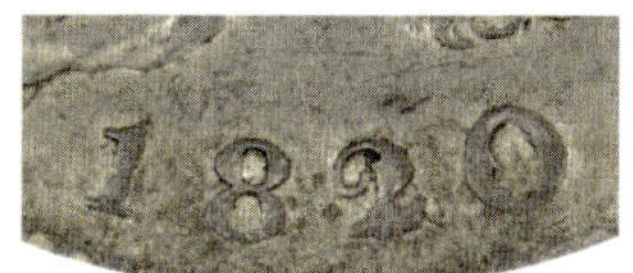
1820, 20 Over 19, Square Base 2

1820, 20 Over 19, Curl Base 2

1820, Curl Base, No Knob 2, Small Date

| Mintage | G-4 | F-12 | VF-20 | EF-40 | AU-50 | MS-60 | MS-63 |
|---|---|---|---|---|---|---|---|
| 1820, All kinds. . . . . . . . . . . . . .751,122 | | | | | | | |
| 1820, 20 Over 19, Square 2 . . . . . . . | $100 | $150 | $250 | $650 | $1,500 | $4,750 | $10,000 |
| 1820, 20 Over 19, Curl Base 2 . . . . . | 100 | 150 | 250 | 600 | 1,250 | 4,200 | 10,000 |
| 1820, Curl Base 2, Small Date. . . . . . | 100 | 200 | 275 | 500 | 1,000 | 3,800 | 8,000 |

Square Base, Knob 2, Large Date

Square Base, No Knob 2, Large Date

| Mintage | G-4 | F-12 | VF-20 | EF-40 | AU-50 | MS-60 | MS-63 |
|---|---|---|---|---|---|---|---|
| 1820, Sq Base Knob 2, Lg Dt. . . . . . . . . | $100 | $175 | $250 | $500 | $950 | $3,250 | $6,000 |
| 1820, Sq Base No Knob 2, Lg Dt . . . . . . | 100 | 175 | 250 | 500 | 950 | 3,250 | 6,500 |
| 1820, No Serifs on E's. . . . . . . . . . . . . . | 500 | 1,250 | 3,250 | 6,500 | 10,000 | 25,000 | |
| 1821 . . . . . . . . . . . . . . . . . . . . .1,305,797 | 70 | 100 | 145 | 275 | 650 | 2,000 | 4,000 |
| 1822, All kinds. . . . . . . . . . . . . . 1,559,573 | | | | | | | |
| 1822 . . . . . . . . . . . . . . . . . . . . . . . . . . | 70 | 100 | 155 | 300 | 500 | 1,800 | 3,500 |
| 1822, So-Called 2 Over 1 . . . . . . . . . . . | 100 | 140 | 225 | 600 | 1,100 | 2,500 | 5,500 |

1823, Broken 3

1823, Patched 3

1823, Ugly 3

| | Mintage | G-4 | F-12 | VF-20 | EF-40 | AU-50 | MS-60 | MS-63 |
|---|---|---|---|---|---|---|---|---|
| 1823, All kinds | 1,694,200 | | | | | | | |
| 1823, Broken 3 | | $120 | $225 | $400 | $750 | $2,250 | $5,500 | $11,000 |
| 1823, Patched 3 | | 100 | 150 | 275 | 700 | 1,600 | 4,250 | 6,500 |
| 1823, Ugly 3 | | 100 | 150 | 250 | 650 | 2,250 | 5,500 | 12,500 |
| 1823, Normal | | 70 | 100 | 130 | 250 | 500 | 1,500 | 3,400 |

"Various Dates"
*Probably 4 over 2 over 0.*

1824, 4 Over 1

1824, 4 Over 4

1824, 4 Over 4

*4 Over 4 varieties are easily mistaken for scarcer 4 Over 1. Note distance between 2's and 4's in each.*

1827, 7 Over 6

| | Mintage | G-4 | F-12 | VF-20 | EF-40 | AU-50 | MS-60 | MS-63 |
|---|---|---|---|---|---|---|---|---|
| 1824, All kinds | 3,504,954 | | | | | | | |
| 1824, 4 Over Various Dates | | $70 | $145 | $175 | $350 | $1,250 | $3,250 | $5,500 |
| 1824, 4 Over 1 | | 75 | 115 | 175 | 350 | 750 | 2,500 | 6,500 |
| 1824, 4 Over 4 *(2 varieties)* | | 75 | 110 | 140 | 210 | 700 | 2,000 | 3,500 |
| 1824, Normal | | 75 | 100 | 115 | 175 | 500 | 1,150 | 2,500 |
| 1825 | 2,943,166 | 75 | 100 | 115 | 175 | 425 | 1,150 | 2,500 |
| 1826 | 4,004,180 | 75 | 100 | 115 | 175 | 350 | 1,150 | 2,000 |
| 1827, All kinds | 5,493,400 | | | | | | | |
| 1827, 7 Over 6 | | 100 | 150 | 200 | 450 | 800 | 2,350 | 4,250 |
| 1827, Square Base 2 | | 75 | 100 | 115 | 175 | 400 | 1,350 | 2,500 |
| 1827, Curl Base 2 | | 75 | 100 | 130 | 300 | 550 | 1,800 | 3,500 |

1828, Curl Base, No Knob 2

1828, Curl Base, Knob 2

1828, Square Base 2, Large 8's

1828, Square Base 2, Small 8's

1828, Large Letters

1828, Small Letters

| | Mintage | G-4 | F-12 | VF-20 | EF-40 | AU-50 | MS-60 | MS-63 |
|---|---|---|---|---|---|---|---|---|
| 1828, All kinds | 3,075,200 | | | | | | | |
| 1828, Curl Base No Knob 2 | | $70 | $100 | $130 | $200 | $450 | $1,350 | $2,250 |
| 1828, Curl Base Knob 2 | | 70 | 115 | 150 | 250 | 700 | 2,000 | 4,500 |
| 1828, Square Base 2, Large 8's | | 70 | 95 | 115 | 175 | 400 | 1,500 | 3,000 |

| | Mintage | G-4 | F-12 | VF-20 | EF-40 | AU-50 | MS-60 | MS-63 |
|---|---|---|---|---|---|---|---|---|
| 1828, Square Base 2, Small 8's, Large Letters. . . . . . . . . | | $65 | $90 | $115 | $165 | $350 | $1,150 | $2,000 |
| 1828, Square Base 2, Small 8's and Letters . . . . . . . . . . | | 75 | 105 | 150 | 250 | 600 | 2,500 | 5,000 |
| 1829, All kinds. . . . . . . . . . . . | 3,712,156 | | | | | | | |
| 1829, 9 Over 7 . . . . . . . . . . . . . . . . . | | 70 | 120 | 165 | 350 | 750 | 1,500 | 3,500 |
| 1829 . . . . . . . . . . . . . . . . . . . . . . . . | | 60 | 80 | 110 | 180 | 400 | 1,150 | 2,000 |
| 1829, Large Letters. . . . . . . . . . . . . . | | 65 | 90 | 120 | 200 | 400 | 1,200 | 2,500 |

1830, Small 0

1832, Large Letters Reverse

*Raised segment lines to right, 1830.*

*Raised segment lines to left, 1830–1831.*

*Adopted edge, 1830–1836.*

| | Mintage | G-4 | F-12 | VF-20 | EF-40 | AU-50 | MS-60 | MS-63 |
|---|---|---|---|---|---|---|---|---|
| 1830, All kinds. . . . . . . . . | 4,764,800 | | | | | | | |
| 1830, Small 0 . . . . . . . . . . . . . . . | | $65 | $90 | $120 | $180 | $375 | $1,100 | $2,100 |
| 1830, Large 0 . . . . . . . . . . . . . . . | | 65 | 90 | 120 | 180 | 375 | 1,000 | 2,100 |
| 1830, Large Letters. . . . . . . . . . . | | 1,100 | 2,400 | 3,250 | 4,000 | 6,000 | 12,000 | 22,000 |
| 1831 . . . . . . . . . . . . . . . . | 5,873,660 | 65 | 90 | 110 | 180 | 375 | 1,100 | 2,000 |
| 1832, All kinds. . . . . . . . . | 4,797,000 | | | | | | | |
| 1832 . . . . . . . . . . . . . . . . . . . . . . | | 65 | 90 | 110 | 180 | 375 | 1,100 | 2,000 |
| 1832, Large Letters. . . . . . . . . . . | | 65 | 90 | 110 | 180 | 400 | 1,250 | 2,250 |
| 1833 . . . . . . . . . . . . . . . . | 5,206,000 | 65 | 90 | 110 | 180 | 375 | 1,100 | 2,000 |

## Slightly Modified Portrait (1834–1836)

1834, Large Date

1834, Small Date

1834, Large Letters Reverse

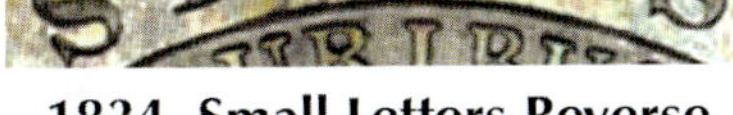

1834, Small Letters Reverse

1836, 50 Over 00

*Proofs of 1833, 1834, and 1835 with crushed edge-lettering use the same reverse die as the 1836 with beaded-border reverse. All are very rare.*

| | Mintage | G-4 | F-12 | VF-20 | EF-40 | AU-50 | MS-60 | MS-63 |
|---|---|---|---|---|---|---|---|---|
| 1834, All kinds. . . . . . . . . . . . . | 6,412,004 | | | | | | | |
| 1834, Large Dt and Letters . . . . . . . . . . | | $60 | $80 | $110 | $180 | $375 | $1,100 | $2,000 |
| 1834, Large Dt, Small Letters . . . . . . . . | | 60 | 80 | 110 | 180 | 375 | 1,100 | 2,000 |
| 1834, Small Dt, Stars, Letters . . . . . . . . | | 60 | 80 | 110 | 180 | 375 | 1,100 | 2,000 |

*Chart continued on next page.*

| | Mintage | G-4 | F-12 | VF-20 | EF-40 | AU-50 | MS-60 | MS-63 |
|---|---|---|---|---|---|---|---|---|
| 1835 | 5,352,006 | $60 | $80 | $110 | $180 | $375 | $1,100 | $2,000 |
| 1836, All kinds | 6,545,000 | | | | | | | |
| 1836 | | 60 | 80 | 110 | 180 | 375 | 1,100 | 2,000 |
| 1836 Over 1336 | | 80 | 100 | 130 | 225 | 475 | 1,200 | 2,500 |
| 1836, 50 Over 00 | | 125 | 200 | 350 | 500 | 925 | 2,750 | 5,000 |
| 1836, Beaded Border on Reverse | | 85 | 120 | 140 | 250 | 525 | 1,300 | 3,000 |

## CAPPED BUST, REEDED EDGE (1836–1839)

*Designer Christian Gobrecht; weight 13.36 grams; composition .900 silver, .100 copper; diameter 30 mm; reeded edge; mints: Philadelphia, New Orleans.*

**G-4 Good**—LIBERTY barely discernible on headband.
**VG-8 Very Good**—Some letters in LIBERTY clear.
**F-12 Fine**—LIBERTY complete but faint.
**VF-20 Very Fine**—LIBERTY sharp. Shoulder clasp clear.
**EF-40 Extremely Fine**—LIBERTY sharp and strong. Hair details visible.
**AU-50 About Uncirculated**—Slight trace of wear on cap, cheek, and hair above forehead, and on eagle's claws, wing tops, and head.
**MS-60 Uncirculated**—No trace of wear. Light blemishes.
**MS-63 Choice Uncirculated**—Some distracting contact marks or blemishes in prime focal areas. Impaired luster possible.

### Reverse 50 CENTS (1836–1837)

| | Mintage | G-4 | VG-8 | F-12 | VF-20 | EF-40 | AU-50 | MS-60 | MS-63 |
|---|---|---|---|---|---|---|---|---|---|
| 1836 | *1,200+* | $1,000 | $1,250 | $1,750 | $2,150 | $3,500 | $5,000 | $9,500 | $20,000 |
| 1837 | 3,629,820 | 65 | 85 | 100 | 125 | 220 | 450 | 1,150 | 2,500 |

### Reverse HALF DOL. (1838–1839)

The 1838-O was the first branch mint half dollar, though not mentioned in the Mint director's report. The New Orleans chief coiner stated that only 20 were struck. In 1838 and 1839 the mintmark appears on the obverse, above the date; thereafter, through 1915, all mintmarks are on the reverse.

| | Mintage | G-4 | VG-8 | F-12 | VF-20 | EF-40 | AU-50 | MS-60 | MS-63 |
|---|---|---|---|---|---|---|---|---|---|
| 1838 | 3,546,000 | $65 | $85 | $100 | $125 | $220 | $450 | $1,150 | $2,750 |

| | Mintage | G-4 | VG-8 | F-12 | VF-20 | EF-40 | AU-50 | MS-60 | MS-63 |
|---|---|---|---|---|---|---|---|---|---|
| 1838O | 20 | | | | | $350,000 | $400,000 | $500,000 | $600,000 |
| *$763,750, PF-64, Heritage auction, January 2014* | | | | | | | | | |
| 1839 | 1,392,976 | $75 | $90 | $110 | $140 | 275 | 500 | 1,400 | 3,100 |
| 1839, Sm Ltrs Rev. | | 15,000 | 20,000 | 40,000 | 55,000 | 60,000 | 75,000 | | 150,000 |
| 1839O | 116,000 | 425 | 600 | 950 | 1,200 | 2,000 | 2,500 | 6,500 | 12,500 |

## LIBERTY SEATED (1839–1891)

**G-4 Good**—Scant rim. LIBERTY on shield worn off. Date and letters legible.
**VG-8 Very Good**—Rim fairly defined. Some letters in LIBERTY evident.
**F-12 Fine**—LIBERTY complete, but weak.
**VF-20 Very Fine**—LIBERTY mostly sharp.
**EF-40 Extremely Fine**—LIBERTY entirely sharp. Scroll edges and clasp distinct.
**AU-50 About Uncirculated**—Slight trace of wear on Liberty's breast and knees, and on eagle's head, claws, and wing tops.
**MS-60 Uncirculated**—No trace of wear. Light blemishes.
**MS-63 Choice Uncirculated**—Some distracting marks or blemishes in focal areas. Impaired luster possible.

### Variety 1 – No Motto Above Eagle (1839–1853)

*Designer Christian Gobrecht; weight 13.36 grams; composition .900 silver, .100 copper; diameter 30.6 mm; reeded edge; mints: Philadelphia, New Orleans.*

No Drapery From Elbow

| | Mintage | G-4 | VG-8 | F-12 | VF-20 | EF-40 | AU-50 | MS-60 | MS-63 |
|---|---|---|---|---|---|---|---|---|---|
| 1839, No Drapery From Elbow | * | $125 | $250 | $500 | $750 | $1,850 | $3,250 | $7,500 | $27,500 |

* Included in "1839, Drapery From Elbow" mintage.

Drapery From Elbow (Starting 1839)

Small Letters in Legend (1839–1841)

1840 (Only), Medium Letters, Large Eagle

| | Mintage | G-4 | VG-8 | F-12 | VF-20 | EF-40 | AU-50 | MS-60 | MS-63 |
|---|---|---|---|---|---|---|---|---|---|
| 1839, Drapery From Elbow | 1,972,400 | $50 | $75 | $100 | $200 | $275 | $450 | $1,300 | $2,300 |
| 1840, Small Letters | 1,435,008 | 50 | 75 | 100 | 150 | 350 | 400 | 800 | 1,400 |
| 1840, Medium Letters **(a)** | * | 200 | 350 | 600 | 900 | 1,500 | 2,250 | 5,000 | 10,000 |
| 1840O | 855,100 | 60 | 75 | 100 | 200 | 325 | 450 | 1,650 | 4,500 |
| 1841 | 310,000 | 65 | 110 | 150 | 250 | 400 | 600 | 1,400 | 2,800 |
| 1841O | 401,000 | 50 | 75 | 115 | 200 | 350 | 600 | 1,450 | 3,500 |

* Included in number below. **a.** Struck at the New Orleans Mint from a reverse die of the previous style without mintmark.

*Chart continued on next page.*

| | Mintage | G-4 | VG-8 | F-12 | VF-20 | EF-40 | AU-50 | MS-60 | MS-63 |
|---|---|---|---|---|---|---|---|---|---|
| 1842, Sm Dt, Sm Ltrs *(4 known)* | * | $17,000 | | | $30,000 | | $40,000 | | |
| 1842O, Sm Dt, Sm Ltrs | 203,000 | 700 | $1,000 | $1,500 | 2,250 | $3,500 | 6,500 | $16,500 | $35,000 |

* Included in "1842, Medium Date" mintage.

## *Modified Reverse With Large Letters in Legend (1842–1853)*

Small Date

Medium Date

Large Letters in Legend (1842–1853)

1844-O, Doubled Date

| | Mintage | G-4 | VG-8 | F-12 | VF-20 | EF-40 | AU-50 | MS-60 | MS-63 |
|---|---|---|---|---|---|---|---|---|---|
| 1842, Medium Date | 2,012,764 | $50 | $75 | $100 | $150 | $225 | $350 | $975 | $2,000 |
| 1842, Small Date | * | 65 | 110 | 135 | 200 | 300 | 450 | 1,300 | 3,750 |
| 1842O, Medium Date | 754,000 | 65 | 75 | 100 | 200 | 300 | 700 | 1,600 | 4,500 |
| 1843 | 3,844,000 | 50 | 75 | 100 | 150 | 200 | 300 | 900 | 2,000 |
| 1843O | 2,268,000 | 50 | 75 | 100 | 175 | 300 | 400 | 1,400 | 3,250 |
| 1844 | 1,766,000 | 50 | 75 | 100 | 150 | 200 | 300 | 700 | 1,700 |
| 1844O | 2,005,000 | 50 | 75 | 100 | 175 | 275 | 400 | 1,350 | 3,000 |
| 1844O, Doubled Date | * | 600 | 1,000 | 1,500 | 1,850 | 3,250 | 5,500 | 8,500 | |
| 1845 | 589,000 | 75 | 100 | 150 | 250 | 325 | 600 | 1,000 | 3,500 |
| 1845O | 2,094,000 | 50 | 75 | 100 | 200 | 300 | 500 | 1,000 | 3,000 |
| 1845O, No Drapery **(a)** | * | 100 | 125 | 150 | 325 | 480 | 800 | 1,400 | 4,500 |

* Included in number above. **a.** Drapery missing because of excessive die polishing.

In 1846 the date size was again enlarged. The 1846 Medium Date is approximately the size of the 1842 Medium Date shown. Tall Date is similar to 1853. See illustrations of large cents on page 112.

| | Mintage | G-4 | VG-8 | F-12 | VF-20 | EF-40 | AU-50 | MS-60 | MS-63 |
|---|---|---|---|---|---|---|---|---|---|
| 1846, All kinds | 2,210,000 | | | | | | | | |
| 1846, Medium Date | | $50 | $75 | $100 | $175 | $250 | $350 | $1,000 | $2,600 |
| 1846, Tall Date | | 75 | 110 | 175 | 250 | 325 | 400 | 1,300 | 2,750 |
| 1846, 6 Over Horizontal 6 | | 225 | 300 | 500 | 1,000 | 1,650 | 2,500 | 4,750 | 10,000 |
| 1846O, Medium Date | 2,304,000 | 75 | 110 | 200 | 300 | 400 | 500 | 1,500 | 3,600 |
| 1846O, Tall Date | * | 250 | 450 | 600 | 900 | 1,850 | 2,500 | 7,500 | 15,000 |
| 1847, 7 Over 6 | ** | 1,500 | 2,250 | 3,500 | 5,000 | 9,000 | 11,500 | 27,500 | |
| 1847 | 1,156,000 | 50 | 75 | 100 | 150 | 250 | 350 | 850 | 1,650 |
| 1847O | 2,584,000 | 50 | 75 | 100 | 150 | 250 | 450 | 1,000 | 2,750 |
| 1848 | 580,000 | 75 | 125 | 175 | 250 | 425 | 650 | 1,200 | 2,500 |
| 1848O | 3,180,000 | 50 | 75 | 100 | 150 | 250 | 450 | 1,200 | 2,200 |
| 1849 | 1,252,000 | 75 | 100 | 150 | 200 | 300 | 450 | 1,000 | 2,250 |
| 1849O | 2,310,000 | 50 | 75 | 100 | 150 | 300 | 750 | 1,600 | 2,700 |
| 1850 | 227,000 | 275 | 375 | 600 | 800 | 1,200 | 1,450 | 2,000 | 3,500 |
| 1850O | 2,456,000 | 50 | 75 | 100 | 200 | 300 | 400 | 1,000 | 1,500 |
| 1851 | 200,750 | 750 | 1,000 | 1,500 | 1,750 | 2,350 | 2,850 | 3,500 | 5,000 |
| 1851O | 402,000 | 65 | 110 | 175 | 325 | 450 | 850 | 1,650 | 3,250 |

* Included in number above. ** Included in number below.

| | Mintage | G-4 | VG-8 | F-12 | VF-20 | EF-40 | AU-50 | MS-60 | MS-63 |
|---|---|---|---|---|---|---|---|---|---|
| 1852 | 77,130 | $500 | $750 | $1,000 | $1,250 | $2,000 | $2,350 | $2,850 | $3,500 |
| 1852O | 144,000 | 275 | 450 | 600 | 800 | 1,100 | 1,800 | 3,500 | 10,000 |
| 1853O *(4 known)* | | 150,000 | 175,000 | 325,000 | 500,000 | | | | |
| *$246,750, G-6, Stack's-Bowers auction, October 2014* | | | | | | | | | |

## Variety 2 – Arrows at Date, Rays Around Eagle (1853)

*Weight 12.44 grams; composition .900 silver, .100 copper; diameter 30.6 mm; reeded edge; mints: Philadelphia, New Orleans.*

| | Mintage | G-4 | VG-8 | F-12 | VF-20 | EF-40 | AU-50 | MS-60 | MS-63 |
|---|---|---|---|---|---|---|---|---|---|
| 1853 | 3,532,708 | $50 | $75 | $95 | $125 | $225 | $450 | $1,500 | $3,500 |
| 1853O | 1,328,000 | 60 | 75 | 95 | 180 | 400 | 750 | 2,750 | 5,500 |

## Variety 3 – Arrows at Date, No Rays (1854–1855)

*Weight 12.44 grams; composition .900 silver, .100 copper; diameter 30.6 mm; reeded edge; mints: Philadelphia, New Orleans, San Francisco.*

| | Mintage | G-4 | VG-8 | F-12 | VF-20 | EF-40 | AU-50 | MS-60 | MS-63 |
|---|---|---|---|---|---|---|---|---|---|
| 1854 | 2,982,000 | $50 | $75 | $95 | $125 | $175 | $300 | $625 | $1,500 |
| 1854O | 5,240,000 | 50 | 75 | 95 | 125 | 175 | 300 | 650 | 1,500 |
| 1855, All kinds | 759,500 | | | | | | | | |
| 1855 Over 1854 | | 75 | 90 | 175 | 360 | 500 | 1,200 | 2,250 | 3,600 |
| 1855, Normal Date | | 50 | 75 | 100 | 140 | 200 | 400 | 800 | 1,750 |
| 1855O | 3,688,000 | 50 | 75 | 95 | 125 | 175 | 300 | 650 | 1,500 |
| 1855S | 129,950 | 500 | 1,000 | 1,350 | 1,750 | 3,500 | 7,000 | 35,000 | 50,000 |

## Variety 1 Resumed, With Weight Standard of Variety 2 (1856–1866)

| | Mintage | G-4 | VG-8 | F-12 | VF-20 | EF-40 | AU-50 | MS-60 | MS-63 | PF-63 |
|---|---|---|---|---|---|---|---|---|---|---|
| 1856 | 938,000 | $50 | $75 | $95 | $125 | $185 | $250 | $600 | $1,200 | $6,500 |
| 1856O | 2,658,000 | 50 | 75 | 95 | 125 | 185 | 250 | 500 | 1,100 | |
| 1856S | 211,000 | 95 | 150 | 240 | 450 | 1,100 | 2,250 | 5,000 | 13,000 | |
| 1857 | 1,988,000 | 50 | 75 | 95 | 125 | 185 | 250 | 600 | 1,100 | 4,500 |
| 1857O | 818,000 | 50 | 75 | 100 | 175 | 300 | 500 | 1,350 | 3,500 | |
| 1857S | 158,000 | 150 | 180 | 250 | 425 | 1,100 | 2,000 | 4,500 | 13,500 | |
| 1858 *(300+)* | 4,225,700 | 50 | 75 | 95 | 125 | 185 | 250 | 600 | 1,100 | 2,250 |
| 1858O | 7,294,000 | 50 | 75 | 95 | 125 | 185 | 250 | 600 | 1,200 | |
| 1858S | 476,000 | 60 | 100 | 150 | 200 | 350 | 500 | 1,700 | 4,000 | |
| 1859 (800) | 747,200 | 50 | 75 | 95 | 125 | 185 | 250 | 500 | 1,100 | 1,600 |
| 1859O | 2,834,000 | 50 | 75 | 95 | 125 | 185 | 250 | 650 | 1,800 | |
| 1859S | 566,000 | 60 | 100 | 150 | 200 | 400 | 600 | 1,300 | 3,000 | |
| 1860 (1,000) | 302,700 | 60 | 75 | 95 | 125 | 200 | 300 | 735 | 1,450 | 1,600 |
| 1860O | 1,290,000 | 50 | 75 | 100 | 140 | 250 | 350 | 650 | 1,300 | |
| 1860S | 472,000 | 60 | 100 | 150 | 200 | 275 | 500 | 1,400 | 3,750 | |

The 1861-O quantity includes 330,000 struck under the U.S. government, 1,240,000 for the State of Louisiana after its secession, and 962,633 after Louisiana joined the

Confederate States of America; all were struck from regular U.S. dies. A late die state has a crack from Liberty's nose to the border; 1861-O coins with this crack can be attributed to the Confederacy. They should not be confused with the very rare 1861 Confederate half dollar, which has a distinctive reverse (see page 428).

| | Mintage | G-4 | VG-8 | F-12 | VF-20 | EF-40 | AU-50 | MS-60 | MS-63 | PF-63 |
|---|---|---|---|---|---|---|---|---|---|---|
| 1861 . . . . . . (1,000) | 2,887,400 | $50 | $75 | $95 | $125 | $185 | $250 | $575 | $1,200 | $1,600 |
| 1861O | 2,532,633 | 70 | 90 | 120 | 180 | 300 | 900 | 1,500 | 2,800 | |
| 1861O, Cracked Obv **(a)** | * | 360 | 500 | 775 | 1,250 | 2,850 | 4,250 | 12,000 | — | |
| 1861S | 939,500 | 60 | 75 | 95 | 200 | 350 | 500 | 1,200 | 3,000 | |
| 1862 . . . . . . . . (550) | 253,000 | 100 | 150 | 200 | 350 | 500 | 650 | 1,250 | 1,950 | 1,600 |
| 1862S | 1,352,000 | 60 | 90 | 120 | 180 | 300 | 425 | 1,150 | 2,700 | |
| 1863 . . . . . . . . (460) | 503,200 | 100 | 125 | 150 | 200 | 350 | 600 | 1,250 | 1,750 | 1,600 |
| 1863S | 916,000 | 60 | 75 | 95 | 150 | 300 | 550 | 1,300 | 2,500 | |
| 1864 . . . . . . . . (470) | 379,100 | 100 | 125 | 175 | 300 | 400 | 750 | 1,300 | 1,800 | 1,600 |
| 1864S | 658,000 | 100 | 125 | 175 | 300 | 400 | 750 | 1,800 | 4,250 | |
| 1865 . . . . . . . . (500) | 511,400 | 100 | 125 | 175 | 300 | 450 | 800 | 1,400 | 2,100 | 1,600 |
| 1865S | 675,000 | 100 | 125 | 175 | 300 | 500 | 750 | 2,000 | 4,500 | |
| 1866S, No Motto | 60,000 | 450 | 600 | 875 | 1,250 | 2,300 | 3,500 | 9,500 | 20,000 | |
| 1866 *(unique, not a regular issue)* | | | | | | | | | | — |

* Included in number above. **a.** Crack from nose to border; same obverse die used to coin pattern Confederate half dollars (see page 428).

## Variety 4 – Motto Above Eagle (1866–1873)

*Standards same as Variety 1, Resumed. Mints: Philadelphia, San Francisco, Carson City.*

*Circulation strike.* *Proof strike.*

| | Mintage | G-4 | VG-8 | F-12 | VF-20 | EF-40 | AU-50 | MS-60 | MS-63 | PF-63 |
|---|---|---|---|---|---|---|---|---|---|---|
| 1866 . . . . . . . . (725) | 744,900 | $60 | $100 | $150 | $200 | $300 | $500 | $1,000 | $2,100 | $1,350 |
| 1866S | 994,000 | 60 | 100 | 175 | 225 | 350 | 600 | 1,150 | 2,250 | |
| 1867 . . . . . . . . (625) | 449,300 | 100 | 125 | 150 | 200 | 300 | 550 | 1,150 | 1,600 | 1,500 |
| 1867S | 1,196,000 | 60 | 100 | 150 | 200 | 300 | 500 | 1,250 | 3,000 | |
| 1868 . . . . . . . . (600) | 417,600 | 100 | 125 | 175 | 250 | 450 | 550 | 1,000 | 2,000 | 1,350 |
| 1868S | 1,160,000 | 60 | 100 | 125 | 175 | 275 | 450 | 1,000 | 2,100 | |
| 1869 . . . . . . . . (600) | 795,300 | 60 | 100 | 125 | 175 | 250 | 300 | 1,000 | 1,600 | 1,350 |
| 1869S | 656,000 | 60 | 100 | 125 | 175 | 350 | 475 | 1,000 | 2,600 | |
| 1870 . . . . . . (1,000) | 633,900 | 60 | 75 | 100 | 150 | 250 | 325 | 725 | 1,500 | 1,350 |
| 1870CC | 54,617 | 1,750 | 2,750 | 4,000 | 5,500 | 10,000 | 30,000 | 85,000 | 225,000 | |
| 1870S | 1,004,000 | 100 | 125 | 150 | 300 | 500 | 650 | 1,950 | 4,500 | |
| 1871 . . . . . . . . (960) | 1,203,600 | 60 | 75 | 100 | 150 | 250 | 325 | 725 | 1,300 | 1,300 |
| 1871CC | 153,950 | 500 | 750 | 1,250 | 1,650 | 3,250 | 5,500 | 30,000 | 55,000 | |
| 1871S | 2,178,000 | 60 | 75 | 100 | 150 | 250 | 400 | 1,000 | 1,850 | |
| 1872 . . . . . . . . (950) | 880,600 | 60 | 100 | 150 | 200 | 300 | 325 | 725 | 2,300 | 1,300 |
| 1872CC | 257,000 | 300 | 600 | 750 | 1,300 | 2,250 | 3,850 | 23,500 | 70,000 | |
| 1872S | 580,000 | 100 | 150 | 200 | 300 | 400 | 700 | 1,750 | 3,000 | |

| | Mintage | G-4 | VG-8 | F-12 | VF-20 | EF-40 | AU-50 | MS-60 | MS-63 | PF-63 |
|---|---|---|---|---|---|---|---|---|---|---|
| 1873, Close 3 . .(600) | 587,000 | $60 | $100 | $175 | $225 | $350 | $600 | $1,000 | $1,500 | $1,300 |
| 1873, Open 3 | 214,200 | 3,250 | 4,500 | 5,500 | 6,750 | 8,000 | 13,500 | 50,000 | 95,000 | |
| 1873CC | 122,500 | 400 | 725 | 1,150 | 1,650 | 3,750 | 6,000 | 12,000 | 32,500 | |
| 1873S, No Arrows | 5,000 | | | | *(unknown in any collection)* | | | | | |

## Variety 5 – Arrows at Date (1873–1874)

*Weight 12.50 grams; composition .900 silver, .100 copper; diameter 30.6 mm; reeded edge; mints: Philadelphia, Carson City, San Francisco.*

**Arrows placed at date to show change in weight from 12.44 to 12.50 grams.**

| | Mintage | G-4 | VG-8 | F-12 | VF-20 | EF-40 | AU-50 | MS-60 | MS-63 | PF-63 |
|---|---|---|---|---|---|---|---|---|---|---|
| 1873 . . . . . . . .(800) | 1,815,200 | $50 | $60 | $75 | $150 | $300 | $475 | $950 | $1,800 | $2,200 |
| 1873CC | 214,560 | 300 | 475 | 800 | 1,150 | 2,000 | 3,500 | 8,250 | 18,500 | |
| 1873S | 228,000 | 100 | 150 | 200 | 350 | 550 | 1,000 | 3,500 | 8,000 | |
| 1874 . . . . . . . .(700) | 2,359,600 | 50 | 60 | 75 | 150 | 300 | 450 | 950 | 1,875 | 2,200 |
| 1874CC | 59,000 | 1,150 | 1,650 | 2,350 | 3,250 | 5,750 | 8,000 | 14,000 | 32,500 | |
| 1874S | 394,000 | 100 | 180 | 225 | 250 | 375 | 700 | 1,700 | 3,000 | |

## Variety 4 Resumed, With Weight Standard of Variety 5 (1875–1891)

| | Mintage | G-4 | VG-8 | F-12 | VF-20 | EF-40 | AU-50 | MS-60 | MS-63 | PF-63 |
|---|---|---|---|---|---|---|---|---|---|---|
| 1875 . . . . . .(700) | 6,026,800 | $50 | $75 | $100 | $140 | $200 | $300 | $475 | $800 | $1,150 |
| 1875CC | 1,008,000 | 85 | 125 | 225 | 325 | 550 | 1,000 | 2,000 | 3,000 | |
| 1875S | 3,200,000 | 50 | 75 | 100 | 140 | 200 | 300 | 475 | 800 | |
| 1876 . . . . (1,150) | 8,418,000 | 50 | 75 | 100 | 140 | 200 | 300 | 475 | 800 | 1,150 |
| 1876CC | 1,956,000 | 85 | 110 | 165 | 200 | 400 | 700 | 1,600 | 2,400 | |
| 1876S | 4,528,000 | 40 | 45 | 65 | 80 | 120 | 225 | 450 | 800 | |
| 1877 . . . . . .(510) | 8,304,000 | 40 | 60 | 70 | 80 | 120 | 225 | 450 | 800 | 1,150 |
| 1877, 7/6 | * | | | | | 1,200 | 2,200 | 3,750 | 12,000 | |
| 1877CC | 1,420,000 | 85 | 135 | 160 | 225 | 400 | 550 | 1,150 | 2,350 | |
| 1877S | 5,356,000 | 40 | 45 | 65 | 80 | 100 | 225 | 475 | 800 | |
| 1878 . . . . . .(800) | 1,377,600 | 45 | 90 | 120 | 135 | 150 | 240 | 425 | 1,100 | 1,150 |
| 1878CC | 62,000 | 1,050 | 1,450 | 2,000 | 3,000 | 3,750 | 5,500 | 12,500 | 25,000 | |
| 1878S | 12,000 | 32,500 | 40,000 | 45,000 | 55,000 | 67,500 | 70,000 | 100,000 | 150,000 | |
| 1879 . . . . (1,100) | 4,800 | 350 | 450 | 550 | 650 | 750 | 900 | 1,050 | 1,300 | 1,150 |
| 1880 . . . . (1,355) | 8,400 | 350 | 450 | 550 | 650 | 750 | 900 | 1,050 | 1,500 | 1,150 |
| 1881 . . . . . .(975) | 10,000 | 350 | 450 | 550 | 650 | 750 | 900 | 1,050 | 1,500 | 1,150 |
| 1882 . . . . (1,100) | 4,400 | 350 | 450 | 550 | 650 | 750 | 900 | 1,050 | 1,600 | 1,150 |
| 1883 . . . . (1,039) | 8,000 | 350 | 450 | 550 | 650 | 750 | 900 | 1,050 | 1,500 | 1,150 |
| 1884 . . . . . .(875) | 4,400 | 425 | 475 | 550 | 650 | 775 | 925 | 1,100 | 1,500 | 1,150 |
| 1885 . . . . . .(930) | 5,200 | 500 | 550 | 625 | 725 | 800 | 900 | 1,050 | 1,500 | 1,150 |
| 1886 . . . . . .(886) | 5,000 | 500 | 550 | 625 | 725 | 800 | 900 | 1,100 | 1,500 | 1,150 |

* Included in number above.

*Chart continued on next page.*

| | Mintage | G-4 | VG-8 | F-12 | VF-20 | EF-40 | AU-50 | MS-60 | MS-63 | PF-63 |
|---|---|---|---|---|---|---|---|---|---|---|
| 1887 . . . . . . . .(710) . . . . . | 5,000 | $525 | $575 | $650 | $750 | $950 | $1,000 | $1,100 | $1,400 | $1,150 |
| 1888 . . . . . . . .(832) . . . . | 12,001 | 350 | 450 | 550 | 650 | 750 | 900 | 1,000 | 1,350 | 1,150 |
| 1889 . . . . . . . .(711) . . . . | 12,000 | 350 | 450 | 550 | 650 | 750 | 900 | 1,000 | 1,250 | 1,150 |
| 1890 . . . . . . . .(590) . . . . | 12,000 | 350 | 450 | 550 | 650 | 750 | 900 | 1,000 | 1,150 | 1,150 |
| 1891 . . . . . . . .(600) . . . | 200,000 | 100 | 150 | 200 | 350 | 500 | 700 | 800 | 1,200 | 1,150 |

## BARBER OR LIBERTY HEAD (1892–1915)

Like the dime and quarter dollar, this type was designed by Charles E. Barber, whose initial B is at the truncation of the neck.

*Designer Charles E. Barber; weight 12.50 grams; composition .900 silver, .100 copper; diameter 30.6 mm; reeded edge; mints: Philadelphia, Denver, New Orleans, San Francisco.*

**G-4 Good**—Date and legends legible. LIBERTY worn off headband.
**VG-8 Very Good**—Some letters legible in LIBERTY.
**F-12 Fine**—LIBERTY nearly completely legible, but worn.
**VF-20 Very Fine**—All letters in LIBERTY evenly plain.
**EF-40 Extremely Fine**—LIBERTY bold, and its ribbon distinct.
**AU-50 About Uncirculated**—Slight trace of wear above forehead, leaf tips, and cheek, and on eagle's head, tail, and wing tips.
**MS-60 Uncirculated**—No trace of wear. Light blemishes.
**MS-63 Choice Uncirculated**—Some distracting contact marks or blemishes in prime focal areas. Impaired luster possible.
**PF-63 Choice Proof**—Reflective surfaces with only a few blemishes in secondary focal places. No major flaws.

*Mintmark location is on reverse, below eagle.*

| | Mintage | G-4 | VG-8 | F-12 | VF-20 | EF-40 | AU-50 | MS-60 | MS-63 | PF-63 |
|---|---|---|---|---|---|---|---|---|---|---|
| 1892 . . . . . . (1,245) . . . | 934,000 | $24 | $35 | $80 | $135 | $200 | $325 | $550 | $800 | $1,000 |
| 1892O . . . . . . . . . . . . . . | 390,000 | 250 | 425 | 550 | 625 | 700 | 825 | 1,025 | 1,650 | |
| 1892O, Micro O **(a)** . . . . . . . . . . | * | 3,650 | 7,500 | 10,000 | 12,500 | 15,500 | 18,000 | 30,000 | 45,000 | |
| 1892S . . . . . . . . . . . . . | 1,029,028 | 275 | 340 | 400 | 500 | 700 | 875 | 1,200 | 2,000 | |
| 1893 . . . . . . . .(792) . . | 1,826,000 | 25 | 30 | 70 | 140 | 210 | 350 | 600 | 1,000 | 1,100 |
| 1893O . . . . . . . . . . . . . | 1,389,000 | 40 | 75 | 135 | 250 | 350 | 450 | 800 | 1,250 | |
| 1893S . . . . . . . . . . . . . . | 740,000 | 150 | 210 | 500 | 750 | 1,200 | 1,600 | 2,250 | 4,300 | |
| 1894 . . . . . . . .(972) . . | 1,148,000 | 30 | 50 | 115 | 200 | 275 | 375 | 650 | 1,000 | 1,100 |
| 1894O . . . . . . . . . . . . . | 2,138,000 | 25 | 40 | 100 | 180 | 300 | 400 | 700 | 1,200 | |
| 1894S . . . . . . . . . . . . . | 4,048,690 | 22 | 35 | 90 | 180 | 240 | 375 | 650 | 1,300 | |
| 1895 . . . . . . . .(880) . . | 1,834,338 | 28 | 40 | 80 | 140 | 210 | 350 | 600 | 900 | 1,100 |
| 1895O . . . . . . . . . . . . . | 1,766,000 | 50 | 70 | 160 | 200 | 260 | 410 | 750 | 1,450 | |
| 1895S . . . . . . . . . . . . . | 1,108,086 | 30 | 75 | 160 | 250 | 450 | 550 | 775 | 1,150 | |
| 1896 . . . . . . . .(762) . . . | 950,000 | 40 | 60 | 115 | 175 | 240 | 400 | 650 | 1,050 | 1,100 |
| 1896O . . . . . . . . . . . . . . | 924,000 | 50 | 95 | 180 | 500 | 1,900 | 3,300 | 6,000 | 12,000 | |
| 1896S . . . . . . . . . . . . . | 1,140,948 | 115 | 165 | 240 | 450 | 1,000 | 1,450 | 2,350 | 3,750 | |
| 1897 . . . . . . . .(731) . . | 2,480,000 | 25 | 35 | 65 | 110 | 240 | 375 | 600 | 950 | 1,100 |
| 1897O . . . . . . . . . . . . . . | 632,000 | 160 | 230 | 450 | 750 | 1,200 | 1,600 | 2,500 | 4,000 | |

* Included in number above. **a.** Normal and "microscopic" mintmarks; see page 22.

| | Mintage | G-4 | VG-8 | F-12 | VF-20 | EF-40 | AU-50 | MS-60 | MS-63 | PF-63 |
|---|---|---|---|---|---|---|---|---|---|---|
| 1897S | 933,900 | $175 | $250 | $400 | $550 | $1,150 | $1,850 | $2,750 | $3,750 | |
| 1898 | (735) . . 2,956,000 | 15 | 20 | 50 | 100 | 200 | 325 | 650 | 950 | $1,100 |
| 1898O | 874,000 | 38 | 90 | 210 | 500 | 675 | 775 | 1,500 | 2,300 | |
| 1898S | 2,358,550 | 30 | 50 | 140 | 185 | 340 | 500 | 1,000 | 2,500 | |
| 1899 | (846) . . 5,538,000 | 15 | 20 | 45 | 120 | 200 | 325 | 575 | 800 | 1,100 |
| 1899O | 1,724,000 | 25 | 40 | 80 | 140 | 240 | 350 | 1,000 | 1,600 | |
| 1899S | 1,686,411 | 25 | 40 | 100 | 175 | 300 | 450 | 850 | 2,000 | |
| 1900 | (912) . . 4,762,000 | 15 | 20 | 45 | 95 | 180 | 325 | 550 | 850 | 1,100 |
| 1900O | 2,744,000 | 30 | 45 | 100 | 170 | 300 | 500 | 1,000 | 2,750 | |
| 1900S | 2,560,322 | 17 | 35 | 60 | 160 | 240 | 325 | 800 | 2,200 | |
| 1901 | (813) . . 4,268,000 | 15 | 20 | 50 | 95 | 180 | 280 | 550 | 850 | 1,100 |
| 1901O | 1,124,000 | 30 | 45 | 125 | 270 | 1,100 | 1,500 | 2,400 | 4,000 | |
| 1901S | 847,044 | 42 | 75 | 225 | 475 | 1,250 | 1,700 | 3,500 | 6,500 | |
| 1902 | (777) . . 4,922,000 | 15 | 20 | 45 | 110 | 200 | 325 | 500 | 850 | 1,100 |
| 1902O | 2,526,000 | 15 | 20 | 60 | 105 | 250 | 350 | 800 | 2,000 | |
| 1902S | 1,460,670 | 25 | 40 | 110 | 200 | 400 | 550 | 1,100 | 3,000 | |
| 1903 | (755) . . 2,278,000 | 15 | 20 | 45 | 125 | 180 | 325 | 550 | 850 | 1,100 |
| 1903O | 2,100,000 | 15 | 30 | 70 | 125 | 210 | 325 | 700 | 1,700 | |
| 1903S | 1,920,772 | 25 | 35 | 80 | 155 | 300 | 600 | 1,000 | 1,700 | |
| 1904 | (670) . . 2,992,000 | 15 | 30 | 45 | 85 | 200 | 325 | 550 | 850 | 1,100 |
| 1904O | 1,117,600 | 30 | 55 | 110 | 350 | 550 | 900 | 1,700 | 3,750 | |
| 1904S | 553,038 | 65 | 180 | 400 | 1,150 | 2,000 | 7,000 | 10,000 | 19,000 | |
| 1905 | (727) . . . 662,000 | 35 | 65 | 100 | 185 | 265 | 425 | 700 | 1,250 | 1,100 |
| 1905O | 505,000 | 40 | 60 | 150 | 250 | 400 | 550 | 1,050 | 1,750 | |
| 1905S | 2,494,000 | 15 | 20 | 48 | 140 | 200 | 400 | 700 | 1,600 | |
| 1906 | (675) . . 2,638,000 | 15 | 20 | 60 | 115 | 180 | 325 | 500 | 900 | 1,100 |
| 1906D | 4,028,000 | 15 | 20 | 60 | 125 | 180 | 325 | 500 | 800 | |
| 1906O | 2,446,000 | 15 | 20 | 45 | 100 | 180 | 350 | 800 | 1,400 | |
| 1906S | 1,740,154 | 15 | 25 | 75 | 140 | 210 | 375 | 625 | 1,600 | |
| 1907 | (575) . . 2,598,000 | 15 | 25 | 55 | 95 | 180 | 300 | 425 | 700 | 1,100 |
| 1907D | 3,856,000 | 15 | 25 | 60 | 115 | 180 | 300 | 450 | 850 | |
| 1907O | 3,946,600 | 15 | 20 | 45 | 105 | 180 | 300 | 500 | 900 | |
| 1907S | 1,250,000 | 30 | 50 | 100 | 240 | 425 | 800 | 2,000 | 5,500 | |
| 1908 | (545) . . 1,354,000 | 15 | 20 | 40 | 85 | 180 | 300 | 425 | 750 | 1,100 |
| 1908D | 3,280,000 | 15 | 20 | 45 | 85 | 180 | 300 | 450 | 800 | |
| 1908O | 5,360,000 | 15 | 20 | 45 | 85 | 180 | 300 | 500 | 1,000 | |
| 1908S | 1,644,828 | 15 | 20 | 65 | 160 | 400 | 600 | 900 | 2,300 | |
| 1909 | (650) . . 2,368,000 | 15 | 20 | 45 | 85 | 180 | 300 | 450 | 825 | 1,100 |
| 1909O | 925,400 | 25 | 45 | 90 | 175 | 325 | 650 | 975 | 1,900 | |
| 1909S | 1,764,000 | 15 | 35 | 45 | 80 | 350 | 400 | 650 | 1,150 | |
| 1910 | (551) . . . 418,000 | 30 | 40 | 100 | 175 | 320 | 410 | 600 | 1,100 | 1,100 |
| 1910S | 1,948,000 | 15 | 20 | 55 | 95 | 240 | 450 | 800 | 1,800 | |
| 1911 | (543) . . 1,406,000 | 15 | 25 | 45 | 95 | 180 | 300 | 425 | 775 | 1,100 |
| 1911D | 695,080 | 20 | 35 | 80 | 130 | 240 | 325 | 500 | 800 | |
| 1911S | 1,272,000 | 18 | 20 | 40 | 120 | 240 | 475 | 800 | 1,500 | |
| 1912 | (700) . . 1,550,000 | 15 | 25 | 45 | 120 | 180 | 300 | 500 | 775 | 1,100 |
| 1912D | 2,300,800 | 20 | 35 | 85 | 140 | 200 | 350 | 500 | 775 | |
| 1912S | 1,370,000 | 15 | 25 | 45 | 150 | 250 | 375 | 750 | 1,100 | |
| 1913 | (627) . . . 188,000 | 75 | 90 | 210 | 400 | 800 | 1,200 | 1,750 | 2,100 | 1,100 |
| 1913D | 534,000 | 15 | 25 | 60 | 110 | 200 | 375 | 625 | 900 | |
| 1913S | 604,000 | 20 | 35 | 60 | 120 | 300 | 450 | 800 | 1,700 | |
| 1914 | (380) . . . 124,230 | 100 | 140 | 400 | 550 | 1,100 | 1,150 | 1,550 | 2,100 | 1,200 |

*Chart continued on next page.*

| | Mintage | G-4 | VG-8 | F-12 | VF-20 | EF-40 | AU-50 | MS-60 | MS-63 | PF-63 |
|---|---|---|---|---|---|---|---|---|---|---|
| 1914S | 992,000 | $16 | $20 | $45 | $100 | $200 | $400 | $650 | $1,300 | |
| 1915 (450) | 138,000 | 85 | 150 | 300 | 375 | 650 | 1,000 | 1,500 | 2,250 | $1,200 |
| 1915D | 1,170,400 | 20 | 30 | 70 | 130 | 200 | 300 | 550 | 850 | |
| 1915S | 1,604,000 | 20 | 30 | 70 | 110 | 200 | 300 | 550 | 900 | |

## LIBERTY WALKING (1916–1947)

This type was designed by Adolph A. Weinman, whose monogram, AW, appears under the tips of the tail feathers. On the 1916 coins and some of the 1917 coins the mintmark is located on the obverse below the motto. The Mint also created a 2016 gold Liberty Walking half dollar at a smaller dimension. See page 225.

*Designer Adolph A. Weinman; weight 12.50 grams; composition .900 silver, .100 copper (net weight: .36169 oz. pure silver); diameter 30.6 mm; reeded edge; mints: Philadelphia, Denver, San Francisco.*

**G-4 Good**—Rims defined. Motto IN GOD WE TRUST legible.
**VG-8 Very Good**—Motto distinct. About half of skirt lines at left clear.
**F-12 Fine**—All skirt lines evident, but worn in spots. Clear details in sandal below motto.
**VF-20 Very Fine**—Skirt lines sharp, including leg area. Little wear on breast and right arm.
**EF-40 Extremely Fine**—Nearly all gown lines visible.
**AU-50 About Uncirculated**—Slight trace of wear on Liberty's head, knee, and breasts, and on eagle's claws and head.
**MS-60 Uncirculated**—No trace of wear. Light blemishes.
**MS-63 Choice Uncirculated**—Some distracting contact marks or blemishes in prime focal areas. Impaired luster possible.
**PF-65 Gem Proof**—Brilliant surfaces with no noticeable blemishes or flaws. A few scattered, barely noticeable marks or hairlines possible.

Mintmark Locations

*Choice Uncirculated, well-struck specimens are worth more than values listed.*

| | Mintage | G-4 | VG-8 | F-12 | VF-20 | EF-40 | AU-50 | MS-60 | MS-63 |
|---|---|---|---|---|---|---|---|---|---|
| 1916 | 608,000 | $50 | $55.00 | $90.00 | $175 | $250 | $265 | $450 | $650 |
| 1916D, Obverse Mintmark | 1,014,400 | 50 | 60.00 | 85.00 | 135 | 215 | 240 | 450 | 725 |
| 1916S, Obverse Mintmark | 508,000 | 100 | 140.00 | 250.00 | 450 | 650 | 950 | 1,600 | 2,500 |
| 1917 | 12,292,000 | 18 | 19.00 | 19.50 | 21 | 40 | 70 | 150 | 210 |
| 1917D, Obverse Mintmark | 765,400 | 25 | 35.00 | 80.00 | 150 | 240 | 325 | 800 | 1,150 |
| 1917D, Reverse Mintmark | 1,940,000 | 18 | 19.00 | 45.00 | 145 | 280 | 515 | 1,200 | 2,200 |
| 1917S, Obverse Mintmark | 952,000 | 27 | 50.00 | 140.00 | 375 | 750 | 1,300 | 3,250 | 5,500 |
| 1917S, Reverse Mintmark | 5,554,000 | 18 | 19.00 | 20.00 | 35 | 70 | 170 | 700 | 1,800 |
| 1918 | 6,634,000 | 18 | 19.00 | 20.00 | 65 | 155 | 265 | 625 | 1,250 |
| 1918D | 3,853,040 | 18 | 19.00 | 38.00 | 100 | 250 | 475 | 1,500 | 3,500 |
| 1918S | 10,282,000 | 18 | 19.00 | 20.00 | 35 | 80 | 200 | 600 | 2,150 |
| 1919 | 962,000 | 25 | 32.00 | 78.00 | 265 | 515 | 950 | 2,350 | 3,500 |
| 1919D | 1,165,000 | 26 | 40.00 | 115.00 | 345 | 825 | 1,900 | 4,750 | 12,000 |
| 1919S | 1,552,000 | 20 | 30.00 | 85.00 | 275 | 815 | 1,600 | 4,000 | 8,750 |
| 1920 | 6,372,000 | 18 | 19.00 | 20.00 | 45 | 80 | 160 | 425 | 700 |
| 1920D | 1,551,000 | 18 | 20.00 | 75.00 | 250 | 450 | 925 | 3,000 | 5,500 |
| 1920S | 4,624,000 | 18 | 18.50 | 23.00 | 90 | 230 | 600 | 1,200 | 3,250 |

| | Mintage | G-4 | VG-8 | F-12 | VF-20 | EF-40 | AU-50 | MS-60 | MS-63 | PF-65 |
|---|---|---|---|---|---|---|---|---|---|---|
| 1921 | 246,000 | $135 | $200 | $325 | $775 | $2,000 | $2,900 | $6,000 | $8,000 | |
| 1921D | 208,000 | 200 | 350 | 550 | 850 | 2,850 | 5,500 | 9,250 | 12,500 | |
| 1921S | 548,000 | 48 | 80 | 250 | 800 | 4,500 | 8,000 | 20,000 | 32,000 | |
| 1923S | 2,178,000 | 13 | 15 | 30 | 110 | 365 | 1,400 | 2,750 | 4,250 | |
| 1927S | 2,392,000 | 13 | 15 | 18 | 50 | 160 | 450 | 1,200 | 2,500 | |
| 1928S **(a,b)** | 1,940,000 | 13 | 15 | 19 | 75 | 180 | 500 | 1,250 | 3,000 | |
| 1929D | 1,001,200 | 12 | 15 | 18 | 30 | 100 | 190 | 450 | 800 | |
| 1929S | 1,902,000 | 12 | 15 | 18 | 35 | 115 | 230 | 500 | 1,150 | |
| 1933S | 1,786,000 | 12 | 15 | 18 | 20 | 60 | 240 | 750 | 1,350 | |
| 1934 | 6,964,000 | 8 | 9 | 10 | 15 | 19 | 26 | 75 | 100 | |
| 1934D **(b)** | 2,361,000 | 8 | 9 | 10 | 15 | 35 | 85 | 140 | 250 | |
| 1934S | 3,652,000 | 8 | 9 | 10 | 15 | 30 | 90 | 365 | 750 | |
| 1935 | 9,162,000 | 8 | 9 | 10 | 15 | 19 | 25 | 40 | 70 | |
| 1935D | 3,003,800 | 8 | 9 | 10 | 15 | 30 | 65 | 140 | 300 | |
| 1935S | 3,854,000 | 8 | 9 | 10 | 15 | 26 | 95 | 275 | 465 | |
| 1936 (3,901) | 12,614,000 | 8 | 9 | 10 | 15 | 18 | 25 | 45 | 75 | $3,000 |
| 1936D | 4,252,400 | 8 | 9 | 10 | 15 | 20 | 50 | 85 | 120 | |
| 1936S | 3,884,000 | 8 | 9 | 10 | 15 | 22 | 60 | 130 | 200 | |
| 1937 (5,728) | 9,522,000 | 8 | 9 | 10 | 15 | 18 | 25 | 40 | 70 | 850 |
| 1937D | 1,676,000 | 8 | 9 | 10 | 18 | 32 | 100 | 215 | 265 | |
| 1937S | 2,090,000 | 8 | 9 | 10 | 15 | 25 | 60 | 165 | 210 | |
| 1938 (8,152) | 4,110,000 | 8 | 9 | 10 | 15 | 20 | 45 | 70 | 160 | 675 |
| 1938D | 491,600 | 50 | 60 | 90 | 100 | 160 | 235 | 475 | 650 | |
| 1939 (8,808) | 6,812,000 | 8 | 9 | 10 | 15 | 18 | 26 | 40 | 65 | 700 |
| 1939D | 4,267,800 | 8 | 9 | 10 | 15 | 18 | 25 | 43 | 75 | |
| 1939S | 2,552,000 | 8 | 9 | 10 | 15 | 26 | 70 | 150 | 175 | |
| 1940 (11,279) | 9,156,000 | 8 | 9 | 10 | 15 | 18 | 22 | 35 | 55 | 600 |
| 1940S | 4,550,000 | 8 | 9 | 10 | 15 | 18 | 35 | 45 | 80 | |
| 1941 **(c)** (15,412) | 24,192,000 | 8 | 9 | 10 | 15 | 18 | 22 | 35 | 55 | 600 |
| 1941D | 11,248,400 | 8 | 9 | 10 | 15 | 18 | 22 | 38 | 65 | |
| 1941S | 8,098,000 | 8 | 9 | 10 | 15 | 18 | 26 | 75 | 120 | |
| 1942 (21,120) | 47,818,000 | 8 | 9 | 10 | 15 | 18 | 22 | 40 | 60 | 600 |
| 1942D | 10,973,800 | 8 | 9 | 10 | 15 | 18 | 20 | 40 | 80 | |
| 1942S **(b)** | 12,708,000 | 8 | 9 | 10 | 15 | 18 | 22 | 40 | 80 | |
| 1943 | 53,190,000 | 8 | 9 | 10 | 15 | 18 | 20 | 35 | 50 | |
| 1943D | 11,346,000 | 8 | 9 | 10 | 15 | 18 | 24 | 48 | 75 | |
| 1943S | 13,450,000 | 8 | 9 | 10 | 15 | 18 | 25 | 42 | 60 | |
| 1944 | 28,206,000 | 8 | 9 | 10 | 15 | 18 | 20 | 35 | 50 | |
| 1944D | 9,769,000 | 8 | 9 | 10 | 15 | 18 | 20 | 40 | 60 | |
| 1944S | 8,904,000 | 8 | 9 | 10 | 15 | 18 | 24 | 40 | 63 | |
| 1945 | 31,502,000 | 8 | 9 | 10 | 15 | 18 | 20 | 35 | 50 | |
| 1945D | 9,966,800 | 8 | 9 | 10 | 15 | 18 | 20 | 35 | 60 | |
| 1945S | 10,156,000 | 8 | 9 | 10 | 15 | 18 | 24 | 38 | 55 | |
| 1946 | 12,118,000 | 8 | 9 | 10 | 15 | 18 | 20 | 37 | 50 | |
| 1946, DblDie Rev. | * | 20 | 24 | 28 | 40 | 65 | 125 | 275 | 550 | |
| 1946D | 2,151,000 | 8 | 9 | 10 | 15 | 22 | 32 | 47 | 60 | |
| 1946S | 3,724,000 | 8 | 9 | 10 | 15 | 18 | 25 | 43 | 58 | |
| 1947 | 4,094,000 | 8 | 9 | 10 | 15 | 18 | 25 | 48 | 60 | |
| 1947D | 3,900,600 | 8 | 9 | 10 | 15 | 18 | 30 | 45 | 60 | |

* Included in number above. **a.** Pieces dated 1928-D are counterfeit. **b.** Large and small mintmark varieties; see page 22. **c.** Proofs struck with and without designer's initials.

## FRANKLIN (1948–1963)

The Benjamin Franklin half dollar and the Roosevelt dime were both designed by John R. Sinnock, whose initials appear below the shoulder. Mint Director Nellie Tayloe Ross had long been a proponent of memorializing Franklin on a U.S. coin. On the reverse, the tiny eagle was included to satisfy the Mint Act of 1873.

*Designer John R. Sinnock; weight 12.50 grams; composition .900 silver, .100 copper (net weight .36169 oz. pure silver); diameter 30.6 mm; reeded edge; mints: Philadelphia, Denver, San Francisco.*

**VF-20 Very Fine**—At least half of the lower and upper incused lines on rim of Liberty Bell on reverse visible.
**EF-40 Extremely Fine**—Wear spots at top of end of Franklin's curls and hair at back of ears. Wear evident at top and on lettering of Liberty Bell.
**MS-63 Choice Uncirculated**—Some distracting contact marks or blemishes in prime focal areas. Impaired luster possible.
**MS-65 Gem Uncirculated**—Only light, scattered contact marks that are not distracting. Strong luster, good eye appeal.
**PF-65 Gem Proof**—Brilliant surfaces with no noticeable blemishes or flaws. A few scattered, barely noticeable marks or hairlines possible.

Mintmark Location

*Choice, well-struck Uncirculated halves with full bell lines command higher prices.*

| | Mintage | VF-20 | EF-40 | MS-60 | MS-63 | MS-65 | PF-65 |
|---|---|---|---|---|---|---|---|
| 1948 | 3,006,814 | $8 | $11 | $20 | $27 | $70 | |
| 1948D | 4,028,600 | 8 | 11 | 20 | 24 | 135 | |
| 1949 | 5,614,000 | 12 | 18 | 40 | 75 | 130 | |
| 1949D | 4,120,600 | 12 | 18 | 45 | 75 | 325 | |
| 1949S | 3,744,000 | 12 | 20 | 65 | 95 | 165 | |
| 1950 (51,386) | 7,742,123 | 8 | 11 | 30 | 35 | 100 | $575 |
| 1950D | 8,031,600 | 8 | 11 | 26 | 40 | 200 | |
| 1951 (57,500) | 16,802,102 | 8 | 11 | 14 | 24 | 55 | 400 |
| 1951D | 9,475,200 | 8 | 11 | 30 | 45 | 140 | |
| 1951S | 13,696,000 | 8 | 11 | 25 | 35 | 55 | |
| 1952 (81,980) | 21,192,093 | 8 | 11 | 14 | 23 | 55 | 275 |
| 1952D | 25,395,600 | 8 | 11 | 14 | 23 | 115 | |
| 1952S | 5,526,000 | 12 | 17 | 50 | 70 | 110 | |
| 1953 (128,800) | 2,668,120 | 8 | 10 | 14 | 27 | 110 | 190 |
| 1953D | 20,900,400 | 8 | 10 | 14 | 23 | 105 | |
| 1953S | 4,148,000 | 8 | 10 | 25 | 35 | 55 | |
| 1954 (233,300) | 13,188,202 | 8 | 10 | 14 | 20 | 45 | 85 |
| 1954D | 25,445,580 | 8 | 10 | 14 | 24 | 75 | |
| 1954S | 4,993,400 | 12 | 14 | 16 | 24 | 35 | |
| 1955 (378,200) | 2,498,181 | 18 | 22 | 25 | 30 | 42 | 75 |
| 1956 (669,384) | 4,032,000 | 8 | 10 | 14 | 25 | 32 | 45 |
| 1957 (1,247,952) | 5,114,000 | 8 | 10 | 14 | 19 | 32 | 28 |
| 1957D | 19,966,850 | 8 | 10 | 14 | 19 | 33 | |
| 1958 (875,652) | 4,042,000 | 8 | 10 | 14 | 19 | 33 | 30 |
| 1958D | 23,962,412 | 8 | 10 | 14 | 18 | 33 | |

1961, Doubled Die Proof

| | Mintage | VF-20 | EF-40 | MS-60 | MS-63 | MS-65 | PF-65 |
|---|---|---|---|---|---|---|---|
| 1959 . . . . . . . . . . . . (1,149,291) | . . . . 6,200,000 | $8 | $10 | $14 | $18 | $60 | $25 |
| 1959D . . . . . . . . . . . . . . . . . . . . . . | 13,053,750 | 8 | 10 | 14 | 18 | 75 | |
| 1960 . . . . . . . . . . . . (1,691,602) | . . . . 6,024,000 | 8 | 10 | 14 | 18 | 80 | 25 |
| 1960D . . . . . . . . . . . . . . . . . . . . . . | 18,215,812 | 8 | 10 | 14 | 18 | 160 | |
| 1961 . . . . . . . . . . . . (3,028,244) | . . . . 8,290,000 | 8 | 10 | 14 | 18 | 50 | 25 |
| 1961, Doubled Die Proof . . . . . * . . . . . . . . . . . . | | | | | | | 2,900 |
| 1961D . . . . . . . . . . . . . . . . . . . . . . | 20,276,442 | 8 | 10 | 14 | 18 | 100 | |
| 1962 . . . . . . . . . . . . (3,218,019) | . . . . 9,714,000 | 8 | 10 | 14 | 18 | 80 | 25 |
| 1962D . . . . . . . . . . . . . . . . . . . . . . | 35,473,281 | 8 | 10 | 14 | 18 | 80 | |
| 1963 . . . . . . . . . . . . (3,075,645) | . . . 22,164,000 | 8 | 10 | 14 | 18 | 30 | 25 |
| 1963D . . . . . . . . . . . . . . . . . . . . . . | 67,069,292 | 8 | 10 | 14 | 18 | 30 | |

* Included in number above.

## KENNEDY (1964 TO DATE)

Gilroy Roberts, chief engraver of the Mint from 1948 to 1964, designed the obverse of this coin. His stylized initials are on the truncation of the forceful bust of President John F. Kennedy. The reverse, which uses the presidential coat of arms for the motif, is the work of Frank Gasparro, who was appointed chief engraver in February 1965. A few of the pieces dated 1971-D and 1977-D were struck in silver clad composition by error.

*Designers Gilroy Roberts and Frank Gasparro. 1964—Standards same as for previous issue (net weight .36169 oz. pure silver). 1965–1970—Weight 11.50 grams; composition, outer layers of .800 silver and .200 copper bonded to inner core of .209 silver, .791 copper (net weight .1479 oz. pure silver; net composition .400 silver, .600 copper). 1971 to date—Weight 11.34 grams; composition, outer layers of copper-nickel (.750 copper, .250 nickel) bonded to inner core of pure copper; diameter 30.6 mm; reeded edge. Mints: Philadelphia, Denver, San Francisco, West Point..*

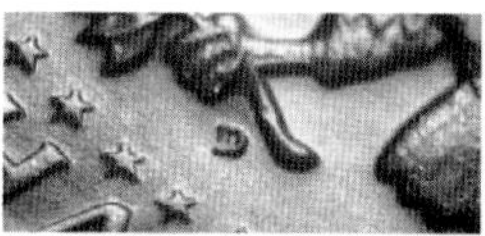

Mintmark Location (1964)

Mintmark Location (1968 to Date)

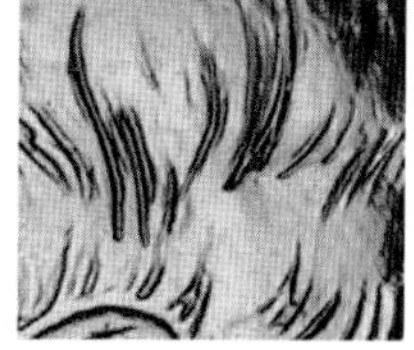

1964, Heavily Accented Hair

### Silver Coinage (1964)

| | Mintage | MS-60 | MS-63 | MS-65 | PF-65 |
|---|---|---|---|---|---|
| 1964 . . . . . . . . . . . . . . . . . . . . . . . . . . (3,950,762) | . . 273,304,004 | $10 | $12 | $25 | $20 |
| 1964, Heavily Accented Hair . . . . . . . . . . . . . . . . . . * . . . . . . . . . . . . | | | | | 75 |
| 1964D . . . . . . . . . . . . . . . . . . . . . . . . . . . . . . . . . . . | 156,205,446 | 10 | 12 | 25 | |

* Included in number above.

## Silver Clad Coinage (1965–1970)

| | Mintage | MS-63 | MS-65 | PF-65 |
|---|---|---|---|---|
| 1965 | 65,879,366 | $6 | $30 | |
| 1966 | 108,984,932 | 6 | 35 | |
| 1967 | 295,046,978 | 6 | 33 | |
| 1968D | 246,951,930 | 6 | 18 | |
| 1968S | (3,041,506) | | | $8 |
| 1969D | 129,881,800 | $6 | $30 | |
| 1969S | (2,934,631) | | | $8 |
| 1970D **(a)** | 2,150,000 | 20 | 45 | |
| 1970S | (2,632,810) | | | 15 |

**a.** Issued only in Mint sets.

## Clad Coinage and Silver Proofs (1971 to Date)

The design was slightly modified several times between 1971 and the present.

**1974-D, Doubled Die Obverse**
*Note prominent doubling of RUS.*

| | Mintage | MS-63 | PF-65 |
|---|---|---|---|
| 1971 | 155,164,000 | $3 | |
| 1971D | 302,097,424 | 3 | |
| 1971S | (3,220,733) | | $4 |
| 1972 | 153,180,000 | 3 | |
| 1972D | 141,890,000 | 3 | |
| 1972S | (3,260,996) | | 4 |
| 1973 | 64,964,000 | 3 | |
| 1973D | 83,171,400 | $3 | |
| 1973S | (2,760,339) | | $3 |
| 1974 | 201,596,000 | 3 | |
| 1974D | 79,066,300 | 3 | |
| 1974D, DblDie Obverse | * | 40 | |
| 1974S | (2,612,568) | | 4 |

* Included in number above.

### *Bicentennial (1776–1976)*

In an open contest for the selection of suitable designs for the special Bicentennial reverses of the quarter, half dollar, and dollar, Seth G. Huntington's winning entry was featured on the half dollar. It shows Independence Hall in Philadelphia as the center device. The obverse was unchanged except for the dual dating 1776–1976. Bicentennial half dollars were struck during 1975 and 1976 and were used for general circulation as well as being included in Proof and Uncirculated sets for 1975 and 1976.

*Designers Gilroy Roberts and Seth Huntington; diameter 30.6 mm; reeded edge. Silver clad—Weight 11.50 grams; composition, outer layers of .800 silver, .200 copper bonded to inner core of .209 silver, .791 copper (net weight .14792 oz. pure silver). Copper-nickel clad—Weight 11.34 grams; composition, outer layers of copper-nickel (.750 copper, .250 nickel) bonded to inner core of pure copper. Mints: Philadelphia, Denver, San Francisco.*

| | Mintage | MS-63 | PF-65 |
|---|---|---|---|
| 1976 | 234,308,000 | $3 | |
| 1976D | 287,565,248 | 3 | |
| 1976S | (7,059,099) | | $4 |
| 1976S, Silver Clad | *11,000,000* | $8 | |
| 1976S, Silver Clad | *(4,000,000)* | | $12 |

*Note:* Mintage figures for 1976-S silver coins are approximate; many were melted in 1982.

## Eagle Reverse Resumed (1977 to Date)

*Copper-nickel clad coinage. Silver Proofs: 1992–2018—weight 12.50 grams; composition .900 silver, .100 copper (net weight .36169 oz. pure silver); 2019 to date—weight 12.685 grams; composition .999 silver, .001 copper (net weight .364 oz. pure silver). Mints: San Francisco, West Point.*

| | Mintage | MS-63 | PF-65 |
|---|---|---|---|
| 1977 | 43,598,000 | $3 | |
| 1977D | 31,449,106 | 3 | |
| 1977S | (3,251,152) | | $4 |
| 1978 | 14,350,000 | 3 | |
| 1978D | 13,765,799 | 3 | |
| 1978S | (3,127,781) | | 3 |
| 1979 | 68,312,000 | 3 | |
| 1979D | 15,815,422 | 3 | |
| 1979S, All kinds | (3,677,175) | | |
| 1979S, Type 1 **(a)** | | | 3 |
| 1979S, Type 2 **(a)** | | | 25 |
| 1980P | 44,134,000 | 3 | |
| 1980D | 33,456,449 | 3 | |
| 1980S | (3,554,806) | | 3 |
| 1981P | 29,544,000 | 3 | |
| 1981D | 27,839,533 | 3 | |
| 1981S, All kinds | (4,063,083) | | |
| 1981S, Type 1 **(a)** | | | 3 |
| 1981S, Type 2 **(a)** | | | 30 |
| 1982P | 10,819,000 | 7 | |
| 1982D | 13,140,102 | 7 | |
| 1982S | (3,857,479) | | 4 |
| 1983P | 34,139,000 | 8 | |
| 1983D | 32,472,244 | 7 | |
| 1983S | (3,279,126) | | 4 |
| 1984P | 26,029,000 | 3 | |
| 1984D | 26,262,158 | 3 | |
| 1984S | (3,065,110) | | 4 |
| 1985P | 18,706,962 | 5 | |
| 1985D | 19,814,034 | 5 | |
| 1985S | (3,362,821) | | 4 |
| 1986P | 13,107,633 | 6 | |
| 1986D | 15,336,145 | 5 | |
| 1986S | (3,010,497) | | 4 |
| 1987P **(b)** | 2,890,758 | 5 | |
| 1987D **(b)** | 2,890,758 | 5 | |
| 1987S | (4,227,728) | | 4 |
| 1988P | 13,626,000 | 5 | |
| 1988D | 12,000,096 | 4 | |
| 1988S | (3,262,948) | | 4 |
| 1989P | 24,542,000 | 4 | |
| 1989D | 23,000,216 | 3 | |
| 1989S | (3,220,194) | | 5 |
| 1990P | 22,278,000 | $3 | |
| 1990D | 20,096,242 | 3 | |
| 1990S | (3,299,559) | | $5 |
| 1991P | 14,874,000 | 4 | |
| 1991D | 15,054,678 | 4 | |
| 1991S | (2,867,787) | | 10 |
| 1992P | 17,628,000 | 3 | |
| 1992D | 17,000,106 | 3 | |
| 1992S | (2,858,981) | | 5 |
| 1992S, Silver | (1,317,579) | | 17 |
| 1993P | 15,510,000 | 3 | |
| 1993D | 15,000,006 | 3 | |
| 1993S | (2,633,439) | | 8 |
| 1993S, Silver | (761,353) | | 27 |
| 1994P | 23,718,000 | 3 | |
| 1994D | 23,828,110 | 3 | |
| 1994S | (2,484,594) | | 8 |
| 1994S, Silver | (785,329) | | 26 |
| 1995P | 26,496,000 | 3 | |
| 1995D | 26,288,000 | 3 | |
| 1995S | (2,117,496) | | 16 |
| 1995S, Silver | (679,985) | | 38 |
| 1996P | 24,442,000 | 3 | |
| 1996D | 24,744,000 | 3 | |
| 1996S | (1,750,244) | | 10 |
| 1996S, Silver | (775,021) | | 30 |
| 1997P | 20,882,000 | 3 | |
| 1997D | 19,876,000 | 3 | |
| 1997S | (2,055,000) | | 12 |
| 1997S, Silver | (741,678) | | 30 |
| 1998P | 15,646,000 | 3 | |
| 1998D | 15,064,000 | 3 | |
| 1998S | (2,086,507) | | 10 |
| 1998S, Silver | (878,792) | | 18 |
| 1998S, Silver, Matte Finish **(c)** | *(62,000)* | | 125 |
| 1999P | 8,900,000 | 3 | |
| 1999D | 10,682,000 | 3 | |
| 1999S | (2,543,401) | | 13 |
| 1999S, Silver | (804,565) | | 25 |
| 2000P | 22,600,000 | 3 | |
| 2000D | 19,466,000 | 3 | |
| 2000S | (3,082,483) | | 5 |

**a.** See page 246 for illustrations. **b.** Not issued for circulation; included with Mint and Souvenir sets. **c.** Included in commemorative set (see page 359).

2014-W gold 50th-anniversary half dollar.

| | Mintage | MS-63 | PF-65 |
|---|---|---|---|
| 2000S, Silver | (965,421) | | $14 |
| 2001P | 21,200,000 | $3 | |
| 2001D | 19,504,000 | 3 | |
| 2001S | (2,294,909) | | 6 |
| 2001S, Silver | (889,697) | | 15 |
| 2002P **(d)** | 3,100,000 | 3 | |
| 2002D **(d)** | 2,500,000 | 3 | |
| 2002S | (2,319,766) | | 5 |
| 2002S, Silver | (892,229) | | 14 |
| 2003P **(d)** | 2,500,000 | 3 | |
| 2003D **(d)** | 2,500,000 | 3 | |
| 2003S | (2,172,684) | | 5 |
| 2003S, Silver | (1,125,755) | | 14 |
| 2004P **(d)** | 2,900,000 | 3 | |
| 2004D **(d)** | 2,900,000 | 3 | |
| 2004S | (1,789,488) | | 13 |
| 2004S, Silver | (1,175,934) | | 20 |
| 2005P **(d)** | 3,800,000 | 4 | |
| 2005D **(d)** | 3,500,000 | 4 | |
| 2005S | (2,275,000) | | 5 |
| 2005S, Silver | (1,069,679) | | 12 |
| 2006P **(d)** | 2,400,000 | 2 | |
| 2006D **(d)** | 2,000,000 | 2 | |
| 2006S | (2,000,428) | | 5 |
| 2006S, Silver | (1,054,008) | | 12 |
| 2007P **(d)** | 2,400,000 | 2 | |
| 2007D **(d)** | 2,400,000 | 2 | |
| 2007S | (1,702,116) | | 5 |
| 2007S, Silver | (875,050) | | 14 |
| 2008P **(d)** | 1,700,000 | 2 | |
| 2008D **(d)** | 1,700,000 | 2 | |
| 2008S | (1,405,674) | | 5 |
| 2008S, Silver | (763,887) | | 14 |
| 2009P **(d)** | 1,900,000 | 2 | |
| 2009D **(d)** | 1,900,000 | 2 | |

| | Mintage | MS-63 | PF-65 |
|---|---|---|---|
| 2009S | (1,482,502) | | $5 |
| 2009S, Silver | 697,365 | | 14 |
| 2010P **(d)** | 1,800,000 | $2 | |
| 2010D **(d)** | 1,700,000 | 2 | |
| 2010S | (1,103,815) | | 5 |
| 2010S, Silver | (585,401) | | 14 |
| 2011P **(d)** | 1,750,000 | 3 | |
| 2011D **(d)** | 1,700,000 | 3 | |
| 2011S | (1,098,835) | | 5 |
| 2011S, Silver | (574,175) | | 14 |
| 2012P **(d)** | 1,800,000 | 3 | |
| 2012D **(d)** | 1,700,000 | 3 | |
| 2012S | (843,705) | | 5 |
| 2012S, Silver | (445,612) | | 14 |
| 2013P **(d)** | 5,000,000 | 3 | |
| 2013D **(d)** | 4,600,000 | 3 | |
| 2013S | *(854,785)* | | 5 |
| 2013S, Silver | (467,691) | | 14 |
| 2014P **(d)** | 2,500,000 | 3 | |
| 2014P, High Relief **(e)** | 197,608 | 15 | |
| 2014P, Silver **(f)** | *(219,173)* | | 15 |
| 2014D **(d)** | 2,100,000 | 3 | |
| 2014D, High Relief **(e)** | 197,608 | 15 | |
| 2014D, Silver **(f)** | *219,173* | 10 | |
| 2014S, Silver Enhanced **(f)** | *219,173* | 10 | |
| 2014S | *(767,977)* | | 15 |
| 2014S, Silver | (472,107) | | 15 |
| 2014W, Reverse Proof, Silver **(f)** | *(219,173)* | | 20 |
| 2014W, 50th Anniversary, Gold **(g)** | (73,772) | | 900 |
| 2015P **(d)** | 2,300,000 | 3 | |
| 2015D **(d)** | 2,300,000 | 3 | |
| 2015S | *(662,854)* | | 5 |
| 2015S, Silver | *(387,310)* | | 14 |

*Note:* Uncirculated Mint Sets for 2005–2010 were made with Satin Finish coins not included in the listings here. See page 369 for their mintages. **d.** Not issued for circulation. The U.S. Mint produces circulation-quality half dollar coins at its Philadelphia and Denver facilities each year. Since 2002, these coins have been made available to the public only through direct purchase from the Mint in Mint sets and rolls of 20 coins or bags of 200 coins. They are not available through banks for general distribution, and are sold by the Mint for approximately 1.5 to 2 times their face value. **e.** For the 50th anniversary of the Kennedy half dollar, in 2014 the U.S. Mint issued an Uncirculated two-coin set featuring a Kennedy half dollar from Philadelphia and one from Denver. **f.** Featured in the 2014 half dollar silver-coin collection released by the U.S. Mint for the 50th anniversary of the Kennedy half dollar. **g.** First gold half dollar offered by the U.S. Mint. It commemorates the 50th anniversary of the first release of the Kennedy half dollar in 1964.

Along with the regular Kennedy half dollars of the year, in 2016 a special gold striking of the Liberty Walking half dollar was created to celebrate the 100th anniversary of its introduction. Similar strikings were made for the 1916 dime and quarter designs.

*Designer Adolph A. Weinman; weight 15.552 grams; composition .9999 gold; diameter 27 mm; reeded edge; mint: West Point.*

| | Mintage | SP-67 | SP-70 |
|---|---|---|---|
| 2016W, Liberty Walking Centennial Gold Coin | *65,509* | $800 | $1,000 |

Normally scheduled production of clad and silver Kennedy half dollars continued in 2016 and beyond, and was not disrupted by the gold Liberty Walking half dollar.

| | Mintage | MS-63 | PF-65 |
|---|---|---|---|
| 2016P **(d)** | 2,100,000 | $3 | |
| 2016D **(d)** | 2,100,000 | 2 | |
| 2016S | *(641,775)* | | $5 |
| 2016S, Silver | *(419,256)* | | 14 |
| 2017P **(d)** | 1,800,000 | 2 | |
| 2017D **(d)** | 2,900,000 | 2 | |
| 2017S **(h)** | *(621,384)* | | 5 |
| 2017S, Silver | *(406,994)* | | 14 |
| 2018P **(d)** | *4,800,000* | 2 | |
| 2018D **(d)** | *6,100,000* | 2 | |
| 2018S | *(535,221)* | | 5 |
| 2018S, Silver | *(350,820)* | | $14 |
| 2019P **(d)** | *1,700,000* | $2 | |
| 2019D **(d)** | *1,700,000* | 2 | |
| 2019S | | | 5 |
| 2019S, Silver | | | 14 |
| 2019S, Enhanced RevPf **(i)** | | | |
| 2020P **(d)** | | 2 | |
| 2020D **(d)** | | 2 | |
| 2020S | | | 5 |
| 2020S, Silver | | | 14 |

**d.** Not issued for circulation. The U.S. Mint produces circulation-quality half dollar coins at its Philadelphia and Denver facilities each year. In 2002 and the years since, these coins have been made available to the public only through direct purchase from the Mint in Mint sets and rolls of 20 coins or bags of 200 coins. The rolled and bagged coins are not available through banks for general distribution, and are sold by the Mint for approximately 1.5 to 2 times their face value. **h.** For its 225th anniversary, the Mint issued a special set of Enhanced Uncirculated coins from the San Francisco Mint; they are not included in the listings here. **i.** Included in the Apollo 11 50th Anniversary Proof Half Dollar Set.

The silver dollar was authorized by Congress on April 2, 1792. Weight and fineness were specified at 416 grains and .8924 fine. The first issues appeared in 1794, and until 1804 all silver dollars had the value stamped on the edge: HUNDRED CENTS, ONE DOLLAR OR UNIT. After a lapse in coinage of the silver dollar during the period 1804 through 1835, in 1836 coins were made with plain edges and the value was placed on the reverse.

The weight was changed by the law of January 18, 1837, to 412-1/2 grains, .900 fineness. The coinage was discontinued by the Act of February 12, 1873, and reauthorized by the Act of February 28, 1878. The silver dollar was again discontinued after 1935, and since then only base-metal pieces have been coined for circulation (also see Silver Bullion on pages 371–375).

## ORIGIN OF THE DOLLAR

The word *dollar* evolves from the German *thaler,* the name given to the first large-sized European silver coin. Designed as a substitute for the gold florin, the coin originated in the Tyrol in 1484. So popular did these large silver coins become during the 16th century that many other countries struck similar pieces, giving them names derived from *thaler.* In the Netherlands the coin was called *rijksdaalder,* in Denmark *rigsdaler,* in Italy *tallero,* in Poland *talar,* in France *jocandale,* in Russia *jefimok.* All these names are abbreviations of *joachimsthaler.* Until the discovery of the great silver deposits in Mexico and South America, the mint with the greatest output of large silver coins was that of Joachimsthal in the Bohemian Erzgebirge.

The Spanish dollar, or piece of eight, was widely used and familiar to everyone in the British American colonies. It was only natural, therefore, that the word *dollar* was adopted officially for the standard monetary unit of the United States by Congress on July 6, 1785. The Continental dollar of 1776 is described on page 87.

*Note: Values of common-date silver coins have been based on a silver bullion price of $18 per ounce, and may vary with the prevailing spot price. To determine the intrinsic value of common silver coins, see page 445.*

## FLOWING HAIR (1794–1795)

Varieties listed are those most significant to collectors, but numerous minor variations may be found because each of the early dies was individually made. Blanks were weighed before the dollars were struck and overweight pieces were filed to remove excess silver. Coins with adjustment marks from this process may be worth less than values shown here. Some Flowing Hair type dollars of 1794 and 1795 were weight-adjusted through insertion of a small (8 mm) silver plug in the center of the blank planchet before the coin was struck. Values of varieties not listed in this guide depend on rarity and collector interest.

*Engraver Robert Scot; weight 26.96 grams; composition .900 silver, .100 copper; approx. diameter 39–40 mm; edge: HUNDRED CENTS ONE DOLLAR OR UNIT with decorations between words.*

**AG-3 About Good**—Clear enough to identify.
**G-4 Good**—Date and letters legible. Main devices outlined, but lacking in detail.
**VG-8 Very Good**—Major details discernible. Letters well formed but worn.
**F-12 Fine**—Hair ends distinguishable. Top hair lines visible, but otherwise worn smooth.
**VF-20 Very Fine**—Some detail visible in hair in center. Other details more bold.
**EF-40 Extremely Fine**—Hair well defined but with some wear.
**AU-50 About Uncirculated**—Slight trace of wear on tips of highest curls; feathers on eagle's breast usually weak.
**MS-60 Uncirculated**—No trace of wear. Light blemishes.

*Values shown for Uncirculated pieces of this type are for well-struck, attractive coins with minimal surface marks.*

| | Mintage | AG-3 | G-4 | VG-8 | F-12 | VF-20 | EF-40 | AU-50 | MS-60 |
|---|---|---|---|---|---|---|---|---|---|
| 1794 . . . . . . . . . . . . . . . | 1,758 | $40,000 | $67,500 | $105,000 | $135,000 | $165,000 | $325,000 | $525,000 | $1,000,000 |
| *$4,993,750, MS-66+, Sotheby's/ Stack's Bowers auction, September 2015* | | | | | | | | | |
| 1794, Silver Plug *(unique)* . . | * | | | | | | | | |
| *$10,016,875, SP-66, Stack's Bowers auction, January 2013* | | | | | | | | | |

* Included in number above.

**Two Leaves Beneath Each Wing**

**Three Leaves Beneath Each Wing**

**Silver Plug (1795)**

| | Mintage | AG-3 | G-4 | VG-8 | F-12 | VF-20 | EF-40 | AU-50 | MS-60 |
|---|---|---|---|---|---|---|---|---|---|
| 1795, All kinds. . . . . . . . . . | 160,295 | | | | | | | | |
| 1795, Two Leaves . . . . . . . . . . . . | | $1,100 | $2,250 | $2,600 | $4,000 | $5,750 | $12,500 | $20,000 | $65,000 |
| *$822,500, SP-64, Stack's Bowers auction, August 2014* | | | | | | | | | |
| 1795, Three Leaves. . . . . . . . . . . | | 1,100 | 2,250 | 2,500 | 4,000 | 5,250 | 11,000 | 19,500 | 55,000 |
| *$646,250, MS-65, Heritage auction, November 2013* | | | | | | | | | |
| 1795, Silver Plug. . . . . . . . . . . . . | | 1,500 | 3,250 | 5,250 | 8,500 | 16,000 | 22,500 | 45,000 | 130,000 |
| *$1,265,000, V Ch Gem MS, Bullowa auction, December 2005* | | | | | | | | | |

# DRAPED BUST (1795–1804)

## Small Eagle Reverse (1795–1798)

*Designer Robert Scot; weight 26.96 grams; composition .8924 silver, .1076 copper; approx. diameter 39–40 mm; edge: HUNDRED CENTS ONE DOLLAR OR UNIT with decorations between words.*

**AG-3 About Good**—Clear enough to identify.
**G-4 Good**—Bust outlined, no detail. Date legible, some leaves evident.
**VG-8 Very Good**—Drapery worn except deepest folds. Hair lines smooth.
**F-12 Fine**—All drapery lines distinguishable. Some detail visible in hair lines near cheek and neck.
**VF-20 Very Fine**—Left side of drapery worn smooth.
**EF-40 Extremely Fine**—Drapery distinctly visible. Hair well outlined and detailed.
**AU-50 About Uncirculated**—Slight trace of wear on the bust shoulder and hair to left of forehead, as well as on eagle's breast and top edges of wings.
**MS-60 Uncirculated**—No trace of wear. Light blemishes.

| | Mintage | AG-3 | G-4 | VG-8 | F-12 | VF-20 | EF-40 | AU-50 | MS-60 |
|---|---|---|---|---|---|---|---|---|---|
| 1795, All kinds | *42,738* | | | | | | | | |
| 1795, Uncentered Bust | | $960 | $1,850 | $2,350 | $3,500 | $5,100 | $9,500 | $14,500 | $60,000 |
| *$1,057,500, SP-66, Sotheby's / Stack's Bowers auction, May 2016* | | | | | | | | | |
| 1795, Centered Bust | | 960 | 1,850 | 2,150 | 3,500 | 5,100 | 9,500 | 15,500 | 55,000 |
| *$373,750, MS-65, Heritage auction, January 2007* | | | | | | | | | |

Small Date

Large Date

Small Letters

Large Letters

| | Mintage | AG-3 | G-4 | VG-8 | F-12 | VF-20 | EF-40 | AU-50 | MS-60 |
|---|---|---|---|---|---|---|---|---|---|
| 1796, All kinds | 79,920 | | | | | | | | |
| 1796, Small Date, Small Letters *(3 varieties)* | | $825 | $1,850 | $2,100 | $3,800 | $5,500 | $9,500 | $14,000 | $62,500 |
| *$1,175,000, MS-65, Heritage auction, April 2013* | | | | | | | | | |
| 1796, Small Date, Large Letters | | 825 | 1,850 | 2,100 | 3,800 | 5,500 | 9,500 | 14,000 | 75,000 |
| 1796, Large Date, Small Letters | | 825 | 1,850 | 2,100 | 3,400 | 5,250 | 9,500 | 14,000 | 62,500 |
| 1797, All kinds | 7,776 | | | | | | | | |
| 1797, 10 Stars Left, 6 Right | | 850 | 1,850 | 2,000 | 3,000 | 5,000 | 9,000 | 13,750 | 62,000 |
| 1797, 9 Stars Left, 7 Right, Lg Ltrs | | 850 | 1,850 | 2,000 | 3,100 | 6,000 | 9,500 | 13,500 | 63,000 |
| 1797, 9 Stars Left, 7 Right, Sm Ltrs | | 1,200 | 2,100 | 2,750 | 3,900 | 8,200 | 15,000 | 32,500 | 105,000 |

| | Mintage | AG-3 | G-4 | VG-8 | F-12 | VF-20 | EF-40 | AU-50 | MS-60 |
|---|---|---|---|---|---|---|---|---|---|
| 1798, Small Eagle, All kinds | 327,536 | | | | | | | | |
| 1798, Sm Eagle, 15 Stars Obv. | | $1,100 | $2,150 | $2,650 | $3,800 | $8,000 | $13,500 | $22,500 | $82,500 |
| 1798, Sm Eagle, 13 Stars Obv. | | 1,000 | 1,850 | 2,100 | 3,500 | 7,750 | 12,500 | 20,000 | 150,000 |

## Heraldic Eagle Reverse (1798–1804)

Heraldic Eagle Reverse silver dollars exist with many minute die varieties, such as those with four or five vertical lines in the shield or differing numbers of berries on the branch in the eagle's claw. Such items were listed in past editions of the Red Book but today are sought only by specialists.

**G-4 Good**—Letters and date legible. E PLURIBUS UNUM illegible.
**VG-8 Very Good**—Motto partially legible. Only deepest drapery details visible. All other lines smooth.
**F-12 Fine**—All drapery lines distinguishable. Some detail visible in hair lines near cheek and neck.
**VF-20 Very Fine**—Left side of drapery worn smooth.
**EF-40 Extremely Fine**—Drapery distinct. Hair well detailed.
**AU-50 About Uncirculated**—Slight trace of wear on the bust shoulder and hair to left of forehead, as well as on eagle's breast and top edges of wings.
**MS-60 Uncirculated**—No trace of wear. Light blemishes.

1798, Knob 9

1798, Pointed 9

| | | G-4 | VG-8 | F-12 | VF-20 | EF-40 | AU-50 | MS-60 |
|---|---|---|---|---|---|---|---|---|
| 1798, All kinds | 327,536 | | | | | | | |
| 1798, Knob 9 | | $850 | $1,050 | $1,450 | $2,600 | $4,500 | $7,500 | $25,000 |
| 1798, Pointed 9 | | 850 | 1,050 | 1,450 | 2,600 | 4,500 | 7,500 | 22,000 |

1799 Over 98, Stars 7 and 6

Stars 8 and 5

*See next page for chart.*

| | Mintage | G-4 | VG-8 | F-12 | VF-20 | EF-40 | AU-50 | MS-60 |
|---|---|---|---|---|---|---|---|---|
| 1799, All kinds | 423,515 | | | | | | | |
| 1799, 99 Over 98, 15-Star Reverse | | $960 | $1,250 | $1,800 | $2,850 | $5,200 | $8,700 | $23,000 |
| 1799, 99 Over 98, 13-Star Reverse | | 950 | 1,150 | 1,750 | 2,700 | 4,700 | 8,500 | 22,400 |
| 1799, Normal Date | | 900 | 1,050 | 1,550 | 2,550 | 4,700 | 8,250 | 22,400 |
| *$822,500, MS-67, Heritage auction, November 2013* | | | | | | | | |
| 1799, 8 Stars Left, 5 Right | | 1,000 | 1,250 | 1,900 | 3,100 | 5,750 | 13,500 | 32,500 |
| 1800, All kinds | 220,920 | | | | | | | |
| 1800, Very Wide Date, Low 8 | | 900 | 1,050 | 1,600 | 2,350 | 4,500 | 8,500 | 24,500 |
| 1800, "Dotted Date" *(from die breaks)* | | 900 | 1,050 | 1,650 | 2,500 | 5,200 | 8,500 | 24,500 |
| 1800, Only 12 Arrows | | 900 | 1,050 | 1,600 | 2,400 | 4,600 | 8,500 | 24,500 |
| 1800, Normal Dies | | 900 | 1,050 | 1,600 | 2,400 | 4,600 | 8,500 | 24,000 |
| 1800, AMERICAI | | 900 | 1,050 | 1,600 | 2,400 | 4,600 | 8,000 | 26,500 |
| 1801 | 54,454 | 900 | 1,050 | 1,600 | 2,400 | 4,900 | 8,350 | 29,500 |
| 1801, Proof Restrike *(reverse struck from first die of 1804 dollar) (2 known)* | | | | | | | | 650,000 |

1802, 2 Over 1, Narrow Date

1802, 2 Over 1, Wide Date

1803, Small 3

1803, Large 3

| | Mintage | G-4 | VG-8 | F-12 | VF-20 | EF-40 | AU-50 | MS-60 |
|---|---|---|---|---|---|---|---|---|
| 1802, All kinds | 41,650 | | | | | | | |
| 1802, 2 Over 1, Narrow Date | | $950 | $1,100 | $1,800 | $2,500 | $5,000 | $9,100 | $30,000 |
| 1802, 2 Over 1, Wide Date | | 1,000 | 1,150 | 1,900 | 2,600 | 5,250 | 9,500 | 32,000 |
| 1802, Proof Restrike *(4 known)* | | | | | | | | 250,000 |
| *$920,000, PF-65 Cam, Heritage auction, April 2008* | | | | | | | | |
| 1803, All kinds | 85,634 | | | | | | | |
| 1803, Small 3 | | 1,000 | 1,050 | 1,800 | 2,650 | 5,250 | 9,000 | 27,000 |
| 1803, Large 3 | | 1,000 | 1,050 | 1,800 | 2,650 | 5,250 | 9,000 | 27,000 |
| *$705,000, MS-65+, Heritage auction, November 2013* | | | | | | | | |
| 1803, Proof Restrike *(4 known)* | | | | | | | | 250,000 |
| *$851,875, PF-66, Stack's Bowers auction, January 2013* | | | | | | | | |

## 1804 DOLLAR

The 1804 dollar is one of the most publicized rarities in the entire series of United States coins. There are specimens known as originals (first reverse), of which eight are known; and restrikes (second reverse), of which seven are known, one of which has a plain edge.

Numismatists have found that the 1804 original dollars were first struck at the Mint in the 1834 through 1835 period, for use in presentation Proof sets. The first coin to be owned by a collector, a Proof, was obtained from a Mint officer by Matthew Stickney on May 9, 1843, in exchange for an Immune Columbia piece in gold. Later, beginning in 1859, the pieces known as *restrikes* and *electrotypes* were made at the Mint to supply the needs of collectors who wanted examples of these dollars.

Evidence that these pieces were struck during the later period is based on the fact that the 1804 dollars differ from issues of 1803 or earlier and conform more closely to those struck after 1836, their edges or borders having beaded segments and raised rims, not elongated denticles such as are found on the earlier dates.

Although the Mint record states that 19,570 dollars were coined in 1804, in no place does it mention that they were dated 1804. It was the practice in those days to use old dies as long as they were serviceable with no regard in the annual reports for the dating of the coins. It is probable that the 1804 total for dollars actually covered coins that were dated 1803.

**First Reverse** **Second Reverse**

***Note position of words STATES OF in relation to clouds.***

| | PF-63 |
|---|---|
| 1804 First Reverse, Class I *(8 known)* | $2,750,000 |
| *$4,140,000, PF-68, Stack's Bowers auction, August 1999* | |
| 1804 Second Reverse, Class III *(6 known)* | |
| *$2,300,000, PF-58, Heritage auction, April 2009* | |
| 1804 Second Reverse, Class II *(unique)* *(Smithsonian Collection)* | |

## GOBRECHT DOLLARS (1836–1839)

Suspension of silver dollar coinage was lifted in 1831, but it was not until 1835 that steps were taken to resume coinage. Late that year, Mint Director R.M. Patterson had engraver Christian Gobrecht prepare a pair of dies based on motifs by Thomas Sully and Titian Peale. The first obverse die, dated 1836, bore the seated figure of Liberty with the inscription C. GOBRECHT F. ("F." for the Latin word *Fecit,* or "made it") in the field above the date. On the reverse die was a large eagle flying left, surrounded by 26 stars and the legend UNITED STATES OF AMERICA • ONE DOLLAR •. It is unknown whether coins were struck from these dies at that time. A new obverse die with Gobrecht's name on the base of Liberty was prepared, and in December 1836, a thousand plain-edged pieces were struck for circulation. These coins weighed 416 grains, the standard enacted in 1792.

The feeder mechanism that was used, apparently designed for coins of half dollar size or smaller, damaged the reverse die's rim. Attempts were made to solve the problem by rotating the reverse die at various times during the striking run, but this only extended the damage to both sides of the rim. The original 1836 issue is thus known in multiple die alignments:

Die Alignment I—head of Liberty opposite DO in DOLLAR; eagle flying upward.
Die Alignment II—head of Liberty opposite ES in STATES; eagle flying upward.
Die Alignment III—head of Liberty opposite N of ONE; eagle flying level.
Die Alignment IV—head of Liberty opposite F in OF; eagle flying level.

*Original 1836 die orientation using either "coin" or "medal" turn.*

*Die alignment of original issues dated 1838 and 1839.*

Restrikes were made from the late 1850s through the early 1870s. They were struck using the original obverse die and a different reverse die with cracks through NITED STATES O and OLLA, and in Die Alignment III.

In January 1837, the standard weight for the dollar was lowered to 412-1/2 grains, and on January 8, 1837, Benjamin Franklin Peale wrote an internal memorandum to Mint Director Patterson noting, among other things, that the new dollar had received much criticism for looking too medallic. Peale felt this was due to the "smooth" edge and suggested striking with a segmented, lettered-edge collar like one he had seen in France. In March 1837, the dies of 1836 were used to strike 600 pieces (whether with plain or reeded edge is unknown). According to reports, the results were unsatisfactory and were destroyed—although a single example, with a reeded edge, is known; it is unclear whether it was part of the March striking, from an earlier 1837 striking caused by the Peale memo, or struck at some later period.

Pattern pieces were struck in 1838 using modified dies with Gobrecht's name removed from the base, 13 stars added to the obverse, and the 26 stars removed from the reverse. These were struck in alignment IV using a reeded-edge collar. In 1839, 300 pieces were struck for circulation, also in alignment IV. Both of these were restruck in alignment III and possibly alignment IV in the late 1850s through early 1870s.

*Designer Christian Gobrecht; weight 26.73–26.96 grams; composition .8924 silver, .1076 copper; approx. diameter 39–40 mm; edge: plain or reeded.*

## Circulation Issues and Patterns

| | VF-20 | EF-40 | AU-50 | MS-60 |
|---|---|---|---|---|
| 1836, C. GOBRECHT F. on base. Stars on reverse. Plain edge. | | | | |
| Die alignment I (↑↓). Circulation issue. 1,000 struck. | $12,500 | $15,000 | $18,000 | $25,000 |
| Struck in 1837. Die alignment II (↑↑) and IV (↑↑). Circulation issue. 600 struck. | 13,000 | 16,000 | 21,000 | 25,000 |

| | VF-20 | EF-40 | AU-50 | MS-60 |
|---|---|---|---|---|
| 1838, Similar obverse, designer's name omitted, stars added around border. Reverse, eagle flying in plain field. Reeded edge. Die alignment IV, ↑↑. Pattern | | | | $55,000 |
| 1839, As above. Reeded edge. Die alignment IV, ↑↑. Circulation issue. 300 struck. | $15,000 | $17,500 | $22,500 | 29,000 |

## Restrikes

| | PF-60 |
|---|---|
| 1836, Name below base; eagle in starry field; plain edge | $75,000 |
| 1836, Name on base; plain edge | 26,000 |
| 1838, Designer's name omitted; reeded edge | 47,500 |
| 1839, Designer's name omitted; eagle in plain field; reeded edge | 42,500 |

## LIBERTY SEATED (1840–1873)

Starting again in 1840, silver dollars were issued for general circulation. The seated figure of Liberty was adopted for the obverse, but the flying eagle design was rejected in favor of the more familiar form with olive branch and arrows used for certain other silver denominations. By the early 1850s the silver content of these pieces was worth more than their face value, and later issues were not seen in circulation but were used mainly in export trade. This situation continued through 1873.

The 1866 Proof quarter, half, and dollar without motto are not mentioned in the Mint director's report, and were not issued for circulation.

*Designer Christian Gobrecht; weight 26.73 grams; composition .900 silver, .100 copper (net weight .77344 oz. pure silver); diameter 38.1 mm; reeded edge; mints: Philadelphia, New Orleans, Carson City, San Francisco.*

**VG-8 Very Good**—Any three letters of LIBERTY at least two-thirds complete.
**F-12 Fine**—All seven letters of LIBERTY visible, though weak.
**VF-20 Very Fine**—LIBERTY strong, but slight wear visible on its ribbon.
**EF-40 Extremely Fine**—Horizontal lines of shield complete. Eagle's eye plain.
**AU-50 About Uncirculated**—Traces of light wear on only the high points of the design. Half of mint luster present.
**MS-60 Uncirculated**—No trace of wear. Light marks or blemishes.
**PF-60 Proof**—Several contact marks, hairlines, or light rubs possible on surface. Luster possibly dull and eye appeal lacking.
**PF-63 Choice Proof**—Reflective surfaces with few blemishes in secondary focal places. No major flaws.

### No Motto (1840–1865)

*Location of mintmark, when present, is on reverse, below eagle.*

| | Mintage | VG-8 | F-12 | VF-20 | EF-40 | AU-50 | MS-60 | PF-60 | PF-63 |
|---|---|---|---|---|---|---|---|---|---|
| 1840 | 61,005 | $450 | $500 | $575 | $850 | $1,500 | $5,500 | $12,500 | $25,000 |
| 1841 | 173,000 | 400 | 475 | 550 | 700 | 1,050 | 2,750 | 30,000 | 70,000 |
| *$94,000, PF-64, Heritage auction, October 2014* | | | | | | | | | |
| 1842 | 184,618 | 400 | 475 | 550 | 600 | 950 | 2,400 | 15,000 | 35,000 |
| 1843 | 165,100 | 400 | 475 | 550 | 600 | 950 | 2,400 | 15,000 | 30,000 |
| 1844 | 20,000 | 450 | 500 | 575 | 800 | 1,300 | 5,000 | 12,500 | 30,000 |
| 1845 | 24,500 | 450 | 500 | 575 | 800 | 1,500 | 9,000 | 12,500 | 30,000 |
| 1846 | 110,600 | 450 | 475 | 525 | 650 | 1,000 | 2,500 | 12,500 | 30,000 |
| 1846O | 59,000 | 450 | 500 | 575 | 800 | 1,400 | 7,250 | | |
| 1847 | 140,750 | 450 | 500 | 575 | 600 | 850 | 2,700 | 22,000 | 30,000 |
| 1848 | 15,000 | 450 | 650 | 750 | 1,400 | 1,900 | 4,750 | 30,000 | 40,000 |
| 1849 | 62,600 | 450 | 500 | 575 | 700 | 1,000 | 2,600 | 34,000 | 40,000 |
| 1850 | 7,500 | 600 | 800 | 1,250 | 1,800 | 2,500 | 6,500 | 25,000 | 30,000 |
| 1850O | 40,000 | 450 | 500 | 750 | 1,450 | 3,200 | 11,500 | | |
| 1851, Original, High Date | 1,300 | 16,500 | 19,500 | 22,000 | 25,000 | 27,500 | 32,500 | | |
| 1851, Restrike, Date Centered | | | | | | | | 20,000 | 30,000 |
| 1852, Original | 1,100 | 13,500 | 16,500 | 20,000 | 24,000 | 27,500 | 40,000 | 27,500 | 43,500 |
| 1852, Restrike | | | | | | | | 17,500 | 30,000 |

| | Mintage | VG-8 | F-12 | VF-20 | EF-40 | AU-50 | MS-60 | PF-60 | PF-63 |
|---|---|---|---|---|---|---|---|---|---|
| 1853 | 46,110 | $350 | $450 | $650 | $1,100 | $1,300 | $3,200 | $20,000 | $37,000 |
| 1854 | 33,140 | 1,500 | 2,500 | 4,000 | 5,000 | 6,000 | 9,000 | 12,500 | 16,500 |
| 1855 | 26,000 | 1,250 | 2,500 | 4,000 | 5,000 | 6,500 | 8,000 | 12,500 | 16,000 |
| 1856 | 63,500 | 500 | 700 | 900 | 2,300 | 3,500 | 5,000 | 5,500 | 13,000 |
| 1857 | 94,000 | 500 | 625 | 850 | 2,200 | 2,500 | 3,250 | 7,000 | 13,500 |
| 1858 | (210) | 5,000 | 6,000 | 7,000 | 8,000 | 9,000 | | 10,000 | 14,000 |

| | Mintage | VG-8 | F-12 | VF-20 | EF-40 | AU-50 | MS-60 | MS-63 | PF-63 |
|---|---|---|---|---|---|---|---|---|---|
| 1859 | (800) 255,700 | $400 | $425 | $525 | $750 | $1,225 | $2,500 | $6,000 | $4,750 |
| 1859O | 360,000 | 400 | 425 | 475 | 600 | 850 | 2,050 | 5,000 | |
| 1859S | 20,000 | 600 | 850 | 1,100 | 1,600 | 3,350 | 13,000 | 29,000 | |
| 1860 | (1,330) 217,600 | 450 | 500 | 575 | 700 | 900 | 2,100 | 5,000 | 4,750 |
| 1860O | 515,000 | 400 | 425 | 475 | 600 | 785 | 1,900 | 3,750 | |
| 1861 | (1,000) 77,500 | 775 | 1,100 | 1,650 | 2,750 | 3,000 | 3,750 | 5,850 | 4,750 |
| 1862 | (550) 11,540 | 900 | 1,300 | 1,900 | 2,750 | 3,750 | 5,500 | 9,000 | 4,750 |
| 1863 | (460) 27,200 | 900 | 1,300 | 2,000 | 2,500 | 2,800 | 3,575 | 7,000 | 4,750 |
| 1864 | (470) 30,700 | 500 | 650 | 1,000 | 1,400 | 2,100 | 3,575 | 7,500 | 4,750 |
| 1865 | (500) 46,500 | 475 | 575 | 950 | 1,800 | 2,400 | 3,575 | 7,500 | 4,750 |
| 1866, No Motto *(2 known)* | | | | | | | | | — |
| *$1,207,500, PF-63, Stack's Bowers auction, January 2005* | | | | | | | | | |

## With Motto IN GOD WE TRUST (1866–1873)

| | Mintage | VG-8 | F-12 | VF-20 | EF-40 | AU-50 | MS-60 | MS-63 | PF-63 |
|---|---|---|---|---|---|---|---|---|---|
| 1866 | (725) 48,900 | $425 | $450 | $600 | $1,100 | $1,400 | $2,300 | $5,500 | $3,800 |
| 1867 | (625) 46,900 | 425 | 450 | 600 | 1,000 | 1,200 | 2,200 | 5,300 | 3,900 |
| 1868 | (600) 162,100 | 425 | 450 | 500 | 800 | 1,150 | 2,400 | 7,000 | 3,800 |
| 1869 | (600) 423,700 | 425 | 450 | 500 | 750 | 1,050 | 2,300 | 5,250 | 3,800 |
| 1870 | (1,000) 415,000 | 425 | 450 | 525 | 600 | 950 | 2,100 | 4,750 | 3,800 |
| 1870CC | 11,758 | 1,000 | 1,350 | 2,100 | 4,250 | 5,500 | 25,000 | 42,500 | |
| 1870S | | 200,000 | 250,000 | 400,000 | 525,000 | 800,000 | 1,750,000 | — | |
| *$1,092,500, BU PL, Stack's Bowers auction, May 2003* | | | | | | | | | |
| 1871 | (960) 1,073,800 | 400 | 450 | 500 | 600 | 1,050 | 2,100 | 4,650 | 3,800 |
| 1871CC | 1,376 | 3,750 | 5,000 | 6,500 | 12,000 | 17,500 | 75,000 | 175,000 | |
| 1872 | (950) 1,105,500 | 400 | 450 | 500 | 600 | 950 | 2,050 | 4,700 | 3,800 |
| 1872CC | 3,150 | 2,500 | 3,250 | 4,250 | 6,000 | 10,000 | 28,000 | 100,000 | |
| 1872S | 9,000 | 650 | 800 | 1,000 | 1,750 | 3,000 | 12,000 | 37,500 | |
| 1873 | (600) 293,000 | 475 | 500 | 550 | 650 | 975 | 2,100 | 4,850 | 3,800 |
| 1873CC | 2,300 | 9,000 | 13,000 | 17,000 | 27,500 | 40,000 | 115,000 | 190,000 | |
| 1873S | 700 | *(Despite the official Mint records none of these coins are known to exist.)* | | | | | | | |

## TRADE DOLLARS (1873–1885)

This coin was issued for circulation in Asia to compete with dollar-sized coins of other countries. They were legal tender in the United States, but when silver prices declined, Congress repealed the provision and authorized the Treasury to limit coinage to export demand. Many pieces that circulated in the Orient were counterstamped with Oriental characters, known as *chop marks.* In 1887, the Treasury redeemed trade dollars that were not mutilated. The law authorizing trade dollars was repealed in February 1887. Modifications to the trade dollar design are distinguished as follows:

- **Reverse 1:** Berry under eagle's left (viewer's right) talon; arrowhead ends over 0. Used on all coins from all mints in 1873 and 1874, and occasionally in 1875 and 1876.
- **Reverse 2:** Without extra berry under talon; arrowhead ends over 2. Used occasionally at all mints from 1875 through 1876, and on all coins from all mints 1877 through 1885.
- **Obverse 1:** Ends of scroll point to left; extended hand has only three fingers. Used on coins at all mints 1873 through 1876.
- **Obverse 2:** Ends of scroll point downward; hand has four fingers. Used in combination with Reverse 2 on varieties of 1876 and 1876-S, and on all coins at all mints from 1877 through 1885.

*Designer William Barber; weight 27.22 grams; composition .900 silver, .100 copper (net weight .7874 oz. pure silver); diameter 38.1 mm; reeded edge; mints: Philadelphia, Carson City, San Francisco.*

**VG-8 Very Good**—About half of mottoes IN GOD WE TRUST (on Liberty's pedestal) and E PLURIBUS UNUM (on reverse ribbon) visible. Rim on both sides well defined.
**F-12 Fine**—Mottoes and LIBERTY legible but worn.
**VF-20 Very Fine**—More than half the details of Liberty's dress visible. Details of wheat sheaf mostly intact.
**EF-40 Extremely Fine**—Mottoes and LIBERTY sharp. Only slight wear on rims.
**AU-50 About Uncirculated**—Slight trace of wear on Liberty's left breast and left knee and on hair above ear, as well as on eagle's head, knee, and wing tips.
**MS-60 Uncirculated**—No trace of wear. Light blemishes.
**MS-63 Choice Uncirculated**—Some distracting contact marks or blemishes in prime focal areas. Impaired luster possible.
**PF-63 Choice Proof**—Reflective surfaces with few blemishes in secondary focal places. No major flaws.

*Mintmark location is on reverse, above D in DOLLAR.*

**1875-S, S Over CC**

| | Mintage | VG-8 | F-12 | VF-20 | EF-40 | AU-50 | MS-60 | MS-63 | PF-63 |
|---|---|---|---|---|---|---|---|---|---|
| 1873 | (600). .396,900 | $150 | $185 | $225 | $300 | $550 | $1,100 | $2,850 | $3,000 |
| 1873CC | 124,500 | 375 | 675 | 900 | 1,650 | 2,750 | 7,000 | 25,000 | |
| 1873S | 703,000 | 175 | 200 | 300 | 450 | 600 | 1,450 | 3,800 | |
| 1874 | (700). .987,100 | 170 | 185 | 225 | 350 | 500 | 1,200 | 2,400 | 3,000 |
| 1874CC | 1,373,200 | 300 | 425 | 525 | 700 | 950 | 2,500 | 5,000 | |
| 1874S | 2,549,000 | 170 | 185 | 200 | 250 | 325 | 900 | 2,000 | |

| | Mintage | VG-8 | F-12 | VF-20 | EF-40 | AU-50 | MS-60 | MS-63 | PF-63 |
|---|---|---|---|---|---|---|---|---|---|
| 1875 . . . . . . . . . . . . . . . (700). . . | 218,200 | $350 | $450 | $650 | $1,000 | $1,350 | $2,500 | $4,500 | $3,000 |
| 1875, Reverse 2 . . . . . . . . . . . . . . . . . . | * | 240 | 375 | 525 | 750 | 1,250 | 2,600 | 4,650 | |
| 1875CC, All kinds . . . . . . . . . . . | 1,573,700 | | | | | | | | |
| 1875CC. . . . . . . . . . . . . . . . . . . . . . . . . | | 275 | 375 | 475 | 575 | 850 | 2,250 | 4,500 | |
| 1875CC, Reverse 2 . . . . . . . . . . . . . . . . | | 275 | 375 | 475 | 650 | 925 | 2,500 | 5,500 | |
| 1875S, All kinds. . . . . . . . . . . . . | 4,487,000 | | | | | | | | |
| 1875S. . . . . . . . . . . . . . . . . . . . . . . . . . | | 165 | 185 | 225 | 300 | 350 | 900 | 1,600 | |
| 1875S, Reverse 2 . . . . . . . . . . . . . . . . . | | 165 | 185 | 200 | 325 | 400 | 1,175 | 2,350 | |
| 1875S, S Over CC . . . . . . . . . . . . . . . . . | | 265 | 400 | 525 | 1,000 | 1,700 | 5,000 | 14,500 | |
| 1876 . . . . . . . . . . . . . .(1,150). . . | 455,000 | 165 | 185 | 200 | 300 | 335 | 900 | 1,450 | |
| 1876, Obverse 2, Reverse 2 *(extremely rare)* . . . . . . . | * | | | | | | — | | |
| 1876, Reverse 2 . . . . . . . . . . . . . . . . . . | * | 165 | 185 | 225 | 300 | 335 | 900 | 2,000 | 3,000 |
| 1876CC, All kinds . . . . . . . . . . . . | 509,000 | | | | | | | | |
| 1876CC. . . . . . . . . . . . . . . . . . . . . . . . . | | 350 | 450 | 575 | 775 | 1,750 | 5,500 | 21,500 | |
| 1876CC, Reverse 1 . . . . . . . . . . . . . . . . | | 325 | 450 | 600 | 875 | 2,150 | 7,250 | 25,000 | |
| 1876CC, DblDie Rev | | 400 | 500 | 750 | 1,200 | 1,900 | 9,000 | 22,500 | |
| 1876S, All kinds. . . . . . . . . . . . . | 5,227,000 | | | | | | | | |
| 1876S. . . . . . . . . . . . . . . . . . . . . . . . . . | | 165 | 185 | 200 | 300 | 350 | 900 | 1,600 | |
| 1876S, Reverse 2 . . . . . . . . . . . . . . . . . | | 165 | 185 | 200 | 300 | 350 | 900 | 1,950 | |
| 1876S, Obverse 2, Reverse 2 | | 165 | 200 | 300 | 500 | 850 | 1,500 | 2,650 | |
| 1877 . . . . . . . . . . . . . . . (510). . | 3,039,200 | 165 | 200 | 225 | 300 | 350 | 900 | 1,600 | 3,500 |
| 1877CC. . . . . . . . . . . . . . . . . . . . . | 534,000 | 285 | 425 | 600 | 950 | 1,250 | 4,000 | 8,500 | |
| 1877S . . . . . . . . . . . . . . . . . . . . | 9,519,000 | 165 | 185 | 200 | 300 | 325 | 900 | 1,450 | |
| 1878 . . . . . . . . . . . . . . . (900). . . . . . . . . . | | | | | 1,500 | | | | 3,000 |
| 1878CC **(a)** . . . . . . . . . . . . . . . . . . | 97,000 | 700 | 1,175 | 1,675 | 3,750 | 5,000 | 13,500 | 35,000 | |
| 1878S . . . . . . . . . . . . . . . . . . . . | 4,162,000 | 165 | 185 | 200 | 275 | 350 | 800 | 1,450 | |
| 1879 . . . . . . . . . . . . . .(1,541). . . . . . . . . . | | | | | 1,250 | | | | 3,000 |
| 1880 . . . . . . . . . . . . . .(1,987). . . . . . . . . . | | | | | 1,250 | | | | 3,000 |
| 1881 . . . . . . . . . . . . . . . (960). . . . . . . . . . | | | | | 1,250 | | | | 3,000 |
| 1882 . . . . . . . . . . . . . .(1,097). . . . . . . . . . | | | | | 1,250 | | | | 3,000 |
| 1883 . . . . . . . . . . . . . . . (979). . . . . . . . . . | | | | | 1,250 | | | | 3,000 |
| 1884 **(b)** . . . . . . . . . . . . (10). . . . . . . . . . | | | | | | | | | 600,000 |
| *$1,140,000, PF-66, Heritage auction, January 2019* | | | | | | | | | |
| 1885 **(b)** . . . . . . . . . . . . . . (5). . . . . . . . . . | | | | | | | | | 2,000,000 |
| *$3,960,000, PF-66, Heritage auction, January 2019* | | | | | | | | | |

* Included in number above. **a.** 44,148 trade dollars were melted on July 19, 1878. Many of these may have been 1878-CC. **b.** The trade dollars of 1884 and 1885 were unknown to collectors until 1908. None are listed in the Mint director's report, and numismatists believe that they are not a part of the regular Mint issue.

## MORGAN (1878–1921)

The coinage law of 1873 made no provision for the standard silver dollar. During the lapse in coinage of this denomination, the gold dollar became the unit coin, and the trade dollar was used for commercial transactions with the Orient.

Resumption of coinage of the silver dollar was authorized by the Act of February 28, 1878, known as the Bland-Allison Act. The weight (412-1/2 grains) and fineness (.900) were to conform with the Act of January 18, 1837.

George T. Morgan, formerly a pupil of William Wyon in the Royal Mint in London, designed the new dollar. His initial M is found at the truncation of the neck, at the last tress. It also appears on the reverse on the left-hand loop of the ribbon.

Coinage of the silver dollar was suspended after 1904, when demand was low and the bullion supply became exhausted. Under provisions of the Pittman Act of 1918,

270,232,722 silver dollars were melted, and later, in 1921, coinage of the silver dollar was resumed. The Morgan design, with some slight refinements, was employed until the new Peace design was adopted later in that year.

Varieties listed are those most significant to collectors. Numerous other variations exist. Values are shown for the most common pieces. Prices of variations not listed in this guide depend on collector interest and rarity.

Sharply struck, prooflike Morgan dollars have highly reflective surfaces and are very scarce, usually commanding substantial premiums.

*Designer George T. Morgan; weight 26.73 grams; composition .900 silver, .100 copper (net weight .77344 oz. pure silver); diameter 38.1 mm; reeded edge; mints: Philadelphia, New Orleans, Carson City, Denver, San Francisco.*

**VF-20 Very Fine**—Two thirds of hair lines from top of forehead to ear visible. Ear well defined. Feathers on eagle's breast worn.

**EF-40 Extremely Fine**—All hair lines strong and ear bold. Eagle's feathers all plain but with slight wear on breast and wing tips.

**AU-50 About Uncirculated**—Slight trace of wear on the bust shoulder and hair left of forehead, and on eagle's breast and top edges of wings.

**MS-60 Uncirculated**—No trace of wear. Full mint luster present, but may be noticeably marred by scuff marks or bag abrasions.

**MS-63 Choice Uncirculated**—No trace of wear; full mint luster; few noticeable surface marks.

**MS-64 Uncirculated**—A few scattered contact marks. Good eye appeal and attractive luster.

**MS-65 Gem Uncirculated**—Only light, scattered contact marks that are not distracting. Strong luster, good eye appeal.

**PF-63 Choice Proof**—Reflective surfaces with only a few blemishes in secondary focal places. No major flaws.

*Location of mintmark, when present, is on reverse, below wreath.*

**First Reverse, 8 Tail Feathers**

**Second Reverse**
*Parallel top arrow feather, concave breast.*

**Third Reverse**
*Slanted top arrow feather, convex breast.*

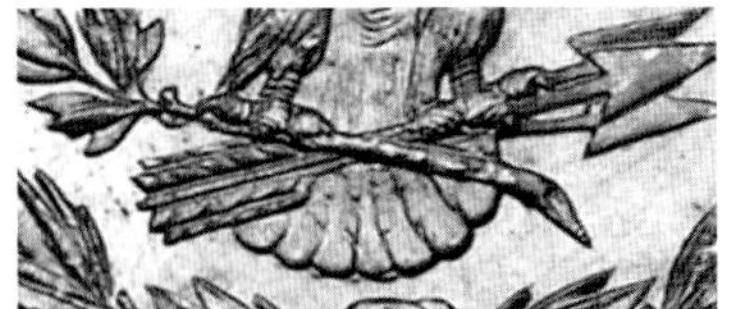

**1878, Doubled Tail Feathers**

| | Mintage | VF-20 | EF-40 | AU-50 | MS-60 | MS-63 | MS-64 | MS-65 | PF-63 |
|---|---|---|---|---|---|---|---|---|---|
| 1878, 8 Feathers . . . . . . . . . (500) | *749,500* | $85 | $100 | $120 | $200 | $250 | $425 | $1,000 | $3,500 |
| 1878, 7 Feathers, All kinds. . (250) | *9,759,300* | | | | | | | | |
| 1878, 7 Over 8 Clear Doubled Feathers . . . . . . . . . . . . . . . . . . | | 50 | 55 | 75 | 200 | 275 | 500 | 1,500 | |
| 1878, 7 Feathers, 2nd Reverse . . . . . . . . . . | | 45 | 48 | 60 | 90 | 135 | 225 | 900 | 3,750 |
| 1878, 7 Feathers, 3rd Reverse. . . . . . . . . . . | | 45 | 48 | 50 | 110 | 250 | 450 | 1,750 | 85,000 |

| | Mintage | VF-20 | EF-40 | AU-50 | MS-60 | MS-63 | MS-64 | MS-65 | PF-63 |
|---|---|---|---|---|---|---|---|---|---|
| 1878CC | 2,212,000 | $125 | $150 | $240 | $400 | $420 | $475 | $1,200 | |
| 1878S | 9,774,000 | 45 | 47 | 48 | 65 | 85 | 110 | 265 | |
| 1879 . . . . (1,100) | 14,806,000 | 30 | 33 | 50 | 55 | 90 | 130 | 450 | $3,200 |
| 1879CC, CC Over CC | 756,000 | 335 | 750 | 1,850 | 4,200 | 6,500 | 8,500 | 42,500 | |
| 1879CC, Clear CC | * | 375 | 950 | 2,500 | 4,500 | 7,250 | 9,500 | 22,500 | |
| 1879O . . . . *(4–8)* | 2,887,000 | 42 | 45 | 47 | 90 | 240 | 485 | 2,450 | |
| 1879S, 2nd Reverse | 9,110,000 | 65 | 75 | 90 | 250 | 675 | 1,250 | 4,500 | |
| 1879S, 3rd Reverse | * | 32 | 35 | 39 | 55 | 60 | 65 | 120 | |
| 1880 . . . . (1,355) | 12,600,000 | 40 | 42 | 46 | 50 | 85 | 125 | 525 | 3,000 |
| 1880, 80 Over 79 **(a)** | * | 55 | 100 | 200 | 550 | 875 | 7,000 | | |

* Included in number above. **a.** Several die varieties. Values shown are for the most common.

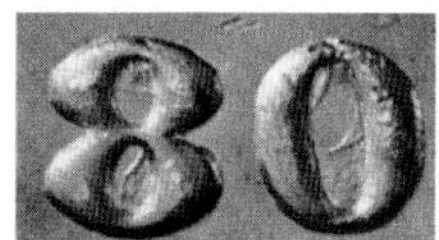

**1880-CC, 80 Over 79**

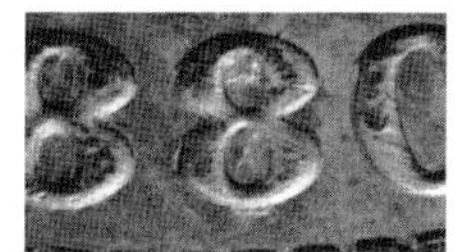

**1880-CC, 8 Over High 7**

**1880-CC, 8 Over Low 7**

| | Mintage | VF-20 | EF-40 | AU-50 | MS-60 | MS-63 | MS-64 | MS-65 | PF-63 |
|---|---|---|---|---|---|---|---|---|---|
| 1880CC, All kinds | 495,000 | | | | | | | | |
| 1880CC, 80 Over 79, 2nd Reverse **(b)** | | $220 | $285 | $350 | $500 | $600 | $1,000 | $2,000 | |
| 1880CC, 8 Over 7, 2nd Reverse **(a)** | | 210 | 285 | 325 | 550 | 600 | 1,000 | 2,000 | |
| 1880CC, 8/High 7, 3rd Reverse **(a)** | | 210 | 275 | 325 | 500 | 575 | 700 | 1,550 | |
| 1880CC, 8/Low 7, 3rd Reverse **(a)** | | 210 | 275 | 325 | 500 | 575 | 700 | 1,550 | |
| 1880CC, 3rd Reverse | | 225 | 260 | 325 | 500 | 575 | 700 | 1,000 | |
| 1880O, All kinds | 5,305,000 | | | | | | | | |
| 1880O, 80/79 **(a)** | | 40 | 65 | 75 | 200 | 500 | 2,000 | 16,000 | |
| 1880O | | 40 | 42 | 45 | 90 | 350 | 1,250 | 14,000 | |
| 1880S, All kinds | 8,900,000 | | | | | | | | |
| 1880S, 80 Over 79 | | 30 | 60 | 65 | 75 | 150 | 175 | 450 | |
| 1880S, 0 Over 9 | | 35 | 75 | 85 | 125 | 200 | 250 | 550 | |
| 1880S | | 30 | 33 | 39 | 45 | 50 | 65 | 120 | |
| 1881 . . . . (984) | 9,163,000 | 30 | 37 | 45 | 53 | 80 | 125 | 450 | $3,000 |
| 1881CC | 296,000 | 400 | 425 | 440 | 475 | 495 | 550 | 750 | |
| 1881O | 5,708,000 | 40 | 42 | 45 | 50 | 75 | 150 | 875 | |
| 1881S | 12,760,000 | 30 | 33 | 39 | 45 | 50 | 65 | 120 | |
| 1882 . . . . (1,100) | 11,100,000 | 30 | 33 | 39 | 50 | 75 | 115 | 330 | 3,000 |
| 1882CC | 1,133,000 | 110 | 130 | 150 | 210 | 235 | 250 | 400 | |
| 1882O | 6,090,000 | 37 | 39 | 45 | 50 | 75 | 125 | 650 | |
| 1882O, O Over S **(a)** | * | 50 | 55 | 70 | 150 | 450 | 1,500 | 50,000 | |
| 1882S | 9,250,000 | 30 | 33 | 39 | 45 | 55 | 65 | 120 | |
| 1883 . . . . (1,039) | 12,290,000 | 30 | 33 | 39 | 50 | 75 | 90 | 150 | 3,000 |
| 1883CC | 1,204,000 | 100 | 125 | 145 | 210 | 215 | 240 | 365 | |
| 1883O . . . . *(4–8)* | 8,725,000 | 30 | 33 | 39 | 45 | 50 | 70 | 120 | 100,000 |
| 1883S | 6,250,000 | 30 | 50 | 115 | 750 | 2,200 | 4,250 | 30,000 | |
| 1884 . . . . (875) | 14,070,000 | 30 | 33 | 39 | 50 | 75 | 95 | 240 | 3,000 |
| 1884CC | 1,136,000 | 150 | 160 | 165 | 210 | 225 | 245 | 365 | |

* Included in number above. **a.** Several die varieties. Values shown are for the most common. **b.** The 7 and 9 show within the 80; no tip below second 8.

1887, 7 Over 6

1888-O, Doubled Die Obverse
*Lips especially prominent ("Hot Lips" variety).*

| | Mintage | VF-20 | EF-40 | AU-50 | MS-60 | MS-63 | MS-64 | MS-65 | PF-63 |
|---|---|---|---|---|---|---|---|---|---|
| 1884O | 9,730,000 | $30 | $33 | $39 | $50 | $55 | $70 | $120 | |
| 1884S | 3,200,000 | 32 | 75 | 200 | 7,800 | 38,000 | 130,000 | 225,000 | |
| 1885 | (930). . 17,787,000 | 30 | 33 | 39 | 50 | 55 | 70 | 120 | $3,000 |
| 1885CC | 228,000 | 575 | 600 | 625 | 650 | 675 | 750 | 875 | |
| 1885O | 9,185,000 | 30 | 33 | 39 | 50 | 55 | 70 | 120 | |
| 1885S | 1,497,000 | 45 | 60 | 95 | 270 | 350 | 575 | 1,500 | |
| 1886 | (886). . 19,963,000 | 30 | 33 | 39 | 50 | 55 | 70 | 120 | 3,000 |
| 1886O | 10,710,000 | 42 | 45 | 80 | 875 | 2,650 | 8,000 | 150,000 | |
| 1886S | 750,000 | 78 | 115 | 150 | 350 | 450 | 650 | 1,600 | |
| 1887, 7 Over 6 | * | 45 | 75 | 150 | 275 | 425 | 550 | 1,500 | |
| 1887 | (710). . 20,290,000 | 30 | 33 | 39 | 50 | 55 | 65 | 120 | 3,000 |
| 1887O, 7 Over 6 | * | 50 | 75 | 155 | 500 | 1,500 | 3,750 | 17,500 | |
| 1887O | 11,550,000 | 30 | 33 | 42 | 70 | 140 | 350 | 1,500 | |
| 1887S | 1,771,000 | 30 | 33 | 43 | 135 | 225 | 575 | 1,450 | |
| 1888 | (833). . 19,183,000 | 30 | 33 | 40 | 50 | 65 | 75 | 150 | 3,000 |
| 1888O | 12,150,000 | 30 | 33 | 45 | 50 | 75 | 115 | 325 | |
| 1888O, DblDie Obv | ** | 150 | 300 | 750 | 5,000 | | — | | |
| 1888S | 657,000 | 125 | 140 | 150 | 315 | 400 | 750 | 2,250 | |
| 1889 | (811). . 21,726,000 | 30 | 33 | 39 | 50 | 60 | 65 | 200 | 3,000 |
| 1889CC | 350,000 | 1,150 | 2,750 | 7,500 | 24,000 | 40,000 | 80,000 | 300,000 | 100,000 |
| *$881,250, MS-68, Stack's Bowers auction, August 2013* | | | | | | | | | |
| 1889O | 11,875,000 | 30 | 37 | 57 | 185 | 350 | 750 | 3,450 | |
| 1889S | 700,000 | 60 | 75 | 95 | 275 | 325 | 550 | 1,350 | |
| 1890 | (590). . 16,802,000 | 30 | 33 | 40 | 53 | 75 | 125 | 750 | 3,000 |
| 1890CC | 2,309,041 | 110 | 150 | 230 | 540 | 875 | 1,150 | 3,000 | |
| 1890O | 10,701,000 | 30 | 33 | 49 | 75 | 125 | 275 | 1,100 | |
| 1890S | 8,230,373 | 30 | 33 | 43 | 70 | 115 | 225 | 850 | |
| 1891 | (650). . . 8,693,556 | 30 | 33 | 45 | 75 | 145 | 450 | 2,500 | 3,000 |
| 1891CC | 1,618,000 | 110 | 140 | 240 | 490 | 775 | 1,050 | 3,250 | |
| 1891O | 7,954,529 | 30 | 33 | 40 | 240 | 375 | 600 | 4,500 | |
| 1891S | 5,296,000 | 30 | 33 | 43 | 70 | 150 | 340 | 1,150 | |
| 1892 | (1,245). . . 1,036,000 | 45 | 55 | 85 | 320 | 425 | 850 | 2,500 | 3,000 |
| 1892CC | 1,352,000 | 250 | 450 | 700 | 1,400 | 1,950 | 2,350 | 5,750 | |
| 1892O | 2,744,000 | 35 | 42 | 85 | 275 | 400 | 775 | 3,250 | |
| 1892S | 1,200,000 | 125 | 275 | 1,450 | 41,000 | 95,000 | 175,000 | 225,000 | |
| *$460,000, MS-67, Heritage auction, January 2009* | | | | | | | | | |
| 1893 | (792). . . . 378,000 | 225 | 250 | 350 | 875 | 1,350 | 2,100 | 4,250 | 3,000 |
| 1893CC | 677,000 | 625 | 1,350 | 2,500 | 4,900 | 6,750 | 15,500 | 100,000 | |

* Included in number below. ** Included in number above.

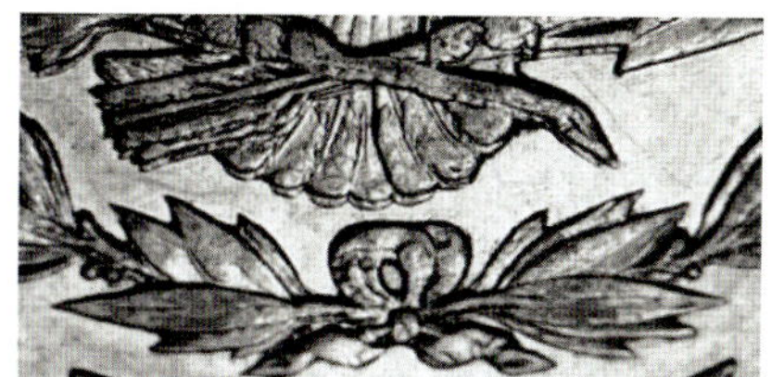

**1901, Doubled Die Reverse**
*Note tail feathers.*

| | Mintage | VF-20 | EF-40 | AU-50 | MS-60 | MS-63 | MS-64 | MS-65 | PF-63 |
|---|---|---|---|---|---|---|---|---|---|
| 1893O | 300,000 | $300 | $475 | $775 | $3,500 | $7,000 | $16,500 | $175,000 | |
| 1893S **(c)** | 100,000 | 5,200 | 8,500 | 20,750 | 145,000 | 275,000 | 330,000 | 600,000 | |
| *$646,250, MS-65, Legend auction, October 2014* | | | | | | | | | |
| 1894 **(c)** (972) | 110,000 | 925 | 1,000 | 1,050 | 3,100 | 4,700 | 7,250 | 35,000 | $3,500 |
| 1894O | 1,723,000 | 55 | 95 | 160 | 1,375 | 4,250 | 7,500 | 57,500 | |
| 1894S | 1,260,000 | 95 | 175 | 425 | 850 | 1,400 | 2,300 | 6,000 | |
| 1895, Proof **(d)** (880) | | | | | | | | | 50,000 |
| 1895O | 450,000 | 350 | 500 | 1,100 | 16,000 | 55,000 | 85,000 | 195,000 | |
| *$575,000, MS-67, Heritage auction, November 2005* | | | | | | | | | |
| 1895S | 400,000 | 675 | 1,000 | 1,500 | 4,500 | 6,500 | 9,000 | 20,000 | |
| 1896 (762) | 9,976,000 | 30 | 33 | 39 | 40 | 50 | 65 | 135 | 3,000 |
| 1896O | 4,900,000 | 42 | 45 | 125 | 1,700 | 6,000 | 36,000 | 160,000 | |
| 1896S | 5,000,000 | 70 | 250 | 850 | 2,300 | 3,750 | 5,000 | 13,500 | |
| *$402,500, MS-69, Heritage auction, November 2005* | | | | | | | | | |
| 1897 (731) | 2,822,000 | 30 | 33 | 39 | 50 | 65 | 85 | 240 | 3,000 |
| 1897O | 4,004,000 | 30 | 50 | 85 | 975 | 4,000 | 12,500 | 60,000 | |
| 1897S | 5,825,000 | 30 | 33 | 48 | 85 | 145 | 185 | 475 | |
| 1898 (735) | 5,884,000 | 30 | 33 | 39 | 50 | 65 | 75 | 190 | 3,000 |
| 1898O | 4,440,000 | 30 | 33 | 39 | 50 | 70 | 75 | 120 | |
| 1898S | 4,102,000 | 45 | 50 | 90 | 275 | 500 | 700 | 1,400 | |
| 1899 (846) | 330,000 | 175 | 185 | 195 | 260 | 275 | 325 | 700 | 3,000 |
| 1899O | 12,290,000 | 30 | 33 | 39 | 50 | 65 | 75 | 120 | |
| 1899S | 2,562,000 | 45 | 65 | 180 | 425 | 575 | 775 | 1,850 | |
| 1900 (912) | 8,830,000 | 30 | 33 | 39 | 45 | 50 | 65 | 120 | 3,000 |
| 1900O | 12,590,000 | 30 | 33 | 39 | 45 | 50 | 65 | 120 | |
| 1900O, O/CC **(e)** | * | 80 | 115 | 150 | 300 | 650 | 850 | 1,850 | |
| 1900S | 3,540,000 | 45 | 55 | 85 | 290 | 400 | 575 | 1,300 | |
| 1901 **(c)** (813) | 6,962,000 | 55 | 95 | 225 | 3,500 | 13,000 | 55,000 | 350,000 | 3,000 |
| 1901, DblDie Rev. | * | 150 | 1,000 | 1,500 | 12,000 | 40,000 | | | |
| 1901O | 13,320,000 | 40 | 42 | 48 | 50 | 55 | 65 | 120 | |
| 1901S | 2,284,000 | 48 | 65 | 200 | 550 | 875 | 1,200 | 2,150 | |
| 1902 (777) | 7,994,000 | 43 | 50 | 53 | 55 | 175 | 200 | 325 | 3,000 |
| 1902O | 8,636,000 | 40 | 43 | 45 | 50 | 55 | 65 | 160 | |
| 1902S | 1,530,000 | 140 | 190 | 250 | 380 | 625 | 750 | 1,850 | |
| 1903 (755) | 4,652,000 | 50 | 53 | 55 | 78 | 100 | 120 | 225 | 3,000 |
| 1903O | 4,450,000 | 350 | 375 | 385 | 415 | 440 | 475 | 650 | |
| 1903S | 1,241,000 | 275 | 375 | 1,600 | 5,000 | 7,250 | 8,250 | 11,500 | |
| 1904 (650) | 2,788,000 | 40 | 47 | 50 | 100 | 250 | 475 | 1,750 | 3,000 |
| 1904O | 3,720,000 | 43 | 45 | 48 | 50 | 65 | 75 | 120 | |
| 1904S | 2,304,000 | 80 | 200 | 600 | 2,600 | 4,250 | 4,750 | 7,500 | |
| 1921 | 44,690,000 | 28 | 30 | 32 | 35 | 45 | 65 | 135 | — |
| 1921D | 20,345,000 | 32 | 34 | 35 | 50 | 70 | 140 | 250 | |
| 1921S | 21,695,000 | 32 | 34 | 35 | 50 | 75 | 125 | 600 | |

* Included in number above. **c.** Authentication is recommended. Beware of altered mintmark. **d.** Beware of removed mintmark. Value is for Proofs; circulation strikes are not known to exist. **e.** Several die varieties.

## PEACE (1921–1935)

The dollar of new design issued from December 1921 through 1935 was a commemorative peace coin. The Peace dollar was issued without congressional sanction, under the terms of the Pittman Act, which referred to the bullion and in no way affected the design. Anthony de Francisci, a medalist, designed this dollar. His monogram is located in the field of the coin under the neck of Liberty.

The new Peace dollar was placed in circulation on January 3, 1922; 1,006,473 pieces had been struck in December 1921.

The high relief of the 1921 design was found impractical for coinage and was modified to low or shallow relief in 1922, after 35,401 coins had been made and most of them melted at the mint. The rare Matte and Satin Finish Proofs of 1922 are of both the high-relief style of 1921 and the normal-relief style.

Legislation dated August 3, 1964, authorized the coinage of 45 million silver dollars, and 316,076 dollars of the Peace design dated 1964 were struck at the Denver Mint in 1965. Plans for completing this coinage were subsequently abandoned and all of these coins were melted. None were preserved or released for circulation. Many deceptive reproductions exist.

*Designer Anthony de Francisci; weight 26.73 grams; composition .900 silver, .100 copper (net weight .77344 oz. pure silver); diameter 38.1 mm; reeded edge; mints: Philadelphia, Denver, San Francisco.*

**VF-20 Very Fine**—Hair over eye well worn. Some strands over ear well defined. Some eagle feathers on top and outside edge of right wing visible.

**EF-40 Extremely Fine**—Hair lines over brow and ear are strong, though slightly worn. Outside wing feathers at right and those at top visible but faint.

**AU-50 About Uncirculated**—Slight trace of wear. Most of mint luster present, although marred by contact marks.

**MS-60 Uncirculated**—No trace of wear. Full mint luster, but possibly noticeably marred by stains, surface marks, or bag abrasions.

**MS-63 Choice Uncirculated**—Some distracting contact marks or blemishes in prime focal areas. Impaired luster possible.

**MS-64 Uncirculated**—A few scattered contact marks. Good eye appeal and attractive luster.

**MS-65 Gem Uncirculated**—Only light, scattered contact marks that are not distracting. Strong luster, good eye appeal.

*Location of mintmark, when present, is on reverse, below ONE.*

| | Mintage | VF-20 | EF-40 | AU-50 | MS-60 | MS-63 | MS-64 | MS-65 | MS-66 | MATTE PF-65 |
|---|---|---|---|---|---|---|---|---|---|---|
| 1921, High Relief | 1,006,473 | $110 | $125 | $150 | $260 | $425 | $850 | $1,600 | $5,000 | $85,000 |
| 1922, High Relief | 35,401 | | | — | | | | | | 200,000 |
| 1922, Normal Relief | 51,737,000 | 25 | 27 | 28 | 30 | 33 | 45 | 100 | 375 | — |

| | Mintage | VF-20 | EF-40 | AU-50 | MS-60 | MS-63 | MS-64 | MS-65 | MS-66 |
|---|---|---|---|---|---|---|---|---|---|
| 1922D | 15,063,000 | $28 | $30 | $33 | $50 | $75 | $125 | $500 | $1,500 |
| 1922S | 17,475,000 | 28 | 30 | 33 | 50 | 90 | 225 | 1,500 | 32,500 |
| 1923 | 30,800,000 | 25 | 27 | 28 | 30 | 33 | 45 | 100 | 325 |
| 1923D | 6,811,000 | 28 | 30 | 40 | 75 | 155 | 350 | 950 | 3,500 |
| 1923S | 19,020,000 | 28 | 30 | 36 | 50 | 85 | 325 | 1,850 | 30,000 |
| 1924 | 11,811,000 | 25 | 28 | 29 | 30 | 33 | 45 | 100 | 350 |
| 1924S | 1,728,000 | 28 | 40 | 60 | 235 | 450 | 950 | 6,500 | 50,000 |
| 1925 | 10,198,000 | 25 | 28 | 29 | 30 | 35 | 45 | 100 | 350 |
| 1925S | 1,610,000 | 28 | 32 | 45 | 90 | 250 | 625 | 22,500 | 70,000 |
| 1926 | 1,939,000 | 28 | 32 | 37 | 50 | 100 | 125 | 385 | 1,250 |
| 1926D | 2,348,700 | 28 | 32 | 44 | 100 | 225 | 410 | 875 | 2,000 |
| 1926S | 6,980,000 | 28 | 32 | 38 | 60 | 100 | 240 | 675 | 2,750 |
| 1927 | 848,000 | 39 | 42 | 50 | 80 | 185 | 410 | 1,400 | 22,500 |
| 1927D | 1,268,900 | 39 | 45 | 75 | 200 | 400 | 1,000 | 3,300 | 30,000 |
| 1927S | 866,000 | 39 | 45 | 75 | 190 | 500 | 900 | 7,500 | 45,000 |
| 1928 | 360,649 | 275 | 320 | 340 | 425 | 600 | 850 | 3,250 | 30,000 |
| 1928S | 1,632,000 | 39 | 48 | 65 | 210 | 375 | 975 | 18,500 | 65,000 |
| 1934 | 954,057 | 44 | 45 | 50 | 120 | 195 | 325 | 650 | 2,000 |
| 1934D **(a)** | 1,569,500 | 44 | 45 | 50 | 130 | 325 | 500 | 1,250 | 3,000 |
| 1934D, DblDie Obv | * | 115 | 185 | 375 | 750 | 1,650 | | | |
| 1934S | 1,011,000 | 80 | 175 | 500 | 2,300 | 4,250 | 6,300 | 8,250 | 27,500 |
| 1935 | 1,576,000 | 44 | 45 | 50 | 80 | 120 | 250 | 625 | 1,900 |
| 1935S **(b)** | 1,964,000 | 44 | 50 | 88 | 260 | 425 | 525 | 1,075 | 2,650 |

* Included in number above. Value is for variety with small mintmark on reverse. A second variety with larger, filled D mintmark is worth only about 20% more than the normal coin. **a.** Large and small mintmark varieties; see page 22. **b.** Varieties exist with either three or four rays below ONE, and are of equal value.

## EISENHOWER (1971–1978)

### Eagle Reverse (1971–1974)

Honoring both President Dwight D. Eisenhower and the first landing of man on the moon, this design is the work of Chief Engraver Frank Gasparro, whose initials are on the truncation of the president's neck, below the eagle. The reverse is an adaptation of the official *Apollo 11* insignia. Collectors' coins were struck in 40% silver composition, and the circulation issue in copper-nickel.

After 1971, the dies for the Eisenhower dollar were modified several times by changing the relief, strengthening the design, and making Earth above the eagle more clearly defined. Low-relief (Variety I) dies, with flattened Earth and three islands off Florida, were used for all copper-nickel issues of 1971, Uncirculated silver coins of 1971, and most copper-nickel coins of 1972. High-relief (Variety II) dies, with round Earth and weak or indistinct islands, were used for most Proofs of 1971, all silver issues of 1972, and the reverse of some scarce Philadelphia copper-nickel coins of 1972. Improved high-relief reverse dies (Variety III) were used for late-1972 Philadelphia copper-nickel coins and for all subsequent issues. Modified high-relief dies were also used on all issues beginning in 1973.

A few 1974-D and 1977-D dollars in silver clad composition were made in error.

*Designer Frank Gasparro; diameter 38.1 mm; reeded edge. Silver issue: weight 24.59 grams; composition, outer layers of .800 silver, .200 copper bonded to inner core of .209 silver, .791 copper (net weight .3161 oz. pure silver). Copper-nickel issue: weight 22.68 grams; composition, outer layers of .750 copper, .250 nickel bonded to inner core of pure copper. Mints: Philadelphia, Denver, San Francisco.*

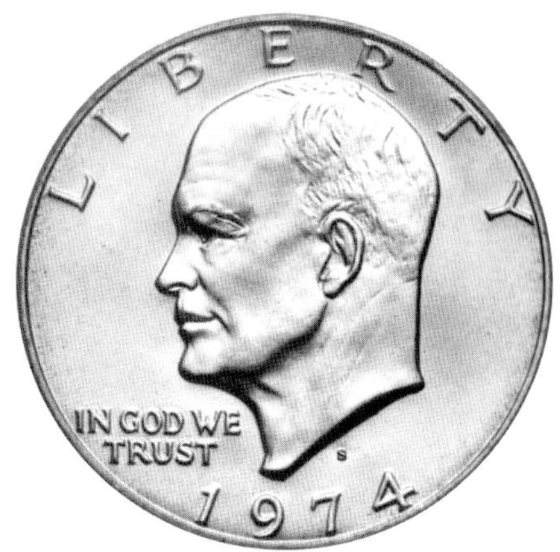

*Mintmark location is above date.*

| | Mintage | EF-40 | MS-63 | MS-65 | PF-65 |
|---|---|---|---|---|---|
| 1971, Copper-Nickel Clad | 47,799,000 | $3.00 | $6 | $85 | |
| 1971D, Copper-Nickel Clad, Variety 1 | 68,587,424 | 3.50 | 15 | 50 | |
| 1971D, Copper-Nickel Clad, Variety 2 **(a)** | * | 2.00 | 5 | 18 | |
| 1971S, Silver Clad (4,265,234) | 6,868,530 | | 13 | 18 | $14 |
| 1972, Copper-Nickel Clad, Variety 1 | 75,890,000 | 2.00 | 5 | 95 | |
| 1972, Copper-Nickel Clad, Variety 2 | * | 10.00 | 110 | 1,500 | |
| 1972, Copper-Nickel Clad, Variety 3 | * | 2.50 | 5 | 95 | |
| 1972D, Copper-Nickel Clad | 92,548,511 | 2.00 | 5 | 10 | |
| 1972S, Silver Clad (1,811,631) | 2,193,056 | | 13 | 18 | 14 |
| 1973, Copper-Nickel Clad **(b)** | 2,000,056 | | 13 | 40 | |
| 1973D, Copper-Nickel Clad **(b)** | 2,000,000 | | 13 | 25 | |
| 1973S, Copper-Nickel Clad (2,760,339) | **(c)** | | | | 14 |
| 1973S, Silver Clad (1,013,646) | 1,883,140 | | 14 | 18 | 35 |
| 1974, Copper-Nickel Clad | 27,366,000 | 2.00 | 6 | 25 | |
| 1974D, Copper-Nickel Clad | 45,517,000 | 2.00 | 6 | 16 | |
| 1974S, Copper-Nickel Clad (2,612,568) | | | | | 7 |
| 1974S, Silver Clad (1,306,579) | 1,900,156 | | 13 | 18 | 15 |

* Included in number above. **a.** Modified with accented crater lines. **b.** 1,769,258 of each sold only in sets and not released for circulation. Unissued coins destroyed at mint. **c.** Two circulation-strike examples are reported to exist.

## Bicentennial (1776–1976)

The national significance of the Bicentennial of the United States was highlighted with the adoption of new reverse designs for the quarter, half dollar, and dollar. Nearly a thousand entries were submitted after the Treasury announced in October 1973 that an open contest was to be held for the selection of the new designs. After the field was narrowed down to 12 semifinalists, the judges chose the rendition of the Liberty Bell superimposed on the moon to appear on the dollar coins. This design is the work of Dennis R. Williams.

The obverse remained unchanged except for the dual date "1776–1976," which appeared on these dollars made during 1975 and 1976. These dual-dated coins were included in the various offerings of Proof and Uncirculated coins made by the Mint. They were also struck for general circulation. The lettering was modified early in 1975 to produce a more attractive design.

*Designers Frank Gasparro and Dennis R. Williams; diameter 38.1 mm; reeded edge. Silver issue—Weight 24.59 grams; composition, outer layers of .800 silver, .200 copper bonded to inner core of .209 silver, .791 copper (net weight .3161 oz. pure silver). Copper-nickel issue—Weight 22.68 grams; composition, outer layers of .750 copper, .250 nickel bonded to inner core of pure copper. Mints: Philadelphia, Denver, San Francisco.*

**Variety 1**
*Design in low relief, bold lettering on reverse.*

**Variety 2**
*Sharp design, delicate lettering on reverse.*

| | Mintage | EF-40 | MS-63 | MS-65 | PF-65 |
|---|---|---|---|---|---|
| 1776–1976, Copper-Nickel Clad, Variety 1 | 4,019,000 | $2 | $8 | $160 | |
| 1776–1976, Copper-Nickel Clad, Variety 2 | 113,318,000 | 2 | 5 | 30 | |
| 1776–1976D, Copper-Nickel Clad, Variety 1 | 21,048,710 | 2 | 5 | 50 | |
| 1776–1976D, Copper-Nickel Clad, Variety 2 | 82,179,564 | 2 | 5 | 28 | |
| 1776–1976S, Copper-Nickel Clad, Variety 1 | (2,845,450) | | | | $12 |
| 1776–1976S, Copper-Nickel Clad, Variety 2 | (4,149,730) | | | | 8 |
| 1776–1976, Silver Clad, Variety 2 *(1 known)* | | | | | — |
| 1776–1976S, Silver Clad, Variety 1 **(a)** | *11,000,000* | | 17 | 20 | |
| 1776–1976S, Silver Clad, Variety 1 **(a)** | *(4,000,000)* | | | | 19 |

**a.** Mintage is approximate.

## Eagle Reverse Resumed (1977–1978)

| | Mintage | EF-40 | MS-63 | MS-65 | PF-65 |
|---|---|---|---|---|---|
| 1977, Copper-Nickel Clad | 12,596,000 | $2 | $6.00 | $35 | |
| 1977D, Copper-Nickel Clad | 32,983,006 | 2 | 6.00 | 35 | |
| 1977S, Copper-Nickel Clad | (3,251,152) | | | | $5 |
| 1978, Copper-Nickel Clad | 25,702,000 | 2 | 6.00 | 45 | |
| 1978D, Copper-Nickel Clad | 33,012,890 | 2 | 5.50 | 40 | |
| 1978S, Copper-Nickel Clad | (3,127,781) | | | | 5 |

# SUSAN B. ANTHONY (1979–1999)

Intended to honor this pioneer in women's rights, legislation dated October 10, 1978, provided for the issuance of the Susan B. Anthony dollar coin. Both obverse and reverse designs were the work of the chief engraver of the U.S. Mint, Frank Gasparro, whose initials FG are located below the portrait and the eagle.

Placement of Susan B. Anthony's likeness on the dollar represented the first time that a woman other than a model or a mythical figure has appeared on a circulating U.S. coin. The reverse design is the same as that used on the Eisenhower dollar. Mintmarks P, D, or S appear on the obverse, slightly above Anthony's right shoulder.

The size of this coin, its silver color, and its edge reeding caused it to be confused with the quarter, and it failed to gain widespread public acceptance. No coins were made for circulation from 1981 to 1998. In 1999 additional pieces were made as a safeguard in anticipation of increased public demand before the Sacagawea dollar debuted in 2000.

*Designer Frank Gasparro; weight 8.1 grams; composition, outer layers of copper-nickel (.750 copper, .250 nickel) bonded to inner core of pure copper; diameter 26.5 mm; reeded edge; mints: Philadelphia, Denver, San Francisco.*

1979, Narrow Rim (Far Date)

1979, Wide Rim (Near Date)

1979-S, Filled S (Type 1)

1979-S, Clear S (Type 2, Rounded)
1981-S, First S (Type 1, Rounded)

1981-S, Clear S
(Type 2, Flat)

| | Mintage | MS-63 | PF-67 |
|---|---|---|---|
| 1979P, Narrow Rim **(a)** | 360,222,000 | $6 | |
| 1979P, Wide Rim **(a)** | * | 38 | |
| 1979D | 288,015,744 | 7 | |
| 1979S | 109,576,000 | 6 | |
| 1979S, Proof, Type 1 | (3,677,175) | | $8 |
| 1979S, Proof, Type 2 | * | | 55 |
| 1980P | 27,610,000 | 5 | |
| 1980D | 41,628,708 | 5 | |
| 1980S | 20,422,000 | 10 | |

| | Mintage | MS-63 | PF-67 |
|---|---|---|---|
| 1980S, Proof | (3,554,806) | | $8 |
| 1981P **(b)** | 3,000,000 | $12 | |
| 1981D **(b)** | 3,250,000 | 10 | |
| 1981S **(b)** | 3,492,000 | 20 | |
| 1981S, Proof, Type 1 | (4,063,083) | | 8 |
| 1981S, Proof, Type 2 | * | | 135 |
| 1999P | 29,592,000 | 3 | |
| 1999P, Proof | *(750,000)* | | 24 |
| 1999D | 11,776,000 | 3 | |

* Included in number above. **a.** The obverse design was modified in 1979 to widen the border rim. Late issues of 1979-P and subsequent issues have the wide rim. Dies for the 1999 coins were further modified to strengthen details on the reverse. **b.** Issued only in Mint Sets.

## SACAGAWEA (2000–2008)

The design of this coin was selected in national competition from among 120 submissions that were considered by a panel appointed by Treasury Secretary Robert Rubin. The adopted motif depicts Sacagawea, a young Native American Shoshone, as conceived by artist Glenna Goodacre. On her back she carries Jean Baptiste, her infant son. The reverse shows an eagle in flight designed by Mint sculptor-engraver Thomas D. Rogers Sr.

The composition exemplifies the spirit of liberty, peace, and freedom shown by Sacagawea in her conduct as interpreter and guide to explorers Meriwether Lewis and William Clark during their famed journey westward from the great northern plains to the Pacific.

These coins have a distinctive golden color and a plain edge to distinguish them from other denominations or coins of a similar size. The change in composition and appearance was mandated under the United States Dollar Coin Act of 1997.

Several distinctive finishes can be identified on the Sacagawea dollars as a result of the Mint's attempts to adjust the dies, blanks, strikes, or finishing to produce coins with minimum spotting and better surface color. One group of 5,000 pieces, dated 2000 and with a special finish, were presented to sculptor Glenna Goodacre in payment for the obverse design. Unexplained error coins made from mismatched dies (a State quarter obverse combined with a Sacagawea dollar reverse) are extremely rare.

*Designers: obv. Glenna Goodacre; rev. Thomas D. Rogers Sr.; weight 8.1 grams; composition, pure copper core with outer layer of manganese brass (.770 copper, .120 zinc, .070 manganese, and .040 nickel); diameter 26.5 mm; plain edge; mints: Philadelphia, Denver, San Francisco; 22-karat gold numismatic specimens dated 2000-W were struck at West Point in 1999 using a prototype reverse design with boldly detailed tail feathers. Some of the early 2000-P circulation strikes were also made using that same prototype design.*

| | Mintage | MS-65 | PF-65 |
|---|---|---|---|
| 2000P | 767,140,000 | $5 | |
| 2000P, Boldly Detailed Tail Feathers **(a)** | 5,500 | 3,000 | |
| 2000P, Goodacre Presentation Finish | 5,000 | 500 | |
| 2000D | 518,916,000 | 8 | |
| 2000S | (4,047,904) | | $6 |
| 2001P | 62,468,000 | 4 | |
| 2001D | 70,939,500 | 4 | |
| 2001S | (3,183,740) | | 6 |
| 2002P **(b)** | 3,865,610 | 4 | |
| 2002D **(b)** | 3,732,000 | 4 | |
| 2002S | (3,211,995) | | 6 |
| 2003P **(b)** | 3,080,000 | 5 | |
| 2003D **(b)** | 3,080,000 | 5 | |
| 2003S | (3,298,439) | | 6 |
| 2004P **(b)** | 2,660,000 | $4 | |
| 2004D **(b)** | 2,660,000 | 4 | |
| 2004S | (2,965,422) | | $6 |
| 2005P **(b)** | 2,520,000 | 10 | |
| 2005D **(b)** | 2,520,000 | 10 | |
| 2005S | (3,344,679) | | 6 |
| 2006P **(b)** | 4,900,000 | 4 | |
| 2006D **(b)** | 2,800,000 | 4 | |
| 2006S | (3,054,436) | | 6 |
| 2007P **(b)** | 3,640,000 | 5 | |
| 2007D **(b)** | 3,920,000 | 5 | |
| 2007S | (2,577,166) | | 6 |
| 2008P **(b)** | 1,820,000 | 5 | |
| 2008D **(b)** | 1,820,000 | 5 | |
| 2008S | (2,169,561) | | 6 |

*Note:* Uncirculated Mint Sets for 2005–2010 were made with Satin Finish coins not included in the listings here. See page 369 for their mintages. **a.** Released as a promotion with the breakfast cereal Cheerios, this variety was not noted as distinct until years later. About 100 are known today. **b.** Not issued for circulation. The U.S. Mint produced circulation-quality Sacagawea dollar coins at its Philadelphia and Denver facilities in 2002, 2007, and 2008. These were never issued for circulation through banks, but were made available to the general public by direct sales from the Mint.

## PRESIDENTIAL (2007–2016, 2020)

Former U.S. presidents are honored on this series of dollar coins, issued (in the order that the presidents served) for circulation from 2007 through 2011 and only for numismatic sales thereafter. The common reverse features the Statue of Liberty. As with the Native American dollars, some error coins have been found that lack the usual edge lettering. The motto IN GOD WE TRUST was moved to the obverse starting in 2009. In 2020 the original program was expanded to include George H.W. Bush, who died in 2018.

A companion series of ten-dollar gold coins honors the spouses of each president during that president's term of service. These coins are made of 24-karat gold, and on the obverse have an image of the spouse (or a representation of Liberty if the president had no spouse while in office), and on the reverse a theme symbolic of the spouse's life and work (or one from the president's life if he was unmarried). See pages 381–386 for more information on the First Spouse gold coins.

*Designers: obv. various; rev. Don Everhart; lettered edge; weight, composition, diameter, and mints identical to those for the Sacagawea dollar.*

**Error coins with wrong or missing edge lettering are valued higher than normal coins.**

Reverse

Date, Mintmark, and Mottos Incused on Edge

| | Mintage | MS-65 | PF-65 |
|---|---|---|---|
| 2007P, Washington | 176,680,000 | $3 | |
| 2007D, Washington | 163,680,000 | 3 | |
| 2007S, Washington | (3,965,989) | | $4 |
| 2007P, J. Adams | 112,420,000 | 3 | |
| 2007D, J. Adams | 112,140,000 | 3 | |
| 2007S, J. Adams | (3,965,989) | | 4 |

| | Mintage | MS-65 | PF-65 |
|---|---|---|---|
| 2007P, Jefferson | 100,800,000 | $3 | |
| 2007D, Jefferson | 102,810,000 | 3 | |
| 2007S, Jefferson | (3,965,989) | | $4 |
| 2007P, Madison | 84,560,000 | 3 | |
| 2007D, Madison | 87,780,000 | 3 | |
| 2007S, Madison | (3,965,989) | | 4 |

*Note:* Uncirculated Mint Sets for 2005–2010 were made with Satin Finish coins not included in the listings here. See page 369 for their mintages.

| | Mintage | MS-65 | PF-65 |
|---|---|---|---|
| 2008P, Monroe | 64,260,000 | $3 | |
| 2008D, Monroe | 60,230,000 | 3 | |
| 2008S, Monroe | (3,083,940) | | $4 |
| 2008P, J.Q. Adams | 57,540,000 | 3 | |
| 2008D, J.Q. Adams | 57,720,000 | 3 | |
| 2008S, J.Q. Adams | (3,083,940) | | 4 |

| | Mintage | MS-65 | PF-65 |
|---|---|---|---|
| 2008P, Jackson | 61,180,000 | $3 | |
| 2008D, Jackson | 61,070,000 | 3 | |
| 2008S, Jackson | (3,083,940) | | $4 |
| 2008P, Van Buren | 51,520,000 | 3 | |
| 2008D, Van Buren | 50,960,000 | 3 | |
| 2008S, Van Buren | (3,083,940) | | 4 |

*Note:* Uncirculated Mint Sets for 2005–2010 were made with Satin Finish coins not included in the listings here. See page 369 for their mintages.

**Error coins with wrong or missing edge lettering are valued higher than normal coins.**

| | Mintage | MS-65 | PF-65 |
|---|---|---|---|
| 2009P, W.H. Harrison . . | 43,260,000 | $3 | |
| 2009D, W.H. Harrison. . | 55,160,000 | 3 | |
| 2009S, W.H. Harrison. . | (2,809,452) | | $4 |
| 2009P, Tyler. . . . . . . . . | 43,540,000 | 3 | |
| 2009D, Tyler . . . . . . . . | 43,540,000 | 3 | |
| 2009S, Tyler . . . . . . . . | (2,809,452) | | 4 |

| | Mintage | MS-65 | PF-65 |
|---|---|---|---|
| 2009P, Polk . . . . . . . . . | 46,620,000 | $3 | |
| 2009D, Polk. . . . . . . . . | 41,720,000 | 3 | |
| 2009S, Polk. . . . . . . . . | (2,809,452) | | $4 |
| 2009P, Taylor. . . . . . . . | 41,580,000 | 3 | |
| 2009D, Taylor . . . . . . . | 36,680,000 | 3 | |
| 2009S, Taylor. . . . . . . . | (2,809,452) | | 4 |

*Note:* Uncirculated Mint Sets for 2005–2010 were made with Satin Finish coins not included in the listings here. See page 369 for their mintages.

| | Mintage | MS-65 | PF-65 |
|---|---|---|---|
| 2010P, Fillmore . . . . . . | 37,520,000 | $3 | |
| 2010D, Fillmore. . . . . . | 36,960,000 | 3 | |
| 2010S, Fillmore . . . . . . | (2,224,613) | | $6 |
| 2010P, Pierce. . . . . . . . | 38,220,000 | 3 | |
| 2010D, Pierce . . . . . . . | 38,360,000 | 3 | |
| 2010S, Pierce . . . . . . . | (2,224,613) | | 6 |

| | Mintage | MS-65 | PF-65 |
|---|---|---|---|
| 2010P, Buchanan. . . . . | 36,820,000 | $3 | |
| 2010D, Buchanan . . . . | 36,540,000 | 3 | |
| 2010S, Buchanan . . . . | (2,224,613) | | $6 |
| 2010P, Lincoln. . . . . . . | 49,000,000 | 3 | |
| 2010D, Lincoln . . . . . . | 48,020,000 | 3 | |
| 2010S, Lincoln . . . . . . | (2,224,613) | | 6 |

*Note:* Uncirculated Mint Sets for 2005–2010 were made with Satin Finish coins not included in the listings here. See page 369 for their mintages.

| | Mintage | MS-65 | PF-65 |
|---|---|---|---|
| 2011P, Johnson . . . . . . | 35,560,000 | $3 | |
| 2011D, Johnson . . . . . | 37,100,000 | 3 | |
| 2011S, Johnson. . . . . . | (1,972,863) | | $8 |
| 2011P, Grant . . . . . . . . | 38,080,000 | 3 | |
| 2011D, Grant. . . . . . . . | 37,940,000 | 3 | |
| 2011S, Grant. . . . . . . . | (1,972,863) | | 8 |

| | Mintage | MS-65 | PF-65 |
|---|---|---|---|
| 2011P, Hayes. . . . . . . . | 37,660,000 | $3 | |
| 2011D, Hayes . . . . . . . | 36,820,000 | 3 | |
| 2011S, Hayes . . . . . . . | (1,972,863) | | $8 |
| 2011P, Garfield . . . . . . | 37,100,000 | 3 | |
| 2011D, Garfield . . . . . . | 37,100,000 | 3 | |
| 2011S, Garfield . . . . . . | (1,972,863) | | 8 |

**Error coins with wrong or missing edge lettering are valued higher than normal coins.**

| | Mintage | MS-65 | PF-65 |
|---|---|---|---|
| 2012P, Arthur **(a)** | 6,020,000 | $3 | |
| 2012D, Arthur **(a)** | 4,060,000 | 3 | |
| 2012S, Arthur | (1,438,743) | | $17 |
| 2012P, Cleveland, Var 1 **(a)** | 5,460,000 | | |
| 2012D, Cleveland, Var 1 **(a)** | 4,060,000 | 3 | |
| 2012S, Cleveland, Var 1 | (1,438,743) | | 17 |

| | Mintage | MS-65 | PF-65 |
|---|---|---|---|
| 2012P, B. Harrison **(a)** | 5,640,000 | $3 | |
| 2012D, B. Harrison **(a)** | 4,200,000 | 3 | |
| 2012S, B. Harrison | (1,438,743) | | $17 |
| 2012P, Cleveland, Var 2 **(a)** | 10,680,000 | 3 | |
| 2012D, Cleveland, Var 2 **(a)** | 3,920,000 | 3 | |
| 2012S, Cleveland, Var 1 | (1,438,743) | | 17 |

**a.** Not issued for circulation.

| | Mintage | MS-65 | PF-65 |
|---|---|---|---|
| 2013P, McKinley **(a)** | 4,760,000 | $3 | |
| 2013D, McKinley **(a)** | 3,365,100 | 3 | |
| 2013S, McKinley | (1,488,798) | | $7 |
| 2013P, T. Roosevelt **(a)** | 5,310,700 | 3 | |
| 2013D, T. Roosevelt **(a)** | 3,920,000 | 3 | |
| 2013S, T. Roosevelt | (1,503,943) | | 7 |

| | Mintage | MS-65 | PF-65 |
|---|---|---|---|
| 2013P, Taft **(a)** | 4,760,000 | $3 | |
| 2013D, Taft **(a)** | 3,360,000 | 3 | |
| 2013S, Taft | (1,488,798) | | $7 |
| 2013P, Wilson **(a)** | 4,620,000 | 3 | |
| 2013D, Wilson **(a)** | 3,360,000 | 3 | |
| 2013S, Wilson | (1,488,798) | | 7 |

**a.** Not issued for circulation.

| | Mintage | MS-65 | PF-65 |
|---|---|---|---|
| 2014P, Harding **(a)** | 6,160,000 | $3 | |
| 2014D, Harding **(a)** | 3,780,000 | 3 | |
| 2014S, Harding | (1,373,569) | | $7 |
| 2014P, Coolidge **(a)** | 4,480,000 | 3 | |
| 2014D, Coolidge **(a)** | 3,780,000 | 3 | |
| 2014S, Coolidge | (1,373,569) | | 7 |

| | Mintage | MS-65 | PF-65 |
|---|---|---|---|
| 2014P, Hoover **(a)** | 4,480,000 | $3 | |
| 2014D, Hoover **(a)** | 3,780,000 | 3 | |
| 2014S, Hoover | (1,373,569) | | $7 |
| 2014P, F.D. Roosevelt **(a)** | 4,760,000 | 3 | |
| 2014D, F.D. Roosevelt **(a)** | 3,920,000 | 3 | |
| 2014S, F.D. Roosevelt | (1,392,619) | | 7 |

**a.** Not issued for circulation.

**Error coins with wrong or missing edge lettering are valued higher than normal coins.**

| | Mintage | MS-65 | PF-65 |
|---|---|---|---|
| 2015P, Truman **(a)** | 4,900,000 | $3 | |
| 2015P, Truman, RevPf | (16,812) | | $175 |
| 2015D, Truman **(a)** | 3,500,000 | 3 | |
| 2015S, Truman | *(662,854)* | | 6 |
| 2015P, Eisenhower **(a)** | 4,900,000 | 3 | |
| 2015P, Eisenhower, RevPf. | (16,744) | | 150 |
| 2015D, Eisenhower **(a)** | 3,645,998 | 3 | |
| 2015S, Eisenhower | *(662,854)* | | 6 |
| 2015P, Kennedy **(a)** | 6,160,000 | $3 | |
| 2015P, Kennedy, RevPf | (49,051) | | $80 |
| 2015D, Kennedy **(a)** | 5,180,000 | 3 | |
| 2015S, Kennedy | *(662,854)* | | 6 |
| 2015P, L.B. Johnson **(a)** | 7,840,000 | 3 | |
| 2015P, L.B. Johnson, RevPf | (23,905) | | 75 |
| 2015D, L.B. Johnson **(a)** | 4,200,000 | 3 | |
| 2015S, L.B. Johnson | *(662,854)* | | 6 |

**a.** Not issued for circulation.

| | Mintage | MS-65 | PF-65 |
|---|---|---|---|
| 2016P, Nixon **(a)** | 5,460,000 | $3 | |
| 2016D, Nixon **(a)** | 4,340,000 | 3 | |
| 2016S, Nixon | *(1,196,582)* | | $8 |
| 2016P, Ford **(a)** | 5,460,000 | 3 | |
| 2016D, Ford **(a)** | 5,040,000 | 3 | |
| 2016S, Ford | *(1,196,582)* | | 8 |
| 2016P, Reagan **(a)** | 7,140,000 | 3 | |
| 2016D, Reagan **(a)** | 5,880,000 | $3 | |
| 2016S, Reagan | *(1,196,582)* | | $6 |
| 2016S, Reagan, RevPf | *(47,447)* | | 60 |
| 2020P, G.H.W. Bush **(a)** | | 3 | |
| 2020D, G.H.W. Bush **(a)** | | 3 | |
| 2020S, G.H.W. Bush | | | 6 |

**a.** Not issued for circulation.

## NATIVE AMERICAN (2009 TO DATE)

Since 2009, the reverse of the golden dollar has featured an annually changing design that memorializes Native Americans and, in the words of the authorizing legislation, "the important contributions made by Indian tribes and individual Native Americans to the development [and history] of the United States."

The Native American $1 Coin Act also calls for edge marking. The year of minting and mintmark are incused on the edge, as is the inscription E PLURIBUS UNUM.

The coins' designs are chosen by the secretary of the Treasury after consultation with the Committee on Indian Affairs of the Senate, the Congressional Native American Caucus of the House of Representatives, the Commission of Fine Arts, and the National Congress of American Indians. They are also reviewed by the Citizens Coinage Advisory Committee.

The original act allowed for the minting of Uncirculated and Proof coins in each design. It also specified that at least 20% of the total mintage of dollar coins in any given year will be Native American dollars. Production of all dollar coins minted after 2011 is limited to numismatic sales; none will be issued for circulation.

*Designers: obv. Glenna Goodacre (date removed); rev. Norm Nemeth (2009), Thomas Cleveland (2010), Richard Masters (2011), Thomas Cleveland (2012), Susan Gamble (2013), Chris Costello (2014), Ronald Sanders (2015), Thomas D. Rogers Sr. (2016), Chris Costello (2017), Michael Gaudioso (2018), Emily Damstra (2019), Phebe Hemphill (2020); lettered edge; weight, composition, diameter, and mints identical to those for the Sacagawea dollar, plus West Point.*

Obverse

Three Sisters (2009)

Great Law of Peace (2010)

Wampanoag Treaty (2011)

Trade Routes in the 17th Century (2012)

Treaty With the Delawares (2013)

Native Hospitality (2014)

Mohawk Ironworkers (2015)

Code Talkers (2016)

Sequoyah (2017)

Jim Thorpe (2018)

American Indians in Space (2019)

Elizabeth Peratrovich and Alaska's Anti-Discrimination Law (2020)

| | Mintage | MS-65 | PF-65 |
|---|---|---|---|
| 2009P, Three Sisters | 39,200,000 | $5 | |
| 2009D, Three Sisters | 35,700,000 | 5 | |
| 2009S, Three Sisters | *(2,179,867)* | | $8 |
| 2010P, Great Law | 32,060,000 | 5 | |
| 2010D, Great Law | 48,720,000 | 5 | |
| 2010S, Great Law | (1,689,216) | | 8 |

| | Mintage | MS-65 | PF-65 |
|---|---|---|---|
| 2011P, Wampanoag Treaty | 29,400,000 | $5 | |
| 2011D, Wampanoag Treaty | 48,160,000 | 5 | |
| 2011S, Wampanoag Treaty | *(1,673,010)* | | $8 |
| 2012P, Trade Routes | 2,800,000 | 5 | |
| 2012D, Trade Routes | 3,080,000 | 5 | |
| 2012S, Trade Routes | (1,189,445) | | 15 |

*Note:* Uncirculated Mint Sets for 2005–2010 were made with Satin Finish coins not included in the listings here. See page 369 for their mintages.

| | Mintage | MS-65 | PF-65 |
|---|---|---|---|
| 2013P, Treaty, Delawares | 1,820,000 | $5 | |
| 2013D, Treaty, Delawares | 1,820,000 | 5 | |
| 2013S, Treaty, Delawares | (1,222,180) | | $8 |
| 2014P, Native Hospitality | 3,080,000 | 6 | |
| 2014D, Native Hospitality | 2,800,000 | 6 | |
| 2014D, Native Hospitality, Enhanced Unc. **(a)** | | 10 | |
| 2014S, Native Hospitality | (1,144,154) | | 8 |
| 2015P, Mohawk Ironworkers | 2,800,000 | 5 | |
| 2015D, Mohawk Ironworkers | 2,240,000 | 5 | |
| 2015S, Mohawk Ironworkers | *(1,050,164)* | | 8 |
| 2015W, Mohawk Ironworkers, Enhanced Unc. **(a)** | *(88,805)* | 20 | |
| 2016P, Code Talkers | 2,800,000 | 5 | |
| 2016D, Code Talkers | 2,100,000 | 5 | |
| 2016S, Code Talkers | *(965,033)* | | 8 |
| 2016S, Code Talkers, Enhanced Unc. **(a)** | *50,737* | 20 | |
| 2017P, Sequoyah | 1,820,000 | 5 | |
| 2017D, Sequoyah | 1,540,000 | 5 | |
| 2017S, Sequoyah **(b)** | (926,774) | | $8 |
| 2018P, Jim Thorpe | *1,400,000* | $5 | |
| 2018D, Jim Thorpe | *1,400,000* | 5 | |
| 2018S, Jim Thorpe | (799,413) | | 8 |
| 2019P, American Indians in Space | *1,400,000* | 5 | |
| 2019P, American Indians in Space. Enhanced Unc. **(a)** | | 20 | |
| 2019D, American Indians in Space | *1,400,000* | 5 | |
| 2019S, American Indians in Space | | | 8 |
| 2020P, Elizabeth Peratrovich and Alaska's Anti-Discrimination Law | | 5 | |
| 2020D, Elizabeth Peratrovich and Alaska's Anti-Discrimination Law | | 5 | |
| 2020S, Elizabeth Peratrovich and Alaska's Anti-Discrimination Law | | | 8 |
| 2020S, Elizabeth Peratrovich and Alaska's Anti-Discrimination Law, Enhanced Unc. **(a)** | | 20 | |

*Note:* Uncirculated Mint Sets for 2005–2010 were made with Satin Finish coins not included in the listings here. See page 369 for their mintages. **a.** Special Native American dollars with Enhanced Uncirculated finish were struck for inclusion in Native American $1 Coin and Currency sets (see pages 361 and 362). **b.** For its 225th anniversary, the Mint issued a special set of Enhanced Uncirculated coins from the San Francisco Mint; they are not included in the listings here.

## AMERICAN INNOVATION (2018 TO DATE)

In 2018, the U.S. Mint issued the first coin in a new, 15-year series: the American Innovation $1 Coin Program. Authorized by Public Law 115-197, each of the golden dollars in the program features a reverse design that "symbolizes quintessentially American traits—the willingness to explore, to discover, and to create one's own destiny." Four new designs, in Uncirculated and Proof finishes, are issued each year from 2019 through 2032—one for each state, in the order in which the states ratified the Constitution or were admitted to the Union, and then for the District of Columbia and each of the five U.S. territories (Puerto Rico, Guam, American Samoa, the U.S. Virgin Islands, and the Northern Mariana Islands). They are issued for numismatic sales only; none are distributed for circulation.

The reverse designs are selected by the same process the Mint has followed for other recent coin programs, including the America the Beautiful quarter-dollar series.

Coins in the series bear the following required inscriptions: on the obverse, IN GOD WE TRUST and the denomination; on the reverse, the name of the state, the District of Columbia, or territory (as appropriate), along with UNITED STATES OF AMERICA; and incused into the edge, the date, the mintmark, and the inscription E PLURIBUS UNUM. The common obverse depicts a left-facing profile of the Statue of Liberty, as designed by Justin Kunz and sculpted by Phebe Hemphill. Below the motto on coins from 2019 onward is a gear-like privy mark representing the series.

While each issue from 2019 through 2032 represents an individual state, district, or territory, the 2018 inaugural issue (designed by Donna Weaver and sculpted by Renata Gordon) represents the program in general. A pattern of gears and cogs represents American industry; below, a facsimile of George Washington's signature with SIGNED FIRST PATENT beneath it together represent the presidential signature on the first-ever U.S. patent, issued July 31, 1790. On a cartouche at the right, an eagle crouches on an angled shield, its wings spread behind it, with tools representing innovation (hammer, plow, wheel, etc.) below it.

*Designers: obv. Justin Kunz; rev. various; lettered edge; weight, composition, diameter, and mints identical to those for the Sacagawea dollar.*

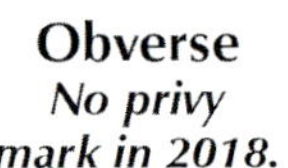

**Obverse**
***No privy mark in 2018.***

**American Innovators (2018)**

**Delaware: Classifying the Stars (2019)**

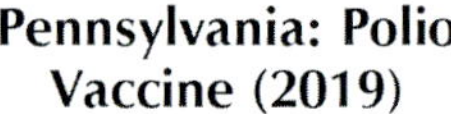

**Pennsylvania: Polio Vaccine (2019)**

**New Jersey: Light Bulb (2019)**

**Georgia: Trustees' Garden (2019)**

| | Mintage | MS-65 | PF-65 |
|---|---|---|---|
| 2018P, Innovators | *700,500* | $5 | |
| 2018D, Innovators | *680,525* | 5 | |
| 2018S, Innovators | *(206,886)* | | $8 |
| 2018S, Innovators, RevPf. | *(74,720)* | | |
| 2019P, Delaware | *346,850* | 5 | |
| 2019D, Delaware | *358,450* | 5 | |
| 2019S, Delaware | *(85,839)* | | 8 |
| 2019S, Delaware, RevPf | *(53,724)* | | |
| 2019P, Pennsylvania | *317,550* | 5 | |
| 2019D, Pennsylvania | *309,375* | 5 | |
| 2019S, Pennsylvania | *(85,839)* | | 8 |
| 2019S, Pennsylvania, RevPf | *(36,337)* | | |
| 2019P, New Jersey | *334,500* | 5 | |
| 2019D, New Jersey | *310,675* | 5 | |
| 2019S, New Jersey | *(85,839)* | | 8 |
| 2019S, New Jersey, RevPf | *(21,101)* | | |
| 2019P, Georgia | *399,900* | 5 | |
| 2019D, Georgia | *368,475* | 5 | |

| | Mintage | MS-65 | PF-65 |
|---|---|---|---|
| 2019S, Georgia | | | $8 |
| 2019S, Georgia, RevPf | | | |
| 2020P, Connecticut | | $5 | |
| 2020D, Connecticut | | 5 | |
| 2020S, Connecticut | | | 8 |
| 2020S, Connecticut, RevPf | | | |
| 2020P, Massachusetts | | 5 | |
| 2020D, Massachusetts | | 5 | |
| 2020S, Massachusetts | | | 8 |
| 2020S, Massachusetts, RevPf | | | |
| 2020P, Maryland | | 5 | |
| 2020D, Maryland | | 5 | |
| 2020S, Maryland | | | 8 |
| 2020S, Maryland, RevPf | | | |
| 2020P, South Carolina | | 5 | |
| 2020D, South Carolina | | 5 | |
| 2020S, South Carolina | | | 8 |
| 2020S, South Carolina, RevPf | | | |

Gold served as money or established the monetary value of currencies longer than any other material. The use of gold coins was widespread in Europe by 300 B.C. In what became the United States, the earliest coins circulated were foreign, mostly silver and gold, brought from Europe, as well as made in Spanish possessions in the New World. The Coinage Act in 1792 established an independent monetary system with the dollar as the basic U.S. monetary unit containing 24-3/4 grains of fine gold, based on the world price of $19.39 a troy ounce (480 grains). Congress changed the gold specification in 1834 and again in 1837, when it set the dollar price of gold at $20.67 an ounce.

In 1933, U.S. citizens were prohibited from holding monetary gold in the United States; this was extended in 1961 to gold held abroad as well. The dollar price was set at $35 per ounce in 1934. Use of gold in international trade was further restricted as the price rose. The government revalued it at $38 per ounce in 1972, then $42.22 in 1973. The price has fluctuated widely in recent years. All restrictions on holding gold were removed on December 31, 1974.

Coinage of the gold dollar was authorized by the Act of March 3, 1849. The weight was 25.8 grains, .900 fineness. The first type, struck until 1854, is known as the Liberty Head or small-sized type (Type 1). All those made after 1849 have the Close Wreath reverse.

In 1854, the dollar coins were made larger in diameter and thinner. The design was changed to a feather headdress on a female, generally referred to as the Indian Princess Head or large-sized type (Type 2). In 1856, the type was changed slightly by enlarging the size of the head (Type 3).

*Note: Values of common gold coins have been based on a gold bullion price of $1,500 per ounce, and may vary with the prevailing spot price. The net weight and content listed may be used to recalculate bullion value.*

## LIBERTY HEAD (1849–1854)

*Designer James B. Longacre; weight 1.672 grams; composition .900 gold, .100 copper (net weight .04837 oz. pure gold); diameter 13 mm; reeded edge; mints: Philadelphia, Charlotte, Dahlonega, New Orleans, San Francisco.*

**VF-20 Very Fine**—LIBERTY on headband complete and legible. Knobs on coronet defined.
**EF-40 Extremely Fine**—Slight wear on hair; knobs on coronet sharp.
**AU-50 About Uncirculated**—Trace of wear on headband. Nearly full luster.
**AU-55 Choice About Uncirculated**—Evidence of friction on design high points.
**MS-60 Uncirculated**—No trace of wear. Light marks and blemishes.
**MS-63 Choice Uncirculated**—Some distracting contact marks or blemishes in prime focal areas. Impaired luster possible.

**Liberty Head (Type 1)**
***Mintmark is below wreath.***

Obverse

Open Wreath Reverse

Close Wreath Reverse

| | Mintage | VF-20 | EF-40 | AU-50 | AU-55 | MS-60 | MS-63 |
|---|---|---|---|---|---|---|---|
| 1849, Open Wreath, No L | 688,567 | $225 | $275 | $300 | $325 | $800 | $1,600 |
| 1849, Open Wreath, With L **(a)** | * | 225 | 250 | 275 | 300 | 350 | 1,400 |
| 1849, Close Wreath (Ends Closer to Numeral) | * | 215 | 250 | 275 | 295 | 650 | 1,500 |
| 1849C, Close Wreath | 11,634 | 1,300 | 1,800 | 2,500 | 4,000 | 9,000 | 17,500 |
| 1849C, Open Wreath *(extremely rare)* | * | 200,000 | 225,000 | 250,000 | 300,000 | 450,000 | 650,000 |
| *$690,000, MS-63 PL, DLRC auction, July 2004* | | | | | | | |

* Included in number above. **a.** Liberty's head appears slightly smaller than normal on some variations.

*Chart continued on next page.*

| | Mintage | VF-20 | EF-40 | AU-50 | AU-55 | MS-60 | MS-63 |
|---|---|---|---|---|---|---|---|
| 1849D, Open Wreath | 21,588 | $1,500 | $2,100 | $2,600 | $2,900 | $5,500 | $13,000 |
| 1849O, Open Wreath | 215,000 | 265 | 325 | 400 | 485 | 1,000 | 3,500 |
| 1850 | 481,953 | 215 | 250 | 265 | 285 | 425 | 775 |
| 1850C | 6,966 | 1,600 | 2,000 | 3,000 | 4,000 | 6,750 | 23,500 |
| 1850D | 8,382 | 1,500 | 2,200 | 3,400 | 5,000 | 10,500 | 25,000 |
| 1850O | 14,000 | 300 | 500 | 900 | 1,150 | 3,150 | 6,000 |
| 1851 | 3,317,671 | 200 | 225 | 240 | 250 | 325 | 500 |
| 1851C | 41,267 | 1,350 | 1,650 | 2,000 | 2,250 | 3,200 | 6,250 |
| 1851D | 9,882 | 1,500 | 2,000 | 2,500 | 3,000 | 5,000 | 14,500 |
| 1851O | 290,000 | 225 | 265 | 325 | 425 | 750 | 1,900 |
| 1852 | 2,045,351 | 200 | 225 | 240 | 250 | 325 | 500 |
| 1852C | 9,434 | 1,400 | 1,850 | 2,250 | 2,750 | 4,600 | 10,500 |
| 1852D | 6,360 | 1,500 | 2,250 | 2,750 | 3,750 | 8,250 | 30,000 |
| 1852O | 140,000 | 225 | 265 | 400 | 600 | 1,300 | 4,200 |
| 1853 | 4,076,051 | 200 | 225 | 240 | 250 | 325 | 500 |
| 1853C | 11,515 | 1,350 | 1,600 | 2,100 | 2,600 | 4,750 | 13,000 |
| 1853D | 6,583 | 1,500 | 2,000 | 2,500 | 3,750 | 8,000 | 22,000 |
| 1853O | 290,000 | 225 | 255 | 335 | 425 | 700 | 1,800 |
| 1854 | 855,502 | 200 | 225 | 240 | 250 | 325 | 500 |
| 1854D | 2,935 | 2,000 | 2,500 | 5,250 | 6,500 | 11,000 | 35,000 |
| 1854S | 14,632 | 450 | 650 | 1,000 | 1,400 | 2,600 | 6,500 |

## INDIAN PRINCESS HEAD, SMALL HEAD (1854–1856)

*Standards same as for previous issue, except diameter changed to 15 mm.*

Indian Princess Head, Small Head (Type 2)

**VF-20 Very Fine**—Feather-curl tips on headdress outlined but details worn.
**EF-40 Extremely Fine**—Slight wear on tips of feather curls on headdress.
**AU-50 About Uncirculated**—Trace of wear on feathers, nearly full luster.
**AU-55 Choice About Uncirculated**—Evidence of friction on design high points. Most of original mint luster present.
**MS-60 Uncirculated**—No trace of wear. Light marks and blemishes.
**MS-63 Choice Uncirculated**—Some distracting contact marks or blemishes in prime focal areas. Impaired luster possible.
**PF-63 Choice Proof**—Reflective surfaces with only a few blemishes in secondary focal areas. No major flaws.

| | Mintage | VF-20 | EF-40 | AU-50 | AU-55 | MS-60 | MS-63 | PF-63 |
|---|---|---|---|---|---|---|---|---|
| 1854 | 783,943 | $325 | $425 | $500 | $625 | $1,250 | $5,000 | $200,000 |
| 1855 | 758,269 | 325 | 425 | 500 | 625 | 1,250 | 5,000 | 165,000 |
| *$373,750, PF-66 DC, Heritage auction, January 2008* | | | | | | | | |
| 1855C | 9,803 | 2,350 | 4,750 | 6,000 | 9,000 | 20,000 | | |
| 1855D | 1,811 | 12,500 | 25,000 | 35,000 | 40,000 | 60,000 | 100,000 | |
| 1855O | 55,000 | 775 | 1,300 | 1,750 | 2,750 | 8,000 | 30,000 | |
| 1856S | 24,600 | 850 | 1,500 | 2,250 | 3,500 | 7,500 | 25,000 | |

## INDIAN PRINCESS HEAD, LARGE HEAD (1856–1889)

Indian Princess Head, Large Head (Type 3)

**VF-20 Very Fine**—Slight detail in curled feathers in headdress. Details worn smooth at eyebrow, hair below headdress, and behind ear and bottom curl.
**EF-40 Extremely Fine**—Slight wear above and to right of eye and on top of curled feathers.
**AU-50 About Uncirculated**—Trace of wear on feathers, nearly full luster.
**AU-55 Choice About Uncirculated**—Evidence of friction on design high points. Most of original mint luster present.
**MS-60 Uncirculated**—No trace of wear. Light marks and blemishes.
**MS-63 Choice Uncirculated**—Some distracting contact marks or blemishes in prime focal areas. Impaired luster possible.
**PF-63 Choice Proof**—Reflective surfaces with few blemishes in secondary focal places. No major flaws.

| | Mintage | VF-20 | EF-40 | AU-50 | AU-55 | MS-60 | MS-63 | PF-63 |
|---|---|---|---|---|---|---|---|---|
| 1856, All kinds | 1,762,936 | | | | | | | |
| 1856, Upright 5 | | $275 | $300 | $375 | $450 | $650 | $1,500 | |
| 1856, Slant 5 | | 245 | 250 | 265 | 285 | 475 | 750 | $30,000 |
| 1856D | 1,460 | 5,000 | 8,000 | 9,500 | 12,000 | 27,500 | 80,000 | |
| 1857 | 774,789 | 245 | 250 | 265 | 285 | 475 | 750 | 20,000 |
| 1857C | 13,280 | 1,350 | 1,750 | 3,250 | 5,000 | 10,000 | | |
| 1857D | 3,533 | 1,500 | 2,400 | 3,750 | 5,000 | 10,500 | | |
| 1857S | 10,000 | 450 | 750 | 1,250 | 2,000 | 5,250 | 20,000 | |
| 1858 | 117,995 | 245 | 250 | 265 | 285 | 400 | 1,050 | 13,500 |
| 1858D | 3,477 | 1,500 | 2,250 | 3,250 | 4,250 | 7,750 | 21,500 | |
| 1858S | 10,000 | 425 | 750 | 1,200 | 1,600 | 5,250 | 15,000 | |
| 1859 (80) | 168,244 | 245 | 250 | 255 | 285 | 325 | 800 | 10,000 |
| 1859C | 5,235 | 2,000 | 3,250 | 4,000 | 5,000 | 7,000 | 25,000 | |
| 1859D | 4,952 | 1,600 | 2,250 | 3,250 | 5,000 | 8,750 | 21,500 | |
| 1859S | 15,000 | 300 | 575 | 1,250 | 1,900 | 4,750 | 14,500 | |
| 1860 (154) | 36,514 | 245 | 250 | 275 | 300 | 525 | 1,250 | 8,000 |
| 1860D | 1,566 | 3,750 | 6,500 | 10,000 | 12,000 | 20,000 | 50,000 | |
| 1860S | 13,000 | 350 | 500 | 775 | 1,100 | 2,650 | 6,000 | |
| 1861 (349) | 527,150 | 245 | 250 | 265 | 285 | 575 | 800 | 8,000 |
| 1861D **(a)** | *1,250* | 25,000 | 30,000 | 40,000 | 57,500 | 75,000 | 125,000 | |
| 1862 (35) | 1,361,355 | 245 | 250 | 265 | 285 | 485 | 750 | 8,000 |
| 1863 (50) | 6,200 | 1,600 | 2,300 | 3,750 | 4,750 | 6,750 | 12,000 | 10,000 |
| 1864 (50) | 5,900 | 650 | 850 | 1,250 | 1,300 | 1,500 | 3,750 | 10,000 |
| 1865 (25) | 3,700 | 750 | 1,000 | 1,100 | 1,350 | 2,000 | 4,750 | 10,000 |
| 1866 (30) | 7,100 | 450 | 600 | 750 | 825 | 1,250 | 2,500 | 10,000 |
| 1867 (50) | 5,200 | 450 | 625 | 750 | 850 | 1,200 | 2,250 | 10,000 |
| 1868 (25) | 10,500 | 450 | 600 | 700 | 800 | 1,000 | 2,000 | 10,000 |
| 1869 (25) | 5,900 | 450 | 600 | 700 | 800 | 1,150 | 2,000 | 10,000 |
| 1870 (35) | 6,300 | 450 | 600 | 700 | 800 | 1,000 | 2,000 | 10,000 |
| 1870S | 3,000 | 700 | 875 | 1,250 | 1,750 | 2,750 | 8,000 | |
| 1871 (30) | 3,900 | 350 | 450 | 575 | 675 | 900 | 1,600 | 10,000 |
| 1872 (30) | 3,500 | 350 | 425 | 575 | 700 | 1,000 | 2,250 | 10,000 |
| 1873, Close 3 (25) | 1,800 | 425 | 750 | 1,100 | 1,150 | 1,700 | 4,000 | 15,000 |
| 1873, Open 3 | 123,300 | 245 | 250 | 265 | 285 | 350 | 575 | |
| 1874 (20) | 198,800 | 245 | 250 | 265 | 285 | 350 | 525 | 12,000 |
| 1875 (20) | 400 | 3,500 | 5,000 | 6,000 | 6,500 | 10,000 | 16,000 | 18,500 |
| 1876 (45) | 3,200 | 325 | 375 | 500 | 600 | 750 | 1,350 | 7,000 |
| 1877 (20) | 3,900 | 300 | 375 | 525 | 600 | 800 | 1,400 | 8,000 |
| 1878 (20) | 3,000 | 300 | 350 | 400 | 500 | 775 | 1,500 | 7,500 |
| 1879 (30) | 3,000 | 265 | 300 | 325 | 350 | 650 | 1,150 | 6,500 |
| 1880 (36) | 1,600 | 265 | 300 | 325 | 350 | 575 | 900 | 5,500 |
| 1881 (87) | 7,620 | 250 | 285 | 325 | 350 | 575 | 900 | 5,000 |
| 1882 (125) | 5,000 | 250 | 285 | 325 | 350 | 575 | 900 | 5,000 |
| 1883 (207) | 10,800 | 250 | 285 | 325 | 350 | 575 | 900 | 5,000 |
| 1884 (1,006) | 5,230 | 250 | 285 | 325 | 350 | 575 | 900 | 5,000 |
| 1885 (1,105) | 11,156 | 250 | 285 | 325 | 350 | 575 | 900 | 5,000 |
| 1886 (1,016) | 5,000 | 250 | 285 | 325 | 350 | 575 | 900 | 5,000 |
| 1887 (1,043) | 7,500 | 250 | 285 | 300 | 315 | 575 | 900 | 5,000 |
| 1888 (1,079) | 15,501 | 250 | 285 | 300 | 315 | 575 | 650 | 5,000 |
| 1889 (1,779) | 28,950 | 250 | 265 | 275 | 285 | 575 | 650 | 5,000 |

**a.** All were struck under the auspices of the state of Georgia and the Confederate States of America after the Dahlonega Mint had been seized by Rebel troops.

Authorized by the Act of April 2, 1792, quarter eagles weighed 67.5 grains, .9167 fineness, until the weight was changed to 64.5 grains, .8992 fineness, by the Act of June 28, 1834. The Act of January 18, 1837, established fineness at .900. Most dates before 1834 are rare. The first issue was struck in 1796; most of these had no stars on the obverse. Proofs of some dates prior to 1855 are known to exist, and all are rare.

*Note: Values of common gold coins have been based on a gold bullion price of $1,500 per ounce, and may vary with the prevailing spot price. The net weight and content listed may be used to recalculate bullion value.*

## CAPPED BUST TO RIGHT (1796–1807)

*Designer Robert Scot; weight 4.37 grams; composition .9167 gold, .0833 silver and copper; approx. diameter 20 mm; reeded edge.*

**F-12 Fine**—Hair worn smooth on high spots. E PLURIBUS UNUM on ribbon weak but legible.
**VF-20 Very Fine**—Some wear on high spots.
**EF-40 Extremely Fine**—Only slight wear on Liberty's hair and cheek.
**AU-50 About Uncirculated**—Trace of wear on cap, hair, cheek, and drapery.
**AU-55 Choice About Uncirculated**—Evidence of friction on design high points. Some original mint luster present.
**MS-60 Uncirculated**—No trace of wear. Light blemishes.

**No Stars on Obverse (1796)** **Stars on Obverse (1796–1807)**

| | Mintage | F-12 | VF-20 | EF-40 | AU-50 | AU-55 | MS-60 |
|---|---|---|---|---|---|---|---|
| 1796, No Stars on Obverse | 963 | $60,000 | $77,500 | $95,000 | $130,000 | $150,000 | $250,000 |
| *$1,725,000, MS-65, Heritage auction, January 2008* | | | | | | | |
| 1796, Stars on Obverse | 432 | 52,500 | 65,000 | 87,500 | 100,000 | 135,000 | 200,000 |
| *$1,006,250, MS-65, Heritage auction, January 2008* | | | | | | | |
| 1797 | 427 | 13,500 | 20,000 | 35,000 | 60,000 | 115,000 | 185,000 |
| 1798 | 1,094 | 5,000 | 10,000 | 15,500 | 27,500 | 35,000 | 65,000 |
| *$763,750, MS-65, Sotheby's / Stack's Bowers auction, May 2015* | | | | | | | |
| 1802 | 3,035 | 5,000 | 7,250 | 12,500 | 17,500 | 20,000 | 30,000 |
| 1804, 13-Star Reverse | * | 65,000 | 95,000 | 150,000 | 200,000 | 350,000 | |
| 1804, 14-Star Reverse | 3,327 | 6,750 | 9,000 | 14,000 | 17,000 | 20,000 | 32,500 |
| 1805 | 1,781 | 5,000 | 8,000 | 13,000 | 16,500 | 19,000 | 35,000 |
| 1806, 6 Over 4, 8 Stars Left, 5 Right | 1,136 | 5,000 | 8,250 | 14,000 | 18,000 | 22,500 | 35,000 |
| 1806, 6 Over 5, 7 Stars Left, 6 Right | 480 | 8,500 | 11,500 | 25,000 | 35,000 | 50,000 | 85,000 |
| 1807 | 6,812 | 5,000 | 7,500 | 12,000 | 16,500 | 22,500 | 31,500 |
| *$587,500, MS-65, Sotheby's / Stack's Bowers auction, May 2015* | | | | | | | |

* Included in number below.

## DRAPED BUST TO LEFT, LARGE SIZE (1808)

*Designer John Reich; standards same as for previous issue.*

**F-12 Fine**—E PLURIBUS UNUM on reverse, and LIBERTY on headband, legible but weak.
**VF-20 Very Fine**—Motto and LIBERTY clear.
**EF-40 Extremely Fine**—All details of hair plain.
**AU-50 About Uncirculated**—Trace of wear above eye, on top of cap, and on cheek, and hair.
**AU-55 Choice About Uncirculated**—Evidence of friction on design high points. Some original mint luster present.
**MS-60 Uncirculated**—No trace of wear. Light blemishes.

| | Mintage | F-12 | VF-20 | EF-40 | AU-50 | AU-55 | MS-60 |
|---|---|---|---|---|---|---|---|
| 1808 | 2,710 | $27,500 | $40,000 | $67,500 | $90,000 | $105,000 | $175,000 |
| *$2,350,000, MS-65, Sotheby's / Stack's Bowers auction, May 2015* | | | | | | | |

## CAPPED HEAD TO LEFT (1821–1834)

### Large Diameter (1821–1827)

*Standards same as for previous issue, except diameter changed to approximately 18.5 mm in 1821.*

| | Mintage | F-12 | VF-20 | EF-40 | AU-50 | AU-55 | MS-60 |
|---|---|---|---|---|---|---|---|
| 1821 | 6,448 | $6,250 | $9,000 | $14,500 | $16,000 | $17,500 | $35,000 |
| 1824, 4 Over 1 | 2,600 | 6,250 | 9,500 | 14,000 | 16,500 | 18,750 | 32,500 |
| 1825 | 4,434 | 6,250 | 7,750 | 14,000 | 16,500 | 17,500 | 30,000 |
| 1826, 6 Over 6 | 760 | 10,000 | 12,500 | 16,500 | 25,000 | 35,000 | 62,500 |
| 1827 | 2,800 | 6,500 | 9,000 | 13,100 | 17,500 | 19,500 | 35,000 |

### Reduced Diameter (1829–1834)

Quarter eagles dated 1829 through 1834 are smaller in diameter (18.2 mm) than the 1821 through 1827 pieces. They also have smaller letters, dates, and stars.

| | Mintage | F-12 | VF-20 | EF-40 | AU-50 | AU-55 | MS-60 |
|---|---|---|---|---|---|---|---|
| 1829 | 3,403 | $6,000 | $7,250 | $9,500 | $13,000 | $17,000 | $22,500 |
| 1830 | 4,540 | 6,000 | 7,250 | 9,500 | 13,000 | 17,000 | 22,500 |
| 1831 | 4,520 | 6,000 | 7,250 | 9,500 | 13,000 | 17,000 | 22,500 |
| 1832 | 4,400 | 6,000 | 7,250 | 9,500 | 13,000 | 17,000 | 22,500 |
| 1833 | 4,160 | 6,000 | 7,250 | 9,500 | 13,000 | 17,000 | 22,500 |
| 1834, With Motto | 4,000 | 22,500 | 27,500 | 55,000 | 90,000 | 135,000 | 200,000 |

## CLASSIC HEAD, NO MOTTO ON REVERSE (1834–1839)

In 1834, a ribbon binding Liberty's hair, bearing the word LIBERTY, replaced the liberty cap. The motto was omitted from the reverse. In 1840 a coronet and smaller head were designed to conform with the appearance of the larger gold coins.

*Designer William Kneass; weight 4.18 grams; composition .8992 gold, .1008 silver and copper (changed to .900 gold in 1837); diameter 18.2 mm; reeded edge; mints: Philadelphia, Charlotte, Dahlonega, New Orleans.*

**F-12 Fine**—LIBERTY on headband legible and complete. Curl under ear outlined but no detail.
**VF-20 Very Fine**—LIBERTY plain; detail in hair curl.
**EF-40 Extremely Fine**—Small amount of wear on top of hair and below L in LIBERTY. Wear evident on wing.
**AU-50 About Uncirculated**—Trace of wear on coronet and hair above ear.
**AU-55 Choice About Uncirculated**—Evidence of friction on design high points. Some of original mint luster present.
**MS-60 Uncirculated**—No trace of wear. Light blemishes.
**MS-63 Choice Uncirculated**—Some distracting contact marks or blemishes in prime focal areas. Impaired luster possible.

Mintmark Location

| | Mintage | F-12 | VF-20 | EF-40 | AU-50 | AU-55 | MS-60 | MS-63 |
|---|---|---|---|---|---|---|---|---|
| 1834, No Motto | 112,234 | $365 | $600 | $800 | $1,250 | $1,650 | $3,250 | $9,500 |
| 1835 | 131,402 | 365 | 600 | 800 | 1,250 | 1,650 | 3,250 | 10,000 |
| 1836, All kinds | 547,986 | | | | | | | |
| 1836, Script 8 | | 365 | 600 | 800 | 1,250 | 1,650 | 3,250 | 9,500 |
| 1836, Block 8 | | 365 | 600 | 800 | 1,250 | 1,650 | 3,250 | 9,500 |
| 1837 | 45,080 | 450 | 750 | 1,200 | 1,750 | 2,000 | 4,500 | 13,500 |
| 1838 | 47,030 | 385 | 625 | 1,000 | 1,500 | 1,750 | 4,250 | 11,500 |
| 1838C | 7,880 | 2,500 | 4,500 | 7,500 | 10,000 | 12,500 | 26,500 | 50,000 |
| 1839 | 27,021 | 650 | 1,000 | 1,650 | 3,000 | 4,000 | 9,500 | 35,000 |
| 1839C | 18,140 | 1,750 | 3,500 | 5,500 | 9,000 | 10,000 | 25,000 | 65,000 |
| 1839D | 13,674 | 2,500 | 4,500 | 6,750 | 9,000 | 14,000 | 30,000 | 55,000 |
| 1839O | 17,781 | 1,000 | 1,650 | 3,000 | 4,250 | 7,000 | 10,000 | 30,000 |

*Note:* So-called 9 Over 8 varieties for P, C, and D mints are made from defective punches.

## LIBERTY HEAD (1840–1907)

*Designer Christian Gobrecht; weight 4.18 grams; composition .900 gold, .100 copper (net weight .12094 oz. pure gold); diameter 18 mm; reeded edge; mints: Philadelphia, Charlotte, Dahlonega, New Orleans, San Francisco.*

See previous type for grading standards.

Mintmark Location

| | Mintage | VF-20 | EF-40 | AU-50 | AU-55 | MS-60 | MS-63 |
|---|---|---|---|---|---|---|---|
| 1840 | 18,859 | $850 | $1,350 | $2,400 | $3,250 | $6,500 | $15,000 |
| 1840C | 12,822 | 1,750 | 3,250 | 4,250 | 5,750 | 10,000 | 30,000 |
| 1840D | 3,532 | 3,250 | 8,500 | 11,000 | 18,000 | 35,000 | |
| 1840O | 33,580 | 500 | 1,250 | 2,100 | 3,250 | 9,000 | 28,000 |
| 1841 **(a)** | *(unknown)* | 75,000 | 125,000 | 150,000 | 160,000 | 225,000 | |
| 1841C | 10,281 | 1,500 | 2,350 | 4,750 | 6,000 | 15,000 | |
| 1841D | 4,164 | 2,500 | 4,750 | 9,000 | 12,000 | 26,500 | 55,000 |
| 1842 | 2,823 | 1,250 | 3,250 | 6,250 | 8,000 | 17,500 | |
| 1842C | 6,729 | 2,000 | 3,250 | 6,750 | 9,250 | 22,500 | |

**a.** Values are for circulated Proofs; recent research suggests circulation strikes were produced.

| | Mintage | VF-20 | EF-40 | AU-50 | AU-55 | MS-60 | MS-63 |
|---|---|---|---|---|---|---|---|
| 1842D | 4,643 | $2,500 | $5,500 | $8,500 | $11,000 | $30,000 | |
| 1842O | 19,800 | 525 | 1,350 | 2,250 | 4,000 | 8,500 | $30,000 |
| 1843, Large Date | 100,546 | 350 | 450 | 700 | 900 | 2,500 | 6,500 |
| 1843C, Small Date, Crosslet 4 | 2,988 | 2,500 | 5,250 | 7,500 | 10,000 | 22,500 | |
| 1843C, Large Date, Plain 4 | 23,076 | 1,500 | 2,000 | 3,000 | 4,250 | 8,000 | 21,000 |
| 1843D, Small Date, Crosslet 4 | 36,209 | 2,000 | 2,250 | 3,250 | 4,500 | 6,500 | 30,000 |
| 1843O, Small Date, Crosslet 4 | 288,002 | 350 | 375 | 475 | 750 | 1,750 | 7,000 |
| 1843O, Large Date, Plain 4 | 76,000 | 400 | 600 | 1,750 | 2,750 | 6,250 | 25,000 |
| 1844 | 6,784 | 450 | 800 | 2,000 | 3,000 | 8,500 | 22,500 |
| 1844C | 11,622 | 1,500 | 2,500 | 5,500 | 6,500 | 15,000 | 40,000 |
| 1844D | 17,332 | 1,650 | 2,500 | 3,250 | 4,250 | 7,000 | 25,000 |
| 1845 | 91,051 | 375 | 400 | 500 | 600 | 1,250 | 4,750 |
| 1845D | 19,460 | 1,650 | 2,350 | 3,250 | 4,250 | 10,000 | 40,000 |
| 1845O | 4,000 | 1,250 | 2,500 | 6,500 | 8,750 | 22,500 | 50,000 |
| 1846 | 21,598 | 360 | 550 | 900 | 1,100 | 5,000 | 20,000 |
| 1846C | 4,808 | 1,700 | 3,000 | 6,000 | 8,500 | 16,000 | 35,000 |
| 1846D | 19,303 | 1,750 | 2,750 | 3,500 | 4,650 | 9,500 | 28,500 |
| 1846O | 62,000 | 400 | 525 | 1,100 | 1,900 | 5,500 | 18,500 |
| 1847 | 29,814 | 375 | 450 | 850 | 1,200 | 3,000 | 8,500 |
| 1847C | 23,226 | 1,500 | 2,250 | 3,000 | 3,500 | 5,750 | 15,000 |
| 1847D | 15,784 | 1,650 | 2,500 | 3,250 | 4,500 | 8,750 | 24,000 |
| 1847O | 124,000 | 375 | 425 | 1,000 | 1,650 | 4,000 | 16,000 |

## CAL. Gold Quarter Eagle (1848)

In 1848, about 230 ounces of gold were sent to Secretary of War Marcy by Colonel R.B. Mason, military governor of California. The gold was turned over to the Mint and made into quarter eagles. The distinguishing mark CAL. was punched above the eagle on the reverse side, while the coins were in the die. Several specimens with prooflike surfaces are known.

CAL. Above Eagle on Reverse (1848)

| | Mintage | VF-20 | EF-40 | AU-50 | AU-55 | MS-60 | MS-63 |
|---|---|---|---|---|---|---|---|
| 1848 | 6,500 | $550 | $950 | $2,250 | $3,250 | $5,500 | $15,000 |
| 1848, CAL. Above Eagle | 1,389 | 37,500 | 45,000 | 55,000 | 65,000 | 90,000 | 150,000 |
| *$402,500, MS-68★, Heritage auction, January 2006* | | | | | | | |
| 1848C | 16,788 | 1,500 | 2,500 | 3,500 | 4,500 | 11,500 | 32,500 |
| 1848D | 13,771 | 1,650 | 2,650 | 3,750 | 4,250 | 8,000 | 28,000 |
| 1849 | 23,294 | 450 | 700 | 950 | 1,250 | 2,750 | 7,500 |
| 1849C | 10,220 | 1,650 | 2,500 | 5,000 | 7,500 | 15,000 | |
| 1849D | 10,945 | 2,000 | 2,750 | 3,750 | 5,500 | 14,000 | — |
| 1850 | 252,923 | 360 | 375 | 400 | 500 | 1,000 | 3,500 |
| 1850C | 9,148 | 1,500 | 2,500 | 3,500 | 5,000 | 12,500 | 35,000 |
| 1850D | 12,148 | 1,600 | 2,750 | 3,750 | 5,500 | 12,500 | 45,000 |
| 1850O | 84,000 | 350 | 550 | 1,250 | 1,500 | 4,000 | 16,500 |
| 1851 | 1,372,748 | 325 | 350 | 375 | 400 | 550 | 1,100 |
| 1851C | 14,923 | 1,500 | 2,450 | 3,750 | 5,000 | 8,500 | 35,000 |
| 1851D | 11,264 | 1,650 | 2,500 | 4,000 | 5,500 | 10,500 | 32,500 |
| 1851O | 148,000 | 400 | 450 | 800 | 1,500 | 4,500 | 11,500 |
| 1852 | 1,159,681 | 325 | 350 | 375 | 400 | 550 | 1,100 |
| 1852C | 9,772 | 1,500 | 2,500 | 4,000 | 5,750 | 11,000 | 32,500 |
| 1852D | 4,078 | 1,850 | 3,250 | 6,000 | 8,000 | 15,750 | 42,500 |
| 1852O | 140,000 | 400 | 450 | 950 | 1,300 | 4,750 | 11,000 |

*Chart continued on next page.*

| | Mintage | VF-20 | EF-40 | AU-50 | AU-55 | MS-60 | MS-63 | PF-63 |
|---|---|---|---|---|---|---|---|---|
| 1853 | 1,404,668 | $300 | $325 | $350 | $365 | $475 | $1,000 | |
| 1853D | 3,178 | 2,000 | 3,500 | 5,000 | 6,000 | 15,000 | 50,000 | |
| 1854 | 596,258 | 300 | 325 | 350 | 365 | 550 | 1,250 | |
| 1854C | 7,295 | 1,850 | 2,850 | 5,000 | 6,500 | 10,000 | 37,500 | |
| 1854D | 1,760 | 3,500 | 7,500 | 10,000 | 12,500 | 27,500 | 80,000 | |
| 1854O | 153,000 | 385 | 425 | 575 | 800 | 1,500 | 9,000 | |
| 1854S | 246 | 200,000 | 300,000 | 450,000 | | | | |
| *$345,000, EF-45, Heritage auction, February 2007* | | | | | | | | |
| 1855 | 235,480 | 300 | 325 | 350 | 365 | 550 | 1,600 | |
| 1855C | 3,677 | 2,250 | 4,250 | 6,000 | 8,500 | 20,000 | 42,500 | |
| 1855D | 1,123 | 4,500 | 8,000 | 13,500 | 20,000 | 50,000 | | |
| 1856 | 384,240 | 300 | 325 | 350 | 365 | 450 | 1,250 | $55,000 |
| 1856C | 7,913 | 1,650 | 2,750 | 4,000 | 6,000 | 11,500 | 25,000 | |
| 1856D | 874 | 10,000 | 15,000 | 30,000 | 37,500 | 75,000 | | |
| 1856O | 21,100 | 385 | 800 | 1,650 | 2,250 | 8,250 | | |
| 1856S | 72,120 | 385 | 450 | 850 | 1,250 | 5,000 | 12,000 | |
| 1857 | 214,130 | 300 | 325 | 350 | 365 | 450 | 1,250 | 57,500 |
| 1857D | 2,364 | 1,750 | 2,800 | 4,000 | 5,500 | 12,000 | | |
| 1857O | 34,000 | 385 | 400 | 1,250 | 1,700 | 4,250 | 14,000 | |
| 1857S | 69,200 | 385 | 475 | 1,200 | 2,000 | 5,500 | 13,500 | |
| 1858 | 47,377 | 375 | 390 | 450 | 500 | 1,100 | 3,000 | 45,000 |
| 1858C | 9,056 | 1,500 | 2,250 | 3,500 | 4,250 | 8,000 | 25,000 | |

A modified reverse design (with smaller letters and arrowheads) was used on Philadelphia quarter eagles from 1859 through 1907, and on San Francisco issues of 1877 through 1879. A few Philadelphia Mint pieces were made in 1859, 1860, and 1861 with the old Large Letters reverse design.

Old Reverse

New Reverse

| | Mintage | VF-20 | EF-40 | AU-50 | AU-55 | MS-60 | MS-63 | PF-63 |
|---|---|---|---|---|---|---|---|---|
| 1859, Old Reverse | (80) . . . 39,364 | $375 | $550 | $850 | $1,000 | $2,000 | $6,000 | $30,000 |
| 1859, New Reverse | *(1 known)* . . . * | 360 | 370 | 500 | 650 | 1,200 | 3,000 | — |
| 1859D | 2,244 | 2,200 | 3,250 | 4,250 | 5,750 | 17,500 | | |
| 1859S | 15,200 | 475 | 1,000 | 2,000 | 2,750 | 5,500 | 17,500 | |
| 1860, Old Reverse | 22,563 | 1,250 | 2,000 | 2,750 | 4,000 | 5,000 | 10,000 | |
| 1860, New Reverse | (112) . . . * | 350 | 370 | 500 | 600 | 1,100 | 3,000 | 22,500 |
| 1860C | 7,469 | 1,850 | 2,500 | 3,250 | 6,000 | 12,000 | | |
| 1860S | 35,600 | 425 | 675 | 1,250 | 1,750 | 3,750 | 20,000 | |
| 1861, Old Reverse | (90) 1,283,788 | 525 | 1,000 | 1,500 | 1,850 | 3,750 | 10,000 | 20,000 |
| 1861, New Reverse | * | 300 | 325 | 350 | 365 | 700 | 1,750 | |
| 1861S | 24,000 | 500 | 900 | 3,250 | 4,500 | 9,000 | | |
| 1862, 2 Over 1 | ** | 1,000 | 1,850 | 3,000 | 4,750 | 8,500 | 32,500 | |
| 1862 | (35) . . . 98,508 | 400 | 600 | 1,350 | 2,250 | 4,750 | 11,000 | 20,000 |
| 1862S | 8,000 | 1,650 | 2,250 | 4,250 | 6,000 | 16,000 | | |
| 1863, Proof only | (30) | | | | | | | 75,000 |
| 1863S | 10,800 | 700 | 2,000 | 4,500 | 6,500 | 15,000 | | |
| 1864 | (50) . . . 2,774 | 8,500 | 20,000 | 40,000 | 60,000 | 100,000 | | 25,000 |
| 1865 | (25) . . . 1,520 | 4,500 | 10,000 | 20,000 | 27,500 | 40,000 | 60,000 | 20,000 |
| 1865S | 23,376 | 750 | 1,300 | 2,000 | 2,500 | 4,500 | 15,000 | |
| 1866 | (30) . . . 3,080 | 1,150 | 3,000 | 5,250 | 7,500 | 12,500 | 25,000 | 17,500 |
| 1866S | 38,960 | 450 | 750 | 1,500 | 2,250 | 6,500 | 22,500 | |
| 1867 | (50) . . . 3,200 | 350 | 750 | 1,350 | 3,000 | 8,000 | 23,000 | 16,000 |

* Included in number above. ** Included in number below.

| | Mintage | VF-20 | EF-40 | AU-50 | AU-55 | MS-60 | MS-63 | PF-63 |
|---|---|---|---|---|---|---|---|---|
| 1867S | 28,000 | $350 | $650 | $1,250 | $1,600 | $4,000 | $12,000 | |
| 1868 | (25)... 3,600 | 375 | 450 | 700 | 850 | 2,250 | 8,000 | $16,500 |
| 1868S | 34,000 | 350 | 425 | 700 | 1,000 | 3,000 | 8,500 | |
| 1869 | (25)... 4,320 | 375 | 450 | 800 | 1,150 | 3,000 | 10,000 | 15,000 |
| 1869S | 29,500 | 325 | 475 | 700 | 1,350 | 3,500 | 9,250 | |
| 1870 | (35)... 4,520 | 325 | 400 | 750 | 1,250 | 3,250 | 8,000 | 15,000 |
| 1870S | 16,000 | 325 | 400 | 900 | 1,500 | 4,000 | 12,500 | |
| 1871 | (30)... 5,320 | 325 | 400 | 750 | 1,000 | 2,000 | 4,000 | 15,000 |
| 1871S | 22,000 | 325 | 400 | 550 | 1,000 | 2,000 | 4,350 | |
| 1872 | (30)... 3,000 | 400 | 700 | 1,100 | 2,000 | 4,350 | 15,000 | 15,000 |
| 1872S | 18,000 | 325 | 400 | 950 | 1,250 | 4,000 | 10,500 | |
| 1873, Close 3 | (25)... 55,200 | 325 | 375 | 400 | 425 | 500 | 1,250 | 15,000 |
| 1873, Open 3 | 122,800 | 300 | 350 | 375 | 385 | 500 | 825 | |
| 1873S | 27,000 | 325 | 400 | 975 | 1,000 | 2,000 | 6,500 | |
| 1874 | (20)... 3,920 | 325 | 375 | 650 | 1,050 | 2,000 | 6,000 | 17,500 |
| 1875 | (20)... 400 | 5,500 | 7,500 | 12,500 | 15,000 | 27,500 | | 50,000 |
| 1875S | 11,600 | 325 | 375 | 650 | 1,100 | 3,500 | 7,250 | |
| 1876 | (45)... 4,176 | 350 | 600 | 950 | 1,750 | 3,250 | 7,500 | 15,000 |
| 1876S | 5,000 | 325 | 525 | 950 | 1,350 | 3,000 | 8,500 | |
| 1877 | (20)... 1,632 | 400 | 750 | 1,000 | 1,500 | 3,000 | 9,500 | 15,000 |
| 1877S | 35,400 | 325 | 350 | 375 | 400 | 650 | 2,350 | |
| 1878 | (20)... 286,240 | 300 | 325 | 350 | 375 | 450 | 700 | 15,000 |
| 1878S | 178,000 | 300 | 365 | 375 | 385 | 500 | 1,500 | |
| 1879 | (30)... 88,960 | 300 | 365 | 375 | 425 | 525 | 800 | 13,000 |
| 1879S | 43,500 | 300 | 365 | 550 | 850 | 1,750 | 4,500 | |
| 1880 | (36)... 2,960 | 375 | 425 | 650 | 800 | 1,500 | 3,750 | 12,500 |
| 1881 | (51)... 640 | 2,000 | 3,000 | 5,000 | 6,000 | 10,000 | 20,000 | 13,500 |
| 1882 | (67)... 4,000 | 375 | 425 | 550 | 700 | 1,250 | 2,750 | 9,500 |
| 1883 | (82)... 1,920 | 1,000 | 1,750 | 2,750 | 4,500 | 6,000 | 12,500 | 9,500 |
| 1884 | (73)... 1,950 | 375 | 500 | 800 | 1,000 | 2,000 | 3,500 | 9,500 |
| 1885 | (87)... 800 | 950 | 2,000 | 2,750 | 3,250 | 5,500 | 10,000 | 9,000 |
| 1886 | (88)... 4,000 | 375 | 400 | 550 | 600 | 1,250 | 3,500 | 9,500 |
| 1887 | (122)... 6,160 | 375 | 400 | 450 | 500 | 800 | 1,500 | 9,500 |
| 1888 | (97)... 16,001 | 325 | 365 | 375 | 385 | 450 | 900 | 8,500 |
| 1889 | (48)... 17,600 | 325 | 365 | 375 | 385 | 450 | 950 | 8,500 |
| 1890 | (93)... 8,720 | 325 | 375 | 385 | 400 | 650 | 1,500 | 8,500 |
| 1891 | (80)... 10,960 | 350 | 385 | 400 | 425 | 550 | 1,450 | 8,000 |
| 1892 | (105)... 2,440 | 350 | 400 | 475 | 525 | 900 | 2,250 | 8,000 |
| 1893 | (106)... 30,000 | 325 | 350 | 375 | 385 | 550 | 1,250 | 7,500 |
| 1894 | (122)... 4,000 | 360 | 365 | 375 | 475 | 750 | 1,350 | 7,500 |
| 1895 | (119)... 6,000 | 360 | 365 | 375 | 385 | 575 | 1,100 | 7,500 |
| 1896 | (132)... 19,070 | 300 | 325 | 375 | 385 | 500 | 800 | 7,500 |
| 1897 | (136)... 29,768 | 300 | 325 | 375 | 385 | 500 | 700 | 7,500 |
| 1898 | (165)... 24,000 | 300 | 315 | 325 | 350 | 475 | 675 | 7,500 |
| 1899 | (150)... 27,200 | 295 | 300 | 325 | 350 | 425 | 575 | 7,500 |
| 1900 | (205)... 67,000 | 295 | 300 | 305 | 325 | 400 | 475 | 7,500 |
| 1901 | (223)... 91,100 | 295 | 300 | 305 | 325 | 400 | 475 | 7,500 |
| 1902 | (193)... 133,540 | 295 | 300 | 305 | 325 | 400 | 475 | 7,500 |
| 1903 | (197)... 201,060 | 295 | 300 | 305 | 325 | 400 | 475 | 7,500 |
| 1904 | (170)... 160,790 | 295 | 300 | 305 | 325 | 400 | 475 | 7,500 |
| 1905 **(a)** | (144)... 217,800 | 295 | 300 | 305 | 325 | 400 | 475 | 7,500 |
| 1906 | (160)... 176,330 | 295 | 300 | 305 | 325 | 400 | 475 | 7,500 |
| 1907 | (154)... 336,294 | 295 | 300 | 305 | 325 | 400 | 475 | 7,500 |

**a.** Pieces dated 1905-S are counterfeit.

## INDIAN HEAD (1908–1929)

This new type represents a departure from all precedents in United States coinage. Its design features no raised edge, and the main devices and legends are in sunken relief below the surface of the coin.

Boston sculptor Bela Lyon Pratt was the designer of this and the similar half eagle piece. A pupil of the famous Augustus Saint-Gaudens, Pratt based his "standing eagle" motif on the reverse of his teacher's gold ten-dollar coin of 1907. (That eagle was itself derived from the reverse of Theodore Roosevelt's 1905 unofficial inaugural medal, designed by Saint-Gaudens and engraved by Adolph A. Weinman, who would later create the Liberty Walking half dollar. The general style had antecedents in coins of the ancient world.)

Among the public, there was some concern that the recessed design of Pratt's quarter eagle would collect germs—an unfounded fear. The artistry of the design was condemned loudly by some numismatists. Few people were interested in saving the coin for their collections. The result is a series with relatively few examples surviving in higher grades. Any initial disfavor has mellowed with time; today Pratt's design is recognized as part of the early 20th-century renaissance of American coinage.

*Designer Bela Lyon Pratt; weight 4.18 grams; composition .900 gold, .100 copper (net weight .12094 oz. pure gold); diameter 18 mm; reeded edge; mints: Philadelphia, Denver.*

**VF-20 Very Fine**—Hair-cord knot distinct. Feathers at top of head clear. Cheekbone worn.
**EF-40 Extremely Fine**—Cheekbone, war bonnet, and headband feathers slightly worn.
**AU-50 About Uncirculated**—Trace of wear on cheekbone and headdress.
**MS-60 Uncirculated**—No trace of wear. Light blemishes.
**MS-63 Choice Uncirculated**—Some distracting contact marks or blemishes in prime focal areas. Impaired luster possible.
**MS-64 Uncirculated**—A few scattered contact marks visible. Good eye appeal and attractive luster.
**MATTE PF-63 Choice Matte Proof**—Few blemishes in secondary focal areas. No major flaws.

***Mintmark location is on reverse, to left of arrows.***

| | Mintage | VF-20 | EF-40 | AU-50 | MS-60 | MS-63 | MS-64 | MATTE PF-63 |
|---|---|---|---|---|---|---|---|---|
| 1908 | (236). . 564,821 | $300 | $325 | $350 | $400 | $700 | $1,100 | $10,250 |
| 1909 | (139). . 441,760 | 300 | 325 | 350 | 385 | 1,050 | 1,600 | |
| 1910 | (682). . 492,000 | 300 | 325 | 350 | 385 | 800 | 1,150 | |
| 1911 | (191). . 704,000 | 300 | 325 | 350 | 385 | 625 | 1,000 | 11,000 |
| 1911D **(a)** | 55,680 | 2,600 | 3,300 | 4,100 | 7,000 | 11,000 | 17,500 | |
| 1912 | (197). . 616,000 | 325 | 350 | 375 | 400 | 1,150 | 1,950 | 11,000 |
| 1913 | (165). . 722,000 | 325 | 350 | 375 | 400 | 575 | 950 | 11,500 |
| 1914 | (117). . 240,000 | 350 | 375 | 450 | 550 | 1,850 | 4,000 | 11,750 |
| 1914D | 448,000 | 325 | 350 | 375 | 450 | 900 | 2,000 | |
| 1915 | (100). . 606,000 | 300 | 325 | 350 | 400 | 600 | 1,250 | 12,000 |
| 1925D | 578,000 | 300 | 325 | 350 | 400 | 475 | 675 | |
| 1926 | 446,000 | 300 | 325 | 350 | 400 | 475 | 675 | |
| 1927 | 388,000 | 300 | 325 | 350 | 400 | 475 | 675 | |
| 1928 | 416,000 | 300 | 325 | 350 | 400 | 475 | 675 | |
| 1929 | 532,000 | 300 | 325 | 350 | 400 | 500 | 800 | |

**a.** Values are for coins with bold mintmark; weak D pieces are worth less. Beware of counterfeits.

## INDIAN PRINCESS HEAD (1854–1889)

The three-dollar gold piece was authorized by the Act of February 21, 1853. First struck in 1854, the coin was never popular with the general public and saw very little circulation. Today, some numismatists theorize that the $3 denomination would have been useful for purchasing postage stamps of the day (with their face value of 3¢) or for acquiring 100 silver three-cent pieces ("trimes"), which were also in circulation at the time.

These gold coins changed hands in the East and Midwest until 1861, after which they disappeared from circulation; through the 1860s, fewer than 10,000 were struck annually. In 1874 and 1878, mintages were increased significantly in anticipation of the coins going into broader circulation. On the West Coast, the three-dollar gold piece did see circulation throughout the series' minting, though they probably weren't seen in change very often after the 1860s.

The head on the obverse represents an Indian princess with hair tightly curling over the neck, her head crowned with a circle of feathers (the band of which is inscribed LIBERTY). A wreath of tobacco, wheat, corn, and cotton occupies the field of the reverse, with the denomination and date within it. The coin weighed 77.4 grains, and was struck in .900 fine gold.

In the year 1854 only, the word DOLLARS is in much smaller letters than in later years. The 1856 Proof has DOLLARS in large letters cut over the same word in small letters. Restrikes of some years were made, particularly Proofs of 1865 and 1873.

Although these coins did not see extensive day-to-day circulation, collector interest was high, and many three-dollar gold pieces were saved by speculators beginning about 1879. As a result, Mint State examples are fairly numerous today. The 1870-S coin is unique, currently residing in the Harry W. Bass Jr. Collection on loan to the American Numismatic Association.

*Designer James B. Longacre; weight 5.015 grams; composition .900 gold, .100 copper (net weight .14512 oz. pure gold); diameter 20.5 mm; reeded edge; mints: Philadelphia, Dahlonega, New Orleans, San Francisco.*

**VF-20 Very Fine**—Eyebrow, hair about forehead and ear, and bottom curl all worn smooth. Faint details visible on curled feather-ends of headdress.
**EF-40 Extremely Fine**—Light wear above and to right of eye, and on top of curled feathers.
**AU-50 About Uncirculated**—Trace of wear on top of curled feathers and in hair above and to right of eye.
**AU-55 Choice About Uncirculated**—Evidence of friction on design high points. Much of original mint luster present.
**MS-60 Uncirculated**—No trace of wear. Light blemishes.
**MS-63 Choice Uncirculated**—Some distracting contact marks or blemishes in prime focal areas. Impaired luster possible.
**PF-63 Choice Proof**—Reflective surfaces with only a few blemishes in secondary focal places. No major flaws.

*Circulation strike.*

*Proof strike.*

*Mintmark location is on reverse, below wreath.*

| | Mintage | VF-20 | EF-40 | AU-50 | AU-55 | MS-60 | MS-63 | PF-63 |
|---|---|---|---|---|---|---|---|---|
| 1854 | 138,618 | $850 | $1,000 | $1,100 | $1,250 | $1,950 | $3,600 | $80,000 |
| 1854D | 1,120 | 20,000 | 27,500 | 47,500 | 55,000 | 110,000 | | |
| 1854O | 24,000 | 2,000 | 3,250 | 3,750 | 8,500 | 47,500 | 115,000 | |
| 1855 | 50,555 | 950 | 1,000 | 1,150 | 1,250 | 2,000 | 4,500 | 75,000 |

*Chart continued on next page.*

| Mintage | VF-20 | EF-40 | AU-50 | AU-55 | MS-60 | MS-63 | PF-63 |
|---|---|---|---|---|---|---|---|
| 1855S . . . . . . . . . . . . . . . . . . 6,600 | $1,500 | $3,000 | $6,000 | $12,000 | $34,500 | $100,000 | |
| *$1,322,500, PF-64 Cam, Heritage auction, August 2011* | | | | | | | |
| 1856 . . . . . . . . . . . . . . . . . . 26,010 | 850 | 1,000 | 1,150 | 1,300 | 2,850 | 6,750 | $45,000 |
| 1856S **(a)** . . . . . . . . . . . . . . 34,500 | 1,000 | 1,500 | 2,250 | 3,500 | 12,500 | 30,000 | |
| 1857 . . . . . . . . . . . . . . . . . . 20,891 | 850 | 1,100 | 1,350 | 1,500 | 3,250 | 6,500 | 30,000 |
| 1857S . . . . . . . . . . . . . . . . . 14,000 | 1,300 | 2,250 | 5,000 | 9,000 | 22,500 | 60,000 | |
| 1858 . . . . . . . . . . . . . . . . . . . 2,133 | 1,300 | 2,250 | 3,750 | 5,500 | 12,000 | 23,500 | 30,000 |
| 1859 . . . . . . . . . . . . (80). . . 15,558 | 1,000 | 1,250 | 1,350 | 1,750 | 3,100 | 6,500 | 20,000 |
| 1860 . . . . . . . . . . . (119). . . . 7,036 | 1,000 | 1,300 | 1,800 | 1,950 | 3,500 | 7,000 | 16,000 |
| 1860S . . . . . . . . . . . . . . . . . . 7,000 | 1,300 | 2,750 | 6,500 | 11,500 | 25,000 | | |
| 1861 . . . . . . . . . . . (113). . . . 5,959 | 1,500 | 2,500 | 3,750 | 4,500 | 8,500 | 13,000 | 16,000 |
| 1862 . . . . . . . . . . . . (35). . . . 5,750 | 1,650 | 2,750 | 4,250 | 4,750 | 8,750 | 13,500 | 16,000 |
| 1863 . . . . . . . . . . . . (39). . . . 5,000 | 1,500 | 2,500 | 4,000 | 4,500 | 8,500 | 15,000 | 16,000 |
| 1864 . . . . . . . . . . . . (50). . . . 2,630 | 1,650 | 3,000 | 4,750 | 6,000 | 8,000 | 15,000 | 16,000 |
| 1865 . . . . . . . . . . . . (25). . . . 1,140 | 2,750 | 4,500 | 7,500 | 9,500 | 16,500 | 26,500 | 20,000 |
| 1866 . . . . . . . . . . . . (30). . . . 4,000 | 1,150 | 1,350 | 2,250 | 2,500 | 4,500 | 10,000 | 16,500 |
| 1867 . . . . . . . . . . . . (50). . . . 2,600 | 1,300 | 1,650 | 2,500 | 3,250 | 5,500 | 15,000 | 16,500 |
| 1868 **(b)** . . . . . . . . . (25). . . . 4,850 | 1,150 | 1,350 | 2,000 | 2,500 | 4,000 | 10,000 | 16,500 |
| 1869 **(b)** . . . . . . . . . (25). . . . 2,500 | 1,150 | 1,400 | 2,200 | 2,800 | 4,300 | 13,500 | 16,500 |
| 1870 . . . . . . . . . . . . (35). . . . 3,500 | 1,150 | 1,550 | 2,250 | 2,750 | 4,300 | 15,000 | 16,500 |
| 1870S . . . . . . . . . . . . . . . . . . . . . . . | *5,000,000* | | *(unique, in Bass Foundation Collection)* | | | | |
| *$687,500, EF-40, B&R auction, October 1982* | | | | | | | |
| 1871 . . . . . . . . . . . . (30). . . . 1,300 | 1,150 | 1,650 | 2,250 | 3,000 | 4,500 | 10,000 | 16,500 |
| 1872 . . . . . . . . . . . . (30). . . . 2,000 | 1,150 | 1,650 | 2,500 | 3,000 | 4,750 | 12,500 | 16,500 |
| 1873, Open 3 (Orig.) (25). . . . . . . . . | | 17,500 | 20,000 | | | | 32,500 |
| *$161,000, PF-65 DC, Goldberg auction, February 2007* | | | | | | | |
| 1873, Close 3 . . . . . . . . . . . . . . **(c)** | 5,500 | 9,500 | 13,500 | 18,000 | 30,000 | 55,000 | 37,500 |
| 1874 . . . . . . . . . . . . (20). . . 41,800 | 850 | 1,000 | 1,050 | 1,150 | 1,850 | 3,650 | 28,000 |
| 1875, Proof only . . . (20). . . . . . . . . | | | 75,000 | | | | 165,000 |
| *$218,500, PF-64, Heritage auction, January 2012* | | | | | | | |
| 1876, Proof only . . . (45). . . . . . . . . | | | 22,500 | | | | 50,000 |
| 1877 . . . . . . . . . . . . (20). . . . 1,468 | 4,500 | 7,500 | 12,500 | 15,000 | 30,000 | 50,000 | 30,000 |
| 1878 **(b)** . . . . . . . . . (20). . . 82,304 | 850 | 1,000 | 1,050 | 1,150 | 1,850 | 3,500 | 27,500 |
| 1879 . . . . . . . . . . . . (30). . . . 3,000 | 1,000 | 1,300 | 2,000 | 2,750 | 3,500 | 6,000 | 17,000 |
| 1880 . . . . . . . . . . . . (36). . . . 1,000 | 1,450 | 2,000 | 3,500 | 3,750 | 5,000 | 8,000 | 17,000 |
| 1881 . . . . . . . . . . . . (54). . . . . .500 | 3,000 | 5,000 | 8,000 | 9,500 | 14,000 | 22,500 | 17,000 |
| 1882 . . . . . . . . . . . . (76). . . . 1,500 | 1,250 | 1,750 | 2,500 | 3,000 | 4,000 | 8,500 | 13,500 |
| 1883 . . . . . . . . . . . . (89). . . . . .900 | 1,500 | 2,500 | 3,000 | 3,500 | 4,500 | 8,500 | 13,500 |
| 1884 . . . . . . . . . . . (106). . . . 1,000 | 1,750 | 2,500 | 3,500 | 4,000 | 5,000 | 10,000 | 13,500 |
| 1885 . . . . . . . . . . . (110). . . . . .800 | 1,650 | 2,500 | 3,750 | 4,500 | 6,000 | 12,000 | 13,500 |
| 1886 . . . . . . . . . . . (142). . . . 1,000 | 1,500 | 1,950 | 2,750 | 3,750 | 5,000 | 12,000 | 13,500 |
| 1887 . . . . . . . . . . . (160). . . . 6,000 | 1,000 | 1,350 | 2,000 | 2,250 | 3,000 | 5,500 | 13,500 |
| 1888 . . . . . . . . . . . (291). . . . 5,000 | 950 | 1,250 | 1,750 | 1,850 | 3,000 | 4,500 | 12,500 |
| 1889 . . . . . . . . . . . (129). . . . 2,300 | 850 | 1,150 | 1,450 | 1,650 | 3,000 | 4,500 | 12,500 |

**a.** Small S and Medium S varieties exist. **b.** Varieties showing traces of possible overdating include 1868, 8 Over 7; 1869, 9 Over 8; and 1878, 8 Over 7. **c.** The mintage of the 1873, Close 3, coins is unknown. Research suggests that Proofs only may have been struck (none for circulation), and those perhaps as late as 1879. Mint records report 25 Proof coins, with no reference to the style of the 3 (Open or Close); however, the actual mintage may be as high as 100 to 1,000 coins.

## STELLA (1879–1880)

These pattern coins were first suggested by John A. Kasson, then U.S. envoy extraordinary and minister plenipotentiary to Austria-Hungary. It was through the efforts of W.W. Hubbell, who patented the alloy *goloid* (used in making another pattern piece, the goloid metric dollar), that we have these beautiful and interesting coins.

The four-dollar Stella—so called because the Latin word for *star* is *stella,* and the coin bears a five-pointed star on the reverse—was envisioned by Kasson as America's answer to various foreign gold coins popular in the international market. The British sovereign, Italy's 20 lire, and the 20 pesetas of Spain were three such coins: each smaller than a U.S. five-dollar gold piece, they were used widely in international trade.

The Stella was one of many proposals made to Congress for an international trade coin, and one of only several that made it to pattern-coin form (others include the 1868 five-dollar piece and 1874 Bickford ten-dollar piece).

Odds were stacked against the Stella from the start. The denomination of four U.S. dollars didn't match any of the coin's European counterparts, and at any rate the U.S. double eagle (twenty-dollar coin)—already used in international commerce—was a more convenient medium of exchange. The Stella was never minted for circulation. Those dated 1879 were struck for congressmen to examine. The 1880 coins were secretly made by Mint officials for sale to private collectors.

There are two distinct types in both years of issue. Charles E. Barber is thought to have designed the Flowing Hair type, and George T. Morgan the Coiled Hair. They were struck as patterns in gold, aluminum, copper, and white metal. (Only those struck in gold are listed here.)

Precise mintage numbers are unknown. The estimates given below are based on surviving pieces, certified population reports, and auction records.

Some of the finest Stella specimens are housed in the National Numismatic Collection in the Smithsonian Institution. Others are in private collections, and cross the auction block from time to time. Recent auction activity for Stellas certified PF-60 and up:

- 1879 Flowing Hair: $115,000 (PF-62 Cam) Stack's Bowers May 2010
- 1879 Coiled Hair: $881,250 (PF-65) Heritage April 2015
- 1880 Flowing Hair: $750,000 (PF-67 Cam) Heritage January 2018
- 1880 Coiled Hair: $1,821,250 (PF-67) Heritage April 2015

Flowing Hair Obverse

Coiled Hair Obverse

Reverse

| | Mintage | PF-40 | PF-50 | PF-60 | PF-63 | PF-65 | PF-66 | PF-67 |
|---|---|---|---|---|---|---|---|---|
| 1879, Flowing Hair . . . . . . . | *(425+)* | $90,000 | $95,000 | $120,000 | $165,000 | $225,000 | $275,000 | $375,000 |
| *$116,625, PF-61, Heritage auction, January 2017* | | | | | | | | |
| 1879, Coiled Hair *(12 known)* . . . . . | | | | 300,000 | 450,000 | 800,000 | 1,100,000 | 1,250,000 |
| *$1,050,000, PF-66 Cam, Heritage auction, January 2019* | | | | | | | | |
| 1880, Flowing Hair *(17 known)* . . . . | | | | 175,000 | 325,000 | 450,000 | 550,000 | 750,000 |
| *$959,400, PF-67★, Bonhams auction, September 2013* | | | | | | | | |
| 1880, Coiled Hair *(8 known)* . . . . . . | | | | 600,000 | 775,000 | 1,250,000 | 1,750,000 | 2,000,000 |
| *$2,574,000, PF-67 Cam, Bonhams auction, September 2013* | | | | | | | | |

The half eagle was the first gold coin actually struck for the United States. The five-dollar piece was authorized to be coined by the Act of April 2, 1792, and the first type weighed 135 grains, .9167 fineness. The Act of June 28, 1834, changed the weight to 129 grains, .8992 fineness. Fineness became .900 by the Act of January 18, 1837.

There are many varieties among the early dates, caused by changes in the number of stars and style of eagle, by overdates, and by differences in the size of figures in the dates. Those dated prior to 1807 do not bear any mark of value. The 1822 half eagle is considered one of the most valuable regular-issue coins of the entire United States series. Proofs of some dates prior to 1855 are known to exist, and all are rare. Commemorative and bullion five-dollar coins have been made at West Point since 1986 and 1994, respectively; thus this is the only U.S. denomination made at all eight U.S. mints.

*Note: Values of common gold coins have been based on a gold bullion price of $1,500 per ounce, and may vary with the prevailing spot price. The net weight and content listed may be used to recalculate bullion value.*

## CAPPED BUST TO RIGHT (1795–1807)

*Designer Robert Scot; weight 8.75 grams; composition .9167 gold, .0833 silver and copper; approx. diameter 25 mm; reeded edge.*

**F-12 Fine**—Liberty's hair worn smooth but distinctly outlined. Heraldic type: E PLURIBUS UNUM faint but legible.
**VF-20 Very Fine**—Slight to noticeable wear on high spots such as hair, turban, and eagle's head and wings.
**EF-40 Extremely Fine**—Slight wear on hair and highest part of cheek.
**AU-50 About Uncirculated**—Trace of wear on cap, hair, cheek, and drapery.
**MS-60 Uncirculated**—No trace of wear. Light blemishes.
**MS-63 Choice Uncirculated**—Some distracting contact marks or blemishes in prime focal areas. Impaired luster possible.

### Small Eagle Reverse (1795–1798)

This type was struck from mid-1795 through early 1798, when the Small Eagle reverse was changed to the Large or "Heraldic" Eagle. Note that the 1795 and 1797 dates exist for both types, but that the Heraldic Eagle reverses of these dates were probably struck in 1798 using serviceable 1795 and 1797 dies.

| | Mintage | F-12 | VF-20 | EF-40 | AU-50 | AU-55 | MS-60 | MS-63 |
|---|---|---|---|---|---|---|---|---|
| 1795, Small Eagle | 8,707 | $21,500 | $25,000 | $32,500 | $42,500 | $52,500 | $77,500 | $165,000 |
| *$646,250, MS-65, Sotheby's / Stack's Bowers auction, September 2015* | | | | | | | | |

*Note:* One variety has the final S in STATES punched over an erroneous D.

1796, 6 Over 5

1797, 15 Stars

1797, 16 Stars

| | Mintage | F-12 | VF-20 | EF-40 | AU-50 | AU-55 | MS-60 | MS-63 |
|---|---|---|---|---|---|---|---|---|
| 1796, 6 Over 5 | 6,196 | $22,500 | $30,000 | $40,000 | $55,000 | $70,000 | $105,000 | $250,000 |
| 1797, All kinds | 3,609 | | | | | | | |
| 1797, 15 Stars | | 27,000 | 40,000 | 65,000 | 125,000 | 155,000 | 260,000 | |
| 1797, 16 Stars | | 25,000 | 40,000 | 65,000 | 115,000 | 145,000 | 240,000 | |
| 1798, Small Eagle *(6 known)* | | | 450,000 | 550,000 | 750,000 | 1,250,000 | — | |

## Heraldic Eagle Reverse (1795–1807)

| | Mintage | F-12 | VF-20 | EF-40 | AU-50 | AU-55 | MS-60 | MS-63 |
|---|---|---|---|---|---|---|---|---|
| 1795, Heraldic Eagle | (a) | $15,000 | $23,000 | $35,000 | $60,000 | $85,000 | $115,000 | $250,000 |
| 1797, 7 Over 5 | (a) | 22,500 | 32,500 | 45,000 | 80,000 | 135,000 | 200,000 | |
| 1797, 16-Star Obverse | (a) | | | — | *(unique, in Smithsonian collection)* | | | |
| 1797, 15-Star Obverse | (a) | | | — | *(unique, in Smithsonian collection)* | | | |
| 1798, All kinds | 24,867 | | | | | | | |
| 1798, Small 8 | | 5,500 | 7,750 | 12,500 | 18,500 | 22,000 | 32,500 | 77,500 |
| 1798, Large 8, 13-Star Reverse | | 5,000 | 6,000 | 10,000 | 16,000 | 20,000 | 30,000 | 60,000 |
| 1798, Large 8, 14-Star Reverse | | 5,500 | 7,000 | 15,000 | 22,500 | 35,000 | 115,000 | |
| 1799 | 7,451 | 5,000 | 6,000 | 8,500 | 13,000 | 18,000 | 27,500 | 65,000 |

**a.** Thought to have been struck in 1798 and included in the mintage figure for that year.

**1802, 2 Over 1**

**1803, 3 Over 2**

**1804, Small 8 Over Large 8**

| | Mintage | F-12 | VF-20 | EF-40 | AU-50 | AU-55 | MS-60 | MS-63 |
|---|---|---|---|---|---|---|---|---|
| 1800 | 37,628 | $4,500 | $5,500 | $7,500 | $10,000 | $12,000 | $17,500 | $40,000 |
| 1802, 2 Over 1 | 53,176 | 4,500 | 5,000 | 7,000 | 10,000 | 11,500 | 16,000 | 33,500 |
| 1803, 3 Over 2 | 33,506 | 4,500 | 5,000 | 7,000 | 10,000 | 12,500 | 17,500 | 30,000 |
| 1804, All kinds | 30,475 | | | | | | | |
| 1804, Small 8 | | 4,500 | 5,000 | 8,000 | 10,000 | 11,500 | 16,500 | 35,000 |
| 1804, Small 8 Over Large 8 | | 4,500 | 5,000 | 8,000 | 10,500 | 12,500 | 19,000 | 42,500 |
| 1805 | 33,183 | 4,500 | 5,500 | 7,750 | 10,500 | 12,500 | 16,000 | 32,500 |

**1806, Pointed-Top 6, Stars 8 and 5**

**1806, Round-Top 6, Stars 7 and 6**

*See next page for chart.*

| | Mintage | F-12 | VF-20 | EF-40 | AU-50 | AU-55 | MS-60 | MS-63 |
|---|---|---|---|---|---|---|---|---|
| 1806, Pointed-Top 6 | 9,676 | $4,500 | $4,750 | $7,000 | $10,000 | $12,000 | $16,500 | $34,500 |
| 1806, Round-Top 6 | 54,417 | 4,500 | 4,750 | 7,000 | 10,000 | 11,500 | 15,500 | 30,000 |
| 1807 | 32,488 | 4,500 | 5,500 | 7,000 | 10,000 | 11,500 | 15,500 | 28,500 |

## DRAPED BUST TO LEFT (1807–1812)

*Designer John Reich; standards same as for previous issue.*

**F-12 Fine**—LIBERTY on cap legible but partly weak.
**VF-20 Very Fine**—Headband edges slightly worn. LIBERTY bold.
**EF-40 Extremely Fine**—Slight wear on highest portions of hair; 80% of major curls plain.
**AU-50 About Uncirculated**—Trace of wear above eye and on top of cap, cheek, and hair.
**AU-55 Choice About Uncirculated**—Evidence of friction on design high points. Some mint luster present.
**MS-60 Uncirculated**—No trace of wear. Light blemishes.
**MS-63 Choice Uncirculated**—Some distracting contact marks or blemishes in prime focal areas. Impaired luster possible.

1808, 8 Over 7 | 1808, Normal Date | 1809, 9 Over 8

| | Mintage | F-12 | VF-20 | EF-40 | AU-50 | AU-55 | MS-60 | MS-63 |
|---|---|---|---|---|---|---|---|---|
| 1807 | 51,605 | $3,250 | $4,750 | $5,750 | $8,000 | $9,750 | $14,000 | $24,500 |
| 1808, All kinds | 55,578 | | | | | | | |
| 1808, 8 Over 7 | | 3,250 | 4,750 | 6,500 | 8,500 | 11,500 | 18,500 | 35,000 |
| 1808 | | 3,000 | 4,250 | 5,750 | 8,000 | 9,500 | 13,500 | 27,500 |
| 1809, 9 Over 8 | 33,875 | 3,000 | 4,250 | 5,750 | 8,000 | 10,500 | 14,000 | 28,500 |

1810, Small Date

1810, Large Date

Large 5

Tall 5

| | Mintage | F-12 | VF-20 | EF-40 | AU-50 | AU-55 | MS-60 | MS-63 |
|---|---|---|---|---|---|---|---|---|
| 1810, All kinds | 100,287 | | | | | | | |
| 1810, Small Date, Small 5 | | $20,000 | $35,000 | $45,000 | $65,000 | $85,000 | $100,000 | |
| 1810, Small Date, Tall 5 | | 3,000 | 4,250 | 5,500 | 8,000 | 9,500 | 14,000 | $29,000 |
| 1810, Large Date, Small 5 | | 25,000 | 55,000 | 75,000 | 110,000 | 130,000 | 200,000 | |
| 1810, Large Date, Large 5 | | 3,000 | 4,250 | 5,500 | 8,000 | 9,500 | 13,000 | 25,000 |

| | Mintage | F-12 | VF-20 | EF-40 | AU-50 | AU-55 | MS-60 | MS-63 |
|---|---|---|---|---|---|---|---|---|
| 1811, All kinds | 99,581 | | | | | | | |
| 1811, Small 5 | | $3,000 | $4,250 | $5,500 | $8,000 | $9,500 | $13,000 | $25,000 |
| 1811, Tall 5 | | 3,000 | 4,250 | 5,500 | 8,000 | 9,500 | 13,000 | 30,000 |
| 1812 | 58,087 | 3,000 | 4,250 | 5,500 | 8,000 | 9,500 | 13,000 | 25,000 |

## CAPPED HEAD TO LEFT (1813–1834)
### Bold Relief (1813–1815), Large Diameter (1813–1829)

| | Mintage | F-12 | VF-20 | EF-40 | AU-50 | AU-55 | MS-60 | MS-63 |
|---|---|---|---|---|---|---|---|---|
| 1813 | 95,428 | $4,750 | $5,750 | $7,000 | $9,500 | $11,000 | $15,000 | $26,500 |
| 1814, 4 Over 3 | 15,454 | 4,750 | 6,000 | 8,000 | 10,000 | 13,000 | 20,000 | 40,000 |
| 1815 *(11 known)* | 635 | | | 200,000 | 275,000 | 325,000 | 400,000 | 600,000 |
| *$822,500, MS-65, Sotheby's / Stack's Bowers auction, February 2016* | | | | | | | | |
| 1818, All kinds | 48,588 | | | | | | | |
| 1818 | | 4,750 | 6,000 | 7,000 | 13,500 | 16,500 | 25,000 | 45,000 |
| 1818, STATESOF one word | | 5,500 | 7,000 | 9,000 | 15,000 | 17,000 | 22,500 | 45,000 |
| 1818, I Over 0 | | 5,000 | 6,500 | 8,000 | 11,000 | 15,000 | 30,000 | 50,000 |
| 1819, All kinds | 51,723 | | | | | | | |
| 1819 | | | | 55,000 | 70,000 | 95,000 | 150,000 | |
| 1819, I Over 0 | | | | 50,000 | 65,000 | 80,000 | 125,000 | 225,000 |

1820, Curved-Base 2

1820, Square-Base 2

1820, Small Letters

1820, Large Letters

| | Mintage | F-12 | VF-20 | EF-40 | AU-50 | AU-55 | MS-60 | MS-63 |
|---|---|---|---|---|---|---|---|---|
| 1820, All kinds | 263,806 | | | | | | | |
| 1820, Curved-Base 2, Sm Ltrs | | $5,250 | $7,000 | $11,000 | $20,000 | $25,000 | $40,000 | $85,000 |
| 1820, Curved-Base 2, Lg Ltrs | | 5,000 | 6,750 | 8,500 | 12,500 | 17,500 | 25,000 | 60,000 |
| 1820, Square-Base 2 | | 5,500 | 7,000 | 11,000 | 16,000 | 20,000 | 27,500 | 45,000 |
| 1821 | 34,641 | 25,000 | 36,500 | 60,000 | 100,000 | 150,000 | 215,000 | 400,000 |
| 1822 *(3 known)* | 17,796 | | | | | 8,000,000 | | |
| *$687,500, VF-30/EF-40, B&R auction, October 1982* | | | | | | | | |
| 1823 | 14,485 | 8,500 | 10,000 | 15,000 | 20,000 | 25,000 | 30,000 | 50,000 |
| 1824 | 17,340 | 14,000 | 20,000 | 30,000 | 37,500 | 50,000 | 75,000 | 130,000 |

1825, 5 Over Partial 4

1825, 5 Over 4

| | Mintage | F-12 | VF-20 | EF-40 | AU-50 | AU-55 | MS-60 | MS-63 |
|---|---|---|---|---|---|---|---|---|
| 1825, 5 Over Partial 4 | 29,060 | $14,000 | $20,000 | $30,000 | $37,500 | $47,500 | $75,000 | $130,000 |
| 1825, 5 Over 4 *(2 known)* | * | | | 500,000 | 700,000 | | | |
| *$940,000, MS-64, Sotheby's / Stack's Bowers auction, May 2016* | | | | | | | | |
| 1826 | 18,069 | 10,000 | 15,000 | 20,000 | 30,000 | 40,000 | 70,000 | 115,000 |
| *$763,750, MS-66, Heritage auction, January 2014* | | | | | | | | |
| 1827 | 24,913 | 20,000 | 25,000 | 30,000 | 40,000 | 50,000 | 65,000 | 125,000 |

* Included in number above.

Large Date

| | Mintage | VF-20 | EF-40 | AU-50 | AU-55 | MS-60 | MS-63 |
|---|---|---|---|---|---|---|---|
| 1828, 8 Over 7 *(5 known)* | * | | | $100,000 | $175,000 | $275,000 | $350,000 |
| *$632,500, MS-64, Heritage auction, January 2012* | | | | | | | |
| 1828 | 28,029 | $50,000 | $70,000 | 80,000 | 100,000 | 200,000 | 325,000 |
| *$499,375, MS-64, Heritage auction, April 2013* | | | | | | | |
| 1829, Large Date | 57,442 | | — | — | | 225,000 | 425,000 |
| *$1,380,000, PF-64, Heritage auction, January 2012* | | | | | | | |

* Included in number below.

## Reduced Diameter (1829–1834)

The half eagles dated 1829 (small date) through 1834 are smaller in diameter than the earlier pieces. They also have smaller letters, dates, and stars.

*Design modified by William Kneass; standards same as before; diameter 23.8 mm.*

1829, Small Date

1830, Large 5 D.

1830, Small 5 D.

1832, 13 Stars, Square-Base 2

| | Mintage | F-12 | VF-20 | EF-40 | AU-50 | AU-55 | MS-60 | MS-63 |
|---|---|---|---|---|---|---|---|---|
| 1829, Small Date | * | $75,000 | $100,000 | $150,000 | $200,000 | $250,000 | $375,000 | $500,000 |
| *$881,250, MS-65+, Sotheby's / Stack's Bowers auction, May 2016* | | | | | | | | |
| 1830, Small or Large 5 D. | 126,351 | 20,000 | 27,500 | 40,000 | 45,000 | 52,500 | 75,000 | 100,000 |
| 1831, Small or Large 5 D. | 140,594 | 20,000 | 27,500 | 40,000 | 45,000 | 52,500 | 75,000 | 100,000 |
| 1832, Curved-Base 2, 12 Stars *(5 known)* | ** | | 300,000 | 350,000 | 450,000 | 500,000 | | |
| *$822,500, MS-63, Sotheby's / Stack's Bowers auction, May 2016* | | | | | | | | |
| 1832, Square-Base 2, 13 Stars | 157,487 | 20,000 | 27,500 | 40,000 | 45,000 | 55,000 | 80,000 | 110,000 |
| 1833, Large Date | 193,630 | 20,000 | 27,500 | 40,000 | 45,000 | 52,500 | 65,000 | 115,000 |
| *$1,351,250, PF-67, Sotheby's / Stack's Bowers auction, May 2016* | | | | | | | | |
| 1833, Small Date | *** | 20,000 | 27,500 | 40,000 | 45,000 | 52,500 | 70,000 | 125,000 |

* Included in "1829, Large Date" mintage. ** Included in number below. *** Included in number above.

Plain 4

Crosslet 4

| | Mintage | F-12 | VF-20 | EF-40 | AU-50 | AU-55 | MS-60 | MS-63 |
|---|---|---|---|---|---|---|---|---|
| 1834, All kinds | 50,141 | | | | | | | |
| 1834, Plain 4 | | $20,000 | $27,500 | $40,000 | $45,000 | $52,500 | $75,000 | $100,000 |
| 1834, Crosslet 4 | | 21,500 | 30,000 | 40,000 | 47,500 | 57,000 | 85,000 | 140,000 |

## CLASSIC HEAD, NO MOTTO (1834–1838)

As on the quarter eagle of 1834, the motto E PLURIBUS UNUM was omitted from the new, reduced-size half eagle in 1834, to distinguish the old coins that had become worth more than face value.

*Designer William Kneass; weight 8.36 grams; composition (1834–1836) .8992 gold, .1008 silver and copper, (1837–1838) .900 gold, .100 copper; diameter 22.5 mm; reeded edge; mints: Philadelphia, Charlotte, Dahlonega.*

**Mintmark is above date.**

| | Mintage | VF-20 | EF-40 | AU-50 | AU-55 | MS-60 | MS-63 |
|---|---|---|---|---|---|---|---|
| 1834, Plain 4 **(a)** | 657,460 | $600 | $750 | $1,250 | $1,750 | $3,500 | $10,750 |
| 1834, Crosslet 4 | * | 2,100 | 3,750 | 6,000 | 9,500 | 23,500 | 50,000 |
| 1835 **(a)** | 371,534 | 600 | 775 | 1,250 | 1,800 | 3,500 | 11,000 |
| *$822,500, PF-67+DC, Sotheby's / Stack's Bowers auction, May 2016* | | | | | | | |
| 1836 **(a)** | 553,147 | 600 | 775 | 1,250 | 1,900 | 3,500 | 11,000 |
| *$690,300, PF-67★ UC, Bonhams auction, September 2013* | | | | | | | |
| 1837 **(a)** | 207,121 | 650 | 850 | 1,550 | 2,100 | 5,500 | 20,000 |
| 1838 | 286,588 | 650 | 850 | 1,500 | 2,050 | 4,250 | 11,500 |
| 1838C | 17,179 | 6,000 | 10,000 | 15,000 | 22,500 | 75,000 | 250,000 |
| 1838D | 20,583 | 6,500 | 8,500 | 12,500 | 20,000 | 35,000 | 85,000 |

* Included in number above. **a.** Varieties have either script 8 or block-style 8 in date.

## LIBERTY HEAD (1839–1908)

### Variety 1 – No Motto Above Eagle (1839–1866)

*Designer Christian Gobrecht; weight 8.359 grams; composition .900 gold, .100 copper (net weight .24187 oz. pure gold); diameter (1839–1840) 22.5 mm, (1840–1866) 21.6 mm; reeded edge; mints: Philadelphia, Charlotte, Dahlonega, New Orleans, San Francisco.*

**VF-20 Very Fine**—LIBERTY on coronet bold. Major lines show in curls on neck.
**EF-40 Extremely Fine**—Details clear in curls on neck. Slight wear on top and lower part of coronet and on hair.
**AU-50 About Uncirculated**—Trace of wear on coronet and hair above eye.
**AU-55 Choice About Uncirculated**—Evidence of friction on design high points. Some original mint luster.
**MS-60 Uncirculated**—No trace of wear. Light blemishes.
**MS-63 Choice Uncirculated**—Some distracting contact marks or blemishes in prime focal areas. Impaired luster possible.
**PF-63 Choice Proof**—Attractive reflective surfaces with only a few blemishes in secondary focal places. No major flaws.

**Mintmark: 1839, above date; 1840–1908, below eagle.**

*See next page for chart.*

| | Mintage | VF-20 | EF-40 | AU-50 | AU-55 | MS-60 | MS-63 |
|---|---|---|---|---|---|---|---|
| 1839 | 118,143 | $700 | $1,150 | $1,800 | $2,500 | $7,000 | $27,500 |
| 1839C | 17,205 | 2,750 | 5,000 | 9,500 | 14,000 | 25,000 | 65,000 |
| 1839D | 18,939 | 3,000 | 5,750 | 9,500 | 16,500 | 30,000 | |
| 1840 **(a)** | 137,382 | 550 | 650 | 1,000 | 1,350 | 3,250 | 9,000 |
| 1840C | 18,992 | 2,000 | 4,000 | 6,000 | 7,000 | 16,000 | 55,000 |
| 1840D | 22,896 | 2,250 | 3,500 | 6,000 | 7,500 | 14,000 | 45,000 |
| 1840O **(a)** | 40,120 | 600 | 1,200 | 2,250 | 3,000 | 9,500 | 40,000 |
| 1841 | 15,833 | 550 | 950 | 1,600 | 1,850 | 4,500 | 12,000 |
| 1841C | 21,467 | 1,850 | 2,500 | 4,500 | 6,000 | 15,000 | 40,000 |
| 1841D | 29,392 | 2,250 | 3,000 | 4,500 | 5,250 | 12,500 | 22,000 |
| 1841O *(not known to exist)* | *50* | | | | | | |

**a.** Scarce varieties of these 1840 coins have the fine edge-reeding and wide rims of the 1839 issues. These are known as "broad mill."

1842, Large Date

Small Letters

Large Letters

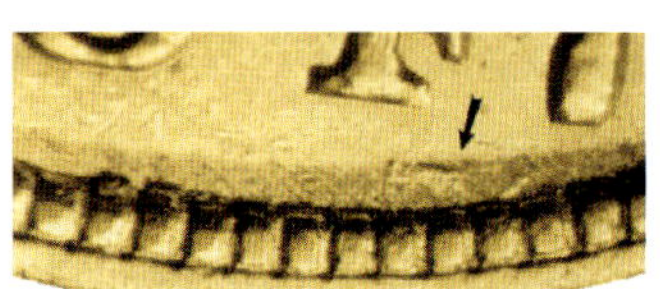
1847, Extra 7 at Border

| | Mintage | VF-20 | EF-40 | AU-50 | AU-55 | MS-60 | MS-63 | PF-63 |
|---|---|---|---|---|---|---|---|---|
| 1842, All kinds | 27,578 | | | | | | | |
| 1842, Small Letters | | $650 | $1,250 | $2,500 | $6,000 | $11,000 | | |
| 1842, Large Letters | | 725 | 1,600 | 3,750 | 6,000 | 11,500 | $25,000 | |
| 1842C, All kinds | 27,432 | | | | | | | |
| 1842C, Small Date | | 9,000 | 17,500 | 25,000 | 35,000 | 75,000 | 150,000 | |
| 1842C, Large Date | | 2,000 | 2,550 | 4,000 | 5,000 | 12,500 | 30,000 | |
| 1842D, All kinds | 59,608 | | | | | | | |
| 1842D, Small Date | | 2,000 | 2,600 | 4,250 | 5,000 | 13,000 | 30,000 | |
| 1842D, Large Date | | 3,500 | 7,500 | 11,000 | 20,000 | 45,000 | | |
| 1842O | 16,400 | 2,500 | 4,000 | 9,500 | 12,500 | 27,500 | | |
| 1843 | 611,205 | 500 | 525 | 575 | 650 | 1,400 | 9,500 | |
| 1843C | 44,277 | 1,800 | 2,500 | 3,750 | 4,500 | 9,500 | 27,500 | |
| 1843D | 98,452 | 2,000 | 2,500 | 3,500 | 4,250 | 10,000 | 28,500 | |
| 1843O, Small Letters | 19,075 | 850 | 1,650 | 2,250 | 4,500 | 17,500 | 38,000 | |
| 1843O, Large Letters | 82,000 | 650 | 1,250 | 2,000 | 3,500 | 10,000 | 30,000 | |
| 1844 | 340,330 | 500 | 525 | 575 | 625 | 1,950 | 10,000 | |
| 1844C | 23,631 | 2,250 | 3,250 | 5,000 | 7,000 | 14,000 | 35,000 | |
| 1844D | 88,982 | 2,000 | 2,750 | 3,750 | 4,000 | 8,500 | 25,000 | |
| 1844O | 364,600 | 550 | 600 | 875 | 1,350 | 4,500 | 17,500 | |
| 1845 | 417,099 | 500 | 550 | 625 | 700 | 2,000 | 8,000 | |
| 1845D | 90,629 | 2,000 | 2,500 | 3,500 | 4,500 | 9,000 | 22,500 | |
| 1845O | 41,000 | 750 | 1,200 | 2,500 | 4,500 | 10,000 | 27,500 | |
| 1846, All kinds | 395,942 | | | | | | | |
| 1846, Large Date | | 450 | 500 | 650 | 700 | 2,000 | 13,000 | |
| 1846, Small Date | | 500 | 650 | 850 | 1,100 | 3,500 | 13,500 | |
| 1846C | 12,995 | 2,000 | 3,750 | 5,000 | 7,000 | 15,500 | 60,000 | |
| 1846D, All kinds | 80,294 | | | | | | | |
| 1846D | | 2,000 | 2,750 | 3,750 | 4,750 | 12,000 | | |
| 1846D, High 2nd D Over Mmk. | | 2,250 | 2,500 | 4,000 | 5,000 | 11,000 | 27,500 | |
| 1846O | 58,000 | 675 | 1,000 | 3,250 | 4,750 | 11,000 | | |

| | Mintage | VF-20 | EF-40 | AU-50 | AU-55 | MS-60 | MS-63 | PF-63 |
|---|---|---|---|---|---|---|---|---|
| 1847, All kinds | 915,981 | | | | | | | |
| 1847 | | $450 | $550 | $600 | $625 | $1,650 | $6,000 | |
| 1847, Top of Extra 7 Very Low at Border | | 575 | 600 | 700 | 1,150 | 2,250 | 8,750 | |
| 1847C | 84,151 | 2,000 | 2,350 | 3,500 | 4,500 | 9,500 | 27,500 | |
| 1847D | 64,405 | 2,000 | 2,500 | 3,500 | 5,000 | 8,500 | 20,000 | |
| 1847O | 12,000 | 3,000 | 7,500 | 11,500 | 15,000 | 47,500 | | |
| 1848 | 260,775 | 450 | 525 | 600 | 700 | 1,750 | 9,500 | |
| 1848C | 64,472 | 2,000 | 2,500 | 3,500 | 5,500 | 15,000 | 40,000 | |
| 1848D | 47,465 | 1,850 | 2,750 | 3,500 | 5,500 | 12,500 | 25,000 | |
| 1849 | 133,070 | 450 | 525 | 675 | 825 | 2,750 | 10,000 | |
| 1849C | 64,823 | 2,000 | 2,500 | 3,250 | 4,750 | 8,500 | 26,000 | |
| 1849D | 39,036 | 2,000 | 2,750 | 3,500 | 4,500 | 11,500 | 35,000 | |
| 1850 | 64,491 | 450 | 525 | 975 | 1,250 | 3,000 | 12,500 | |
| 1850C | 63,591 | 2,000 | 2,350 | 3,250 | 4,250 | 10,000 | 18,500 | |
| 1850D | 43,984 | 2,000 | 2,750 | 3,950 | 5,000 | 23,500 | | |
| 1851 | 377,505 | 450 | 525 | 600 | 650 | 2,500 | 8,500 | |
| 1851C | 49,176 | 2,000 | 2,500 | 3,500 | 4,500 | 11,000 | 37,500 | |
| 1851D | 62,710 | 2,000 | 2,500 | 3,750 | 5,500 | 12,000 | 25,000 | |
| 1851O | 41,000 | 850 | 1,500 | 4,750 | 5,750 | 10,000 | 25,000 | |
| 1852 | 573,901 | 450 | 500 | 575 | 600 | 1,500 | 6,500 | |
| 1852C | 72,574 | 2,000 | 2,500 | 3,500 | 4,250 | 6,000 | 20,000 | |
| 1852D | 91,584 | 2,000 | 2,600 | 3,750 | 5,000 | 9,500 | 25,000 | |
| 1853 | 305,770 | 450 | 500 | 575 | 600 | 1,500 | 5,750 | |
| 1853C | 65,571 | 2,000 | 2,500 | 3,500 | 4,250 | 6,750 | 21,500 | |
| 1853D | 89,678 | 2,000 | 2,400 | 3,400 | 4,500 | 6,750 | 15,000 | |
| 1854 | 160,675 | 450 | 500 | 575 | 850 | 2,000 | 8,500 | |
| 1854C | 39,283 | 2,000 | 2,500 | 4,000 | 5,000 | 10,000 | 37,500 | |
| 1854D | 56,413 | 2,000 | 2,500 | 3,750 | 4,500 | 8,000 | 23,500 | |
| 1854O | 46,000 | 550 | 800 | 1,350 | 2,250 | 8,000 | 22,500 | |
| 1854S *(2 known)* | 268 | | 2,500,000 | | | | | |
| 1855 | 117,098 | 450 | 550 | 600 | 650 | 1,650 | 7,500 | — |
| 1855C | 39,788 | 2,250 | 2,500 | 4,000 | 4,750 | 12,000 | 45,000 | |
| 1855D | 22,432 | 2,000 | 2,750 | 3,600 | 5,000 | 13,500 | 35,000 | |
| 1855O | 11,100 | 1,250 | 2,750 | 4,750 | 7,000 | 20,000 | | |
| 1855S | 61,000 | 750 | 1,250 | 2,250 | 4,000 | 12,500 | | |
| 1856 | 197,990 | 475 | 525 | 600 | 650 | 2,000 | 8,000 | — |
| 1856C | 28,457 | 2,000 | 2,500 | 3,750 | 5,000 | 13,500 | 45,000 | |
| 1856D | 19,786 | 2,000 | 2,500 | 3,750 | 5,750 | 8,500 | 27,500 | |
| 1856O | 10,000 | 1,000 | 1,850 | 4,250 | 6,500 | 12,500 | | |
| 1856S | 105,100 | 575 | 750 | 1,250 | 2,000 | 7,500 | 25,000 | — |
| 1857 | 98,188 | 450 | 475 | 575 | 625 | 1,850 | 6,000 | |
| 1857C | 31,360 | 2,000 | 2,500 | 3,500 | 4,250 | 7,500 | 27,500 | |
| 1857D | 17,046 | 2,000 | 2,600 | 3,750 | 5,000 | 10,000 | | |
| 1857O | 13,000 | 1,000 | 1,700 | 4,000 | 5,500 | 13,500 | | |
| 1857S | 87,000 | 600 | 800 | 1,100 | 2,250 | 10,500 | 30,000 | |
| 1858 | 15,136 | 550 | 575 | 800 | 1,250 | 3,250 | 8,000 | $75,000 |
| 1858C | 38,856 | 2,000 | 2,500 | 3,750 | 4,500 | 9,000 | 30,000 | |
| 1858D | 15,362 | 2,000 | 2,500 | 3,750 | 4,750 | 10,500 | 32,500 | |
| 1858S | 18,600 | 1,500 | 3,000 | 5,250 | 9,000 | | | |
| 1859 (80) | 16,734 | 550 | 750 | 1,650 | 1,750 | 6,000 | 18,000 | 45,000 |
| 1859C | 31,847 | 2,000 | 2,500 | 3,500 | 5,000 | 10,500 | 35,000 | |

*Chart continued on next page.*

| | Mintage | VF-20 | EF-40 | AU-50 | AU-55 | MS-60 | MS-63 | PF-63 |
|---|---|---|---|---|---|---|---|---|
| 1859D | 10,366 | $2,000 | $2,750 | $3,750 | $5,000 | $10,000 | | |
| 1859S | 13,220 | 1,500 | 3,500 | 5,000 | 6,500 | 25,000 | | |
| 1860 (62) | 19,763 | 600 | 1,000 | 1,500 | 2,000 | 3,500 | $17,500 | $37,500 |
| 1860C | 14,813 | 2,000 | 2,750 | 4,250 | 6,500 | 11,000 | 27,500 | |
| 1860D | 14,635 | 2,250 | 3,500 | 4,500 | 6,500 | 13,000 | 40,000 | |
| 1860S | 21,200 | 2,000 | 3,500 | 6,500 | 9,500 | 29,500 | | |
| 1861 (66) | 688,084 | 450 | 475 | 575 | 675 | 1,750 | 6,000 | 35,000 |
| 1861C | 6,879 | 6,000 | 9,500 | 13,000 | 16,000 | 30,000 | 100,000 | |
| 1861D | 1,597 | 25,000 | 40,000 | 45,000 | 60,000 | 90,000 | 200,000 | |
| 1861S | 18,000 | 3,250 | 6,500 | 8,500 | 12,000 | | | |
| 1862 (35) | 4,430 | 2,500 | 5,000 | 8,500 | 13,500 | 25,000 | | 35,000 |
| 1862S | 9,500 | 4,250 | 8,500 | 10,500 | 17,500 | | | |
| 1863 (30) | 2,442 | 3,500 | 8,500 | 18,500 | 27,500 | | | 35,000 |
| 1863S | 17,000 | 3,500 | 5,000 | 12,500 | 17,500 | | | |
| 1864 (50) | 4,170 | 2,500 | 4,000 | 8,500 | 11,000 | 20,000 | | 35,000 |
| 1864S | 3,888 | 20,000 | 45,000 | 75,000 | 85,000 | | | |
| 1865 (25) | 1,270 | 6,500 | 12,000 | 20,000 | 25,000 | 35,000 | | 35,000 |
| 1865S | 27,612 | 2,750 | 4,250 | 7,000 | 8,000 | 14,500 | | |
| 1866S, No Motto | 9,000 | 2,250 | 5,000 | 8,500 | 11,000 | 30,000 | | |

## Variety 2 – Motto Above Eagle (1866–1908)

*Designer Christian Gobrecht; weight 8.359 grams; composition .900 gold, .100 copper (net weight .24187 oz. pure gold); diameter 21.6 mm; reeded edge; mints: Philadelphia, Carson City, Denver, New Orleans, San Francisco.*

**VF-20 Very Fine**—Half of hair lines above coronet missing. Hair curls under ear evident, but worn. Motto and its ribbon sharp.
**EF-40 Extremely Fine**—Small amount of wear on top of hair and below L in LIBERTY. Wear evident on wing tips and neck of eagle.
**AU-50 About Uncirculated**—Trace of wear on tip of coronet and hair above eye.
**AU-55 Choice About Uncirculated**—Evidence of friction on design high points. Some original mint luster present.
**MS-60 Uncirculated**—No trace of wear. Light blemishes.
**MS-63 Choice Uncirculated**—Some distracting contact marks or blemishes in prime focal areas. Impaired luster possible.
**PF-63 Choice Proof**—Reflective surfaces with only a few blemishes in secondary focal places. No major flaws.

*Circulation strike.*

*Proof strike.*

| | Mintage | VF-20 | EF-40 | AU-50 | AU-55 | MS-60 | MS-63 | PF-63 |
|---|---|---|---|---|---|---|---|---|
| 1866 (30) | 6,700 | $1,000 | $2,000 | $3,000 | $5,000 | $11,500 | $40,000 | $25,000 |
| 1866S | 34,920 | 1,250 | 2,750 | 7,000 | 10,000 | 25,000 | | |
| 1867 (50) | 6,870 | 1,000 | 1,750 | 3,000 | 5,000 | 10,000 | | 25,000 |
| 1867S | 29,000 | 1,100 | 2,000 | 5,500 | 10,000 | | | |
| 1868 (25) | 5,700 | 600 | 1,000 | 2,500 | 4,750 | 10,000 | | 25,000 |
| 1868S | 52,000 | 525 | 1,250 | 3,000 | 4,500 | 20,000 | | |
| 1869 (25) | 1,760 | 1,100 | 2,750 | 5,000 | 7,500 | 15,000 | | 25,000 |
| 1869S | 31,000 | 600 | 1,500 | 3,000 | 5,000 | 16,000 | | |

| | Mintage | VF-20 | EF-40 | AU-50 | AU-55 | MS-60 | MS-63 | PF-63 |
|---|---|---|---|---|---|---|---|---|
| 1870 . . . . . . . . . . . (35) | 4,000 | $900 | $2,000 | $3,250 | $5,000 | $15,000 | | $25,000 |
| 1870CC | 7,675 | 25,000 | 35,000 | 55,000 | 70,000 | 110,000 | | |
| 1870S | 17,000 | 1,000 | 2,350 | 5,500 | 8,500 | | | |
| 1871 . . . . . . . . . . . (30) | 3,200 | 1,150 | 1,600 | 2,650 | 4,500 | 10,000 | | 25,000 |
| 1871CC | 20,770 | 4,750 | 10,000 | 16,000 | 25,000 | 55,000 | | |
| 1871S | 25,000 | 525 | 1,100 | 2,500 | 4,000 | 13,500 | | |
| 1872 . . . . . . . . . . . (30) | 1,660 | 1,000 | 2,000 | 4,500 | 5,500 | 10,500 | $20,000 | 22,500 |
| 1872CC | 16,980 | 3,500 | 9,000 | 18,000 | 25,000 | | | |
| 1872S | 36,400 | 750 | 1,100 | 2,600 | 4,000 | 12,000 | | |
| 1873, Close 3 . . . . (25) | 112,480 | 395 | 405 | 475 | 550 | 950 | 4,000 | 22,500 |
| 1873, Open 3 | 112,505 | 395 | 405 | 450 | 500 | 1,000 | 3,500 | |
| 1873CC | 7,416 | 7,500 | 15,000 | 25,000 | 38,000 | 75,000 | | |
| 1873S | 31,000 | 600 | 1,100 | 2,250 | 4,250 | 18,500 | | |
| 1874 . . . . . . . . . . . (20) | 3,488 | 850 | 1,400 | 2,250 | 3,000 | 10,000 | 22,500 | 27,500 |
| 1874CC | 21,198 | 2,750 | 4,500 | 12,000 | 17,000 | 35,000 | | |
| 1874S | 16,000 | 800 | 1,650 | 3,000 | 4,750 | | | |
| 1875 . . . . . . . . . . . (20) | 200 | 85,000 | 100,000 | 150,000 | 225,000 | | | 150,000 |
| 1875CC | 11,828 | 3,750 | 8,000 | 16,000 | 25,000 | 45,000 | | |
| 1875S | 9,000 | 1,250 | 2,500 | 4,250 | 7,500 | 18,500 | | |
| 1876 . . . . . . . . . . . (45) | 1,432 | 1,750 | 4,500 | 5,500 | 7,500 | 14,000 | 25,000 | 20,000 |
| 1876CC | 6,887 | 4,500 | 8,000 | 14,000 | 17,500 | 50,000 | | |
| *$477,250, MS-66, Stack's Bowers auction, August 2012* | | | | | | | | |
| 1876S | 4,000 | 3,250 | 5,500 | 10,000 | 12,500 | 30,000 | | |
| 1877 . . . . . . . . . . . (20) | 1,132 | 2,250 | 3,750 | 5,000 | 6,000 | 12,500 | | 22,500 |
| 1877CC | 8,680 | 3,000 | 7,000 | 13,000 | 20,000 | 50,000 | | |
| 1877S | 26,700 | 500 | 650 | 1,500 | 3,000 | 8,500 | 20,000 | |
| 1878 . . . . . . . . . . . (20) | 131,720 | 395 | 400 | 405 | 410 | 575 | 1,750 | 22,500 |
| 1878CC | 9,054 | 5,500 | 11,000 | 17,500 | 32,000 | | | |
| 1878S | 144,700 | 395 | 400 | 405 | 410 | 650 | 4,000 | |
| 1879 . . . . . . . . . . . (30) | 301,920 | 395 | 400 | 405 | 410 | 450 | 1,500 | 22,500 |
| 1879CC | 17,281 | 1,750 | 2,750 | 4,000 | 7,500 | 25,000 | | |
| 1879S | 426,200 | 395 | 400 | 405 | 410 | 600 | 1,750 | |
| 1880 . . . . . . . . . . . (36) | 3,166,400 | 395 | 400 | 405 | 410 | 450 | 650 | 17,500 |
| 1880CC | 51,017 | 1,250 | 1,500 | 2,000 | 4,500 | 12,500 | 45,000 | |
| 1880S | 1,348,900 | 395 | 400 | 405 | 410 | 450 | 650 | |
| 1881, Final 1 Over 0 | * | 475 | 500 | 550 | 675 | 1,350 | 2,500 | |
| 1881 . . . . . . . . . . . (42) | 5,708,760 | 395 | 400 | 405 | 410 | 450 | 600 | 16,500 |
| 1881CC | 13,886 | 1,750 | 3,500 | 7,000 | 10,500 | 25,000 | 55,000 | |
| 1881S | 969,000 | 395 | 400 | 405 | 410 | 450 | 650 | |
| 1882 . . . . . . . . . . . (48) | 2,514,520 | 395 | 400 | 405 | 410 | 450 | 650 | 15,500 |
| 1882CC | 82,817 | 1,000 | 1,500 | 2,000 | 4,000 | 11,500 | 35,000 | |
| 1882S | 969,000 | 395 | 400 | 405 | 410 | 500 | 600 | |
| 1883 . . . . . . . . . . . (61) | 233,400 | 395 | 400 | 405 | 410 | 500 | 1,250 | 15,500 |
| 1883CC | 12,598 | 2,000 | 3,000 | 4,500 | 6,750 | 18,500 | 50,000 | |
| 1883S | 83,200 | 395 | 400 | 405 | 410 | 700 | 1,650 | |
| 1884 . . . . . . . . . . . (48) | 191,030 | 395 | 400 | 405 | 410 | 550 | 1,650 | 15,500 |
| 1884CC | 16,402 | 1,500 | 2,500 | 4,500 | 7,500 | 20,000 | | |
| 1884S | 177,000 | 395 | 400 | 405 | 410 | 450 | 1,150 | |
| 1885 . . . . . . . . . . . (66) | 601,440 | 395 | 400 | 405 | 410 | 450 | 600 | 15,500 |
| 1885S | 1,211,500 | 395 | 400 | 405 | 410 | 450 | 600 | |
| 1886 . . . . . . . . . . . (72) | 388,360 | 395 | 400 | 405 | 410 | 450 | 700 | 15,500 |

* Included in number below.

*Chart continued on next page.*

| | Mintage | VF-20 | EF-40 | AU-50 | AU-55 | MS-60 | MS-63 | PF-63 |
|---|---|---|---|---|---|---|---|---|
| 1886S | 3,268,000 | $395 | $400 | $405 | $410 | $450 | $550 | |
| 1887, Proof only | (87) | | | | | | | $65,000 |
| 1887S | 1,912,000 | 395 | 400 | 405 | 410 | 450 | 600 | |
| 1888 | (95) 18,201 | 395 | 400 | 405 | 410 | 650 | 1,750 | 13,500 |
| 1888S | 293,900 | 395 | 400 | 405 | 450 | 1,000 | 3,500 | |
| 1889 | (45) 7,520 | 500 | 600 | 700 | 950 | 1,250 | 4,500 | 14,000 |
| 1890 | (88) 4,240 | 550 | 675 | 850 | 1,250 | 2,250 | 6,000 | 14,000 |
| 1890CC | 53,800 | 800 | 950 | 1,100 | 1,450 | 2,250 | 8,500 | |
| 1891 | (53) 61,360 | 395 | 400 | 405 | 410 | 500 | 1,250 | 13,500 |
| 1891CC | 208,000 | 875 | 950 | 1,150 | 1,350 | 2,000 | 4,500 | |
| 1892 | (92) 753,480 | 395 | 400 | 405 | 410 | 450 | 600 | 13,500 |
| 1892CC | 82,968 | 750 | 850 | 1,100 | 1,300 | 2,500 | 9,000 | |
| 1892O | 10,000 | 1,750 | 2,250 | 2,500 | 3,000 | 5,000 | 18,500 | |
| 1892S | 298,400 | 395 | 400 | 405 | 410 | 450 | 1,800 | |
| 1893 | (77) 1,528,120 | 395 | 400 | 405 | 410 | 450 | 575 | 13,500 |
| 1893CC | 60,000 | 950 | 1,100 | 1,300 | 1,800 | 3,000 | 10,000 | |
| 1893O | 110,000 | 400 | 450 | 500 | 550 | 1,000 | 5,000 | |
| 1893S | 224,000 | 395 | 400 | 405 | 410 | 450 | 550 | |
| 1894 | (75) 957,880 | 395 | 400 | 405 | 410 | 450 | 550 | 13,500 |
| 1894O | 16,600 | 425 | 450 | 550 | 800 | 2,000 | 8,500 | |
| 1894S | 55,900 | 400 | 425 | 450 | 650 | 2,500 | 9,000 | |
| 1895 | (81) 1,345,855 | 395 | 400 | 405 | 410 | 425 | 550 | 12,500 |
| 1895S | 112,000 | 395 | 425 | 450 | 650 | 1,500 | 5,000 | |
| 1896 | (103) 58,960 | 395 | 400 | 405 | 410 | 425 | 550 | 12,500 |
| 1896S | 155,400 | 395 | 400 | 405 | 410 | 1,100 | 5,500 | |
| 1897 | (83) 867,800 | 395 | 400 | 405 | 410 | 425 | 550 | 12,500 |
| 1897S | 354,000 | 395 | 400 | 405 | 410 | 800 | 4,500 | |
| 1898 | (75) 633,420 | 395 | 400 | 405 | 410 | 425 | 550 | 12,500 |
| 1898S | 1,397,400 | 395 | 400 | 405 | 410 | 450 | 1,100 | |
| 1899 | (99) 1,710,630 | 395 | 400 | 405 | 410 | 425 | 550 | 12,500 |
| 1899S | 1,545,000 | 395 | 400 | 405 | 410 | 450 | 1,000 | |
| 1900 | (230) 1,405,500 | 395 | 400 | 405 | 410 | 425 | 525 | 12,500 |
| 1900S | 329,000 | 395 | 400 | 405 | 410 | 450 | 850 | |
| 1901 | (140) 615,900 | 395 | 400 | 405 | 410 | 425 | 525 | 12,500 |
| 1901S, All kinds | 3,648,000 | | | | | | | |
| 1901S, Final 1/0 | | 395 | 400 | 475 | 500 | 550 | 1,250 | |
| 1901S | | 395 | 400 | 405 | 410 | 425 | 525 | |
| 1902 | (162) 172,400 | 395 | 400 | 405 | 410 | 425 | 525 | 12,500 |
| 1902S | 939,000 | 395 | 400 | 405 | 410 | 425 | 525 | |
| 1903 | (154) 226,870 | 395 | 400 | 405 | 410 | 425 | 525 | 12,500 |
| 1903S | 1,855,000 | 395 | 400 | 405 | 410 | 425 | 525 | |
| 1904 | (136) 392,000 | 395 | 400 | 405 | 410 | 425 | 525 | 12,500 |
| 1904S | 97,000 | 395 | 400 | 405 | 450 | 800 | 3,000 | |
| 1905 | (108) 302,200 | 395 | 400 | 405 | 410 | 425 | 525 | 12,500 |
| 1905S | 880,700 | 395 | 400 | 425 | 475 | 650 | 1,500 | |
| 1906 | (85) 348,735 | 395 | 400 | 405 | 410 | 425 | 525 | 12,500 |
| 1906D | 320,000 | 395 | 400 | 405 | 410 | 425 | 525 | |
| 1906S | 598,000 | 395 | 400 | 405 | 450 | 500 | 1,000 | |
| 1907 | (92) 626,100 | 395 | 400 | 405 | 410 | 425 | 525 | 12,500 |
| 1907D | 888,000 | 395 | 400 | 405 | 410 | 425 | 525 | |
| 1908 | 421,874 | 395 | 400 | 405 | 410 | 425 | 525 | |

## INDIAN HEAD (1908–1929)

This type conforms to the quarter eagle of the same date. The sunken-relief designs and lettering make these two series unique in United States coinage.

*Designer Bela Lyon Pratt; weight 8.359 grams; composition .900 gold, .100 copper (net weight .24187 oz. pure gold); diameter 21.6 mm; reeded edge; mints: Philadelphia, Denver, New Orleans, San Francisco.*

**VF-20 Very Fine**—Noticeable wear on large middle feathers and tip of eagle's wing.
**EF-40 Extremely Fine**—Cheekbone, war bonnet, and headband feathers slightly worn. Feathers on eagle's upper wing show considerable wear.
**AU-50 About Uncirculated**—Trace of wear on cheekbone and headdress.
**AU-55 Choice About Uncirculated**—Evidence of friction on design high points. Much of original mint luster present.
**MS-60 Uncirculated**—No trace of wear. Light blemishes.
**MS-63 Choice Uncirculated**—Some distracting contact marks or blemishes in prime focal areas. Impaired luster possible.

Mintmark Location

*Scarcer coins with well-struck mintmarks command higher prices.*

| | Mintage | VF-20 | EF-40 | AU-50 | AU-55 | MS-60 | MS-63 | MATTE PF-63 |
|---|---|---|---|---|---|---|---|---|
| 1908 . . . . . . . . . . . (167) | 577,845 | $405 | $420 | $440 | $460 | $500 | $1,000 | $15,000 |
| 1908D | 148,000 | 405 | 420 | 440 | 460 | 600 | 1,050 | |
| 1908S | 82,000 | 575 | 700 | 1,000 | 1,350 | 3,000 | 9,000 | |
| 1909 . . . . . . . . . . . (78) | 627,060 | 405 | 420 | 440 | 460 | 525 | 1,000 | 16,750 |
| 1909D | 3,423,560 | 405 | 420 | 440 | 460 | 525 | 900 | |
| 1909O **(a)** | 34,200 | 4,750 | 7,500 | 10,000 | 13,500 | 35,000 | 85,000 | |
| *$690,000, MS-66, Heritage auction, January 2011* | | | | | | | | |
| 1909S | 297,200 | 425 | 450 | 475 | 550 | 2,100 | 10,000 | |
| 1910 . . . . . . . . . . . (250) | 604,000 | 405 | 420 | 440 | 460 | 525 | 1,000 | 16,500 |
| 1910D | 193,600 | 405 | 420 | 440 | 460 | 525 | 2,300 | |
| 1910S | 770,200 | 425 | 450 | 475 | 500 | 1,250 | 9,000 | |
| 1911 . . . . . . . . . . . (139) | 915,000 | 405 | 420 | 440 | 460 | 525 | 1,000 | 15,500 |
| 1911D | 72,500 | 750 | 1,000 | 1,600 | 2,750 | 7,750 | 37,500 | |
| *$299,000, MS-65+, Heritage auction, January 2011* | | | | | | | | |
| 1911S | 1,416,000 | 425 | 450 | 475 | 500 | 825 | 3,500 | |
| 1912 . . . . . . . . . . . (144) | 790,000 | 405 | 420 | 440 | 460 | 525 | 1,000 | 15,500 |
| 1912S | 392,000 | 425 | 450 | 475 | 600 | 1,500 | 14,000 | |
| 1913 . . . . . . . . . . . . (99) | 915,901 | 405 | 420 | 440 | 460 | 525 | 1,000 | 16,000 |
| 1913S | 408,000 | 525 | 575 | 625 | 800 | 2,000 | 12,500 | |
| 1914 . . . . . . . . . . . (125) | 247,000 | 405 | 420 | 440 | 460 | 525 | 1,550 | 16,500 |
| 1914D | 247,000 | 405 | 420 | 440 | 460 | 600 | 2,000 | |
| 1914S | 263,000 | 425 | 450 | 475 | 525 | 1,650 | 7,700 | |
| 1915 **(b)** . . . . . . . . . (75) | 588,000 | 405 | 420 | 440 | 460 | 525 | 1,050 | 17,000 |
| 1915S | 164,000 | 425 | 450 | 500 | 700 | 2,300 | 10,500 | |
| 1916S | 240,000 | 450 | 485 | 525 | 625 | 1,150 | 3,500 | |
| 1929 | 662,000 | 18,500 | 20,000 | 23,500 | 25,000 | 33,500 | 42,500 | |

**a.** Beware spurious "O" mintmark. **b.** Pieces dated 1915-D are counterfeit.

Coinage authority, including weights and fineness, of the eagle is specified by the Act of April 2, 1792. The Small Eagle reverse was used until 1797, when the large Heraldic Eagle replaced it. The early dates vary in the number of stars, the rarest date being 1798. Many of these early pieces show file scratches from the Mint's practice of adjusting planchet weight before coining. No eagles were struck dated 1805 to 1837. Proofs of some dates prior to 1855 are known to exist, and all are rare.

*Note: Values of common gold coins have been based on a gold bullion price of $1,500 per ounce, and may vary with the prevailing spot price. The net weight and content listed may be used to recalculate bullion value.*

## CAPPED BUST TO RIGHT (1795–1804)

### Small Eagle Reverse (1795–1797)

*Designer Robert Scot; weight 17.50 grams; composition .9167 gold, .0833 silver and copper; approx. diameter 33 mm; reeded edge.*

**F-12 Fine**—Details on turban and head obliterated.
**VF-20 Very Fine**—Hair lines in curls on neck and details under turban and over forehead worn but distinguishable.
**EF-40 Extremely Fine**—Definite wear on hair to left of eye and strand of hair across and around turban, as well as on eagle's wing tips.
**AU-50 About Uncirculated**—Trace of wear on cap, hair, cheek, and drapery.
**AU-55 Choice About Uncirculated**—Evidence of friction on design high points. Most of original mint luster present.
**MS-60 Uncirculated**—No trace of wear. Light blemishes.
**MS-63 Choice Uncirculated**—Some distracting contact marks or blemishes in prime focal areas. Impaired luster possible.

13 Leaves

9 Leaves

| | Mintage | F-12 | VF-20 | EF-40 | AU-50 | AU-55 | MS-60 | MS-63 |
|---|---|---|---|---|---|---|---|---|
| 1795, 13 Leaves Below Eagle . . . . *$2,585,000, MS-66+, Sotheby's/ Stack's Bowers auction, September 2015* | 5,583 | $27,500 | $35,000 | $50,000 | $57,500 | $72,500 | $105,000 | $300,000 |
| 1795, 9 Leaves Below Eagle . . . . . . . . . *$1,057,500, MS-63+, Sotheby's/ Stack's Bowers auction, September 2015* | * | 55,000 | 65,000 | 80,000 | 130,000 | 180,000 | 250,000 | 750,000 |
| 1796 . . . . . . . . . . . . . . . . . . . . . . . | 4,146 | 30,000 | 35,000 | 50,000 | 57,500 | 67,500 | 125,000 | 425,000 |
| 1797, Small Eagle . . . . . . . . . . . . . *$448,500, MS-63, Goldberg auction, May 2007* | 3,615 | 40,000 | 55,000 | 70,000 | 105,000 | 140,000 | 225,000 | 450,000 |

* Included in number above.

## Heraldic Eagle Reverse (1797–1804)

1803, Small Reverse Stars

| | Mintage | F-12 | VF-20 | EF-40 | AU-50 | AU-55 | MS-60 | MS-63 |
|---|---|---|---|---|---|---|---|---|
| 1797, Large Eagle | 10,940 | $11,000 | $15,000 | $20,000 | $32,500 | $40,000 | $52,500 | $150,000 |
| 1798, 8 Over 7, 9 Stars Left, 4 Right | 900 | 22,500 | 27,500 | 38,000 | 52,500 | 75,000 | 120,000 | 325,000 |
| 1798, 8 Over 7, 7 Stars Left, 6 Right | 842 | 45,000 | 65,000 | 105,000 | 185,000 | 275,000 | 475,000 | |
| 1799, Small Obverse Stars | 37,449 | 9,000 | 12,500 | 16,000 | 20,000 | 23,500 | 32,500 | 72,500 |
| 1799, Large Obverse Stars | * | 9,000 | 12,500 | 16,000 | 20,000 | 23,500 | 32,500 | 72,500 |
| 1800 | 5,999 | 9,500 | 13,000 | 16,500 | 19,000 | 21,500 | 32,500 | 87,500 |
| 1801 | 44,344 | 9,000 | 11,000 | 15,500 | 18,500 | 20,000 | 28,500 | 60,000 |
| 1803, Small Reverse Stars | 15,017 | 9,500 | 12,000 | 16,000 | 20,000 | 22,500 | 35,000 | 65,000 |
| 1803, Large Reverse Stars **(a)** | * | 9,500 | 12,000 | 16,000 | 20,000 | 22,500 | 35,000 | 65,000 |
| 1804, Crosslet 4 | 3,757 | 20,000 | 23,500 | 37,500 | 50,000 | 65,000 | 85,000 | 185,000 |
| 1804, Plain 4, Proof, Restrike *(4 known)* | | | | | | | | 4,000,000 |

* Included in number above. **a.** Variety without tiny 14th star in cloud is very rare.

# LIBERTY HEAD (1838–1907)

## Variety 1 – No Motto Above Eagle (1838–1866)

In 1838, the weight and diameter of the eagle were reduced and the obverse and reverse were redesigned. Liberty now faces left and the word LIBERTY is placed on the coronet. A more natural-appearing eagle is used on the reverse. The value, TEN D., is shown for the first time on this denomination.

*Designer Christian Gobrecht; weight 16.718 grams; composition .900 gold, .100 copper (net weight: .48375 oz. pure gold); diameter 27 mm; reeded edge; mints: Philadelphia, New Orleans, San Francisco.*

**VF-20 Very Fine**—Hair lines above coronet partly worn. Curls under ear worn but defined.
**EF-40 Extremely Fine**—Small amount of wear on top of hair and below L in LIBERTY. Wear evident on wing tips and neck of eagle.
**AU-50 About Uncirculated**—Trace of wear on tip of coronet and hair above eye.
**AU-55 Choice About Uncirculated**—Evidence of friction on design high points. Some of original mint luster present.
**MS-60 Uncirculated**—No trace of wear. Light blemishes.
**MS-63 Choice Uncirculated**—Some distracting contact marks or blemishes in prime focal areas. Impaired luster possible.
**PF-63 Choice Proof**—Attractive reflective surfaces with only a few blemishes in secondary focal places. No major flaws.

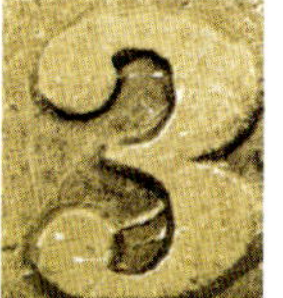

*Mintmark is on reverse, below eagle.*

1853, 3 Over 2

*See next page for chart.*

| | Mintage | VF-20 | EF-40 | AU-50 | AU-55 | MS-60 | MS-63 |
|---|---|---|---|---|---|---|---|
| 1838 **(a)** | 7,200 | $4,000 | $9,000 | $17,500 | $25,000 | $62,500 | $125,000 |
| *$550,000, PF-63, Akers auction, May 1998* | | | | | | | |
| 1839, Large Letters **(a)** | 25,801 | 2,000 | 5,000 | 6,500 | 11,500 | 32,500 | 85,000 |
| 1839, Lg Ltrs, 9 Over 8, Type of 1838 | | | | | | | |
| *$1,610,000, PF-67 UC, Heritage auction, January 2007* | | | | | | | |
| 1839, Small Letters | 12,447 | 4,000 | 12,000 | 20,000 | 35,000 | 75,000 | |
| 1840 | 47,338 | 1,150 | 1,500 | 1,850 | 2,750 | 13,500 | |
| 1841 | 63,131 | 1,000 | 1,100 | 1,350 | 2,500 | 11,000 | 45,000 |
| 1841O | 2,500 | 7,000 | 15,000 | 30,000 | 75,000 | | |
| 1842, Small Date, Plain 4 | 18,623 | 1,000 | 1,150 | 1,750 | 3,000 | 12,500 | 65,000 |
| 1842, Large Date, Crosslet 4 | 62,884 | 1,000 | 1,150 | 1,650 | 2,750 | 15,000 | 45,000 |
| 1842O | 27,400 | 1,250 | 1,650 | 3,500 | 7,500 | 70,000 | 250,000 |
| 1843 | 75,462 | 1,050 | 1,150 | 1,850 | 4,000 | 20,000 | |
| 1843O | 175,162 | 1,050 | 1,200 | 1,800 | 3,250 | 14,000 | 55,000 |
| 1844 | 6,361 | 2,500 | 4,500 | 7,000 | 16,000 | | 85,000 |
| 1844O | 118,700 | 1,050 | 1,350 | 1,850 | 4,750 | 15,000 | |
| 1845 | 26,153 | 1,000 | 1,450 | 2,750 | 7,000 | 22,500 | |
| 1845O | 47,500 | 1,050 | 1,650 | 3,250 | 7,500 | 22,000 | |
| 1846 | 20,095 | 1,150 | 1,350 | 4,250 | 7,000 | 30,000 | |
| 1846O | 81,780 | 1,200 | 2,000 | 3,500 | 6,000 | 25,000 | |
| 1847 | 862,258 | 900 | 1,000 | 1,050 | 1,100 | 3,500 | 21,500 |
| 1847O | 571,500 | 950 | 1,050 | 1,150 | 1,600 | 6,000 | 30,000 |
| 1848 | 145,484 | 850 | 950 | 1,050 | 1,350 | 6,000 | 30,000 |
| 1848O | 35,850 | 1,500 | 3,250 | 4,000 | 6,500 | 15,000 | 50,000 |
| 1849 | 653,618 | 850 | 1,100 | 1,300 | 1,400 | 3,750 | 18,000 |
| 1849O | 23,900 | 1,750 | 3,500 | 5,500 | 9,500 | 35,000 | |
| 1850, All kinds | 291,451 | | | | | | |
| 1850, Large Date | | 900 | 1,000 | 1,100 | 1,250 | 4,500 | |
| 1850, Small Date | | 950 | 1,200 | 1,850 | 2,750 | 8,000 | |
| 1850O | 57,500 | 1,350 | 2,000 | 3,500 | 6,500 | 30,000 | |
| 1851 | 176,328 | 875 | 1,000 | 1,100 | 1,250 | 4,250 | 32,500 |
| 1851O | 263,000 | 1,000 | 1,200 | 1,750 | 2,750 | 9,500 | 40,000 |
| 1852 | 263,106 | 875 | 1,000 | 1,050 | 1,250 | 4,250 | 25,000 |
| 1852O | 18,000 | 1,650 | 2,500 | 6,000 | 11,000 | 85,000 | |
| 1853, All kinds | 201,253 | | | | | | |
| 1853, 3 Over 2 | | 1,000 | 1,500 | 2,000 | 3,250 | 13,000 | |
| 1853 | | 875 | 1,000 | 1,050 | 1,150 | 3,500 | 17,000 |

**a.** The Liberty Head style of 1838 and 1839 (Large Letters) differs from that used for subsequent issues.

| | Mintage | VF-20 | EF-40 | AU-50 | AU-55 | MS-60 | MS-63 | PF-63 |
|---|---|---|---|---|---|---|---|---|
| 1853O | 51,000 | $1,200 | $1,600 | $2,250 | $4,500 | $15,000 | | |
| 1854 | 54,250 | 900 | 1,050 | 1,250 | 1,650 | 6,500 | $27,500 | |
| 1854O, Large or Small Date | 52,500 | 1,150 | 1,350 | 2,000 | 3,250 | 10,500 | | |
| 1854S | 123,826 | 1,150 | 1,400 | 2,000 | 3,250 | 12,500 | | |
| 1855 | 121,701 | 900 | 1,100 | 1,200 | 1,350 | 4,750 | 17,500 | |
| 1855O | 18,000 | 1,250 | 3,500 | 5,500 | 10,000 | | | |
| 1855S | 9,000 | 2,750 | 4,000 | 7,000 | 20,000 | | | |
| 1856 | 60,490 | 900 | 1,000 | 1,150 | 1,250 | 4,000 | 15,000 | |
| 1856O | 14,500 | 1,350 | 2,500 | 4,500 | 7,000 | 45,000 | | |
| 1856S | 68,000 | 900 | 1,150 | 1,500 | 2,750 | 11,500 | | |

| | Mintage | VF-20 | EF-40 | AU-50 | AU-55 | MS-60 | MS-63 | PF-63 |
|---|---|---|---|---|---|---|---|---|
| 1857 | 16,606 | $900 | $1,000 | $1,650 | $3,000 | $16,000 | | |
| *$396,000, PF-66, Goldberg auction, May 1999* | | | | | | | | |
| 1857O | 5,500 | 2,500 | 4,500 | 8,500 | 12,500 | — | | |
| 1857S | 26,000 | 1,350 | 1,850 | 2,500 | 4,500 | 11,000 | | |
| 1858 **(b)** | 2,521 | 5,500 | 7,500 | 12,500 | 17,500 | 35,000 | | |
| 1858O | 20,000 | 1,250 | 1,600 | 2,750 | 3,750 | 11,000 | $40,000 | |
| 1858S | 11,800 | 1,600 | 4,000 | 7,000 | 18,000 | | | |
| 1859 (80) | 16,013 | 1,000 | 1,250 | 1,500 | 2,250 | 17,500 | 70,000 | $75,000 |
| 1859O | 2,300 | 6,000 | 15,000 | 30,000 | 40,000 | | | |
| 1859S | 7,000 | 3,000 | 8,000 | 20,000 | 30,000 | | | |
| 1860 (50) | 15,055 | 900 | 1,100 | 1,750 | 2,500 | 7,500 | 25,000 | 50,000 |
| 1860O | 11,100 | 1,450 | 2,750 | 4,000 | 6,000 | 17,500 | | |
| 1860S | 5,000 | 4,750 | 12,500 | 17,500 | 27,500 | 75,000 | | |
| 1861 (69) | 113,164 | 925 | 1,050 | 1,500 | 2,500 | 6,500 | 20,000 | 45,000 |
| 1861S | 15,500 | 4,000 | 8,500 | 12,500 | 17,500 | 65,000 | | |
| 1862 (35) | 10,960 | 1,000 | 2,250 | 5,500 | 6,500 | 18,500 | | 42,500 |
| 1862S | 12,500 | 2,500 | 5,000 | 10,000 | 22,500 | 100,000 | | |
| 1863 (30) | 1,218 | 15,000 | 32,500 | 50,000 | 70,000 | | — | 42,500 |
| 1863S | 10,000 | 5,500 | 15,000 | 20,000 | 35,000 | | | |
| 1864 (50) | 3,530 | 6,500 | 10,000 | 22,500 | 35,000 | 75,000 | | 42,500 |
| 1864S | 2,500 | 45,000 | 100,000 | 150,000 | 195,000 | | | |
| 1865 (25) | 3,980 | 4,500 | 9,000 | 15,000 | 20,000 | 65,000 | | 42,500 |
| *$528,750, PF-66+ DC, Stack's Bowers auction, August 2013* | | | | | | | | |
| 1865S, All kinds | 16,700 | | | | | | | |
| 1865S | | 6,500 | 12,500 | 19,500 | 27,500 | 95,000 | | |
| 1865S, 865/Inverted 186 | | 7,500 | 10,000 | 17,500 | 25,000 | 45,000 | | |
| 1866S | 8,500 | 5,000 | 15,000 | 20,000 | 25,000 | 65,000 | | |

**b.** Beware of fraudulently removed mintmark.

## Variety 2 – Motto Above Eagle (1866–1907)

*Designer Christian Gobrecht; weight 16.718 grams; composition .900 gold, .100 copper (net weight: .48375 oz. pure gold); diameter 27 mm; reeded edge; mints: Philadelphia, Carson City, Denver, New Orleans, San Francisco.*

**VF-20 Very Fine**—Half of hair lines over coronet visible. Curls under ear worn but defined. IN GOD WE TRUST and its ribbon sharp.

**EF-40 Extremely Fine**—Small amount of wear on top of hair and below L in LIBERTY. Wear evident on wing tips and neck of eagle.

**AU-50 About Uncirculated**—Trace of wear on hair above eye and on coronet.

**AU-55 Choice About Uncirculated**—Evidence of friction on design high points. Some of original mint luster present.

*Mintmark is on reverse, below eagle.*

**MS-60 Uncirculated**—No trace of wear. Light blemishes.

**MS-63 Choice Uncirculated**—Some distracting contact marks or blemishes in prime focal areas. Impaired luster possible.

**PF-63 Choice Proof**—Reflective surfaces with only a few blemishes in secondary focal areas. No major flaws.

| | Mintage | VF-20 | EF-40 | AU-50 | AU-55 | MS-60 | MS-63 | PF-63 |
|---|---|---|---|---|---|---|---|---|
| 1866 (30) | 3,750 | $1,500 | $3,000 | $5,000 | $10,000 | $42,500 | | $35,000 |
| 1866S | 11,500 | 2,500 | 4,500 | 7,250 | 10,000 | | | |
| 1867 (50) | 3,090 | 2,000 | 3,000 | 6,500 | 11,500 | 40,000 | | 35,000 |
| 1867S | 9,000 | 4,000 | 6,500 | 9,000 | 20,000 | | | |

*Chart continued on next page.*

| | Mintage | VF-20 | EF-40 | AU-50 | AU-55 | MS-60 | MS-63 | PF-63 |
|---|---|---|---|---|---|---|---|---|
| 1868 (25) | 10,630 | $850 | $1,250 | $1,850 | $3,500 | $17,500 | | $35,000 |
| 1868S | 13,500 | 1,800 | 2,500 | 4,000 | 7,000 | | | |
| 1869 (25) | 1,830 | 1,650 | 4,000 | 5,500 | 11,500 | 35,000 | | 35,000 |
| 1869S | 6,430 | 2,200 | 3,500 | 6,250 | 11,000 | 35,000 | | |
| 1870 (35) | 3,990 | 1,100 | 1,750 | 3,000 | 10,000 | 35,000 | | 35,000 |
| 1870CC | 5,908 | 40,000 | 60,000 | 85,000 | 150,000 | | | |
| 1870S | 8,000 | 1,650 | 4,000 | 5,500 | 11,000 | | | |
| 1871 (30) | 1,790 | 1,400 | 3,000 | 5,500 | 8,500 | | | 35,000 |
| 1871CC | 8,085 | 5,500 | 15,000 | 22,500 | 32,500 | | | |
| 1871S | 16,500 | 1,500 | 2,250 | 4,500 | 8,250 | | | |
| 1872 (30) | 1,620 | 3,000 | 5,000 | 9,250 | 11,000 | 25,000 | | 35,000 |
| 1872CC | 4,600 | 8,500 | 15,000 | 27,500 | 42,500 | | | |
| 1872S | 17,300 | 1,000 | 1,600 | 2,000 | 4,250 | 25,000 | | |
| 1873 (25) | 800 | 10,000 | 20,000 | 35,000 | 47,500 | 75,000 | | 37,500 |
| 1873CC | 4,543 | 12,500 | 25,000 | 52,500 | 75,000 | | | |
| 1873S | 12,000 | 1,250 | 2,750 | 4,250 | 7,000 | 30,000 | | |
| 1874 (20) | 53,140 | 800 | 850 | 900 | 925 | 1,650 | $10,000 | 35,000 |
| 1874CC | 16,767 | 3,500 | 6,000 | 12,500 | 20,000 | 70,000 | 200,000 | |
| 1874S | 10,000 | 1,500 | 2,250 | 4,750 | 8,000 | | | |
| 1875 (20) | 100 | 150,000 | 200,000 | 350,000 | 450,000 | | | 165,000 |
| *$345,000, AU-55+, Stack's Bowers auction, August 2011* | | | | | | | | |
| 1875CC | 7,715 | 6,000 | 10,000 | 17,500 | 45,000 | 100,000 | 185,000 | |
| 1876 (45) | 687 | 5,000 | 10,000 | 27,500 | 35,000 | 100,000 | | 32,500 |
| 1876CC | 4,696 | 5,500 | 13,500 | 22,500 | 40,000 | | | |
| 1876S | 5,000 | 2,000 | 5,000 | 10,000 | 25,000 | | | |
| 1877 (20) | 797 | 4,250 | 7,000 | 10,000 | 13,500 | 65,000 | | 35,000 |
| 1877CC | 3,332 | 8,500 | 12,500 | 25,000 | 50,000 | | | |
| 1877S | 17,000 | 900 | 1,350 | 2,000 | 4,500 | 30,000 | | |
| 1878 (20) | 73,780 | 800 | 805 | 815 | 820 | 975 | 5,500 | 27,500 |
| 1878CC | 3,244 | 7,500 | 20,000 | 40,000 | 65,000 | 135,000 | | |
| 1878S | 26,100 | 875 | 950 | 1,350 | 2,000 | 11,500 | 25,000 | |
| 1879 (30) | 384,740 | 800 | 805 | 815 | 820 | 900 | 3,000 | 25,000 |
| 1879CC | 1,762 | 17,500 | 25,000 | 40,000 | 55,000 | | | |
| 1879O | 1,500 | 10,000 | 17,500 | 25,000 | 35,000 | 85,000 | | |
| 1879S | 224,000 | 875 | 900 | 925 | 935 | 1,200 | 6,000 | |
| 1880 (36) | 1,644,840 | 800 | 805 | 815 | 820 | 900 | 1,500 | 22,500 |
| 1880CC | 11,190 | 2,000 | 2,750 | 4,000 | 6,500 | 37,500 | | |
| 1880O | 9,200 | 1,500 | 2,500 | 4,250 | 5,500 | 20,000 | | |
| 1880S | 506,250 | 800 | 805 | 815 | 820 | 900 | 2,000 | |
| 1881 (40) | 3,877,220 | 800 | 805 | 815 | 820 | 850 | 1,000 | 22,500 |
| 1881CC | 24,015 | 1,750 | 2,500 | 3,500 | 4,500 | 8,500 | | |
| 1881O | 8,350 | 1,150 | 1,500 | 3,000 | 5,000 | 15,000 | | |
| 1881S | 970,000 | 800 | 805 | 815 | 820 | 850 | 1,500 | |
| 1882 (40) | 2,324,440 | 800 | 805 | 815 | 820 | 850 | 1,000 | 20,000 |
| 1882CC | 6,764 | 2,000 | 3,500 | 5,500 | 11,500 | 35,000 | | |
| 1882O | 10,820 | 1,150 | 1,500 | 2,500 | 4,500 | 12,500 | 45,000 | |
| 1882S | 132,000 | 800 | 805 | 815 | 820 | 850 | 2,500 | |
| 1883 (40) | 208,700 | 800 | 805 | 815 | 820 | 850 | 1,350 | 20,000 |
| 1883CC | 12,000 | 1,650 | 2,500 | 4,500 | 8,500 | 37,500 | | |
| 1883O | 800 | 12,500 | 27,500 | 55,000 | 80,000 | 125,000 | | |
| 1883S | 38,000 | 800 | 805 | 815 | 820 | 1,150 | 8,500 | |
| 1884 (45) | 76,860 | 800 | 805 | 815 | 820 | 950 | 4,250 | 20,000 |

| | Mintage | VF-20 | EF-40 | AU-50 | AU-55 | MS-60 | MS-63 | PF-63 |
|---|---|---|---|---|---|---|---|---|
| 1884CC | 9,925 | $1,750 | $3,000 | $5,500 | $7,500 | $17,500 | $65,000 | |
| 1884S | 124,250 | 800 | 805 | 815 | 820 | 850 | 4,500 | |
| 1885 (65) | 253,462 | 800 | 805 | 815 | 820 | 850 | 2,000 | $20,000 |
| 1885S | 228,000 | 800 | 805 | 815 | 820 | 850 | 1,150 | |
| 1886 (60) | 236,100 | 800 | 805 | 815 | 820 | 850 | 2,000 | 18,500 |
| 1886S | 826,000 | 800 | 805 | 815 | 820 | 850 | 1,000 | |
| 1887 (80) | 53,600 | 800 | 805 | 815 | 820 | 1,000 | 4,500 | 18,500 |
| 1887S | 817,000 | 800 | 805 | 815 | 820 | 850 | 1,500 | |
| 1888 (75) | 132,921 | 800 | 805 | 815 | 820 | 850 | 3,250 | 18,500 |
| 1888O | 21,335 | 825 | 835 | 850 | 1,000 | 1,250 | 7,500 | |
| 1888S | 648,700 | 800 | 805 | 815 | 820 | 850 | 1,200 | |
| 1889 (45) | 4,440 | 900 | 925 | 950 | 1,350 | 4,250 | 10,000 | 18,000 |
| 1889S | 425,400 | 800 | 805 | 815 | 820 | 850 | 1,250 | |
| 1890 (63) | 57,980 | 800 | 805 | 815 | 820 | 900 | 3,500 | 16,500 |
| 1890CC | 17,500 | 1,250 | 1,550 | 2,250 | 2,750 | 4,500 | 20,000 | |
| 1891 (48) | 91,820 | 800 | 805 | 815 | 820 | 900 | 2,500 | 16,500 |
| 1891CC | 103,732 | 1,250 | 1,450 | 1,650 | 2,250 | 2,850 | 8,500 | |
| 1892 (72) | 797,480 | 800 | 805 | 815 | 820 | 850 | 1,000 | 16,500 |
| 1892CC | 40,000 | 1,250 | 1,500 | 2,000 | 2,750 | 5,500 | 35,000 | |
| 1892O | 28,688 | 800 | 805 | 850 | 900 | 1,300 | 8,000 | |
| 1892S | 115,500 | 800 | 805 | 815 | 820 | 1,050 | 2,000 | |
| 1893 (55) | 1,840,840 | 800 | 805 | 815 | 820 | 850 | 950 | 16,500 |
| 1893CC | 14,000 | 1,650 | 2,000 | 3,500 | 5,500 | 20,000 | — | |
| 1893O | 17,000 | 825 | 835 | 850 | 975 | 1,350 | 5,000 | |
| 1893S | 141,350 | 800 | 805 | 815 | 820 | 850 | 2,000 | |
| 1894 (43) | 2,470,735 | 800 | 805 | 815 | 820 | 850 | 1,000 | 16,500 |
| 1894O | 107,500 | 825 | 835 | 850 | 975 | 1,250 | 5,500 | |
| 1894S | 25,000 | 825 | 835 | 950 | 1,100 | 3,500 | | |
| 1895 (56) | 567,770 | 800 | 805 | 815 | 820 | 850 | 1,000 | 16,000 |
| 1895O | 98,000 | 825 | 835 | 850 | 975 | 1,200 | 6,500 | |
| 1895S | 49,000 | 850 | 925 | 975 | 1,000 | 2,000 | 8,000 | |
| 1896 (78) | 76,270 | 800 | 805 | 815 | 820 | 850 | 1,200 | 16,000 |
| 1896S | 123,750 | 800 | 815 | 825 | 850 | 1,850 | 8,000 | |
| 1897 (69) | 1,000,090 | 800 | 805 | 815 | 820 | 850 | 925 | 16,000 |
| 1897O | 42,500 | 825 | 835 | 850 | 900 | 1,500 | 6,500 | |
| 1897S | 234,750 | 800 | 805 | 815 | 820 | 850 | 5,500 | |
| 1898 (67) | 812,130 | 800 | 805 | 815 | 820 | 850 | 950 | 16,000 |
| 1898S | 473,600 | 800 | 805 | 815 | 820 | 850 | 2,000 | |
| 1899 (86) | 1,262,219 | 800 | 805 | 815 | 820 | 850 | 950 | 15,000 |
| 1899O | 37,047 | 825 | 835 | 845 | 950 | 1,450 | 7,500 | |
| 1899S | 841,000 | 800 | 805 | 815 | 820 | 850 | 1,750 | |
| 1900 (120) | 293,840 | 800 | 805 | 815 | 820 | 835 | 950 | 15,000 |
| 1900S | 81,000 | 800 | 805 | 815 | 820 | 1,000 | 5,500 | |
| 1901 (85) | 1,718,740 | 800 | 805 | 815 | 820 | 835 | 950 | 15,000 |
| 1901O | 72,041 | 825 | 835 | 845 | 925 | 1,150 | 3,250 | |
| 1901S | 2,812,750 | 800 | 805 | 815 | 820 | 835 | 950 | |
| 1902 (113) | 82,400 | 800 | 805 | 815 | 820 | 850 | 1,300 | 15,000 |
| 1902S | 469,500 | 800 | 805 | 815 | 820 | 835 | 950 | |
| 1903 (96) | 125,830 | 800 | 805 | 815 | 820 | 850 | 950 | 15,000 |

*Chart continued on next page.*

| | Mintage | VF-20 | EF-40 | AU-50 | AU-55 | MS-60 | MS-63 | PF-63 |
|---|---|---|---|---|---|---|---|---|
| 1903O | 112,771 | $825 | $835 | $845 | $925 | $1,200 | $2,500 | |
| 1903S | 538,000 | 800 | 805 | 815 | 820 | 850 | 950 | |
| 1904 | (108). . . 161,930 | 800 | 805 | 815 | 820 | 850 | 1,500 | $15,000 |
| 1904O | 108,950 | 825 | 835 | 845 | 925 | 1,200 | 3,000 | |
| 1905 | (86). . . 200,992 | 800 | 805 | 815 | 820 | 850 | 1,200 | 15,000 |
| 1905S | 369,250 | 800 | 805 | 815 | 820 | 850 | 3,500 | |
| 1906 | (77). . . 165,420 | 800 | 805 | 815 | 820 | 850 | 1,250 | 15,000 |
| 1906D | 981,000 | 800 | 805 | 815 | 820 | 850 | 1,000 | |
| 1906O | 86,895 | 825 | 835 | 845 | 925 | 1,100 | 4,750 | |
| 1906S | 457,000 | 800 | 805 | 815 | 820 | 850 | 2,500 | |
| 1907 | (74). .1,203,899 | 800 | 805 | 815 | 820 | 850 | 950 | 15,000 |
| 1907D | 1,030,000 | 800 | 805 | 815 | 820 | 850 | 1,650 | |
| 1907S | 210,500 | 800 | 805 | 815 | 820 | 850 | 3,500 | |

## INDIAN HEAD (1907–1933)

Augustus Saint-Gaudens, considered by many the greatest of modern sculptors, introduced a new high standard of art in United States coins evidenced by his eagle and double eagle types of 1907. The obverse of the eagle shows the head of Liberty crowned with an Indian war bonnet while an impressively majestic eagle dominates the reverse side. A departure from older standards is found on the edge of the piece, where 46 raised stars (48 stars in 1912 and later) are arranged signifying the states of the Union, instead of there being a lettered or reeded edge.

The first of these coins struck had no motto IN GOD WE TRUST, unlike the later issues, starting in 1908. President Theodore Roosevelt personally objected to the use of the Deity's name on coins. The motto was restored to the coins by an act of Congress in 1908.

*Designer Augustus Saint-Gaudens; weight 16.718 grams; composition .900 gold, .100 copper (net weight: .48375 oz. pure gold); diameter 27 mm; edge: (1907–1911) 46 raised stars (one specimen of the 1907 with periods variety with plain edge is known), (1912–1933) 48 raised stars; mints: Philadelphia, Denver, San Francisco.*

**VF-20 Very Fine**—Bonnet feathers worn near band. Wear visible on high points of hair.
**EF-40 Extremely Fine**—Slight wear on cheekbone and headdress feathers. Slight wear visible on eagle's eye and left wing.
**AU-50 About Uncirculated**—Trace of wear on hair above eye and on forehead.
**AU-55 Choice About Uncirculated**—Evidence of friction on design high points. Much of original mint luster present.
**MS-60 Uncirculated**—No trace of wear. Light blemishes.
**MS-63 Choice Uncirculated**—Some distracting contact marks or blemishes in prime focal areas. Impaired luster possible.

### Variety 1 – No Motto on Reverse (1907–1908)

***Mintmark is above left tip of branch on 1908-D, No Motto, and at left of arrow points thereafter.***

*Gem Uncirculated (MS-65) coins are rare and worth substantial premiums.*

| | Mintage | VF-20 | EF-40 | AU-50 | AU-55 | MS-60 | MS-63 | PF-63 |
|---|---|---|---|---|---|---|---|---|
| 1907, Wire Rim, Periods | 500 | | $25,000 | $27,500 | $29,500 | $35,000 | $45,000 | |
| *$230,000, MS-67, Stack's Bowers auction, January 2011* | | | | | | | | |
| 1907, Rounded Rim, Periods, •E•PLURIBUS•UNUM• **(a)** | 50 | | 60,000 | 65,000 | 70,000 | 85,000 | 165,000 | |
| *$2,185,000, PF-67, Heritage auction, January 2011* | | | | | | | | |
| 1907, No Periods | 239,406 | $800 | 825 | 850 | 925 | 1,100 | 2,000 | |
| 1908, No Motto | 33,500 | 800 | 850 | 875 | 975 | 1,400 | 4,250 | |
| 1908D, No Motto | 210,000 | 800 | 825 | 850 | 950 | 1,250 | 4,500 | |

**a.** 31,500 were minted; all but 50 were melted at the mint.

## Variety 2 – Motto on Reverse (1908–1933)

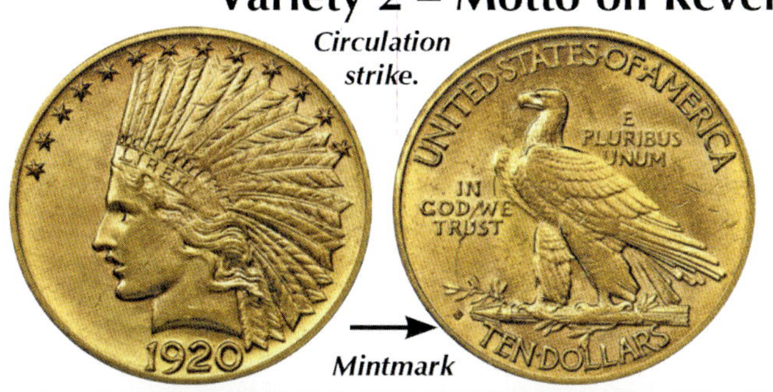


*Circulation strike.* *Mintmark*

*Proof strike.*

| | Mintage | VF-20 | EF-40 | AU-50 | AU-55 | MS-60 | MS-63 | MATTE PF-63 |
|---|---|---|---|---|---|---|---|---|
| 1908 | (116) 341,370 | $800 | $805 | $815 | $820 | $975 | $1,300 | $20,000 |
| 1908D | 836,500 | 800 | 805 | 815 | 820 | 1,100 | 4,000 | |
| 1908S | 59,850 | 975 | 1,100 | 1,200 | 1,500 | 4,500 | 13,000 | |
| 1909 | (74) 184,789 | 800 | 805 | 815 | 820 | 900 | 1,500 | 22,500 |
| 1909D | 121,540 | 800 | 850 | 925 | 975 | 1,100 | 3,000 | |
| 1909S | 292,350 | 800 | 805 | 815 | 820 | 1,500 | 4,250 | |
| 1910 | (204) 318,500 | 800 | 805 | 815 | 820 | 850 | 1,100 | 20,000 |
| 1910D | 2,356,640 | 800 | 805 | 815 | 820 | 850 | 1,000 | |
| 1910S | 811,000 | 800 | 805 | 815 | 820 | 1,000 | 5,000 | |
| 1911 | (95) 505,500 | 800 | 805 | 815 | 820 | 850 | 1,050 | 20,000 |
| 1911D | 30,100 | 1,250 | 1,750 | 2,750 | 3,500 | 11,500 | 30,000 | |
| 1911S | 51,000 | 800 | 850 | 1,100 | 1,125 | 3,000 | 11,000 | |
| 1912 | (83) 405,000 | 800 | 805 | 815 | 820 | 875 | 1,050 | 20,000 |
| 1912S | 300,000 | 800 | 815 | 820 | 825 | 1,250 | 4,750 | |
| 1913 | (71) 442,000 | 800 | 805 | 815 | 820 | 875 | 1,100 | 20,000 |
| 1913S | 66,000 | 1,000 | 1,100 | 1,200 | 2,250 | 6,000 | 21,000 | |
| 1914 | (50) 151,000 | 800 | 805 | 815 | 820 | 875 | 1,500 | 20,000 |
| 1914D | 343,500 | 800 | 805 | 815 | 820 | 875 | 1,400 | |
| 1914S | 208,000 | 800 | 805 | 815 | 825 | 1,750 | 4,500 | |
| 1915 | (75) 351,000 | 800 | 805 | 815 | 820 | 900 | 1,300 | 25,000 |
| 1915S | 59,000 | 900 | 1,000 | 1,500 | 2,250 | 6,000 | 20,000 | |
| 1916S | 138,500 | 950 | 985 | 1,000 | 1,100 | 1,500 | 5,750 | |
| 1920S | 126,500 | 20,000 | 25,000 | 32,500 | 40,000 | 60,000 | 105,000 | |
| *$1,725,000, MS-67, Heritage auction, March 2007* | | | | | | | | |
| 1926 | 1,014,000 | 800 | 805 | 810 | 815 | 875 | 950 | |
| 1930S | 96,000 | 20,000 | 22,500 | 25,000 | 30,000 | 40,000 | 55,000 | |
| 1932 | 4,463,000 | 800 | 805 | 810 | 815 | 875 | 950 | |
| 1933 **(a)** | 312,500 | | | | | 300,000 | 400,000 | |
| *$881,250, MS-66, Goldberg auction, June 2016* | | | | | | | | |

**a.** Nearly all were melted at the mint.

*Note: Values of common gold coins have been based on a gold bullion price of $1,500 per ounce, and may vary with the prevailing spot price. The net weight and content listed may be used to recalculate bullion value.*

## LIBERTY HEAD (1849–1907)

This largest denomination of all regular United States issues was authorized to be coined by the Act of March 3, 1849. Its weight was 516 grains, .900 fine. The 1849 double eagle is a unique specimen and reposes in the Smithsonian. The 1861 reverse design by Anthony C. Paquet was withdrawn soon after being struck. Very few pieces are known.

*Designer James B. Longacre; weight 33.436 grams; composition .900 gold, .100 copper (net weight: .96750 oz. pure gold); diameter 34 mm; reeded edge; mints: Philadelphia, Carson City, Denver, New Orleans, San Francisco.*

**VF-20 Very Fine**—LIBERTY on crown bold; prongs on crown defined; lower half worn flat. Hair worn about ear.
**EF-40 Extremely Fine**—Trace of wear on rounded prongs of crown and down hair curls. Minor bagmarks.
**AU-50 About Uncirculated**—Trace of wear on hair over eye and on coronet.
**AU-55 Choice About Uncirculated**—Evidence of friction on design high points. Some of original mint luster present.
**MS-60 Uncirculated**—No trace of wear. Light blemishes.
**MS-63 Choice Uncirculated**—Some distracting contact marks or blemishes in prime focal areas. Impaired luster possible.
**PF-63 Choice Proof**—Reflective surfaces with only a few blemishes in secondary focal areas. No major flaws.

### Without Motto on Reverse (1849–1866)

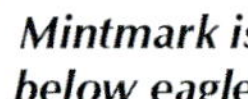

*Mintmark is below eagle.*

**1853, "3 Over 2"**

| | Mintage | VF-20 | EF-40 | AU-50 | AU-55 | MS-60 | MS-63 |
|---|---|---|---|---|---|---|---|
| 1849 *(pattern)* | 1 | | | *(Smithsonian collection)* | | | |
| 1850 | 1,170,261 | $2,500 | $3,500 | $4,500 | $7,000 | $16,500 | $60,000 |
| 1850O | 141,000 | 5,500 | 7,250 | 15,000 | 26,000 | 75,000 | |
| 1851 | 2,087,155 | 2,000 | 2,250 | 2,600 | 3,000 | 5,750 | 25,000 |
| 1851O | 315,000 | 2,750 | 4,250 | 6,000 | 10,000 | 28,500 | 125,000 |
| 1852 | 2,053,026 | 2,000 | 2,100 | 2,300 | 3,100 | 5,750 | 22,500 |
| 1852O | 190,000 | 2,500 | 4,000 | 6,500 | 10,000 | 37,500 | 95,000 |
| 1853, All kinds | 1,261,326 | | | | | | |
| 1853, "3 Over 2" **(a)** | | 3,000 | 3,750 | 5,500 | 10,000 | 42,500 | |
| 1853 | | 2,000 | 2,250 | 2,600 | 3,000 | 5,750 | 30,000 |
| 1853O | 71,000 | 3,000 | 7,000 | 10,000 | 17,500 | 37,500 | |
| 1854, All kinds | 757,899 | | | | | | |
| 1854, Small Date | | 2,000 | 2,250 | 2,500 | 3,500 | 7,500 | 35,000 |
| 1854, Large Date | | 3,500 | 4,250 | 8,500 | 15,000 | 37,500 | 65,000 |
| 1854O | 3,250 | 135,000 | 215,000 | 350,000 | 425,000 | — | |
| *$603,750, AU-55, Heritage auction, October 2008* | | | | | | | |

**a.** Overlaid photographs indicate this is not a true overdate.

| | Mintage | VF-20 | EF-40 | AU-50 | AU-55 | MS-60 | MS-63 | PF-63 |
|---|---|---|---|---|---|---|---|---|
| 1854S | 141,468 | $3,000 | $4,250 | $10,500 | $17,500 | $30,000 | $50,000 | |
| 1855 | 364,666 | 2,000 | 2,250 | 2,750 | 3,750 | 12,000 | 60,000 | |
| 1855O | 8,000 | 13,500 | 35,000 | 50,000 | 67,500 | 125,000 | | |
| 1855S | 879,675 | 2,000 | 2,100 | 2,300 | 3,350 | 7,000 | 25,000 | |
| 1856 | 329,878 | 2,150 | 2,250 | 2,850 | 3,750 | 8,000 | 35,000 | |
| 1856O | 2,250 | 145,000 | 225,000 | 350,000 | 385,000 | | | |
| *$1,437,500, SP-63, Heritage auction, May 2009* | | | | | | | | |
| 1856S | 1,189,750 | 2,000 | 2,200 | 2,500 | 3,000 | 6,250 | 16,500 | |
| 1857 | 439,375 | 2,000 | 2,250 | 2,500 | 3,000 | 6,750 | 40,000 | |
| 1857O | 30,000 | 4,750 | 9,500 | 15,000 | 21,500 | 50,000 | 250,000 | |
| 1857S **(b)** | 970,500 | 2,000 | 2,100 | 2,300 | 2,750 | 5,000 | 8,500 | |
| *$138,000, MS-67, Heritage auction, January 2012* | | | | | | | | |
| 1858 | 211,714 | 2,150 | 2,500 | 3,000 | 4,000 | 9,000 | 45,000 | |
| 1858O | 35,250 | 5,000 | 9,500 | 20,000 | 32,500 | 60,000 | | |
| 1858S | 846,710 | 2,000 | 2,250 | 2,600 | 3,000 | 8,000 | 45,000 | |
| 1859 (80) | 43,597 | 3,250 | 6,500 | 11,000 | 16,000 | 32,000 | | $250,000 |
| 1859O | 9,100 | 9,500 | 25,000 | 47,500 | 65,000 | 125,000 | | |
| 1859S | 636,445 | 2,000 | 2,100 | 2,500 | 3,500 | 11,000 | 57,500 | |
| 1860 (59) | 577,611 | 2,000 | 2,150 | 2,350 | 2,750 | 5,500 | 20,000 | 125,000 |
| 1860O | 6,600 | 12,500 | 37,500 | 55,000 | 67,500 | | | |
| 1860S | 544,950 | 2,000 | 2,250 | 2,500 | 3,500 | 8,000 | 35,000 | |

**b.** Different size mintmark varieties exist; the Large S variety is rarest.

**1861-S, Normal Reverse**

**1861-S, Paquet Reverse**

| | Mintage | VF-20 | EF-40 | AU-50 | AU-55 | MS-60 | MS-63 | PF-63 |
|---|---|---|---|---|---|---|---|---|
| 1861 (66) | 2,976,387 | $2,000 | $2,150 | $2,300 | $2,650 | $4,500 | $18,500 | $125,000 |
| 1861, Paquet Rev (Tall Ltrs) | | | | | | 2,000,000 | | |
| *$1,645,000, MS-61, Heritage auction, August 2014* | | | | | | | | |
| 1861O | 17,741 | 15,000 | 35,000 | 55,000 | 67,500 | 165,000 | | |
| 1861S | 768,000 | 2,000 | 2,250 | 2,750 | 4,000 | 15,000 | 47,500 | |
| 1861S, Paquet Rev (Tall Ltrs) | 19,250 | 35,000 | 65,000 | 90,000 | 115,000 | | | |
| 1862 (35) | 92,098 | 4,500 | 12,000 | 15,000 | 20,000 | 40,000 | 70,000 | 125,000 |
| 1862S | 854,173 | 2,000 | 2,500 | 3,000 | 4,000 | 12,000 | 50,000 | |
| 1863 (30) | 142,760 | 3,000 | 5,500 | 11,500 | 15,000 | 32,500 | 85,000 | 125,000 |
| 1863S | 966,570 | 2,150 | 2,500 | 3,000 | 4,000 | 8,000 | 35,000 | |
| 1864 (50) | 204,235 | 3,250 | 5,500 | 9,000 | 11,000 | 25,000 | 75,000 | 125,000 |
| 1864S | 793,660 | 2,000 | 2,250 | 2,500 | 3,250 | 8,000 | 45,000 | |
| 1865 (25) | 351,175 | 2,250 | 2,750 | 3,000 | 3,750 | 7,250 | 22,500 | 125,000 |
| 1865S | 1,042,500 | 2,000 | 2,150 | 2,500 | 3,000 | 6,750 | 13,500 | |
| 1866S | 120,000 | 10,000 | 22,500 | 35,000 | 57,500 | 155,000 | | |

## Motto Above Eagle
### *Value TWENTY D. (1866–1876)*

| | Mintage | VF-20 | EF-40 | AU-50 | AU-55 | MS-60 | MS-63 | PF-63 |
|---|---|---|---|---|---|---|---|---|
| 1866 . . . . . . . . . . . (30). . . | 698,745 | $1,700 | $2,400 | $3,500 | $5,000 | $10,000 | $65,000 | $57,500 |
| 1866S **(a)** . . . . . . . . . . . . . | 842,250 | 1,950 | 2,250 | 3,000 | 8,250 | 16,500 | | |
| 1867 . . . . . . . . . . . (50). . . | 251,015 | 1,700 | 1,850 | 2,250 | 3,250 | 5,500 | 30,000 | 57,500 |
| 1867S . . . . . . . . . . . . . . . . | 920,750 | 1,700 | 1,800 | 1,850 | 4,000 | 10,000 | | |
| 1868 . . . . . . . . . . . (25). . . . | 98,575 | 2,000 | 2,500 | 4,250 | 9,500 | 21,500 | 70,000 | 65,000 |
| 1868S . . . . . . . . . . . . . . . . | 837,500 | 1,700 | 1,750 | 1,775 | 2,250 | 6,000 | | |
| 1869 . . . . . . . . . . . (25). . . | 175,130 | 1,700 | 1,750 | 2,250 | 3,500 | 10,500 | 40,000 | 65,000 |
| *$299,000, MS-65, Heritage auction, January 2008* | | | | | | | | |
| 1869S . . . . . . . . . . . . . . . . | 686,750 | 1,700 | 1,800 | 1,850 | 2,500 | 5,000 | 35,000 | |
| 1870 . . . . . . . . . . . (35). . . | 155,150 | 1,700 | 2,000 | 2,850 | 4,850 | 11,750 | 57,500 | 65,000 |
| *$503,100, PF-67 UC, Bonhams auction, September 2013* | | | | | | | | |
| 1870CC . . . . . . . . . . . . . . . . | 3,789 | 185,000 | 250,000 | 325,000 | 500,000 | | | |
| *$414,000, AU-55, Stack's Bowers auction, March 2009* | | | | | | | | |
| 1870S . . . . . . . . . . . . . . . . | 982,000 | 1,700 | 1,750 | 1,775 | 1,850 | 5,000 | 57,500 | |
| 1871 . . . . . . . . . . . (30). . . . | 80,120 | 1,700 | 1,750 | 3,000 | 5,000 | 9,000 | 50,000 | 65,000 |
| 1871CC . . . . . . . . . . . . . . . . | 17,387 | 27,500 | 42,500 | 57,500 | 75,000 | 130,000 | | |
| *$414,000, MS-64, Heritage auction, April 2008* | | | | | | | | |
| 1871S . . . . . . . . . . . . . . . . | 928,000 | 1,700 | 1,750 | 1,775 | 1,800 | 3,500 | 22,500 | |
| 1872 . . . . . . . . . . . (30). . . | 251,850 | 1,700 | 1,750 | 1,775 | 2,200 | 3,750 | 25,000 | 65,000 |
| 1872CC . . . . . . . . . . . . . . . . | 26,900 | 5,500 | 10,500 | 16,500 | 22,500 | 65,000 | | |
| 1872S . . . . . . . . . . . . . . . . | 780,000 | 1,700 | 1,750 | 1,775 | 1,800 | 3,000 | 30,000 | |
| 1873, Close 3 . . . . (25). . | 1,709,800 | 1,700 | 1,750 | 1,775 | 2,250 | 4,250 | | 65,000 |
| 1873, Open 3 . . . . . . . . . . . . . . . . | * | 1,700 | 1,750 | 1,775 | 1,800 | 1,875 | 5,500 | |
| 1873CC, Close 3 . . . . . . . . . | 22,410 | 4,250 | 8,500 | 17,500 | 24,500 | 52,500 | 155,000 | |
| 1873S, Close 3 . . . . . . . . | 1,040,600 | 1,700 | 1,750 | 1,775 | 1,800 | 2,400 | 20,000 | |
| 1873S, Open 3 . . . . . . . . . . . . . . . | * | 1,700 | 1,750 | 1,775 | 2,000 | 4,500 | | |
| 1874 . . . . . . . . . . . (20). . . | 366,780 | 1,700 | 1,750 | 1,775 | 1,800 | 2,000 | 22,500 | 75,000 |
| 1874CC . . . . . . . . . . . . . . . | 115,085 | 2,850 | 3,500 | 4,500 | 8,750 | 25,500 | | |
| 1874S . . . . . . . . . . . . . . . | 1,214,000 | 1,700 | 1,750 | 1,775 | 1,800 | 2,000 | 28,500 | |
| 1875 . . . . . . . . . . . (20). . . | 295,720 | 1,700 | 1,750 | 1,775 | 1,800 | 2,000 | 6,500 | 100,000 |
| 1875CC . . . . . . . . . . . . . . . | 111,151 | 2,850 | 3,250 | 4,000 | 5,750 | 9,500 | 37,500 | |
| 1875S . . . . . . . . . . . . . . . | 1,230,000 | 1,700 | 1,750 | 1,775 | 1,800 | 2,000 | 10,000 | |
| 1876 **(b)** . . . . . . . . (45). . . | 583,860 | 1,700 | 1,750 | 1,775 | 1,800 | 2,000 | 7,500 | 55,000 |
| 1876CC . . . . . . . . . . . . . . . | 138,441 | 2,750 | 3,250 | 3,750 | 5,500 | 8,500 | 42,500 | |
| 1876S . . . . . . . . . . . . . . . | 1,597,000 | 1,700 | 1,750 | 1,775 | 1,800 | 2,000 | 5,500 | |

* Included in number above. **a.** The 1866-S was also produced Without Motto; see listing on previous page. **b.** A transitional Proof pattern also exists dated 1876 but of the type of 1877.

## Value TWENTY DOLLARS (1877–1907)

| | Mintage | VF-20 | EF-40 | AU-50 | AU-55 | MS-60 | MS-63 | PF-63 |
|---|---|---|---|---|---|---|---|---|
| 1877 . . . . . . . . . . . . (20) | 397,650 | $1,600 | $1,650 | $1,665 | $1,675 | $2,100 | $15,000 | $40,000 |
| 1877CC | 42,565 | 3,000 | 3,500 | 6,750 | 11,000 | 30,000 | | |
| 1877S | 1,735,000 | 1,600 | 1,650 | 1,665 | 1,675 | 1,850 | 16,000 | |
| 1878 . . . . . . . . . . . . (20) | 543,625 | 1,600 | 1,650 | 1,665 | 1,675 | 1,750 | 11,000 | 40,000 |
| 1878CC | 13,180 | 5,750 | 8,750 | 16,000 | 26,500 | 50,000 | | |
| 1878S | 1,739,000 | 1,600 | 1,650 | 1,665 | 1,675 | 1,750 | 16,500 | |
| 1879 . . . . . . . . . . . . (30) | 207,600 | 1,600 | 1,650 | 1,665 | 1,675 | 2,150 | 17,500 | 40,000 |
| 1879CC | 10,708 | 6,500 | 11,500 | 16,500 | 28,500 | 55,000 | | |
| 1879O | 2,325 | 30,000 | 55,000 | 65,000 | 75,000 | 140,000 | | |
| 1879S | 1,223,800 | 1,600 | 1,650 | 1,665 | 1,675 | 2,250 | 40,000 | |
| 1880 . . . . . . . . . . . . (36) | 51,420 | 1,600 | 1,650 | 1,750 | 1,850 | 8,500 | 32,500 | 40,000 |
| 1880S | 836,000 | 1,600 | 1,650 | 1,665 | 1,675 | 1,800 | 22,500 | |
| 1881 . . . . . . . . . . . . (61) | 2,199 | 18,500 | 32,500 | 45,000 | 67,500 | 125,000 | | 40,000 |
| 1881S | 727,000 | 1,600 | 1,650 | 1,665 | 1,675 | 2,000 | 22,500 | |
| 1882 . . . . . . . . . . . . (59) | 571 | 30,000 | 55,000 | 100,000 | 110,000 | 135,000 | 250,000 | 40,000 |
| 1882CC | 39,140 | 2,850 | 3,500 | 4,500 | 6,000 | 9,500 | 100,000 | |
| 1882S | 1,125,000 | 1,600 | 1,650 | 1,665 | 1,675 | 1,750 | 14,000 | |
| 1883, Proof only . . . (92) | | | | | | | | 115,000 |
| 1883CC | 59,962 | 2,850 | 3,250 | 4,000 | 5,500 | 10,000 | 50,000 | |
| 1883S | 1,189,000 | 1,600 | 1,650 | 1,665 | 1,675 | 1,750 | 5,500 | |
| 1884, Proof only . . . (71) | | | | | | | | 110,000 |
| 1884CC | 81,139 | 2,850 | 3,250 | 3,750 | 5,500 | 9,000 | 47,500 | |
| 1884S | 916,000 | 1,600 | 1,650 | 1,665 | 1,675 | 1,850 | 4,500 | |
| 1885 . . . . . . . . . . . . (77) | 751 | 22,500 | 32,500 | 50,000 | 65,000 | 85,000 | 135,000 | 50,000 |
| 1885CC | 9,450 | 6,500 | 12,500 | 17,500 | 25,000 | 42,500 | | |
| 1885S | 683,500 | 1,600 | 1,650 | 1,665 | 1,675 | 1,800 | 3,250 | |
| 1886 . . . . . . . . . . . (106) | 1,000 | 40,000 | 80,000 | 95,000 | 115,000 | 135,000 | 165,000 | 45,000 |
| 1887, Proof only . . (121) | | | | | | | | 67,500 |
| *$411,250, PF-67+ Cam, Heritage auction, August 2012* | | | | | | | | |
| 1887S | 283,000 | 1,600 | 1,650 | 1,665 | 1,675 | 1,800 | 12,500 | |
| 1888 . . . . . . . . . . . (105) | 226,161 | 1,600 | 1,650 | 1,665 | 1,675 | 2,100 | 12,000 | 32,500 |
| 1888S | 859,600 | 1,600 | 1,650 | 1,665 | 1,675 | 1,750 | 4,000 | |
| 1889 . . . . . . . . . . . . (41) | 44,070 | 1,600 | 1,650 | 1,665 | 1,675 | 2,150 | 15,000 | 32,500 |
| 1889CC | 30,945 | 3,000 | 3,250 | 4,500 | 6,500 | 11,500 | 45,000 | |
| 1889S | 774,700 | 1,600 | 1,650 | 1,665 | 1,675 | 1,800 | 3,250 | |
| 1890 . . . . . . . . . . . . (55) | 75,940 | 1,600 | 1,650 | 1,665 | 1,675 | 1,750 | 10,000 | 32,500 |
| 1890CC | 91,209 | 2,750 | 3,250 | 3,500 | 5,000 | 9,500 | 45,000 | |
| 1890S | 802,750 | 1,600 | 1,650 | 1,665 | 1,675 | 1,700 | 4,500 | |
| 1891 . . . . . . . . . . . . (52) | 1,390 | 15,000 | 22,500 | 40,000 | 50,000 | 85,000 | | 32,500 |
| *$655,200, PF-68★ UC, Bonhams auction, September 2013* | | | | | | | | |
| 1891CC | 5,000 | 8,500 | 16,000 | 24,500 | 30,000 | 47,500 | | |

*Chart continued on next page.*

| | Mintage | VF-20 | EF-40 | AU-50 | AU-55 | MS-60 | MS-63 | PF-63 |
|---|---|---|---|---|---|---|---|---|
| 1891S | 1,288,125 | $1,600 | $1,650 | $1,665 | $1,675 | $1,700 | $2,750 | |
| 1892 | (93) 4,430 | 4,500 | 7,000 | 10,000 | 14,500 | 22,500 | 40,000 | $32,500 |
| 1892CC | 27,265 | 2,750 | 3,500 | 4,500 | 5,500 | 12,500 | 57,500 | |
| 1892S | 930,150 | 1,600 | 1,650 | 1,665 | 1,675 | 1,700 | 2,500 | |
| 1893 | (59) 344,280 | 1,600 | 1,650 | 1,665 | 1,675 | 1,700 | 2,500 | 32,500 |
| 1893CC | 18,402 | 2,850 | 5,000 | 6,000 | 8,000 | 12,000 | 50,000 | |
| 1893S | 996,175 | 1,600 | 1,650 | 1,665 | 1,675 | 1,700 | 3,250 | |
| 1894 | (50) 1,368,940 | 1,600 | 1,650 | 1,665 | 1,675 | 1,700 | 2,000 | 32,500 |
| 1894S | 1,048,550 | 1,600 | 1,650 | 1,665 | 1,675 | 1,700 | 2,750 | |
| 1895 | (51) 1,114,605 | 1,600 | 1,650 | 1,665 | 1,675 | 1,700 | 2,100 | 32,500 |
| 1895S | 1,143,500 | 1,600 | 1,650 | 1,665 | 1,675 | 1,700 | 2,000 | |
| 1896 | (128) 792,535 | 1,600 | 1,650 | 1,665 | 1,675 | 1,700 | 2,000 | 32,500 |
| 1896S | 1,403,925 | 1,600 | 1,650 | 1,665 | 1,675 | 1,700 | 2,000 | |
| 1897 | (86) 1,383,175 | 1,600 | 1,650 | 1,665 | 1,675 | 1,700 | 2,000 | 32,500 |
| 1897S | 1,470,250 | 1,600 | 1,650 | 1,665 | 1,675 | 1,700 | 2,250 | |
| 1898 | (75) 170,395 | 1,600 | 1,650 | 1,665 | 1,675 | 2,000 | 3,250 | 32,500 |
| 1898S | 2,575,175 | 1,600 | 1,650 | 1,665 | 1,675 | 1,700 | 2,000 | |
| 1899 | (84) 1,669,300 | 1,600 | 1,650 | 1,665 | 1,675 | 1,700 | 1,750 | 32,500 |
| 1899S | 2,010,300 | 1,600 | 1,650 | 1,665 | 1,675 | 1,700 | 2,500 | |
| 1900 | (124) 1,874,460 | 1,600 | 1,650 | 1,665 | 1,675 | 1,700 | 1,750 | 30,000 |
| 1900S | 2,459,500 | 1,600 | 1,650 | 1,665 | 1,675 | 1,700 | 2,250 | |
| 1901 | (96) 111,430 | 1,600 | 1,650 | 1,665 | 1,675 | 1,700 | 1,750 | 30,000 |
| 1901S | 1,596,000 | 1,600 | 1,650 | 1,665 | 1,675 | 1,700 | 3,750 | |
| 1902 | (114) 31,140 | 1,600 | 1,675 | 1,685 | 1,700 | 2,500 | 10,000 | 30,000 |
| 1902S | 1,753,625 | 1,600 | 1,650 | 1,665 | 1,675 | 1,700 | 3,250 | |
| 1903 | (158) 287,270 | 1,600 | 1,650 | 1,665 | 1,675 | 1,700 | 1,750 | 30,000 |
| 1903S | 954,000 | 1,600 | 1,650 | 1,665 | 1,675 | 1,700 | 2,250 | |
| 1904 | (98) 6,256,699 | 1,600 | 1,650 | 1,665 | 1,675 | 1,700 | 1,750 | 30,000 |
| 1904S | 5,134,175 | 1,600 | 1,650 | 1,665 | 1,675 | 1,700 | 1,750 | |
| 1905 | (92) 58,919 | 1,600 | 1,700 | 1,725 | 1,750 | 2,500 | 15,000 | 30,000 |
| 1905S | 1,813,000 | 1,600 | 1,650 | 1,665 | 1,675 | 1,700 | 3,500 | |
| 1906 | (94) 69,596 | 1,600 | 1,650 | 1,665 | 1,675 | 1,800 | 8,500 | 30,000 |
| 1906D | 620,250 | 1,600 | 1,650 | 1,665 | 1,675 | 1,700 | 4,000 | |
| 1906S | 2,065,750 | 1,600 | 1,650 | 1,665 | 1,675 | 1,700 | 2,250 | |
| 1907 | (78) 1,451,786 | 1,600 | 1,650 | 1,665 | 1,675 | 1,700 | 1,750 | 30,000 |
| 1907D | 842,250 | 1,600 | 1,650 | 1,665 | 1,675 | 1,700 | 3,500 | |
| 1907S | 2,165,800 | 1,600 | 1,650 | 1,665 | 1,675 | 1,700 | 3,000 | |

## SAINT-GAUDENS (1907–1933)

Many consider the twenty-dollar gold piece designed by Augustus Saint-Gaudens to be the most beautiful U.S. coin. The first coins issued were slightly more than 12,000 high-relief pieces struck for general circulation. Their relief is much higher than for later issues, and the date 1907 is in Roman numerals (MCMVII). A few of the Proof coins were made using the lettered-edge collar from the ultra high relief version. These can be distinguished by a pronounced bottom left serif on the N in UNUM, and other minor differences. High-relief Proofs are trial or experimental pieces. Flat-relief double eagles were issued later in 1907 with Arabic numerals, and continued through 1933.

The field of the rare, ultra high relief experimental pieces is exceedingly concave and connects directly with the edge without any border, giving it a sharp, knifelike appearance; Liberty's skirt shows two folds on the side of her right leg; the Capitol building in the background at left is very small; the sun, on the reverse side, has 14 rays, as opposed to the 13 rays on regular high-relief coins.

The Proof finish of 1908 and 1911 through 1915 coins was originally referred to by the Mint as Sand Blast Proof. Proof coins minted in 1909 and 1910 have a different finish described as Satin Proof. In addition, double eagles from 1907 through 1911 have 46 stars on the obverse; and from 1912 through 1933, 48 stars.

*Designer Augustus Saint-Gaudens; weight 33.436 grams; composition .900 gold, .100 copper (net weight: .96750 oz. pure gold); diameter 34 mm; edge: E PLURIBUS UNUM with words divided by stars (one specimen of the high-relief variety with plain edge is known); mints: Philadelphia, Denver, San Francisco.*

**VF-20 Very Fine**—Minor wear on Liberty's legs and toes. Eagle's left wing and breast feathers worn.
**EF-40 Extremely Fine**—Drapery lines on chest visible. Wear on left breast, knee, and below. Eagle's feathers on breast and right wing bold.
**AU-50 About Uncirculated**—Trace of wear on nose, breast, and knee. Wear visible on eagle's wings.
**MS-60 Uncirculated**—No trace of wear. Light marks or blemishes.

## Ultra High Relief Pattern, MCMVII (1907)

| | PF-67 |
|---|---|
| 1907, Ultra High Relief, Plain Edge *(unique)* | |
| 1907, Ultra High Relief, Lettered Edge | $2,500,000 |
| *$2,990,000, PF-69, Heritage auction, November 2005* | |

## Without Motto IN GOD WE TRUST (1907–1908)

### *High Relief, MCMVII (1907)*

| | Mintage | VF-20 | EF-40 | AU-50 | AU-55 | MS-60 | MS-63 |
|---|---|---|---|---|---|---|---|
| 1907, High Relief, Roman Numerals (MCMVII), Wire Rim | 12,367 | $9,000 | $10,500 | $11,500 | $12,500 | $15,000 | $22,500 |
| *$575,000, MS-69, Heritage auction, November 2005* | | | | | | | |
| 1907, Same, Flat Rim | * | 9,000 | 10,500 | 11,500 | 12,500 | 15,000 | 23,500 |
| *$534,750, PF-69, Heritage auction, November 2005* | | | | | | | |

* Included in number above.

## *Arabic Numerals, No Motto (1907–1908)*

*Mintmark is on obverse, above date.*

| | Mintage | VF-20 | EF-40 | AU-50 | AU-55 | MS-60 | MS-63 |
|---|---|---|---|---|---|---|---|
| 1907, Arabic Numerals | 361,667 | $1,600 | $1,625 | $1,635 | $1,650 | $1,700 | $2,000 |
| 1908 | 4,271,551 | 1,600 | 1,625 | 1,635 | 1,640 | 1,650 | 1,675 |
| 1908D | 663,750 | 1,600 | 1,625 | 1,635 | 1,640 | 1,675 | 1,750 |

## With Motto IN GOD WE TRUST (1908–1933)

1909, 9 Over 8

| | Mintage | VF-20 | EF-40 | AU-50 | AU-55 | MS-60 | MS-63 | MATTE PF-63 |
|---|---|---|---|---|---|---|---|---|
| 1908 (101) | 156,258 | $1,600 | $1,625 | $1,635 | $1,675 | $1,875 | $2,250 | $30,000 |
| 1908D | 349,500 | 1,600 | 1,625 | 1,635 | 1,640 | 1,650 | 2,000 | |
| 1908S | 22,000 | 2,500 | 3,750 | 5,500 | 6,500 | 11,000 | 22,500 | |
| *$161,000, MS-67, Heritage auction, January 2012* | | | | | | | | |
| 1909, All kinds (67) | 161,282 | | | | | | | |
| 1909, 9 Over 8 | | 1,600 | 1,625 | 1,635 | 1,675 | 2,000 | 4,000 | |
| 1909 | | 1,600 | 1,625 | 1,635 | 1,675 | 1,700 | 2,750 | 32,500 |
| 1909D | 52,500 | 1,600 | 1,700 | 1,750 | 2,000 | 3,000 | 6,000 | |
| 1909S | 2,774,925 | 1,600 | 1,625 | 1,635 | 1,640 | 1,650 | 1,675 | |
| 1910 (167) | 482,000 | 1,600 | 1,625 | 1,635 | 1,640 | 1,650 | 1,675 | 32,500 |
| 1910D | 429,000 | 1,600 | 1,625 | 1,635 | 1,640 | 1,650 | 1,675 | |
| 1910S | 2,128,250 | 1,600 | 1,625 | 1,635 | 1,640 | 1,650 | 1,700 | |
| 1911 (100) | 197,250 | 1,600 | 1,625 | 1,635 | 1,640 | 1,650 | 2,500 | 30,000 |
| *$184,000, MS-67, Heritage auction, January 2012* | | | | | | | | |
| 1911D | 846,500 | 1,600 | 1,625 | 1,635 | 1,640 | 1,650 | 1,675 | |
| 1911S | 757,750 | 1,600 | 1,625 | 1,635 | 1,640 | 1,650 | 1,675 | |

| | Mintage | VF-20 | EF-40 | AU-50 | AU-55 | MS-60 | MS-63 | MATTE PF-63 |
|---|---|---|---|---|---|---|---|---|
| 1912 . . . . . . . . . . . . (74) | 149,750 | $1,600 | $1,625 | $1,635 | $1,640 | $1,650 | $2,250 | $30,000 |
| 1913 . . . . . . . . . . . . (58) | 168,780 | 1,600 | 1,625 | 1,635 | 1,640 | 1,650 | 2,500 | 30,000 |
| 1913D . . . . . . . . . . . . . . . . | 393,500 | 1,600 | 1,625 | 1,635 | 1,640 | 1,650 | 1,750 | |
| 1913S . . . . . . . . . . . . . . . . | 34,000 | 1,750 | 1,850 | 2,000 | 2,100 | 2,350 | 4,500 | |
| 1914 . . . . . . . . . . . . (70) | 95,250 | 1,600 | 1,625 | 1,635 | 1,640 | 1,650 | 2,750 | 30,000 |
| 1914D . . . . . . . . . . . . . . . . | 453,000 | 1,600 | 1,625 | 1,635 | 1,640 | 1,650 | 1,675 | |
| 1914S . . . . . . . . . . . . . . . | 1,498,000 | 1,600 | 1,625 | 1,635 | 1,640 | 1,650 | 1,675 | |
| 1915 . . . . . . . . . . . . (50) | 152,000 | 1,600 | 1,625 | 1,635 | 1,640 | 1,650 | 2,000 | 45,000 |
| 1915S . . . . . . . . . . . . . . . . | 567,500 | 1,600 | 1,625 | 1,635 | 1,640 | 1,650 | 1,675 | |
| 1916S . . . . . . . . . . . . . . . . | 796,000 | 1,600 | 1,625 | 1,635 | 1,640 | 1,650 | 1,800 | |
| 1920 . . . . . . . . . . . . . . . . . | 228,250 | 1,600 | 1,625 | 1,635 | 1,640 | 1,650 | 1,700 | |
| 1920S . . . . . . . . . . . . . . . . | 558,000 | 16,500 | 20,000 | 25,000 | 32,500 | 50,000 | 85,000 | |
| *$575,000, MS-66, Heritage auction, January 2012* | | | | | | | | |
| 1921 . . . . . . . . . . . . . . . . . | 528,500 | 25,000 | 37,500 | 55,000 | 65,000 | 100,000 | 225,000 | |
| *$1,495,000, MS-63, Stack's Bowers auction, August 2006* | | | | | | | | |
| 1922 . . . . . . . . . . . . . . . . | 1,375,500 | 1,600 | 1,625 | 1,635 | 1,640 | 1,650 | 1,675 | |
| 1922S . . . . . . . . . . . . . . . | 2,658,000 | 1,850 | 1,900 | 2,000 | 2,150 | 2,650 | 4,500 | |
| 1923 . . . . . . . . . . . . . . . . . | 566,000 | 1,600 | 1,625 | 1,635 | 1,640 | 1,650 | 1,675 | |
| 1923D . . . . . . . . . . . . . . . | 1,702,250 | 1,600 | 1,625 | 1,635 | 1,640 | 1,650 | 1,675 | |
| 1924 . . . . . . . . . . . . . . . . | 4,323,500 | 1,600 | 1,625 | 1,635 | 1,640 | 1,650 | 1,675 | |
| 1924D . . . . . . . . . . . . . . . | 3,049,500 | 2,200 | 2,500 | 2,650 | 3,250 | 4,250 | 7,500 | |
| 1924S . . . . . . . . . . . . . . . | 2,927,500 | 2,200 | 2,500 | 2,650 | 3,250 | 4,500 | 9,500 | |
| *$172,500, MS-65, Heritage auction, January 2012* | | | | | | | | |
| 1925 . . . . . . . . . . . . . . . . | 2,831,750 | 1,600 | 1,625 | 1,635 | 1,640 | 1,650 | 1,675 | |
| 1925D . . . . . . . . . . . . . . . | 2,938,500 | 2,600 | 3,200 | 3,750 | 4,250 | 5,500 | 10,000 | |
| 1925S . . . . . . . . . . . . . . . | 3,776,500 | 2,250 | 3,000 | 4,000 | 5,500 | 9,500 | 15,500 | |
| 1926 . . . . . . . . . . . . . . . . . | 816,750 | 1,600 | 1,625 | 1,635 | 1,640 | 1,650 | 1,675 | |
| 1926D . . . . . . . . . . . . . . . . | 481,000 | 8,000 | 11,000 | 12,500 | 13,500 | 14,500 | 25,000 | |
| *$402,500, MS-66+, Heritage auction, January 2012* | | | | | | | | |
| 1926S . . . . . . . . . . . . . . . | 2,041,500 | 2,150 | 2,450 | 2,750 | 2,950 | 3,500 | 5,500 | |
| 1927 . . . . . . . . . . . . . . . . | 2,946,750 | 1,600 | 1,625 | 1,635 | 1,640 | 1,650 | 1,675 | |
| 1927D . . . . . . . . . . . . . . . . | 180,000 | | | 500,000 | 550,000 | 750,000 | 1,300,000 | |
| *$2,160,000, MS-65+, Heritage auction, January 2020* | | | | | | | | |
| 1927S . . . . . . . . . . . . . . . | 3,107,000 | | | 14,000 | 16,000 | 26,000 | 45,000 | |
| *$276,000, MS-67, Heritage auction, January 2012* | | | | | | | | |
| 1928 . . . . . . . . . . . . . . . . | 8,816,000 | 1,600 | 1,625 | 1,635 | 1,640 | 1,650 | 1,675 | |
| 1929 . . . . . . . . . . . . . . . . | 1,779,750 | | | 13,500 | 15,500 | 20,000 | 35,000 | |
| 1930S . . . . . . . . . . . . . . . . . | 74,000 | | | 42,000 | 45,000 | 65,000 | 90,000 | |
| 1931 . . . . . . . . . . . . . . . . | 2,938,250 | | | 22,500 | 25,000 | 35,000 | 65,000 | |
| *$322,000, MS-67, Heritage auction, August 2010* | | | | | | | | |
| 1931D . . . . . . . . . . . . . . . . | 106,500 | | | 22,500 | 25,000 | 35,000 | 65,000 | |
| *$230,000, MS-66, Heritage auction, January 2012* | | | | | | | | |
| 1932 . . . . . . . . . . . . . . . . | 1,101,750 | | | 22,500 | 25,000 | 35,000 | 65,000 | |
| 1933 *(extremely rare)* **(a)** | 445,500 | | | — | | | | |
| *$7,590,020, Gem BU, Sotheby's / Stack's Bowers auction, July 2002* | | | | | | | | |

*Note:* Most of the double eagles of the 1920s were returned to the Mint and melted in the 1930s. Some, however, were unofficially saved by Treasury employees. Estimates of the quantities saved range from a few dozen to several hundred thousand, depending on the date. This explains the high values for coins that, judged only by their initial mintages, should otherwise be more common. **a.** All were to have been melted at the mint. Today at least 13 are known to have survived. Only one, the King Farouk specimen, has ever been sold at auction.

Commemorative coins have been popular since the days of the ancient Greeks and Romans. In the beginning they recorded and honored important events and passed along the news of the day. Many modern nations have issued commemorative coins, and they are highly esteemed by collectors. No nation has surpassed the United States when it comes to commemorative coins.

The unique position occupied by commemoratives in United States coinage is largely due to the fact that, with few exceptions, all commemorative coins have real historical significance. The progress and advance of people in the New World are presented in an interesting and instructive manner on the commemorative issues. Such a record of facts artistically presented on U.S. gold, silver, and other memorial issues appeals strongly to the collector who favors the historical side of numismatics. It is the historical features of the commemoratives, in fact, that create interest among many people who would otherwise have little interest in coins.

Proposed coin programs are considered by two congressional committees: the Senate Committee on Banking, Housing, and Urban Affairs; and the House Financial Services Committee. Once a program is approved by Congress, the independent Citizens Coinage Advisory Committee (ccac.gov) and the U.S. Commission of Fine Arts (cfa.gov) advise the secretary of the Treasury on its coin designs.

These special coins are usually issued either to commemorate events or to help pay for monuments or celebrations that commemorate historical persons, places, or things. Pre-1982 commemorative coins were offered in most instances by a commission in charge of the event to be commemorated and sold at a premium over face value.

Commemorative coins are popularly collected either by major types or in sets with mintmark varieties. During many years, no special commemorative coins were issued. Some regular coins, such as the Lincoln cent of 1909, quarters of 1999 through 2021, and Bicentennial issues of 1976, are also commemorative in nature.

**A note about mintages:** Unless otherwise stated, the coinage figures given in each "Distribution" column represent the total released mintage: the original total mintage (including assay coins), minus the quantity of unsold coins. In many cases, larger quantities were minted but not all were sold. The unsold coins were usually returned to the mint and melted, although some were placed in circulation at face value. A limited number of Proof strikings or presentation pieces were made for some of the 1892 through 1954 issues. All are very rare and valuable. For modern commemoratives (1982 to date), this edition of the *Red Book* has been updated with the latest data as provided by the U.S. Mint. Some of the updated modern mintage figures reflect substantial changes from numbers earlier released by the Mint.

### *Price Performance*

Few people would ever guess, or even believe, that this country once issued an official half dollar bearing the portrait of P.T. Barnum, the famous impresario to whom the saying "There's a sucker born every minute" was misattributed. He had nothing to do with the coins, which were made in 1936 (long after his death), but the exceptional honor and the fact that the fifty-cent coins were sold to the public for $2 each would have made him smile about bilking the public one last time.

Barnum did not have the last laugh in this matter. Those fortunate enough to buy one of the original coins in 1936, and to save it in Mint State, find that today their treasure is worth more than $125! Only 25,015 of the pieces were made, and at the time they were not very popular even with the few people who ever heard about them.

The Bridgeport commemorative half dollar with P.T. Barnum's portrait is but one of many different designs that have been used on special coins made for collectors since 1892. During that time, commemorative coins have been issued to celebrate the founding of cities, to mark expositions, to honor famous citizens and presidents, and even to promote Olympic contests in recent years. These coins were not normally placed in circulation and were usually distributed by some agency at a price over face value, with the surplus going to fund the event being celebrated. All commemorative coins made since 1982 have been distributed through the Mint with proceeds going directly to the government, and from there, to the various benefiting organizations.

It has mostly been in recent years that the general public has learned about commemorative coins. They have long been popular with coin collectors who enjoy the artistry and history associated with them, as well as the tremendous profit that they have made from owning these rare pieces. Very few ever reached circulation, as all were originally sold above face value, and because they are all so rare. Most early issues were of the half dollar denomination, often made in quantities of fewer than 20,000 pieces. This is minuscule when compared to the regular half dollar pieces that are made by the millions each year, and still rarely seen in circulation.

At the beginning of 1988, prices of classic commemoratives in MS-65 condition had risen so high that most collectors had to content themselves with pieces in lower grades. Investors continued to apply pressure to the high-quality pieces, driving prices even higher, while the collector community went after coins in grades from About Uncirculated to MS-63. For several months the pressure from both influences caused prices to rise very rapidly for all issues and grades of commemoratives without even taking the price-adjustment breather that usually goes along with such activity.

By 1990, prices dropped to the point that several of the commemoratives began to look like bargains once again. Many of the MS-65 pieces held firm at price levels above the $3,000 mark, but others were still available at under $500 even for coins of similar mintage. Coins in MS-63 or MS-64 were priced at but a fraction of the MS-65 prices, which would seem to make them reasonably priced because the demand for these pieces is universal, and not keyed simply to grade, rarity, or speculator pressure.

Historically, the entire series of commemorative coins has frequently undergone a roller-coaster cycle of price adjustments. These cycles have usually been of short duration, lasting from months to years, with prices always recovering and eventually exceeding previous levels.

## CLASSIC COMMEMORATIVE SILVER AND GOLD

### (1892–1893) World's Columbian Exposition Half Dollar

The first United States commemorative coin was the Columbian half dollar designed by Olin Lewis Warner. Charles E. Barber engraved the obverse, showing the bust of Columbus; and George T. Morgan engraved the reverse, a representation of Columbus's flagship the *Santa Maria* above two hemispheres. The coins were sold for $1 each at the World's Columbian Exposition in Chicago during 1893. A great many remained unsold and a substantial quantity was later released for circulation at face value or melted. Approximately 100 brilliant Proofs were struck for each date.

| | Distribution | AU-50 | MS-60 | MS-63 | MS-65 | MS-66 |
|---|---|---|---|---|---|---|
| 1892, World's Columbian Exposition | 950,000 | $20 | $27 | $70 | $275 | $650 |
| 1893, Same type | 1,550,405 | 20 | 27 | 70 | 275 | 650 |

## (1893) World's Columbian Exposition, Isabella Quarter

In 1893, the Board of Lady Managers of the World's Columbian Exposition petitioned for a souvenir quarter dollar. Authority was granted March 3, 1893. The coin known as the *Isabella quarter* was designed by Charles E. Barber. These souvenir quarters were sold for $1. The obverse has the crowned bust of Queen Isabella I of Spain. The kneeling female on the reverse with distaff and spindle is emblematic of women's industry.

| | Distribution | AU-50 | MS-60 | MS-63 | MS-65 | MS-66 |
|---|---|---|---|---|---|---|
| 1893, World's Columbian Exposition, Chicago | 24,214 | $325 | $375 | $500 | $1,600 | $2,500 |

## (1900) Lafayette Dollar

The heads of George Washington and the marquis de Lafayette appear on this issue, which was the first commemorative coin of one-dollar denomination, and the first authorized United States coin to bear a portrait of a U.S. president. The dies were prepared by Charles E. Barber. The statue on the reverse is similar to the monument of General Lafayette that was later erected in Paris as a gift of the American people. The coins were sold by the Lafayette Memorial Commission for $2 each.

| | Distribution | AU-50 | MS-60 | MS-63 | MS-65 | MS-66 |
|---|---|---|---|---|---|---|
| 1900, Lafayette | 36,026 | $450 | $775 | $1,400 | $5,500 | $11,000 |

## (1903) Louisiana Purchase Exposition

The first commemorative U.S. gold coins were authorized for the Louisiana Purchase Exposition, held in St. Louis in 1904. There are two varieties of the gold dollar, each dated 1903—one with the head of Thomas Jefferson, who was president when the Louisiana Territory was purchased from France, and the other with President William McKinley, who sanctioned the exposition. The reverse is the same for each variety. The designs were by Charles E. Barber.

| | Distribution | AU-50 | MS-60 | MS-63 | MS-65 | MS-66 |
|---|---|---|---|---|---|---|
| 1903, Louisiana Purchase / Thomas Jefferson | 17,500 | $550 | $625 | $800 | $1,050 | $1,550 |
| 1903, Louisiana Purchase / William McKinley | 17,500 | 550 | 600 | 700 | 1,100 | 1,250 |

## (1904–1905) Lewis and Clark Exposition

The Lewis and Clark Centennial Exposition was held in Portland, Oregon, in 1905. A souvenir issue of gold dollars was struck to mark the event with the dates 1904 and 1905. The two famous explorers are represented on either side of the coin, which was designed by Charles E. Barber. A bronze memorial of the Indian guide, Sacagawea, who assisted in the famous expedition, was erected in Portland, Oregon, and financed by the sale of these coins.

| | Distribution | AU-50 | MS-60 | MS-63 | MS-65 | MS-66 |
|---|---|---|---|---|---|---|
| 1904, Lewis and Clark Exposition | 10,025 | $750 | $900 | $1,000 | $3,500 | $6,500 |
| 1905, Lewis and Clark Exposition | 10,041 | 750 | 900 | 1,150 | 4,500 | 9,500 |

## (1915) Panama-Pacific International Exposition

This half dollar was designed by Charles E. Barber (obverse) and George T. Morgan (reverse). The exposition held in San Francisco in 1915 celebrated the opening of the Panama Canal. The coins were struck at the San Francisco Mint and were sold at $1 each during the exposition. A representation of Columbia with the golden gate in the background is the principal feature of the obverse. The Panama-Pacific coins were the first commemorative coins to carry the motto IN GOD WE TRUST, which appears above the eagle.

| | Distribution | AU-50 | MS-60 | MS-63 | MS-65 | MS-66 |
|---|---|---|---|---|---|---|
| 1915S, Panama-Pacific International Exposition | 27,134 | $375 | $500 | $700 | $1,325 | $2,500 |

Charles Keck designed the gold dollar, the obverse of which has the head of a man, representing a Panama Canal laborer. Two dolphins encircle ONE DOLLAR on the reverse.

The quarter eagle was the work of Charles E. Barber and George T. Morgan. The obverse shows Columbia with a caduceus in her left hand seated on a hippocampus, signifying the use of the Panama Canal. An American eagle with raised wings is shown on the reverse.

| | Distribution | AU-50 | MS-60 | MS-63 | MS-65 | MS-66 |
|---|---|---|---|---|---|---|
| 1915S, Panama-Pacific Internat'l Exposition, gold $1 | 15,000 | $450 | $550 | $625 | $1,000 | $1,500 |
| 1915S, Panama-Pacific Internat'l Exposition, $2.50 | 6,749 | 1,550 | 2,000 | 3,250 | 4,250 | 5,000 |

The fifty-dollar gold piece was designed by Robert Aitken and was issued in both round and octagonal form. The obverse bears a helmeted head of Minerva; the owl, symbol of wisdom, is on the reverse. The octagonal issue has eight dolphins in the angles on both sides. Other devices are smaller on the octagonal variety.

*Entry continued on next page.* 

| | Distribution | AU-50 | MS-60 | MS-63 | MS-65 | MS-66 |
|---|---|---|---|---|---|---|
| 1915S, Panama-Pacific Internat'l Exposition, Round ..... | 483 | $55,000 | $70,000 | $95,000 | $190,000 | $255,000 |
| 1915S, Panama-Pacific Internat'l Exposition, Octagonal... | 645 | 55,000 | 67,500 | 90,000 | 190,000 | 265,000 |

## (1916–1917) McKinley Memorial

The sale of the McKinley dollars aided in paying for a memorial building at Niles, Ohio, the martyred president's birthplace. The obverse, showing a profile of McKinley, was designed by Charles E. Barber; the reverse, with the memorial building, was designed by George T. Morgan.

| | Distribution | AU-50 | MS-60 | MS-63 | MS-65 | MS-66 |
|---|---|---|---|---|---|---|
| 1916, McKinley Memorial .................... | *15,000* | $450 | $500 | $575 | $850 | $1,000 |
| 1917, McKinley Memorial .................... | *5,000* | 500 | 550 | 600 | 1,000 | 1,400 |

## (1918) Illinois Centennial

This coin was authorized to commemorate the 100th anniversary of the admission of Illinois into the Union, and was the first souvenir piece for such an event. The obverse was designed by George T. Morgan and the reverse by J.R. Sinnock. The obverse shows the head of Lincoln taken from the statue by Andrew O'Connor in Springfield, Illinois. The reverse is based on the Illinois State Seal.

| | Distribution | AU-50 | MS-60 | MS-63 | MS-65 | MS-66 |
|---|---|---|---|---|---|---|
| 1918, Illinois Centennial | 100,058 | $130 | $150 | $170 | $325 | $685 |

## (1920) Maine Centennial

Congress authorized the Maine Centennial half dollar on May 10, 1920, to be sold at the centennial celebration at Portland. They were received too late for this event and were sold by the state treasurer for many years. Anthony de Francisci modeled this coin from a design by Harry H. Cochrane. The obverse device is the arms of the state of Maine; the Latin word DIRIGO means "I Direct."

| | Distribution | AU-50 | MS-60 | MS-63 | MS-65 | MS-66 |
|---|---|---|---|---|---|---|
| 1920, Maine Centennial | 50,028 | $120 | $140 | $160 | $395 | $525 |

## (1920–1921) Pilgrim Tercentenary

To commemorate the landing of the Pilgrims at Plymouth, Massachusetts, in 1620, Congress authorized a special half dollar on May 12, 1920. Cyrus E. Dallin, a Boston sculptor, executed the designs furnished to him by the commission. His initial D is below the elbow of Governor William Bradford, on the obverse. The reverse shows the *Mayflower*. The first issue had no date on the obverse. The coins struck in 1921 show that date in addition to 1620–1920. There was a large coinage of both issues, and not all were sold. A total of 128,000 were returned to the mint and melted.

| | Distribution | AU-50 | MS-60 | MS-63 | MS-65 | MS-66 |
|---|---|---|---|---|---|---|
| 1920, Pilgrim Tercentenary | 152,112 | $80 | $90 | $100 | $200 | $475 |
| 1921, Same, With Date Added in Field | 20,053 | 165 | 180 | 195 | 275 | 650 |

## (1921) Missouri Centennial

The 100th anniversary of the admission of Missouri to the Union was celebrated in Sedalia during August 1921. To mark the occasion, Congress authorized the coinage of a fifty-cent piece. Robert Aitken designed the coin, which shows the bust of a frontiersman on the obverse, and a frontiersman and Indian on the reverse. The first coins struck show 2★4 incused, indicating that Missouri was the 24th star in the flag. The type without this marking was struck later, but was the first to be sold.

2★4 in Field

| | Distribution | AU-50 | MS-60 | MS-63 | MS-65 | MS-66 |
|---|---|---|---|---|---|---|
| 1921, Missouri Centennial, "2★4" in Field | 9,400 | $575 | $625 | $950 | $2,100 | $5,400 |
| 1921, Missouri Centennial, Plain | 11,400 | 400 | 525 | 675 | 2,000 | 4,900 |

## (1921) Alabama Centennial

2X2 in Field

The Alabama half dollars were authorized in 1920 for the statehood centennial, which was celebrated in 1919, but they were not struck until 1921. The coins, designed by Laura Gardin Fraser, were offered first during President Warren Harding's visit to Birmingham, October 26, 1921. The St. Andrew's cross, an emblem on the state flag, appears on a part of the issue between the numbers in "2X2," indicating it was the 22nd state of the Union. The obverse has busts of William Wyatt Bibb, first governor of Alabama, and T.E. Kilby, governor at the time of the centennial. This is the first instance of the use of a living person's portrait on a United States coin.

| | Distribution | AU-50 | MS-60 | MS-63 | MS-65 | MS-66 |
|---|---|---|---|---|---|---|
| 1921, Alabama Centennial, With "2X2" in Field of Obverse | *6,006* | $285 | $325 | $400 | $1,000 | $2,000 |
| 1921, Alabama Centennial, Plain | *16,014* | 160 | 200 | 385 | 900 | 1,500 |

## (1922) Grant Memorial

This coin was struck during 1922 as a centenary souvenir of Ulysses S. Grant's birth. An incuse (recessed) star that appeared on the first issues was later removed, creating a second variety. The star has no particular significance. The reverse shows the frame house in Point Pleasant, Ohio, where Grant was born on April 27, 1822. Laura Gardin Fraser designed both the Grant half dollar and gold dollar.

**Star in Obverse Field**
*Fake stars usually have flattened spot on reverse.*

| | Distribution | AU-50 | MS-60 | MS-63 | MS-65 | MS-66 |
|---|---|---|---|---|---|---|
| 1922, Grant Memorial, Star in Obverse Field | 4,256 | $900 | $1,200 | $1,675 | $5,000 | $6,500 |
| 1922, Same type, No Star in Field | 67,405 | 110 | 120 | 150 | 550 | 900 |

Like the half-dollar commemorative coins, the gold dollars were first issued with a star, which was removed for the later issues. The designs by Laura Gardin Fraser are the same as for the half-dollar coinage.

| | Distribution | AU-50 | MS-60 | MS-63 | MS-65 | MS-66 |
|---|---|---|---|---|---|---|
| 1922, Grant Memorial, With Star | 5,016 | $950 | $1,050 | $1,100 | $1,500 | $1,900 |
| 1922, Grant Memorial, No Star | 5,016 | 1,000 | 1,050 | 1,200 | 1,500 | 1,900 |

## (1923) Monroe Doctrine Centennial

The California film industry promoted this issue in conjunction with a motion picture exposition held in June 1923. The obverse shows the heads of James Monroe and John Quincy Adams, who were identified with the Monroe Doctrine. The Western Hemisphere is portrayed on the reverse in forms that suggest two female figures. Chester Beach prepared the models for this coin. Many unsold coins were released into circulation at face value.

| | Distribution | AU-50 | MS-60 | MS-63 | MS-65 | MS-66 |
|---|---|---|---|---|---|---|
| 1923S, Monroe Doctrine Centennial | 274,077 | $50 | $75 | $120 | $800 | $1,500 |

## (1924) Huguenot-Walloon Tercentenary

Settling of the Huguenots and Walloons in the New World was the occasion commemorated by this issue. New Netherland, now New York, was founded in 1624 by a group of Dutch colonists. The persons represented on the obverse were not directly concerned with the occasion, however. They are Admiral Coligny and William the Silent. The reverse shows the vessel *Nieuw Nederland.* George T. Morgan prepared the models for this coin.

| | Distribution | AU-50 | MS-60 | MS-63 | MS-65 | MS-66 |
|---|---|---|---|---|---|---|
| 1924, Huguenot-Walloon Tercentenary | 142,080 | $125 | $130 | $160 | $240 | $525 |

## (1925) Lexington-Concord Sesquicentennial

The two famous battles fought in 1775 are commemorated on this coin. A statue of the familiar Minute Man is depicted on the obverse, and the Old Belfry at Lexington is the reverse device. Chester Beach designed the coin. The famous statue by Daniel Chester French located in Concord was used for the design.

| | Distribution | AU-50 | MS-60 | MS-63 | MS-65 | MS-66 |
|---|---|---|---|---|---|---|
| 1925, Lexington-Concord Sesquicentennial | 162,013 | $75 | $85 | $100 | $325 | $550 |

## (1925) Stone Mountain Memorial

The models for this coin were prepared by Gutzon Borglum, who would later sculpt Mount Rushmore. The first coins were struck at Philadelphia on January 21, 1925, General Thomas "Stonewall" Jackson's birthday. Generals Robert E. Lee and Jackson, mounted, are shown on the obverse. The funds received from the sale of this large issue of half dollars were devoted to the expense of carving figures of Confederate leaders and soldiers on Stone Mountain in Georgia. The carving was completed and dedicated in 1970. Some of these coins were counterstamped on the reverse by the issuing commission, with letters and numbers for distribution to individual state sales agencies. These are valued much higher than normal coins.

| | Distribution | AU-50 | MS-60 | MS-63 | MS-65 | MS-66 |
|---|---|---|---|---|---|---|
| 1925, Stone Mountain Memorial | 1,314,709 | $55 | $65 | $80 | $185 | $250 |

## (1925) California Diamond Jubilee

The California half dollar was designed by Jo Mora, a noted California sculptor. The obverse bears a kneeling figure of a Forty-Niner. The reverse shows a walking grizzly bear, the state emblem. The celebration for which these coins were struck marked the 75th anniversary of the admission of California into the Union.

| | Distribution | AU-50 | MS-60 | MS-63 | MS-65 | MS-66 |
|---|---|---|---|---|---|---|
| 1925S, California Diamond Jubilee | 86,594 | $185 | $200 | $210 | $450 | $650 |

## (1925) Fort Vancouver Centennial

John McLoughlin, shown on the obverse of this coin, built Fort Vancouver (Washington) on the Columbia River in 1825. The sale of the coins at $1 each helped to finance the pageant staged for the celebration. Laura Gardin Fraser prepared the models for this coin, which was minted in San Francisco. The S mintmark was omitted. The reverse has a pioneer settler in buckskin suit with a musket in his hands. Fort Vancouver is in the background.

| | Distribution | AU-50 | MS-60 | MS-63 | MS-65 | MS-66 |
|---|---|---|---|---|---|---|
| 1925, Fort Vancouver Centennial | 14,994 | $300 | $325 | $375 | $600 | $900 |

## (1926) Sesquicentennial of American Independence

The 150th anniversary of the signing of the Declaration of Independence was the occasion for an international fair held in Philadelphia in 1926. To help raise funds for financing the fair, special issues of half dollars and quarter eagles were authorized by Congress. For the first time, a portrait of a president appeared on a coin struck during his own lifetime. Presidents Calvin Coolidge and George Washington are depicted on the obverse of the half dollar. The reverse bears an accurate model of the Liberty Bell. John R. Sinnock, chief engraver of the United States Mint, modeled the sesquicentennial coins from designs by John Frederick Lewis. The dies were in very low relief, causing much loss of detail.

| | Distribution | AU-50 | MS-60 | MS-63 | MS-65 | MS-66 |
|---|---|---|---|---|---|---|
| 1926, Sesquicentennial of American Independence | 141,120 | $75 | $90 | $130 | $1,250 | $20,000 |

The obverse of this special gold quarter eagle has a standing female figure symbolic of Liberty, holding in one hand a scroll representing the Declaration of Independence and in the other the Torch of Freedom. The reverse bears a representation of Independence Hall in Philadelphia. The coin was designed by John R. Sinnock.

| | Distribution | AU-50 | MS-60 | MS-63 | MS-65 | MS-66 |
|---|---|---|---|---|---|---|
| 1926, Sesquicentennial of American Independence | 46,019 | $400 | $450 | $550 | $1,350 | $4,000 |

## (1926–1939) Oregon Trail Memorial

This memorial coin was struck in commemoration of the Oregon Trail and in memory of the pioneers, many of whom lie buried along the famous 2,000-mile highway of history. James Earle Fraser and his wife, Laura Gardin Fraser, prepared the designs. The original issue was struck at Philadelphia and San Francisco in 1926. Coinage was resumed in 1928 (released in 1933), and in 1933, 1934, and 1936 through 1939. The 1933 half dollar was the first commemorative coin struck at the Denver Mint.

| | Distribution | AU-50 | MS-60 | MS-63 | MS-65 | MS-66 |
|---|---|---|---|---|---|---|
| 1926, Oregon Trail Memorial | 47,955 | $135 | $160 | $190 | $250 | $325 |
| 1926S, Same type, S Mint | 83,055 | 135 | 160 | 190 | 260 | 350 |
| 1928, Oregon Trail Memorial (same as 1926) | 6,028 | 160 | 180 | 200 | 300 | 435 |
| 1933D, Oregon Trail Memorial | 5,008 | 350 | 370 | 400 | 450 | 550 |
| 1934D, Oregon Trail Memorial | 7,006 | 190 | 200 | 210 | 300 | 450 |
| 1936, Oregon Trail Memorial | 10,006 | 160 | 180 | 200 | 260 | 280 |
| 1936S, Same type, S Mint | 5,006 | 170 | 180 | 200 | 260 | 335 |
| 1937D, Oregon Trail Memorial | 12,008 | 165 | 180 | 195 | 250 | 315 |
| 1938, Oregon Trail Memorial (same as 1926) | 6,006 | | | | | |
| 1938D, Same type, D Mint | 6,005 | *Set:* | 575 | 600 | 850 | 1,100 |
| 1938S, Same type, S Mint | 6,006 | | | | | |
| 1939, Oregon Trail Memorial (same as 1926) | 3,004 | | | | | |
| 1939D, Same type, D Mint | 3,004 | *Set:* | 1,450 | 1,550 | 1,800 | 2,000 |
| 1939S, Same type, S Mint | 3,005 | | | | | |
| Oregon Trail Memorial, single type coin | | 135 | 160 | 190 | 250 | 325 |

## (1927) Vermont Sesquicentennial

This souvenir issue commemorates the 150th anniversary of the Battle of Bennington and the independence of Vermont. Authorized in 1925, it was not coined until 1927. The models were prepared by Charles Keck. The obverse shows the head of Ira Allen, founder of Vermont. The reverse bears a catamount walking left.

| | Distribution | AU-50 | MS-60 | MS-63 | MS-65 | MS-66 |
|---|---|---|---|---|---|---|
| 1927, Vermont Sesquicentennial (Battle of Bennington) | 28,142 | $250 | $265 | $275 | $460 | $650 |

## (1928) Hawaiian Sesquicentennial

This issue was struck to commemorate the 150th anniversary of the arrival on the Hawaiian Islands of Captain James Cook in 1778. The design was sketched by Juliette May Fraser of Honolulu and executed by Chester Beach. Captain Cook is shown on the obverse and a native chief on the reverse. The coins were distributed in 1928 and sold for $2 each, the highest initial sale price up to that time.

| | Distribution | AU-50 | MS-60 | MS-63 | MS-65 | MS-66 |
|---|---|---|---|---|---|---|
| 1928, Hawaiian Sesquicentennial | 10,008 | $1,800 | $2,100 | $2,475 | $3,500 | $5,250 |
| 1928, Hawaiian Sesquicentennial, Sandblast Proof Presentation Piece . . . (50) | | | | | 50,000 | — |

## (1934) Maryland Tercentenary

The 300th anniversary of the founding of the Maryland Colony by Cecil Calvert (known as Lord Baltimore) was the occasion for this special coin. The profits from the sale of this issue were used to finance the celebration in Baltimore during 1934. Hans Schuler designed the coin, which shows the facing head of Lord Baltimore on the obverse and the arms of Maryland on the reverse, reminiscent of the Maryland colonial pieces.

| | Distribution | AU-50 | MS-60 | MS-63 | MS-65 | MS-66 |
|---|---|---|---|---|---|---|
| 1934, Maryland Tercentenary | 25,015 | $130 | $140 | $165 | $185 | $275 |

## (1934–1938) Texas Independence Centennial

This issue commemorated the independence of Texas in 1836. The first of several dates was offered in 1934. The later dates were struck at all three mints. The models were prepared by Pompeo Coppini. The reverse shows the kneeling figure of winged Victory, and on each side, medallions with portraits of General Sam Houston and Stephen Austin, founders of the Republic and State of Texas. The large five-pointed star behind the eagle on the obverse carries out the Lone Star tradition.

*See next page for chart.*

| | Distribution | AU-50 | MS-60 | MS-63 | MS-65 | MS-66 |
|---|---|---|---|---|---|---|
| 1934, Texas Independence Centennial | 61,463 | $130 | $140 | $150 | $200 | $300 |
| 1935, Texas Independence Centennial (same as 1934) | 9,996 | | | | | |
| 1935D, Same type, D Mint | 10,007 | *Set:* | 425 | 465 | 600 | 900 |
| 1935S, Same type, S Mint | 10,008 | | | | | |
| 1936, Texas Independence Centennial (same as 1934) | 8,911 | | | | | |
| 1936D, Same type, D Mint | 9,039 | *Set:* | 450 | 525 | 725 | 875 |
| 1936S, Same type, S Mint | 9,055 | | | | | |
| 1937, Texas Independence Centennial (same as 1934) | 6,571 | | | | | |
| 1937D, Same type, D Mint | 6,605 | *Set:* | 450 | 550 | 800 | 1,000 |
| 1937S, Same type, S Mint | 6,637 | | | | | |
| 1938, Texas Independence Centennial (same as 1934) | 3,780 | | | | | |
| 1938D, Same type, D Mint | 3,775 | *Set:* | 800 | 900 | 1,200 | 1,800 |
| 1938S, Same type, S Mint | 3,814 | | | | | |
| Texas Independence Centennial, single type coin | | 130 | 140 | 150 | 200 | 300 |

## (1934–1938) Daniel Boone Bicentennial

This coin type, which was minted for five years, was first struck in 1934 to commemorate the 200th anniversary of the famous frontiersman's birth. The change of date to 1935 for the second year's coinage brought about the addition of the commemorative date 1934 above the words PIONEER YEAR. Coinage covered several years, similar to the schedule for the Texas issues. The models for this coin were prepared by Augustus Lukeman. The obverse bears a portrait of Daniel Boone; the reverse shows Boone with Blackfish, war chief of the Chillicothe band of the Shawnee tribe.

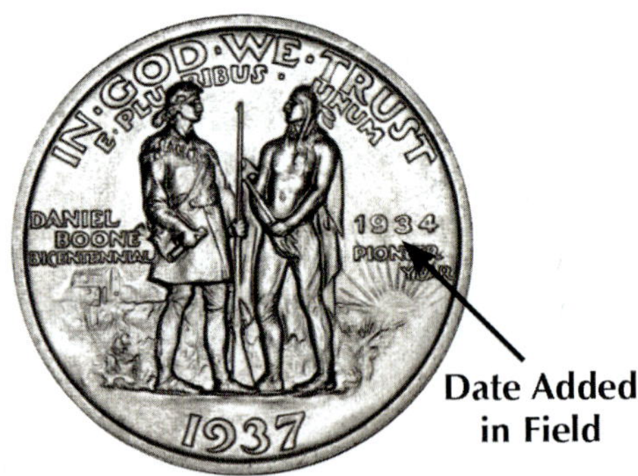


Date Added in Field

| | Distribution | AU-50 | MS-60 | MS-63 | MS-65 | MS-66 |
|---|---|---|---|---|---|---|
| 1934, Daniel Boone Bicentennial | 10,007 | $130 | $135 | $150 | $180 | $275 |
| 1935, Same type | 10,010 | | | | | |
| 1935D, Same type, D Mint | 5,005 | *Set:* | 405 | 450 | 625 | 875 |
| 1935S, Same type, S Mint | 5,005 | | | | | |
| 1935, Same as 1934, Small 1934 on Reverse | 10,008 | | | | | |
| 1935D, Same type, D Mint | 2,003 | *Set:* | 675 | 800 | 1,550 | 1,950 |
| 1935S, Same type, S Mint | 2,004 | | | | | |
| 1936, Daniel Boone Bicentennial (same as above) | 12,012 | | | | | |
| 1936D, Same type, D Mint | 5,005 | *Set:* | 415 | 450 | 650 | 875 |
| 1936S, Same type, S Mint | 5,006 | | | | | |
| 1937, Daniel Boone Bicentennial (same as above) | 9,810 | | | | | |
| 1937D, Same type, D Mint | 2,506 | *Set:* | 410 | 450 | 650 | 950 |
| 1937S, Same type, S Mint | 2,506 | | | | | |

| | Distribution | AU-50 | MS-60 | MS-63 | MS-65 | MS-66 |
|---|---|---|---|---|---|---|
| 1938, Daniel Boone Bicentennial (same as above) | 2,100 | | | | | |
| 1938D, Same type, D Mint | 2,100 | *Set:* | $800 | $1,000 | $1,400 | $2,000 |
| 1938S, Same type, S Mint | 2,100 | | | | | |
| Daniel Boone Bicentennial, single type coin | | $130 | 135 | 150 | 180 | 275 |

## (1935) Connecticut Tercentenary

In commemoration of the 300th anniversary of the founding of the colony of Connecticut, a souvenir half dollar was struck. Henry Kreis designed the coin. The famous Charter Oak is the main device on the reverse—according to legend, the Royal Charter was secreted in the tree during the reign of James II, who wished to revoke it. The charter was produced after the king's overthrow in 1688, and the colony continued under its protection.

| | Distribution | AU-50 | MS-60 | MS-63 | MS-65 | MS-66 |
|---|---|---|---|---|---|---|
| 1935, Connecticut Tercentenary | 25,018 | $215 | $220 | $235 | $400 | $550 |

## (1935–1939) Arkansas Centennial

This souvenir issue marked the 100th anniversary of the admission of Arkansas into the Union. Edward Everett Burr designed the piece, and models were prepared by Emily Bates of Arkansas. Although 1936 was the centennial year, the first of several issues was brought out in 1935 from all three mints. The 1936 through 1939 issues were the same as those of 1935 except for the dates. They were sold by the distributors at $8.75 per set of three coins. The reverse shows accolated heads of an Indian chief of 1836 and an American girl of 1935. During 1936, a second design was authorized by Congress. Senator Joseph T. Robinson consented to have his portrait placed on the reverse side of the coins, which were struck at the Philadelphia Mint (see listing on next page).

| | Distribution | AU-50 | MS-60 | MS-63 | MS-65 | MS-66 |
|---|---|---|---|---|---|---|
| 1935, Arkansas Centennial | 13,012 | | | | | |
| 1935D, Same type, D Mint | 5,505 | *Set:* | $300 | $330 | $525 | $1,400 |
| 1935S, Same type, S Mint | 5,506 | | | | | |
| 1936, Arkansas Centennial (same as 1935; date 1936 on reverse) | 9,660 | | | | | |
| 1936D, Same type, D Mint | 9,660 | *Set:* | 285 | 330 | 475 | 1,900 |
| 1936S, Same type, S Mint | 9,662 | | | | | |
| 1937, Arkansas Centennial (same as 1935) | 5,505 | | | | | |
| 1937D, Same type, D Mint | 5,505 | *Set:* | 345 | 375 | 725 | 1,875 |
| 1937S, Same type, S Mint | 5,506 | | | | | |

*Chart continued on next page.*

| | Distribution | AU-50 | MS-60 | MS-63 | MS-65 | MS-66 |
|---|---|---|---|---|---|---|
| 1938, Arkansas Centennial (same as 1935) | 3,156 | | | | | |
| 1938D, Same type, D Mint | 3,155 | *Set:* | $435 | $500 | $1,075 | $2,800 |
| 1938S, Same type, S Mint | 3,156 | | | | | |
| 1939, Arkansas Centennial (same as 1935) | 2,104 | | | | | |
| 1939D, Same type, D Mint | 2,104 | *Set:* | 725 | 800 | 2,200 | 4,500 |
| 1939S, Same type, S Mint | 2,105 | | | | | |
| Arkansas Centennial, single type coin | | $110 | 120 | 140 | 200 | 350 |

### *(1936) Arkansas Centennial – Robinson*

A new reverse design for the Arkansas Centennial coin (see prior page) was authorized by the Act of June 26, 1936. Senator Joseph T. Robinson, still living at the time his portrait was used, was the subject for the new issue engraved by Henry Kreis. The obverse, designed by Everett Burr, was unchanged. The law specified a change in the reverse, because of the fact that the obverse side is that which bears the date. From a numismatic viewpoint, however, the side that has the portrait is usually considered the obverse. Thus, in this instance, the side with the eagle device is often considered the reverse.

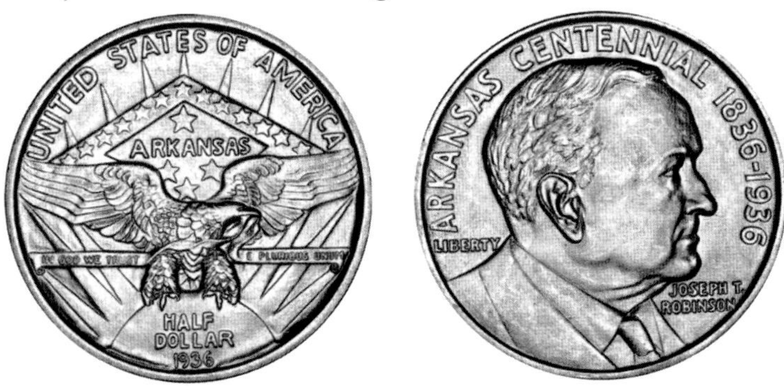


| | Distribution | AU-50 | MS-60 | MS-63 | MS-65 | MS-66 |
|---|---|---|---|---|---|---|
| 1936, Arkansas Centennial (Robinson) | 25,265 | $105 | $125 | $135 | $215 | $375 |

### (1935) Hudson, New York, Sesquicentennial

This souvenir half dollar marked the 150th anniversary of the founding of Hudson, New York, which was named after the explorer Henry Hudson. The designs, by Chester Beach, show Hudson's flagship, the *Half Moon,* on the obverse and the seal of the City of Hudson on the reverse. Details of the seal include representations of Neptune with trident on a spouting whale and a mermaid blowing a conch shell.

| | Distribution | AU-50 | MS-60 | MS-63 | MS-65 | MS-66 |
|---|---|---|---|---|---|---|
| 1935, Hudson, New York, Sesquicentennial | 10,008 | $650 | $700 | $800 | $1,000 | $1,250 |

## (1935–1936) California Pacific International Exposition

Congress approved the coinage of souvenir half dollars for the exposition on May 3, 1935. Robert Aitken designed the coin, which was struck at the San Francisco Mint. The same type with date 1936 was struck at the Denver Mint, under authority of the special Recoinage Act of May 6, 1936, which specified that 180,000 pieces could be recoined with the date 1936 irrespective of the year of issue. The obverse displays a seated female with spear and a bear in the left background. The reverse shows the observation tower and the State of California building at the exposition.

| | Distribution | AU-50 | MS-60 | MS-63 | MS-65 | MS-66 |
|---|---|---|---|---|---|---|
| 1935S, California Pacific International Exposition. . . | 70,132 | $100 | $105 | $115 | $135 | $160 |
| 1936D, California Pacific International Exposition . . | 30,092 | 100 | 105 | 115 | 140 | 200 |

## (1935) Old Spanish Trail

This coin commemorated the 400th anniversary of the overland trek of the Cabeza de Vaca Expedition through the Gulf states in 1535. The coin was designed by L.W. Hoffecker, and models were prepared by Edmund J. Senn. The explorer's name literally translated means "head of a cow"; therefore this device was chosen for the obverse. The reverse bears a yucca tree and a map showing the Old Spanish Trail.

| | Distribution | AU-50 | MS-60 | MS-63 | MS-65 | MS-66 |
|---|---|---|---|---|---|---|
| 1935, Old Spanish Trail. . . . . . . . . . . . . . . . . . . . . . | 10,008 | $1,050 | $1,100 | $1,150 | $1,275 | $1,450 |

## (1936) Providence, Rhode Island, Tercentenary

The 300th anniversary of Roger Williams's founding of Providence was the occasion for this special half dollar in 1936. The designs were the work of Arthur Graham Carey and John Howard Benson. The obverse shows Roger Williams in a canoe, being welcomed by an Indian. The reverse has the anchor of Hope with a shield and mantling in the background. Although the founding of Providence was being celebrated, no mention of the city is to be found on the coin.

| | Distribution | AU-50 | MS-60 | MS-63 | MS-65 | MS-66 |
|---|---|---|---|---|---|---|
| 1936, Providence, Rhode Island, Tercentenary . . . . | 20,013 | | | | | |
| 1936D, Same type, D Mint . . . . . . . . . . . . . . . . . . . | 15,010 | *Set:* | $325 | $360 | $500 | $675 |
| 1936S, Same type, S Mint. . . . . . . . . . . . . . . . . . . . | 15,011 | | | | | |
| Providence, Rhode Island, Tercentenary, single type coin . . | | $95 | 105 | 120 | 150 | 210 |

## (1936) Cleveland Centennial / Great Lakes Exposition

A special coinage of fifty-cent pieces was authorized in commemoration of the centennial celebration of Cleveland, Ohio, on the occasion of the Great Lakes Exposition held there in 1936. The designs were prepared by Brenda Putnam. Although half the coinage was struck in 1937, all were dated 1936. The obverse has a bust of Moses Cleaveland, and the reverse displays a map of the Great Lakes region with a compass point at the city of Cleveland. Nine Great Lakes cities are marked by stars.

| | Distribution | AU-50 | MS-60 | MS-63 | MS-65 | MS-66 |
|---|---|---|---|---|---|---|
| 1936, Cleveland Centennial / Great Lakes Exposition.... | 50,030 | $100 | $110 | $130 | $150 | $230 |

## (1936) Wisconsin Territorial Centennial

The 100th anniversary of the Wisconsin territorial government was the occasion for this issue. The original design was made by David Parsons, a University of Wisconsin student. Benjamin Hawkins, a New York artist, made changes to conform with technical requirements. The reverse has the territorial seal, which includes a forearm holding a pickaxe over a mound of lead ore, and the inscription 4TH DAY OF JULY ANNO DOMINI 1836. The obverse shows a badger on a log, the state emblem, and arrows representing the Black Hawk War of the 1830s.

| | Distribution | AU-50 | MS-60 | MS-63 | MS-65 | MS-66 |
|---|---|---|---|---|---|---|
| 1936, Wisconsin Territorial Centennial........... | 25,015 | $175 | $180 | $195 | $230 | $250 |

## (1936) Cincinnati Music Center

Although the head of Stephen Foster, "America's Troubadour," dominates the obverse of this special issue, the anniversary celebrated bears no relation to him. The coins, designed by Constance Ortmayer of Washington, D.C., were supposedly struck to commemorate the 50th anniversary in 1936 of Cincinnati as a center of music. The coins were struck at the three mints and were sold only in sets at $7.75, the highest initial cost of a new type at that time.

| | Distribution | AU-50 | MS-60 | MS-63 | MS-65 | MS-66 |
|---|---|---|---|---|---|---|
| 1936, Cincinnati Music Center.................. | 5,005 | | | | | |
| 1936D, Same type, D Mint .................... | 5,005 | *Set:* | $900 | $1,100 | $1,375 | $2,500 |
| 1936S, Same type, S Mint..................... | 5,006 | | | | | |
| Cincinnati Music Center, single type coin............... | | $285 | 300 | 360 | 450 | 650 |

## (1936) Long Island Tercentenary

This souvenir issue was authorized to commemorate the 300th anniversary of the first white settlement on Long Island, which was made at Jamaica Bay by Dutch colonists. The design was prepared by Howard Kenneth Weinman, son of the sculptor A.A. Weinman, who designed the regular Liberty Walking type half dollar. Accolated heads depicting a Dutch settler and an Indian are shown on the obverse, while a Dutch sailing vessel is the reverse device. This was the first issue for which a date was specified (1936) irrespective of the year minted or issued, as a safeguard against extending the coinage over a period of years.

| | Distribution | AU-50 | MS-60 | MS-63 | MS-65 | MS-66 |
|---|---|---|---|---|---|---|
| 1936, Long Island Tercentenary | 81,826 | $85 | $95 | $110 | $195 | $375 |

## (1936) York County, Maine, Tercentenary

A souvenir half dollar was authorized by Congress upon the 300th anniversary of the founding of York County, Maine. Brown's Garrison on the Saco River was the site of a town that was settled in 1636. The designs were made by Walter H. Rich of Portland. The obverse design shows a stockade, and the reverse has an adaptation of the York County seal.

| | Distribution | AU-50 | MS-60 | MS-63 | MS-65 | MS-66 |
|---|---|---|---|---|---|---|
| 1936, York County, Maine, Tercentenary | 25,015 | $160 | $165 | $180 | $200 | $220 |

## (1936) Bridgeport, Connecticut, Centennial

In commemoration of the 100th anniversary of the incorporation of the city of Bridgeport, a special fifty-cent piece was authorized on May 15, 1936. Henry Kreis designed this coin. The head of P.T. Barnum, Bridgeport's best-known citizen, occupies the obverse. An Art Deco eagle dominates the reverse.

| | Distribution | AU-50 | MS-60 | MS-63 | MS-65 | MS-66 |
|---|---|---|---|---|---|---|
| 1936, Bridgeport, Connecticut, Centennial | 25,015 | $120 | $125 | $135 | $180 | $280 |

## (1936) Lynchburg, Virginia, Sesquicentennial

The issuance of a charter to the city of Lynchburg in 1786 was commemorated in 1936 by a special coinage of half dollars. The models for the coin were prepared by Charles Keck. The obverse bears a portrait of Senator Carter Glass, a native of Lynchburg and former secretary of the Treasury, who objected to the idea of using portraits of living men on coins. Despite his mild protests, his likeness was incorporated on the coin. The reverse shows Liberty standing, with the old Lynchburg courthouse in the background.

| | Distribution | AU-50 | MS-60 | MS-63 | MS-65 | MS-66 |
|---|---|---|---|---|---|---|
| 1936, Lynchburg, Virginia, Sesquicentennial | 20,013 | $220 | $230 | $240 | $275 | $350 |

## (1936) Elgin, Illinois, Centennial

The 100th anniversary of the founding of Elgin was marked by a special issue of half dollars in 1936. The proceeds were devoted to financing a Pioneer Memorial statue, which is depicted on the reverse of the coin. The year 1673 bears no relation to the event but refers to the year in which Louis Joliet and Jacques Marquette entered Illinois Territory. The designs were prepared by Trygve Rovelstad, who also designed the Pioneer Memorial (which was not dedicated until 2001).

| | Distribution | AU-50 | MS-60 | MS-63 | MS-65 | MS-66 |
|---|---|---|---|---|---|---|
| 1936, Elgin, Illinois, Centennial | 20,015 | $180 | $190 | $200 | $230 | $255 |

## (1936) Albany, New York, Charter

The 250th anniversary of the granting of a charter to the city of Albany was the occasion for this commemorative half dollar. The reverse design shows Governor Thomas Dongan, Peter Schuyler, and Robert Livingston. The obverse depicts a beaver gnawing on a maple branch. Gertrude K. Lathrop of Albany was the designer.

| | Distribution | AU-50 | MS-60 | MS-63 | MS-65 | MS-66 |
|---|---|---|---|---|---|---|
| 1936, Albany, New York, Charter | 17,671 | $210 | $230 | $240 | $275 | $350 |

## (1936) San Francisco – Oakland Bay Bridge Opening

The opening of the San Francisco Bay Bridge was the occasion for a special souvenir fifty-cent piece. The designs were the work of Jacques Schnier, a San Francisco artist. A California grizzly bear dominates the obverse. The famous landmark bridge is shown on the reverse. The coins were struck at the San Francisco Mint in November 1936. The bear depicted was a composite of animals in local zoos.

| | Distribution | AU-50 | MS-60 | MS-63 | MS-65 | MS-66 |
|---|---|---|---|---|---|---|
| 1936S, San Francisco–Oakland Bay Bridge Opening.... | 71,424 | $145 | $150 | $175 | $200 | $300 |

## (1936) Columbia, South Carolina, Sesquicentennial

Souvenir half dollars were authorized to help finance the extensive celebrations marking the sesquicentennial of the founding of Columbia in 1786. A. Wolfe Davidson designed the coin, which was struck at all three mints and sold in sets. The obverse bears the figure of Justice with sword and scales. At the left is the capitol of 1786, and at the right, the capitol of 1936. A palmetto tree, the state emblem, is the reverse device.

| | Distribution | AU-50 | MS-60 | MS-63 | MS-65 | MS-66 |
|---|---|---|---|---|---|---|
| 1936, Columbia, South Carolina, Sesquicentennial ...... | 9,007 | | | | | |
| 1936D, Same type, D Mint ........................ | 8,009 | *Set:* | $650 | $675 | $750 | $875 |
| 1936S, Same type, S Mint......................... | 8,007 | | | | | |
| Columbia, South Carolina, Sesquicentennial, single type coin ... | | $180 | 215 | 225 | 245 | 300 |

## (1936) Delaware Tercentenary

The 300th anniversary of the landing of the Swedes in Delaware was the occasion for a souvenir issue of half dollars. The colonists landed on the spot that is now Wilmington and established a church, which is the oldest Protestant church in the United States still used for worship. Their ship, *Kalmar Nyckel,* is shown on the reverse of the coin, and the Old Swedes Church is on the obverse. Designs were chosen from a competition that was won by Carl L. Schmitz. This coin was authorized in 1936, struck in 1937, and dated 1938 on the reverse and 1936 on the obverse. The anniversary was celebrated in 1938 in both Sweden and the United States. A two-krona coin was issued in Sweden to commemorate the same event.

| | Distribution | AU-50 | MS-60 | MS-63 | MS-65 | MS-66 |
|---|---|---|---|---|---|---|
| 1936, Delaware Tercentenary ................. | 20,993 | $210 | $225 | $230 | $250 | $350 |

## (1936) Battle of Gettysburg Anniversary

On June 16, 1936, Congress authorized a coinage of fifty-cent pieces in commemoration of the 1863 Battle of Gettysburg. The models were prepared by Frank Vittor, a Pittsburgh sculptor. Portraits of a Union and a Confederate veteran are shown on the obverse. On the reverse are two shields, representing the Union and Confederate armies, separated by a double-bladed fasces.

| | Distribution | AU-50 | MS-60 | MS-63 | MS-65 | MS-66 |
|---|---|---|---|---|---|---|
| 1936, Battle of Gettysburg Anniversary | 26,928 | $435 | $450 | $490 | $775 | $1,000 |

## (1936) Norfolk, Virginia, Bicentennial

To provide funds for the celebration of Norfolk's anniversary of its growth from a township in 1682 to a royal borough in 1736, Congress first passed a law for the striking of medals. The proponents, however, being dissatisfied, finally succeeded in winning authority for half dollars commemorating the 300th anniversary of the original Norfolk land grant and the 200th anniversary of the establishment of the borough. William Marks Simpson and his wife, Marjorie Emory Simpson, designed the piece. The obverse shows the Seal of the City of Norfolk with a three-masted ship as the central device. The reverse features the Royal Mace of Norfolk, presented by Lieutenant Governor Dinwiddie in 1753.

| | Distribution | AU-50 | MS-60 | MS-63 | MS-65 | MS-66 |
|---|---|---|---|---|---|---|
| 1936, Norfolk, Virginia, Bicentennial | 16,936 | $250 | $280 | $300 | $340 | $350 |

## (1937) Roanoke Island, North Carolina, 350th Anniversary

A celebration was held in Old Fort Raleigh in 1937 to commemorate the 350th anniversary of Sir Walter Raleigh's "Lost Colony" and the birth of Virginia Dare, the first white child born in British North America. A special half dollar for the occasion was designed by William Marks Simpson of Baltimore. The obverse bears a portrait of Sir Walter Raleigh, and the reverse has a figure representing Ellinor Dare holding her child Virginia.

| | Distribution | AU-50 | MS-60 | MS-63 | MS-65 | MS-66 |
|---|---|---|---|---|---|---|
| 1937, Roanoke Island, North Carolina, 350th Anniversary | 29,030 | $135 | $150 | $185 | $230 | $250 |

## (1937) Battle of Antietam Anniversary

A souvenir half dollar was designed by William Marks Simpson and struck in 1937 to commemorate the 75th anniversary of the famous Civil War battle to thwart Lee's invasion of Maryland. The opposing generals McClellan and Lee are featured on the obverse, while the Burnside Bridge, an important tactical objective, is shown on the reverse. The Battle of Antietam, on September 17, 1862, was one of the bloodiest single-day battles of the war, with more than 23,000 men killed, wounded, or missing.

| | Distribution | AU-50 | MS-60 | MS-63 | MS-65 | MS-66 |
|---|---|---|---|---|---|---|
| 1937, Battle of Antietam Anniversary | 18,028 | $525 | $550 | $575 | $600 | $650 |

## (1938) New Rochelle, New York, 250th Anniversary

To observe the founding of New Rochelle in 1688 by French Huguenots, a special half dollar was issued in 1938. The title to the land that the Huguenots purchased from John Pell provided that a fattened calf be given away every year on June 20. This is represented by a calf and figure of John Pell on the obverse of the coin. The fleur-de-lis, which is shown on the reverse, is adapted from the seal of the city. Both sides of the coin were designed by Gertrude K. Lathrop.

| | Distribution | AU-50 | MS-60 | MS-63 | MS-65 | MS-66 |
|---|---|---|---|---|---|---|
| 1938, New Rochelle, New York, 250th Anniversary | 15,266 | $300 | $310 | $325 | $375 | $400 |

## (1946) Iowa Centennial

This half dollar, commemorating the 100th anniversary of Iowa's statehood, was designed by Adam Pietz of Philadelphia. The reverse shows the Iowa state seal, and the obverse shows the first stone capitol building at Iowa City. This issue was sold first to the residents of Iowa and only a small remainder to others. Nearly all of the issue was disposed of quickly, except for 500 that were held back to be distributed in 1996, and another 500 in 2046.

| | Distribution | AU-50 | MS-60 | MS-63 | MS-65 | MS-66 |
|---|---|---|---|---|---|---|
| 1946, Iowa Centennial | 100,057 | $85 | $90 | $100 | $110 | $130 |

## (1946–1951) Booker T. Washington Memorial

This commemorative coin was issued to perpetuate the ideals and teachings of Booker T. Washington and to construct memorials to his memory. Issued from all mints, it received wide distribution from the start. The reverse has the legend FROM SLAVE CABIN TO HALL OF FAME. His log-cabin birthplace is shown beneath. This coin was designed by Isaac Scott Hathaway, as was the Carver/Washington half dollar.

| | Distribution | AU-50 | MS-60 | MS-63 | MS-65 | MS-66 |
|---|---|---|---|---|---|---|
| 1946, Booker T. Washington Memorial **(a)** | 700,546 | | | | | |
| 1946D, Same type, D Mint | 50,000 | *Set:* | $60 | $75 | $180 | $425 |
| 1946S, Same type, S Mint | 500,279 | | | | | |
| 1947, Same type as 1946 | 6,000 | | | | | |
| 1947D, Same type, D Mint | 6,000 | *Set:* | 85 | 165 | 225 | 700 |
| 1947S, Same type, S Mint | 6,000 | | | | | |
| 1948, Same type as 1946 | 8,005 | | | | | |
| 1948D, Same type, D Mint | 8,005 | *Set:* | 85 | 185 | 250 | 525 |
| 1948S, Same type, S Mint | 8,005 | | | | | |
| 1949, Same type as 1946 | 6,004 | | | | | |
| 1949D, Same type, D Mint | 6,004 | *Set:* | 60 | 75 | 400 | 525 |
| 1949S, Same type, S Mint | 6,004 | | | | | |
| 1950, Same type as 1946 | 6,004 | | | | | |
| 1950D, Same type, D Mint | 6,004 | *Set:* | 60 | 75 | 300 | 500 |
| 1950S, Same type, S Mint | 62,091 | | | | | |
| 1951, Same type as 1946 | 210,082 | | | | | |
| 1951D, Same type, D Mint | 7,004 | *Set:* | 95 | 160 | 275 | 450 |
| 1951S, Same type, S Mint | 7,004 | | | | | |
| Booker T. Washington Memorial, single type coin | | $18 | 20 | 25 | 60 | 100 |

**a.** Minted; quantity melted unknown.

## (1951–1954) Carver/Washington Commemorative

Designed by Isaac Scott Hathaway, this coin portrays the conjoined busts of two prominent black Americans. Booker T. Washington was a lecturer, educator, and principal of Tuskegee Institute. He urged training to advance independence and efficiency for his race. George Washington Carver was an agricultural chemist who worked to improve the economy of the South. He spent part of his life teaching crop improvement and new uses for soybeans, peanuts, sweet potatoes, and cotton waste. Money obtained from the sale of these commemoratives was to be used "to oppose the spread of communism among Negroes in the interest of national defense."

| | Distribution | AU-50 | MS-60 | MS-63 | MS-65 | MS-66 |
|---|---|---|---|---|---|---|
| 1951, Carver/Washington | 20,018 | | | | | |
| 1951D, Same type, D Mint | 10,004 | *Set:* | $70 | $110 | $350 | $1,150 |
| 1951S, Same type, S Mint | 10,004 | | | | | |
| 1952, Same type as 1951 | 1,106,292 | | | | | |
| 1952D, Same type, D Mint | 8,006 | *Set:* | 85 | 115 | 285 | 1,025 |
| 1952S, Same type, S Mint | 8,006 | | | | | |
| 1953, Same type as 1951 | 8,003 | | | | | |
| 1953D, Same type, D Mint | 8,003 | *Set:* | 95 | 120 | 270 | 1,500 |
| 1953S, Same type, S Mint | 88,020 | | | | | |
| 1954, Same type as 1951 | 12,006 | | | | | |
| 1954D, Same type, D Mint | 12,006 | *Set:* | 80 | 100 | 210 | 1,350 |
| 1954S, Same type, S Mint | 42,024 | | | | | |
| Carver/Washington, single type coin | | $20 | 25 | 30 | 60 | 150 |

# MODERN COMMEMORATIVES

## (1982) George Washington 250th Anniversary of Birth

This coin, the first commemorative half dollar issued since 1954, commemorated the 250th anniversary of the birth of George Washington. It was also the first 90% silver coin produced by the U.S. Mint since 1964. Designed by Elizabeth Jones, chief sculptor and engraver of the Mint, the obverse features George Washington astride a horse. The reverse depicts the eastern facade of Washington's home, Mount Vernon. The Uncirculated version was struck at Denver and the Proof at San Francisco.

| | Distribution | MS-67 | PF-67 |
|---|---|---|---|
| 1982D, George Washington, 250th Anniversary silver half dollar | 2,210,458 | $11 | |
| 1982S, Same type, S Mint, Proof | (4,894,044) | | $11 |

## (1983–1984) Los Angeles Olympiad

Three distinctive coins were issued to commemorate the 1984 Los Angeles Summer Olympic Games. The silver dollar dated 1983 was designed by Elizabeth Jones, chief engraver of the Mint. On the obverse is a representation of the traditional Greek discus thrower inspired by the ancient work of the sculptor Myron. The reverse depicts the head and upper body of an American eagle.

The 1984 Olympic silver dollar was designed by Robert Graham, an American sculptor who created the controversial headless sculpture placed at the entrance to the Los Angeles Memorial Coliseum. The obverse depicts Graham's sculpture with the coliseum in the background. The reverse features an American eagle.

The commemorative gold coin minted for the 1984 Olympics was the first U.S. gold piece issued in more than 50 years. The weight, size, and fineness are the same as for the previous ten-dollar coin, issued in 1933: weight, 16.718 grams; composition, .900 gold, .100 copper (net weight, .4837 oz. pure gold). It is the first coin ever to bear the W mintmark for West Point. The obverse depicts two runners bearing the Olympic torch aloft, and was designed by John Mercanti from a concept by James Peed, an artist at the Mint. The eagle on the reverse is modeled after that on the Great Seal.

| | | Distribution | MS-67 | PF-67 |
|---|---|---|---|---|
| 1983P, Discus Thrower silver dollar | | 294,543 | $22 | |
| 1983D, Same type, D Mint | | 174,014 | 22 | |
| 1983S, Same type, S Mint | (1,577,025) | 174,014 | 22 | $22 |
| 1984P, Olympic Coliseum silver dollar | | 217,954 | 22 | |
| 1984D, Same type, D Mint | | 116,675 | 23 | |
| 1984S, Same type, S Mint | (1,801,210) | 116,675 | 23 | 24 |
| 1984P, Olympic Torch Bearers gold $10 | (33,309) | | | 750 |
| 1984D, Same type, D Mint | (34,533) | | | 750 |
| 1984S, Same type, S Mint | (48,551) | | | 750 |
| 1984W, Same type, W Mint | (381,085) | 75,886 | 750 | 750 |

## (1986) Statue of Liberty Centennial

The first copper-nickel clad half dollar commemorative depicts the United States' heritage as a nation of immigrants. The obverse, designed by Edgar Steever, pictures a ship of immigrants steaming into New York Harbor, with the Statue of Liberty greeting them in the foreground and the New York skyline in the distance. The reverse, designed by Sherl Joseph Winter, has a scene of an immigrant family with their belongings on the threshold of America.

Designed by Mint artist John Mercanti, the Statue of Liberty silver dollar commemorates Ellis Island as the "Gateway to America." The obverse features a classic pose of Liberty in the foreground, with the Ellis Island Immigration Center behind her. On the reverse is a depiction of Liberty's torch, along with the words GIVE ME YOUR TIRED, YOUR POOR, YOUR HUDDLED MASSES YEARNING TO BREATHE FREE.

The commemorative half eagle was also the first of this denomination to be minted in more than 50 years. Standards for weight and size are the same as for previous half eagle gold coins: weight, 8.359 grams; composition, .900 gold, .100 copper (net weight .2418 oz. pure gold). The design is the creation of the Mint's chief engraver, Elizabeth Jones. The obverse features a compelling close-up view of Liberty's face in sharp relief, with the inscription 1986 LIBERTY. An eagle in flight adorns the reverse. All were minted at West Point and bear the W mintmark.

| | Distribution | MS-67 | PF-67 |
|---|---|---|---|
| 1986D, Statue of Liberty Centennial clad half dollar | 928,008 | $5 | |
| 1986S, Same type, S Mint, Proof | (6,925,627) | | $5 |
| 1986P, Statue of Liberty Centennial silver dollar | 723,635 | 24 | |
| 1986S, Same type, S Mint, Proof | (6,414,638) | | 24 |
| 1986W, Statue of Liberty Centennial gold $5 | (404,013) 95,248 | 375 | 375 |

## (1987) U.S. Constitution Bicentennial

The silver dollar commemorating the 200th anniversary of the United States Constitution was designed by Patricia Lewis Verani using standard weight, size, and fineness. A quill pen, a sheaf of parchment, and the words WE THE PEOPLE are depicted on the obverse. The reverse portrays a cross-section of Americans from various periods representing contrasting lifestyles.

A modernistic design by Marcel Jovine was selected for the five-dollar gold coin of standard weight, size, and fineness. The obverse portrays a stylized eagle holding a massive quill pen. Another large quill pen is featured on the reverse. To the left are nine stars, signifying the first colonies that ratified the Constitution. Four stars to the right represent the remaining original states. Both Uncirculated and Proof versions were minted at West Point.

| | Distribution | MS-67 | PF-67 |
|---|---|---|---|
| 1987P, U.S. Constitution Bicentennial silver dollar | 451,629 | $22 | |
| 1987S, Same type, S Mint, Proof | (2,747,116) | | $22 |
| 1987W, U.S. Constitution Bicentennial gold $5 | (651,659) 214,225 | 375 | 375 |

## (1988) Seoul Olympiad

The 1988 Olympic silver dollar commemorates U.S. participation in the Seoul Olympiad. Its size and weight are identical to those of other silver dollars. Design of the obverse is by Patricia Lewis Verani. The reverse is by Mint sculptor-engraver Sherl Joseph Winter.

The 1988 five-dollar gold Olympic coin was designed by Elizabeth Jones, chief sculptor and engraver of the U.S. Mint. The obverse features Nike, goddess of Victory, wearing a crown of olive leaves. The reverse features Marcel Jovine's stylized Olympic flame, evoking the spectacle of the Olympic Games and the renewal of the Olympic spirit every four years.

| | Distribution | MS-67 | PF-67 |
|---|---|---|---|
| 1988D, Seoul Olympiad silver dollar | 191,368 | $22 | |
| 1988S, Same type, S Mint, Proof | (1,359,366) | | $22 |
| 1988W, Seoul Olympiad gold $5 | (281,465) 62,913 | 375 | 375 |

## (1989) Congress Bicentennial

The Bicentennial of the Congress was commemorated on three coins. The obverse of the half dollar was designed by sculptor Patricia L. Verani and features a detailed bust of the Statue of Freedom. The reverse, designed by William Woodward, offers a full view of the Capitol Building accented by a wreath of stars.

Designed by muralist William Woodward, the obverse of the dollar features the Statue of Freedom that towers atop the Capitol dome. The reverse shows the Mace of the House of Representatives, which resides in the House Chamber whenever the House is in session. The mace's staff is topped by an eagle astride a globe. A scarce variety of the 1989-D dollar shows the dies aligned the same way, rather than the normal "coin turn" of 180 degrees.

The Capitol dome is depicted on the obverse of the five-dollar gold coin. The design is the work of Mint engraver John Mercanti. The reverse features a majestic eagle atop the canopy overlooking the Old Senate Chamber.

| | Distribution | MS-67 | PF-67 |
|---|---|---|---|
| 1989D, Congress Bicentennial clad half dollar | 163,753 | $8 | |
| 1989S, Same type, S Mint, Proof | (767,897) | | $8 |
| 1989D, Congress Bicentennial silver dollar | 135,203 | 22 | |
| 1989D, Same type, inverted reverse | | 1,800 | |
| 1989S, Same type, S Mint, Proof | (762,198) | | 24 |
| 1989W, Congress Bicentennial gold $5 | (164,690) 46,899 | 375 | 375 |

## (1990) Eisenhower Centennial

The unusual design on this coin features the profile of President Dwight Eisenhower facing right, superimposed over his own left-facing profile as a five-star general. It is the creation of Mint engraver John Mercanti. The reverse shows the Eisenhower home at Gettysburg, a national historic site, and was designed by Marcel Jovine. The coin was issued to celebrate the 100th anniversary of the birth of the 34th president.

| | Distribution | MS-67 | PF-67 |
|---|---|---|---|
| 1990W, Eisenhower Centennial silver dollar | 241,669 | $27 | |
| 1990P, Same type, P Mint, Proof | (1,144,461) | | $25 |

## (1991) Mount Rushmore Golden Anniversary

The 50th anniversary of the Mount Rushmore National Memorial was commemorated on three coins. Surcharges from the sale of these pieces were divided between the Treasury Department and the Mount Rushmore National Memorial Society of Black Hills, South Dakota, with money going to finance restoration work on the national landmark.

The obverse of the copper-nickel half dollar was designed by New Jersey artist Marcel Jovine and features a view of the famous carving by Gutzon Borglum. The reverse, designed by Mint sculptor-engraver James Ferrell, shows an American bison with the words GOLDEN ANNIVERSARY.

The Mount Rushmore Golden Anniversary silver dollar obverse was designed by Marika Somogyi. It displays the traditional portraits of presidents George Washington, Thomas Jefferson, Theodore Roosevelt, and Abraham Lincoln as sculptured on the mountain by Gutzon Borglum, who earlier had modeled the figures shown on the Stone Mountain commemorative coin. The reverse,

which was designed by former chief sculptor-engraver of the Mint Frank Gasparro, features a small outline map of the continental United States with the Great Seal above.

The five-dollar gold coin commemorating the 50th anniversary of the Mount Rushmore National Memorial features an American eagle flying above the monument with LIBERTY and the date in the field. The obverse was designed by Mint sculptor-engraver John Mercanti, and the reverse was designed by Rhode Island artist Robert Lamb and engraved by Mint sculptor-engraver William Cousins. The size, weight, and fineness are the same as for all other half eagle coins.

| | Distribution | MS-67 | PF-67 |
|---|---|---|---|
| 1991D, Mount Rushmore Golden Anniversary clad half dollar | 172,754 | $13 | |
| 1991S, Same type, S Mint, Proof | (753,257) | | $10 |
| 1991P, Mount Rushmore Golden Anniversary silver dollar | 133,139 | 28 | |
| 1991S, Same type, S Mint, Proof | (738,419) | | 25 |
| 1991W, Mount Rushmore Golden Anniversary gold $5 | (111,991) 31,959 | 375 | 375 |

## (1991) Korean War Memorial

The 38th anniversary of the end of the Korean War was the occasion for striking this coin, which commemorates the end of the conflict and honors those who served in combat. The design has been criticized as being cluttered, and the occasion no more than a fund-raising opportunity for the creation of a national monument in Washington. The obverse, designed by sculptor-engraver of the U.S. Mint John Mercanti, features an Army infantryman in full gear. On the reverse is an outline map of Korea with North and South divided at the 38th parallel, designed by Mint sculptor-engraver James Ferrell.

| | Distribution | MS-67 | PF-67 |
|---|---|---|---|
| 1991D, Korean War Memorial silver dollar | 213,049 | $25 | |
| 1991P, Same type, P Mint, Proof | (618,488) | | $23 |

## (1991) United Service Organizations

A special commemorative silver dollar was struck to honor the 50th anniversary of United Service Organizations. The group was founded in 1941 to supply social, recreational, welfare, and spiritual facilities to armed services personnel. Surcharges on sales of the coins were divided equally between the USO and the Department of the Treasury. The coins were launched on Flag Day, June 14, using designs selected in a limited competition between Mint staff and five outside, invited artists. The obverse uses a banner inscribed USO, designed by Rhode Island artist Robert Lamb. On the reverse is a globe with an eagle on top, the work of Mint sculptor-engraver John Mercanti.

| | Distribution | MS-67 | PF-67 |
|---|---|---|---|
| 1991D, USO silver dollar | 124,958 | $25 | |
| 1991S, Same type, S Mint, Proof | (321,275) | | $23 |

## (1992) XXV Olympiad

The XXV Olympiad held Winter Olympic games in Albertville and Savoie, France, and Summer Olympic games in Barcelona, Spain. United States commemorative coins were issued to honor the participation of American athletes and to finance their training. Competitive designs were selected from 1,107 entries.

The clad half dollar obverse, designed by Mint sculptor-engraver William Cousins, depicts a gymnast in motion. The reverse, by Steven M. Bieda, has the inscription CITIUS, ALTIUS, FORTIUS (the Olympic motto: "Faster, Higher, Stronger") with an olive branch crossing the Olympic torch.

The 1992 Olympic silver dollar obverse is a rendering by John R. Deecken of a pitcher firing a ball to home plate. The reverse, by sculptor Marcel Jovine, combines the Olympic rings, olive branches, and stars and stripes with a bold USA. Uncirculated dollars minted at Denver have the phrase XXV OLYMPIAD impressed four times around the edge, alternately inverted, on a reeded background, making this the first commemorative dollar to be edge-incused.

The obverse of the 1992 Olympic five-dollar gold was designed by James Sharpe, and modeled by T. James Ferrell. It depicts a sprinter

in a burst of speed. The reverse, by James Peed, unites two impressive symbols, the Olympic rings and the American bald eagle. **Size and fineness for these coins are the same as for other United States gold and silver issues of these denominations.**

| | Distribution | MS-67 | PF-67 |
|---|---|---|---|
| 1992P, XXV Olympiad clad half dollar | 161,607 | $8 | |
| 1992S, Same type, S Mint, Proof | (519,645) | | $7 |
| 1992D, XXV Olympiad silver dollar | 187,552 | 25 | |
| 1992S, Same type, S Mint, Proof | (504,505) | | 23 |
| 1992W, XXV Olympiad gold $5 | (77,313) 27,732 | 375 | 375 |

## (1992) White House 200th Anniversary

The obverse of this coin, designed by Mint sculptor Edgar Z. Steever IV, depicts the north portico of the White House. The reverse, by Mint sculptor Chester Y. Martin, features a bust of James Hoban, the original architect, and the main entrance he designed.

| | Distribution | MS-67 | PF-67 |
|---|---|---|---|
| 1992D, White House 200th Anniversary silver dollar | 123,803 | $25 | |
| 1992W, Same type, W Mint, Proof | (375,851) | | $23 |

## (1992) Christopher Columbus Quincentenary

The Columbus quincentenary was honored on three U.S. coins. The copper-nickel half dollar, designed by Mint sculptor T. James Ferrell, depicts Columbus landing in the New World on the obverse, and his three ships on the reverse. Mint sculptor John Mercanti designed the silver dollar obverse, which features a full-length figure of Columbus beside a globe, with his ships above. The reverse, by Mint sculptor Thomas D. Rogers Sr., is a split image of the *Santa Maria* and the U.S. space shuttle *Discovery*.

*Entry continued on next page.*

The five-dollar gold coin obverse, designed by Mint sculptor T. James Ferrell, bears a portrait of Columbus facing a map of the New World. The reverse, by Mint sculptor Thomas D. Rogers Sr., shows the Crest of the Admiral of the Ocean Sea.

| | Distribution | MS-67 | PF-67 |
|---|---|---|---|
| 1992D, Christopher Columbus Quincentenary clad half dollar | 135,702 | $12 | |
| 1992S, Same type, S Mint, Proof | (390,154) | | $12 |
| 1992D, Christopher Columbus Quincentenary silver dollar | 106,949 | 30 | |
| 1992P, Same type, P Mint, Proof | (385,241) | | 25 |
| 1992W, Christopher Columbus Quincentenary gold $5 | (79,730) 24,329 | 375 | 375 |

## (1993) Bill of Rights

The silver half dollar in this series depicts James Madison penning the Bill of Rights. It was designed by Mint sculptor T. James Ferrell. The reverse, by Dean McMullen, displays the torch of freedom. Some 9,656 of the Uncirculated version were privately marked on the edge with a serial number and the initials of the Madison Foundation and the American Numismatic Association.

A portrait of James Madison is shown on the obverse of this silver dollar, designed by William Krawczewicz. Dean McMullen designed the reverse, which shows Montpelier, the Virginia home of James and Dolley Madison.

The obverse of the five-dollar gold coin was designed by Scott R. Blazek. It features Madison studying the Bill of Rights. On the reverse, by Joseph D. Peña, is a quotation from Madison, accented by an eagle, torch, and laurel branch.

| | Distribution | MS-67 | PF-67 |
|---|---|---|---|
| 1993W, Bill of Rights clad half dollar | 193,346 | $18 | |
| 1993S, Same type, S Mint, Proof | (586,315) | | $15 |
| 1993D, Bill of Rights silver dollar | 98,383 | 30 | |
| 1993S, Same type, S Mint, Proof | (534,001) | | 25 |
| 1993W, Bill of Rights gold $5 | (78,651) 23,266 | 375 | 375 |

## (1991–1995) 50th Anniversary of World War II

Each of the three coins in this series is dated 1991–1995 and commemorates the 50th anniversary of U.S. involvement in World War II, which lasted from 1941 to 1945. Pieces were coined and issued in 1993. The obverse of the clad half dollar was designed by George Klauba. It depicts the faces of three members of the armed services superimposed upon the "V for victory" symbol. The reverse, by Bill J. Leftwich, portrays a Pacific island battle scene.

U.S. Mint sculptor-engraver Thomas D. Rogers Sr. designed the silver dollar showing an American soldier on the beach at Normandy. The reverse depicts the shoulder sleeve insignia of the Supreme Headquarters Allied Expeditionary Force, with a quotation from Dwight D. Eisenhower.

Both Proof and Uncirculated versions of the five-dollar gold coin were struck at the West Point Mint. The obverse, designed by Charles J. Madsen, depicts an American serviceman with rifle raised in victory. The reverse, by Edward Southworth Fisher, features a "V for victory" in the center with Morse code for the letter superimposed.

*See next page for chart.*

| | Distribution | MS-67 | PF-67 |
|---|---|---|---|
| (1993P) 1991–1995 World War II clad half dollar . . . . . . . . . . . . . . (317,396) . . . . . . | 197,072 | $15 | $15 |
| (1993D) 1991–1995 World War II silver dollar . . . . . . . . . . . . . . . . . . . . . . . . . . . . . . | 107,240 | 35 | |
| (1993W) Same type, W Mint, Proof . . . . . . . . . . . . . . . . . . . . . . . . (342,041) . . . . . . . . . . . . | | | 35 |
| (1993W) 1991–1995 World War II gold $5 . . . . . . . . . . . . . . . . . . . . (67,026) . . . . . . . | 23,672 | 375 | 375 |

## (1994) World Cup Tournament

The 1994 World Cup Tournament was the culmination of soccer games among 141 nations. The United States was selected to host the XV FIFA World Cup playoff, and three commemorative coins were issued to celebrate the event. Each of the coins employs a shared design on the reverse.

The obverse of the clad half dollar depicts a soccer player in action. It was designed by Richard T. LaRoche. The reverse, designed by Dean McMullen, features the official World Cup USA 1994 logo flanked by laurel branches.

The obverse of the silver dollar coin features two competing players converging on a soccer ball. It was designed by Dean McMullen, who also executed the reverse design, the official logo that is used on all of the World Cup coins.

Both Proof and Uncirculated versions of the five-dollar gold coin were struck at the West Point Mint. The obverse, designed by William J. Krawczewicz, depicts the modernistic gold World Cup trophy. The reverse was designed by Dean McMullen and shows the same logo used on other World Cup coins.

| | Distribution | MS-67 | PF-67 |
|---|---|---|---|
| 1994D, World Cup Tournament clad half dollar . . . . . . . . . . . . . . . . . . . . . . . . . . . . . | 168,208 | $8 | |
| 1994P, Same type, P Mint, Proof. . . . . . . . . . . . . . . . . . . . . . . . . (609,354) . . . . . . . . . . . . | | | $8 |
| 1994D, World Cup Tournament silver dollar. . . . . . . . . . . . . . . . . . . . . . . . . . . . . . . . | 81,524 | 30 | |
| 1994S, Same type, S Mint, Proof. . . . . . . . . . . . . . . . . . . . . . . . . (577,090) . . . . . . . . . . . . | | | 35 |
| 1994W, World Cup Tournament gold $5 . . . . . . . . . . . . . . . . . . . . . (89,614) . . . . . . . | 22,447 | 375 | 375 |

## (1993 [1994]) Thomas Jefferson

| | Distribution | MS-67 | PF-67 |
|---|---|---|---|
| 1993 (1994) Thomas Jefferson silver dollar, P Mint | 266,927 | $25 | |
| 1993 (1994) Same type, S Mint, Proof | (332,891) | | $23 |

## (1994) Vietnam Veterans Memorial

| | Distribution | MS-67 | PF-67 |
|---|---|---|---|
| 1994W, Vietnam Veterans Memorial silver dollar | 57,290 | $50 | |
| 1994P, Same type, P Mint, Proof | (227,671) | | $55 |

## (1994) U.S. Prisoner of War Museum

| | Distribution | MS-67 | PF-67 |
|---|---|---|---|
| 1994W, U.S. Prisoner of War Museum silver dollar | 54,893 | $50 | |
| 1994P, Same type, P Mint, Proof | (224,449) | | $55 |

## (1994) Women in Military Service Memorial

| | Distribution | MS-67 | PF-67 |
|---|---|---|---|
| 1994W, Women in Military Service Memorial silver dollar | 69,860 | $32 | |
| 1994P, Same type, P Mint, Proof | (241,278) | | $38 |

## (1994) U.S. Capitol Bicentennial

| | Distribution | MS-67 | PF-67 |
|---|---|---|---|
| 1994D, U.S. Capitol Bicentennial silver dollar | 68,332 | $30 | |
| 1994S, Same type, S Mint, Proof | (279,579) | | $30 |

## (1995) Civil War Battlefield Preservation

| | Distribution | MS-67 | PF-67 |
|---|---|---|---|
| 1995S, Civil War Battlefield Preservation clad half dollar | 119,520 | $25 | |
| 1995S, Same type, Proof | (330,002) | | $25 |
| 1995P, Civil War Battlefield Preservation silver dollar | 45,866 | 50 | |
| 1995S, Same type, S Mint, Proof | (437,114) | | 40 |
| 1995W, Civil War Battlefield Preservation gold $5 | 12,735 | 400 | |
| 1995W, Same type, Proof | (55,246) | | 375 |

## (1995) XXVI Olympiad

| | Distribution | MS-67 | PF-67 |
|---|---|---|---|
| 1995S, XXVI Olympiad, Basketball clad half dollar | 171,001 | $18 | |
| 1995S, Same type, Proof | (169,655) | | $18 |
| 1995S, XXVI Olympiad, Baseball clad half dollar | 164,605 | 16 | |
| 1995S, Same type, Proof | (118,087) | | 20 |
| 1996S, XXVI Olympiad, Swimming clad half dollar | 49,533 | 75 | |
| 1996S, Same type, Proof | (114,315) | | 25 |
| 1996S, XXVI Olympiad, Soccer clad half dollar | 52,836 | 75 | |
| 1996S, Same type, Proof | (112,412) | | 60 |

*Entry continued on next page.*

| | Distribution | MS-67 | PF-67 |
|---|---|---|---|
| 1995D, XXVI Olympiad, Gymnastics silver dollar | 42,497 | $35 | |
| 1995P, Same type, P Mint, Proof | (182,676) | | $30 |
| 1995D, XXVI Olympiad, Paralympics silver dollar | 28,649 | 55 | |
| 1995P, Same type, P Mint, Proof | (138,337) | | 30 |
| 1995D, XXVI Olympiad, Track and Field silver dollar | 24,976 | 65 | |
| 1995P, Same type, P mint, Proof | (136,935) | | 35 |
| 1995D, XXVI Olympiad, Cycling silver dollar | 19,662 | 75 | |
| 1995P, Same type, P Mint, Proof | (118,795) | | 38 |
| 1996D, XXVI Olympiad, Tennis silver dollar | 15,983 | 140 | |
| 1996P, Same type, P Mint, Proof | (92,016) | | 65 |
| 1996D, XXVI Olympiad, Paralympics silver dollar | 14,497 | 140 | |
| 1996P, Same type, P Mint, Proof | (84,280) | | 35 |
| 1996D, XXVI Olympiad, Rowing silver dollar | 16,258 | 145 | |
| 1996P, Same type, P Mint, Proof | (151,890) | | 60 |
| 1996D, XXVI Olympiad, High Jump silver dollar | 15,697 | 150 | |
| 1996P, Same type, P Mint, Proof | (124,502) | | 45 |

| | Distribution | MS-67 | PF-67 |
|---|---|---|---|
| 1995W, XXVI Olympiad, Torch Runner gold $5 | 14,675 | $400 | |
| 1995W, Same type, Proof | (57,442) | | $400 |
| 1995W, XXVI Olympiad, Stadium gold $5 | 10,579 | 425 | |
| 1995W, Same type, Proof | (43,124) | | 400 |
| 1996W, XXVI Olympiad, Flag Bearer gold $5 | 9,174 | 425 | |
| 1996W, Same type, Proof | (32,886) | | 400 |
| 1996W, XXVI Olympiad, Cauldron gold $5 | 9,210 | 600 | |
| 1996W, Same type, Proof | (38,555) | | 400 |

## (1995) Special Olympics World Games

| | Distribution | MS-67 | PF-67 |
|---|---|---|---|
| 1995W, Special Olympics World Games silver dollar | 89,301 | $30 | |
| 1995P, Same type, P Mint, Proof | (351,764) | | $30 |

## (1996) National Community Service

| | Distribution | MS-67 | PF-67 |
|---|---|---|---|
| 1996S, National Community Service silver dollar | 23,500 | $75 | |
| 1996S, Same type, Proof | (101,543) | | $34 |

## (1996) Smithsonian Institution 150th Anniversary

| | Distribution | MS-67 | PF-67 |
|---|---|---|---|
| 1996D, Smithsonian Institution 150th Anniversary silver dollar | 31,320 | $60 | |
| 1996P, Same type, P Mint, Proof | (129,152) | | $40 |

*Chart continued on next page.*

| | Distribution | MS-67 | PF-67 |
|---|---|---|---|
| 1996W, Smithsonian Institution 150th Anniversary gold $5 | 9,068 | $375 | |
| 1996W, Same type, Proof | (21,772) | | $375 |

## (1997) U.S. Botanic Garden

| | Distribution | MS-67 | PF-67 |
|---|---|---|---|
| 1997P, Botanic Garden silver dollar | 58,505 | $27 | |
| 1997P, Same type, Proof | (189,671) | | $35 |

## (1997) Jackie Robinson

| | Distribution | MS-67 | PF-67 |
|---|---|---|---|
| 1997S, Jackie Robinson silver dollar | 30,180 | $60 | |
| 1997S, Same type, Proof | (110,002) | | $55 |
| 1997W, Jackie Robinson gold $5 | 5,174 | 900 | |
| 1997W, Same type, Proof | (24,072) | | 450 |

## (1997) Franklin D. Roosevelt

| | Distribution | MS-67 | PF-67 |
|---|---|---|---|
| 1997W, Franklin D. Roosevelt gold $5 | 11,894 | $400 | |
| 1997W, Same type, Proof | (29,474) | | $375 |

## (1997) National Law Enforcement Officers Memorial

| | Distribution | MS-67 | PF-67 |
|---|---|---|---|
| 1997P, National Law Enforcement Officers Memorial silver dollar | 28,575 | $115 | |
| 1997P, Same type, Proof | (110,428) | | $60 |

## (1998) Robert F. Kennedy

| | Distribution | MS-67 | PF-67 |
|---|---|---|---|
| 1998S, Robert F. Kennedy silver dollar | 106,422 | $30 | |
| 1998S, Same type, Proof | (99,020) | | $40 |

## (1998) Black Revolutionary War Patriots

| | Distribution | MS-67 | PF-67 |
|---|---|---|---|
| 1998S, Black Revolutionary War Patriots silver dollar | 37,210 | $60 | |
| 1998S, Same type, Proof | (75,070) | | $50 |

## (1999) Dolley Madison

| | Distribution | MS-67 | PF-67 |
|---|---|---|---|
| 1999P, Dolley Madison silver dollar | 89,104 | $30 | |
| 1999P, Same type, Proof | (224,403) | | $30 |

## (1999) George Washington Death Bicentennial

| | Distribution | MS-67 | PF-67 |
|---|---|---|---|
| 1999W, George Washington Death Bicentennial gold $5 | 22,511 | $375 | |
| 1999W, Same type, Proof | (41,693) | | $375 |

## (1999) Yellowstone National Park

| | Distribution | MS-67 | PF-67 |
|---|---|---|---|
| 1999P, Yellowstone National Park silver dollar | 82,563 | $38 | |
| 1999P, Same type, Proof | (187,595) | | $40 |

## (2000) Library of Congress Bicentennial

| | Distribution | MS-67 | PF-67 |
|---|---|---|---|
| 2000P, Library of Congress Bicentennial silver dollar | 53,264 | $24 | |
| 2000P, Same type, Proof | (198,503) | | $27 |
| 2000W, Library of Congress Bicentennial bimetallic (gold/platinum) $10 | 7,261 | 1,100 | |
| 2000W, Same type, Proof | (27,445) | | 850 |

## (2000) Leif Ericson Millennium

| | Distribution | MS-67 | PF-67 |
|---|---|---|---|
| 2000P, Leif Ericson Millennium silver dollar | 28,150 | $65 | |
| 2000P, Same type, Proof | (144,748) | | $55 |

## (2001) American Buffalo

| | Distribution | MS-67 | PF-67 |
|---|---|---|---|
| 2001D, American Buffalo silver dollar | 227,131 | $125 | |
| 2001P, Same type, P Mint, Proof | (272,869) | | $120 |

## (2001) U.S. Capitol Visitor Center

| | Distribution | MS-67 | PF-67 |
|---|---|---|---|
| 2001P, U.S. Capitol Visitor Center clad half dollar | 99,157 | $16 | |
| 2001P, Same type, Proof | (77,962) | | $20 |
| 2001P, U.S. Capitol Visitor Center silver dollar | 35,380 | 30 | |
| 2001P, Same type, Proof | (143,793) | | 36 |
| 2001W, U.S. Capitol Visitor Center gold $5 | 6,761 | 550 | |
| 2001W, Same type, Proof | (27,652) | | 375 |

## (2002) Salt Lake City Olympic Games

| | Distribution | MS-67 | PF-67 |
|---|---|---|---|
| 2002P, Salt Lake City Olympics silver dollar | 40,257 | $35 | |
| 2002P, Same type, Proof | (166,864) | | $30 |
| 2002W, Salt Lake City Olympics gold $5 | 10,585 | 375 | |
| 2002W, Same type, Proof | (32,877) | | 375 |

## (2002) West Point Bicentennial

| | Distribution | MS-67 | PF-67 |
|---|---|---|---|
| 2002W, West Point Bicentennial silver dollar | 103,201 | $25 | |
| 2002W, Same type, Proof | (288,293) | | $35 |

## (2003) First Flight Centennial

| | Distribution | MS-67 | PF-67 |
|---|---|---|---|
| 2003P, First Flight Centennial clad half dollar | 57,122 | $16 | |
| 2003P, Same type, Proof | (109,710) | | $18 |
| 2003P, First Flight Centennial silver dollar | 53,533 | 40 | |
| 2003P, Same type, Proof | (190,240) | | 42 |
| 2003W, First Flight Centennial gold $10 | 10,009 | 750 | |
| 2003W, Same type, Proof | (21,676) | | 750 |

## (2004) Thomas Alva Edison

| | Distribution | MS-67 | PF-67 |
|---|---|---|---|
| 2004P, Thomas Alva Edison silver dollar | 92,510 | $35 | |
| 2004P, Same type, Proof | (211,055) | | $32 |

## (2004) Lewis and Clark Bicentennial

| | Distribution | MS-67 | PF-67 |
|---|---|---|---|
| 2004P, Lewis and Clark Bicentennial silver dollar | 142,015 | $32 | |
| 2004P, Same type, Proof | (351,989) | | $30 |

## (2005) Chief Justice John Marshall

| | Distribution | MS-67 | PF-67 |
|---|---|---|---|
| 2005P, Chief Justice John Marshall silver dollar | 67,096 | $35 | |
| 2005P, Same type, Proof | (196,753) | | $35 |

## (2005) Marine Corps 230th Anniversary

| | Distribution | MS-67 | PF-67 |
|---|---|---|---|
| 2005P, Marine Corps 230th Anniversary silver dollar | 49,671 | $45 | |
| 2005P, Same type, Proof | (548,810) | | $43 |

## (2006) Benjamin Franklin Tercentenary

| | Distribution | MS-67 | PF-67 |
|---|---|---|---|
| 2006P, Benjamin Franklin "Scientist" silver dollar | 58,000 | $32 | |
| 2006P, Same type, Proof | (142,000) | | $28 |
| 2006P, Benjamin Franklin "Founding Father" silver dollar | 58,000 | 35 | |
| 2006P, Same type, Proof | (142,000) | | 32 |

## (2006) San Francisco Old Mint Centennial

| | Distribution | MS-67 | PF-67 |
|---|---|---|---|
| 2006S, San Francisco Old Mint Centennial silver dollar | 67,100 | $37 | |
| 2006S, Same type, Proof | (160,870) | | $35 |
| 2006S, San Francisco Old Mint Centennial gold $5 | 17,500 | 375 | |
| 2006S, Same type, Proof | (44,174) | | 375 |

## (2007) Jamestown 400th Anniversary

| | Distribution | MS-67 | PF-67 |
|---|---|---|---|
| 2007P, Jamestown 400th Anniversary silver dollar | 81,034 | $30 | |
| 2007P, Same type, Proof | (260,363) | | $30 |
| 2007W, Jamestown 400th Anniversary gold $5 | 18,623 | 375 | |
| 2007W, Same type, Proof | (47,123) | | 375 |

## (2007) Little Rock Central High School Desegregation

| | Distribution | MS-67 | PF-67 |
|---|---|---|---|
| 2007P, Little Rock Central High School Desegregation silver dollar | 124,678 | $28 | |
| 2007P, Same type, Proof | (66,093) | | $25 |

## (2008) Bald Eagle Recovery and National Emblem

*Entry continued on next page.*

| | Distribution | MS-67 | PF-67 |
|---|---|---|---|
| 2008S, Bald Eagle Recovery and National Emblem clad half dollar | 120,180 | $15 | |
| 2008S, Same type, Proof | (220,577) | | $18 |
| 2008P, Bald Eagle Recovery and National Emblem silver dollar | 119,204 | 28 | |
| 2008P, Same type, Proof | (294,601) | | 25 |
| 2008W, Bald Eagle Recovery and National Emblem gold $5 | 15,009 | 375 | |
| 2008W, Same type, Proof | (59,269) | | 375 |

## (2009) Louis Braille Bicentennial

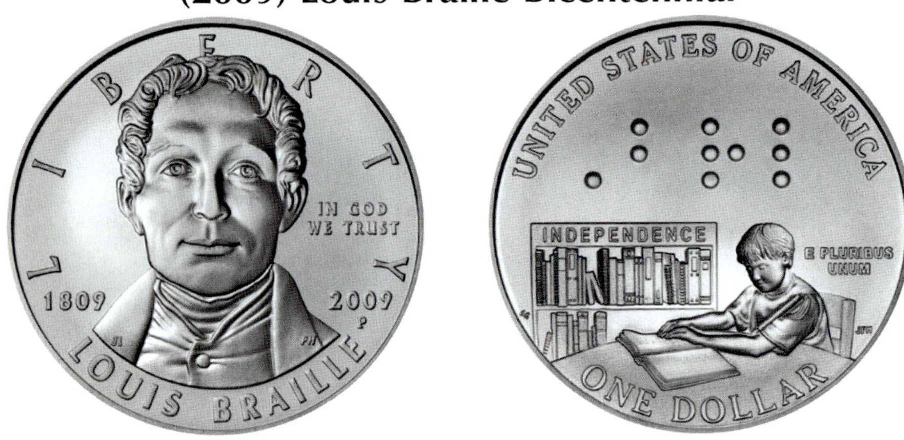

| | Distribution | MS-67 | PF-67 |
|---|---|---|---|
| 2009P, Louis Braille Bicentennial silver dollar | 82,639 | $27 | |
| 2009P, Same type, Proof | (135,235) | | $25 |

## (2009) Abraham Lincoln Bicentennial

| | Distribution | MS-67 | PF-67 |
|---|---|---|---|
| 2009P, Abraham Lincoln Bicentennial silver dollar | 125,000 | $30 | |
| 2009P, Same type, Proof | (325,000) | | $35 |

## (2010) American Veterans Disabled for Life

| | Distribution | MS-67 | PF-67 |
|---|---|---|---|
| 2010W, American Veterans Disabled for Life silver dollar | 78,301 | $32 | |
| 2010W, Same type, Proof | (202,770) | | $32 |

## (2010) Boy Scouts of America Centennial

| | Distribution | MS-67 | PF-67 |
|---|---|---|---|
| 2010P, Boy Scouts Centennial silver dollar | 105,020 | $27 | |
| 2010P, Same type, Proof | (244,963) | | $30 |

## (2011) Medal of Honor

*See next page for chart.*

| | Distribution | MS-67 | PF-67 |
|---|---|---|---|
| 2011S, Medal of Honor silver dollar | 44,752 | $45 | |
| 2011P, Same type, P Mint, Proof | (112,833) | | $45 |
| 2011P, Medal of Honor gold $5 | 8,233 | 400 | |
| 2011W, Same type, W Mint, Proof | (17,999) | | 375 |

## (2011) U.S. Army

| | Distribution | MS-67 | PF-67 |
|---|---|---|---|
| 2011D, U.S. Army clad half dollar | 39,442 | $30 | |
| 2011S, Same type, S Mint, Proof | (68,332) | | $50 |
| 2011S, U.S. Army silver dollar | 43,512 | 42 | |
| 2011P, Same type, P Mint, Proof | (119,829) | | 42 |
| 2011P, U.S. Army gold $5 | 8,052 | 375 | |
| 2011W, Same type, W Mint, Proof | (17,148) | | 375 |

## (2012) Infantry Soldier

| | Distribution | MS-67 | PF-67 |
|---|---|---|---|
| 2012W, Infantry Soldier silver dollar | 44,348 | $40 | |
| 2012W, Same type, Proof | (161,151) | | $50 |

## (2012) Star-Spangled Banner

| | Distribution | MS-67 | PF-67 |
|---|---|---|---|
| 2012P, Star-Spangled Banner silver dollar | 41,686 | $40 | |
| 2012P, Same type, Proof | (169,065) | | $40 |
| 2012W, Star-Spangled Banner gold $5 | 7,027 | 420 | |
| 2012W, Same type, Proof | (18,313) | | 375 |

## (2013) Girl Scouts of the U.S.A. Centennial

| | Distribution | MS-67 | PF-67 |
|---|---|---|---|
| 2013W, Girl Scouts of the U.S.A. Centennial silver dollar | 37,462 | $40 | |
| 2013W, Same type, Proof | (86,355) | | $42 |

## (2013) 5-Star Generals

| | Distribution | MS-67 | PF-67 |
|---|---|---|---|
| 2013D, 5-Star Generals clad half dollar | 38,095 | $22 | |
| 2013S, Same type, S Mint, Proof | (47,326) | | $35 |

*Entry continued on next page.*

| | Distribution | MS-67 | PF-67 |
|---|---|---|---|
| 2013W, 5-Star Generals silver dollar | 34,638 | $55 | |
| 2013P, Same type, P Mint, Proof | (69,283) | | $55 |
| 2013P, 5-Star Generals gold $5 | 5,667 | 475 | |
| 2013W, Same type, W Mint, Proof | (15,844) | | 425 |

## (2014) National Baseball Hall of Fame

| | Distribution | MS-67 | PF-67 |
|---|---|---|---|
| 2014D, National Baseball Hall of Fame clad half dollar | *142,405* | $30 | |
| 2014S, Same type, S Mint, Proof | *(249,049)* | | $24 |
| 2014P, National Baseball Hall of Fame silver dollar | *131,910* | 50 | |
| 2014P, Same type, Proof | *(267,847)* | | 48 |
| 2014W, National Baseball Hall of Fame gold $5 | *17,674* | 400 | |
| 2014W, Same type, Proof | *(32,428)* | | 400 |

*Note:* The obverse of each denomination is concave; the reverse is convex.

## (2014) Civil Rights Act of 1964

| | Distribution | MS-67 | PF-67 |
|---|---|---|---|
| 2014P, Civil Rights Act of 1964 silver dollar | 24,720 | $50 | |
| 2014P, Same type, Proof | (61,992) | | $55 |

## (2015) U.S. Marshals Service 225th Anniversary

| | Distribution | MS-67 | PF-67 |
|---|---|---|---|
| 2015D, U.S. Marshals Service 225th Anniversary clad half dollar | 30,231 | $20 | |
| 2015S, Same type, S Mint, Proof | (76,549) | | $22 |
| 2015P, U.S. Marshals Service 225th Anniversary silver dollar | 38,149 | 47 | |
| 2015P, Same type, Proof | (124,329) | | 52 |
| 2015W, U.S. Marshals Service 225th Anniversary $5 gold | 6,743 | 400 | |
| 2015W, Same type, Proof | (24,959) | | 400 |

## (2015) March of Dimes 75th Anniversary

| | Distribution | MS-67 | PF-67 |
|---|---|---|---|
| 2015P, March of Dimes 75th Anniversary silver dollar | 24,742 | $47 | |
| 2015W, Same type, W Mint, Proof | (32,030) | | $40 |

## (2016) Mark Twain

| | Distribution | MS-67 | PF-67 |
|---|---|---|---|
| 2016P, Mark Twain silver dollar | 26,281 | $45 | |
| 2016P, Same type, Proof | (78,536) | | $40 |
| 2016W, Mark Twain $5 gold | 5,695 | 400 | |
| 2016W, Same type, Proof | (13,266) | | 400 |

## (2016) National Park Service 100th Anniversary

| | Distribution | MS-67 | PF-67 |
|---|---|---|---|
| 2016D, National Park Service 100th Anniversary clad half dollar | 21,019 | $30 | |
| 2016S, Same type, S Mint, Proof | (54,844) | | $35 |

| | Distribution | MS-67 | PF-67 |
|---|---|---|---|
| 2016P, National Park Service 100th Anniversary silver dollar | 20,994 | $40 | |
| 2016P, Same type, Proof | (77,309) | | $38 |
| 2016W, National Park Service 100th Anniversary $5 gold | 5,150 | 400 | |
| 2016W, Same type, Proof | (19,506) | | 400 |

## (2017) Lions Club International Century of Service

| | Distribution | MS-67 | PF-67 |
|---|---|---|---|
| 2017P, Lions Club International Century of Service silver dollar | *17,247* | $50 | |
| 2017P, Same type, Proof | *(68,519)* | | $48 |

## (2017) Boys Town Centennial

| | Distribution | MS-67 | PF-67 |
|---|---|---|---|
| 2017S, Boys Town Centennial clad half dollar | *15,525* | $32 | |
| 2017D, Same type, D Mint, Proof | *(23,164)* | | $34 |

*Entry continued on next page.*

| | Distribution | MS-67 | PF-67 |
|---|---|---|---|
| 2017P, Boys Town Centennial silver dollar | 12,234 | $42 | |
| 2017P, Same type, Proof | (31,610) | | $45 |
| 2017W, Boys Town Centennial$5 gold | 2,947 | 400 | |
| 2017W, Same type, Proof | (7,347) | | 400 |

## (2018) World War I Centennial

| | Distribution | MS-67 | PF-67 |
|---|---|---|---|
| 2018P, World War I Centennial silver dollar | 22,340 | $50 | |
| 2018P, Same type, Proof | (127,848) | | $55 |

## (2018) Breast Cancer Awareness

| | Distribution | MS-67 | PF-67 |
|---|---|---|---|
| 2018D, Breast Cancer Awareness clad half dollar | 11,301 | $22 | |
| 2018S, Same type, S Mint, Proof | (22,393) | | $22 |

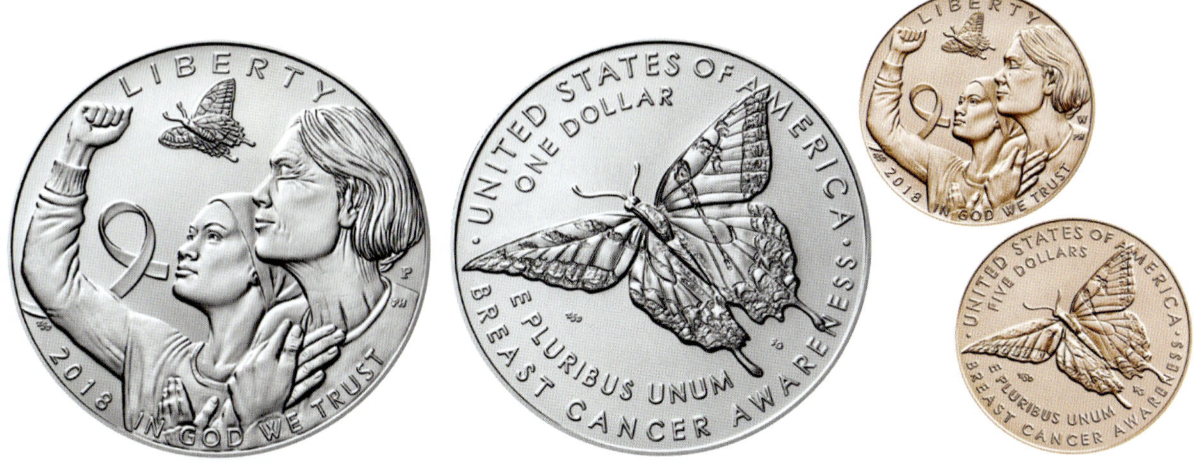

| | Distribution | MS-67 | PF-67 |
|---|---|---|---|
| 2018P, Breast Cancer Awareness silver dollar | *12,526* | $50 | |
| 2018P, Same type, Proof | *(34,543)* | | $50 |
| 2018W, Breast Cancer Awareness$5 gold **(a)** | *4,477* | 375 | |
| 2018W, Same type, Proof | *(10,387)* | | 370 |

**a.** Produced in "rose pink" gold, composed of .850 gold, .148 copper, and .002 zinc.

## (2019) Apollo 11 50th Anniversary

| | Distribution | MS-67 | PF-67 |
|---|---|---|---|
| 2019D, Apollo 11 50th Anniversary clad half dollar | | $26 | |
| 2019S, Same type, S Mint, Proof | | | $28 |
| 2019P, Apollo 11 50th Anniversary silver dollar **(a)** | | 52 | |
| 2019P, Same type, Proof **(a)** | | | 55 |
| 2019P, Apollo 11 50th Anniversary 5-oz. silver dollar, Proof **(a,b)** | | | 225 |

*Note:* The obverse of each denomination is concave; the reverse is convex. **a.** In 2019, the fineness of U.S. Mint silver coins increased from .900 to .999. **b.** Identical in design to the regular-issue dollar coin, but enlarged to 3 inches in diameter.

*Chart continued on next page.*

| | Distribution | MS-67 | PF-67 |
|---|---|---|---|
| 2019W, Apollo 11 50th Anniversary $5 gold | | $375 | |
| 2019W, Same type, Proof | | | $370 |

*Note:* The obverse is concave; the reverse is convex.

## (2019) American Legion 100th Anniversary

| | Distribution | MS-67 | PF-67 |
|---|---|---|---|
| 2019D, American Legion 100th Anniversary clad half dollar | | $26 | |
| 2019S, Same type, S Mint, Proof | | | $28 |
| 2019P, American Legion 100th Anniversary silver dollar **(a)** | | 52 | |
| 2019P, Same type, Proof **(a)** | | | 55 |
| 2019W, American Legion 100th Anniversary $5 gold | | 375 | |
| 2019W, Same type, Proof | | | 370 |

**a.** In 2019, the fineness of U.S. Mint silver coins increased from .900 to .999.

## (2020) Naismith Memorial Basketball Hall of Fame 60th Anniversary

| | Distribution | MS-67 | PF-67 |
|---|---|---|---|
| 2020D, Naismith Memorial Basketball Hall of Fame 60th Anniversary clad half dollar | *11,301* | $26 | |
| 2020S, Same type, S Mint, Proof | *(22,393)* | | $28 |

*Note:* The obverse is concave; the reverse is convex. The half dollar and silver dollar are colorized.

| | Distribution | MS-67 | PF-67 |
|---|---|---|---|
| 2020P, Naismith Memorial Basketball Hall of Fame 60th Anniversary silver dollar **(a)** | | $52 | |
| 2020P, Same type, Proof **(a)** | | | $55 |
| 2020W, Naismith Memorial Basketball Hall of Fame 60th Anniversary $5 gold | | 375 | |
| 2020W, Same type, Proof | | | 370 |

*Note:* The obverse is concave; the reverse is convex. The half dollar and silver dollar are colorized. **a.** In 2019, the fineness of U.S. Mint silver coins increased from .900 to .999.

## (2020) Women's Suffrage Centennial

| | Distribution | MS-67 | PF-67 |
|---|---|---|---|
| 2020, Women's Suffrage Centennial, silver dollar **(a)** | | | |

**a.** Details of this program have not been publicized as of press time.

# GOVERNMENT COMMEMORATIVE SETS

| | Value |
|---|---|
| **(1983–1984) Los Angeles Olympiad** | |
| 1983 and 1984 Proof dollars | $50 |
| 1983 and 1984 6-coin set. One each of 1983 and 1984 dollars, both Proof and Uncirculated gold $10 **(a)** | 1,650 |
| 1983 3-piece collector set. 1983 P, D, and S Uncirculated dollars | 70 |
| 1984 3-piece collector set. 1984 P, D, and S Uncirculated dollars | 75 |
| 1983 and 1984 gold and silver Uncirculated set. One each of 1983 and 1984 Uncirculated dollar and one 1984 Uncirculated gold $10 | 850 |
| 1983 and 1984 gold and silver Proof set. One each of 1983 and 1984 Proof dollars and one 1984 Proof gold $10 | 850 |
| **(1986) Statue of Liberty** | |
| 2-coin set. Proof silver dollar and clad half dollar | 30 |
| 3-coin set. Proof silver dollar, clad half dollar, and gold $5 | 420 |
| 2-coin set. Uncirculated silver dollar and clad half dollar | 30 |
| 2-coin set. Uncirculated and Proof gold $5 | 750 |
| 3-coin set. Uncirculated silver dollar, clad half dollar, and gold $5 | 420 |
| 6-coin set. One each of Proof and Uncirculated half dollar, silver dollar, and gold $5 **(a)** | 900 |
| **(1987) Constitution** | |
| 2-coin set. Uncirculated silver dollar and gold $5 | 400 |
| 2-coin set. Proof silver dollar and gold $5 | 400 |
| 4-coin set. One each of Proof and Uncirculated silver dollar and gold $5 **(a)** | 800 |
| **(1988) Seoul Olympiad** | |
| 2-coin set. Uncirculated silver dollar and gold $5 | 400 |
| 2-coin set. Proof silver dollar and gold $5 | 400 |
| 4-coin set. One each of Proof and Uncirculated silver dollar and gold $5 **(a)** | 800 |

**a.** Packaged in cherrywood box.

*Chart continued on next page.*

| | Value |
|---|---|
| **(1989) Congress** | |
| 2-coin set. Proof clad half dollar and silver dollar | $320 |
| 3-coin set. Proof clad half dollar, silver dollar, and gold $5 | 410 |
| 2-coin set. Uncirculated clad half dollar and silver dollar | 30 |
| 3-coin set. Uncirculated clad half dollar, silver dollar, and gold $5 | 405 |
| 6-coin set. One each of Proof and Uncirculated clad half dollar, silver dollar, and gold $5 **(a)** | 825 |
| **(1991) Mount Rushmore** | |
| 2-coin set. Uncirculated clad half dollar and silver dollar | 45 |
| 2-coin set. Proof clad half dollar and silver dollar | 40 |
| 3-coin set. Uncirculated clad half dollar, silver dollar, and gold $5 | 425 |
| 3-coin set. Proof half dollar, silver dollar, and gold $5 | 425 |
| 6-coin set. One each of Proof and Uncirculated clad half dollar, silver dollar, and gold $5 **(a)** | 850 |
| **(1992) XXV Olympiad** | |
| 2-coin set. Uncirculated clad half dollar and silver dollar | 40 |
| 2-coin set. Proof clad half dollar and silver dollar | 40 |
| 3-coin set. Uncirculated clad half dollar, silver dollar, and gold $5 | 425 |
| 3-coin set. Proof half dollar, silver dollar, and gold $5 | 425 |
| 6-coin set. One each of Proof and Uncirculated clad half dollar, silver dollar, and gold $5 **(a)** | 850 |
| **(1992) Christopher Columbus** | |
| 2-coin set. Uncirculated clad half dollar and silver dollar | 45 |
| 2-coin set. Proof clad half dollar and silver dollar | 40 |
| 3-coin set. Uncirculated clad half dollar, silver dollar, and gold $5 | 425 |
| 3-coin set. Proof half dollar, silver dollar, and gold $5 | 425 |
| 6-coin set. One each of Proof and Uncirculated clad half dollar, silver dollar, and gold $5 **(a)** | 850 |
| **(1993) Bill of Rights** | |
| 2-coin set. Uncirculated silver half dollar and silver dollar | 50 |
| 2-coin set. Proof silver half dollar and silver dollar | 40 |
| 3-coin set. Uncirculated silver half dollar, silver dollar, and gold $5 | 425 |
| 3-coin set. Proof half dollar, silver dollar, and gold $5 | 425 |
| 6-coin set. One each of Proof and Uncirculated silver half dollar, silver dollar, and gold $5 **(a)** | 850 |
| "Young Collector" set. Silver half dollar | 35 |
| Educational set. Silver half dollar and James Madison medal | 35 |
| Proof silver half dollar and 25-cent stamp | 20 |
| **(1993) World War II** | |
| 2-coin set. Uncirculated clad half dollar and silver dollar | 50 |
| 2-coin set. Proof clad half dollar and silver dollar | 50 |
| 3-coin set. Uncirculated clad half dollar, silver dollar, and gold $5 | 425 |
| 3-coin set. Proof clad half dollar, silver dollar, and gold $5 | 425 |
| 6-coin set. One each of Proof and Uncirculated clad half dollar, silver dollar, and gold $5 **(a)** | 850 |
| "Young Collector" set. Clad half dollar | 30 |
| Victory Medal set. Uncirculated clad half dollar and reproduction medal | 40 |
| **(1993) Thomas Jefferson** | |
| "Coinage and Currency" set. (issued in 1994). Silver dollar, Jefferson nickel, and $2 note | 110 |
| **(1994) World Cup Soccer** | |
| 2-coin set. Uncirculated clad half dollar and silver dollar | 40 |
| 2-coin set. Proof clad half dollar and silver dollar | 40 |
| 3-coin set. Uncirculated clad half dollar, silver dollar, and gold $5 | 425 |
| 3-coin set. Proof clad half dollar, silver dollar, and gold $5 | 425 |
| 6-coin set. One each of Proof and Uncirculated clad half dollar, silver dollar, and gold $5 **(a)** | 850 |
| "Young Collector" set. Uncirculated clad half dollar | 20 |
| "Special Edition" set. Proof clad half dollar and silver dollar | 50 |

**a.** Packaged in cherrywood box.

| | Value |
|---|---|
| **(1994) U.S. Veterans** | |
| 3-coin set. Uncirculated POW, Vietnam, and Women in Military Service silver dollars | $150 |
| 3-coin set. Proof POW, Vietnam, and Women in Military Service silver dollars | 125 |
| **(1995) Special Olympics** | |
| 2-coin set. Proof Special Olympics silver dollar, 1995S Kennedy half dollar | 75 |
| **(1995) Civil War Battlefield Preservation** | |
| 2-coin set. Uncirculated clad half dollar and silver dollar | 80 |
| 2-coin set. Proof clad half dollar and silver dollar | 80 |
| 3-coin set. Uncirculated clad half dollar, silver dollar, and gold $5 | 475 |
| 3-coin set. Proof clad half dollar, silver dollar, and gold $5 | 450 |
| 6-coin set. One each of Proof and Uncirculated clad half dollar, silver dollar, and gold $5 **(a)** | 925 |
| "Young Collector" set. Uncirculated clad half dollar | 50 |
| 2-coin "Union" set. Clad half dollar and silver dollar | 125 |
| 3-coin "Union" set. Clad half dollar, silver dollar, and gold $5 | 485 |
| **(1995–1996) Centennial Olympic Games** | |
| 4-coin set #1. Uncirculated half dollar (Basketball), dollars (Gymnastics, Paralympics), gold $5 (Torch Bearer) | 600 |
| 4-coin set #2. Proof half dollar (Basketball), dollars (Gymnastics, Paralympics), gold $5 (Torch Bearer) | 550 |
| 4-coin set #3. Proof half dollar (Baseball), dollars (Cyclist, Track Runner), gold $5 (Olympic Stadium) | 550 |
| 2-coin set #1: Proof silver dollars (Gymnastics, Paralympics) | 70 |
| "Young Collector" set. Uncirculated Basketball half dollar | 35 |
| "Young Collector" set. Uncirculated Baseball half dollar | 35 |
| "Young Collector" set. Uncirculated Swimming half dollar | 200 |
| "Young Collector" set. Uncirculated Soccer half dollar | 175 |
| 1995–1996 16-coin Uncirculated set. One each of all Uncirculated coins **(a)** | 2,700 |
| 1995–1996 16-coin Proof set. One each of all Proof coins **(a)** | 2,100 |
| 1995–1996 8-coin Proof silver dollars set | 400 |
| 1995–1996 32-coin set. One each of all Uncirculated and Proof coins **(a)** | 4,800 |
| **(1996) National Community Service** | |
| Proof silver dollar and Saint-Gaudens stamp | 100 |
| **(1996) Smithsonian Institution 150th Anniversary** | |
| 2-coin set. Proof silver dollar and gold $5 | 425 |
| 4-coin set. One each of Proof and Uncirculated silver dollar and gold $5 **(a)** | 900 |
| "Young Collector" set. Proof silver dollar | 100 |
| **(1997) U.S. Botanic Garden** | |
| "Coinage and Currency" set. Uncirculated silver dollar, Jefferson nickel, and $1 note | 200 |
| **(1997) Jackie Robinson** | |
| 2-coin set. Proof silver dollar and gold $5 | 500 |
| 4-coin set. One each of Proof and Uncirculated silver dollar and gold $5 **(a)** | 1,475 |
| 3-piece "Legacy" set. Baseball card, pin, and gold $5 **(a)** | 650 |
| **(1997) Franklin D. Roosevelt** | |
| 2-coin set. One each of Proof and Uncirculated gold $5 | 800 |
| **(1997) National Law Enforcement Officers Memorial** | |
| Insignia set. Silver dollar, lapel pin, and patch | |
| **(1998) Robert F. Kennedy** | |
| 2-coin set. RFK silver dollar and JFK silver half dollar | 200 |
| 2-coin set. Proof and Uncirculated RFK silver dollars | 100 |
| **(1998) Black Revolutionary War Patriots** | |
| 2-coin set. Proof and Uncirculated silver dollars | 125 |
| "Young Collector" set. Uncirculated silver dollar | 125 |
| Black Revolutionary War Patriots set. Silver dollar and four stamps | 150 |

**a.** Packaged in cherrywood box.

*Chart continued on next page.*

| | Value |
|---|---|
| **(1999) Dolley Madison** | |
| 2-coin set. Proof and Uncirculated silver dollars | $75 |
| **(1999) George Washington Death** | |
| 2-coin set. One each of Proof and Uncirculated gold $5 | 750 |
| **(1999) Yellowstone National Park** | |
| 2-coin set. One each of Proof and Uncirculated silver dollars | 100 |
| **(2000) Leif Ericson Millennium** | |
| 2-coin set. Proof silver dollar and Icelandic 1,000 kronur | 100 |
| **(2000) Millennium Coin and Currency Set** | |
| 3-piece set. Uncirculated 2000 Sacagawea dollar; Uncirculated 2000 Silver Eagle; George Washington $1 note, series 1999 | 100 |
| **(2001) American Buffalo** | |
| 2-coin set. One each of Proof and Uncirculated silver dollar | 300 |
| "Coinage and Currency" set. Uncirculated American Buffalo silver dollar, face reprint of 1899 $5 Indian Chief Silver Certificate, 1987 Chief Red Cloud 10¢ stamp, 2001 Bison 21¢ stamp | 200 |
| **(2001) U.S. Capitol Visitor Center** | |
| 3-coin set. Proof clad half dollar, silver dollar, and gold $5 | 435 |
| **(2002) Salt Lake Olympic Games** | |
| 2-coin set. Proof silver dollar and gold $5 | 420 |
| 4-coin set. One each of Proof and Uncirculated silver dollar and gold $5 | 850 |
| **(2003) First Flight Centennial** | |
| 3-coin set. Proof clad half dollar, silver dollar, and gold $10 | 825 |
| **(2003) Legacies of Freedom™** | |
| Uncirculated 2003 $1 American Eagle silver bullion coin and an Uncirculated 2002 £2 Silver Britannia coin | 75 |
| **(2004) Thomas A. Edison** | |
| Edison set. Uncirculated silver dollar and light bulb (with working light bulb) | 85 |
| **(2004) Lewis and Clark** | |
| Coin and Pouch set. Proof silver dollar and beaded pouch | 200 |
| "Coinage and Currency" set. Uncirculated silver dollar, Sacagawea golden dollar, two 2005 nickels, replica 1901 $10 Bison note, silver-plated Peace Medal replica, three stamps, two booklets | 100 |
| **(2004) Westward Journey Nickel Series™** | |
| Westward Journey Nickel Series™ Coin and Medal set. Proof Sacagawea golden dollar, two 2004 Proof nickels, silver-plated Peace Medal replica | 60 |
| **(2005) Westward Journey Nickel Series™** | |
| Westward Journey Nickel Series™ Coin and Medal set. Proof Sacagawea golden dollar, two 2005 Proof nickels, silver-plated Peace Medal replica | 40 |
| **(2005) Chief Justice John Marshall** | |
| "Coin and Chronicles" set. Uncirculated silver dollar, booklet, BEP intaglio portrait | 60 |
| **(2005) American Legacy** | |
| American Legacy Collection. Proof Marine Corps dollar, Proof John Marshall dollar, 11-piece Proof set | 100 |
| **(2005) Marine Corps 230th Anniversary** | |
| Marine Corps Uncirculated silver dollar and stamp set | 100 |
| **(2006) Benjamin Franklin** | |
| "Coin and Chronicles" set. Uncirculated "Scientist" silver dollar, four stamps, *Poor Richard's Almanack* replica, intaglio print | 75 |
| **(2006) American Legacy** | |
| American Legacy Collection. Proof 2006P Benjamin Franklin, Founding Father silver dollar; Proof 2006S San Francisco Old Mint silver dollar; Proof cent, nickel, dime, quarter, half dollar, and dollar | 90 |
| **(2007) American Legacy** | |
| American Legacy Collection. 16 Proof coins for 2007: five State quarters; four Presidential dollars; Jamestown and Little Rock Central High School Desegregation silver dollars; Proof cent, nickel, dime, half dollar, and dollar | 140 |

| | Value |
|---|---|
| **(2007) Little Rock Central High School Desegregation** | |
| Little Rock Coin and Medal set. Uncirculated silver dollar, bronze medal | $175 |
| **(2008) Bald Eagle** | |
| 3-piece set. Proof clad half dollar, silver dollar, and gold $5 | 425 |
| Bald Eagle Coin and Medal Set. Uncirculated silver dollar, bronze medal | 70 |
| "Young Collector" set. Uncirculated clad half dollar | 18 |
| **(2008) American Legacy** | |
| American Legacy Collection. 15 Proof coins for 2008: cent, nickel, dime, half dollar, and dollar; | 15 |
| five State quarters; four Presidential dollars; Bald Eagle dollar | 150 |
| **(2009) Louis Braille** | |
| Uncirculated silver dollar in tri-fold package | 50 |
| **(2009) Abraham Lincoln Coin and Chronicles** | |
| Four Proof 2009S cents and Abraham Lincoln Proof silver dollar | 150 |
| **(2012) Star-Spangled Banner** | |
| 2-coin set. Proof silver dollar and gold $5 | 425 |
| **(2013) 5-Star Generals** | |
| 3-coin set. Proof clad half dollar, silver dollar, and gold $5 | 550 |
| Profile Collection. Uncirculated half dollar and silver dollar, replica of 1962 General MacArthur Congressional Gold Medal | 80 |
| **(2013) Theodore Roosevelt Coin and Chronicles** | |
| Theodore Roosevelt Proof Presidential dollar; silver Presidential medal; National Wildlife Refuge System Centennial bronze medal; and Roosevelt print | 60 |
| **(2013) Girl Scouts of the U.S.A.** | |
| "Young Collector" set. Uncirculated silver dollar | 60 |
| **(2014) Franklin D. Roosevelt Coin and Chronicles** | |
| Franklin D. Roosevelt Proof dime and Presidential dollar; bronze Presidential medal; silver Presidential medal; four stamps; companion booklet | 100 |
| **(2014) National Baseball Hall of Fame** | |
| "Young Collector" set. Uncirculated half dollar | 30 |
| **(2014) American $1 Coin and Currency Set** | |
| 2014D Native American – Native Hospitality Enhanced Uncirculated dollar and $1 Federal Reserve Note | 50 |
| **(2015) Harry S. Truman Coin and Chronicles** | |
| Harry S. Truman Reverse Proof Presidential dollar, silver Presidential medal, one stamp, information booklet | 300 |
| **(2015) Dwight D. Eisenhower Coin and Chronicles** | |
| Dwight D. Eisenhower Reverse Proof Presidential dollar, silver Presidential medal, one stamp, information booklet | 150 |
| **(2015) John F. Kennedy Coin and Chronicles** | |
| John F. Kennedy Reverse Proof Presidential dollar, silver Presidential medal, one stamp, information booklet | 100 |
| **(2015) Lyndon B. Johnson Coin and Chronicles** | |
| Lyndon B. Johnson Reverse Proof Presidential dollar, silver Presidential medal, one stamp, information booklet | 100 |
| **(2015) March of Dimes Special Silver Set** | |
| Proof dime and March of Dimes silver dollar, Reverse Proof dime | 80 |
| **(2015) American $1 Coin and Currency Set** | |
| 2015W Native American – Mohawk Ironworkers Enhanced Uncirculated dollar and $1 Federal Reserve Note | 25 |
| **(2016) National Park Service 100th Anniversary** | |
| 3-coin set. Proof clad half dollar, silver dollar, and gold $5 | 500 |
| **(2016) Ronald Reagan Coin and Chronicles** | |
| Ronald Reagan Reverse Proof Presidential dollar, 2016W American Eagle silver Proof dollar, Ronald and Nancy Reagan bronze medal, engraved Ronald Reagan Presidential portrait, information booklet | 125 |

*Chart continued on next page.*

| | Value |
|---|---|
| **(2016) American $1 Coin and Currency Set** | |
| 2016S Native American – Code Talkers Enhanced Uncirculated dollar and $1 Federal Reserve Note | $25 |
| **(2017) Boys Town Centennial** | |
| 3-coin set. Proof clad half dollar, silver dollar, and gold $5 | 500 |
| **(2018) Breast Cancer Awareness** | |
| Coin and Stamp Set. Breast Cancer Awareness Proof half dollar and Breast Cancer Research stamp | 100 |
| **(2018) World War I Centennial** | |
| Silver Dollar and Air Service Medal Set. Proof World War I Centennial silver dollar and Proof silver Air Service medal | 100 |
| Silver Dollar and Army Medal Set. Proof World War I Centennial silver dollar and Proof silver Army medal | 100 |
| Silver Dollar and Coast Guard Medal Set. Proof World War I Centennial silver dollar and Proof silver Coast Guard medal | 100 |
| Silver Dollar and Marine Corps Medal Set. Proof World War I Centennial silver dollar and Proof silver Marine Corps medal | 100 |
| Silver Dollar and Navy Medal Set. Proof World War I Centennial silver dollar and Proof silver Navy medal | 100 |
| **(2019) Apollo 11 50th Anniversary** | |
| 2-coin set. Uncirculated and Proof clad half dollars | |
| **(2019) American Legion 100th Anniversary** | |
| 3-coin set. Proof clad half dollar, silver dollar, and gold $5 **(b)** | 475 |
| Silver Dollar and Medal Set. American Legion 100th Anniversary Proof silver dollar and American Veterans medal **(b)** | 100 |
| **(2019) American $1 Coin and Currency Set** | |
| 2019P Native American – American Indians in Space Enhanced Uncirculated dollar and $1 Federal Reserve Note | 75 |
| **(2019) Youth Coin and Currency Set** | |
| Five Proof clad America the Beautiful™ quarters and $2 Federal Reserve Note | 30 |
| **(2020) American $1 Coin and Currency Set** | |
| 2020S Native American – Elizabeth Peratrovich and Alaska's Anti-Discrimination Law Enhanced Uncirculated dollar and $1 Federal Reserve Note | |
| **(2020) Naismith Memorial Basketball Hall of Fame 60th Anniversary** | |
| "Kids Set." 2020S Proof clad half dollar | |

**b.** In 2019, the fineness of U.S. Mint silver coins increased from .900 to .999.

## PROOF COINS AND SETS

A Proof is a specimen striking of coinage for presentation, souvenir, exhibition, or numismatic purposes. Pre-1968 Proofs were made only at the Philadelphia Mint, except in a few rare instances in which presentation pieces were struck at branch mints. Current Proofs are made at San Francisco and West Point.

The term *Proof* refers to the method of manufacture and not the condition of a coin. Regular-production coins in Mint State have coruscating, frosty luster; and, often, minor imperfections due to handling during the minting process. A Proof coin can usually be distinguished by its sharpness of detail, high wire edge, and extremely brilliant, mirrorlike surface. All Proofs are originally sold by the Mint at a premium.

Very few Proof coins were made prior to 1856. Because of their rarity and infrequent sales, they are not all listed in this guide book.

*Frosted Proofs* were issued prior to 1936 and starting again in the late 1970s. These have a brilliant, mirrorlike field with contrasting satiny or frosted letters and motifs.

*Matte Proofs* have a granular, "sandblast" surface instead of the mirror finish. Matte Proof cents, nickels, and gold coins were issued from 1908 to 1916; a few 1921 and 1922 silver dollars and a 1998-S silver half dollar were also struck in this manner.

*Brilliant Proofs* have been issued from 1936 to date. These have a uniformly brilliant, mirrorlike surface and sharp, high-relief details.

"Prooflike" coins are occasionally seen. These are examples from dies that have been lightly polished, often inadvertently during the removal of lines, contact marks, or other marks in the fields. In other instances, such as with certain New Orleans gold coins of the 1850s, the dies were polished in the machine shop of the mint. They are not true Proofs, but may have most of the characteristics of a Proof coin and generally command a premium. Collectors should beware of coins that have been buffed to look like Proofs; magnification will reveal polishing lines and lack of detail.

### How Modern Proof Coins Are Made

Selected dies are inspected for perfection and are highly polished and cleaned. They are again wiped clean or polished after every 15 to 25 impressions and are replaced frequently to avoid imperfections from worn dies. Coinage blanks are polished and cleaned to assure high quality in striking. They are then hand fed into the coinage press one at a time, each blank receiving two or more blows from the dies to bring up sharp, high-relief details. The coinage operation is done at slow speed with extra pressure. Finished Proofs are individually inspected and are handled with gloves or tongs. They also receive a final inspection by packers before being sonically sealed in special plastic cases.

After a lapse of 20 years, Proof coins were struck at the Philadelphia Mint from 1936 to 1942, inclusive. In 1942, when the composition of the five-cent piece was changed, there were two types of this denomination available to collectors. The striking of Proof coins was temporarily suspended from 1943 through 1949, and again from 1965 through 1967; during the latter period, Special Mint Sets were struck. Proof sets were resumed in 1968.

Sets from 1936 through 1972 include the cent, nickel, dime, quarter, and half; from 1973 through 1981 the dollar was also included, and again from 2000 on. Regular Proof sets issued from 1982 to 1998 contain the cent through half dollar. Special Prestige sets containing commemorative coins were sold from 1983 through 1997 at an additional premium. From 1999 to 2009, sets contain five different State or six Territorial quarters. 1999 Proof dollars were sold separately. Four-piece Presidential dollar sets have been issued since 2007. In 2019, the Mint increased the fineness of all silver coins from .900 to .999. American Legacy Collection sets containing Proof and commemorative coins are listed on pages 360 and 361.

## *Proof Set Values*

*Values are for sets in average unspotted condition and after 1955 in original government packaging. Figures in parentheses are the total number of full sets minted.*

| | Mintage | Issue Price | Current Value |
|---|---|---|---|
| 1936 | (3,837) | $1.89 | $6,000 |
| 1937 | (5,542) | 1.89 | 2,850 |
| 1938 | (8,045) | 1.89 | 1,175 |
| 1939 | (8,795) | 1.89 | 1,125 |
| 1940 | (11,246) | 1.89 | 925 |
| 1941 | (15,287) | 1.89 | 875 |
| 1942, Both nickels | (21,120) | 1.89 | 1,000 |
| 1942, One nickel | * | 1.89 | 850 |
| 1950 | (51,386) | 2.10 | 535 |
| 1951 | (57,500) | 2.10 | 485 |
| 1952 | (81,980 | 2.10 | 240 |
| 1953 | (128,800) | 2.10 | 190 |
| 1954 | (233,300) | 2.10 | 100 |
| 1955, Box pack | (378,200) | 2.10 | 100 |
| 1955, Flat pack | * | 2.10 | 120 |
| 1956 | (669,384) | 2.10 | 65 |
| 1957 | (1,247,952) | 2.10 | 30 |
| 1958 | (875,652) | 2.10 | 32 |
| 1959 | (1,149,291) | 2.10 | 28 |
| 1960, With Large Date cent | (1,691,602) | 2.10 | 28 |
| 1960, With Small Date cent | * | 2.10 | 32 |
| 1961 | (3,028,244) | 2.10 | 22 |
| 1962 | (3,218,019) | 2.10 | 22 |
| 1963 | (3,075,645) | 2.10 | 22 |
| 1964 | (3,950,762) | 2.10 | 22 |
| 1968S | (3,041,506) | 5.00 | 7 |
| 1968S, With No S dime | * | 5.00 | 15,000 |
| 1969S | (2,934,631) | 5.00 | 7 |
| 1970S | (2,632,810) | 5.00 | 11 |
| 1970S, With Small Date cent | * | 5.00 | 85 |
| 1970S, With No S dime *(estimated mintage: 2,200)* | * | 5.00 | 900 |
| 1971S | (3,220,733) | 5.00 | 4 |
| 1971S, With No S nickel *(estimated mintage: 1,655)* | * | 5.00 | 1,200 |
| 1972S | (3,260,996) | 5.00 | 5 |
| 1973S | (2,760,339) | 7.00 | 8 |
| 1974S | (2,612,568) | 7.00 | 10 |
| 1975S, With 1976 quarter, half, and dollar | (2,845,450) | 7.00 | 9 |
| 1975S, With No S dime | * | 7.00 | 250,000 |
| 1976S | (4,149,730) | 7.00 | 9 |
| 1976S, Silver clad, 3-piece set | (3,998,621) | 15.00 | 24 |
| 1977S | (3,251,152) | 9.00 | 7 |
| 1978S | (3,127,781) | 9.00 | 7 |
| 1979S, Type 1 **(a)** | (3,677,175) | 9.00 | 8 |
| 1979S, Type 2 **(a)** | * | 9.00 | 50 |
| 1980S | (3,554,806) | 10.00 | 5 |
| 1981S, Type 1 **(a)** | (4,063,083) | 11.00 | 5 |
| 1981S, Type 2 (all six coins in set) **(a)** | * | 11.00 | 275 |
| 1982S | (3,857,479) | 11.00 | 5 |
| 1983S | (3,138,765) | 11.00 | 5 |

* Included in number above. **a.** See illustrations on page 246 for clarification.

| | Mintage | Issue Price | Current Value |
|---|---|---|---|
| 1983S, With No S dime | * | $11.00 | $700 |
| 1983S, Prestige set (Olympic dollar) | (140,361) | 59.00 | 42 |
| 1984S | (2,748,430) | 11.00 | 6 |
| 1984S, Prestige set (Olympic dollar) | (316,680) | 59.00 | 25 |
| 1985S | (3,362,821) | 11.00 | 4 |
| 1986S | (2,411,180) | 11.00 | 6 |
| 1986S, Prestige set (Statue of Liberty half, dollar) | (599,317) | 48.50 | 28 |
| 1987S | (3,792,233) | 11.00 | 5 |
| 1987S, Prestige set (Constitution dollar) | (435,495) | 45.00 | 27 |
| 1988S | (3,031,287) | 11.00 | 5 |
| 1988S, Prestige set (Olympic dollar) | (231,661) | 45.00 | 25 |
| 1989S | (3,009,107) | 11.00 | 5 |
| 1989S, Prestige set (Congressional half, dollar) | (211,807) | 45.00 | 30 |
| 1990S | (2,793,433) | 11.00 | 5 |
| 1990S, With No S cent | (3,555) | 11.00 | 4,250 |
| 1990S, With No S cent (Prestige set) | * | 45.00 | 4,750 |
| 1990S, Prestige set (Eisenhower dollar) | (506,126) | 45.00 | 30 |
| 1991S | (2,610,833) | 11.00 | 5 |
| 1991S, Prestige set (Mt. Rushmore half, dollar) | (256,954) | 59.00 | 45 |
| 1992S | (2,675,618) | 11.00 | 5 |
| 1992S, Prestige set (Olympic half, dollar) | (183,293) | 56.00 | 48 |
| 1992S, Silver | (1,009,586) | 11.00 | 22 |
| 1992S, Silver Premier set | (308,055) | 37.00 | 24 |
| 1993S | (2,409,394) | 12.50 | 6 |
| 1993S, Prestige set (Bill of Rights half, dollar) | (224,045) | 57.00 | 36 |
| 1993S, Silver | (570,213) | 21.00 | 28 |
| 1993S, Silver Premier set | (191,140) | 37.50 | 35 |
| 1994S | (2,308,701) | 12.50 | 5 |
| 1994S, Prestige set (World Cup half, dollar) | (175,893) | 57.00 | 35 |
| 1994S, Silver | (636,009) | 21.00 | 28 |
| 1994S, Silver Premier set | (149,320) | 37.50 | 36 |
| 1995S | (2,010,384) | 12.50 | 10 |
| 1995S, Prestige set (Civil War half, dollar) | (107,112) | 57.00 | 80 |
| 1995S, Silver | (549,878) | 21.00 | 50 |
| 1995S, Silver Premier set | (130,107) | 37.50 | 52 |
| 1996S | (1,695,244) | 12.50 | 8 |
| 1996S, Prestige set (Olympic half, dollar) | (55,000) | 57.00 | 320 |
| 1996S, Silver | (623,655) | 21.00 | 28 |
| 1996S, Silver Premier set | (151,366) | 37.50 | 32 |
| 1997S | (1,975,000) | 12.50 | 8 |
| 1997S, Prestige set (Botanic dollar) | (80,000) | 57.00 | 60 |
| 1997S, Silver | (605,473) | 21.00 | 34 |
| 1997S, Silver Premier set | (136,205) | 37.50 | 38 |
| 1998S | (2,086,507) | 12.50 | 10 |
| 1998S, Silver | (638,134) | 21.00 | 24 |
| 1998S, Silver Premier set | (240,658) | 37.50 | 28 |
| 1999S, 9-piece set | (2,543,401) | 19.95 | 9 |
| 1999S, 5-piece quarter set | (1,169,958) | 13.95 | 5 |
| 1999S, Silver 9-piece set | (804,565) | 31.95 | 90 |
| 2000S, 10-piece set | (3,082,572) | 19.95 | 6 |
| 2000S, 5-piece quarter set | (937,600) | 13.95 | 5 |
| 2000S, Silver 10-piece set | (965,421) | 31.95 | 38 |
| 2001S, 10-piece set | (2,294,909) | 19.95 | 11 |

* Included in number above.

*Chart continued on next page.*

| | Mintage | Issue Price | Current Value |
|---|---|---|---|
| 2001S, 5-piece quarter set | (799,231) | $13.95 | $5 |
| 2001S, Silver 10-piece set | (889,697) | 31.95 | 45 |
| 2002S, 10-piece set | (2,319,766) | 19.95 | 8 |
| 2002S, 5-piece quarter set | (764,479) | 13.95 | 6 |
| 2002S, Silver 10-piece set | (892,229) | 31.95 | 38 |
| 2003S, 10-piece set | (2,172,684) | 19.95 | 6 |
| 2003S, 5-piece quarter set | (1,235,832) | 13.95 | 5 |
| 2003S, Silver 10-piece set | (1,125,755) | 31.95 | 35 |
| 2004S, 11-piece set | (1,789,488) | 22.95 | 11 |
| 2004S, 5-piece quarter set | (951,196) | 15.95 | 5 |
| 2004S, Silver 11-piece set | (1,175,934) | 37.95 | 35 |
| 2004S, Silver 5-piece quarter set | (593,852) | 23.95 | 24 |
| 2005S, 11-piece set | (2,275,000) | 22.95 | 5 |
| 2005S, 5-piece quarter set | (987,960) | 15.95 | 4 |
| 2005S, Silver 11-piece set | (1,069,679) | 37.95 | 38 |
| 2005S, Silver 5-piece quarter set | (608,970) | 23.95 | 24 |
| 2006S, 10-piece set | (2,000,428) | 22.95 | 8 |
| 2006S, 5-piece quarter set | (882,000) | 15.95 | 4 |
| 2006S, Silver 10-piece set | (1,054,008) | 37.95 | 36 |
| 2006S, Silver 5-piece quarter set | (531,000) | 23.95 | 24 |
| 2007S, 14-piece set | (1,702,116) | 26.95 | 16 |
| 2007S, 5-piece quarter set | (672,662) | 13.95 | 7 |
| 2007S, 4-piece Presidential set | (1,285,972) | 14.95 | 6 |
| 2007S, Silver 14-piece set | (875,050) | 44.95 | 42 |
| 2007S, Silver 5-piece quarter set | (672,662) | 25.95 | 24 |
| 2008S, 14-piece set | (1,382,017) | 26.95 | 28 |
| 2008S, 5-piece quarter set | (672,438) | 13.95 | 22 |
| 2008S, 4-piece Presidential set | (836,730) | 14.95 | 12 |
| 2008S, Silver 14-piece set | (763,887) | 44.95 | 45 |
| 2008S, Silver 5-piece quarter set | (429,021) | 25.95 | 24 |
| 2009S, 18-piece set | (1,482,502) | 29.95 | 25 |
| 2009S, 6-piece quarter set | (630,976) | 14.95 | 6 |
| 2009S, 4-piece Presidential set | (629,585) | 14.95 | 9 |
| 2009S, Silver 18-piece set | (697,365) | 52.95 | 50 |
| 2009S, Silver 6-piece quarter set | (299,183) | 29.95 | 30 |
| 2009S, 4-piece Lincoln Bicentennial set | (201,107) | 7.95 | 10 |
| 2010S, 14-piece set | (1,103,815) | 31.95 | 35 |
| 2010S, 5-piece quarter set | (276,296) | 14.95 | 13 |
| 2010S, 4-piece Presidential set | (535,397) | 15.95 | 15 |
| 2010S, Silver 14-piece set | (585,401) | 56.95 | 52 |
| 2010S, Silver 5-piece quarter set | (274,034) | 32.95 | 24 |
| 2011S, 14-piece set | *(1,098,835)* | 31.95 | 36 |
| 2011S, 5-piece quarter set | *(152,302)* | 14.95 | 14 |
| 2011S, 4-piece Presidential set | *(299,853)* | 19.95 | 28 |
| 2011S, Silver 14-piece set | *(574,175)* | 67.95 | 60 |
| 2011S, Silver 5-piece quarter set | *(147,901)* | 39.95 | 28 |
| 2012S, 14-piece set | *(794,002)* | 31.95 | 125 |
| 2012S, 5-piece quarter set | *(148,498)* | 14.95 | 15 |
| 2012S, 4-piece Presidential set | *(249,265)* | 18.95 | 65 |
| 2012S, Silver 14-piece set | *(395,443)* | 67.95 | 230 |
| 2012S, Silver 8-piece Limited Edition set | (44,952) | 149.95 | 235 |
| 2012S, Silver 5-piece quarter set | *(162,448)* | 41.95 | 30 |
| 2013S, 14-piece set | (802,460) | 31.95 | 35 |
| 2013S, 5-piece quarter set | (128,377) | 14.95 | 14 |

| | Mintage | Issue Price | Current Value |
|---|---|---|---|
| 2013S, 4-piece Presidential set | (266,677) | $18.95 | $18 |
| 2013S, Silver 14-piece set | (419,720) | 67.95 | 70 |
| 2013S, Silver 8-piece Limited Edition set | (47,971) | 139.95 | 120 |
| 2013S, Silver 5-piece quarter set | (138,451) | 41.95 | 30 |
| 2014S, 14-piece set | (802,460) | 31.95 | 35 |
| 2014S, 5-piece quarter set | *(109,423)* | 14.95 | 16 |
| 2014S, 4-piece Presidential set | *(218,976)* | 18.95 | 18 |
| 2014S, Silver 14-piece set | *(404,665)* | 67.95 | 58 |
| 2014S, Silver 8-piece Limited Edition set | *(41,609)* | 139.95 | 160 |
| 2014S, Silver 5-piece quarter set | *(111,172)* | 41.95 | 35 |
| 2015S, 14-piece set | *(662,854)* | 32.95 | 38 |
| 2015S, 5-piece quarter set | *(99,466)* | 14.95 | 14 |
| 2015S, 4-piece Presidential set | *(222,068)* | 18.95 | 20 |
| 2015S, Silver 14-piece set | *(387,310)* | 53.95 | 60 |
| 2015S, Silver 5-piece quarter set | *(103,311)* | 31.95 | 32 |
| 2016S, 13-piece set | (595,184) | 31.95 | 48 |
| 2016S, 5-piece quarter set | *(91,754)* | 14.95 | 14 |
| 2016S, 3-piece Presidential set | *(231,549)* | 17.95 | 18 |
| 2016S, Silver 13-piece set | (369,849) | 52.95 | 65 |
| 2016S, Silver 8-piece Limited Edition set | *(49,647)* | 139.95 | 135 |
| 2016S, Silver 5-piece quarter set | *(95,649)* | 31.95 | 28 |
| 2017S, 10-piece set | *(568,681)* | 26.95 | 30 |
| 2017S, 5-piece quarter set | *(85,238)* | 14.95 | 15 |
| 2017S, Silver 10-piece set | *(358,093)* | 47.95 | 48 |
| 2017S, Silver 5-piece quarter set | *(84,258)* | 31.95 | 33 |
| 2017S, Silver 8-piece Limited Edition set | *(48,901)* | 139.95 | 185 |
| 2018S, 10-piece set | *(490,414)* | 27.95 | 28 |
| 2018S, 5-piece quarter set | *(80,812)* | 15.95 | 15 |
| 2018S, Silver 10-piece set | *(308,999)* | 49.95 | 50 |
| 2018S, Silver 5-piece quarter set | *(74,874)* | 33.95 | 33 |
| 2018S, 50th Anniversary silver 10-piece Reverse Proof set | *(199,116)* | 54.95 | 60 |
| 2018S, Silver 8-piece Limited Edition set | *(41,821)* | 144.95 | 175 |
| 2019S, 10-piece set, plus 2019W Proof cent | | 27.95 | 35 |
| 2019S, 5-piece quarter set | | 15.95 | 15 |
| 2019S, 4-piece American Innovation set | | 20.95 | 20 |
| 2019S, Silver 10-piece set, plus 2019W Reverse Proof cent **(b)** | | 54.95 | 60 |
| 2019S, Silver 5-piece quarter set **(b)** | | 36.95 | 38 |
| 2019S, Silver 8-piece Limited Edition set **(b)** | | 149.95 | |
| 2020S, 10-piece set, plus 2020W Proof nickel | | 32.00 | |
| 2020S, 5-piece quarter set | | 18.50 | |
| 2020S, 4-piece American Innovation set | | | |
| 2020S, Silver 10-piece set, plus 2020W Reverse Proof nickel **(b)** | | | |
| 2020S, Silver 5-piece quarter set **(b)** | | 42.50 | |
| 2020S, Silver 8-piece Limited Edition set **(b)** | | | |

**b.** In 2019, the fineness of U.S. Mint silver coins increased from .900 to .999.

## UNCIRCULATED MINT SETS

Official Uncirculated Mint sets are specially packaged by the government for sale to collectors. They contain Uncirculated specimens of each year's coins for every denomination issued from each mint. In previous years, the coins were the same as those normally intended for circulation and were not minted with any special consideration for quality. From 2005 through 2010, Mint sets were made with a Satin Finish rather than the traditional Uncirculated luster. As in the past, coins struck only as Proofs are not included.

Prior to 1942 the Mint sold Uncirculated coins individually to collectors upon request. From 1942 to 1946, groups of two coins from each mint were sold in a cloth shipping bag with only minimal protection. Very few of those mailing packages were ever saved by collectors.

Uncirculated Mint sets sold by the Treasury from 1947 through 1958 contained two examples of each regular-issue coin. These were packaged in cardboard holders that did not protect the coins from tarnish. Nicely preserved early sets generally command a 10 to 20% premium above listed values. No official Uncirculated Mint sets were produced in 1950, 1982, or 1983.

Since 1959, sets have been sealed in protective plastic envelopes. In 1965, 1966, and 1967, Special Mint Sets of higher-than-normal quality were made to substitute for Proof sets, which were not made during that period. Similar coins dated 1964 also exist (see page 369). The 1966 and 1967 sets were packaged in hard plastic holders.

Privately assembled Mint sets, and Souvenir sets produced for sale at the Philadelphia or Denver mints or for special occasions, are valued according to the individual pieces they contain. Only the official, government-sealed full sets are included in this list.

Current-year sets may be ordered by telephoning 1-800-USA-MINT.

### *Uncirculated Mint Set Values*

| | Mintage | Issue Price | Face Value | Current Value |
|---|---|---|---|---|
| 1947 P-D-S | *5,000* | $4.87 | $4.46 | $1,500.00 |
| 1948 P-D-S | *6,000* | 4.92 | 4.46 | 1,100.00 |
| 1949 P-D-S | *5,000* | 5.45 | 4.96 | 1,225.00 |
| 1951 P-D-S | 8,654 | 6.75 | 5.46 | 950.00 |
| 1952 P-D-S | 11,499 | 6.14 | 5.46 | 900.00 |
| 1953 P-D-S | 15,538 | 6.14 | 5.46 | 775.00 |
| 1954 P-D-S | 25,599 | 6.19 | 5.46 | 450.00 |
| 1955 P-D-S | 49,656 | 3.57 | 2.86 | 375.00 |
| 1956 P-D | 45,475 | 3.34 | 2.64 | 375.00 |
| 1957 P-D | 34,324 | 4.40 | 3.64 | 375.00 |
| 1958 P-D | 50,314 | 4.43 | 3.64 | 300.00 |
| 1959 P-D | 187,000 | 2.40 | 1.82 | 55.00 |
| 1960 P-D | 260,485 | 2.40 | 1.82 | 40.00 |
| 1961 P-D | 223,704 | 2.40 | 1.82 | 42.00 |
| 1962 P-D | 385,285 | 2.40 | 1.82 | 42.00 |
| 1963 P-D | 606,612 | 2.40 | 1.82 | 37.00 |
| 1964 P-D | 1,008,108 | 2.40 | 1.82 | 35.00 |
| 1968 P-D-S | 2,105,128 | 2.50 | 1.33 | 7.00 |
| 1969 P-D-S | 1,817,392 | 2.50 | 1.33 | 7.00 |
| 1970 P-D-S, With Large Date cent | 2,038,134 | 2.50 | 1.33 | 20.00 |
| 1970 P-D-S, With Small Date cent | * | 2.50 | 1.33 | 50.00 |
| 1971 P-D-S (no Eisenhower dollar) | 2,193,396 | 3.50 | 1.83 | 5.00 |
| 1972 P-D-S (no Eisenhower dollar) | 2,750,000 | 3.50 | 1.83 | 5.00 |
| 1973 P-D-S | 1,767,691 | 6.00 | 3.83 | 12.00 |
| 1974 P-D-S | 1,975,981 | 6.00 | 3.83 | 6.00 |
| 1975 P-D, With 1976 quarter, half, dollar | 1,921,488 | 6.00 | 3.82 | 8.00 |
| 1976S, Silver clad, 3-piece set | 4,908,319 | 9.00 | 1.75 | 18.00 |
| 1976 P-D | 1,892,513 | 6.00 | 3.82 | 9.00 |
| 1977 P-D | 2,006,869 | 7.00 | 3.82 | 6.00 |
| 1978 P-D | 2,162,609 | 7.00 | 3.82 | 7.50 |
| 1979 P-D **(a)** | 2,526,000 | 8.00 | 3.82 | 7.00 |
| 1980 P-D-S | 2,815,066 | 9.00 | 4.82 | 7.50 |
| 1981 P-D-S | 2,908,145 | 11.00 | 4.82 | 9.00 |

* Included in number above. **a.** S-mint dollar not included.

| | Mintage | Issue Price | Face Value | Current Value |
|---|---|---|---|---|
| 1984 P-D | 1,832,857 | $7.00 | $1.82 | $5.00 |
| 1985 P-D | 1,710,571 | 7.00 | 1.82 | 5.00 |
| 1986 P-D | 1,153,536 | 7.00 | 1.82 | 7.50 |
| 1987 P-D | 2,890,758 | 7.00 | 1.82 | 5.00 |
| 1988 P-D | 1,646,204 | 7.00 | 1.82 | 5.00 |
| 1989 P-D | 1,987,915 | 7.00 | 1.82 | 5.00 |
| 1990 P-D | 1,809,184 | 7.00 | 1.82 | 5.00 |
| 1991 P-D | 1,352,101 | 7.00 | 1.82 | 5.00 |
| 1992 P-D | 1,500,143 | 7.00 | 1.82 | 5.00 |
| 1993 P-D | 1,297,431 | 8.00 | 1.82 | 5.50 |
| 1994 P-D | 1,234,813 | 8.00 | 1.82 | 5.00 |
| 1995 P-D | 1,038,787 | 8.00 | 1.82 | 5.50 |
| 1996 P-D, plus 1996W dime | 1,457,949 | 8.00 | 1.92 | 15.00 |
| 1997 P-D | 950,473 | 8.00 | 1.82 | 5.50 |
| 1998 P-D | 1,187,325 | 8.00 | 1.82 | 5.00 |
| 1999 P-D (18 pieces) **(b)** | 1,243,867 | 14.95 | 3.82 | 8.00 |
| 2000 P-D (20 pieces) | 1,490,160 | 14.95 | 5.82 | 8.00 |
| 2001 P-D (20 pieces) | 1,116,915 | 14.95 | 5.82 | 8.00 |
| 2002 P-D (20 pieces) | 1,139,388 | 14.95 | 5.82 | 8.00 |
| 2003 P-D (20 pieces) | 1,001,532 | 14.95 | 5.82 | 8.00 |
| 2004 P-D (22 pieces) | 842,507 | 16.95 | 5.92 | 8.00 |
| 2005 P-D (22 pieces) | 1,160,000 | 16.95 | 5.92 | 8.00 |
| 2006 P-D (20 pieces) | 847,361 | 16.95 | 5.82 | 8.00 |
| 2007 P-D (28 pieces) | 895,628 | 22.95 | 13.82 | 17.50 |
| 2008 P-D (28 pieces) | 745,464 | 22.95 | 13.82 | 30.00 |
| 2009 P-D (36 pieces) | 784,614 | 27.95 | 14.38 | 24.00 |
| 2010 P-D (28 pieces) | 583,897 | 31.95 | 13.82 | 24.00 |
| 2011 P-D (28 pieces) | *533,529* | 31.95 | 13.82 | 24.00 |
| 2012 P-D (28 pieces) | *392,224* | 27.95 | 13.82 | 65.00 |
| 2013 P-D (28 pieces) | 376,844 | 27.95 | 13.82 | 24.00 |
| 2014 P-D (28 pieces) | *327,969* | 27.95 | 13.82 | 24.00 |
| 2015 P-D (28 pieces) | *314,029* | 28.95 | 13.82 | 25.00 |
| 2016 P-D (26 pieces) | *296,582* | 27.95 | 11.82 | 40.00 |
| 2017 P-D (20 pieces) | *286,813* | 20.95 | 5.82 | 25.00 |
| 2017S, 225th Anniversary Enhanced Uncirculated Set (10 pieces) | *210,419* | 29.95 | 2.91 | 40.00 |
| 2018 P-D (20 pieces) | *240,470* | 21.95 | 5.82 | 25.00 |
| 2019 P-D, plus 2019W cent (21 pieces) | | 21.95 | 5.83 | 25.00 |
| 2020 P-D, plus 2020W nickel (21 pieces) | | | 5.87 | |

*Note:* Sets issued from 2005 through 2010 have a special Satin Finish that is somewhat different from the finish on Uncirculated coins made for general circulation. **b.** Dollar not included.

## Special Mint Sets

In mid-1964 the Treasury Department announced that the Mint would not offer Proof sets or Mint sets the following year. This was prompted by a nationwide shortage of circulating coins, which was wrongly blamed on coin collectors.

In 1966 the San Francisco Assay Office began striking coins dated 1965, for inclusion in so-called United States Special Mint Sets. These were issued in pliofilm packaging similar to that of recent Proof sets. The coins in early 1965 Special Mint Sets are semi-brilliant or satiny (distinctive, but not equal in quality to Proofs); the coins in later 1965 sets feature very brilliant fields (but again not reaching Proof brilliance).

The San Francisco Assay Office started striking 1966-dated coins in August of that year, and its Special Mint Sets were packaged in rigid, sonically sealed plastic holders.

The coins were struck once on unpolished planchets, unlike Proof coins (which are struck twice on polished planchets). Also unlike Proofs, the SMS coins were allowed to come into contact with each other during production, which accounts for minor contact marks and abrasions. To achieve a brilliant finish, Mint technicians overpolished the coinage dies. The result was a trade-off: most of the coins have prooflike brilliance, but many are missing polished-off design details, such as Frank Gasparro's initials on the half dollar.

1967 Special Mint Set

All 1967-dated coinage was struck in that calendar year. Nearly all SMS coins of 1967 have fully brilliant, prooflike finishes. This brilliance was achieved without overpolishing the dies, resulting in coins that approach the quality of true Proofs. Sales of the 1967 sets were lackluster, however. The popularity of coin collecting had dropped from its peak in 1964. Also, collectors did not anticipate much secondary-market profit from the sets, which had an issue price of $4.00, compared to $2.10 for a 1964 Proof set. As a result, fewer collectors bought multiples of the 1967 sets, and today they are worth more than those of 1966 and 1965.

| | Mintage | Issue Price | Face Value | Current Value |
|---|---|---|---|---|
| 1965 | 2,360,000 | $4 | $0.91 | $10 |
| 1966 | 2,261,583 | 4 | 0.91 | 10 |
| 1967 | 1,863,344 | 4 | 0.91 | 11 |

## 1964 Special Strikes

In addition to the normal SMS coins dated 1965–1967, there are other, very similar pieces dated 1964. These coins are unlike ordinary Uncirculated and Proof coins made that year and have characteristics akin to the SMS pieces. Collectors generally refer to the 1964 pieces as *Special Strikes.* All denominations are very rare, whether sold as single pieces or in sets. It is unknown why these pieces are rare (whether sold as single pieces or in sets), why they were made, or how they left the Mint.

| | |
|---|---|
| 1964 Special Strike coins. Cent through half dollar | *$15,000–$20,000* |

## Souvenir Sets

Uncirculated Souvenir sets were packaged and sold in gift shops at the Philadelphia and Denver mints in 1982 and 1983 in place of the "official Mint sets," which were not made in those years. A bronze Mint medal is packaged with each set. Similar sets were also made in other years and sold at several locations.

| | Issue Price | Face Value | Current Value |
|---|---|---|---|
| 1982P | $4 | $0.91 | $60 |
| 1982D | 4 | 0.91 | 60 |
| 1983P | 4 | 0.91 | 80 |
| 1983D | 4 | 0.91 | 80 |

## AMERICA THE BEAUTIFUL™ SILVER BULLION COINS

**Weight and purity incused on edge.**
*Actual size 3 inches.*

In conjunction with the America the Beautiful™ quarter dollar circulating coins, the Mint also produces a companion series of bullion pieces with matching designs. Five different sites of "natural or historic significance" are being honored each year from 2010 through 2021.

The bullion coins contain five ounces of pure silver and have designs nearly identical to those of the America the Beautiful quarters, struck in a larger size (3 inches in diameter) and with their edge marked .999 FINE SILVER 5.0 OUNCE, instead of being reeded like the standard quarters. All are coined at the Philadelphia Mint, but only the Burnished versions have a mintmark. These coins are not intended for circulation. Burnished pieces are sold by the Mint directly to collectors, and bullion pieces to authorized distributors.

| | Mintage | MS | SP |
|---|---|---|---|
| 25¢, 2010(P), Hot Springs National Park (Arkansas) | 33,000 | $140 | |
| 25¢, 2010P, Hot Springs National Park (Arkansas) | (26,788) | | $160 |
| 25¢ 2010(P), Yellowstone National Park (Wyoming) | 33,000 | 140 | |
| 25¢ 2010P, Yellowstone National Park (Wyoming) | (26,711) | | 150 |
| 25¢ 2010(P), Yosemite National Park (California) | 33,000 | 150 | |
| 25¢ 2010P, Yosemite National Park (California) | (26,716) | | 155 |
| 25¢ 2010(P), Grand Canyon National Park (Arizona) | 33,000 | 140 | |
| 25¢ 2010P, Grand Canyon National Park (Arizona) | (25,967) | | 155 |
| 25¢ 2010(P), Mount Hood National Park (Oregon) | 33,000 | 155 | |
| 25¢ 2010P, Mount Hood National Park (Oregon) | (26,637) | | 155 |
| 25¢, 2011(P), Gettysburg National Military Park (Pennsylvania) | 126,700 | 140 | |
| 25¢, 2011P, Gettysburg National Military Park (Pennsylvania) | *(24,625)* | | 255 |
| 25¢, 2011(P), Glacier National Park (Montana) | 126,700 | 140 | |
| 25¢, 2011P, Glacier National Park (Montana) | *(20,805)* | | 170 |
| 25¢, 2011(P), Olympic National Park (Washington) | 104,900 | 135 | |
| 25¢, 2011P, Olympic National Park (Washington) | *(18,345)* | | 155 |
| 25¢, 2011(P), Vicksburg National Military Park (Mississippi) | 58,100 | 135 | |
| 25¢, 2011P, Vicksburg National Military Park (Mississippi) | *(18,528)* | | 155 |
| 25¢, 2011(P), Chickasaw National Recreation Area (Oklahoma) | 48,700 | 135 | |
| 25¢, 2011P, Chickasaw National Recreation Area (Oklahoma) | *(16,746)* | | 215 |
| 25¢, 2012(P), El Yunque National Forest (Puerto Rico) | 24,000 | 215 | |
| 25¢, 2012P, El Yunque National Forest (Puerto Rico) | (17,314) | | 400 |
| 25¢, 2012(P), Chaco Culture National Historical Park (New Mexico) | 24,400 | 235 | |
| 25¢, 2012P, Chaco Culture National Historical Park (New Mexico) | (17,146) | | 355 |
| 25¢, 2012(P), Acadia National Park (Maine) | 25,400 | 350 | |
| 25¢, 2012P, Acadia National Park (Maine) | (14,978) | | 550 |
| 25¢, 2012(P), Hawai'i Volcanoes National Park (Hawaii) | 20,000 | 350 | |
| 25¢, 2012P, Hawai'i Volcanoes National Park (Hawaii) | (14,863) | | 650 |

*Note:* The U.S. Mint produces the America the Beautiful™ 5-oz. silver coins in bullion and numismatic versions. The bullion version, which lacks the P mintmark, has a brilliant Uncirculated finish and is sold only through dealers. The numismatic version, with the mintmark, has a matte or burnished finish (although it is not marketed by the Mint as "Burnished"). These coins, designated Specimens (SP) by grading services, are sold directly to the public.

| | Mintage | MS | SP |
|---|---|---|---|
| 25¢, 2012(P), Denali National Park and Preserve (Alaska) | 20,000 | $235 | |
| 25¢, 2012P, Denali National Park and Preserve (Alaska) | (15,225) | | $475 |
| 25¢, 2013(P), White Mountain National Forest (New Hampshire) | 35,000 | 135 | |
| 25¢, 2013P, White Mountain National Forest (New Hampshire) | (20,530) | | 180 |
| 25¢, 2013(P), Perry's Victory and Int'l Peace Memorial (Ohio) | 30,000 | 135 | |
| 25¢, 2013P, Perry's Victory and Int'l Peace Memorial (Ohio) | (17,707) | | 165 |
| 25¢, 2013(P), Great Basin National Park (Nevada) | 30,000 | 135 | |
| 25¢, 2013P, Great Basin National Park (Nevada) | (17,792) | | 165 |
| 25¢, 2013(P), Fort McHenry Nat'l Mon't and Historic Shrine (Maryland) | 30,000 | 135 | |
| 25¢, 2013P, Fort McHenry Nat'l Mon't and Historic Shrine (Maryland) | (19,802) | | 165 |
| 25¢, 2013(P), Mount Rushmore National Memorial (South Dakota) | 35,000 | 135 | |
| 25¢, 2013P, Mount Rushmore National Memorial (South Dakota) | (23,547) | | 165 |
| 25¢, 2014(P), Great Smoky Mountains National Park (Tennessee) | 33,000 | 140 | |
| 25¢, 2014P, Great Smoky Mountains National Park (Tennessee) | (24,710) | | 135 |
| 25¢, 2014(P), Shenandoah National Park (Virginia) | 25,000 | 140 | |
| 25¢, 2014P, Shenandoah National Park (Virginia) | (28,451) | | 125 |
| 25¢, 2014(P), Arches National Park (Utah) | 22,000 | 140 | |
| 25¢, 2014P, Arches National Park (Utah) | (28,424) | | 140 |
| 25¢, 2014(P), Great Sand Dunes National Park (Colorado) | 22,000 | 140 | |
| 25¢, 2014P, Great Sand Dunes National Park (Colorado) | (24,103) | | 140 |
| 25¢, 2014(P), Everglades National Park (Florida) | 34,000 | 140 | |
| 25¢, 2014P, Everglades National Park (Florida) | (19,772) | | 135 |
| 25¢, 2015(P), Homestead Nat'l Monument of America (Nebraska) | 35,000 | 140 | |
| 25¢, 2015P, Homestead Nat'l Monument of America (Nebraska) | (21,286) | | 160 |
| 25¢, 2015(P), Kisatchie National Forest (Louisiana) | 42,000 | 140 | |
| 25¢, 2015P, Kisatchie National Forest (Louisiana) | (19,449) | | 160 |
| 25¢, 2015(P), Blue Ridge Parkway (North Carolina) | 45,000 | 140 | |
| 25¢, 2015P, Blue Ridge Parkway (North Carolina) | (17,461) | | 160 |
| 25¢, 2015(P), Bombay Hook National Wildlife Refuge (Delaware) | 45,000 | 140 | |
| 25¢, 2015P, Bombay Hook National Wildlife Refuge (Delaware) | (17,309) | | 160 |
| 25¢, 2015(P), Saratoga National Historical Park (New York) | 45,000 | 140 | |
| 25¢, 2015P, Saratoga National Historical Park (New York) | (17,563) | | 160 |
| 25¢, 2016(P), Shawnee National Forest (Illinois) | *105,000* | 140 | |
| 25¢, 2016P, Shawnee National Forest (Illinois) | *(18,781)* | | 160 |
| 25¢, 2016(P), Cumberland Gap National Historical Park (Kentucky) | *75,000* | 140 | |
| 25¢, 2016P, Cumberland Gap National Historical Park (Kentucky) | | | 160 |
| 25¢, 2016(P), Harpers Ferry National Historical Park (West Virginia) | *75,000* | 140 | |
| 25¢, 2016P, Harpers Ferry National Historical Park (West Virginia) | *(18,896)* | | 150 |
| 25¢, 2016(P), Theodore Roosevelt National Park (North Dakota) | *40,000* | 140 | |
| 25¢, 2016P, Theodore Roosevelt National Park (North Dakota) | *(18,917)* | | 160 |
| 25¢, 2016(P), Fort Moultrie at Fort Sumter Nat'l Mon't (SC) | *35,000* | 140 | |
| 25¢, 2016P, Fort Moultrie at Fort Sumter Nat'l Mon't (SC) | *(17,882)* | | 160 |
| 25¢, 2017(P), Effigy Mounds National Monument (Iowa) | *35,000* | 140 | |
| 25¢, 2017P, Effigy Mounds National Monument (Iowa) | *(17,251)* | | 150 |
| 25¢, 2017(P), Frederick Douglass National Historic Site (DC) | *20,000* | 140 | |
| 25¢, 2017P, Frederick Douglass National Historic Site (DC) | *(17,678)* | | 150 |
| 25¢, 2017(P), Ozark National Scenic Riverways (Missouri) | *20,000* | 140 | |
| 25¢, 2017P, Ozark National Scenic Riverways (Missouri) | *(17,694)* | | 150 |

*Note:* The U.S. Mint produces the America the Beautiful™ 5-oz. silver coins in bullion and numismatic versions. The bullion version, which lacks the P mintmark, has a brilliant Uncirculated finish and is sold only through dealers. The numismatic version, with the mintmark, has a matte or burnished finish (although it is not marketed by the Mint as "Burnished"). These coins, designated Specimens (SP) by grading services, are sold directly to the public.

| | Mintage | MS | SP |
|---|---|---|---|
| 25¢, 2017(P), Ellis Island (Statue of Liberty National Monument) (NJ) | 40,000 | $140 | |
| 25¢, 2017P, Ellis Island (Statue of Liberty National Monument) (NJ) | *(17,670)* | | $150 |
| 25¢, 2017(P), George Rogers Clark National Historical Park (Indiana) | 35,000 | 140 | |
| 25¢, 2017P, George Rogers Clark National Historical Park (Indiana) | *(14,731)* | | 150 |
| 25¢, 2018(P), Pictured Rocks National Lakeshore (Michigan) | 30,000 | 140 | |
| 25¢, 2018P, Pictured Rocks National Lakeshore (Michigan) | *(17,770)* | | 150 |
| 25¢, 2018(P), Apostle Islands National Lakeshore (Wisconsin) | 30,000 | 140 | |
| 25¢, 2018P, Apostle Islands National Lakeshore (Wisconsin) | *(16,450)* | | 150 |
| 25¢, 2018(P), Voyageurs National Park (Minnesota) | 30,000 | 140 | |
| 25¢, 2018P, Voyageurs National Park (Minnesota) | *(16,225)* | | 150 |
| 25¢, 2018(P), Cumberland Island National Seashore (Georgia) | 52,500 | 140 | |
| 25¢, 2018P, Cumberland Island National Seashore (Georgia) | *(14,987)* | | 150 |
| 25¢, 2018(P), Block Island National Wildlife Refuge (Rhode Island) | 80,000 | 140 | |
| 25¢, 2018P, Block Island National Wildlife Refuge (Rhode Island) | *(14,760)* | | 150 |
| 25¢, 2019P, Lowell National Historical Park (Massachusetts) | | 140 | |
| 25¢, 2019(P), Lowell National Historical Park (Massachusetts) | | | 150 |
| 25¢, 2019P, American Memorial Park (Northern Mariana Islands) | | 140 | |
| 25¢, 2019(P), American Memorial Park (Northern Mariana Islands) | | | 150 |
| 25¢, 2019P, War in the Pacific National Historical Park (Guam) | | 140 | |
| 25¢, 2019(P), War in the Pacific National Historical Park (Guam) | | | 150 |
| 25¢, 2019P, Frank Church River of No Return Wilderness (Idaho) | | 140 | |
| 25¢, 2019(P), Frank Church River of No Return Wilderness (Idaho) | | | 150 |
| 25¢, 2019P, San Antonio Missions National Historical Park (Texas) | | 140 | |
| 25¢, 2019(P), San Antonio Missions National Historical Park (Texas) | | | 150 |
| 25¢, 2020P, National Park of American Samoa (American Samoa) | | 140 | |
| 25¢, 2020(P), National Park of American Samoa (American Samoa) | | | 180 |
| 25¢, 2020P, Weir Farm National Historic Site (Connecticut) | | 140 | |
| 25¢, 2020(P), Weir Farm National Historic Site (Connecticut) | | | 180 |
| 25¢, 2020P, Salt River Bay National Hist'l Park and Ecological Preserve (USVI) | | 140 | |
| 25¢, 2020(P), Salt River Bay National Hist'l Park and Ecological Preserve (USVI) | | | 180 |
| 25¢, 2020P, Marsh-Billings-Rockefeller National Historical Park (Vermont) | | 140 | |
| 25¢, 2020(P), Marsh-Billings-Rockefeller National Historical Park (Vermont) | | | 180 |
| 25¢, 2020P, Tallgrass Prairie National Preserve (Kansas) | | 140 | |
| 25¢, 2020(P), Tallgrass Prairie National Preserve (Kansas) | | | 180 |

*Note:* The U.S. Mint produces the America the Beautiful™ 5-oz. silver coins in bullion and numismatic versions. The bullion version, which lacks the P mintmark, has a brilliant Uncirculated finish and is sold only through dealers. The numismatic version, with the mintmark, has a matte or burnished finish (although it is not marketed by the Mint as "Burnished"). These coins, designated Specimens (SP) by grading services, are sold directly to the public.

## $1 AMERICAN SILVER EAGLES

The American Silver Eagle is a one-ounce bullion coin with a face value of one dollar. The obverse has a modified rendition of Adolph A. Weinman's Liberty Walking design used on the half dollar coins from 1916 through 1947. His initials are on the hem of the gown. The reverse design is a rendition of a heraldic eagle by John Mercanti.

The U.S. Mint does not release bullion mintage data on a regular basis; the numbers below are the most recent official mintages.

*Designers Adolph A. Weinman (obv) and John Mercanti (rev); composition .999 silver, .001 copper (net weight 1 oz. pure silver); weight 31.101 grams; diameter 40.6 mm; reeded edge; mints: Philadelphia, San Francisco, West Point.*

| | Mintage | Unc. | PF |
|---|---|---|---|
| $1 1986 | 5,393,005 | $40 | |
| $1 1986S | (1,446,778) | | $50 |
| $1 1987 | 11,442,335 | 28 | |
| $1 1987S | (904,732) | | 50 |
| $1 1988 | 5,004,646 | 30 | |
| $1 1988S | (557,370) | | 50 |
| $1 1989 | 5,203,327 | 30 | |
| $1 1989S | (617,694) | | 50 |
| $1 1990 | 5,840,210 | 30 | |
| $1 1990S | (695,510) | | 50 |
| $1 1991 | 7,191,066 | 30 | |
| $1 1991S | (511,925) | | 50 |
| $1 1992 | 5,540,068 | 30 | |
| $1 1992S | (498,654) | | 50 |
| $1 1993 | 6,763,762 | 29 | |
| $1 1993P | (405,913) | | 90 |
| $1 1994 | 4,227,319 | 38 | |
| $1 1994P | (372,168) | | 180 |
| $1 1995 | 4,672,051 | 35 | |
| $1 1995P | (438,511) | | 65 |
| $1 1995W | (30,125) | | 3,500 |
| $1 1996 | 3,603,386 | 65 | |
| $1 1996P | (500,000) | | 50 |
| $1 1997 | 4,295,004 | 32 | |
| $1 1997P | (435,368) | | 50 |
| $1 1998 | 4,847,549 | 30 | |
| $1 1998P | (450,000) | | 50 |
| $1 1999 | 7,408,640 | 30 | |
| $1 1999P | (549,769) | | 50 |
| $1 2000(W) | 9,239,132 | 35 | |
| $1 2000P | (600,000) | | 50 |
| $1 2001(W) | 9,001,711 | 30 | |
| $1 2001W | (746,398) | | 50 |
| $1 2002(W) | 10,539,026 | 30 | |
| $1 2002W | (647,342) | | 50 |

| | Mintage | Unc. | PF |
|---|---|---|---|
| $1 2003(W) | 8,495,008 | $25 | |
| $1 2003W | (747,831) | | $50 |
| $1 2004(W) | 8,882,754 | 25 | |
| $1 2004W | (801,602) | | 50 |
| $1 2005(W) | 8,891,025 | 25 | |
| $1 2005W | (816,663) | | 50 |
| $1 2006(W) | 10,676,522 | 25 | |
| $1 2006W, Burnished **(a)** | 468,020 | 75 | |
| $1 2006W | (1,092,477) | | 50 |
| $1 2006P, Rev Proof **(b)** | (248,875) | | 160 |
| $1 2007(W) | 9,028,036 | 25 | |
| $1 2007W, Burnished | 621,333 | 30 | |
| $1 2007W | (821,759) | | 50 |
| $1 2008(W) | 20,583,000 | 25 | |
| $1 2008W, Burnished | 533,757 | 48 | |
| $1 2008W, Burnished, Reverse of 2007 **(c)** | *47,000* | 450 | |
| $1 2008W | (700,979) | | 50 |
| $1 2009(W) **(d)** | 30,459,000 | 24 | |
| $1 2010(W) | 34,764,500 | 24 | |
| $1 2010W | *(849,861)* | | 65 |
| $1 2011(W)(S) | 40,020,000 | 24 | |
| $1 2011W, Burnished | 409,776 | 38 | |
| $1 2011W | (947,355) | | 50 |
| $1 2011P, Rev Proof **(b)** | (99,882) | | 255 |
| $1 2011S, Burnished | 99,882 | 225 | |
| $1 2012(W)(S) | 33,121,500 | 24 | |
| $1 2012W, Burnished | 226,120 | 50 | |
| $1 2012W | (869,386) | | 50 |
| $1 2012S, Rev Proof **(b)** | (224,981) | | 55 |
| $1 2012S | (285,184) | | 125 |
| $1 2013(W)(S) | 42,675,000 | 24 | |
| $1 2013W, Burnished | 222,091 | 50 | |
| $1 2013W, Enhanced | 281,310 | 90 | |
| $1 2013W | (934,812) | | 50 |

**a.** In celebration of the 20th anniversary of the Bullion Coinage Program, in 2006 the W mintmark was used on bullion coins produced in sets except for the Reverse Proof, which was struck at the Philadelphia Mint. **b.** Reverse Proof coins have brilliant devices, and frosted fields in the background. **c.** Reverse dies of 2007 and earlier have a plain U in UNITED. Modified dies of 2008 and later have a small serif at the bottom right of the U. **d.** No Proof American Silver Eagles were made in 2009. Beware of alterations made privately outside the Mint.

| | Mintage | Unc. | PF |
|---|---|---|---|
| $1 2013W, Rev Proof **(b)** | (281,310) | | $115 |
| $1 2014(W)(S) | 44,006,000 | $24 | |
| $1 2014W, Burnished | 253,169 | 50 | |
| $1 2014W | (944,757) | | 50 |
| $1 2015(W)(S) | 47,000,000 | 24 | |
| $1 2015W, Burnished | 223,879 | 50 | |
| $1 2015W | (707,518) | | 50 |
| $1 2016(W)(S) | *37,701,500* | 24 | |
| $1 2016W, Burnished | *216,501* | 50 | |
| $1 2016W | *(595,843)* | | 50 |
| $1 2017(W)(S) | *18,065,500* | 24 | |
| $1 2017W, Burnished | *176,739* | 50 | |
| $1 2017W | *(440,596)* | | 50 |
| $1 2017S | *(123,799)* | | 100 |
| $1 2018(W)(S) | *15,700,000* | $24 | |
| $1 2018W, Burnished | *131,935* | 50 | |
| $1 2018W | *(361,192)* | | $50 |
| $1 2018S | *(158,791)* | | 50 |
| $1 2019(W)(S) | | 24 | |
| $1 2019W, Burnished | | 50 | |
| $1 2019W, Proof | | | 50 |
| $1 2019W, Enhanced RevPf **(e)** | | | 1,250 |
| $1 2019S, Proof | | | 50 |
| $1 2020(W)(S) **(f)** | | 24 | |
| $1 2020W, Burnished **(f)** | | 50 | |
| $1 2020W, Proof **(f)** | | | 65 |
| $1 2020S, Enhanced RevPf **(f,g)** | | | 900 |
| $1 2020S, Proof **(f)** | | | 65 |

**a.** In celebration of the 20th anniversary of the Bullion Coinage Program, in 2006 the W mintmark was used on bullion coins produced in sets except for the Reverse Proof, which was struck at the Philadelphia Mint. **b.** Reverse Proof coins have brilliant devices, and frosted fields in the background. **c.** Reverse dies of 2007 and earlier have a plain U in UNITED. Modified dies of 2008 and later have a small serif at the bottom right of the U. **d.** No Proof American Silver Eagles were made in 2009. Beware of alterations made privately outside the Mint. **e.** Included in the 2019 Pride of Two Nations set. **f.** Some (but not all) 2020 American Silver Eagles will be privy-marked to observe the 75th anniversary of the end of World War II. As of press date, specific formats, mintmarks, and product options have not been announced. **g.** Included in the 2020 Pride of Nations set.

From 2006 to 2011, special American Eagle Uncirculated coins in silver, gold, and platinum were sold directly from the United States Mint. The term "Uncirculated-burnished" refers to the specialized minting process used to create these coins. Although they are similar in appearance to the ordinary Uncirculated American Eagle bullion coins, the Uncirculated-burnished coins can be distinguished by the addition of a mintmark and by the use of burnished coin blanks. Proof coins, which also have a mintmark, have a highly reflective, mirrorlike surface.

## American Silver Eagle Sets

| Set | Value |
|---|---|
| 1997 Impressions of Liberty Set **(a)** | $3,300 |
| 2006 20th Anniversary Silver Coin Set. Uncirculated, Proof, Reverse Proof | 225 |
| 2006W 20th Anniversary 1-oz. Gold- and Silver-Dollar Set. Uncirculated | 1,600 |
| 2011 25th Anniversary Five-Coin Set. 2011W Uncirculated, Proof; 2011P Reverse Proof; 2011S Uncirculated; 2011 Bullion | 650 |
| 2012 75th Anniversary of San Francisco Mint Two-Piece Set. S-Mint Proof and Reverse Proof silver dollars | 200 |
| 2013 75th Anniversary of West Point Depository Two-Coin Set. W-Mint Enhanced Uncirculated and Reverse Proof silver dollars | 175 |
| 2019 Pride of Two Nations Limited Edition Two-Coin Set. W-Mint Enhanced Reverse Proof and Royal Canadian Mint Silver Maple Leaf modified Proof | 180 |
| 2020 Pride of Nations Two-Coin Set. Enhanced Reverse Proof Silver Eagle and Israel silver coin | 180 |

**a.** See page 380.

# AMERICAN EAGLE GOLD BULLION COINS

The American Eagle gold bullion coins are made in four denominations that contain 1 oz., 1/2 oz., 1/4 oz., and 1/10 oz. of gold. The obverse features a modified rendition of the Augustus Saint-Gaudens design used on U.S. twenty-dollar gold pieces from 1907 until 1933. The reverse displays a "family of eagles" motif designed by Miley Busiek.

Bullion-strike American Eagles are sold by the Mint not directly to the general public, but to approved authorized purchasers. These purchasers obtain the bullion coins based on the current spot price of the metal plus a small premium. They then sell the coins to secondary distributors for sale to other dealers and to the general public. Individuals can buy Proof, Reverse Proof, Burnished (called "Uncirculated" by the Mint), and other collector formats of the coins directly from the Mint.

## $5 Tenth-Ounce Gold

*Designers Augustus Saint-Gaudens (obv), Miley Busiek (rev); weight 3.393 grams; composition .9167 gold, .03 silver, .0533 copper (net weight 1/10 oz. pure gold); diameter 16.5 mm; reeded edge; mints: Philadelphia, West Point.*

*All modern Proof Eagles and sets must contain complete original U.S. Mint packaging for these values.*

| | Mintage | Unc. | PF |
|---|---|---|---|
| $5 MCMLXXXVI (1986) | 912,609 | $170 | |
| $5 MCMLXXXVII (1987) | 580,266 | 180 | |
| $5 MCMLXXXVIII (1988) | 159,500 | 175 | |
| $5 MCMLXXXVIII (1988)P | (143,881) | | $205 |
| $5 MCMLXXXIX (1989) | 264,790 | 180 | |
| $5 MCMLXXXIX (1989)P | (84,647) | | 195 |
| $5 MCMXC (1990) | 210,210 | 190 | |
| $5 MCMXC (1990)P | (99,349) | | 195 |
| $5 MCMXCI (1991) | 165,200 | 190 | |
| $5 MCMXCI (1991)P | (70,334) | | 195 |
| $5 1992 | 209,300 | 185 | |
| $5 1992P | (64,874) | | 185 |
| $5 1993 | 210,709 | 175 | |
| $5 1993P | (58,649) | | 185 |
| $5 1994 | 206,380 | 175 | |
| $5 1994W | (62,849) | | 185 |
| $5 1995 | 223,025 | 170 | |
| $5 1995W | (62,667) | | 185 |
| $5 1996 | 401,964 | 165 | |
| $5 1996W | (57,047) | | 185 |
| $5 1997 | 528,266 | 155 | |
| $5 1997W | (34,977) | | 185 |
| $5 1998 | 1,344,520 | 170 | |
| $5 1998W | (39,395) | | 185 |
| $5 1999 | 2,750,338 | 165 | |
| $5 1999W | (48,428) | | 185 |
| $5 1999W, Unc. made from unpolished Proof dies | *14,500* | | 800 |
| $5 2000 | 569,153 | 165 | |
| $5 2000W | (49,971) | | 185 |
| $5 2001 | 269,147 | 165 | |
| $5 2001W | (37,530) | | 185 |

| | Mintage | Unc. | PF |
|---|---|---|---|
| $5 2002 | 230,027 | $180 | |
| $5 2002W | (40,864) | | $185 |
| $5 2003 | 245,029 | 165 | |
| $5 2003W | (40,027) | | 185 |
| $5 2004 | 250,016 | 165 | |
| $5 2004W | (35,131) | | 185 |
| $5 2005 | 300,043 | 155 | |
| $5 2005W | (49,265) | | 185 |
| $5 2006 | 285,006 | 155 | |
| $5 2006W, Burnished | 20,643 | 190 | |
| $5 2006W | (47,277) | | 175 |
| $5 2007 | 190,010 | 155 | |
| $5 2007W, Burnished | 22,501 | 195 | |
| $5 2007W | (58,553) | | 175 |
| $5 2008 | 305,000 | 155 | |
| $5 2008W, Burnished | 12,657 | 275 | |
| $5 2008W | (28,116) | | 175 |
| $5 2009 | 270,000 | 155 | |
| $5 2010 | 435,000 | 155 | |
| $5 2010W | (54,285) | | 185 |
| $5 2011 | 350,000 | 155 | |
| $5 2011W | (42,697) | | 175 |
| $5 2012 | 290,000 | 155 | |
| $5 2012W | (20,637) | | 175 |
| $5 2013 | 555,000 | 155 | |
| $5 2013W | (21,738) | | 175 |
| $5 2014 | 545,000 | 155 | |
| $5 2014W | (22,725) | | 175 |
| $5 2015 | *980,000* | 155 | |
| $5 2015, Narrow Reeding | * | | |
| $5 2015W | *(16,851)* | | 175 |
| $5 2016 | *925,000* | 155 | |

* Included in number above.

| | Mintage | Unc. | PF |
|---|---|---|---|
| $5 2016W | *(38,788)* | | $175 |
| $5 2017 | *395,000* | $155 | |
| $5 2017W | (11,158) | | 175 |
| $5 2018 | *230,000* | 155 | |
| $5 2018W | *(21,343)* | | 175 |
| $5 2019 | | $155 | |
| $5 2019W | | | $175 |
| $5 2020 | | 155 | |
| $5 2020W | | | 175 |

## $10 Quarter-Ounce Gold

*Designers Augustus Saint-Gaudens (obv), Miley Busiek (rev); weight 8.483 grams; composition .9167 gold, .03 silver, .0533 copper (net weight 1/4 oz. pure gold); diameter 22 mm; reeded edge; mints: Philadelphia, West Point.*

| | Mintage | Unc. | PF |
|---|---|---|---|
| $10 MCMLXXXVI (1986) | 726,031 | $450 | |
| $10 MCMLXXXVII (1987) | 269,255 | 450 | |
| $10 MCMLXXXVIII (1988) | 49,000 | 650 | |
| $10 MCMLXXXVIII (1988)P | (98,028) | | $420 |
| $10 MCMLXXXIX (1989) | 81,789 | 600 | |
| $10 MCMLXXXIX (1989)P | (54,170) | | 420 |
| $10 MCMXC (1990) | 41,000 | 750 | |
| $10 MCMXC (1990)P | (62,674) | | 420 |
| $10 MCMXCI (1991) | 36,100 | 725 | |
| $10 MCMXCI (1991)P | (50,839) | | 420 |
| $10 1992 | 59,546 | 550 | |
| $10 1992P | (46,269) | | 420 |
| $10 1993 | 71,864 | 550 | |
| $10 1993P | (46,464) | | 420 |
| $10 1994 | 72,650 | 550 | |
| $10 1994W | (48,172) | | 420 |
| $10 1995 | 83,752 | 550 | |
| $10 1995W | (47,526) | | 420 |
| $10 1996 | 60,318 | 550 | |
| $10 1996W | (38,219) | | 420 |
| $10 1997 | 108,805 | 400 | |
| $10 1997W | (29,805) | | 420 |
| $10 1998 | 309,829 | 400 | |
| $10 1998W | (29,503) | | 420 |
| $10 1999 | 564,232 | 400 | |
| $10 1999W | (34,417) | | 420 |
| $10 1999W, Unc. made from unpolished Proof dies | *10,000* | 1,600 | |
| $10 2000 | 128,964 | 425 | |
| $10 2000W | (36,036) | | 420 |
| $10 2001 | 71,280 | 550 | |
| $10 2001W | (25,613) | | 420 |
| $10 2002 | 62,027 | 550 | |
| $10 2002W | (29,242) | | 420 |
| $10 2003 | 74,029 | 400 | |
| $10 2003W | (30,292) | | 420 |
| $10 2004 | 72,014 | $385 | |
| $10 2004W | (28,839) | | $420 |
| $10 2005 | 72,015 | 385 | |
| $10 2005W | (37,207) | | 420 |
| $10 2006 | 60,004 | 385 | |
| $10 2006W, Burnished | 15,188 | 650 | |
| $10 2006W | (36,127) | | 420 |
| $10 2007 | 34,004 | 550 | |
| $10 2007W, Burnished | 12,766 | 700 | |
| $10 2007W | (46,189) | | 420 |
| $10 2008 | 70,000 | 385 | |
| $10 2008W, Burnished | 8,883 | 900 | |
| $10 2008W | (18,877) | | 500 |
| $10 2009 | 110,000 | 385 | |
| $10 2010 | *86,000* | 385 | |
| $10 2010W | *(44,507)* | | 450 |
| $10 2011 | *80,000* | 385 | |
| $10 2011W | *(28,782)* | | 450 |
| $10 2012 | 90,000 | 385 | |
| $10 2012W | (13,926) | | 450 |
| $10 2013 | 114,500 | 385 | |
| $10 2013W | (12,782) | | 450 |
| $10 2014 | 90,000 | 385 | |
| $10 2014W | (14,790) | | 450 |
| $10 2015 | *158,000* | 385 | |
| $10 2015W | (15,775) | | 450 |
| $10 2016 | *152,000* | 385 | |
| $10 2016W | *(24,405)* | | 450 |
| $10 2017 | *64,000* | 385 | |
| $10 2017W | *(14,516)* | | 450 |
| $10 2018 | *62,000* | 385 | |
| $10 2018W | *(11,961)* | | 450 |
| $10 2019 | | 385 | |
| $10 2019W | | | 450 |
| $10 2020 | | 385 | |
| $10 2020W | | | 450 |

## $25 Half-Ounce Gold

*Designers Augustus Saint-Gaudens (obv), Miley Busiek (rev); weight 16.966 grams; composition .9167 gold, .03 silver, .0533 copper (net weight 1/2 oz. pure gold); diameter 27 mm; reeded edge; mints: Philadelphia, West Point.*

| | Mintage | Unc. | PF |
|---|---|---|---|
| $25 MCMLXXXVI (1986) | 599,566 | $800 | |
| $25 MCMLXXXVII (1987) | 131,255 | 950 | |
| $25 MCMLXXXVII (1987)P | (143,398) | | $800 |
| $25 MCMLXXXVIII (1988) | 45,000 | 1,500 | |
| $25 MCMLXXXIX (1988)P | (76,528) | | 800 |
| $25 MCMLXXXIX (1989) | 44,829 | 1,500 | |
| $25 MCMLXXXIX (1989)P | (44,798) | | 950 |
| $25 MCMXC (1990) | 31,000 | 1,800 | |
| $25 MCMXC (1990)P | (51,636) | | 850 |
| $25 MCMXCI (1991) | 24,100 | 2,750 | |
| $25 MCMXCI (1991)P | (53,125) | | 850 |
| $25 1992 | 54,404 | 900 | |
| $25 1992P | (40,976) | | 850 |
| $25 1993 | 73,324 | 900 | |
| $25 1993P | (43,819) | | 850 |
| $25 1994 | 62,400 | 900 | |
| $25 1994W | (44,584) | | 850 |
| $25 1995 | 53,474 | 1,000 | |
| $25 1995W | (45,388) | | 850 |
| $25 1996 | 39,287 | 1,350 | |
| $25 1996W | (35,058) | | 850 |
| $25 1997 | 79,605 | 900 | |
| $25 1997W | (26,344) | | 850 |
| $25 1998 | 169,029 | 750 | |
| $25 1998W | (25,374) | | 850 |
| $25 1999 | 263,013 | 900 | |
| $25 1999W | (30,427) | | 850 |
| $25 2000 | 79,287 | 900 | |
| $25 2000W | (32,028) | | 800 |
| $25 2001 | 48,047 | 1,250 | |
| $25 2001W | (23,240) | | 800 |
| $25 2002 | 70,027 | 900 | |
| $25 2002W | (26,646) | | 800 |
| $25 2003 | 79,029 | 800 | |
| $25 2003W | (28,270) | | 800 |
| $25 2004 | 98,040 | 800 | |
| $25 2004W | (27,330) | | $800 |
| $25 2005 | 80,023 | $775 | |
| $25 2005W | (34,311) | | 800 |
| $25 2006 | 66,005 | 775 | |
| $25 2006W, Burnished | 15,164 | 775 | |
| $25 2006W | (34,322) | | 800 |
| $25 2007 | 47,002 | 775 | |
| $25 2007W, Burnished | 11,455 | 1,100 | |
| $25 2007W | (44,025) | | 800 |
| $25 2008 | 61,000 | 775 | |
| $25 2008W, Burnished | 15,682 | 875 | |
| $25 2008W | (22,602) | | 1,000 |
| $25 2009 | 110,000 | 775 | |
| $25 2010 | *81,000* | 775 | |
| $25 2010W | *(44,527)* | | 850 |
| $25 2011 | *70,000* | 775 | |
| $25 2011W | *(26,781)* | | 800 |
| $25 2012 | 43,000 | 775 | |
| $25 2012W | (12,919) | | 800 |
| $25 2013 | 57,000 | 775 | |
| $25 2013W | (12,716) | | 800 |
| $25 2014 | 35,000 | 775 | |
| $25 2014W | (14,693) | | 800 |
| $25 2015 | *78,000* | 775 | |
| $25 2015W | (15,287) | | 800 |
| $25 2016 | *71,000* | 775 | |
| $25 2016W | *(23,585)* | | 800 |
| $25 2017 | *37,000* | 775 | |
| $25 2017W | *(12,717)* | | 800 |
| $25 2018 | *32,000* | 850 | |
| $25 2018W | *(9,204)* | | 800 |
| $25 2019 | | 775 | |
| $25 2019W | | | 800 |
| $25 2020 | | 775 | |
| $25 2020W | | | 800 |

*Note:* Some (but not all) 2020 American Gold Eagles will be privy-marked to observe the 75th anniversary of the end of World War II. As of press date, specific formats, mintmarks, and product options have not been announced.

## $50 One-Ounce Gold

*Designers Augustus Saint-Gaudens (obv), Miley Busiek (rev); weight 33.931 grams; composition .9167 gold, .03 silver, .0533 copper (net weight 1 oz. pure gold); diameter 32.7 mm; reeded edge; mints: Philadelphia, West Point.*

| | Mintage | Unc. | PF |
|---|---|---|---|
| $50 MCMLXXXVI (1986) | 1,362,650 | $1,500 | |
| $50 MCMLXXXVI (1986)W | (446,290) | | $1,700 |
| $50 MCMLXXXVII (1987) | 1,045,500 | 1,500 | |
| $50 MCMLXXXVII (1987)W | (147,498) | | 1,650 |
| $50 MCMLXXXVIII (1988) | 465,000 | 1,500 | |
| $50 MCMLXXXVIII (1988)W | (87,133) | | 1,650 |
| $50 MCMLXXXIX (1989) | 415,790 | 1,500 | |
| $50 MCMLXXXIX (1989)W | (54,570) | | 1,700 |
| $50 MCMXC (1990) | 373,210 | 1,500 | |
| $50 MCMXC (1990)W | (62,401) | | 1,700 |
| $50 MCMXCI (1991) | 243,100 | 1,500 | |
| $50 MCMXCI (1991)W | (50,411) | | 1,700 |
| $50 1992 | 275,000 | 1,500 | |
| $50 1992W | (44,826) | | 1,700 |
| $50 1993 | 480,192 | 1,500 | |
| $50 1993W | (34,369) | | 1,700 |
| $50 1994 | 221,633 | 1,500 | |
| $50 1994W | (46,674) | | 1,650 |
| $50 1995 | 200,636 | 1,500 | |
| $50 1995W | (46,368) | | 1,700 |
| $50 1996 | 189,148 | 1,500 | |
| $50 1996W | (36,153) | | 1,700 |
| $50 1997 | 664,508 | 1,500 | |
| $50 1997W | (32,999) | | 1,700 |
| $50 1998 | 1,468,530 | 1,500 | |
| $50 1998W | (25,886) | | 1,700 |
| $50 1999 | 1,505,026 | 1,500 | |
| $50 1999W | (31,427) | | 1,700 |
| $50 2000 | 433,319 | 1,500 | |
| $50 2000W | (33,007) | | 1,700 |
| $50 2001 | 143,605 | 1,500 | |
| $50 2001W | (24,555) | | 1,700 |
| $50 2002 | 222,029 | 1,500 | |
| $50 2002W | (27,499) | | 1,700 |
| $50 2003 | 416,032 | 1,500 | |
| $50 2003W | (28,344) | | 1,700 |
| $50 2004 | 417,019 | 1,500 | |
| $50 2004W | (28,215) | | 1,700 |
| $50 2005 | 356,555 | 1,500 | |
| $50 2005W | (35,246) | | 1,675 |
| $50 2006 | 237,510 | 1,500 | |
| $50 2006W, Burnished | 45,053 | 1,600 | |
| $50 2006W | (47,092) | | $1,675 |
| $50 2006W, Reverse Proof | (9,996) | | 2,650 |
| $50 2007 | 140,016 | $1,500 | |
| $50 2007W, Burnished | 18,066 | 1,550 | |
| $50 2007W | (51,810) | | 1,675 |
| $50 2008 | 710,000 | 1,500 | |
| $50 2008W, Burnished | 11,908 | 1,900 | |
| $50 2008W | (30,237) | | 1,675 |
| $50 2009 | 1,493,000 | 1,500 | |
| $50 2010 | *1,125,000* | 1,500 | |
| $50 2010W | *(59,480)* | | 1,675 |
| $50 2011 | *857,000* | 1,500 | |
| $50 2011W, Burnished | *8,729* | 2,200 | |
| $50 2011W | *(48,306)* | | 1,675 |
| $50 2012 | 675,000 | 1,500 | |
| $50 2012W, Burnished | 6,118 | 2,200 | |
| $50 2012W | (23,805) | | 1,700 |
| $50 2013 | 758,500 | 1,500 | |
| $50 2013W, Burnished | 7,293 | 1,550 | |
| $50 2013W | (24,709) | | 1,700 |
| $50 2014 | 425,000 | 1,500 | |
| $50 2014W, Burnished | 7,902 | 1,700 | |
| $50 2014W | (28,703) | | 1,700 |
| $50 2015 | *594,000* | 1,500 | |
| $50 2015W, Burnished | 6,533 | 1,700 | |
| $50 2015W | (40,004) | | 1,700 |
| $50 2016 | *817,500* | 1,500 | |
| $50 2016W, Burnished | | 1,700 | |
| $50 2016W | *(24,352)* | | 1,700 |
| $50 2017 | *228,500* | 1,500 | |
| $50 2017W, Burnished | *5,800* | 2,200 | |
| $50 2017W, Proof | *(9,245)* | | 1,700 |
| $50 2018 | *191,000* | 1,500 | |
| $50 2018W, Burnished | *7,913* | 1,700 | |
| $50 2018W | *(13,806)* | | 1,700 |
| $50 2019 | | 1,500 | |
| $50 2019W, Burnished | | 1,700 | |
| $50 2019W | | | 1,700 |
| $50 2020 | | 1,500 | |
| $50 2020W, Burnished | | 1,700 | |
| $50 2020W | | | 1,700 |

*Note:* Some (but not all) 2020 American Gold Eagles will be privy-marked to observe the 75th anniversary of the end of World War II. As of press date, specific formats, mintmarks, and product options have not been announced.

## Gold Bullion Sets

| | PF |
|---|---|
| 1987 Gold Set. $50, $25 | $2,450 |
| 1988 Gold Set. $50, $25, $10, $5 | 3,075 |
| 1989 Gold Set. $50, $25, $10, $5 | 3,265 |
| 1990 Gold Set. $50, $25, $10, $5 | 3,165 |
| 1991 Gold Set. $50, $25, $10, $5 | 3,165 |
| 1992 Gold Set. $50, $25, $10, $5 | 3,000 |
| 1993 Gold Set. $50, $25, $10, $5 | 3,000 |
| 1993 Bicentennial Gold Set. $25, $10, $5, $1 Silver Eagle, and medal | 1,400 |
| 1994 Gold Set. $50, $25, $10, $5 | 3,000 |
| 1995 Gold Set. $50, $25, $10, $5 | 3,000 |
| 1995 Anniversary Gold Set. $50, $25, $10, $5, and $1 Silver Eagle | 6,800 |
| 1996 Gold Set. $50, $25, $10, $5 | 3,000 |
| 1997 Gold Set. $50, $25, $10, $5 | 3,300 |
| 1997 Impressions of Liberty Set. $100 platinum, $50 gold, $1 silver | 3,200 |
| 1998 Gold Set. $50, $25, $10, $5 | 3,200 |
| 1999 Gold Set. $50, $25, $10, $5 | 3,000 |
| 2000 Gold Set. $50, $25, $10, $5 | 3,000 |
| 2001 Gold Set. $50, $25, $10, $5 | $3,000 |
| 2002 Gold Set. $50, $25, $10, $5 | 3,000 |
| 2003 Gold Set. $50, $25, $10, $5 | 3,000 |
| 2004 Gold Set. $50, $25, $10, $5 | 3,000 |
| 2005 Gold Set. $50, $25, $10, $5 | 3,000 |
| 2006 Gold Set. $50, $25, $10, $5 | 3,000 |
| 2007 Gold Set. $50, $25, $10, $5 | 3,000 |
| 2008 Gold Set. $50, $25, $10, $5 | 3,000 |
| 2010 Gold Set. $50, $25, $10, $5 **(a)** | 3,000 |
| 2011 Gold Set. $50, $25, $10, $5 | 3,000 |
| 2012 Gold Set. $50, $25, $10, $5 | 3,000 |
| 2013 Gold Set. $50, $25, $10, $5 | 3,000 |
| 2014 Gold Set. $50, $25, $10, $5 | 3,000 |
| 2015 Gold Set. $50, $25, $10, $5 | 3,000 |
| 2016 Gold Set. $50, $25, $10, $5 | 3,000 |
| 2017 Gold Set. $50, $25, $10, $5 | 3,000 |
| 2018 Gold Set. $50, $25, $10, $5 | 3,000 |
| 2019 Gold Set. $50, $25, $10, $5 | 3,000 |
| 2020 Gold Set. $50, $25, $10, $5 | 3,000 |

**a.** The U.S. Mint did not issue a 2009 gold set.

## 2006 20th Anniversary Sets

| | |
|---|---|
| 2006W $50 Gold Set. Uncirculated, Proof, Reverse Proof | $5,900 |
| 2006W 1-oz. Gold- and Silver-Dollar Set. Uncirculated | 1,800 |

## Gold Bullion Burnished Sets, 2006–2008

| | Unc. |
|---|---|
| 2006W Burnished Gold Set. $50, $25, $10, $5 | $3,000 |
| 2007W Burnished Gold Set. $50, $25, $10, $5 | 2,750 |
| 2008W Burnished Gold Set. $50, $25, $10, $5 | 2,900 |

## AMERICAN BUFFALO .9999 FINE GOLD BULLION COINS

American Buffalo gold bullion coins were the first .9999 fine (24-karat) gold coins made by the U.S. Mint. They are struck at the West Point facility and distributed in the same manner as American Eagle gold bullion coins. In 2006 and 2007, only one-ounce coins (with a $50 face value) were minted. In 2008 the Mint also produced half-ounce ($25 face value), quarter-ounce ($10), and tenth-ounce ($5) pieces in Proof and Uncirculated, individually and in sets.

Values change frequently and are based on prevailing bullion and fabrication costs relative to the weight of each denomination.

| | Mintage | Unc. | PF |
|---|---|---|---|
| $5 2008W, Burnished | 17,429 | $450 | |
| $5 2008W | (18,884) | | $450 |
| $10 2008W, Burnished | 9,949 | 1,000 | |
| $10 2008W | (13,125) | | 1,100 |
| $25 2008W, Burnished | 16,908 | 1,150 | |
| $25 2008W | (12,169) | | 1,600 |
| $50 2006 | 337,012 | 1,500 | |
| $50 2006W | (246,267) | | 1,550 |
| $50 2007 | 136,503 | 1,500 | |
| $50 2007W | (58,998) | | 1,550 |
| $50 2008 | 214,053 **(a)** | 1,500 | |
| $50 2008W | (18,863) | 2,200 | |
| $50 2008W, Burnished | 9,074 | | 2,500 |
| $50 2009 | 200,000 | 1,500 | |
| $50 2009W | (49,306) | | 1,550 |
| $50 2010 | 209,000 | 1,500 | |
| $50 2010W | (49,263) | | 1,550 |
| $50 2011 | 250,000 | 1,500 | |
| $50 2011W | *(28,693)* | | 1,500 |
| $50 2012 | 100,000 | $1,500 | |
| $50 2012W | (19,765) | | $1,650 |
| $50 2013 | 198,500 | 1,500 | |
| $50 2013W | (18,594) | | 1,600 |
| $50 2013W, Reverse Proof | (47,836) | | 1,500 |
| $50 2014 | 180,500 | 1,500 | |
| $50 2014W | (20,557) | | 1,450 |
| $50 2015 | *223,500* | 1,500 | |
| $50 2015W | *(16,591)* | | 1,500 |
| $50 2016 | *211,000* | 1,500 | |
| $50 2016W | | | 1,500 |
| $50 2017 | *99,500* | 1,500 | |
| $50 2017W | *(15,810)* | | 1,500 |
| $50 2018 | *121,500* | 1,500 | |
| $50 2018W | *(15,283)* | | 1,500 |
| $50 2019 | | 1,500 | |
| $50 2019W | | | 1,500 |
| $50 2020 | | 1,500 | |
| $50 2020W | | | 1,500 |

**a.** 24,553 sold as Lunar New Year Celebration coins.

## American Buffalo Gold Bullion Sets

| | Unc. | PF |
|---|---|---|
| 2008W Four-coin set ($5, $10, $25, $50) | | $5,500 |
| 2008W Four-coin set ($5, $10, $25, $50), Burnished | $4,500 | |
| 2008W Double Prosperity set. Uncirculated $25 Buffalo gold and $25 American Eagle coins | 2,000 | |

# FIRST SPOUSE $10 GOLD BULLION COINS

The U.S. Mint's First Spouse gold bullion coins are struck in .9999 fine (24-karat) gold. They weigh one-half ounce and have a $10 face value. The coins honor the nation's first spouses on the same schedule as the Mint's Presidential dollars program. Each features a portrait on the obverse, and on the reverse a unique design symbolic of the spouse's life and work. In instances where a president held office without a first spouse, the coin bears "an obverse image emblematic of Liberty as depicted on a circulating coin of that era and a reverse image emblematic of themes of that president's life."

The U.S. Mint has also issued a series of bronze medals with designs similar to those on the First Spouse bullion gold coins, available directly from the Mint.

*Designers various; composition .9999 gold, .0001 copper (net weight 1/2 oz. pure gold); weight 15.55 grams; diameter 26.5 mm; reeded edge; mint: West Point.*

Martha Washington Abigail Adams

*Entry continued on next page.*

Jefferson's Liberty

Dolley Madison

| | Mintage | Unc. | PF |
|---|---|---|---|
| $10 2007W, Martha Washington | (19,167). . .17,661 | $800 | $800 |
| $10 2007W, Abigail Adams | (17,149). . .17,142 | 800 | 800 |
| $10 2007W, Thomas Jefferson's Liberty | (19,815). . .19,823 | 800 | 800 |
| $10 2007W, Dolley Madison | (17,943). . .12,340 | 800 | 800 |

Elizabeth Monroe

Louisa Adams

Jackson's Liberty

Van Buren's Liberty

| | Mintage | Unc. | PF |
|---|---|---|---|
| $10 2008W, Elizabeth Monroe | (7,800). . . .4,462 | $800 | $800 |
| $10 2008W, Louisa Adams | (6,581). . . .3,885 | 800 | 850 |
| $10 2008W, Andrew Jackson's Liberty | (7,684). . . .4,609 | 850 | 900 |
| $10 2008W, Martin Van Buren's Liberty | (6,807). . . .3,826 | 850 | 1,000 |

Anna Harrison

Letitia Tyler Julia Tyler

Sarah Polk Margaret Taylor

| | Mintage | Unc. | PF |
|---|---|---|---|
| $10 2009W, Anna Harrison | (6,251). . . .3,645 | $800 | $900 |
| $10 2009W, Letitia Tyler | (5,296). . . .3,240 | 900 | 1,000 |
| $10 2009W, Julia Tyler | (4,844). . . .3,143 | 900 | 1,000 |
| $10 2009W, Sarah Polk | (5,151). . . .3,489 | 925 | 800 |
| $10 2009W, Margaret Taylor | (4,936). . . .3,627 | 800 | 800 |

Abigail Fillmore Jane Pierce

Buchanan's Liberty Mary Lincoln

| | Mintage | Unc. | PF |
|---|---|---|---|
| $10 2010W, Abigail Fillmore | (6,130) . . . . . . . .3,482 | $800 | $900 |
| $10 2010W, Jane Pierce | (4,775) . . . . . . . .3,338 | 800 | 950 |
| $10 2010W, James Buchanan's Liberty | (7,110) . . . . . . . .5,162 | 800 | 900 |
| $10 2010W, Mary Lincoln | (6,861) . . . . . . . .3,695 | 800 | 900 |

Eliza Johnson

Julia Grant

Lucy Hayes

Lucretia Garfield

| | Mintage | Unc. | PF |
|---|---|---|---|
| $10 2011W, Eliza Johnson. . . . . . . . . . . . . . . . . . . . . . . . . . . . . . . . . . . .(3,887) . . . . . . . . | *2,905* | $800 | $950 |
| $10 2011W, Julia Grant. . . . . . . . . . . . . . . . . . . . . . . . . . . . . . . . . . . . .(3,943) . . . . . . . . | *2,892* | 800 | 950 |
| $10 2011W, Lucy Hayes . . . . . . . . . . . . . . . . . . . . . . . . . . . . . . . . . . . .(3,868) . . . . . . . . | *2,196* | 950 | 900 |
| $10 2011W, Lucretia Garfield . . . . . . . . . . . . . . . . . . . . . . . . . . . . . . . .(3,653) . . . . . . . . | *2,168* | 950 | 900 |

Alice Paul

Frances Cleveland (Type 1)

Caroline Harrison

Frances Cleveland (Type 2)

| | Mintage | Unc. | PF |
|---|---|---|---|
| $10 2012W, Alice Paul. . . . . . . . . . . . . . . . . . . . . . . . . . . . . . . . . . . . .(3,505) . . . . . . . . | 2,798 | $850 | $875 |
| $10 2012W, Frances Cleveland, Type 1 . . . . . . . . . . . . . . . . . . . . . . . . .(3,158) . . . . . . . . | 2,454 | 850 | 925 |
| $10 2012W, Caroline Harrison . . . . . . . . . . . . . . . . . . . . . . . . . . . . . . .(3,046) . . . . . . . . | 2,436 | 850 | 925 |
| $10 2012W, Frances Cleveland, Type 2 . . . . . . . . . . . . . . . . . . . . . . . . .(3,104) . . . . . . . . | 2,425 | 850 | 925 |

Ida McKinley

Edith Roosevelt

Helen Taft

Ellen Wilson

Edith Wilson

| | Mintage | Unc. | PF |
|---|---|---|---|
| $10 2013W, Ida McKinley . . . . . (2,724) | 2,008 | $825 | $900 |
| $10 2013W, Edith Roosevelt . . . . . (2,840) | 2,027 | 825 | 900 |
| $10 2013W, Helen Taft. . . . . (2,598) | 1,993 | 825 | 900 |
| $10 2013W, Ellen Wilson . . . . . (2,511) | 1,980 | 825 | 900 |
| $10 2013W, Edith Wilson. . . . . (2,464) | 1,974 | 825 | 900 |

Florence Harding

Grace Coolidge

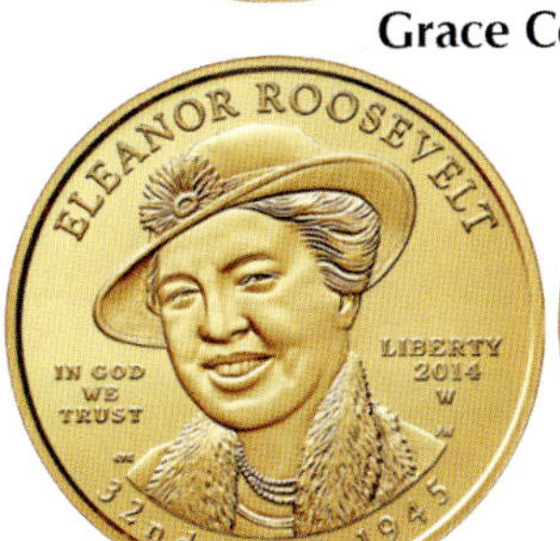

Lou Hoover

Eleanor Roosevelt

*See next page for chart.*

| | Mintage | | Unc. | PF |
|---|---|---|---|---|
| $10 2014W, Florence Harding | (2,372) | 1,944 | $825 | $875 |
| $10 2014W, Grace Coolidge | (2,315) | 1,949 | 825 | 900 |
| $10 2014W, Lou Hoover | (2,392) | 1,936 | 825 | 900 |
| $10 2014W, Eleanor Roosevelt | *(2,377)* | *1,886* | 1,600 | 1,400 |

Elizabeth Truman

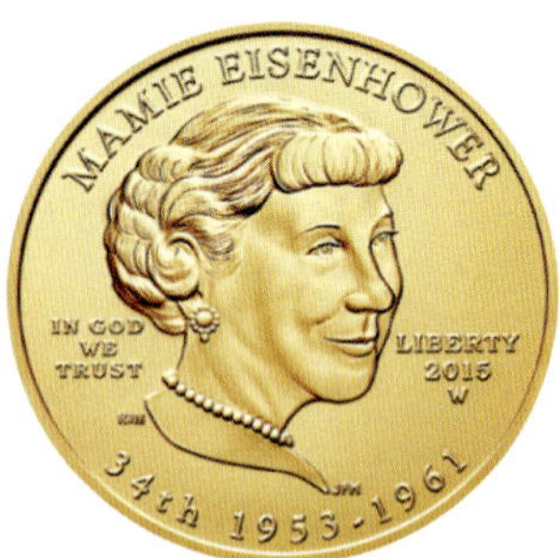

Mamie Eisenhower

Jacqueline Kennedy

Claudia Taylor "Lady Bird" Johnson

| | Mintage | | Unc. | PF |
|---|---|---|---|---|
| $10 2015W, Elizabeth Truman | (2,747) | 1,946 | $825 | $900 |
| $10 2015W, Mamie Eisenhower | (2,704) | 2,102 | 825 | 900 |
| $10 2015W, Jacqueline Kennedy | *(11,222)* | 6,771 | 825 | 900 |
| $10 2015W, Claudia Taylor "Lady Bird" Johnson | (2,653) | 1,927 | 825 | 900 |

Pat Nixon

Betty Ford

Nancy Reagan

| | Mintage | | Unc. | PF |
|---|---|---|---|---|
| $10 2016W, Pat Nixon | *(2,645)* | *1,839* | $825 | $900 |
| $10 2016W, Betty Ford | *(2,471)* | *1,824* | 825 | 900 |
| $10 2016W, Nancy Reagan | *(3,548)* | *2,009* | 825 | 900 |

## MMIX ULTRA HIGH RELIEF GOLD COIN

A modern version of the famous United States 1907 Ultra High Relief double eagle gold pattern was produced in 2009 at the Philadelphia Mint. It was made as a tour de force to demonstrate how technical advances in minting techniques can now accommodate manufacturing such a coin. The original design was never made for commercial use because it was at that time impossible to make it in sufficient quantities.

The original striding-Liberty design used on these coins was the artistry of Augustus Saint-Gaudens. A version of it in much lower relief was used on double eagle coins minted from 1907 to 1933. In recreating the artist's attempt to mint a stunning coin in ultra high relief, the 2009 version was made in a slightly smaller diameter, and composed of 24-karat gold, thus making it easier to strike and maintain the fidelity of the design. Through 21st-century technology the original Saint-Gaudens plasters were digitally mapped by the Mint and used in the die-making process. The date was changed to 2009, and four additional stars were added to represent the current 50 states. Also included was the inscription "In God We Trust," which was not used on the 1907 version.

The MMIX Ultra High Relief gold coins are 4 mm thick and contain one ounce of .999 fine gold. All are Uncirculated (specimen strikes). All were made at the U.S. Mint's West Point facility, and were packaged in a special mahogany box.

**MMIX Ultra High Relief Gold Coin**
*Photographed at an angle to show the edge, lettered E PLURIBUS UNUM, and the depth of relief.*

| | Mintage | Unc. |
|---|---|---|
| MMIX Ultra High Relief $20 Gold Coin | 114,427 | $1,800 |

## 400TH ANNIVERSARY OF THE MAYFLOWER GOLD COIN

In 2020 the United States Mint will recognize the 400th anniversary of the Pilgrims' landing at Plymouth Rock aboard the Mayflower. The Mint will issue a ten-dollar gold coin under authority granted by Congress to the secretary of the Treasury. The coin will have the same fineness (.9167) as the American Gold Eagle. The Mint will also issue a related silver medal. As of press date, specific formats, mintmarks, and product options have not been announced.

## 75TH ANNIVERSARY OF THE END OF WORLD WAR II GOLD COIN

Under the Treasury secretary's authority to issue gold coins "from time to time" without specific commemorative legislation, in 2020 the Mint will issue a .9167 fine gold twenty-five-dollar coin to mark the 75th anniversary of the end of World War II. As of press date, specific formats, mintmarks, and product options have not been announced. The Mint will also issue a related silver medal, privy-marked West Point quarter dollars, and privy-marked gold and silver American Eagles in celebration of the anniversary.

## AMERICAN LIBERTY HIGH RELIEF GOLD COINS

The first American Liberty High Relief .9999-fine gold coin, with a weight of one ounce and a face value of $100, was minted at West Point in 2015. The coin was not congressionally mandated, instead being created under authority granted to the Secretary of the Treasury by federal law—31 U.S.C. Section 5112 (i)(4)(C).

The design was strongly influenced by the Citizens Coinage Advisory Committee, who, according to a Mint spokesperson, "emphasized creating a 'modern' Liberty that reflects the nation's diversity." The U.S. Commission of Fine Arts also reviewed designs and made recommendations.

The designs for the American Liberty High Relief gold coins are created to take full advantage of the same high-relief techniques used to create the MMIX Ultra High Relief gold coin. The design of the 2015 American Liberty High Relief gold coin was adapted for a silver medal in 2016, but in 2017 the Mint continued the series with a 1792–2017 American Liberty High Relief gold coin. The series is slated to continue biennially, with a new design being issued every two years. In the years between new gold one-ounce designs, gold 1/10-ounce coins featuring the same designs are issued. The Mint also strikes high-relief silver medals based on each design.

2015-W

1792–2017-W

2018-W, $10

2019-W

| | Mintage | Unc. | PF |
|---|---|---|---|
| $100 2015W, 1 oz. | *49,325* | $1,950 | |
| $100 1792–2017W, 1 oz. | | | $2,000 |
| $10 2018W, 1/10 oz. | | | 245 |
| $100 2019W, 1 oz. | | | 1,800 |

## AMERICAN EAGLE PLATINUM BULLION COINS

American Eagle platinum coins have been made in four denominations. The one-hundred-dollar coin contains one ounce of pure platinum. Fractional denominations (not minted after 2008) containing 1/2 oz., 1/4 oz., and 1/10 oz. are denominated fifty, twenty-five, and ten dollars, respectively. In their first and twentieth years of issue (1997 and 2017), Proof platinum coins had the same reverse design as regular strikes. Proof coins of 1998 to 2016 featured a unique reverse design each year. Since 2018 Proofs have featured a new common reverse, with changing obverse designs.

As of this printing, the spot price of platinum is about $950 per ounce.

### Proof Platinum Reverse Designs

**1997.**

**1998: Eagle Over New England. "Vistas of Liberty" series.**

**1999: Eagle Above Southeastern Wetlands. "Vistas of Liberty" series.**

**2000: Eagle Above America's Heartland. "Vistas of Liberty" series.**

**2001: Eagle Above America's Southwest. "Vistas of Liberty" series.**

**2002: Eagle Fishing in America's Northwest. "Vistas of Liberty" series.**

**2003.**

**2004.**

**2005.**

2006: Legislative Branch. "Foundations of Democracy" series.

2007: Executive Branch. "Foundations of Democracy" series.

2008. Judicial Branch. "Foundations of Democracy" series.

2009. To Form a More Perfect Union. "Preamble to the Constitution" series.

2010: To Establish Justice. "Preamble to the Constitution" series.

2011: To Insure Domestic Tranquility. "Preamble to the Constitution" series.

2012: To Provide for the Common Defence. "Preamble to the Constitution" series.

2013: To Promote the General Welfare. "Preamble to the Constitution" series.

2014: To Secure the Blessings of Liberty to Ourselves and Our Posterity. "Preamble to the Constitution" series.

2015: Liberty Nurtures Freedom. "Torches of Liberty" series.

2016: Portrait of Liberty. "Torches of Liberty" series.

Common Reverse: "Preamble to the Declaration of Independence" series.

2018: Life. "Preamble to the Declaration of Independence" series.

2019: Liberty. "Preamble to the Declaration of Independence" series.

2020: Pursuit of Happiness. "Preamble to the Declaration of Independence" series.

## $10 Tenth-Ounce Platinum

*Designers John M. Mercanti (obv), Thomas D. Rogers Sr. (orig rev); weight 0.10005 oz.; composition .9995 platinum; diameter 16.5 mm; reeded edge; mints: Philadelphia, West Point.*

| | Mintage | Unc. | PF |
|---|---|---|---|
| $10 1997 | 70,250 | $120 | |
| $10 1997W | (36,993) | | $140 |
| $10 1998 | 39,525 | 120 | |
| $10 1998W | (19,847) | | 140 |
| $10 1999 | 55,955 | 120 | |
| $10 1999W | (19,133) | | 140 |
| $10 2000 | 34,027 | 120 | |
| $10 2000W | (15,651) | | 140 |
| $10 2001 | 52,017 | 120 | |
| $10 2001W | (12,174) | | 140 |
| $10 2002 | 23,005 | 120 | |
| $10 2002W | (12,365) | | 140 |
| $10 2003 | 22,007 | 120 | |
| $10 2003W | (9,534) | | 140 |
| $10 2004 | 15,010 | $120 | |
| $10 2004W | (7,161) | | $150 |
| $10 2005 | 14,013 | 120 | |
| $10 2005W | (8,104) | | 140 |
| $10 2006 | 11,001 | 120 | |
| $10 2006W, Burnished | 3,544 | 410 | |
| $10 2006W | (10,205) | | 140 |
| $10 2007 | 13,003 | 125 | |
| $10 2007W, Burnished | 5,556 | 200 | |
| $10 2007W | (8,176) | | 140 |
| $10 2008 | 17,000 | 120 | |
| $10 2008W, Burnished | 3,706 | 335 | |
| $10 2008W | (5,138) | | 275 |

## $25 Quarter-Ounce Platinum

*Designers John M. Mercanti (obv), Thomas D. Rogers Sr. (orig rev); weight 0.2501 oz.; composition .9995 platinum; diameter 22 mm; reeded edge; mints: Philadelphia, West Point.*

2007 Proof, Frosted FREEDOM variety.

| | Mintage | Unc. | PF |
|---|---|---|---|
| $25 1997 | 27,100 | $300 | |
| $25 1997W | (18,628) | | $320 |
| $25 1998 | 38,887 | 300 | |
| $25 1998W | (14,873) | | $320 |
| $25 1999 | 39,734 | $300 | |
| $25 1999W | (13,507) | | 320 |

*Chart continued on next page.*

| | Mintage | Unc. | PF |
|---|---|---|---|
| $25 2000 | 20,054 | $300 | |
| $25 2000W | (11,995) | | $320 |
| $25 2001 | 21,815 | 300 | |
| $25 2001W | (8,847) | | 320 |
| $25 2002 | 27,405 | 300 | |
| $25 2002W | (9,282) | | 320 |
| $25 2003 | 25,207 | 300 | |
| $25 2003W | (7,044) | | 320 |
| $25 2004 | 18,010 | 300 | |
| $25 2004W | (5,193) | | 500 |
| $25 2005 | 12,013 | 300 | |
| $25 2005W | (6,592) | | 325 |
| $25 2006 | 12,001 | $300 | |
| $25 2006W, Burnished | 2,676 | 600 | |
| $25 2006W | (7,813) | | $320 |
| $25 2007 | 8,402 | 300 | |
| $25 2007W, Burnished | 3,690 | 550 | |
| $25 2007W | (6,017) | | 320 |
| $25 2007W, Frosted FREEDOM | (21) | | — |
| $25 2008 | 22,800 | 300 | |
| $25 2008W, Burnished | 2,481 | 750 | |
| $25 2008W | (4,153) | | 550 |

## $50 Half-Ounce Platinum

*Designers John M. Mercanti (obv), Thomas D. Rogers Sr. (orig rev); weight 0.5003 oz.; composition .9995 platinum; diameter 27 mm; reeded edge; mints: Philadelphia, West Point.*

| | Mintage | Unc. | PF |
|---|---|---|---|
| $50 1997 | 20,500 | $600 | |
| $50 1997W | (15,431) | | $650 |
| $50 1998 | 32,415 | 600 | |
| $50 1998W | (13,836) | | 650 |
| $50 1999 | 32,309 | 600 | |
| $50 1999W | (11,103) | | 650 |
| $50 2000 | 18,892 | 600 | |
| $50 2000W | (11,049) | | 650 |
| $50 2001 | 12,815 | 600 | |
| $50 2001W | (8,254) | | 650 |
| $50 2002 | 24,005 | 600 | |
| $50 2002W | (8,772) | | 650 |
| $50 2003 | 17,409 | 600 | |
| $50 2003W | (7,131) | | 650 |
| $50 2004 | 13,236 | 600 | |
| $50 2004W | (5,063) | | $650 |
| $50 2005 | 9,013 | $600 | |
| $50 2005W | (5,942) | | 650 |
| $50 2006 | 9,602 | 600 | |
| $50 2006W, Burnished | 2,577 | 800 | |
| $50 2006W | (7,649) | | 650 |
| $50 2007 | 7,001 | 650 | |
| $50 2007W, Burnished | 3,635 | 825 | |
| $50 2007W | (25,519) | | 650 |
| $50 2007W, Rev Proof | (19,583) | | 800 |
| $50 2007W, Frosted FREEDOM **(a)** | (21) | | — |
| $50 2008 | 14,000 | 600 | |
| $50 2008W, Burnished | 2,253 | 900 | |
| $50 2008W | (4,020) | | 950 |

**a.** See page 391 for illustration.

## $100 One-Ounce Platinum

*Designers John M. Mercanti (obv), Thomas D. Rogers Sr. (orig rev); weight 1.0005 oz.; composition .9995 platinum; diameter 32.7 mm; reeded edge; mints: Philadelphia, West Point.*

| | Mintage | Unc. | PF |
|---|---|---|---|
| $100 1997 | 56,000 | $1,200 | |
| $100 1997W | (20,851) | | $1,300 |
| $100 1998 | 133,002 | 1,200 | |
| $100 1998W | (14,912) | | 1,300 |
| $100 1999 | 56,707 | 1,200 | |
| $100 1999W | (12,363) | | 1,300 |
| $100 2000 | 10,003 | 1,200 | |
| $100 2000W | (12,453) | | 1,300 |
| $100 2001 | 14,070 | 1,200 | |
| $100 2001W | (8,969) | | 1,300 |
| $100 2002 | 11,502 | 1,200 | |
| $100 2002W | (9,834) | | 1,300 |
| $100 2003 | 8,007 | 1,200 | |
| $100 2003W | (8,246) | | 1,300 |
| $100 2004 | 7,009 | 1,200 | |
| $100 2004W | (6,007) | | 1,300 |
| $100 2005 | 6,310 | 1,200 | |
| $100 2005W | (6,602) | | 1,300 |
| $100 2006 | 6,000 | 1,200 | |
| $100 2006W, Burnished | 3,068 | 2,100 | |
| $100 2006W | (9,152) | | 1,300 |
| $100 2007 | 7,202 | 1,200 | |
| $100 2007W, Burnished | 4,177 | 1,900 | |
| $100 2007W | (8,363) | | 1,300 |
| $100 2007W, Frosted FREEDOM **(a)** | (12) | | — |
| $100 2008 | 21,800 | $1,200 | |
| $100 2008W, Burnished | 2,876 | 2,200 | |
| $100 2008W | (4,769) | | $1,900 |
| $100 2009W | (7,945) | | 1,300 |
| $100 2010W | (14,790) | | 1,300 |
| $100 2011W | *(14,835)* | | 1,300 |
| $100 2012W | (10,084) | | 1,300 |
| $100 2013W | (5,745) | | 1,950 |
| $100 2014 | 16,900 | 1,200 | |
| $100 2014W | (4,596) | | 1,850 |
| $100 2015W | (3,881) | | 2,500 |
| $100 2016 | *20,000* | 1,000 | |
| $100 2016W | (9,151) | | 1,200 |
| $100 2017 | *20,000* | 1,200 | |
| $100 2017W | *(8,892)* | | 1,300 |
| $100 2018 | *30,000* | 1,200 | |
| $100 2018W | *(12,411)* | | 1,250 |
| $100 2019 | | 1,200 | |
| $100 2019W | | | 1,250 |
| $100 2020 | | 1,200 | |
| $100 2020W | | | 1,250 |

**a.** See page 391 for illustration.

## Platinum Bullion Sets

| | Unc. | PF |
|---|---|---|
| 1997W Platinum Set. $100, $50, $25, $10 | | $2,500 |
| 1998W Platinum Set. $100, $50, $25, $10 | | 2,500 |
| 1999W Platinum Set. $100, $50, $25, $10 | | 2,500 |
| 2000W Platinum Set. $100, $50, $25, $10 | | 2,500 |
| 2001W Platinum Set. $100, $50, $25, $10 | | 2,500 |
| 2002W Platinum Set. $100, $50, $25, $10 | | 2,500 |
| 2003W Platinum Set. $100, $50, $25, $10 | | 2,500 |
| 2004W Platinum Set. $100, $50, $25, $10 | | 2,500 |
| 2005W Platinum Set. $100, $50, $25, $10 | | 2,500 |
| 2006W Platinum Set. $100, $50, $25, $10 | | 2,500 |
| 2006W Platinum Burnished Set. $100, $50, $25, $10 | $3,800 | |
| 2007W Platinum Set. $100, $50, $25, $10 | | 2,500 |
| 2007W Platinum Burnished Set. $100, $50, $25, $10 | 3,400 | |
| 2008W Platinum Set. $100, $50, $25, $10 | | 3,800 |
| 2008W Platinum Burnished Set. $100, $50, $25, $10 | 3,500 | |

## American Eagle 10th Anniversary Platinum Set

| | PF |
|---|---|
| Two-coin set containing one Proof platinum half-ounce and one Enhanced Reverse Proof half-ounce dated 2007W. Housed in hardwood box with mahogany finish | $1,500 |

## AMERICAN EAGLE PALLADIUM BULLION COINS (2017 TO DATE)

*Designer Adolph A. Weinman; composition .9995 palladium; net weight 1 oz. pure palladium; diameter 32.7 mm; reeded edge; mints: Philadelphia, West Point.*

The American Palladium Eagle features a high-relief obverse design derived from artist Adolph Weinman's Winged Liberty dime of 1916 to 1945. The reverse is a high-relief version of Weinman's 1907 American Institute of Architects gold medal reverse, showing an eagle grasping a branch.

Bullion-strike coins are minted in Philadelphia and distributed through the Mint's authorized purchasers. Proof, Reverse Proof, and Uncirculated numismatic versions struck at the West Point Mint are sold by the Mint directly to collectors.

As of this printing, the spot price of palladium is about $2,400 per ounce.

| | Mintage | Unc. | PF |
|---|---|---|---|
| 2017 | *15,000* | $2,400 | |
| 2018W | *(14,986)* | | $2,700 |
| 2019W, Reverse Proof | *(15,621)* | | 2,750 |
| 2020W | | 2,400 | |

United States patterns are a fascinating part of numismatics that encompass a myriad of designs and experimental pieces made by the U.S. Mint to test new concepts and motifs, to provide coins for numismatists, and for other reasons. The book *United States Pattern Coins,* by J. Hewitt Judd, gives extensive details of the history and characteristics of more than 2,000 different pattern varieties from 1792 to the present era.

Patterns provide students and collectors a chronology of the continuing efforts of engravers and artists to present their work for approval. Throughout the 225+ years of federal coinage production, concepts meant to improve various aspects of circulating coins have been proposed and incorporated into representative patterns. In some instances, changes have been prompted by an outcry for higher aesthetics, a call for a more convenient denomination, or a need to overcome striking deficiencies. In many other instances, the Mint simply created special coins for the numismatic trade—often controversial in their time, but enthusiastically collected today. Certain patterns, bearing particular proposed designs or innovations, provided tangible examples for Mint and Treasury Department officials or members of Congress to evaluate. If adopted, the pattern design became a familiar regular-issue motif; those that were rejected have become part of American numismatic history.

The patterns listed and illustrated in this section are representative of a much larger group. Such pieces generally include die and hub trials, off-metal Proof strikings of regular issues, and various combinations of dies that were sometimes struck at a later date. Certain well-known members of this extended pattern family historically have been included with regular issues in many popular, general-circulation numismatic reference books. The four-dollar gold Stellas of 1879 and 1880; certain Gobrecht dollars of 1836, 1838, and 1839; and the Flying Eagle cents of 1856 are such examples. No official mintage figures of patterns and related pieces were recorded in most instances, and the number extant of each can usually only be estimated from auction appearances and from those found in museum holdings and important private collections. Although most patterns are very rare, the 2,000+ distinct varieties make them unexpectedly collectible—not by one of each, but by selected available examples from favorite types or categories.

Unlike regular coin issues that were emitted through the usual channels of commerce, and Proofs of regular issues that were struck expressly for sale to collectors, patterns were not intended to be officially sold. Yet as a matter of Mint policy in accordance with certain previously established restrictions, countless patterns were secretly and unofficially sold and traded to favorite dealers and collectors, disseminated to government officials, and occasionally made available to numismatic societies. Not until mid-1887 did the Mint enforce stringent regulations prohibiting their sale and distribution, although there had been several misleading statements to this effect earlier. In succeeding decades the Mint, while not making patterns available to numismatists, did place certain examples in the Mint Collection, now called the National Numismatic Collection, in the Smithsonian Institution. On other occasions, selected patterns were obtained by Mint and Treasury officials, or otherwise spared from destruction. Today, with the exception of certain cents and five-cent pieces of 1896, all pattern coins dated after 1885 are extremely rare.

The private possession of patterns has not been without its controversy. Most significant was the 1910 seizure by government agents of a parcel containing some 23 pattern pieces belonging to John W. Haseltine, a leading Philadelphia coin dealer with undisclosed private ties to Mint officials. The government asserted that the patterns had been removed from the Mint without authority, and that they remained the property of the United States. Haseltine's attorney successfully used the Mint's pre-1887 policies in his defense, and recovered the patterns a year after their confiscation.

This set precedent for ownership, at least for the patterns minted prior to 1887, as all of the pieces in question predated that year. Today, pattern coins can be legally held.

Among the grandest impressions ever produced at the U.S. Mint are the two varieties of pattern fifty-dollar gold pieces of 1877. Officially titled *half unions,* these large patterns were created at the request of certain politicians with interests tied to the gold-producing state of California. Specimens were struck in copper, and one of each variety was struck in gold. Both of the gold pieces were purchased around 1908 by numismatist William H. Woodin (who, years later, in 1933, served as President Franklin D. Roosevelt's first secretary of the Treasury). The Mint desired to re-obtain the pieces for its own collection, and through a complex trade deal for quantities of other patterns, did so, adding them to the Mint Collection. Now preserved in the Smithsonian Institution, these half unions are regarded as national treasures.

Special credit is due to the following individuals for contributing to this feature: Q. David Bowers, Marc Crane, Robert Hughes, Julian Leidman, Andy Lustig, Saul Teichman, and Eddie Wilson.

Shown below are just three out of more than 2,000 distinct patterns made by the U.S. Mint over the years. The following sources are recommended for additional information, descriptions, and complete listings:

- *United States Pattern Coins,* 10th ed., J. Hewitt Judd, ed. by Q. David Bowers, 2009.
- *United States Patterns and Related Issues,* Andrew W. Pollock III, 1994. (Out of print)
- www.harrybassfoundation.org
- www.uspatterns.com

Judd-52

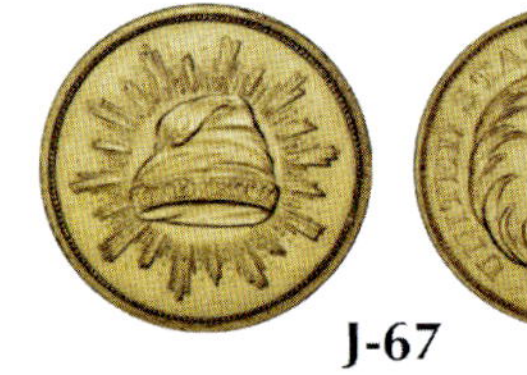

J-67

| | PF-60 | PF-63 | PF-65 |
|---|---|---|---|
| **1836 Two-cent piece (J-52, billon)** This proposal for a two-cent coin is one of the earliest collectible patterns. It was designed by Christian Gobrecht. *(21–30 known)* . . | $3,000 | $5,000 | $8,500 |
| *$8,625, PF-65, Heritage auction, January 2009* | | | |
| **1836 Gold dollar (J-67, gold)** Gobrecht styled the first gold dollar pattern after the familiar Mexican "cap and rays" design, then legal tender in this country. *(31–75 known) $24,725, PF-65, Stack's Bowers auction, November 2010* . . . . . . . | 7,500 | 12,500 | 30,000 |

J-1373

| | PF-60 | PF-63 | PF-65 |
|---|---|---|---|
| **1874 Bickford eagle (J-1373, gold)** Dana Bickford, a manufacturer, proposed a ten-dollar gold coin that would be exchangeable at set rates with other world currencies. Patterns were made, but the idea proved impractical. *(2 known)* . . . . | — | $550,000 | $1,500,000 |
| *$1,265,000, PF-65 DC, Heritage auction, January 2010* | | | |

The expression *private gold,* used with reference to coins struck outside the United States Mint, is a general term. In the sense that no state or territory had authority to coin money, *private gold* simply refers to those interesting necessity pieces of various shapes, denominations, and degrees of intrinsic worth that were circulated in isolated areas of the United States by individuals, assayers, bankers, and so on. Some numismatists use the words *territorial* and *state* to cover certain issues because they were coined and circulated in a territory or state. While the state of California properly sanctioned the ingots stamped by F.D. Kohler as state assayer, in no instance were any of the gold pieces struck by authority of any of the territorial governments.

The stamped fifty-dollar and other gold coins, sometimes called *ingots,* but in coin form, were made by Augustus Humbert, the United States Assayer of Gold, but were not receivable at face value for government payments, despite the fact that Humbert was an official agent. However, such pieces circulated widely in commerce.

Usually, private coins were circulated due to a shortage of regular coinage. In the Western states particularly, money became so scarce that the very commodity the pioneers had come so far to acquire was converted into a local medium of exchange.

Ephraim Brasher's New York doubloon of 1787 is also a private American gold issue and is described on page 67.

## TEMPLETON REID

### Georgia Gold 1830

The first private gold coinage in the 19th century was struck by Templeton Reid, a jeweler and gunsmith, in Milledgeville, Georgia, in July 1830. To be closer to the mines, he moved to Gainesville, where most of his coins were made. Although weights were accurate, Reid's assays were not and his coins were slightly short of claimed value. He was severely attacked in the newspapers and soon lost the public's confidence. He closed his mint before the end of October in 1830; his output had amounted to only about 1,600 coins. Denominations struck were $2.50, $5, and $10.

| | VF | EF | AU |
|---|---|---|---|
| 1830 $2.50 . . . . . . . | $150,000 | $200,000 | $325,000 |

| | VF | EF | AU |
|---|---|---|---|
| 1830 $5 *(7 known)* . . | $400,000 | $575,000 | $725,000 |

| | VF | EF |
|---|---|---|
| 1830 TEN DOLLARS *(6 known)* . . . . . . . . . . . . . | $725,000 | $975,000 |

| | VF | EF |
|---|---|---|
| (No Date) TEN DOLLARS *(3 known)* . . . . . . . . . . . . . | — | |

### California Gold 1849

The enigmatic later issues of Templeton Reid were probably made from California gold. Reid, who never went to California, was then a cotton-gin maker in Columbus, Georgia, where he died in 1851. The coins were in denominations of ten and twenty-five dollars. Struck copies of both exist in various metals. The only example known of the twenty-five-dollar piece was stolen from the cabinet of the U.S. Mint on August 16, 1858. It was never recovered.

| | |
|---|---|
| 1849 TEN DOLLAR CALIFORNIA GOLD | *(unique, in Smithsonian collection)* |
| 1849 TWENTY-FIVE DOLLARS CALIFORNIA GOLD | *(unknown)* |

## THE BECHTLERS
## RUTHERFORD COUNTY, NC, 1831–1852

A skilled German metallurgist, Christopher Bechtler, assisted by his son August and his nephew, also named Christopher, operated a private mint in Rutherford County, North Carolina. Rutherford County and other areas in the Piedmont region of North Carolina and Georgia were the principal sources of the nation's gold supply from 1790 until the California gold strikes in 1848.

The coins minted by the Bechtlers were of only three denominations, but they covered a wide variety of weights and sizes. Rotated dies are common throughout the series. In 1831, the Bechtlers produced the first gold dollar in the United States. (The U.S. Mint struck its first circulating gold dollar in 1849.) Bechtler coins were well accepted by the public and circulated widely in the Southeast.

The inscription AUGUST 1. 1834 on several varieties of five-dollar pieces has a special significance. The secretary of the Treasury recommended to the Mint director that gold coins of the reduced weight bear the authorization date. This was not done on federal gold coinage, but the elder Christopher Bechtler evidently acted on the recommendation to avoid potential difficulty with Treasury authorities.

### Christopher Bechtler

| | VF | EF | AU | Unc. |
|---|---|---|---|---|
| ONE GOLD DOLLAR N. CAROLINA, 30.G., Star | $3,000 | $4,500 | $7,000 | $15,000 |
| ONE GOLD DOLLAR N. CAROLINA, 28.G Centered, No Star | 5,000 | 6,000 | 11,500 | 26,000 |
| ONE GOLD DOLLAR N. CAROLINA, 28.G High, No Star | 9,000 | 15,000 | 23,000 | 35,000 |

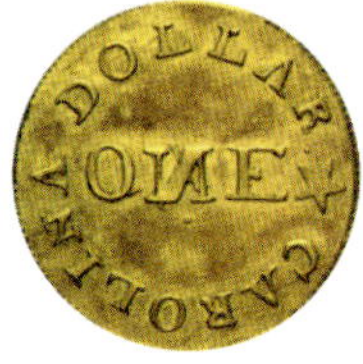

| | VF | EF | AU | Unc. |
|---|---|---|---|---|
| ONE DOLLAR CAROLINA, 28.G, N Reversed | $2,600 | $3,200 | $4,750 | $8,250 |
| 2.50 NORTH CAROLINA, 20 C. Without 75.G. | 28,000 | 38,500 | 57,500 | 120,000 |

| | VF | EF | AU | Unc. |
|---|---|---|---|---|
| 2.50 NORTH CAROLINA, 75.G., 20 C. RUTHERFORD in a Circle. Border of Large Beads. | $26,000 | $36,000 | $52,500 | $115,000 |
| 2.50 NORTH CAROLINA, 20 C. Without 75.G., CAROLINA above 250 instead of GOLD *(unique)*. | | | | — |
| 2.50 NORTH CAROLINA, 20 C. on Obverse, 75.G. and Star on Reverse. Border Finely Serrated. | — | — | — | |
| 2.50 CAROLINA, 67.G., 21 CARATS | 8,000 | 13,000 | 17,500 | 33,000 |

| | VF | EF | AU | Unc. |
|---|---|---|---|---|
| 2.50 GEORGIA, 64.G, 22 CARATS (Uneven "22") | $7,500 | $12,500 | $16,500 | $32,000 |
| 2.50 GEORGIA, 64.G, 22 CARATS (Even "22") | 9,000 | 15,000 | 20,000 | 40,000 |
| 2.50 CAROLINA, 70.G, 20 CARATS. | 7,500 | 12,500 | 16,500 | 32,000 |
| 5 DOLLARS NORTH CAROLINA GOLD, 150.G., 20.CARATS. | 28,000 | 40,000 | 72,000 | 120,000 |
| Similar, Without 150.G. *(1 or 2 known)* | | — | — | |

## Christopher Bechtler – Carolina

*See next page for chart.*

| | VF | EF | AU | Unc. |
|---|---|---|---|---|
| 5 DOLLARS CAROLINA, RUTHERFORD, 140.G., 20 CARATS, Plain Edge | $6,000 | $8,500 | $12,500 | $26,000 |
| 5 DOLLARS CAROLINA, RUTHERFORD, 140.G., 20 CARATS, Reeded Edge | 20,000 | 30,000 | 45,000 | 70,000 |
| 5 DOLLARS CAROLINA GOLD, RUTHERF., 140.G., 20 CARATS, AUGUST 1, 1834 | 11,000 | 18,000 | 30,000 | 50,000 |
| Similar, but "20" Distant From CARATS | 6,500 | 10,000 | 15,000 | 27,500 |
| 5 DOLLARS CAROLINA GOLD, 134.G., 21 CARATS, With Star | 6,000 | 8,000 | 12,000 | 24,000 |

## Georgia

| | VF | EF | AU | Unc. |
|---|---|---|---|---|
| 5 DOLLARS GEORGIA GOLD, RUTHERFORD, 128.G., 22 CARATS | $8,750 | $12,500 | $17,000 | $33,000 |
| 5 DOLLARS GEORGIA GOLD, RUTHERFORD, 128.G:, 22 CARATS, With Colon After G | 16,000 | 26,000 | 38,500 | |
| 5 DOLLARS GEORGIA GOLD, RUTHERF, 128.G., 22 CARATS | 8,250 | 12,000 | 16,000 | 32,000 |

## August Bechtler

| | VF | EF | AU | Unc. | PF |
|---|---|---|---|---|---|
| 1 DOL:, CAROLINA GOLD, 27.G., 21.C. | $1,850 | $2,500 | $3,300 | $5,750 | |
| 5 DOLLARS, CAROLINA GOLD, 134.G:, 21 CARATS | 6,000 | 8,750 | 15,000 | 36,000 | |
| 5 DOLLARS, CAROLINA GOLD, 134 G: 21 CARATS, Reverse of C. Bechtler as Shown Above | — | — | | | |
| Same as above, Restrike | | | | | $30,000 |

| | VF | EF | AU | Unc. | PF |
|---|---|---|---|---|---|
| 5 DOLLARS, CAROLINA GOLD, 128.G., 22 CARATS | $15,000 | $18,000 | $27,500 | $47,500 | |
| 5 DOLLARS, CAROLINA GOLD, 141.G., 20 CARATS | 12,500 | 17,000 | 25,000 | 42,500 | |
| Same as above, Restrike | | | | | $30,000 |

*Note:* Restrikes in "Proof" of this type using original dies were made about 1920.

## NORRIS, GREGG & NORRIS
## SAN FRANCISCO 1849

Collectors consider this piece the first of the California private gold coins. A newspaper account dated May 31, 1849, described a five-dollar gold coin, struck at Benicia City, though with the imprint San Francisco. It mentioned the private stamp of Norris, Gregg & Norris. The initials N.G.&N. were not interpreted until 1902, when the coins of Augustus Humbert were sold.

| | F | VF | EF | AU | Unc. |
|---|---|---|---|---|---|
| 1849 Half Eagle, Plain Edge | $4,750 | $7,000 | $12,000 | $17,000 | $37,000 |
| 1849 Half Eagle, Reeded Edge | 4,750 | 7,000 | 12,000 | 17,000 | 37,000 |
| 1850 Half Eagle, With STOCKTON Beneath Date *(unique, in Smithsonian collection)* | | — | | | |

## MOFFAT & CO.
## SAN FRANCISCO 1849–1853

The firm of Moffat & Co. was perhaps the most important of the California private coiners. The assay office they conducted was semi-official in character. The successors to this firm, Curtis, Perry, and Ward, later sold their coining facility to the Treasury Department, which in March 1854 reopened it as the branch mint of San Francisco.

In June or July 1849, Moffat & Co. began to issue small, rectangular ingots of gold owing to lack of coin in the locality, in values from $9.43 to $264. The $9.43, $14.25, and $16.00 varieties are the only known types.

| | |
|---|---|
| $9.43 Moffat Ingot *(unique, in Smithsonian collection)* | — |
| $14.25 Moffat Ingot *(unique, in Smithsonian collection)* | — |
| $16.00 Moffat Ingot | $235,000 |

The dies for the five-dollar and ten-dollar pieces were cut by a Bavarian, Albrecht Küner. On the coronet of Liberty appear the words MOFFAT & CO., instead of the word LIBERTY as in regular United States issues.

| | F | VF | EF | AU | Unc. |
|---|---|---|---|---|---|
| 1849 FIVE DOL. *(all varieties)* | $2,200 | $3,300 | $4,700 | $7,000 | $15,000 |
| 1850 FIVE DOL. *(all varieties)* | 2,200 | 3,500 | 5,000 | 7,500 | 17,500 |
| 1849 TEN DOL. | 4,000 | 6,500 | 12,500 | 22,500 | 38,000 |
| 1849 TEN D. | 5,000 | 7,000 | 13,500 | 25,000 | 45,000 |

## UNITED STATES ASSAY OFFICE
### Augustus Humbert / United States Assayer of Gold, 1851

Augustus Humbert, a New York watchcase maker, was appointed United States assayer, and he placed his name and the government stamp on the ingots of gold issued by Moffat

& Co. The assay office, a provisional government mint, was a temporary expedient to accommodate the Californians until the establishment of a permanent branch mint.

The fifty-dollar gold piece was accepted by most banks and merchants as legal tender on a par with standard U.S. gold coins and was known variously as a *slug, quintuple eagle,* or *five-eagle piece.* It was officially termed an *ingot.*

### *Lettered-Edge Varieties*

| | F | VF | EF | AU | Unc. |
|---|---|---|---|---|---|
| 1851 50 D C 880 THOUS., No 50 on Reverse. Sunk in Edge: AUGUSTUS HUMBERT UNITED STATES ASSAYER OF GOLD, CALIFORNIA 1851 ............ | $25,000 | $40,000 | $60,000 | $90,000 | $200,000 |
| *$546,250, MS-63, Heritage auction, August 2010* | | | | | |
| 1851 50 D C 880 THOUS, Similar to Last Variety, but 50 on Reverse........................... | 50,000 | 60,000 | 90,000 | 160,000 | 300,000 |
| 1851 50 D C, 887 THOUS., With 50 on Reverse ......... | 32,500 | 50,000 | 75,000 | 115,000 | 250,000 |

### *Reeded-Edge Varieties*

| | F | VF | EF | AU | Unc. |
|---|---|---|---|---|---|
| 1851 FIFTY DOLLS, 880 THOUS., "Target" Reverse. . . . . . . . . . . | $16,500 | $25,000 | $40,000 | $52,000 | $150,000 |
| *$460,000, MS-65, Stack's Bowers auction, September 2008* | | | | | |
| 1851 FIFTY DOLLS, 887 THOUS., "Target" Reverse. . . . . . . . . . . | 16,500 | 25,000 | 40,000 | 52,000 | 150,000 |
| *$500,000, Proof, B&R auction, March 1980* | | | | | |
| 1852 FIFTY DOLLS, 887 THOUS., "Target" Reverse. . . . . . . . . . . | 17,000 | 27,000 | 50,000 | 95,000 | 200,000 |

## *Moffat-Humbert*

In 1851, certain issues of the Miners' Bank, Baldwin, Pacific Company, and others were discredited by newspaper accounts stating they were of reduced gold value. This provided an enhanced opportunity for Moffat and the U.S. Assay Office of Gold. Fractional-currency coins of almost every nation were being pressed into service by the Californians, but the supply was too small to help to any extent. Moffat & Co. proceeded in January 1852 to issue a new ten-dollar gold piece bearing the stamp MOFFAT & CO.

Close Date
Wide Date

| | F | VF | EF | AU | Unc. |
|---|---|---|---|---|---|
| 1852 TEN D. MOFFAT & CO. (Close Date) . . . . . . . . . . . . . . | $4,200 | $7,000 | $25,000 | $65,000 | |
| 1852 TEN D. MOFFAT & CO. (Wide Date). . . . . . . . . . . . . . . | 4,200 | 7,000 | 15,000 | 35,000 | $77,500 |
| *$940,000, SP-63, Heritage auction, January 2014* | | | | | |

1852, Normal Date
1852, 2 Over 1

| | F | VF | EF | AU | Unc. |
|---|---|---|---|---|---|
| 1852 TEN DOLS. . . . . . . . . . . . . . . . . . . . . . . . . . . . . . . . . | $2,750 | $4,250 | $7,500 | $12,000 | $27,500 |
| *$1,057,500, MS-68, Heritage auction, April 2013* | | | | | |
| 1852 TEN DOLS. 1852, 2 Over 1 . . . . . . . . . . . . . . . . . . . . | 3,000 | 5,250 | 9,500 | 20,000 | 50,000 |

*Chart continued on next page.*

| | F | VF | EF | AU | Unc. |
|---|---|---|---|---|---|
| 1852 TWENTY DOLS., 1852, 2 Over 1 | $8,250 | $14,000 | $27,500 | $45,000 | $140,000 |
| *$434,500, PF-64, Superior auction, October 1990* | | | | | |

## United States Assay Office of Gold – 1852

The firm of Moffat & Co. was dissolved in 1852 and a newly reorganized company known as the United States Assay Office of Gold took over the contract. Principals were Curtis, Perry, and Ward.

| | F | VF | EF | AU | Unc. |
|---|---|---|---|---|---|
| 1852 FIFTY DOLLS., 887 THOUS. | $16,500 | $25,000 | $40,000 | $65,000 | $150,000 |
| 1852 FIFTY DOLLS., 900 THOUS. | 17,500 | 27,000 | 42,000 | 55,000 | 125,000 |

| | F | VF | EF | AU | Unc. |
|---|---|---|---|---|---|
| 1852 TEN DOLS., 884 THOUS. | $2,500 | $3,500 | $5,500 | $10,000 | $22,500 |
| 1853 TEN D., 884 THOUS. | 10,000 | 20,000 | 30,000 | 45,000 | 125,000 |
| 1853 TEN D., 900 THOUS. | 4,500 | 6,500 | 10,000 | 16,000 | 25,000 |
| 1853 TWENTY D., 884 THOUS. | 7,800 | 11,500 | 19,000 | 32,000 | 75,000 |

| | F | VF | EF | AU | Unc. |
|---|---|---|---|---|---|
| 1853 TWENTY D., 900 THOUS. | $2,400 | $3,500 | $5,000 | $8,000 | $13,000 |

*Note:* Modern prooflike forgeries exist.

## Moffat & Co. Gold

The last Moffat issue, an 1853 twenty-dollar piece, is very similar to the U.S. double eagle of that period. It was struck after John L. Moffat retired from the Assay Office.

| | F | VF | EF | AU | Unc. |
|---|---|---|---|---|---|
| 1853 TWENTY D. | $4,750 | $7,000 | $11,000 | $20,000 | $65,000 |

## J.H. BOWIE

Joseph H. Bowie joined his cousins in San Francisco in 1849 and possibly produced a limited coinage of gold pieces. A trial piece of the dollar denomination is known in copper, but may never have reached the coinage stage. Little is known about the company or the reason for considering these pieces.

| | |
|---|---|
| 1849 1 DOL. (copper pattern) | — |

## CINCINNATI MINING & TRADING CO. (1849)

The origin and location of this company are unknown.

*See next page for chart.*

| | EF | Unc. |
|---|---|---|
| 1849 FIVE DOLLARS *(unique)*. . . . . . . . | | |
| 1849 TEN DOLLARS *(5 known) $431,250, EF, Stack's Bowers auction, May 2004*. . . . . . . . | $800,000 | — |

*Note:* Beware of spurious specimens cast in base metal with the word TRACING in place of TRADING.

## MASSACHUSETTS AND CALIFORNIA COMPANY

This company was believed to have been organized in Northampton, Massachusetts, in May 1849. Pieces with 5D are not genuine.

| | EF |
|---|---|
| 1849 FIVE D. *(5–7 known)*. . . . . . . . | $475,000 |

## MINERS' BANK
## SAN FRANCISCO 1849

The institution of Wright & Co., exchange brokers located in Portsmouth Square, San Francisco, was known as the Miners' Bank.

A ten-dollar piece was issued in the autumn of 1849, but the coins were not readily accepted because they were worth less than face value. The firm was dissolved on January 14, 1850. Unlike the gold in most California issues, the gold in these coins was alloyed with copper.

| | VF | EF | AU | Unc. |
|---|---|---|---|---|
| (1849) TEN D. . . . . . . . . | $22,500 | $34,000 | $50,000 | $110,000 |

## J.S. ORMSBY
## SACRAMENTO 1849

The initials J.S.O., which appear on certain issues of California privately coined gold pieces, represent the firm of J.S. Ormsby & Co. They struck both five- and ten-dollar denominations, all undated.

| | VF | EF |
|---|---|---|
| (1849) 5 DOLLS, Plain Edge *(possibly unique)*. . . . . . . . | — | |
| (1849) 5 DOLLS, Reeded Edge *(unique, in Smithsonian collection)* . . . . . . . . | — | |
| (1849) 10 DOLLS *(3 known)* . . . . . . . . | | $650,000 |

## PACIFIC COMPANY, SAN FRANCISCO 1849

The origin of the Pacific Company is very uncertain. All data regarding the firm are based on conjecture.

Edgar H. Adams wrote that he believed that the coins bearing the stamp of the Pacific Company were produced by the coining firm of Broderick and Kohler. The coins were probably hand struck with the aid of a sledgehammer.

| | EF | AU | Unc. |
|---|---|---|---|
| 1849 1 DOLLAR *(2 known)* | | | $325,000 |
| 1849 5 DOLLARS *(4 known)* | $500,000 | $750,000 | |
| 1849 10 DOLLARS *(4 known)* | | | 1,000,000 |

## F.D. KOHLER CALIFORNIA STATE ASSAYER 1850

The State Assay Office was authorized on April 12, 1850. That year, Governor Peter Burnett appointed F.D. Kohler, who thereupon sold his assaying business to Baldwin & Co. He served at both the San Francisco and Sacramento offices. The State Assay Offices were discontinued at the time the U.S. Assay Office was established, on February 1, 1851.

Ingots issued ranged from $36.55 to $150. An Extremely Fine specimen sold in the Garrett Sale, 1980, for $200,000. Each is unique.

| | |
|---|---|
| $36.55 Sacramento | — |
| $37.31 San Francisco | — |
| $40.07 San Francisco | — |
| $45.34 San Francisco | — |
| $50.00 San Francisco | — |
| $54.09 San Francisco | — |

*Note:* A $40.07 ingot was stolen from the Mint Cabinet in 1858 and never recovered.

## DUBOSQ & COMPANY SAN FRANCISCO 1850

Theodore Dubosq, a Philadelphia jeweler, took melting and coining equipment to San Francisco in 1849.

| | VF |
|---|---|
| 1850 FIVE D. *(3–5 known)* | — |

| | VF |
|---|---|
| 1850 TEN D. *(8–10 known)* | $300,000 |
| *$329,000, MS-60, Heritage auction, April 2014* | |

## BALDWIN & CO.
## SAN FRANCISCO 1850

George C. Baldwin and Thomas S. Holman were in the jewelry business in San Francisco and were known as Baldwin & Co. They were the successors to F.D. Kohler & Co., taking over its machinery and other equipment in May 1850.

| | F | VF | EF | AU | Unc. |
|---|---|---|---|---|---|
| 1850 FIVE DOL. | $7,500 | $13,000 | $25,000 | $35,000 | $75,000 |
| 1850 TEN DOLLARS, Horseman Type | 45,000 | 80,000 | 125,000 | 175,000 | 350,000 |
| 1851 TEN D. | 16,000 | 34,000 | 50,000 | 85,000 | 225,000 |

The Baldwin & Co. twenty-dollar piece was the first of that denomination issued in California. Baldwin coins are believed to have contained about 2% copper alloy.

| | EF | Unc. |
|---|---|---|
| 1851 TWENTY D. *(4–6 known)* | $650,000 | — |
| *$646,250, EF-45, Heritage auction, April 2014* | | |

## SCHULTZ & COMPANY
## SAN FRANCISCO 1851

The firm of Schultz & Co., a brass foundry, was operated by Judge G.W. Schultz and William T. Garratt. The surname is misspelled Shultz on the coins.

| | F | VF | EF | AU | Unc. |
|---|---|---|---|---|---|
| 1851 FIVE D. | — | $75,000 | $130,000 | $235,000 | $350,000 |

## DUNBAR & COMPANY SAN FRANCISCO 1851

Edward E. Dunbar operated the California Bank in San Francisco. Dunbar later returned to New York City and organized the famous Continental Bank Note Co.

| | VF | EF | Unc. |
|---|---|---|---|
| 1851 FIVE D. *(4–6 known)* | $425,000 | $575,000 | $750,000 |

## WASS, MOLITOR & CO. SAN FRANCISCO 1852–1855

The gold-smelting and assaying plant of Wass, Molitor & Co. was operated by two Hungarians, Count S.C. Wass and A.P. Molitor. They maintained an excellent laboratory and complete apparatus for analysis and coinage of gold.

The company struck five-, ten-, twenty-, and fifty-dollar coins. In 1852 they produced a ten-dollar piece similar in design to the five-dollar denomination. The difference is in the reverse legend, which reads: S.M.V. [Standard Mint Value] CALIFORNIA GOLD TEN D.

No pieces were coined in 1853 or 1854, but they brought out the twenty- and fifty-dollar pieces in 1855. A considerable number of the fifty-dollar coins were made. There was a ten-dollar piece issued in 1855 also, with the Liberty head and small close date.

Small Head, Rounded Bust

Large Head, Pointed Bust

| | F | VF | EF | AU | Unc. |
|---|---|---|---|---|---|
| 1852 FIVE DOLLARS, Small Head, With Rounded Bust | $5,500 | $11,000 | $22,500 | $40,000 | $80,000 |
| 1852 FIVE DOLLARS, Large Head, With Pointed Bust | 5,000 | 10,000 | 20,000 | 36,000 | 70,000 |

Large Head

Small Head

Small Date

1855

*See next page for chart.*

| | F | VF | EF | AU | Unc. |
|---|---|---|---|---|---|
| 1852 TEN D., Large Head | $2,750 | $4,750 | $8,250 | $14,500 | $32,500 |
| 1852 TEN D., Small Head | 6,200 | 8,000 | 19,000 | 32,000 | 80,000 |
| 1852 TEN D., Small Close Date | 12,500 | 28,000 | 47,000 | 90,000 | |
| 1855 TEN D. | 9,500 | 16,000 | 22,000 | 29,000 | 52,500 |

Large Head — Small Head

| | F | VF | EF | AU | Unc. |
|---|---|---|---|---|---|
| 1855 TWENTY DOL., Large Head *(4–6 known)* **(a)** | — | — | $550,000 | $675,000 | — |
| 1855 TWENTY DOL., Small Head | $12,000 | $25,000 | 35,000 | 75,000 | $165,000 |

**a.** A unique variety combines the Large Head obverse with the Small Head reverse shown here.

| | F | VF | EF | AU | Unc. |
|---|---|---|---|---|---|
| 1855 50 DOLLARS | $25,000 | $36,000 | $55,000 | $85,000 | $180,000 |

## KELLOGG & CO. SAN FRANCISCO 1854–1855

John G. Kellogg went to San Francisco on October 12, 1849, from Auburn, New York. At first he was employed by Moffat & Co., and remained with that organization when control passed to Curtis, Perry, and Ward. When the U.S. Assay Office was discontinued, December 14, 1853, Kellogg became associated with G.F. Richter, who had been an assayer in the government assay office. These two set up business as Kellogg & Richter on December 19, 1853.

When the U.S. Assay Office ceased operations, a period ensued during which no private firm was striking gold. The new San Francisco branch mint did not produce coins for some months after Curtis & Perry took the contract for the government (Ward having died). The lack of coin was again keenly felt by businessmen, who petitioned Kellogg & Richter to "supply the vacuum" by issuing private coin. Their plea was soon answered: on February 9, 1854, Kellogg & Co. placed their first twenty-dollar piece in circulation.

The firm dissolved late in 1854 and reorganized as Kellogg & Humbert. The latter partner was Augustus Humbert, for some time identified as U.S. assayer of gold in California. Regardless of the fact that the branch mint was then producing coins, Kellogg & Humbert issued twenty-dollar coins in 1855 in a quantity greater than before.

| | F | VF | EF | AU | Unc. |
|---|---|---|---|---|---|
| 1854 TWENTY D. | $3,500 | $5,000 | $6,500 | $10,000 | $25,000 |

The 1855 twenty-dollar piece is similar to that of 1854. The letters on the reverse are larger and the arrows longer on one 1854 variety. There are die varieties of both.

| | F | VF | EF | AU | Unc. |
|---|---|---|---|---|---|
| 1855 TWENTY D. | $3,750 | $5,250 | $7,000 | $12,000 | $27,500 |

In 1855, Ferdinand Grüner cut the dies for a round-format fifty-dollar gold coin for Kellogg & Co., but coinage seems to have been limited to presentation pieces. Only 13 to 15 pieces are known to exist. A "commemorative restrike" was made in 2001 using transfer dies made from the original and gold recovered from the SS *Central America.* These pieces have the inscription S.S. CENTRAL AMERICA GOLD, C.H.S. on the reverse ribbon.

| | PF |
|---|---|
| 1855 FIFTY DOLLS. *(13–15 known) $763,750, PF-64, Heritage auction, April 2014* | $600,000 |

# OREGON EXCHANGE COMPANY
# OREGON CITY 1849
## The Beaver Coins of Oregon

Upon the discovery of gold in California, a great exodus of Oregonians joined in the hunt for the precious metal. Soon, returning gold seekers offered their gold dust, which became the accepted medium of exchange. As in other Western areas at that time, the uncertain qualities of the gold and weighing devices tended to irk the tradespeople, and petitions were made to the legislature for a standard gold coin issue.

On February 16, 1849, the territorial legislature passed an act providing for a mint and specified five- and ten-dollar gold coins without alloy. Oregon City, the largest city in the territory with a population of about 1,000, was designated as the location for the mint. At the time this act was passed, Oregon had been brought into the United States as a territory by act of Congress. When the new governor arrived on March 2, he declared the coinage act unconstitutional.

The public-spirited people, however, continued to work for a convenient medium of exchange and soon took matters into their own hands by starting a private mint. Eight men of affairs, whose names were Kilborne, Magruder, Taylor, Abernethy, Willson, Rector, Campbell, and Smith, set up the Oregon Exchange Company.

The coins struck were of virgin gold as specified in the original act. Ten-dollar dies were made slightly later, and were of finer design and workmanship.

| | F | VF | EF | AU | Unc. |
|---|---|---|---|---|---|
| 1849 5 D. | $35,000 | $50,000 | $75,000 | $125,000 | $275,000 |
| 1849 TEN.D. | 90,000 | 160,000 | 300,000 | 375,000 | — |

# MORMON GOLD PIECES
# SALT LAKE CITY, UTAH, 1849–1860

The first name given to the organized Mormon Territory was the "State of Deseret," the last word meaning "honeybee." The beehive, which is shown on the reverse of the five-dollar 1860 piece, was a favorite device of the followers of Joseph Smith and Brigham Young. The clasped hands appear on most Mormon coins and exemplify strength in unity. HOLINESS TO THE LORD was an inscription frequently used.

Brigham Young was the instigator of the coinage system and personally supervised the mint, which was housed in a little adobe building in Salt Lake City. The mint was inaugurated late in 1848 as a public convenience.

| | F | VF | EF | AU | Unc. |
|---|---|---|---|---|---|
| 1849 TWO.AND.HALF.DO. | $13,500 | $25,000 | $37,500 | $60,000 | $90,000 |
| 1849 FIVE.DOLLARS | 10,000 | 18,500 | 30,000 | 40,000 | 75,000 |

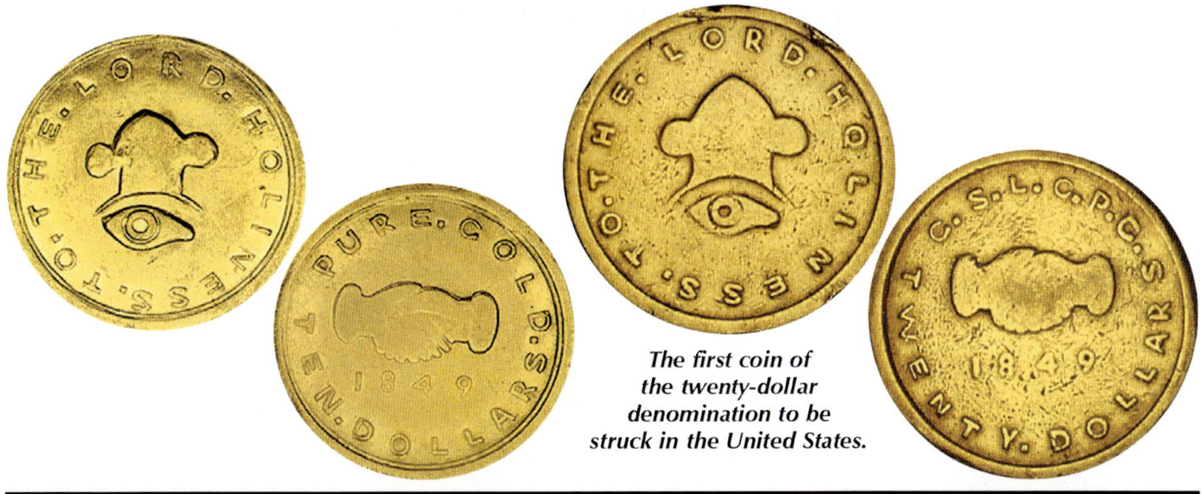
*The first coin of the twenty-dollar denomination to be struck in the United States.*

| | F | VF | EF | AU | Unc. |
|---|---|---|---|---|---|
| 1849 TEN.DOLLARS | $375,000 | $550,000 | $750,000 | $850,000 | $950,000 |
| *$705,000, AU-58, Heritage auction, April 2014* | | | | | |
| 1849 TWENTY.DOLLARS | 95,000 | 175,000 | 275,000 | 375,000 | 525,000 |
| *$558,125, MS-62, Heritage auction, April 2014* | | | | | |

| | F | VF | EF | AU | Unc. |
|---|---|---|---|---|---|
| 1850 FIVE DOLLARS | $13,000 | $22,000 | $34,000 | $47,500 | $85,000 |
| 1860 5.D. | 22,500 | 32,000 | 42,000 | 65,000 | 90,000 |

## COLORADO GOLD PIECES
### Clark, Gruber & Co.
### Denver 1860–1861

Clark, Gruber & Co. was a well-known private minting firm in Denver, Colorado, in the early 1860s.

*See next page for chart.*

| | F | VF | EF | AU | Unc. |
|---|---|---|---|---|---|
| 1860 2 1/2 D. | $2,000 | $3,000 | $4,200 | $5,700 | $13,500 |
| 1860 FIVE D | 2,250 | 3,000 | 4,500 | 6,250 | 14,500 |
| 1860 TEN D. | 9,000 | 15,000 | 21,000 | 30,000 | 55,000 |
| 1860 TWENTY D | 70,000 | 135,000 | 250,000 | 385,000 | 650,000 |
| *$690,000, MS-64, Heritage auction, January 2006* | | | | | |

The $2.50 and $5 pieces of 1861 follow closely the designs of the 1860 issues. The main difference is found in the legends. The reverse side now has CLARK GRUBER & CO. DENVER. PIKES PEAK now appears on the coronet of Liberty.

| | F | VF | EF | AU | Unc. |
|---|---|---|---|---|---|
| 1861 2 1/2 D. | $1,900 | $3,000 | $4,400 | $7,500 | $14,000 |
| 1861 FIVE D | 2,300 | 3,700 | 5,750 | 11,500 | 37,500 |
| 1861 TEN D. | 2,400 | 4,200 | 6,750 | 11,500 | 28,500 |

| | F | VF | EF | AU | Unc. |
|---|---|---|---|---|---|
| 1861 TWENTY D | $22,500 | $40,000 | $60,000 | $100,000 | $235,000 |

Beware of prooflike counterfeits.

## John Parsons & Company
## Tarryall Mines – Colorado, 1861

Very little is known regarding the mint of John Parsons and Co., although it is reasonably certain that it operated in the South Park section of Park County, Colorado, near the original town of Tarryall, in the summer of 1861.

**Pikes Peak Gold**

| | VF | EF |
|---|---|---|
| (1861) Undated 2 1/2 D. *(6–8 known)* | $300,000 | $400,000 |
| (1861) Undated FIVE D. *(5–6 known)* | 450,000 | 650,000 |

## J.J. Conway & Co.
## Georgia Gulch, Colorado, 1861

Records show that the Conway mint operated for a short while in 1861. As in all gold-mining areas the value of gold dust caused disagreement among the merchants and the miners. The firm of J.J. Conway & Co. solved this difficulty by bringing out its gold pieces in August 1861.

| | VF | EF | AU |
|---|---|---|---|
| (1861) Undated 2 1/2 DOLL'S *(8–12 known)* | | $450,000 | $650,000 |
| (1861) Undated FIVE DOLLARS *(5–8 known)* | $475,000 | 650,000 | |

| | |
|---|---|
| (1861) Undated TEN DOLLARS *(3 known)* | — |

## CALIFORNIA SMALL-DENOMINATION GOLD

There was a scarcity of small coins during the California gold rush. Starting in 1852, quarter, half, and dollar coins were privately minted from native gold to alleviate the shortage. Period 1 California fractional gold coins were issued between 1852 and 1857 as Liberty Head denominations of 25 cents, 50 cents, and one dollar, in both octagonal and round formats. There is much credible evidence available to conclude these were used in daily commerce during the early stages of the gold rush. Beginning in 1859, various private entities continued to make them, but more as souvenirs, as charms, or for barter. These are called Period 2 California fractional gold coins and were issued up to 1882. Period 2 has both the Liberty Head and Indian Head designs and the coins are often prooflike. Most have a wreath on the reverse, but some have original designs.

Early coins contained up to 85% of face value in gold. The amount and quality of gold in the coins soon decreased, and some are merely gold plated.

The Coinage Act of April 22, 1864, made private coinage illegal, but the law was not fully enforced until 1883. In compliance with the law, non-denominated tokens were made, and from 1872 until 1883 both coins and tokens were produced. After 1883, most of the production was tokens. To circumvent the law, and to make them more acceptable, some pieces made after 1881 were backdated to the 1850s or 1860s.

About 35,000 pieces are believed to exist. More than 570 different varieties have been identified, many of them very rare. The quality of strike and edge treatment is inconsistent. Many bear their makers' initials: D, DERI, DERIB, DN, FD, G, GG, GL, H, L, N, or NR. Major denominated coins are listed below; values are for the most common variety of each type. Non-denominated tokens are not included in these listings. They are much less valuable. ***Beware of extremely common modern replicas*** (often having a bear in the design), which have little numismatic value.

The values in the following charts are only for coins made before 1883 with the denomination on the reverse expressed as CENTS, DOL., DOLL., or DOLLAR.

### *Quarter Dollar, Octagonal*

| | AU | Unc. | Ch. Unc. | Gem BU |
|---|---|---|---|---|
| **Period 1 (reverse 1/4 DOLLAR unless noted otherwise)** | | | | |
| Small Liberty Head / Circular Value and Date in Beaded Circle, 1853 . . . | $450 | $900 | $4,250 | |
| Large Liberty Head / Circular Value and Date in Beaded Circle, 1853 . . . | 225 | 300 | 525 | |
| Large Liberty Head / Value in Beaded Circle, Date Below, DOLLA, 1853 . . . | 12,500 | 20,000 | 30,000 | |
| Large Liberty Head / Value and Date in Beaded Circle, 1854–1856 . . . . . | 225 | 325 | 450 | |
| Small Liberty Head 1854 / Value in Wreath, DOL. . . . . . . . . . . . . . . . . . . | 225 | 300 | 450 | |
| Small Liberty Head 1854 / Value in Wreath, DOLLAR . . . . . . . . . . . . . . . . | 275 | 450 | 650 | |
| Small Liberty Head / Value and Date in Wreath, 1855–1856 . . . . . . . . . . | 225 | 350 | 450 | |
| **Period 2** | | | | |
| Large Liberty Head / Value and Date in Wreath . . . . . . . . . . . . . . . . . . . . | | 210 | 300 | $700 |
| Washington Head 1872 / Value and CAL in Wreath . . . . . . . . . . . . . . . . | | 1,250 | 2,000 | 3,750 |
| Large Liberty Head and Date / Value and CAL in Wreath . . . . . . . . . . . . | | 250 | 300 | 650 |
| Small Liberty Head / Value and CAL in Wreath. . . . . . . . . . . . . . . . . . . . . | | 300 | 450 | — |
| Small Liberty Head, Initial G / Value in Shield, Date in Wreath . . . . . . . . . | | 300 | 700 | — |
| Small Indian Head / Value and CAL in Wreath . . . . . . . . . . . . . . . . . . . . . | | 225 | 375 | 850 |
| Small Liberty Head / Value in Wreath, Date Below . . . . . . . . . . . . . . . . . . | | 300 | 500 | 1,200 |
| Large Indian Head / Value and CAL in Wreath . . . . . . . . . . . . . . . . . . . . . | | 225 | 350 | 1,100 |
| Large Indian Head and Date / Value in Wreath. . . . . . . . . . . . . . . . . . . . . | | 230 | 375 | 700 |

### *Quarter Dollar, Round*

| | AU | Unc. | Ch. Unc. | Gem BU |
|---|---|---|---|---|
| **Period 1** | | | | |
| Small Liberty Head / 25 CENTS in Wreath, No Date (c. 1853) . . . . . . . . . | $1,750 | $3,250 | $8,500 | |
| Small Liberty Head / Value in Wreath, No Date (c. 1852–1854) . . . . . . . . | 225 | 300 | 425 | |
| Small Liberty Head / Value in Wreath, Star Above, No Date (c. 1853) . . . . . | 400 | 625 | 1,800 | |
| Small Liberty Head / Value in Wreath, Star Below, No Date (c. 1853–1854) | 175 | 255 | 390 | |
| Large Liberty Head / Value in Wreath, Star Above, No Date (c. 1853). . . . | 275 | 425 | 900 | |
| Large Liberty Head / Value and Date in Wreath, 1853–1854 . . . . . . . . . . | 400 | 700 | 2,150 | |
| Large Liberty Head, Initials FD / Value and Date in Wreath, 1853. . . . . . . | 1,750 | 3,000 | 12,000 | |
| Large Liberty Head, Initials GG / Value and Date in Wreath, 1853 . . . . . . | 1,250 | 2,000 | 3,750 | |
| Defiant Eagle and Date / 25 CENTS in Wreath, 1854 . . . . . . . . . . . . . . . . | 20,000 | 30,000 | 75,000 | |
| Small Liberty Head / Value and Date in Wreath, 1855–1856 . . . . . . . . . . | | 250 | 450 | |
| **Period 2** | | | | |
| Large Liberty Head and Date / Value and CAL in Wreath . . . . . . . . . . . . | | 220 | 325 | $675 |
| Liberty Head / Value in Wreath. . . . . . . . . . . . . . . . . . . . . . . . . . . . . . . . | | 200 | 275 | 600 |
| Washington Head 1872 / Value and CAL in Wreath . . . . . . . . . . . . . . . . | | 1,250 | 2,000 | 3,750 |
| Small Liberty Head / Value in Shield, Date in Wreath . . . . . . . . . . . . . . . . | | 340 | 650 | — |
| Small Liberty Head / Value and CAL in Wreath. . . . . . . . . . . . . . . . . . . . . | | 235 | 400 | 1,050 |
| Small Indian Head / Value and CAL in Wreath . . . . . . . . . . . . . . . . . . . . . | | 210 | 350 | 1,200 |
| Large Indian Head / Value and CAL in Wreath . . . . . . . . . . . . . . . . . . . . . | | 235 | 350 | 700 |
| Large Indian Head and Date / Value in Wreath. . . . . . . . . . . . . . . . . . . . . | | 250 | 375 | 750 |

## *Half Dollar, Octagonal*

| | AU | Unc. | Ch. Unc. | Gem BU |
|---|---|---|---|---|
| **Period 1 (reverse CALIFORNIA GOLD)** | | | | |
| Large Liberty Head and FD / Large Eagle with Raised Wings, FIFTY CENTS, 1853 | $17,500 | $32,500 | — | |
| Large Liberty Head Date and FD/ Peacock with Rays, 50 CENTS, 1853 | 1,500 | 2,200 | $4,500 | |
| Large Liberty Head Date and FD / Value in Beaded Circle, 1853 | 300 | 500 | 750 | |
| Large Liberty Head Date / Value in Beaded Circle, 1854 | 225 | 350 | 475 | |
| Large Liberty Head Date / Value in Beaded Circle, Initials FD, 1854 | 225 | 325 | 600 | |
| Large Liberty Head / Value, Date, and Star in Beaded Circle, 1856 | 275 | 425 | 1,300 | |
| Small Liberty Head / Date within Wreath Value Below HALF DOL., Initial N., 1854–1856 | 225 | 325 | 600 | |
| **Period 2** | | | | |
| Large Liberty Head / Value and Date in Wreath | | 250 | 400 | $675 |
| Small Liberty Head / Value and Date in Wreath | | 275 | 425 | 3,000 |
| Large Liberty Head / Value and CAL in Wreath | | 275 | 400 | 950 |
| Small Liberty Head and Date / Value and CAL in Wreath | | 260 | 375 | 1,200 |
| Small Indian Head and Date / Value and CAL in Wreath | | 250 | 400 | 1,250 |
| Large Indian Head and Date / Value in Wreath | | 230 | 400 | 900 |
| Large Indian Head and Date / Value and CAL in Wreath | | 275 | 450 | 875 |

## *Half Dollar, Round*

| | AU | Unc. | Ch. Unc. | Gem BU |
|---|---|---|---|---|
| **Period 1 (reverse CALIFORNIA GOLD except on Eagle reverse issues)** | | | | |
| Small Liberty Head / Date and Value in Wreath, HALF DOL., 1852 | $225 | $400 | $525 | |
| Large Liberty Head / Small Eagle, No Rays, Date Below, 1853 | — | — | 35,000 | |
| Large Liberty Head, Initials FD / Value and Date in Wreath, 1854–1855 | 400 | 650 | 1,250 | |
| Small Liberty Head, Initials DN / Date in Wreath, Value Below, HALF DOL., 1852–1853 | 225 | 350 | 650 | |
| Small Liberty Head, Initials DN / Date in Wreath, Value Below, HALF D, 1853 | 450 | 700 | 2,250 | |
| Small Liberty Head, Initials GG / Small Eagle, No Rays, Date Below, 1853 | 9,500 | 15,000 | 30,000 | |
| Small Liberty Head, Initials GG / Value in Wreath, Date Below, 1853 | 350 | 550 | 1,450 | |
| Large Liberty Head / Date in Wreath, HALF D. 1853–1854 | 225 | 450 | 1,000 | |
| Liberty Head, Initial D / Date in Wreath, HALF D, 1853–1854 | 175 | 300 | 495 | |
| Large Liberty Head / Date in Wreath, HALF DOL, Initial D, 1854 | 1,750 | 3,500 | 5,750 | |
| Small Liberty Head / Date in Wreath, HALF DOL, 1852–1853 | 175 | 275 | 500 | |
| Small Liberty Head / Date Below HALF DOL, 1854 | 275 | 450 | 1,200 | |
| Large Liberty Head / Date in Wreath, HALF DOL, 1855 | 200 | 325 | 450 | |
| Large Liberty Head, Initial N. / Date in Wreath, HALF DOL, 1856 | 175 | 250 | 650 | |
| Arms of California / Small Eagle with Raised Wings, 1853 | 6,500 | 10,000 | 13,000 | |
| Liberty Head / Large Eagle with Raised Wings, 1854 | — | — | 4,300 | |
| **Period 2** | | | | |
| Liberty Head / Value in Wreath | | 230 | 375 | $650 |
| Liberty Head and Date / Value and CAL in Wreath | | 230 | 400 | 1,300 |
| Liberty Head / CALIFORNIA GOLD around Wreath, HALF DOL | | 250 | 600 | 2,000 |
| Liberty Head / Value and Date in Wreath, *HALF DOLLAR | | 260 | 350 | 1,350 |
| Small Indian Head and Date / Value and CAL in Wreath | | 275 | 400 | 1,250 |
| Large Indian Head and Date / Value and CAL in Wreath | | 250 | 375 | 1,200 |
| Large Indian Head and Date / Value in Wreath | | 275 | 450 | 1,200 |

### *Dollar, Octagonal*

| | AU | Unc. | Ch. Unc. | Gem BU |
|---|---|---|---|---|
| **Period 1 (reverse CALIFORNIA GOLD)** | | | | |
| Liberty Head / Large Eagle with Scroll, ONE. DOL., No Date | $3,250 | $5,500 | $14,500 | |
| Liberty Head / Large Eagle with Scroll, ONE DOL, 1853 | 2,500 | 4,500 | 7,800 | |
| Liberty Head / Value and Date in Beaded Circle, Initials FD, 1853–1856 | 800 | 1,200 | 2,150 | |
| Liberty Head / Value and Date in Wreath, Initials GL, 1854 *(about 3 known)* | 875 | 1,350 | — | |
| Liberty Head, Initials DERI / Value and Date in Beaded Circle, 1853–1854 | | — | — | |
| Liberty Head, Initials DERIB / Value and Date in Beaded Circle, 1853–1854 | 475 | 875 | 2,000 | |
| Liberty Head / Value and Date in Beaded Circle, Initial N., 1853–1855 | 550 | 925 | 1,500 | |
| Liberty Head / Large Eagle, No Scroll, 1854 | 7,500 | 12,000 | 17,500 | |
| **Period 2** | | | | |
| Liberty Head / Legend around Wreath | | 800 | 1,500 | $2,000 |
| Small Indian Head and Date / Value and CAL in Wreath | | 825 | 1,400 | 2,000 |
| Large Indian Head and Date / Value in Wreath | | 750 | 1,500 | 2,000 |

### *Dollar, Round*

| | AU | Unc. | Ch. Unc. | Gem BU |
|---|---|---|---|---|
| **Period 1** | | | | |
| Liberty Head / CALIFORNIA GOLD., Value and Date in Wreath, 1854, 1857 | — | — | — | |
| Liberty Head, Initials FD / CALIFORNIA GOLD., Value and Date in Wreath, 1854 | $8,500 | $12,500 | $20,000 | |
| Liberty Head, Initials GG / Eagle Reverse, Date Below, 1853 | 75,000 | 120,000 | — | |
| **Period 2** | | | | |
| Liberty Head / Date Beneath Head | | 2,700 | 4,500 | — |
| Indian Head / Date Beneath Head | | 2,200 | 3,200 | $6,500 |

## COINS OF THE GOLDEN WEST

Small souvenir California gold pieces were made by several manufacturers in the early 20th century. A series of 36 pieces, in the size of 25¢, 50¢, and $1 coins, was made by the M.E. Hart Company of San Francisco to honor Alaska and various Western states. The Hart Company also marketed the official commemorative Panama-Pacific gold coins from the 1915 Exposition and manufactured plush copper cases for them. Similar cases were acquired by Farran Zerbe, who mounted 15 complete sets of what he termed "Coins of the Golden West." Intact, framed 36-piece sets are rare; individual specimens are among the most popular of all souvenir pieces of that era.

| | AU | Unc. | Ch. Unc. |
|---|---|---|---|
| 36-Piece Gold Set: Coins of Alaska, California, Idaho, Montana, Oregon, Washington | — | — | $45,000 |

## CALIFORNIA GOLD INGOT BARS

During the Gold Rush era, gold coins, ingots, and "dust" were sent by steamship from San Francisco to other ports, most importantly to New York City and London, where the gold was sold or, in some instances, sent to mints for conversion into coins. The typical procedure in the mid-1850s was to send the gold by steamship from San Francisco to Panama, where it was sent across 48 miles of land on the Panama Railroad, then loaded aboard another ship at the town of Aspinwall on the Atlantic side. On September 12, 1857, the SS *Central America,* en route from Aspinwall to New York City with more than 475 passengers, over 100 crew members, and an estimated $2.6 million in gold (in an era in which pure gold was valued at $20.67 per ounce) was lost at sea. Miraculously, more than 150 people, including all but one of the women and children, were rescued by passing ships. The SS *Central America* went to the bottom of the Atlantic Ocean off the Carolina coast.

In the 1980s a group of researchers in Ohio formed the Columbus-America Discovery Group and secured financing to search for the long-lost ship. After much study and many explorations, they discovered the wreck of the SS *Central America* 7,200 feet below the surface. The firm used the robotic *Nemo,* a sophisticated device weighing several tons, to photograph the wreck and to carefully bring to the surface many artifacts. A king's ransom in gold ingots was found, along with more than 7,500 coins, the latter mostly consisting of Mint State 1857-S double eagles.

The 500-plus gold ingots furnished a unique opportunity to study specimens that, after conservation, were essentially in the same condition as they had been in 1857. These bore the imprints of five different California assayers, who operated seven offices. With few exceptions, each ingot bears individual stamps, indicating its maker, a serial number, the weight in ounces, the fineness (expressed in thousandths, e.g., .784 indicating 784/1000 pure gold), and the 1857 value in dollars. The smallest bar found was issued by Blake & Co., weighed 4.95 ounces, was .795 fine, and was stamped with a value of $81.34. The largest ingot, dubbed the Eureka bar, bore the imprint of Kellogg & Humbert, and was stamped with a weight of 933.94 ounces, .903 fine, and a value of $17,433.57.

**Blake & Co., Sacramento, California:** From December 28, 1855, to May 1858, Blake & Co. was operated by Gorham Blake and W.R. Waters. • 34 ingots recovered. Serial numbers in the 5100 and 5200 series. Lowest weight and value: 4.95 ounces, $81.34. Highest weight and value: 157.40 ounces, $2,655.05. These bars have beveled or "dressed" edges and may have seen limited use in California commerce.

**Harris, Marchand & Co., Sacramento and Marysville:** Founded in Sacramento in 1855 by Harvey Harris and Desiré Marchand, with Charles L. Farrington as the "& Co." The Marysville office was opened in January 1856. Serial numbers in the 6000 series are attributed to Sacramento, comprising 36 bars; a single bar in the 7000 series (7095) is attributed to Marysville. The Marchand bars each have a circular coin-style counterstamp on the face. Lowest weight and value (Sacramento): 9.87 ounces, $158.53. Highest weight and value (Sacramento): 295.20 ounces, $5,351.73. • Unique Marysville bar: 174.04 ounces, $3,389.06.

**Henry Hentsch, San Francisco:** Henstch, a Swiss, was an entrepreneur involved in banking, real estate, assaying, and other ventures. In February 1856, he opened an assay office as an annex to his bank. It is likely that many of his ingots were exported to Europe, where he had extensive banking connections. • 33 ingots recovered. Lowest weight and value: 12.52 ounces, $251.82. Highest weight and value: 238.84 ounces, $4,458.35.

**Justh & Hunter, San Francisco and Marysville:** Emanuel Justh, a Hungarian, was a lithographer in San Francisco in the early 1850s. In 1854 and 1855 he worked as assistant assayer at the San Francisco Mint. Solomon Hillen Hunter came to California from Baltimore. The Justh & Hunter partnership was announced in May 1855. • Although study is continuing, the 60 ingots in the 4000 series are tentatively attributed to San Francisco, and the 26 ingots in the 9000 series are attributed to Marysville. • San Francisco—Lowest weight and value: 5.24 ounces, $92.18. Highest weight and value: 866.19 ounces, $15,971.93. • Marysville—Lowest weight and value: 19.34 ounces, $356.21. Highest weight and value: 464.65 ounces, $8,759.90.

**Kellogg & Humbert, San Francisco:** John Glover Kellogg and Augustus Humbert, two of the most famous names in the minting of California gold coins, formed the partnership of Kellogg & Humbert in spring 1855. The firm was one of the most active of all California assayers during the mid-1850s. • 346 ingots recovered, constituting the majority of those found. • Lowest weight and value: 5.71 ounces, $101.03. Highest weight and value: 933.94 ounces, $17,433.57.

**A selection of gold ingots from the SS *Central America* treasure (with an 1857S-S $20 double eagle shown for scale, near lower left).** (1) Harris, Marchand & Co., Marysville office, serial number 7095, 174.04 ounces, .942 fine, $3,389.06 (all values as stamped in 1857). (2) Henry Henstch, San Francisco, serial number 3120, 61.93 ounces, .886 fine, $1,134.26. (3) Kellogg & Humbert, San Francisco, serial number 215, .944 fine, $1,045.96. (4) Blake & Co., Sacramento, 19.30 ounces, .946 fine, $297.42. (5) Another Blake & Co. ingot, serial number 5216, .915 fine, $266.12. (6) Justh & Hunter, Marysville office, serial number 9440, 41.79 ounces, $761.07. (7) Justh & Hunter, San Francisco office, serial number 4243, 51.98 ounces, .916 fine, $984.27. (8) Harris, Marchand & Co., Sacramento office, serial number 6514, 35.33 ounces, .807 fine, $589.38. (9) Harris, Marchand & Co., Sacramento office, serial number 6486, 12.64 ounces, .950 fine, $245.00.

## HARD TIMES TOKENS (1832–1844)

Hard Times tokens, as they are called, are mostly the size of a contemporary large copper cent. Privately minted from 1832 to 1844, they display diverse motifs reflecting political campaigns and satire of the era as well as carrying advertisements for merchants, products, and services. For many years these have been a popular specialty within numismatics, helped along with the publication of *Hard Times Tokens* by Lyman H. Low (1899; revised edition, 1906) and later works, continuing to the present day. In 1899 Low commented (adapted) that "the issues commonly called Hard Times tokens . . . had no semblance of authority behind them. They combine the character of political pieces with the catch-words of party cries; of satirical pieces with sarcastic allusions to the sentiments or speeches of the leaders of opposing parties; and in some degree also of necessity pieces, in a time when, to use one of the phrases of the day, 'money was a cash article,' hard to get for daily needs."

Although these are designated as Hard Times tokens, the true Hard Times period began in a serious way on May 10, 1837, when banks began suspending specie payments and would no longer exchange paper currency for coins. This date is memorialized on some of the token inscriptions. Difficult economic conditions continued through 1843; the first full year of recovery was 1844. From March 1837 to March 1841, President Martin Van Buren vowed to "follow in the steps of my illustrious predecessor," President Andrew Jackson, who had been in office from March 1829 until Van Buren's inauguration. Jackson was perhaps the most controversial president up to that time. His veto in 1832 of the impending (1836) recharter of the Bank of the United States set off a political firestorm, made no calmer when his administration shifted deposits to favored institutions, derisively called "pet banks."

The Jackson era was one of unbridled prosperity. Due to sales of land in the West, the expansion of railroads, and a robust economy, so much money piled up in the Treasury that distributions were made in 1835 to all of the states. Seeking to end wild speculation, Jackson issued the "Specie Circular" on July 11, 1836, mandating that purchases of Western land, often done on credit or by other non-cash means, had to be paid in silver or gold coins. Almost immediately, the land boom settled and prices stabilized. A chill began to spread across the economy, which finally warmed in early 1837. Finally, many banks ran short of ready cash, causing the specie suspension.

After May 10, 1837, silver and gold coins completely disappeared from circulation. Copper cents remained, but were in short supply. Various diesinkers and others produced a flood of copper tokens. These were sold at discounts to merchants and banks, with $6 for 1,000 tokens being typical. Afterward, they were paid out in commerce and circulated for the value of one cent.

The actions of Jackson, the financial tribulations that many thought he precipitated, and the policies of Van Buren inspired motifs for the Hard Times tokens known as "politicals." Several hundred other varieties were made with the advertisements of merchants, services, and products and are known as "store cards" or "merchants' tokens." Many of these were illustrated with elements such as a shoe, umbrella, comb, coal stove, storefront, hotel, or carriage.

One of the more famous issues depicts a slave kneeling in chains, with the motto "Am I Not a Woman & a Sister?" This token was issued in 1838, when abolition was a major rallying point for many Americans in the North. The curious small-size Feuchtwanger cents of 1837, made in Feuchtwanger's Composition (a type of German silver), were proposed to Congress as a cheap substitute for copper cents, but no action was taken. Lewis Feuchtwanger produced large quantities on his own account and circulated them extensively. (See pages 423 and 424.)

As the political and commercial motifs of Hard Times tokens are so diverse, and reflect the American economy and political scene of their era, numismatists have found them fascinating to collect and study. Although there are major rarities in the series, most are very affordable. Expanded information concerning more than 500 varieties of Hard Times tokens can be found in Russell Rulau's *Standard Catalog of United States Tokens, 1700–1900* (fourth edition). See also Bowers, *A Guide Book of Hard Times Tokens*. A representative selection is illustrated here.

L1, HT1

L57, HT76

L4, HT6

L56, HT75

L66, HT24

L54, HT81

L55, HT63

L31, HT46

| | VF | EF | AU |
|---|---|---|---|
| L1, HT1. Andrew Jackson. Copper | $5,000 | $8,500 | — |
| L57, HT76. Van Buren, facing left. Brass | 2,200 | 3,250 | $4,250 |
| L4, HT6. Jackson President of the U.S. Brass | 135 | 275 | 750 |
| L56, HT75. Van Buren facing left. Copper | 80 | 160 | 375 |
| L66, HT24. Agriculture. Copper | 225 | 350 | 650 |
| L54, HT81. A Woman & A Sister. Copper | 180 | 275 | 400 |
| L55, HT63. Loco Foco, 1838. Copper | 55 | 160 | 275 |
| L31, HT46. Not One Cent, Motto. Copper | 45 | 60 | 135 |

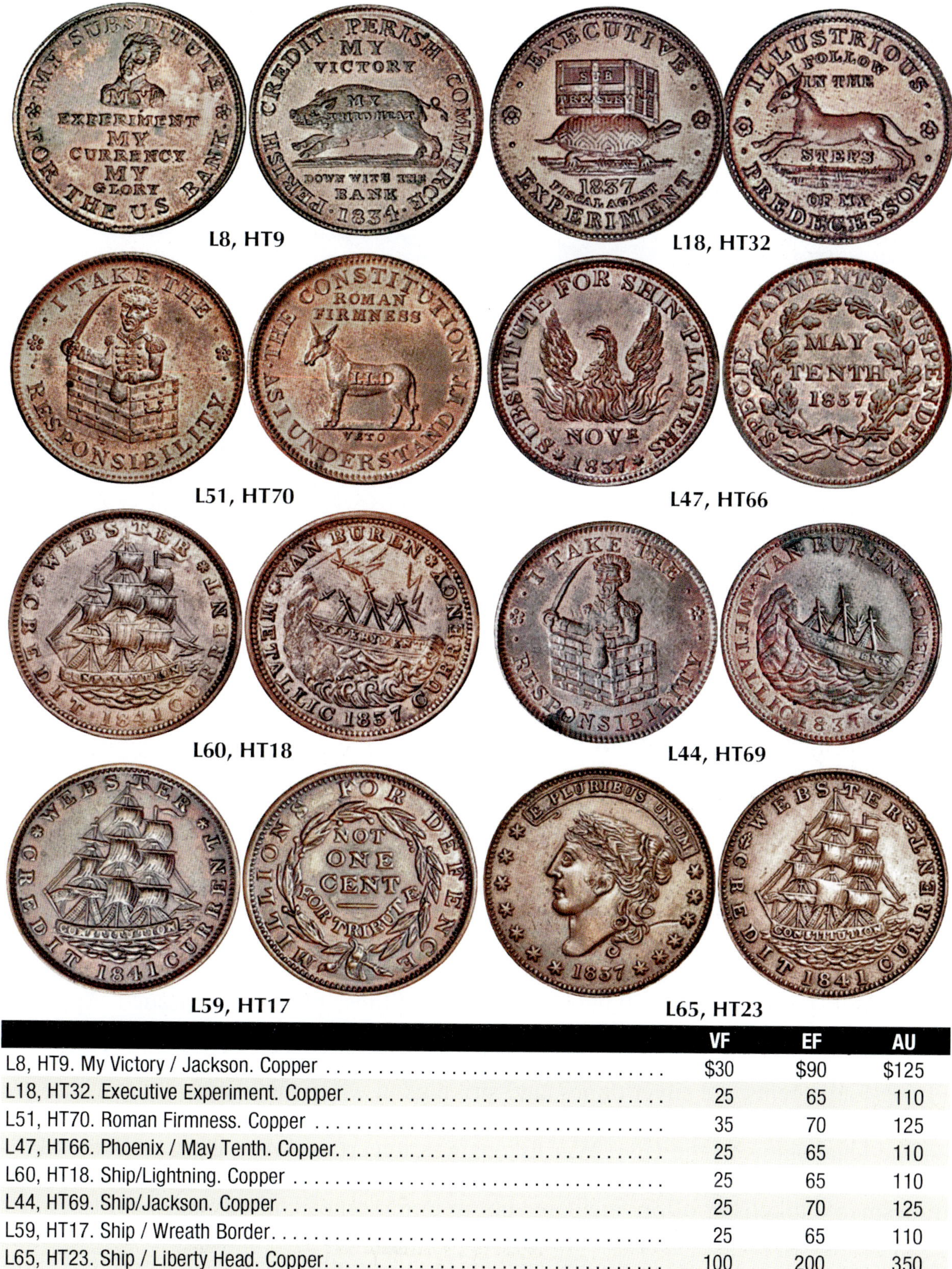


L8, HT9 L18, HT32

L51, HT70 L47, HT66

L60, HT18 L44, HT69

L59, HT17 L65, HT23

| | VF | EF | AU |
|---|---|---|---|
| L8, HT9. My Victory / Jackson. Copper | $30 | $90 | $125 |
| L18, HT32. Executive Experiment. Copper | 25 | 65 | 110 |
| L51, HT70. Roman Firmness. Copper | 35 | 70 | 125 |
| L47, HT66. Phoenix / May Tenth. Copper | 25 | 65 | 110 |
| L60, HT18. Ship/Lightning. Copper | 25 | 65 | 110 |
| L44, HT69. Ship/Jackson. Copper | 25 | 70 | 125 |
| L59, HT17. Ship / Wreath Border | 25 | 65 | 110 |
| L65, HT23. Ship / Liberty Head. Copper | 100 | 200 | 350 |

## FEUCHTWANGER TOKENS (1837–1864)

Lewis Feuchtwanger produced a metal that was really a variety of German silver consisting of nickel, copper, and some zinc. He suggested to Congress as early as 1837 that his metal be substituted for copper, and he made one-cent and three-cent trial pieces that circulated freely during the coin shortage of 1836 through 1844.

| | VF | EF | AU | Unc. |
|---|---|---|---|---|
| 1837 One Cent, Eagle | $135 | $210 | $300 | $500 |
| 1837 Three-Cent, New York Coat of Arms | 750 | 1,600 | 2,750 | 5,250 |
| 1837 Three-Cent, Eagle | 1,700 | 3,600 | 5,500 | 13,000 |
| 1864 Three-Cent, Eagle | 1,300 | 2,800 | 3,800 | 7,500 |

## CIVIL WAR TOKENS (1860s)

Civil War tokens are generally divided into two groups: tradesmen's tokens, also called store cards, and anonymously issued pieces with political or patriotic themes. These were struck during the Civil War, mostly in 1863. In July of that year federal cents disappeared from circulation and were hoarded. Various substitutes appeared, including tokens. Most production ended after bronze federal cents again became plentiful in circulation in the summer of 1864.

The tradesmen's tokens were purchased at a discount by various firms, who distributed them with advertising messages. Some of these were redeemable in goods. Political and patriotic tokens were produced at a profit by private manufacturers and put into circulation, with no identification as to the issuer. As there was no provision to redeem these, tokens of both types remained in circulation for many years, until they gradually disappeared.

These tokens are of great variety in composition and design. A number were more or less faithful imitations of the copper-nickel cent. A few of this type have the word NOT in very small letters above the words ONE CENT.

Many pieces, especially tradesmen's tokens, were individual in device and size, representing any caprice of design or slogan that appealed to the maker. Some were political or patriotic in character, carrying the likeness of some military leader such as McClellan or bearing such inscriptions as "Millions for contractors, not one cent for the widows." An estimated 50,000,000 or more of these pieces were issued. Approximately 10,000 different varieties have been recorded. Among these tokens are many issues made for numismatists of the era, including overstrikes on Indian Head and Flying Eagle cents and silver dimes, and strikings in white metal and silver. These are highly prized today.

The legal status of the Civil War tokens was uncertain. Mint Director James Pollock thought they were illegal; however, there was no law prohibiting the issue of tradesmen's tokens or of private coins not in imitation of United States coins. A law was passed April 22, 1864, prohibiting the private issue of any one- or two-cent coins, tokens, or devices for use as money, and on June 8 another law was passed that abolished private coinage of every kind.

*Values shown are for the most common tokens in each composition.*

| | F | VF | EF | MS-63 |
|---|---|---|---|---|
| Copper or brass | $15 | $25 | $35 | $125 |
| Nickel or German silver | 55 | 75 | 130 | 290 |
| White metal | 80 | 125 | 150 | 275 |
| Copper-nickel | 75 | 125 | 175 | 325 |
| Silver | 200 | 300 | 500 | 1,200 |

## Patriotic Civil War Tokens

Patriotic Civil War tokens feature leaders such as Abraham Lincoln; military images such as cannons or ships; and sociopolitical themes popular in the North, such as flags and slogans. Thousands of varieties are known.

| | F | VF | AU | MS-63 |
|---|---|---|---|---|
| Lincoln | $35 | $70 | $150 | $300 |
| Monitor | 30 | 50 | 125 | 225 |
| "Wealth of the South" **(a)** | 200 | 400 | 600 | 1,000 |
| Various common types | 15 | 25 | 45 | 125 |

**a.** Dated 1860, but sometimes collected along with Civil War tokens.

## Civil War Store Cards

Tradesmen's tokens of the Civil War era are often called *store cards.* These are typically collected by geographical location or by topic. The Fuld text (see bibliography) catalogs store cards by state, city, merchant, die combination, and metal. Values shown below are for the most common tokens for each state.

| | VG | VF | AU | MS-63 |
|---|---|---|---|---|
| Alabama | $1,500 | $3,000 | $4,000 | $6,500 |
| Connecticut | 10 | 25 | 50 | 125 |
| Washington, DC | — | 1,000 | 1,400 | 2,000 |
| Idaho | 400 | 700 | 1,300 | — |

| | VG | VF | AU | MS-63 |
|---|---|---|---|---|
| Illinois | $10 | $25 | $50 | $125 |
| Indiana | 10 | 25 | 50 | 135 |
| Iowa | 150 | 450 | 550 | 1,250 |
| Kansas | 900 | 2,500 | 3,500 | 5,500 |

*Chart continued on next page.*

| | VG | VF | AU | MS-63 |
|---|---|---|---|---|
| Kentucky | $50 | $125 | $200 | $350 |
| Louisiana | 2,000 | 3,500 | 4,500 | — |
| Maine | 50 | 100 | 175 | 275 |
| Maryland | 150 | 350 | 550 | 1,000 |
| Massachusetts | 15 | 35 | 60 | 140 |
| Michigan | 10 | 25 | 50 | 125 |
| Minnesota | 150 | 450 | 550 | 750 |
| Missouri | 40 | 100 | 150 | 250 |
| New Hampshire | 80 | 130 | 175 | 275 |
| New Jersey | 10 | 25 | 50 | 135 |
| New York | $10 | $25 | $50 | $125 |
| Ohio | 10 | 25 | 50 | 125 |
| Pennsylvania | 10 | 25 | 50 | 125 |
| Rhode Island | 10 | 25 | 50 | 135 |
| Tennessee | 300 | 650 | 1,200 | 1,750 |
| Virginia | 250 | 500 | 1,000 | — |
| West Virginia | 45 | 100 | 175 | 400 |
| Wisconsin | 15 | 30 | 60 | 130 |
| Sutlers' **(a)** | 185 | 375 | 500 | 700 |

**a.** Sutlers' tokens were issued by registered contractors who operated camp stores that traveled with the military.

DC500A-1h

IN190D-3a

MI865A-1a

MN980A-1a

MO910A-2a

NY630AQ-4a

NY630Z-1a

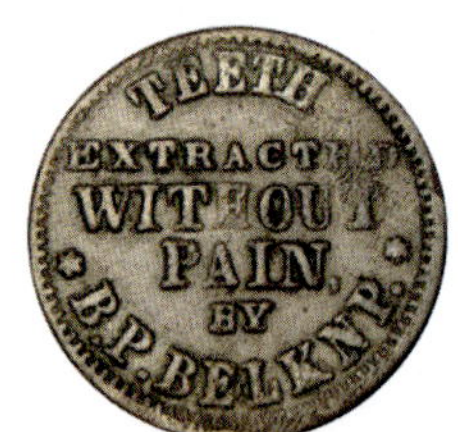

OH165M-1a

| | VG | VF | AU | MS-63 |
|---|---|---|---|---|
| DC500a-1h. H.A. Hall, Washington, DC | — | $1,000 | $1,400 | $2,200 |
| IN190D-3a. J.L. & G.F. Rowe, Corunna, IN, 1863 | $15 | 40 | 75 | 175 |
| MI865A-1a, W. Darling, Saranac, MI, 1864 | 7,500 | 12,000 | 15,000 | — |
| MN980A-1a. C. Benson, Druggist, Winona, MN | 300 | 700 | 900 | 1,500 |
| MO910A-4a. Drovers Hotel, St. Louis, MO, 1863 | 125 | 300 | 600 | 1,250 |
| NY630AQ-4a. Gustavus Lindenmueller, New York, 1863 | 15 | 25 | 50 | 125 |
| NY630Z-1a. Fr. Freise, Undertaker, New York, 1863 | 20 | 35 | 85 | 135 |
| OH165M-1a. B.P. Belknp., "Teeth Extracted Without Pain" | 125 | 250 | 400 | 600 |

NY630BJ-1a

WI510M-1a

PA750F-1a

WV890D-4a

| | VG | VF | AU | MS-63 |
|---|---|---|---|---|
| NY630BJ-1a. Sanitary Commission, New York, 1864 . . . . . . . . . . . . . | $400 | $850 | $1,100 | $1,750 |
| WI510M-1a. Goes & Falk Malt House & Brewery, Milwaukee, WI, 1863 | 25 | 65 | 100 | 175 |
| PA750F-1a. M.C. Campbell's Dancing Academy, Philadelphia, PA. . . . | 20 | 35 | 50 | 130 |
| WV890D-4a. R.C. Graves, News Dealer, Wheeling, WV, 1863 . . . . . . . | 45 | 100 | 175 | 400 |

## LESHER REFERENDUM DOLLARS (1900–1901)

Distributed in 1900 and 1901 by Joseph Lesher of Victor, Colorado, these private tokens were used in trade to some extent, and stocked by various merchants who redeemed them in goods. Coins were numbered and a blank space left at bottom of 1901 issues, in which were stamped names of businessmen who bought them. All are quite rare; many varieties are extremely rare. Composition is .950 fine silver (alloyed with copper).

| | VF | EF | AU | Unc. |
|---|---|---|---|---|
| 1900 First type, no business name . . . . . . . . . . . . . . . . . . . . . . . . . | $2,900 | $3,500 | $4,200 | $6,750 |
| 1900 A.B. Bumstead, with or without scrolls (Victor) . . . . . . . . . . . . . | 1,600 | 2,500 | 2,900 | 4,000 |
| 1900 Bank type . . . . . . . . . . . . . . . . . . . . . . . . . . . . . . . . . . . . . . . . | 15,000 | 22,000 | 35,000 | — |
| 1901 Imprint type, no name . . . . . . . . . . . . . . . . . . . . . . . . . . . . . . | 1,800 | 2,200 | 3,300 | 4,800 |
| 1901 Imprint type, Boyd Park. Denver . . . . . . . . . . . . . . . . . . . . . . . | 1,800 | 2,200 | 3,300 | 4,800 |
| 1901 Imprint type, Slusher. Cripple Creek . . . . . . . . . . . . . . . . . . . . | 2,000 | 2,600 | 3,600 | 5,500 |
| 1901 Imprint type, Mullen. Victor. . . . . . . . . . . . . . . . . . . . . . . . . . . | 3,000 | 4,200 | 7,000 | 12,000 |
| 1901 Imprint type, Cohen. Victor . . . . . . . . . . . . . . . . . . . . . . . . . . . | 5,000 | 7,500 | 11,000 | 16,000 |
| 1901 Imprint type, Klein. Pueblo . . . . . . . . . . . . . . . . . . . . . . . . . . . | 7,000 | 9,500 | 14,000 | 20,000 |
| 1901 Imprint type, Alexander. Salida. . . . . . . . . . . . . . . . . . . . . . . . . | 7,500 | 10,000 | 16,000 | 23,000 |
| 1901 Imprint type, White. Grand Junction . . . . . . . . . . . . . . . . . . . . . | 13,000 | 21,000 | 30,000 | — |
| 1901 Imprint type, Goodspeeds. Colorado Springs. . . . . . . . . . . . . . . | 27,000 | 37,000 | 47,000 | — |
| 1901 Imprint type, Nelson. Holdrege, Nebraska. . . . . . . . . . . . . . . . . | 22,500 | 33,000 | 45,000 | — |
| 1901 Imprint type, A.W. Clark (Denver) *(unique)* . . . . . . . . . . . . . . . . . | | | 42,000 | |

## CONFEDERATE CENTS

The 1861 "Confederate States of America" cent is a fantasy coin, likely by Robert Lovett Jr. of Philadelphia. For years numismatic texts called the 1861-dated copper-nickel coin an original, but the first example appeared in 1873, after which 11 more were revealed and marketed along with "restrikes" in bronze, silver, and gold. The popular story that Lovett designed the coin after being contacted by the Confederacy is untrue—the latter controlled the New Orleans Mint and had their own engraver. Further, the design employs the French Liberty-head punch Lovett used on his store cards.

| | Mintage | Unc. | PF |
|---|---|---|---|
| 1861 Cent, Original, Copper-Nickel, Unc. | *13–16* | $135,000 | |
| 1861 Cent, Haseltine Restrike, Copper, Proof | (55) | | $15,000 |
| 1861 Cent, Haseltine Restrike, Gold, Proof | (7) | | 45,000 |
| 1861 Cent, Haseltine Restrike, Silver, Proof | (12) | | 12,500 |

## CONFEDERATE HALF DOLLARS

According to records, only four original Confederate half dollars were struck (on a hand press). Regular silver planchets were used, as well as a regular federal obverse die. One of the coins was given to Secretary of the Treasury Christopher G. Memminger, who passed it on to President Jefferson Davis for his approval. Another was given to Professor J.L. Riddell of the University of Louisiana. E. Ames of New Orleans received a third specimen. The last was kept by chief coiner B.F. Taylor. Lack of bullion prevented the Confederacy from coining more pieces.

The Confederate half dollar was unknown to collectors until 1879, when a specimen and its reverse die were found in Taylor's possession in New Orleans. E. Mason Jr., of Philadelphia, purchased both and later sold them to J.W. Scott and Company of New York. J.W. Scott acquired 500 genuine 1861 half dollars, routed the reverses, and then restamped them with the Confederate die. Known as restrikes, these usually have slightly flattened obverses. Scott also struck some medals in white metal using the Confederate reverse die and an obverse die bearing this inscription: 4 ORIGINALS STRUCK BY ORDER OF C.S.A. IN NEW ORLEANS 1861 / ******* / REV. SAME AS U.S. (FROM ORIGINAL DIE•SCOTT).

Confederate Reverse

Scott Obverse

| | Mintage | VF-20 | EF-40 | Unc. |
|---|---|---|---|---|
| 1861 HALF DOL. *(4 known)* *$881,250, PF-30, Heritage auction, January 2015* | | — | $1,000,000 | — |
| 1861 HALF DOL., Restrike | 500 | $6,500 | 7,500 | $15,000 |
| 1861 Scott Obverse, Confederate Reverse | 500 | 3,000 | 4,000 | 6,500 |

## HAWAIIAN ISSUES

Five official coins were issued for the Kingdom of Hawaii. These include the 1847 cent issued by King Kamehameha III and the 1883 silver dimes, quarters, halves, and dollars of King Kalakaua I, which bear his portrait. The silver pieces were all designed by Charles Barber and struck at the San Francisco Mint. After Hawaii became a U.S. territory in 1900, the legal-tender status of these coins was removed and most were withdrawn and melted. The 1883 eighth-dollar piece is a pattern. The 1881 five-cent piece is an unofficial issue.

**One Cent, 1847**

**Ten Cents, 1883**

| | Mintage | F-12 | VF-20 | EF-40 | AU-50 | MS-60 | MS-63 | PF-63 |
|---|---|---|---|---|---|---|---|---|
| 1847 Cent* | 100,000 | $350 | $450 | $650 | $850 | $1,000 | $1,600 | |
| 1881 Five Cents** | | 7,000 | 10,000 | 11,000 | 12,000 | 15,000 | 22,000 | $7,000 |
| 1883 Ten Cents. . . . (26) | 250,000 | 65 | 100 | 275 | 400 | 900 | 2,000 | 15,000 |
| 1883 Eighth Dollar. . (20) | | | | | | | | 40,000 |
| 1883 Quarter Dollar (26) | 500,000 | 75 | 100 | 150 | 175 | 250 | 400 | 15,000 |
| 1883 Half Dollar . . . (26) | 700,000 | 125 | 175 | 300 | 450 | 900 | 1,750 | 20,000 |
| 1883 Dollar . . . . . . . (26) | 500,000 | 350 | 500 | 750 | 1,200 | 3,750 | 9,000 | 40,000 |

* Values shown are for the most common of the six known varieties. ** All Proofs were made circa 1900.

### Plantation Tokens

During the 19th century, several private firms issued tokens for use as money in Hawaiian company stores. These are often referred to as Plantation tokens. The unusual denomination of 12-1/2 cents was equivalent to a day's wages in the sugar plantations, and was related to the fractional part of the Spanish eight-reales coin.

**Kahului Railroad, 1891**

**Waterhouse Token (1860)**

**Haiku Plantation, 1882**

*Entry continued on next page.*

Wailuku Plantation (1871)

Wailuku Plantation, 1880

| | F-12 | VF-20 | EF-40 | AU-50 |
|---|---|---|---|---|
| Waterhouse / Kamehameha IV, ca. 1860 | $1,500 | $3,000 | $4,500 | $7,000 |
| Wailuku Plantation, 12-1/2 (cents), (1871), narrow starfish | 750 | 2,000 | 3,750 | 6,200 |
| Similar, broad starfish | 900 | 2,400 | 4,500 | 7,500 |
| Wailuku Plantation, VI (6-1/4 cents), (1871), narrow starfish | 1,800 | 4,750 | 7,000 | 9,500 |
| Similar, broad starfish | 2,200 | 5,500 | 7,500 | 10,500 |
| Thomas H. Hobron, 12-1/2 (cents), 1879 *(Rare varieties exist)* | 600 | 850 | 1,100 | 1,400 |
| Similar, two stars on both sides | 1,600 | 3,000 | 6,000 | 10,000 |
| Thomas H. Hobron, 25 (cents), 1879 *(3 known)* | | | 55,000 | 70,000 |
| Wailuku Plantation, 1 Real, 1880 | 750 | 1,800 | 3,750 | 8,000 |
| Wailuku Plantation, Half Real, 1880 | 2,200 | 5,000 | 8,500 | 11,500 |
| Haiku Plantation, 1 Rial, 1882 | 800 | 1,250 | 1,750 | 2,250 |
| Grove Ranch Plantation, 12-1/2 (cents), 1886 | 1,500 | 3,000 | 5,000 | 7,000 |
| Grove Ranch Plantation, 12-1/2 (cents), 1887 | 3,000 | 4,500 | 8,000 | 10,500 |
| Kahului Railroad, 10 cents, 1891 | 3,000 | 6,000 | 11,000 | 13,500 |
| Kahului Railroad, 15 cents, 1891 | 3,000 | 6,000 | 11,000 | 13,500 |
| Kahului Railroad, 20 cents, 1891 | 3,000 | 6,000 | 11,000 | 13,500 |
| Kahului Railroad, 25 cents, 1891 | 3,000 | 6,000 | 11,000 | 13,500 |
| Kahului Railroad, 35 cents, 1891 | 3,000 | 6,000 | 11,000 | 13,500 |
| Kahului Railroad, 75 cents, 1891 | 3,000 | 6,000 | 11,000 | 13,500 |

## PUERTO RICAN ISSUES

Puerto Rico, the farthest east of the Greater Antilles, lies about 1,000 miles southeast of Florida between the Atlantic Ocean and the Caribbean Sea. Settled by Spain in 1508, the island was ceded to the United States after the Spanish-American War in 1898. Puerto Ricans were granted U.S. citizenship in 1917. Today Puerto Rico is a self-governing territory of the United States with commonwealth status.

Collectors of United States coins often include Puerto Rican coins in their collections, even though they are not U.S. issues. After the Spanish-American War, exchange rates were set for these coins relative to the U.S. dollar, and the island transitioned to a dollar-based currency. Today in Puerto Rico the dollar is still popularly referred to as a "peso."

Puerto Rico 5 Centavos, 1896

Puerto Rico 20 Centavos, 1895

| | Mintage | F | VF | EF | AU | Unc. |
|---|---|---|---|---|---|---|
| 1896 5 Centavos | 600,000 | $30 | $50 | $100 | $150 | $200 |
| 1896 10 Centavos | 700,000 | 40 | 85 | 135 | 200 | 300 |
| 1895 20 Centavos | 3,350,000 | 45 | 100 | 150 | 250 | 400 |
| 1896 40 Centavos | 725,002 | 180 | 300 | 900 | 1,700 | 2,900 |
| 1895 1 Peso | 8,500,021 | 200 | 400 | 950 | 2,000 | 3,250 |

The Philippine Islands were acquired by the United States in 1899 as part of a treaty with Spain ending the Spanish-American War of the previous year. A military government was replaced with a civil administration in 1901, and one of its first tasks was to sponsor a new coinage that was compatible with the old Spanish issues, yet was also legally exchangeable for American money at the rate of two Philippine pesos to the U.S. dollar.

The resulting coins were introduced in 1903 and bear the identities of both the Philippines (*Filipinas* in Spanish) and the United States of America. Following Spanish custom, the peso was divided into 100 centavos. A dollar-size coin valued at one peso was the principal issue in this series, but silver fractions were also minted in values of 50, 20, and 10 centavos. Minor coins included the copper-nickel five-centavo piece, as well as one-centavo and half-centavo coins of bronze.

A rise in the price of silver forced the reduction of the fineness and weight for each silver denomination beginning in 1907, and subsequent issues are smaller in diameter. The smaller size of the new silver issues led to confusion between the silver 20-centavo piece and the copper-nickel five-centavo piece, resulting in a mismatching of dies for these two denominations in 1918 and again in 1928. A solution was found by reducing the diameter of the five-centavo piece beginning in 1930.

In 1935, the Commonwealth of the Philippines was established by an act of Congress, and a three-piece set of commemorative coins was issued the following year to mark this transition. Despite the popularity of United States commemoratives at that time, these sets sold poorly, and thousands remained within the Philippine Treasury at the onset of World War II. The commonwealth arms were adapted to all circulating issues beginning in 1937.

The advance on the Philippines by Japanese forces in 1942 prompted removal of much of the Treasury's bullion to the United States. More than 15 million pesos' worth of silver remained, mostly in the form of one-peso pieces of 1907 through 1912 and the ill-fated 1936 commemoratives. These coins were hastily crated and dumped into Manila's Caballo Bay to prevent their capture. Partially recovered during and after the war, these coins were badly corroded from their exposure to saltwater, adding further to the scarcity of high-grade prewar silver coins.

The Philippines became an independent republic on July 4, 1946, ending a historic and colorful chapter in U.S. history and numismatics.

## PHILIPPINES UNDER U.S. SOVEREIGNTY

**Basic Design for Half-, One-, and Five-Centavos Pieces**
*(Large-size five centavos shown.)*

**Basic Design for Ten-, Twenty-, and Fifty-Centavo and 1-Peso Pieces**
*(Reduced-size twenty centavos shown.)*

Philippine coins of 1903 to 1919 were struck at the Philadelphia and San Francisco mints. Centavos of 1920 were made in Philadelphia and Manila. Coins from 1920 up to the formation of the Commonwealth (and centavos of 1936) were made at the Manila Mint, which continued to strike coins until the 1941 Japanese occupation.

# Bronze Coinage

## *Half Centavo (17.5 mm)*

| | Mintage | EF | MS-60 | MS-63 | PF-65 |
|---|---|---|---|---|---|
| 1903 | 12,084,000 | $2.25 | $20 | $40 | |
| 1903, Pf. | (2,558) | | | | $175 |
| 1904 | 5,654,000 | 3.50 | 25 | 60 | |
| 1904, Pf. | (1,355) | | | | 200 |
| 1905, Pf only | (471) | | $175 | $300 | $550 |
| 1906, Pf only | (500) | | 150 | 250 | 500 |
| 1908, Pf only | (500) | | 150 | 250 | 500 |

## *One Centavo (24 mm)*

| | Mintage | VF | EF | MS-60 | MS-63 |
|---|---|---|---|---|---|
| 1903 | 10,790,000 | $1.25 | $3.00 | $15 | $35 |
| 1903, Pf. | (2,558) | | | 60 | 120 |
| 1904 | 17,040,400 | 1.25 | 3.00 | 25 | 45 |
| 1904, Pf. | (1,355) | | | 75 | 125 |
| 1905 | 10,000,000 | 1.25 | 3.50 | 30 | 45 |
| 1905, Pf. | (471) | | | 175 | 325 |
| 1906, Pf only | (500) | | | 150 | 275 |
| 1908, Pf only | (500) | | | 150 | 275 |
| 1908S | 2,187,000 | 4.00 | 8.00 | 40 | 100 |
| 1908S, S/S | * | 30.00 | 50.00 | 135 | 300 |
| 1909S | 1,737,612 | 10.00 | 20.00 | 110 | 225 |
| 1910S | 2,700,000 | 4.50 | 9.00 | 35 | 60 |
| 1911S | 4,803,000 | 2.50 | 5.00 | 25 | 60 |
| 1912S | 3,001,000 | 7.50 | 15.00 | 75 | 125 |
| 1913S | 5,000,000 | 4.00 | 7.00 | 35 | 75 |
| 1914S | 5,000,500 | 3.50 | 5.00 | 35 | 70 |
| 1915S | 2,500,000 | 50.00 | 125.00 | 525 | 1,000 |
| 1916S | 4,330,000 | 7.50 | 12.50 | 90 | 150 |
| 1917S | 7,070,000 | 4.00 | 10.00 | 75 | 150 |
| 1917S, 7/6 | * | $50.00 | $160.00 | $500 | |
| 1918S | 11,660,000 | 5.00 | 12.00 | 100 | $200 |
| 1918S, Lg S. | * | 150.00 | 275.00 | 1,000 | 1,900 |
| 1919S | 4,540,000 | 5.00 | 15.00 | 75 | 125 |
| 1920S | 2,500,000 | 3.50 | 20.00 | 50 | 175 |
| 1920 | 3,552,259 | 8.00 | 20.00 | 125 | 225 |
| 1921 | 7,282,673 | 2.50 | 5.00 | 35 | 85 |
| 1922 | 3,519,100 | 3.00 | 6.00 | 30 | 70 |
| 1925M. | 9,325,000 | 3.00 | 7.00 | 35 | 65 |
| 1926M. | 9,000,000 | 2.50 | 5.00 | 30 | 55 |
| 1927M. | 9,279,000 | 2.00 | 4.00 | 25 | 45 |
| 1928M. | 9,150,000 | 2.00 | 5.00 | 30 | 75 |
| 1929M. | 5,657,161 | 3.00 | 6.00 | 40 | 85 |
| 1930M. | 5,577,000 | 2.00 | 4.50 | 30 | 50 |
| 1931M. | 5,659,355 | 2.25 | 5.00 | 40 | 60 |
| 1932M. | 4,000,000 | 3.00 | 7.00 | 50 | 75 |
| 1933M. | 8,392,692 | 2.00 | 3.00 | 20 | 50 |
| 1934M. | 3,179,000 | 2.50 | 4.50 | 50 | 75 |
| 1936M. | 17,455,463 | 2.50 | 4.00 | 35 | 65 |

* Included in number above.

# Copper-Nickel Coinage

## *Five Centavos*

***(Large-Size [1903–1928]: 20.5 mm; Reduced-Size [1930–1935]: 19 mm)***

| | Mintage | VF | EF | MS-60 | MS-63 |
|---|---|---|---|---|---|
| 1903 | 8,910,000 | $1.25 | $2.50 | $20 | $35 |
| 1903, Pf. | (2,558) | | | 75 | 130 |
| 1904 | 1,075,000 | 2.50 | 3.00 | 20 | 40 |
| 1904, Pf. | (1,355) | | | 90 | 150 |
| 1905, Pf only | (471) | | | 200 | 400 |
| 1906, Pf only | (500) | | | 175 | 300 |
| 1908, Pf only | (500) | | | 200 | 300 |
| 1916S | 300,000 | 125.00 | 225.00 | 800 | 1,700 |
| 1917S | 2,300,000 | 5.00 | 12.00 | 160 | 350 |
| 1918S | 2,780,000 | 8.00 | 15.00 | 140 | 300 |
| 1918S, S Over S | * | 20.00 | 150.00 | 600 | 1,250 |
| 1918S, Mule **(a)** | * | 575.00 | 1,750.00 | 4,750 | 9,750 |
| 1919S | 1,220,000 | 15.00 | 30.00 | 200 | 450 |
| 1920 | 1,421,078 | $8.50 | $20 | $175 | $375 |
| 1921 | 2,131,529 | 9.00 | 15 | 125 | 300 |
| 1925M. | 1,000,000 | 12.00 | 30 | 175 | 300 |
| 1926M. | 1,200,000 | 5.00 | 25 | 140 | 250 |
| 1927M. | 1,000,000 | 5.00 | 10 | 90 | 150 |
| 1928M. | 1,000,000 | 7.00 | 14 | 75 | 150 |
| 1930M. | 2,905,182 | 2.50 | 6 | 50 | 100 |
| 1931M. | 3,476,790 | 2.50 | 6 | 75 | 150 |
| 1932M. | 3,955,861 | 2.00 | 6 | 50 | 130 |
| 1934M. | 2,153,729 | 3.50 | 10 | 100 | 300 |
| 1934M, Recut 1 | * | 10.00 | 35 | 125 | 300 |
| 1935M. | 2,754,000 | 2.50 | 8 | 85 | 225 |

* Included in number above. **a.** Small-Date Reverse of 20 centavos.

# Silver Coinage

## *Ten Centavos*

*(Large-Size [1903–1906]: 17.5 mm; Reduced-Size [1907–1935]: 16.5 mm)*

| | Mintage | VF | EF | MS-60 | MS-63 |
|---|---|---|---|---|---|
| 1903 | 5,102,658 | $4 | $5.00 | $35 | $75 |
| 1903, Pf. | (2,558) | | | 100 | 150 |
| 1903S | 1,200,000 | 20 | 45.00 | 350 | 1,000 |
| 1904 | 10,000 | 20 | 50.00 | 120 | 250 |
| 1904, Pf. | (1,355) | | | 110 | 150 |
| 1904S | 5,040,000 | 4 | 9.00 | 65 | 120 |
| 1905, Pf only | (471) | | | 225 | 350 |
| 1906, Pf only | (500) | | | 150 | 250 |
| 1907 | 1,500,781 | 4 | 7.50 | 60 | 135 |
| 1907S | 4,930,000 | 2 | 5.00 | 40 | 70 |
| 1908, Pf only | (500) | | | 175 | 250 |
| 1908S | 3,363,911 | 2 | 5.00 | 40 | 70 |
| 1909S | 312,199 | 30 | 65.00 | 450 | 1,200 |
| 1911S | 1,000,505 | $10.00 | $15.00 | $250 | $600 |
| 1912S | 1,010,000 | 6.00 | 12.00 | 150 | 300 |
| 1912S, S/S | * | | 85.00 | 200 | 500 |
| 1913S | 1,360,693 | 4.25 | 13.00 | 140 | 250 |
| 1914S **(a)** | 1,180,000 | 6.00 | 12.00 | 175 | 375 |
| 1915S | 450,000 | 25.00 | 40.00 | 350 | 750 |
| 1917S | 5,991,148 | 2.00 | 3.00 | 20 | 65 |
| 1918S | 8,420,000 | 2.00 | 3.00 | 20 | 75 |
| 1919S | 1,630,000 | 2.50 | 3.50 | 30 | 110 |
| 1920 | 520,000 | 6.00 | 16.00 | 105 | 300 |
| 1921 | 3,863,038 | 2.00 | 3.00 | 25 | 50 |
| 1929M | 1,000,000 | 2.00 | 3.00 | 25 | 45 |
| 1935M | 1,280,000 | 2.00 | 4.00 | 30 | 50 |

* Included in number above. **a.** Long or short crossbar on 4. Long is slightly more valuable.

## *Twenty Centavos*

*(Large-Size [1903–1906]: 23 mm; Reduced-Size [1907–1929]: 20 mm)*

| | Mintage | VF | EF | MS-60 | MS-63 |
|---|---|---|---|---|---|
| 1903 | 5,350,231 | $3.50 | $15 | $45 | $100 |
| 1903, Pf. | (2,558) | | | 125 | 200 |
| 1903S | 150,080 | 25.00 | 50 | 600 | 1,900 |
| 1904 | 10,000 | 45.00 | 60 | 125 | 200 |
| 1904, Pf. | (1,355) | | | 150 | 225 |
| 1904S | 2,060,000 | 7.50 | 11 | 110 | 200 |
| 1905, Pf only | (471) | | | 250 | 450 |
| 1905S | 420,000 | 20.00 | 35 | 425 | 1,250 |
| 1906, Pf only | (500) | | | 225 | 375 |
| 1907 | 1,250,651 | 6.00 | 12 | 200 | 450 |
| 1907S | 3,165,000 | 4.50 | 10 | 75 | 200 |
| 1908, Pf only | (500) | | | 200 | 325 |
| 1908S | 1,535,000 | 3.50 | 10 | 100 | 300 |
| 1909S | 450,000 | 12.50 | 50 | 600 | 1,500 |
| 1910S | 500,259 | 25.00 | 60 | 400 | 1,200 |
| 1911S | 505,000 | $25.00 | $45.00 | $400 | $1,000 |
| 1912S | 750,000 | 10.00 | 30.00 | 200 | 400 |
| 1913S | 795,000 | 10.00 | 15.00 | 175 | 300 |
| 1914S | 795,000 | 12.50 | 30.00 | 300 | 750 |
| 1915S | 655,000 | 20.00 | 50.00 | 500 | 1,800 |
| 1916S **(a)** | 1,435,000 | 10.00 | 17.50 | 225 | 725 |
| 1917S | 3,150,655 | 5.00 | 8.00 | 75 | 200 |
| 1918S | 5,560,000 | 4.00 | 6.00 | 50 | 125 |
| 1919S | 850,000 | 6.00 | 15.00 | 125 | 225 |
| 1920 | 1,045,415 | 8.00 | 20.00 | 135 | 225 |
| 1921 | 1,842,631 | 2.00 | 7.00 | 50 | 90 |
| 1928M, Mule **(b)** | 100,000 | 15.00 | 50.00 | 900 | 1,800 |
| 1929M | 1,970,000 | 3.00 | 5.00 | 40 | 100 |
| 1929M, 2/2/2 | * | | 75.00 | 250 | 400 |

* Included in number above. **a.** Straight or, slightly scarcer, tilted 6 in date. **b.** Reverse of 1928 5 centavos.

## *Fifty Centavos*

*(Large-Size [1903–1906]: 30 mm; Reduced-Size [1907–1921]: 27 mm)*

| | Mintage | VF | EF | MS-60 | MS-63 |
|---|---|---|---|---|---|
| 1903 | 3,099,061 | $7.50 | $10 | $75 | $150 |
| 1903, Pf. | (2,558) | | | 150 | 275 |
| 1903S | | | *30,000* | | |
| 1904 | 10,000 | 35.00 | 75 | 150 | 300 |
| 1904, Pf. | (1,355) | | | 175 | 350 |
| 1904S | 216,000 | 12.00 | 15 | 125 | 225 |
| 1905, Pf only | (471) | | | 275 | 625 |
| 1905S | 852,000 | 20.00 | 75 | 700 | 2,100 |
| 1906, Pf only | (500) | | | 325 | 575 |
| 1907 | 1,200,625 | 15.00 | 40 | 250 | 475 |
| 1907S | 2,112,000 | $12.50 | $30.00 | $225 | $450 |
| 1908, Pf only | (500) | | | 300 | 525 |
| 1908S | 1,601,000 | 15.00 | 40.00 | 500 | 1,800 |
| 1909S | 528,000 | 17.50 | 60.00 | 450 | 1,400 |
| 1917S | 674,369 | 15.00 | 35.00 | 200 | 550 |
| 1918S | 2,202,000 | 7.50 | 15.00 | 125 | 220 |
| 1918S, S/Inv S. | * | 7.50 | 15.00 | 185 | 600 |
| 1919S | 1,200,000 | 7.50 | 15.00 | 100 | 225 |
| 1920 | 420,000 | 7.50 | 12.50 | 120 | 180 |
| 1921 | 2,316,763 | 5.00 | 11.00 | 70 | 110 |

* Included in number above.

## *One Peso*

***(Large-Size [1903–1906]: 38 mm; Reduced-Size [1907–1912]: 35 mm)***

| | Mintage | VF | EF | MS-60 | MS-63 |
|---|---|---|---|---|---|
| 1903 | 2,788,901 | $35 | $45 | $250 | $550 |
| 1903, Proof | (2,558) | | | 350 | 750 |
| 1903S | 11,361,000 | 35 | 40 | 150 | 325 |
| 1904 | 11,355 | 90 | 110 | 300 | 625 |
| 1904, Proof | (1,355) | | | 450 | 750 |
| 1904S | 6,600,000 | 35 | 50 | 175 | 375 |
| 1905, Proof only | (471) | | | 950 | 2,600 |
| 1905S, Curved Serif on "1" | 6,056,000 | 40 | 60 | 350 | 750 |
| 1905S, Straight Serif on "1" | * | 50 | 75 | 900 | 3,500 |
| 1906, Proof only | (500) | | | $900 | $2,200 |
| 1906S | 201,000 | $1,500 | $3,900 | 17,500 | 32,500 |
| 1907, Pf only *(2 known)* | | | | | 160,000 |
| 1907S | 10,278,000 | 10 | 20 | 250 | 450 |
| 1908, Proof only | (500) | | | 900 | 1,800 |
| 1908S | 20,954,944 | 10 | 20 | 225 | 425 |
| 1909S | 7,578,000 | 15 | 24 | 275 | 500 |
| 1909S, S Over S | * | 35 | 100 | 325 | 750 |
| 1910S | 3,153,559 | 24 | 55 | 425 | 850 |
| 1911S | 463,000 | 45 | 75 | 1,250 | 4,250 |
| 1912S | 680,000 | 100 | 220 | 4,000 | 7,000 |

* Included in number above.

## Manila Mint Opening Medal (1920)

These medals were struck to commemorate the opening of the Manila Mint.

***Designer Clifford Hewitt; composition bronze, silver, gold; diameter 38 mm; plain edge; Mint: Manila.***

| | Mintage | VF-20 | EF-40 | AU-50 | MS-60 | MS-63 | MS-65 |
|---|---|---|---|---|---|---|---|
| Manila Mint medal, 1920, bronze | 3,700 | $50 | $125 | $235 | $785 | $1,350 | $4,500 |
| Manila Mint medal, 1920, silver | 2,200 | 100 | 250 | 350 | 600 | 2,000 | 3,250 |
| Manila Mint medal, 1920, gold | 5 | | | (a) | (b) | | |

**a.** The value in AU-55 is $45,000. **b.** The value in MS-62 is $75,000.

# COMMONWEALTH ISSUES

The Manila Mint ceased operation after the Japanese occupation in 1941. Coins of 1944 and 1945 were made at Philadelphia, Denver, and San Francisco.

## Bronze Coinage

### *One Centavo* *(24 mm)*

| | Mintage | VF | EF | MS-60 | MS-63 |
|---|---|---|---|---|---|
| 1937M | 15,790,492 | $2.00 | $3.00 | $15.00 | $50 |
| 1938M | *10,000,000* | 1.50 | 2.50 | 15.00 | 35 |
| 1939M | *6,500,000* | 2.50 | 3.50 | 17.50 | 55 |
| 1940M | *4,000,000* | $1.25 | $3.00 | $15 | $25 |
| 1941M | *5,000,000* | 3.00 | 7.50 | 20 | 45 |
| 1944S | 58,000,000 | 0.25 | 0.50 | 2 | 4 |

## Copper-Nickel Coinage

### *Five Centavos* *(19 mm)*

| | Mintage | VF | EF | MS-60 | MS-63 |
|---|---|---|---|---|---|
| 1937M | 2,493,872 | $5 | $7.00 | $50 | $75 |
| 1938M | *4,000,000* | 1 | 2.25 | 25 | 55 |
| 1941M | *2,750,000* | 4 | 8.00 | 55 | 150 |
| 1944 **(a)** | 21,198,000 | $0.50 | $1.00 | $2 | $3 |
| 1944S **(a)** | 14,040,000 | 0.25 | 0.50 | 1 | 2 |
| 1945S **(a)** | 72,796,000 | 0.25 | 0.50 | 1 | 2 |

**a.** Copper-nickel-zinc alloy.

## Silver Coinage

### *Ten Centavos (16.5 mm)*

| | Mintage | VF | EF | MS-60 | MS-63 |
|---|---|---|---|---|---|
| 1937M | 3,500,000 | $2.25 | $3.50 | $15 | $45.00 |
| 1938M | *3,750,000* | 1.75 | 2.25 | 12 | 20.00 |
| 1941M | *2,500,000* | 1.50 | 2.00 | 7 | 12.50 |

| | Mintage | VF | EF | MS-60 | MS-63 |
|---|---|---|---|---|---|
| 1944D | 31,592,000 | $1.00 | $2 | $2.50 | $3.50 |
| 1945D | 137,208,000 | 1.00 | 2 | 2.50 | 3.50 |
| 1945D, D/D | * | 8.50 | 15 | 25.00 | 50.00 |

* Included in number above.

### *Twenty Centavos (20 mm)*

| | Mintage | VF | EF | MS-60 | MS-63 |
|---|---|---|---|---|---|
| 1937M | 2,665,000 | $3 | $5.00 | $35 | $40 |
| 1938M | 3,000,000 | 3 | 5.00 | 15 | 20 |
| 1941M | *1,500,000* | 3 | 3.50 | 15 | 20 |

| | Mintage | VF | EF | MS-60 | MS-63 |
|---|---|---|---|---|---|
| 1944D | 28,596,000 | $2 | $2.75 | $3 | $5 |
| 1944D, D/S | * | 5 | 9.00 | 25 | 50 |
| 1945D | 82,804,000 | 2 | 2.75 | 3 | 5 |

* Included in number above.

### *Fifty Centavos (27 mm)*

| | Mintage | VF | EF | MS-60 | MS-63 |
|---|---|---|---|---|---|
| 1944S | 19,187,000 | $5 | $6 | $8 | $10 |
| 1945S | 18,120,000 | 5 | 6 | 8 | 10 |

| | Mintage | VF | EF | MS-60 | MS-63 |
|---|---|---|---|---|---|
| 1945S, S Over S | * | $12 | $25 | $80 | $180 |

* Included in number above.

## Commemorative Issues

Silver Fifty Centavos

Silver One Peso, Busts of Murphy and Quezon

Silver One Peso, Busts of Roosevelt and Quezon

| | Mintage | VF | EF | MS-60 | MS-63 |
|---|---|---|---|---|---|
| 1936M, Silver fifty centavos | 20,000 | $30 | $50 | $100 | $155 |
| 1936M, Silver one peso, busts of Murphy and Quezon | 10,000 | 70 | 85 | 200 | 325 |
| 1936M, Silver one peso, busts of Roosevelt and Quezon | 10,000 | 70 | 85 | 200 | 300 |

## ALASKA RURAL REHABILITATION CORPORATION TOKENS OF 1935

These tokens were issued by the U.S. government for the use of the Midwesterners who relocated to Alaska as part of the Matanuska Valley Colonization Project, to supply them with much-needed federal aid. They were redeemable only at the ARRC stores. The "Bingles," as they were called, were in use only about six months during 1935 and 1936, after which they were redeemed for regular U.S. money and destroyed. They were issued on a basis of family dependents. Each token is similar in size to the corresponding U.S. coin, with the exception of the one-cent piece, which is octagonal. The design is the same on both sides of each denomination.

### Aluminum

| | Mintage | EF | Unc. |
|---|---|---|---|
| One Cent | 5,000 | $90 | $160 |
| Five Cents | 5,000 | 90 | 160 |
| Ten Cents | 5,000 | 90 | 160 |
| Twenty-Five Cents | 3,000 | $135 | $265 |
| Fifty Cents | 2,500 | 135 | 265 |
| One Dollar | 2,500 | 225 | 265 |

### Brass

| | Mintage | EF | Unc. |
|---|---|---|---|
| Five Dollars | 1,000 | $225 | $350 |
| Ten Dollars | 1,000 | $250 | $400 |

With the production of millions of coins each year, it is natural that a few abnormal pieces escape inspection and are inadvertently released for circulation, usually in original bags or rolls of new coins. These are not considered regular issues because they were not made intentionally. They are all eagerly sought by collectors for the information they shed on minting techniques, and as a variation from normal date and mint series collecting.

Nearly every misstruck or error coin is unique in some way, and prices may vary from coin to coin. They may all be classified in general groups related to the kinds of errors or manufacturing malfunctions involved. Collectors value these pieces according to the scarcity of each kind of error for each type of coin. Non-collectors usually view them as curios, and often believe that they must be worth much more than normal coins because they look so strange. In reality, the value assigned to various types of errors by collectors and dealers reflects both supply and demand, and is based on recurring transactions between willing buyers and sellers.

The following listings show current average values for the most frequently encountered kinds of error coins. In each case, the values shown are for coins that are unmarred by serious marks or scratches, and in Uncirculated condition for modern issues, and Extremely Fine condition for obsolete types. Exceptions are valued higher or lower. Error coins of rare date issues generally do not command a premium beyond their normal values. In most cases each of these coins is unique in some respect and must be valued according to its individual appearance, quality, and eye appeal.

There are many other kinds of errors and misstruck coins beyond those listed in this guide book. Some are more valuable, and others less valuable, than the most popular pieces that are listed here as examples of what this interesting field contains. The pieces illustrated are general examples of the types described.

Early in 2002 the mints changed their production methods to a new system designed to eliminate deformed planchets, off-center strikes, and similar errors. They also changed the delivery system of bulk coinage, and no longer shipped loose coins in sewn bags to be counted and wrapped by banks or counting rooms, where error coins were often found and sold to collectors. Under the new system, coins are packaged in large quantities and go directly to automated counters that filter out deformed coins. The result has been that very few error coins have entered the market since late 2002, and almost none after that date. The values shown in these listings are for pre-2002 coins; those dated after that, with but a few exceptions, are valued considerably higher.

For additional details and information about these coins, the following books are recommended:

- Margolis, Arnold, and Weinberg, Fred. *The Error Coin Encyclopedia* (4th ed.), 2004.
- Herbert, Alan. *Official Price Guide to Minting Varieties and Errors,* New York, 1991.
- Brown, Nicholas, David Camire, and Fred Weinberg, *100 Greatest U.S. Error Coins*, Atlanta GA, 2010.

The coins discussed in this section must not be confused with others that have been mutilated or damaged after leaving the mint. Examples of such pieces include coins that have been scratched, hammered, engraved, impressed, acid etched, or plated by individuals to simulate something other than a normal coin. Those pieces have no numismatic value, and can only be considered as altered coins not suitable for a collection.

## TYPES OF ERROR COINS

*Clipped Planchet*—**An incomplete coin, missing 10 to 25% of the metal.** Incomplete planchets result from accidents when the steel rods used to punch out blanks from the metal strip overlap a portion of the strip already punched. There are curved, straight, ragged, incomplete, and elliptical clips. Values may be greater or less depending on the nature and size of the clip. Coins with more than one clip usually command higher values.

*Multiple Strike*—**A coin with at least one additional image from being struck again off center.** Value increases with the number of strikes. These minting errors occur when a finished coin goes back into the press and is struck again with the same dies. The presence of a date can bring a higher value.

No Rim With Rim

*Blank or Planchet*—**A blank disc of metal intended for coinage but not struck with dies.** In the process of preparation for coinage, the blanks are first punched from a strip of metal and then milled to upset the rim. In most instances, first-process pieces (blanks without upset rims) are slightly more valuable than the finished planchets. Values shown are for the most common pieces.

*Defective Die*—**A coin showing raised metal from a large die crack, or small rim break.** Coins that show evidence of light die cracks, polishing, or very minor die damage are generally of little or no value. Prices shown here are for coins with very noticeable, raised die-crack lines, or those for which the die broke away, producing an unstruck area known as a *cud.*

*Off Center*—**A coin that has been struck out of collar and incorrectly centered, with part of the design missing.** Values are for coins with approximately 10 to 20% of design missing from obsolete coins, or 20 to 60% missing from modern coins. These are misstruck coins that were made when the planchet did not enter the coinage press properly. Coins that are struck only slightly off center, with none of the design missing, are called broadstrikes (see the next category). Those with nearly all of the impression missing are generally worth more, but those with a readable date and mint are the most valuable.

*Broadstrike*—**A coin that was struck outside the retaining collar.** When coins are struck without being contained in the collar die, they spread out larger than normal pieces. All denominations have a plain edge.

*Lamination*—**A flaw whereby a fragment of metal has peeled off the coin's surface.** This defect occurs when a foreign substance, such as gas oxides or dirt, becomes trapped in the strip as it is rolled out to the proper thickness. Lamination flaws may be missing or still attached to the coin's surface. Minor flaws may only decrease a coin's value, while a clad coin that is missing the full surface of one or both sides is worth more than the values listed here.

*Brockage*—**A mirror image of the design impressed on the opposite side of the same coin.** These errors are caused when a struck coin remains on either die after striking, and impresses its image into the next blank planchet as it is struck, leaving a negative or mirror image. Off-center and partial brockage coins are worth less than those with full impression. Coins with negative impressions on both sides are usually mutilated pieces made outside the mint by the pressing together of coins.

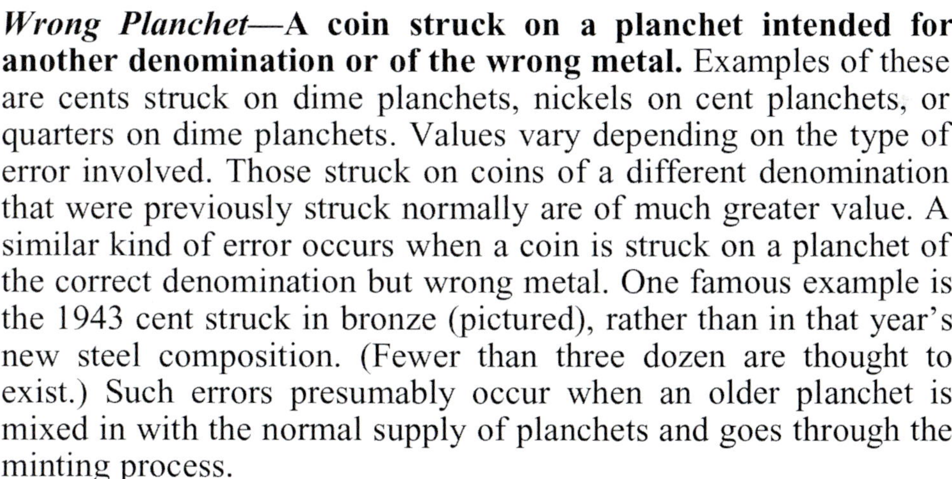

*Wrong Planchet*—**A coin struck on a planchet intended for another denomination or of the wrong metal.** Examples of these are cents struck on dime planchets, nickels on cent planchets, or quarters on dime planchets. Values vary depending on the type of error involved. Those struck on coins of a different denomination that were previously struck normally are of much greater value. A similar kind of error occurs when a coin is struck on a planchet of the correct denomination but wrong metal. One famous example is the 1943 cent struck in bronze (pictured), rather than in that year's new steel composition. (Fewer than three dozen are thought to exist.) Such errors presumably occur when an older planchet is mixed in with the normal supply of planchets and goes through the minting process.

## Mint-Canceled Coins

In mid-2003, the U.S. Mint acquired machines to eliminate security concerns and the cost associated with providing Mint police escorts to private vendors for the melting of scrap, substandard struck coins, planchets, and blanks. Under high pressure, the rollers and blades of these machines cancel the coins and blanks in a manner similar in appearance to the surface of a waffle, and they are popularly known by that term. This process has effectively kept most misstruck coins produced after 2003 from becoming available to collectors. Waffled examples are known for all six 2003-dated coin denominations, from the Lincoln cent through the Sacagawea dollar. The Mint has not objected to these pieces' trading in the open market because they are not considered coins with legal–tender status.

## Misstruck and Error Pieces

| | Clipped Planchet | Multiple Strike | Blank, No Raised Rim | Planchet, Raised Rim | Defective Die | Off Center | Broadstrike | Lamination | Brockage |
|---|---|---|---|---|---|---|---|---|---|
| Large Cent. . . . . . . . . . . | $50 | $1,000 | — | $250 | $25 | $600 | $100 | $25 | $1,000 |
| Indian 1¢. . . . . . . . . . . . | 12 | 600 | — | — | 25 | 150 | 40 | 15 | 400 |
| Lincoln 1¢ (95% Copper) | 3 | 50 | $4 | 3 | 12 | 12 | 8 | 3 | 35 |
| Steel 1¢. . . . . . . . . . . . . | 18 | 250 | 60 | 75 | 15 | 60 | 35 | 15 | 250 |
| Lincoln 1¢ (Zinc) . . . . . . | 4 | 35 | 3 | 2 | 15 | 8 | 5 | 15 | 35 |
| Liberty 5¢ . . . . . . . . . . . | 20 | 700 | — | 250 | 35 | 250 | 110 | 20 | 450 |
| Buffalo 5¢ . . . . . . . . . . . | 20 | 3,250 | — | 600 | 50 | 500 | 300 | 30 | 850 |
| Jefferson 5¢ . . . . . . . . . | 3 | 45 | 15 | 10 | 15 | 12 | 10 | 10 | 40 |
| Wartime 5¢ . . . . . . . . . . | 8 | 450 | 400 | 350 | 25 | 200 | 70 | 15 | 250 |
| Barber 10¢ . . . . . . . . . . | 40 | 750 | — | — | 75 | 325 | 85 | 12 | 400 |
| Mercury 10¢ . . . . . . . . . | 18 | 800 | — | — | 35 | 175 | 55 | 15 | 300 |
| Roosevelt 10¢ (Silver) . . | 7 | 275 | 50 | 40 | 35 | 150 | 45 | 12 | 100 |
| Roosevelt 10¢ (Clad) . . . | 3 | 50 | 4 | 3 | 15 | 12 | 10 | 16 | 40 |
| Washington 25¢ (Silver) | 15 | 400 | 175 | 175 | 25 | 350 | 200 | 15 | 300 |
| Washington 25¢ (Clad). . | 5 | 150 | 8 | 7 | 15 | 70 | 20 | 25 | 50 |
| Bicentennial 25¢ . . . . . . | 25 | 375 | — | — | 65 | 150 | 50 | 50 | 250 |
| Statehood 25¢. . . . . . . . | 20 | 500 | — | — | 25 | 85 | 30 | 150 | 325 |
| Franklin 50¢ . . . . . . . . . | 30 | 2,250 | — | — | 150 | 2,000 | 500 | 25 | 750 |
| Kennedy 50¢ (40% Silver) | 20 | 1,150 | 185 | 150 | 70 | 450 | 200 | 40 | 450 |
| Kennedy 50¢ (Clad) . . . . | 12 | 600 | 135 | 85 | 50 | 250 | 75 | 25 | 300 |
| Bicentennial 50¢ . . . . . . | 40 | 700 | — | — | 90 | 300 | 95 | 40 | 550 |
| Silver $1 . . . . . . . . . . . . | 35 | 5,000 | 1,500 | 1,400 | 950 | 2,250 | 750 | 50 | 600 |
| Eisenhower $1. . . . . . . . | 30 | 1,100 | 150 | 100 | 500 | 600 | 150 | 50 | 950 |
| Bicentennial $1 . . . . . . . | 45 | 1,500 | 135 | — | 750 | 750 | 200 | 50 | 1,100 |
| Anthony $1 . . . . . . . . . . | 20 | 600 | 175 | 100 | 100 | 250 | 75 | 30 | 300 |
| Sacagawea $1. . . . . . . . | 85 | 1,950 | 200 | 60 | 50 | 1,500 | 275 | 50 | 500 |

## Wrong Planchets

| | 1¢ ZN | 1¢ CU | 1¢ Steel | 5¢ | 10¢ (S) | 10¢ (C) | 25¢ (S) | 25¢ (C) | 50¢ (C) |
|---|---|---|---|---|---|---|---|---|---|
| Indian 1¢ | np | — | np | np | $9,500 | np | np | np | np |
| Lincoln 1¢ . . . . . . . . . . . | — | — | — | np | 2,500 | $350 | np | np | np |
| Buffalo 5¢ . . . . . . . . . . . | np | $4,250 | np | — | 7,000 | np | np | np | np |
| Jefferson 5¢ . . . . . . . . . | $300 | 250 | $2,500 | — | 450 | 350 | np | np | np |
| Wartime 5¢ . . . . . . . . . . | np | 2,500 | 3,500 | — | 2,000 | np | np | np | np |
| Washington 25¢ (Silver) | np | 850 | 7,000 | $450 | 750 | — | — | — | np |
| Washington 25¢ (Clad) | — | 750 | np | 225 | — | 350 | — | — | np |
| Bicentennial 25¢ . . . . . . | np | 3,000 | np | 2,500 | — | 3,500 | — | — | np |
| Statehood 25¢. . . . . . . . | 4,500 | np | np | 600 | np | 4,000 | np | — | np |
| Walking Liberty 50¢. . . . | np | — | — | — | — | np | $25,000 | np | np |
| Franklin 50¢ . . . . . . . . . | np | 5,500 | np | 5,000 | 6,000 | np | 1,500 | np | np |
| Kennedy 50¢. . . . . . . . . | np | 3,000 | np | 1,250 | — | 1,750 | — | $650 | — |
| Bicentennial 50¢ . . . . . . | np | 4,000 | np | 3,000 | — | — | — | 1,300 | — |
| Eisenhower $1. . . . . . . . | np | 10,000 | np | 9,000 | — | 10,000 | — | 6,000 | $2,500 |
| Anthony $1 . . . . . . . . . . | — | 3,300 | np | 5,000 | np | — | — | 800 | np |
| Sacagawea $1. . . . . . . . | 10,000 | np | np | 10,000 | np | 10,000 | np | 3,250 | np |

*Note:* ZN = Zinc; CU = Copper; S = Silver; C = Copper-Nickel Clad; np = not possible.

The Kennedy fifty-cent piece struck on an Anthony one-dollar planchet is very rare. Coins struck over other coins of different denominations are usually valued three to five times higher than these prices. Values for State quarter errors vary with each type and state, and are generally much higher than for other quarters. Coins made from mismatched dies (State quarter obverse combined with Sacagawea dollar reverse) are extremely rare.

## THE RED BOOK AS A COLLECTIBLE

The *Guide Book of United States Coins* has long held the record for being the longest-running annual retail coin-price guide. It has passed its 65th anniversary, and collectors seem to be almost as interested in assembling sets of old *Red Book*s as of old coins. The demand for old *Red Book*s has created a solid market. Some who collect these old editions maintain reference libraries of all kinds of coin publications. To them, having one of each edition is essential, because that is the way old books are collected. Others are speculators who believe that the value of old editions will go up as interest and demand increase. Many people who save old *Red Book*s do so to maintain a record of coin prices going back further than any other source.

Following price trends in old *Red Book*s is a good indicator of how well individual coins are doing in comparison to each other. The price information published in this book each year is an average of what collectors are paying for each coin. It is a valuable benchmark, showing how prices have gone up or down over the years. Information like this often gives investors an edge in predicting what the future may hold.

Old *Red Book*s are also a handy resource on collecting trends. They show graphically how grading has changed over the years, what new coins have been discovered and added to the listings, and which areas are growing in popularity. Studying these old books can be educational as well as nostalgic. It's great fun to see what your favorite coins sold for 15 or 25 years ago or more—and a bit frustrating to realize what might have been if we had only bought the right coins at the right time in years past.

Many collectors have asked about the quantities printed of each edition. That information has never been published, and now no company records exist specifying how many were made. The original author, R.S. Yeoman, told inquirers that the first press run in November 1946 was for 9,000 copies. In February 1947 an additional 9,000 copies were printed to satisfy the unexpected demand.

There was a slight difference between the first and second printings. The wording in the first printing, at the bottom of page 135, reads, "which probably accounts for the scarcity of *this* date." Those last few words were changed to "the scarcity of *1903 O*" in the second printing.

The second edition had a press run of 22,000. The printing of each edition thereafter gradually increased, with the highest number ever being reached with the 18th edition, dated 1965. In that year, at the top of a booming coin market, a whopping 1,200,000 copies were produced. Since that time the numbers have decreased, but the *Red Book* still maintains a record of being the world's largest-selling coin publication each year.

In some years a very limited number of *Red Book*s were made for use by price contributors. Those were interleaved with blank pages. No more than 50 copies were ever made for any one year. Perhaps fewer than 20 were made in the first few years. Three of these of the first edition, and one of the second edition, are currently known. Their value is now in four figures. Those made in the 1960s sell for about $300–$500 today.

There are other unusual *Red Book*s that command exceptional prices. One of the most popular is the 1987 special edition that was made for, and distributed only to, people who attended the 1986 American Numismatic Association banquet in Milwaukee. Only 500 of those were printed with a special commemorative cover.

Error books are also popular with collectors. The most common is one with double-stamped printing on the cover. The second most frequently seen are those with an upside-down cover. Probably the best known of the error books is the 1963 16th edition with a missing page. For some uncanny reason, page 239 is duplicated in some of those books, and page 237 is missing. The error was corrected on most of the printing.

The terminology used to describe book condition differs from that utilized in grading coins. A "Very Fine" book is one that is nearly new, with minimal signs of use. Early editions of the *Red Book* are rarely if ever found in anything approaching "New" condition. Exceptionally well-preserved older editions command a substantial premium and are in great demand. Nice used copies that are still clean and in good shape, but slightly worn from use, are also desirable. Only the early editions are worth a premium in badly worn condition.

For a more detailed history and edition-by-edition study of the *Red Book*, see *A Guide Book of The Official Red Book of United States Coins* (Whitman, 2009).

### Classic Hardcover Binding

| Year/Edition | Issue Price | VG | F | VF | New |
|---|---|---|---|---|---|
| 1947 (1st ed.), 1st Printing | $1.50 | $275 | $475 | $775 | $1,500 **(a)** |
| 1947 (1st ed.), 2nd Printing | 1.50 | 225 | 425 | 775 | 1,200 **(a)** |
| 1948 (2nd ed.) | 1.50 | 60 | 125 | 200 | 450 **(a)** |
| 1949 (3rd ed.) | 1.50 | 60 | 135 | 300 | 500 **(a)** |
| 1951/52 (4th ed.) | 1.50 | 50 | 100 | 165 | 300 **(a)** |
| 1952/53 (5th ed.) | 1.50 | 110 | 200 | 385 | 1,200 **(a)** |
| 1953/54 (6th ed.) | 1.75 | 40 | 60 | 85 | 100 |
| 1954/55 (7th ed.) | 1.75 | 35 | 55 | 80 | 100 |
| 1955 (8th ed.) | 1.75 | 30 | 40 | 70 | 80 |
| 1956 (9th ed.) | 1.75 | 20 | 35 | 45 | 70 |
| 1957 (10th ed.) | 1.75 | 10 | 15 | 35 | 50 |
| 1958 (11th ed.) | 1.75 | | 8 | 12 | 20 |
| 1959 (12th ed.) | 1.75 | | 8 | 10 | 20 |
| 1960 (13th ed.) | 1.75 | | 7 | 9 | 20 |
| 1961 (14th ed.) | 1.75 | | 4 | 6 | 20 |
| 1962 (15th ed.) | 1.75 | | 4 | 6 | 15 |
| 1963 (16th ed.) | 1.75 | | 4 | 6 | 15 |
| 1964 (17th ed.) | 1.75 | | 3 | 4 | 10 |
| 1965 (18th ed.) | 1.75 | | 3 | 4 | 10 |
| 1966 (19th ed.) | 1.75 | | 3 | 4 | 10 |
| 1967 (20th ed.) | 1.75 | | 2 | 3 | 8 |
| 1968 (21st ed.) | 2.00 | | 2 | 3 | 8 |
| 1969 (22nd ed.) | 2.00 | | 2 | 3 | 8 |
| 1970 (23rd ed.) | 2.50 | | 2 | 3 | 8 |
| 1971 (24th ed.) | 2.50 | | 2 | 3 | 7 |
| 1972 (25th ed.) | 2.50 | | 2 | 3 | 7 |
| 1973 (26th ed.) | 2.50 | | 2 | 3 | 7 |
| 1974 (27th ed.) | 2.50 | | 2 | 3 | 7 |
| 1975 (28th ed.) | 3.00 | | | 3 | 6 |
| 1976 (29th ed.) | 3.95 | | | 3 | 6 |
| 1977 (30th ed.) | 3.95 | | | 3 | 6 |
| 1978 (31st ed.) | 3.95 | | | 3 | 6 |
| 1979 (32nd ed.) | 3.95 | | | 3 | 6 |
| 1980 (33rd ed.) | 3.95 | | | 3 | 6 |
| 1981 (34th ed.) | 4.95 | | | 2 | 5 |
| 1982 (35th ed.) | 4.95 | | | 2 | 5 |

| Year/Edition | Issue Price | VF | New |
|---|---|---|---|
| 1983 (36th ed.) | $5.95 | $2 | $5 |
| 1984 (37th ed.) | 5.95 | 2 | 5 |
| 1985 (38th ed.) | 5.95 | 2 | 5 |
| 1986 (39th ed.) | 5.95 | 2 | 5 |
| 1987 (40th ed.) | 6.95 | 2 | 5 |
| 1988 (41st ed.) | 6.95 | 2 | 5 |
| 1989 (42nd ed.) | 6.95 | 2 | 5 |
| 1990 (43rd ed.) | 7.95 | 2 | 5 |
| 1991 (44th ed.) | 8.95 | 2 | 5 |
| 1992 (45th ed.) | 8.95 | 2 | 5 |
| 1993 (46th ed.) | 9.95 | | 5 |
| 1994 (47th ed.) | 9.95 | | 3 |
| 1995 (48th ed.) | 10.95 | | 3 |
| 1996 (49th ed.) | 10.95 | | 3 |
| 1997 (50th ed.) | 11.95 | | 3 |
| 1998 (51st ed.) | 11.95 | | 2 |
| 1999 (52nd ed.) | 11.95 | | 2 |
| 2000 (53rd ed.) | 12.95 | | 2 |
| 2001 (54th ed.) | 13.95 | | 2 |
| 2002 (55th ed.) | 14.95 | | 2 |
| 2003 (56th ed.) | 15.95 | | 2 |
| 2004 (57th ed.) | 15.95 | | 2 |
| 2005 (58th ed.) | 15.95 | | 2 |
| 2006 (59th ed.) | 16.95 | | 2 |
| 2007 (60th ed.) | 16.95 | | 2 |
| 2008 (61st ed.) | 16.95 | | 2 |
| 2009 (62nd ed.) | 16.95 | | 2 |
| 2010 (63rd ed.) | 16.95 | | 2 |
| 2011 (64th ed.) | 16.95 | | 2 |
| 2012 (65th ed.) | 16.95 | | 2 |
| 2013 (66th ed.) | 16.95 | | 2 |
| 2014 (67th ed.) | 16.95 | | 2 |
| 2015 (68th ed.) | 16.95 | | 2 |
| 2016 (69th ed.) | 16.95 | | 2 |
| 2017 (70th ed.) | 16.95 | | 2 |
| 2018 (71st ed.) **(b)** | 16.95 | | 2 |
| 2019 (72nd ed.) **(c)** | 17.95 | | 2 |
| 2020 (73rd ed.) | 17.95 | | 2 |

*Note:* Values are for unsigned books. Those signed by R.S. Yeoman are worth substantially more. See pages 443 and 444 for special editions in the classic hardcover binding. **a.** Values are for books in Near Mint condition, as truly New copies are effectively nonexistent. **b.** Features a gold-foil portrait of first Mint director David Rittenhouse. **c.** Features a gold-foil portrait of Editor Emeritus Kenneth Bressett.

### *Softcovers (1993–2007)*

The first softcover (trade paperback) *Red Book* was the 1993 (46th) edition. The softcover binding was offered (alongside other formats) in the 1993, 1994, 1995, and 1996 editions; again in the 1998 edition; and from 2003 through 2007. All are fairly common and easily collectible today. Values in New condition range from $2 up to $3–$4 for the earlier editions.

### *Spiralbound Softcovers (1997 to Date)*

The first spiralbound softcover *Red Book* was the 1997 (50th) edition. The format was next available in the 1999 edition, and it has been an annually offered format since then. Today the spiralbound softcovers all are easily collectible. The 1997 edition is worth $4 in New condition, and later editions are valued around $2.

### *Spiralbound Hardcovers (2008 to Date)*

The first spiralbound hardcover *Red Book* was the 2008 (61st) edition. The format has been available (alongside other formats) every edition since. All spiralbound hardcovers are readily available to collectors, and are valued from $2 to $4.

### *Journal Edition (2009)*

The large-sized Journal Edition, featuring a three-ring binder, color-coded tabbed dividers, and removable pages, was issued only for the 2009 (62nd) edition. Today it is valued at $5 in VF and $30 in New condition.

### *Large Print Editions (2010 to Date)*

An oversized format has been offered annually since the 2010 (63rd) edition. All editions are readily available to collectors and are valued at $5 in New condition.

### *Leather Limited Editions (2005 to Date)*

| Year/Edition | Print Run | Issue Price | New |
|---|---|---|---|
| 2005 (58th ed.) | 3,000 | $69.95 | $75 |
| 2006 (59th ed.) | 3,000 | 69.95 | 75 |
| 2007 (60th ed.) | 3,000 | 69.95 | 75 |
| 2007 1947 Tribute Edition | 500 | 49.95 | 125 |
| 2008 (61st ed.) | 3,000 | 69.95 | 75 |
| 2008 (61st ed.), Numismatic Literary Guild **(a)** | 135* | | 650 |
| 2008 (61st ed.), American Numismatic Society **(b)** | 250* | | 500 |
| 2009 (62nd ed.) | 3,000 | 69.95 | 75 |
| 2010 (63rd ed.) | 1,500 | $69.95 | $75 |
| 2011 (64th ed.) | 1,500 | 69.95 | 75 |
| 2012 (65th ed.) | 1,000 | 69.95 | 75 |
| 2013 (66th ed.) | 1,000 | 69.95 | 75 |
| 2014 (67th ed.) | 1,000 | 69.95 | 75 |
| 2015 (68th ed.) | 500 | 99.95 | 100 |
| 2016 (69th ed.) | 500 | 99.95 | 100 |
| 2017 (70th ed.) | 500 | 99.95 | 100 |
| 2018 (71st ed.) | 500 | 99.95 | 100 |
| 2019 (72nd ed.) | 500 | 99.95 | 100 |

* Included in total print-run quantity. **a.** One hundred thirty-five imprinted copies of the 2008 leather Limited Edition were created. Of these, 125 were distributed to members of the NLG at its 2007 literary awards ceremony; the remaining 10 were distributed from Whitman Publishing headquarters in Atlanta. **b.** Two hundred fifty copies of the 2008 leather Limited Edition were issued with a special bookplate honoring the 150th anniversary of the ANS. They were distributed to attendees of the January 2008 celebratory banquet in New York.

### *Special Editions*

| Year/Edition | Print Run | Issue Price | VF | New |
|---|---|---|---|---|
| 1987 (40th ed.), American Numismatic Association 95th Anniversary | *500* | | $600 | $750 |
| 1992 (45th ed.), American Numismatic Association 100th Anniversary | *600* | | 120 | 225 |
| 1997 (50th ed.), *Red Book* 50th Anniversary | 1,200 | $24.95 | 50 | 100 |
| 2002 (55th ed.), American Numismatic Association "Target 2001" | 500 | 100.00 | 25 | 50 |
| 2002 (55th ed.), SS *Central America* | | 35.00 | 20 | 30 |
| 2005 (58th ed.), FUN (Florida United Numismatists) 50th Anniversary | *1,100* | | 50 | 100 |
| 2007 (60th ed.), American Numismatic Association 115th Anniversary | 500 | | 50 | 100 |
| 2007 (60th ed.), Michigan State Numismatic Society 50th Anniversary | *500* | | 50 | 100 |
| 2007 (1st ed.), 1947 Tribute Edition | | 17.95 | 5 | 20 |

| Year/Edition | Print Run | Issue Price | VF | New |
|---|---|---|---|---|
| 2008 (61st ed.), ANA Milwaukee World's Fair of Money | *1,080* | | $25 | $50 |
| 2008 (61st ed.), Stack's Rare Coins | | | 5 | 15 |
| 2010 (63rd ed.), Hardcover, Philadelphia Expo **(a)** | | $24.95 | 20 | 40 |
| 2011 (64th ed.), Boston Numismatic Society | | 85.00 | 45 | 90 |
| 2012 (65th ed.), American Numismatic Association | 800 | 100.00 | 30 | 60 |
| 2013 (66th ed.), American Numismatic Society **(b)** | 250 | | 100 | 250 |
| 2015 (68th ed.), Central States Numismatic Society | 500 | 15.00 | 25 | 60 |
| 2016 (69th ed.), ANA 125th Anniversary | | 100.00 | 40 | 75 |
| 2018 (71st ed.) NGC 30th Anniversary | | | 60 | 100 |
| 2020 (73rd ed.) Chicago Coin Club 100th Anniversary | 250 | | 50 | 125 |
| 2021 (74th ed.) Philippine Collectors Forum / 100th Anniversary Manila Mint | 250 | | | |

**a.** Two thousand and nine copies of a special 2010 hardcover edition were made for distribution to dealers at the premiere Whitman Coin and Collectibles Philadelphia Expo (September 2009). Extra copies were sold at $50 apiece with proceeds benefiting the National Federation for the Blind. **b.** Two hundred fifty copies of the 2013 hardcover were issued with a special bookplate honoring ANS Trustees' Award recipient (and *Red Book* contributor) Roger Siboni.

## THE BLUE BOOK AS A COLLECTIBLE

The precursor to the *Red Book* was *The Handbook of United States Coins With Premium List,* popularly known as the "Blue Book." Its mastermind was R.S. Yeoman, who had been hired by Western Publishing as a commercial artist in 1932. He distributed Western's Whitman line of "penny boards" to coin collectors, promoting them through department stores, along with children's books and games. He eventually arranged for Whitman to expand the line into other denominations, giving them the reputation of a numismatic endeavor rather than a "game" of filling holes with missing coins. He also developed these flat boards into a line of popular folders.

Yeoman began to compile coin-mintage data and market values to aid collectors. This research grew into the Blue Book: a coin-by-coin guide to the average prices dealers would pay for U.S. coins. The first two editions were both published in 1942.

In the first edition of the *Red Book*, Whitman Publishing would describe the Blue Book as "a low-priced standard reference book of United States coins and kindred issues" for which there had been "a long-felt need among American collectors."

The Blue Book has been published annually (except in 1944 and 1950) since its debut. Past editions offer valuable information about the hobby of yesteryear as well as developments in numismatic research and the marketplace. Old Blue Books are collectible; most editions after the 12th can be found for a few dollars in VF or better condition. Major variants were produced for the third, fourth, and ninth editions, including perhaps the only "overdate" books in American numismatic publishing. Either to conserve the previous years' covers or to correct an error in binding, the cloth on some third-edition covers was overstamped "Fourth Edition," and a number of eighth-edition covers were overstamped "Ninth Edition." The third edition was produced in several shades of blue ranging from light to dark. Some copies of the fourth edition were also produced in black cloth—the only time the Blue Book was bound in other than blue.

### *Valuation Guide for Select Past Editions of the Blue Book*

| Edition | Date* Title-Page | Date* Copyright | VF | New |
|---|---|---|---|---|
| 1st | 1942 | 1942 | $100 | $250 |
| 2nd | 1943 | 1942 | 40 | 60 |
| 3rd | 1944 | 1943 | 25 | 60 |
| 4th | *None* | 1945 | 25 | 50 |
| 5th | *None* | 1946 | 20 | 50 |
| 6th | 1948 | 1947 | 15 | 30 |
| 7th | 1949 | 1948 | $12 | $25 |
| 8th | 1950 | 1949 | 10 | 20 |
| 9th | 1952 | 1951 | 5 | 10 |
| 10th | 1953 | 1952 | 5 | 10 |
| 11th | 1954 | 1953 | 3 | 7 |
| 12th | 1955 | 1954 | 3 | 7 |

* During its early years of production, the Blue Book's date presentation was not standardized. Full information is given here to aid in precise identification of early editions.

These charts show the bullion values of silver and gold U.S. coins. These are intrinsic values and do not reflect any numismatic premium a coin might have. The weight listed under each denomination is its actual silver weight (ASW) or actual gold weight (AGW).

In recent years, the bullion price of silver has fluctuated considerably. You can use the following chart to determine the approximate bullion value of many 19th- and 20th-century silver coins at various price levels—or you can calculate the approximate value by multiplying the current spot price of silver by the ASW for each coin, as indicated. Dealers generally purchase common silver coins at around 15% below bullion value, and sell them at around 15% above bullion value.

Nearly all U.S. gold coins have an additional premium value beyond their bullion content, and thus are not subject to minor bullion-price variations. The premium amount is not necessarily tied to the bullion price of gold, but is usually determined by supply and demand levels in the numismatic marketplace. Because these factors can vary significantly, there is no reliable formula for calculating "percentage below and above bullion" prices that would remain accurate over time. The gold chart below lists bullion values based on AGW only; consult a coin dealer to ascertain current buy and sell prices.

### *Bullion Values of Silver Coins*

| Silver Price Per Ounce | Wartime Nickel .05626 oz. | Dime .07234 oz. | Quarter .18084 oz. | Half Dollar .36169 oz. | Silver Clad Half Dollar .14792 oz. | Silver Dollar .77344 oz. |
|---|---|---|---|---|---|---|
| $14 | $0.79 | $1.01 | $2.53 | $5.06 | $2.07 | $10.83 |
| 15 | 0.84 | 1.09 | 2.71 | 5.43 | 2.22 | 11.60 |
| 16 | 0.90 | 1.16 | 2.89 | 5.79 | 2.37 | 12.38 |
| 17 | 0.96 | 1.23 | 3.07 | 6.15 | 2.51 | 13.15 |
| 18 | 1.01 | 1.30 | 3.26 | 6.51 | 2.66 | 13.92 |
| 19 | 1.07 | 1.37 | 3.44 | 6.87 | 2.81 | 14.70 |
| 20 | 1.13 | 1.45 | 3.62 | 7.23 | 2.96 | 15.47 |
| 21 | 1.18 | 1.52 | 3.80 | 7.60 | 3.11 | 16.24 |
| 22 | 1.24 | 1.59 | 3.98 | 7.96 | 3.25 | 17.02 |
| 23 | 1.29 | 1.66 | 4.16 | 8.32 | 3.40 | 17.79 |
| 24 | 1.35 | 1.74 | 4.34 | 8.68 | 3.55 | 18.56 |

### *Bullion Values of Gold Coins*

| Gold Price Per Ounce | $5.00 Liberty Head 1839–1908 Indian Head 1908–1929 .24187 oz. | $10.00 Liberty Head 1838–1907 Indian Head 1907–1933 .48375 oz. | $20.00 1849–1933 .96750 oz. |
|---|---|---|---|
| $1,550 | $374.90 | $749.81 | $1,499.63 |
| 1,575 | 380.95 | 761.91 | 1,523.81 |
| 1,600 | 386.99 | 774.00 | 1,548.00 |
| 1,625 | 393.04 | 786.09 | 1,572.19 |
| 1,650 | 399.09 | 798.19 | 1,596.38 |
| 1,675 | 405.13 | 810.28 | 1,620.56 |
| 1,700 | 411.18 | 822.38 | 1,644.75 |
| 1,725 | 417.23 | 834.47 | 1,668.94 |
| 1,750 | 423.27 | 846.56 | 1,693.13 |
| 1,775 | 429.32 | 858.66 | 1,717.31 |
| 1,800 | 435.37 | 870.75 | 1,741.50 |

*Note:* The U.S. bullion coins first issued in 1986 are unlike the older regular issues. They contain the following amounts of pure metal: silver $1, 1 oz.; gold $50, 1 oz.; gold $25, 1/2 oz.; gold $10, 1/4 oz.; gold $5, 1/10 oz.

## TOP 250 U.S. COIN PRICES REALIZED AT AUCTION

| Rank | Price | Coin | Grade | Firm | Date |
|---|---|---|---|---|---|
| 1 | $10,016,875 | $1(s), 1794 | PCGS SP-66 | Stack's Bowers | Jan-13 |
| 2 | 7,590,020 | $20, 1933 | Gem BU | Soth/Stack's | Jul-02 |
| 3 | 4,993,750 | $1(s), 1794 | PCGS MS-66+ | Soth/Stack's Bwrs | Sep-15 |
| 4 | 4,582,500 | Prefed, 1787, Brasher dbln, EB on Wing | NGC MS-63 | Heritage | Jan-14 |
| 5 | 4,560,000 | 5¢, 1913, Liberty Head **(U)** | PCGS PF-66 | Stack's Bowers | Aug-18 |
| 6 | 4,140,000 | $1(s), 1804, Class I | PCGS PF-68 | B&M | Aug-99 |
| 7 | 3,960,000 | $1 Trade, 1885 | NGC PF-66 | Heritage | Jan-19 |
| 8 | 3,877,500 | $1(s), 1804, Class I | PCGS PF-62 | Heritage | Aug-13 |
| 9 | 3,737,500 | 5¢, 1913, Liberty Head **(A)** | NGC PF-64 | Heritage | Jan-10 |
| 10 | 3,737,500 | $1(s), 1804, Class I | NGC PF-62 | Heritage | Apr-08 |
| 11 | 3,290,000 | $1(s), 1804, Class I | PCGS PF-65 | Soth/Stack's Bwrs | Mar-17 |
| 12 | 3,290,000 | 5¢, 1913, Liberty Head **(A)** | NGC PF-64 | Heritage | Jan-14 |
| 13 | 3,172,500 | 5¢, 1913, Liberty Head | PCGS PF-63 | Heritage | Apr-13 |
| 14 | 2,990,000 | $20, MCMVII, Ultra HR, LE **(B)** | PCGS PF-69 | Heritage | Nov-05 |
| 15 | 2,990,000 | Prefed, 1787, Brasher, EB on Breast **(C)** | NGC EF-45 | Heritage | Jan-05 |
| 16 | 2,820,000 | $1(s), 1794 | PCGS MS-64 | Stack's Bowers | Aug-17 |
| 17 | 2,760,000 | $20, MCMVII, Ultra HR, LE **(B)** | PCGS PF-69 | Stack's Bowers | Jun-12 |
| 18 | 2,640,000 | $1(s), 1804, Class I **(V)** | PCGS PF-62 | Heritage | Jun-18 |
| 19 | 2,585,000 | $10, 1795, 13 Leaves, BD-4 | PCGS MS-66+ | Soth/Stack's Bwrs | Sep-15 |
| 20 | 2,585,000 | Pattern 1¢, 1792, Birch Cent, LE, J-4 | NGC MS-65RB | Heritage | Jan-15 |
| 21 | 2,574,000 | $4, 1880, Coiled Hair **(D)** | NGC PF-67 Cam | Bonhams | Sep-13 |
| 22 | 2,415,000 | Prefed, 1787, Brasher, EB on Wing | NGC AU-55 | Heritage | Jan-05 |
| 23 | 2,350,000 | $2.50, 1808 | PCGS MS-65 | Soth/Stack's Bwrs | May-15 |
| 24 | 2,350,000 | 1¢, 1793, Chain AMERICA, S-4 | PCGS MS-66BN | Heritage | Jan-15 |
| 25 | 2,300,000 | $1(s), 1804, Class III | PCGS PF-58 | Heritage | Apr-09 |
| 26 | 2,232,500 | Pattern 25¢, 1792, copper, J-12 | NGC MS-63BN | Heritage | Jan-15 |
| 27 | 2,185,000 | $10, 1907, Rounded Rim | NGC Satin PF-67 | Heritage | Jan-11 |
| 28 | 2,160,000 | $20, 1927-D **(W)** | PCGS MS-65+ | Heritage | Jan-20 |
| 29 | 2,160,000 | $5, 1854-S | NGC EF-45 | Heritage | Aug-18 |
| 30 | 2,115,000 | $20, MCMVII, Ultra HR, LE | PCGS PF-68 | Heritage | Jan-15 |
| 31 | 1,997,500 | 10¢, 1894-S | PCGS PF-66 | Heritage | Jan-16 |
| 32 | 1,997,500 | Pattern 1¢, 1792 Silver Center, J-1 | PCGS MS-64BN | Heritage | Aug-14 |
| 33 | 1,997,500 | $20, 1927-D | NGC MS-66 | Heritage | Jan-14 |
| 34 | 1,897,500 | $20, 1927-D | PCGS MS-67 | Heritage | Nov-05 |
| 35 | 1,880,000 | Pattern $20, 1879 Quintuple Stella, J-1643 | PCGS PF-64Dcam | Legend | May-16 |
| 36 | 1,880,000 | $1(s), 1804, Class III | NGC PF-55 | Stack's Bowers | Aug-14 |
| 37 | 1,840,000 | 10¢, 1873-CC, No Arrows | PCGS MS-65 | Stack's Bowers | Aug-12 |
| 38 | 1,840,000 | 5¢, 1913, Liberty Head | NGC PF-66 | Superior | Mar-08 |
| 39 | 1,840,000 | $20, MCMVII, Ultra HR, LE | PCGS PF-68 | Heritage | Jan-07 |
| 40 | 1,840,000 | $1(s), 1804, Class I **(E)** | PCGS PF-64 | Stack's | Oct-00 |
| 41 | 1,821,250 | $4, 1880, Coiled Hair | NGC PF-67 | Heritage | Apr-15 |
| 42 | 1,815,000 | $1(s), 1804, Class I | PF-63 | B&M/Stack's | Apr-97 |
| 43 | 1,740,000 | Pre-Fed, 1792, Washington $10, M-31 | NGC EF-45* | Heritage | Aug-18 |
| 44 | 1,725,000 | $2.50, 1796, No Stars **(F)** | PCGS MS-65 | Heritage | Jan-08 |
| 45 | 1,725,000 | $10, 1920-S | PCGS MS-67 | Heritage | Mar-07 |
| 46 | 1,645,000 | $20, 1861, Paquet Reverse **(G)** | PCGS MS-61 | Heritage | Aug-14 |
| 47 | 1,610,000 | $10, 1839/8, Type of 1838, Lg Letters **(H)** | NGC PF-67 Ucam | Heritage | Jan-07 |
| 48 | 1,610,000 | $20, 1861, Paquet Reverse **(G)** | PCGS MS-61 | Heritage | Aug-06 |
| 49 | 1,552,500 | 10¢, 1894-S | PCGS PF-64 | Stack's | Oct-07 |
| 50 | 1,527,500 | 25¢, 1796, B-2 | PCGS MS-66 | Soth/Stack's Bwrs | May-15 |
| 51 | 1,527,500 | 50¢, 1797, O-101a | PCGS MS-66 | Soth/Stack's Bwrs | May-15 |
| 52 | 1,527,500 | Prefed, 1776, Cont. $1 Silver, N-3D | NGC MS-62 | Heritage | Jan-15 |
| 53 | 1,527,500 | Prefed, 1776, Cont. $1 Silver, N-1C | NGC EF-40 | Heritage | Jan-15 |
| 54 | 1,527,500 | 25¢, 1796, B-2 | NGC MS-67+ | Heritage | Nov-13 |

| Rank | Price | Coin | Grade | Firm | Date |
|---|---|---|---|---|---|
| 55 | $1,500,000 | 1¢, 1793, Chain, S-1 | PCGS MS-64BN+ | Heritage | Jan-19 |
| 56 | 1,495,000 | $20, 1927-D | PCGS MS-66 | Heritage | Jan-10 |
| 57 | 1,495,000 | $20, 1921 | PCGS MS-63 | B&M | Aug-06 |
| 58 | 1,485,000 | 5¢, 1913, Liberty Head | Gem PF-66 | B&M/Stack's | May-96 |
| 59 | 1,437,500 | $20, 1856-O | NGC SP-63 | Heritage | May-09 |
| 60 | 1,410,000 | Prefed, 1776, Cont. $1 Silver, N-3D | NGC MS-63 | Heritage | May-14 |
| 61 | 1,410,000 | Pattern 1¢, 1792, Silver Center, J-1 | NGC MS-63BN+ | Heritage | May-14 |
| 62 | 1,410,000 | Pattern half disme, 1792, J-7 **(I)** | PCGS SP-67 | Heritage | Jan-13 |
| 63 | 1,380,000 | $5, 1829, Large Date | PCGS PF-64 | Heritage | Jan-12 |
| 64 | 1,380,000 | 1¢, 1793, Chain AMERICA, S-4 | PCGS MS-65BN | Heritage | Jan-12 |
| 65 | 1,380,000 | 50¢, 1797, O-101a **(J)** | NGC MS-66 | Stack's | Jul-08 |
| 66 | 1,380,000 | $2.50, 1796, No Stars **(F)** | PCGS MS-65 | Stack's (ANR) | Jun-05 |
| 67 | 1,351,250 | $5, 1833, BD-1 | PCGS PF-67 | Soth/Stack's Bwrs | May-16 |
| 68 | 1,322,500 | $3, 1855-S | NGC PF-64 Cam | Heritage | Aug-11 |
| 69 | 1,322,500 | Pattern half disme, 1792, J-7 **(I)** | PCGS SP-67 | Heritage | Apr-06 |
| 70 | 1,322,500 | $20, 1927-D | NGC MS-65 | Heritage | Jan-06 |
| 71 | 1,322,500 | 10¢, 1894-S | NGC PF-66 | DLRC | Mar-05 |
| 72 | 1,320,000 | 10¢, 1894-S | PCGS PF-63 | Stack's Bowers | Aug-19 |
| 73 | 1,292,500 | Pattern half disme, 1792, J-7 **(I)** | PCGS SP-67 | Heritage | Aug-14 |
| 74 | 1,292,500 | 50¢, 1797, O-101a | PCGS MS-65+ | Heritage | Aug-14 |
| 75 | 1,265,000 | Pattern $10, 1874, Bickford, J-1373 | PCGS PF-65 DCam | Heritage | Jan-10 |
| 76 | 1,265,000 | 1¢, 1795, Reeded Edge, S-79 **(K)** | PCGS VG-10 | Goldberg | Sep-09 |
| 77 | 1,265,000 | $1(s), 1795, Flowing Hair, B-7, BB-18 | V Ch Gem MS | Bullowa | Dec-05 |
| 78 | 1,210,000 | $20, MCMVII, Ultra HR, LE **(L)** | PCGS PF-67 | Goldberg | May-99 |
| 79 | 1,207,500 | $1(s), 1794 | NGC MS-64 | B&M | Aug-10 |
| 80 | 1,207,500 | $1(s), 1866, No Motto | NGC PF-63 | Stack's (ANR) | Jan-05 |
| 81 | 1,207,500 | $1(s), 1804, Class III **(M)** | PCGS PF-58 | B&M | Jul-03 |
| 82 | 1,175,000 | $5, 1798, Small Eagle, BD-1 | PCGS AU-55 | Soth/Stack's Bwrs | Sep-15 |
| 83 | 1,175,000 | Pattern 1¢, 1792, Birch Cent, LE, J-4 | PCGS AU-58 | Stack's Bowers | Mar-15 |
| 84 | 1,175,000 | Prefed, 1783, quint, T-II, Nova Const. | PCGS AU-53 | Heritage | Apr-13 |
| 85 | 1,175,000 | $1(s), 1796, Sm Dt, Sm Ltrs, B-2, BB-63 | NGC MS-65 | Heritage | Apr-13 |
| 86 | 1,150,000 | 1/2¢, 1794, C-7 **(G)** | PCGS MS-67RB | Goldberg | Jan-14 |
| 87 | 1,150,000 | Pattern 1¢, 1792, Silver Center Cent, J-1 | PCGS MS-61BN | Heritage | Apr-12 |
| 88 | 1,150,000 | $1(s), 1794 | NGC MS-64 | Stack's (ANR) | Jun-05 |
| 89 | 1,145,625 | Pattern half disme, 1792, J-7 | NGC MS-68 | Stack's Bowers | Jan-13 |
| 90 | 1,140,000 | $1 Trade, 1884 | NGC PF-66 | Heritage | Jan-19 |
| 91 | 1,121,250 | 1/2¢, 1811, C-1 | PCGS MS-66RB | Goldberg | Jan-14 |
| 92 | 1,116,250 | $4, 1880, Coiled Hair | PCGS PF-65 | Heritage | Jun-15 |
| 93 | 1,092,500 | $20, 1921 | PCGS MS-66 | Heritage | Nov-05 |
| 94 | 1,092,500 | $1(s), 1870-S | BU PL | Stack's | May-03 |
| 95 | 1,057,500 | $1(s), 1795 Draped Bust, BB-51 | PCGS SP-66 | Soth/Stack's Bwrs | May-16 |
| 96 | 1,057,500 | $10, 1795, 9 Leaves, BD-3 | PCGS MS-63+ | Soth/Stack's Bwrs | Sep-15 |
| 97 | 1,057,500 | Pattern disme, 1792, copper, J-11 | NGC MS-64RB | Heritage | Jan-15 |
| 98 | 1,057,500 | Terr, 1852, Humbert, $10, K-10 | NGC MS-68 | Heritage | Apr-13 |
| 99 | 1,057,500 | $20, MCMVII, Ultra HR, LE of 06 | PCGS PF-58 | Heritage | Aug-12 |
| 100 | 1,050,000 | $4, 1879, Coiled Hair | NGC PF-66 Cam | Heritage | Jan-19 |
| 101 | 1,041,300 | $4, 1879, Coiled Hair **(N)** | NGC PF-67 Cam | Bonhams | Sep-13 |
| 102 | 1,035,000 | 10¢, 1894-S | PCGS PF-65 | Heritage | Jan-05 |
| 103 | 1,012,000 | $20, 1921 **(O)** | PCGS MS-65 PQ | Goldberg | Sep-07 |
| 104 | 1,006,250 | $2.50, 1796, Stars, Bass-3003, BD-3 **(P)** | NGC MS-65 | Heritage | Jan-08 |
| 105 | 1,006,250 | $1 Trade, 1885 | NGC PF-62 | DLRC | Nov-04 |
| 106 | 998,750 | 1/2¢, 1811, C-1 | PCGS-MS66RB | Soth/Stack's Bwrs | Mar-17 |
| 107 | 998,750 | Pattern disme, 1792, J-9 | PCGS AU-50 | Heritage | Apr-16 |
| 108 | 998,750 | 1¢, 1793, Chain, S-3 | PCGS MS-65RB | Soth/Stack's Bwrs | Feb-16 |
| 109 | 998,750 | Pattern disme, 1792, J-9 | NGC AU-50 | Heritage | Jan-15 |

| Rank | Price | Coin | Grade | Firm | Date |
|---|---|---|---|---|---|
| 110 | $998,750 | $1 Trade, 1884 | PCGS PF-65 | Heritage | Jan-14 |
| 111 | 998,750 | 1¢, 1793, Chain, S-2 | PCGS MS-65BN | Stack's Bowers | Jan-13 |
| 112 | 990,000 | 1¢, 1793, Chain, AMERICA, S-4 **(T)** | PCGS MS-65BN | Heritage | Jun-18 |
| 113 | 990,000 | $1(s), 1804, Class I **(E)** | Choice Proof | Rarcoa | Jul-89 |
| 114 | 977,500 | 1¢, 1799, S-189 | NGC MS-62BN | Goldberg | Sep-09 |
| 115 | 977,500 | $4, 1880, Coiled Hair **(D)** | NGC PF-66 Cam | Heritage | Jan-05 |
| 116 | 977,500 | $5, 1833, Large Date | PCGS PF-67 | Heritage | Jan-05 |
| 117 | 966,000 | 50¢, 1797, O-101a **(J)** | NGC MS-66 | Stack's (ANR) | Mar-04 |
| 118 | 962,500 | 5¢, 1913, Liberty Head | Proof | Stack's | Oct-93 |
| 119 | 960,000 | Confed, 1861, Original 50¢ | NGC PF-40 | Heritage | Nov-17 |
| 120 | 959,400 | $4, 1880, Flowing Hair | NGC PF-67 | Bonhams | Sep-13 |
| 121 | 948,750 | Terr, 1852, Moffat & Co., $10, Wide Date, K-9 | PCGS SP-67 | Stack's (ANR) | Aug-06 |
| 122 | 940,000 | 1¢, 1793, Liberty Cap, S-13, B-20 | PCGS AU-58 | Soth/Stack's Bwrs | Mar-17 |
| 123 | 940,000 | $5, 1825, Over 4, BD-2 | PCGS MS-64 | Soth/Stack's Bwrs | May-16 |
| 124 | 940,000 | 1/2¢, 1794, C-7 **(G)** | PCGS MS-67RB | Soth/Stack's Bwrs | Feb-16 |
| 125 | 940,000 | Terr, 1852, Moffat & Co., $10, Wide Date, K-9 | PCGS SP-63 | Heritage | Jan-14 |
| 126 | 920,000 | 1/2¢, 1793, C-4 | PCGS MS-66BN | Goldberg | Jan-14 |
| 127 | 920,000 | $1(s), 1802, Restrike | PCGS PF-65 Cam | Heritage | Apr-08 |
| 128 | 920,000 | $20, 1907, Small Edge Letters | PCGS PF-68 | Heritage | Nov-05 |
| 129 | 920,000 | $1 Trade, 1885 | NGC PF-61 | Stack's | May-03 |
| 130 | 910,625 | $1(s), 1794 | PCGS AU-58+ | Stack's Bowers | Mar-17 |
| 131 | 910,625 | $1(s), 1795, Draped, Off-Ctr, B-14, BB-51 | NGC MS-66+ | Heritage | Nov-13 |
| 132 | 907,500 | $1 Trade, 1885 | Gem PF-65 | B&M/Stack's | Apr-97 |
| 133 | 900,000 | Pattern 1¢, 1792 Silver Center, J-1 | PCGS MS-61BN | Stack's Bowers | Nov-17 |
| 134 | 891,250 | 1/2¢, 1796, No Pole, C-1 | PCGS MS-65BN | Goldberg | Jan-14 |
| 135 | 891,250 | 10¢, 1873-CC, No Arrows **(R)** | NGC MS-65 | B&M | Jul-04 |
| 136 | 882,500 | $5, 1815, BD-1 | PCGS MS-65 | Soth/Stack's Bwrs | Feb-16 |
| 137 | 881,250 | $10, 1933 | PCGS MS-66 | Goldberg | Jun-16 |
| 138 | 881,250 | $5, 1829, Small Date, BD-2 | PCGS MS-65+ | Soth/Stack's Bwrs | May-16 |
| 139 | 881,250 | $4, 1879, Coiled Hair | PCGS PF-65 | Heritage | Apr-15 |
| 140 | 881,250 | Confed, 1861, Original 50¢ | NGC PF-30 | Heritage | Jan-15 |
| 141 | 881,250 | 25¢, 1796, B-1 | PCGS SP-66 | Heritage | Aug-14 |
| 142 | 881,250 | $10, 1795, BD-5 | PCGS MS-65 | Heritage | Aug-14 |
| 143 | 881,250 | 10¢, 1796, JR-1 | PCGS MS-67 | Heritage | Jun-14 |
| 144 | 881,250 | $1(s), 1889-CC | PCGS MS-68 | Stack's Bowers | Aug-13 |
| 145 | 881,250 | 1¢, 1794, Head of 93, S-18b | PCGS MS-64BN | Stack's Bowers | Jan-13 |
| 146 | 874,000 | $1(s), 1804, Class III **(M)** | PCGS PF-58 | B&M | Nov-01 |
| 147 | 862,500 | 1¢, 1793, Strawberry Leaf, NC-3 | NGC F-12 | Stack's | Jan-09 |
| 148 | 862,500 | Pattern $4, 1879, Quintuple Stella, J-1643 | PCGS PF-62 | Heritage | Jan-07 |
| 149 | 862,500 | $2.50, 1796, Stars, Bass-3003, BD-3 **(P)** | NGC MS-65 | Heritage | Jan-07 |
| 150 | 851,875 | $4, 1879, Coiled Hair | PCGS PF-66 | Heritage | Jan-14 |
| 151 | 851,875 | $1(s), 1803, Restrike | PCGS PF-66 | Heritage | Jan-13 |
| 152 | 851,875 | $1(s), 1802, Restrike | PCGS PF-65 Cam | Heritage | Aug-12 |
| 153 | 825,000 | $20, MCMVII, Ultra HR, LE | Proof | Sotheby's | Dec-96 |
| 154 | 824,850 | Pattern half disme, 1792, copper, J-8 | NGC AU-55 | Heritage | Jan-15 |
| 155 | 822,500 | $10, 1797, Large Eagle, 13 Leaves | PCGS MS-64+ | Legend | Mar-19 |
| 156 | 822,500 | $5, 1832, 12 Stars, BD-12 | PCGS MS-63 | Soth/Stack's Bwrs | May-16 |
| 157 | 822,500 | $5, 1835, McM-5 | PCGS PF-67+ DCam | Soth/Stack's Bwrs | May-16 |
| 158 | 822,500 | $1(s), 1795, Flowing Hair, B-7, BB-18 | PCGS MS-66 | Soth/Stack's Bwrs | Sep-15 |
| 159 | 822,500 | 50¢, 1796, 16 Stars, O-102 | PCGS MS-66 | Soth/Stack's Bwrs | May-15 |
| 160 | 822,500 | $2.50, 1796, No Stars, BD-2 | PCGS MS-62 | Soth/Stack's Bwrs | May-15 |
| 161 | 822,500 | $10, 1933 | PCGS MS-65 | Heritage | Apr-15 |
| 162 | 822,500 | $1(s), 1795, Flowing Hair, B-2, BB-20 | NGC SP-64 | Stack's Bowers | Aug-14 |
| 163 | 822,500 | $1(s), 1799, B-5, BB-157 | NGC MS-67 | Heritage | Nov-13 |
| 164 | 822,500 | Pattern 1¢, 1792, Silver Center Cent, J-1 **(T)** | NGC MS-61BN+ | Heritage | Apr-13 |

| Rank | Price | Coin | Grade | Firm | Date |
|---|---|---|---|---|---|
| 165 | $805,000 | $1(s), 1870-S | NGC EF-40 | Heritage | Apr-08 |
| 166 | 805,000 | $20, 1921 | PCGS MS-65 | Heritage | Nov-05 |
| 167 | 793,125 | 10¢, 1796, JR-6 | PCGS MS-68 | Heritage | Aug-14 |
| 168 | 793,125 | Pattern half disme, 1792, J-7 | PCGS MS-66 | Stack's Bowers | Aug-13 |
| 169 | 780,000 | $1(s), 1794 | NGC AU-58 | Heritage | Aug-18 |
| 170 | 763,750 | $1(s), 1795, Draped Bust, BB-51 | PCGS MS-66 | Soth/Stack's Bwrs | May-16 |
| 171 | 763,750 | $5, 1829, Large Date, BD-1 | PCGS MS-66+ | Soth/Stack's Bwrs | May-16 |
| 172 | 763,750 | 1/2¢, 1796, No Pole, C-1 | PCGS MS-67RB | Soth/Stack's Bwrs | Feb-16 |
| 173 | 763,750 | 50¢, 1794, O-101a | PCGS MS-64 | Soth/Stack's Bwrs | May-15 |
| 174 | 763,750 | $2.50, 1798, BD-1 | PCGS MS-65 | Soth/Stack's Bwrs | May-15 |
| 175 | 763,750 | Terr, 1849, Pacific Company, $5, K-1 | PCGS AU-58 | Heritage | Apr-14 |
| 176 | 763,750 | Terr, 1855, Kellogg & Co., $50 | PCGS PF-64 Cam | Heritage | Apr-14 |
| 177 | 763,750 | 50¢, 1838-O | NGC PF-64 | Heritage | Jan-14 |
| 178 | 763,750 | $1(s), 1870-S | PCGS EF-40 | Heritage | Jan-14 |
| 179 | 763,750 | $5, 1826, BD-2 | PCGS MS-66 | Heritage | Jan-14 |
| 180 | 750,000 | Pattern, 1792, Silver Center Cent, J-1 | PCGS SP-58BN+ | Heritage | Jan-19 |
| 181 | 750,000 | $4, 1880, Flowing Hair | NGC PF-67 Cam | Heritage | Jan-18 |
| 182 | 747,500 | 1¢, 1793, Chain, S-3 | NGC MS-66BN | Stack's Bowers | Aug-12 |
| 183 | 747,500 | $20, 1921 | PCGS MS-66 | Heritage | Jan-12 |
| 184 | 747,500 | Terr, 1855, Kellogg & Co., $50 | PCGS PF-64 | Heritage | Jan-07 |
| 185 | 747,500 | $1(s), 1794 | NGC MS-61 | Heritage | Jun-05 |
| 186 | 734,375 | 50¢, 1838-O | PCGS PF-64 | Heritage | Jan-13 |
| 187 | 725,000 | Prefed, 1787, Brasher, EB on Wing | MS-63 | B&R | Nov-79 |
| 188 | 718,750 | 1/2¢, 1793, C-3 | PCGS MS-65BN | Goldberg | Jan-14 |
| 189 | 718,750 | 1/2¢, 1796, With Pole, C-2 | PCGS MS-65RB+ | Goldberg | Jan-14 |
| 190 | 718,750 | $10, 1933 | Unc | Stack's | Oct-04 |
| 191 | 705,698 | $1(s), 1870-S | VF-25 | B&M | Feb-08 |
| 192 | 705,000 | 1¢, 1796, Liberty Cap, S-84 | PCGS MS-66RB+ | Soth/Stack's Bwrs | Mar-17 |
| 193 | 705,000 | Pattern disme, 1792, copper, RE, J-10 | PCGS SP-64BN | Heritage | Apr-16 |
| 194 | 705,000 | $1(s), 1795, Flowing Hair, B-7, BB-18 | PCGS MS-65+ | Soth/Stack's Bwrs | Sep-15 |
| 195 | 705,000 | $10, 1798/7, 7x6 Stars, BD-2 | PCGS MS-61 | Soth/Stack's Bwrs | Sep-15 |
| 196 | 705,000 | 25¢, 1827, Original | PCGS PF-66+ Cam | Soth/Stack's Bwrs | May-15 |
| 197 | 705,000 | 50¢, 1794, O-109 | NGC VF-25 | Heritage | Apr-15 |
| 198 | 705,000 | Pattern 1¢, 1792, Silver Center Cent, J-1 **(T)** | NGC MS-61BN+ | Heritage | Sep-14 |
| 199 | 705,000 | Prefed, 1783, Nova Const., PE Bit, W-1820 | NGC AU-55 | Heritage | May-14 |
| 200 | 705,000 | Terr, 1849, Mormon, $10, K-3 | NGC AU-58 | Heritage | Apr-14 |
| 201 | 705,000 | $1(s), 1803, Large 3, B-6, BB-255 | NGC MS-65+ | Heritage | Nov-13 |
| 202 | 690,300 | $5, 1836 | NGC PF-67 UCam | Bonhams | Sep-13 |
| 203 | 690,000 | $5, 1909-O **(S)** | PCGS MS-66 | Heritage | Jan-11 |
| 204 | 690,000 | 1¢, 1796, Liberty Cap, S-84 | PCGS MS-66RB | Goldberg | Sep-08 |
| 205 | 690,000 | Pattern disme, 1792, copper, RE, J-10 | NGC PF-62BN | Heritage | Jul-08 |
| 206 | 690,000 | $5, 1825, 5 Over 4 | NGC AU-50 | Heritage | Jul-08 |
| 207 | 690,000 | $20, MCMVII, Ultra HR, LE of 06 | NGC PF-58 | Stack's | Jul-08 |
| 208 | 690,000 | Terr, 1860, Clark, Gruber & Co., $20 | NGC MS-64 | Heritage | Jan-06 |
| 209 | 690,000 | Prefed, 1742 (1786), Lima Brasher | NGC EF-40 | Heritage | Jan-05 |
| 210 | 690,000 | $5, 1835 | PCGS PF-67 | Heritage | Jan-05 |
| 211 | 690,000 | $1(g), 1849-C, Open Wreath | NGC MS-63 PL | DLRC | Jul-04 |
| 212 | 690,000 | $20, MCMVII, Ultra HR, LE | Proof | Soth/Stack's | Oct-01 |
| 213 | 690,000 | $10, 1839, 9/8, Type of 1838, Lg Letters (H) | NGC PF-67 | Goldberg | Sep-99 |
| 214 | 687,500 | $3, 1870-S | EF-40 | B&R | Oct-82 |
| 215 | 687,500 | $5, 1822 | VF-30/EF-40 | B&R | Oct-82 |
| 216 | 675,525 | $10, 1795, BD-5 | NGC MS-65 | Heritage | Aug-13 |
| 217 | 672,750 | $1(s), 1803, Restrike | PF-66 | B&M | Feb-07 |
| 218 | 661,250 | 1¢, 1804, S-266c | PCGS MS-63BN | Goldberg | Sep-09 |
| 219 | 661,250 | 1/2 dime, 1870-S | NGC MS-63 PL | B&M | Jul-04 |

| Rank | Price | Coin | Grade | Firm | Date |
|---|---|---|---|---|---|
| 220 | $660,000 | Pattern, 1792, Birch Cent, PE, J-3 | PCGS AU-58 | Stack's Bowers | Oct-18 |
| 221 | 660,000 | $20, MCMVII, Ultra HR, LE **(L)** | PF-67 | B&M | Jan-97 |
| 222 | 660,000 | $20, 1861, Paquet Reverse | MS-67 | B&M | Nov-88 |
| 223 | 655,500 | $4, 1879, Coiled Hair **(N)** | NGC PF-67 Cam | Heritage | Jan-05 |
| 224 | 655,200 | $20, 1891 | NGC PF-68 UCam | Bonhams | Sep-13 |
| 225 | 646,250 | $1(s), 1795, Draped Bust, BB-52 | MS-66 | Soth/Stack's Bwrs | May-16 |
| 226 | 646,250 | $5, 1831, Small 5D, BD-1 | MS-67 | Soth/Stack's Bwrs | May-16 |
| 227 | 646,250 | $5, 1795, Small Eagle, BD-3 | PCGS MS-65 | Soth/Stack's Bwrs | Sep-15 |
| 228 | 646,250 | 50¢, 1838-O | NGC PF-64 | Heritage | May-15 |
| 229 | 646,250 | Confed, 1861, Original 50¢ | NGC EF-40 | Stack's Bowers | Mar-15 |
| 230 | 646,250 | $1(s), 1893-S | PCGS MS-65 | Legend | Oct-14 |
| 231 | 646,250 | Prefed, (1652), NE 6 Pence, N-1-A, S-1-A | NGC AU-58 | Heritage | May-14 |
| 232 | 646,250 | Terr, 1851, Baldwin & Co., $20, K-5 | PCGS EF-45 | Heritage | Apr-14 |
| 233 | 646,250 | 1¢, 1795, Reeded Edge, S-79 **(K)** | PCGS VG-10 | Heritage | Jan-14 |
| 234 | 646,250 | $5, 1909-O **(S)** | PCGS MS-66 | Heritage | Jan-14 |
| 235 | 646,250 | $1(s), 1795, 3 Leaves, B-5, BB-27 | NGC MS-65 | Heritage | Nov-13 |
| 236 | 646,250 | $4, 1879, Coiled Hair | PCGS PF-64 Cam | Stack's Bowers | May-13 |
| 237 | 632,500 | $5, 1828, 8 Over 7 | NGC MS-64 | Heritage | Jan-12 |
| 238 | 632,500 | $1(s), 1870-S | PCGS EF-40 | B&M | Aug-10 |
| 239 | 632,500 | 10¢, 1804, 14 Star Reverse, JR-2 | NGC AU-58 | Heritage | Jul-08 |
| 240 | 632,500 | 1¢, 1793, Liberty Cap, S-13, B-20 | PCGS AU-55 | Heritage | Feb-08 |
| 241 | 632,500 | 1¢, 1794, Starred Reverse, S-48, B-38 | PCGS AU-50 | Heritage | Feb-08 |
| 242 | 632,500 | 50¢, 1838-O | PCGS PF-63 BM | Heritage | Feb-08 |
| 243 | 632,500 | Prefed, 1652, Willow Tree Threepence, N-1A | VF | Stack's | Oct-05 |
| 244 | 632,500 | 50¢, 1838-O | PCGS PF-64 BM | Heritage | Jun-05 |
| 245 | 632,500 | Confed, 1861, Original 50¢ | VF | Stack's | Oct-03 |
| 246 | 632,500 | 10¢, 1873-CC, No Arrows **(R)** | PCGS MS-64 | Heritage | Apr-99 |
| 247 | 630,000 | $10, 1795, 9 Leaves, BD-3 | PCGS-MS-63 | Stack's Bowers | Aug-19 |
| 248 | 630,000 | 1/2¢, 1796, With Pole, C-2 | PCGS MS-66+ | Heritage | Aug-18 |
| 249 | 625,000 | Prefed, 1787, Brasher, EB on Breast **(C)** | VF | B&R | Mar-81 |
| 250 | 618,125 | $4, 1880, Coiled Hair | NGC PF-63 | Superior | Jul-05 |

## Key

**Price:** The sale price of the coin, including the appropriate buyer's fee.

**Coin:** The denomination/classification, date, and description of the coin, along with pertinent catalog or reference numbers. B = Baker (for pre-federal), Bolender (for silver dollars), Breen (for gold), or Browning (for quarter dollars); BB = Bowers/Borckardt; BD = Bass-Dannreuther; Confed = Confederate States of America issue; dbln = doubloon; HR = High Relief; J = Judd; JR = John Reich Society; LE = Lettered Edge; N = Newman; NC = Non-Collectible; O = Overton; P = Pollock; Pattern = a pattern, experimental, or trial piece; Prefed = pre-federal issue; S = Sheldon; T = Taraskza; Terr = territorial issue. Letters in parentheses, **(A)** through **(U),** denote instances in which multiple sales of the same coin rank within the Top 250.

**Grade:** The grade of the coin, plus the name of the grading firm (if independently graded). BM = branch mint; NGC = Numismatic Guaranty Corporation of America; PCGS = Professional Coin Grading Service; PQ = premium quality.

**Firm:** The auction firm (or firms) that sold the coin. ANR = American Numismatic Rarities; B&R = Bowers & Ruddy; DLRC = David Lawrence Rare Coins; Soth = Sotheby's; Stack's Bowers, or Stack's Bwrs = Stack's Bowers Galleries (name under which Stack's and B&M merged in 2010; also encompasses the merger of Stack's and ANR in 2006).

**Date:** The month and year of the auction.

***Auction records compiled and edited by P. Scott Rubin.***

Over the years coin collectors have developed a special jargon to describe their coins. The following list includes terms that are used frequently by coin collectors or that have a special meaning other than their ordinary dictionary definitions. You will find them useful when you want to discuss or describe your coins.

***alloy***—A combination of two or more metals.

***altered date***—A false date on a coin; a date altered to make a coin appear to be one of a rarer or more valuable issue.

***bag mark***—A surface mark, usually a small nick, acquired by a coin through contact with others in a mint bag.

***billon***—A low-grade alloy of silver (usually less than 50%) mixed with another metal, typically copper.

***blank***—The formed piece of metal on which a coin design will be stamped.

***bronze***—An alloy of copper, zinc, and tin.

***bullion***—Uncoined gold or silver in the form of bars, ingots, or plate.

***cast coins***—Coins that are made by pouring molten metal into a mold, instead of in the usual manner of striking blanks with dies.

***cent***—One one-hundredth of the standard monetary unit. Also known as a *centavo*, *centimo*, or *centesimo* in some Central American and South American countries; *centime* in France and various former colonies in Africa; and other variations.

***certified coin***—A coin that has been graded, authenticated, and encapsulated in plastic by an independent (neither buyer nor seller) grading service.

***cherrypicker***—A collector who finds scarce and unusual coins by carefully searching through unattributed items in old accumulations or dealers' stocks.

***circulation strike***—An Uncirculated coin intended for eventual use in commerce, as opposed to a Proof coin.

***clad coinage***—Issues of the United States dimes, quarters, halves, and some dollars made since 1965. Each coin has a center core of pure copper and a layer of copper-nickel or silver on both sides.

***collar***—The outer ring, or die chamber, that holds a blank in place in the coinage press while the coin is impressed by the obverse and reverse dies.

***contact marks***—Minor abrasions on an Uncirculated coin, made by contact with other coins in a bag or roll.

***countermark***—A stamp or mark impressed on a coin to verify its use by another government or to indicate revaluation.

***crack-out***—A coin that has been removed from a grading service holder.

***crown***—Any dollar-size coin (c. 38 mm in diameter) in general, often struck in silver; specifically, one from the United Kingdom and some Commonwealth countries.

***cud***—An area of raised metal at the rim of a coin where a portion of the die broke off, leaving a void in the design.

***designer***—The artist who creates a coin's design. An engraver is the person who cuts a design into a coinage die.

***die***—A piece of metal, usually hardened steel, with an incuse reverse image, used for stamping coins.

***die crack***—A fine, raised line on a coin, caused by a broken die.

***die defect***—An imperfection on a coin, caused by a damaged die.

***die variety***—Any minor alteration in the basic design of a coin.

***dipped, dipping***—Refers to chemical cleaning of a coin to remove oxidation or foreign matter.

***double eagle***—The United States twenty-dollar gold coin.

***doubled die***—A die that has been given two misaligned impressions from a hub; also, a coin made from such a die.

***doubloon***—Popular name for a Spanish gold coin originally valued at $16.

***eagle***—A United States ten-dollar gold coin; also refers to U.S. silver, gold, and platinum bullion pieces made from 1986 to the present.

***edge***—Periphery of a coin, often with reeding, lettering, or other decoration.

***electrotype***—A reproduction of a coin or medal made by the electrodeposition process. Electrotypes are frequently used in museum displays.

***electrum***—A naturally occurring mixture of gold and silver. Some of the world's first coins were made of this alloy.

***encapsulated coins***—Coins that have been authenticated, graded, and sealed in plastic by a professional service.

***engraver***—The person who engraves or sculpts a model for use in translating to a coin die.

***error***—A mismade coin not intended for circulation.

***exergue***—That portion of a coin beneath the main design, often separated from it by a line, and typically bearing the date.

***field***—The background portion of a coin's surface not used for a design or inscription.

***filler***—A coin in worn condition but rare enough to be included in a collection.

***fineness***—The purity of gold, silver, or any other precious metal, expressed in terms of one thousand parts. A coin of 90% pure silver is expressed as .900 fine.

***flan***—A blank piece of metal in the size and shape of a coin; also called a *planchet.*

***gem***—A coin of exceptionally high quality, typically considered MS-65 or PF-65 or better.

***half eagle***—The United States five-dollar gold coin minted from 1795 to 1929.

***hub***—A positive-image punch to impress the coin's design into a die for coinage.

***incuse***—The design of a coin that has been impressed below the coin's surface. A design raised above the coin's surface is in relief.

***inscription***—The legend or lettering on a coin.

***intrinsic value***—Bullion or "melt" value of the actual precious metal in a numismatic item.

***investment grade***—Promotional term; generally, a coin in grade MS-65 or better.

***junk silver***—Common-date silver coins taken from circulation; worth only bullion value.

***key coin***—One of the scarcer or more valuable coins in a series.

***laureate***—Head crowned with a laurel wreath.

***legal tender***—Money that is officially issued and recognized for redemption by an authorized agency or government.

***legend***—A principal inscription on a coin.

***lettered edge***—The edge of a coin bearing an inscription, found on some foreign and some older United States coins, modern Presidential dollars, and the MMIX Ultra High Relief gold coin.

***luster***—The brilliant or "frosty" surface quality of an Uncirculated (Mint State) coin.

***milled edge***—The raised rim around the outer surface of a coin, not to be confused with the reeded or serrated narrow edge of a coin.

***mint error***—Any mismade or defective coin produced by a mint.

***mint luster***—Shiny "frost" or brilliance on the surface of an Uncirculated or Mint State coin.

***mintmark***—A small letter or other mark on a coin, indicating the mint at which it was struck.

***Mint set***—A set of Uncirculated coins packaged and sold by the Mint. Each set contains one of each of the coins made for circulation at each of the mints that year.

***motto***—An inspirational word or phrase used on a coin.
***mule***—A coin struck from two dies not originally intended to be used together.

***obverse***—The front or face side of a coin.
***overdate***—Date made by superimposing one or more numerals on a previously dated die.
***overgraded***—A coin in poorer condition than stated.
***overstrike***—An impression made with new dies on a previously struck coin.

***patina***—The green or brown surface film found on ancient copper and bronze coins, caused by oxidation over a long period of time.
***pattern***—Experimental or trial coin, generally of a new design, denomination, or metal.
***pedigree***—The record of previous owners of a rare coin.
***planchet***—The blank piece of metal on which a coin design is stamped.
***Proof***—Coins struck for collectors by the Mint using specially polished dies and planchets.
***Proof set***—A set of each of the Proof coins made during a given year, packaged by the Mint and sold to collectors.

***quarter eagle***—The United States $2.50 gold coin.

***raw***—A coin that has not been encapsulated by an independent grading service.
***reeded edge***—The edge of a coin with grooved lines that run vertically around its perimeter, as seen on modern United States silver and clad coins.
***relief***—Any part of a coin's design that is raised above the coin's field is said to be in relief. The opposite of relief is incuse, meaning sunk into the field.
***restrike***—A coin struck from genuine dies at a later date than the original issue.
***reverse***—The back side of a coin.
***rim***—The raised portion of a coin that protects the design from wear.
***round***—A round one-ounce silver medal or bullion piece.

***series***—A set of one coin of each year of a specific design and denomination issued from each mint. For example, Lincoln cents from 1909 to 1959.
***slab***—A hard plastic case containing a coin that has been graded and encapsulated by a professional service.
***spot price***—The daily quoted market value of precious metals in bullion form.

***token***—A privately issued piece, typically with an exchange value for goods or services, but not an official government coin.
***trade dollar***—Silver dollar issued especially for trade with a foreign country. In the United States, trade dollars were first issued in 1873 to stimulate commerce with the Orient. Many other countries have also issued trade dollars.
***truncation***—The sharply cut-off bottom edge of a bust or portrait.
***type***—A series of coins defined by a shared distinguishing design, composition, denomination, and other elements. For example, Barber dimes or Franklin half dollars.
***type set***—A collection consisting of one representative coin of each type, of a particular series or period.

***Uncirculated***—A circulation-strike coin that has never been used in commerce, and has retained its original surface and luster; also called Mint State.
***unique***—An item of which only one specimen is known to exist.

***variety***—A coin's design that sets it apart from the normal issue of that type.

***wheaties***—Lincoln cents with the wheat ears reverse, issued from 1909 to 1958.

***year set***—A set of coins for any given year, consisting of one of each denomination issued that year.

### COLONIAL AND EARLY AMERICAN ISSUES

Bowers, Q. David. *Whitman Encyclopedia of Colonial and Early American Coins* (2nd ed.), Pelham, AL, 2020.

———. *The Copper Coins of Vermont and Interrelated Issues 1783–1788.* Wolfeboro, NH, Stack's Bowers Galleries, 2017.

Breen, Walter. *Walter Breen's Complete Encyclopedia of U.S. and Colonial Coins*, New York, 1988.

Carlotto, Tony. *The Copper Coins of Vermont*, Chelsea, MI, 1998.

Crosby, S.S. *The Early Coins of America*, Boston, 1875 (reprinted 1945, 1965, 1974, 1983).

Demling, Michael. *New Jersey Coppers*. 2011.

Maris, Edward. *A Historic Sketch of the Coins of New Jersey*, Philadelphia, 1881 (reprinted 1965, 1974, 1987).

Martin, Syd. *French Coinage Specifically for Colonial America*. Ann Arbor, MI, 2015.

———. *The Hibernia Coinage of William Wood (1722–1724)*, n.p., 2007.

———. *The Rosa Americana Coinage of William Wood*, Ann Arbor, MI, 2011.

———. *St. Patrick Coinage for Ireland and New Jersey*, C-4 Publications, 2018.

McDowell, Christopher. *Abel Buell and the History of the Connecticut and Fugio Coppers*, 2015.

Miller, Henry C., and Hillyer, Ryder. *The State Coinages of New England*, New York, 1920.

Moore, Roger. *The Coins of Colonial Virginia*, C-4 Publications, 2019.

———, et al. *Contemporary Counterfeit Halfpenny and Farthing Families*, C-4 Publications, 2018.

Musante, Neil. *Medallic Washington* (2 vols.), London, 2016.

Nelson, Philip. *The Coinage of William Wood 1722–1733*, London, 1903 (reprinted 1959).

Newman, Eric P. *The United States Fugio Copper Coinage of 1787*, Ypsilanti, MI, 2007.

———, and Doty, Richard G. *Studies on Money in Early America*, New York, 1976.

Noe, Sydney P. *The New England and Willow Tree Coinage of Massachusetts*, New York, 1943; *The Oak Tree Coinage of Massachusetts*, New York, 1947; and *The Pine Tree Coinage of Massachusetts*, New York, 1952 (combined reprint as *The Silver Coins of Massachusetts*, 1973).

Rulau, Russell, and Fuld, George. *Medallic Portraits of Washington*, Iola, WI, 1999.

Salmon, Christopher J. *The Silver Coins of Massachusetts*. New York, 2010.

Siboni, Roger, John Howes, and A. Buell Ish. *New Jersey State Coppers: History. Description. Collecting*. New York, 2013.

### HISTORY OF THE U.S. MINT

Augsburger, Leonard, and Joel Orosz. *The Secret History of the First U.S. Mint*, Atlanta, GA, 2011.

Bierly, William. *In God We Trust*, Pelham, AL, 2019.

Bowers, Q. David. *A Guide Book of the United States Mint*, Pelham, AL, 2016.

Evans, George. *Illustrated History of the U.S. Mint* (various eds.), Philadelphia, 1885–1901.

Lange, David W. *History of the United States Mint and Its Coinage*, Atlanta, GA, 2005.

Mishler, Clifford. *Coins: Questions and Answers* (6th ed.), Pelham, AL, 2019.

Smith, Pete, Joel Orosz, and Leonard Augsburger. *1792: Birth of a Nation's Coinage*, Birmingham, AL, 2017.

Stewart, Frank. *History of the First United States Mint, Its People and Its Operations*, 1924 (rpt 1974).

### HALF CENTS

Bowers, Q. David. *A Guide Book of Half Cents and Large Cents*, Atlanta, GA, 2015.

Breen, Walter. *Walter Breen's Encyclopedia of United States Half Cents 1793–1857*, South Gate, CA, 1983.

Cohen, Roger S., Jr. *American Half Cents—The "Little Half Sisters"* (2nd ed.), 1982.

Eckberg, William. *The Half Cent 1793–1857*, West Palm Beach, FL, 2019.

Manley, Ronald P. *The Half Cent Die State Book, 1793–1857*, United States, 1998.

### LARGE CENTS

Bowers, Q. David. *A Guide Book of Half Cents and Large Cents*, Atlanta, GA, 2015.

Breen, Walter. *Walter Breen's Encyclopedia of Early United States Cents 1793–1814*, Wolfeboro, NH, 2001.

Grellman, J.R. *Attribution Guide for United States Large Cents 1840–1857* (3rd ed.), Bloomington, MN, 2002.

Newcomb, H.R. *United States Copper Cents 1816–1857*, New York, 1944 (reprinted 1983).

Noyes, William C. *United States Large Cents (6 vols.)*, Ypsilanti, MI, 2006–2015.

———. *United States Large Cents 1793–1814*, Bloomington, MN, 1991.

———. *United States Large Cents 1816–1839*, Bloomington, MN, 1991.

Sheldon, William H. *Penny Whimsy (1793–1814)*, New York, 1958 (reprinted 1965, 1976).

Wright, John D. *The Cent Book 1816–1839*, Bloomington, MN, 1992.

### SMALL CENTS

Bowers, Q. David. *A Guide Book of Lincoln Cents* (3rd ed.), Pelham, AL, 2018.

Lange, David W. *The Complete Guide to Lincoln Cents*, Wolfeboro, NH, 1996.

Snow, Richard. *A Guide Book of Flying Eagle and Indian Head Cents* (3rd ed.), Atlanta, GA, 2016.

### TWO-CENT PIECES

Bierly, William. *In God We Trust*, Pelham, AL, 2019.

### NICKEL FIVE-CENT PIECES

Bowers, Q. David. *A Guide Book of Buffalo and Jefferson Nickels* (2nd ed.), Pelham, AL, 2007.

———. *A Guide Book of Shield and Liberty Head Nickels*, Atlanta, GA, 2006.

Fletcher, Edward L., Jr. *The Shield Five Cent Series*, Ormond Beach, FL, 1994.

Lange, David W. *The Complete Guide to Buffalo Nickels*, Virginia Beach, VA, 2006.

Peters, Gloria, and Cynthia Mahon. *The Complete Guide to Shield and Liberty Head Nickels*, Virginia Beach, VA, 1995.

### HALF DIMES

Blythe, Al. *The Complete Guide to Liberty Seated Half Dimes*, Virginia Beach, VA, 1992.

Bowers, Q. David. *A Guide Book of Liberty Seated Silver Coins* (2nd ed.), Pelham, AL, 2019.

Logan, Russell, and John McClosky. *Federal Half Dimes 1792–1837*, Manchester, MI, 1998.

### DIMES AND TWENTY-CENT PIECES

Bowers, Q. David. *A Guide Book of Barber Silver Coins* (2nd ed.), Pelham, AL, 2019.

———. *A Guide Book of Liberty Seated Silver Coins*, Atlanta, GA, 2016.

———. *A Guide Book of Mercury Dimes, Standing Liberty Quarters, and Liberty Walking Half Dollars*, Atlanta, GA, 2015.

Brunner, Lane J., and John M. Frost. *Double Dime: The United States Twenty-Cent Piece*, 2014.

Davis, David, Russell Logan, Allen Lovejoy, John McCloskey, and William Subjack. *Early United States Dimes 1796–1837*, Ypsilanti, MI, 1984.

Greer, Brian. *The Complete Guide to Liberty Seated Dimes*, Virginia Beach, VA, 2005.

Lange, David W. *The Complete Guide to Mercury Dimes* (2nd ed.), Virginia Beach, VA, 2005.

Lawrence, David. *The Complete Guide to Barber Dimes*, Virginia Beach, VA, 1991.

### QUARTER DOLLARS

Bowers, Q. David. *A Guide Book of Barber Silver Coins* (2nd ed.), Pelham, AL, 2019.

———. *A Guide Book of Liberty Seated Silver Coins*, Atlanta, GA, 2016.

———. *A Guide Book of Mercury Dimes, Standing Liberty Quarters, and Liberty Walking Half Dollars*, Atlanta, GA, 2015.

———. *A Guide Book of Washington Quarters* (2nd ed.), Pelham, AL, 2017.

Briggs, Larry. *The Comprehensive Encyclopedia of United States Seated Quarters*, Lima, OH, 1991.

Cline, J.H. *Standing Liberty Quarters* (3rd ed.), 1996.

Rea, Rory, Glenn Peterson, Bradley Karoleff, and John Kovach. *Early Quarter Dollars of the U.S. Mint, 1796–1838*, 2010.

Tompkins, Steve M. *Early United States Quarters, 1796–1838*, 2008.

### HALF DOLLARS

Amato, Jon, *The Draped Bust Half Dollars of 1796–1797*, Dallas, TX, 2012.

Bowers, Q. David. *A Guide Book of Barber Silver Coins* (2nd ed.), Pelham, AL, 2019.

———. *A Guide Book of Liberty Seated Silver Coins*, Atlanta, GA, 2016.

———. *A Guide Book of Mercury Dimes, Standing Liberty Quarters, and Liberty Walking Half Dollars*, Atlanta, GA, 2015.

Parsley, Donald L. (Overton, Al). *Early Half Dollar Die Varieties 1794–1836* (5th ed.), Murietta, CA, 2014.

Peterson, Glenn R. *The Ultimate Guide to Attributing Bust Half Dollars*, Rocky River, OH, 2000.

Tomaska, Rick. *A Guide Book of Franklin and Kennedy Half Dollars* (3rd ed.), Atlanta, GA, 2018.

Tompkins, Steve, *Early United States Half Dollars, vol. 1: 1794–1804*, Peculiar, MO, 2015.

Wiley, Randy, and Bugert, Bill. *The Complete Guide to Liberty Seated Half Dollars*, Virginia Beach, VA, 1993.

### SILVER DOLLARS AND RELATED DOLLARS

Bolender, M.H. *The United States Early Silver Dollars From 1794 to 1803* (5th ed.), Iola, WI, 1987.

Bowers, Q. David. *The Encyclopedia of United States Silver Dollars 1794–1804*, Wolfeboro, NH, 2013.

——. *A Guide Book of Liberty Seated Silver Coins*, Atlanta, GA, 2016.

——. *A Guide Book of Modern United States Dollar Coins*, Atlanta, GA, 2016.

——. *The Rare Silver Dollars Dated 1804*, Wolfeboro, NH, 1999.

——. *Silver Dollars and Trade Dollars of the United States: A Complete Encyclopedia*, Wolfeboro, NH, 1993.

——. *A Guide Book of Morgan Silver Dollars* (6th ed.), Pelham, AL, 2019.

Burdette, Roger W. *A Guide Book of Peace Dollars* (4th ed.), Pelham, AL, 2019.

Crum, Adam, Selby Ungar, and Jeff Oxman. *Carson City Morgan Dollars* (5th ed.), Pelham, AL, 2019.

Fey, Michael S., and Jeff Oxman. *The Top 100 Morgan Dollar Varieties*, Morris Planes, NJ, 1997.

Newman, Eric P., and Kenneth E. Bressett. *The Fantastic 1804 Dollar*, Racine, WI, 1962 (Tribute ed. 2009).

Standish, Michael "Miles," with John B. Love. *Morgan Dollar: America's Love Affair With a Legendary Coin*, Atlanta, GA, 2014.

Van Allen, Leroy C., and A. George Mallis. *Comprehensive Catalogue and Encyclopedia of U.S. Morgan and Peace Silver Dollars*, New York, 1997.

### GOLD PIECES ($1 THROUGH $20)

Akers, David W. *Gold Dollars (and Other Gold Denominations)*, Englewood, OH, 1975–1982.

Bowers, Q. David. *A Guide Book of Double Eagle Gold Coins* (2nd ed.), Pelham, AL, 2019.

——. *A Guide Book of Gold Dollars* (2nd ed.), Atlanta, GA, 2011.

——. *A Guide Book of Gold Eagle Coins*, Pelham, AL, 2017.

——. *A Guide Book of Quarter Eagle and Half Eagle Gold Coins*, Pelham, AL, 2019.

——. *United States Gold Coins: An Illustrated History*, Wolfeboro, NH, 1982.

Dannreuther, John. *United States Proof Coins, vol. 4: Gold*, JDRC, Fullerton, CA, 2018.

——, and Harry W. Bass. *Early U.S. Gold Coin Varieties*, Atlanta, GA, 2006.

Fivaz, Bill. *United States Gold Counterfeit Detection Guide*, Atlanta, GA, 2005.

Garrett, Jeff, and Ron Guth. *Encyclopedia of U.S. Gold Coins, 1795–1933* (2nd ed.), Atlanta, GA, 2008.

Schein, Allan. *The $2 1/2 and $5 Gold Indians of Bela Lyon Pratt*, 2016.

### COMMEMORATIVE COINS

Bowers, Q. David. *A Guide Book of United States Commemorative Coins* (2nd ed.), Pelham, AL, 2016.

Swiatek, Anthony J. *Encyclopedia of the Commemorative Coins of the United States*, Chicago, IL, 2012.

### BULLION COINS

Mercanti, John M., with Michael Standish. *American Silver Eagles: A Guide to the U.S. Bullion Coin Program* (3rd ed.), Atlanta, GA, 2016 (reprint, Pelham, AL, 2018).

Moy, Edmund. *American Gold and Platinum Eagles: A Guide to the U.S. Bullion Coin Programs*, Atlanta, GA, 2014.

Tucker, Dennis. *American Gold and Silver: U.S. Mint Collector and Investor Coins and Medals, Bicentennial to Date*, Atlanta, GA, 2016.

Whitman Publishing. *Precious Metal: Investing and Collecting in Today's Silver, Gold, and Platinum Markets* (2nd ed.), Pelham, AL, 2019.

### TOKENS AND MEDALS

Bowers, Q. David. *A Guide Book of Civil War Tokens* (3rd ed.), Pelham, AL, 2018.

——. *A Guide Book of Hard Times Tokens*, Atlanta, GA, 2015.

Fuld, George, and Melvin Fuld. *U.S. Civil War Store Cards* (3rd ed.), Civil War Token Society, 2015.

——. *Patriotic Civil War Tokens* (6th ed.), Civil War Token Society, 2016.

Jaeger, Katherine. *A Guide Book of United States Tokens and Medals*, Atlanta, GA, 2008.

——, and Q. David Bowers. *100 Greatest American Medals and Tokens*, Atlanta, GA, 2007.

Rulau, Russell. *Standard Catalog of United States Tokens 1700–1900*, Iola, WI, 1997.

Leonard, Robert D. Jr., Kenneth L. Hallenbeck, and Adna G. Wilde Jr. *Forgotten Colorado Silver: Joseph Lesher's Defiant Coins*, Charleston, SC, 2017.

Tucker, Dennis. *American Gold and Silver: U.S. Mint Collector and Investor Coins and Medals, Bicentennial to Date*, Atlanta, GA, 2016.

### PATTERNS

Judd, J. Hewitt. *United States Pattern Coins* (10th ed.), Atlanta, GA, 2008.

### PRIVATE AND TERRITORIAL GOLD

Adams, Edgar H. *Private Gold Coinage of California 1849–1855*, Brooklyn, NY, 1913.

Bowers, Q. David. *A California Gold Rush History Featuring Treasure from the* S.S. *Central America*, Wolfeboro, NH, 2001.

Breen, Walter, and Ronald Gillio, *California Pioneer Fractional Pioneer Gold* (2nd ed.), Wolfeboro, NH, 2003.

Kagin, Donald H. *Private Gold Coins and Patterns of the United States*, New York, 1981.

### WORLD ISSUES RELATED TO THE UNITED STATES

Allen, Lyman L. *U.S. Philippine Coins*, Oakland Park, FL, 1998.

Medcalf, Donald, and Ronald Russell. *Hawaiian Money Standard Catalog* (2nd ed.), Mill Creek, WA, 1991.

Shafer, Neil. *United States Territorial Coinage for the Philippine Islands,* Whitman Publishing, 1961.

### PROOF COINS AND PROOF SETS

Lange, David W. *A Guide Book of Modern United States Proof Coin Sets* (2nd ed.), Atlanta, GA, 2010.

### TYPE COINS

Bowers, Q. David. *A Guide Book of United States Type Coins* (3rd ed.), Pelham, AL, 2019.

Burdette, Roger W. *The Renaissance of American Coinage 1905–1908*. Great Falls, VA, 2006.

——. *The Renaissance of American Coinage 1909–1915*. Great Falls, VA, 2007.

——. *The Renaissance of American Coinage 1916–1921*. Great Falls, VA, 2005.

Garrett, Jeff, and Ron Guth. *100 Greatest U.S. Coins* (5th ed.), Pelham, AL, 2019.

Guth, Ron, and Jeff Garrett. *United States Coinage: A Study by Type*, Atlanta, GA, 2005.

### DIE VARIETIES

Fivaz, Bill, and J.T. Stanton. *The Cherrypickers' Guide to Rare Die Varieties* (various editions and volumes), Pelham, AL.

The Numismatist
Vive le franc!
the coins of King Mindon